Practical Baking

Revised Third Edition

Practical Baking

Revised Third Edition

WILLIAM J. SULTAN
Consultant
Tamarac, Florida

THE AVI PUBLISHING COMPANY, INC.
WESTPORT, CONNECTICUT

Library of Congress Catalog Card Number: 76-21453
ISBN-0-87055-394-1

Printed in the United States of America
DEFG 4321098765

Contents

Section III.   Sweet Yeast Dough Products and Specialties

Section IV. Biscuits and Muffins

Section V. Doughnuts and Crullers

Section VI. Pies and Pastries

Section VII.   Cakes and Cake Specialties

Section VIII.   Cookies

Section IX. Specialized Baking

Section X.   Appendix

Preface

The purpose of this book is twofold: to provide the experienced baker or pastry chef with a practical handbook which he can use for ready reference and to offer the teacher and student of baking a text which can be used equally effectively in classroom, vocational training programs, or on-the-job training programs.

To accomplish this dual aim, a "recipe method" or approach has been taken in much the same way as the case method is used in the teaching of law. The numerous recipes contained in this book are basic to the trade and have been tested by repeated use in bakeshops. They represent a cross-section of all types of bakery products.

Of special import are the step-by-step procedures provided with each recipe. This leaves nothing to chance or the lack of experience. Special note is also made of practices, techniques, and procedures related to each of the bakery products. For example, the special factors pertaining to the fermentation and proofing of yeast-raised products, handling of various cake mixes, baking and finishing products, and the retarding of products are explained. The illustrations provide a better insight and understanding of the techniques and skills of makeup of the various products. In addition, the procedures are described in terms of equipment and practices used in both large production plants and the small retail shop.

For the experienced baker, the recipes serve as a vehicle for the improvement of quality bakery products by stressing those principles of production which eliminate failure or poor quality resulting from the lack of understanding. His present recipes may certainly be used to better effect with application of the knowledge and skill derived from the contents of this publication.

To the teachers of baking and food preparation in formal, school situations and to qualified bakers doing on-the-job training, the units are set up in their respective categories in a sequence from the simple to the complex. This makes possible a chronological development and transfer of skills and knowledge from one job or project to the next. Of special interest to teachers is the fact that this publication is an outgrowth of a recently revised course of study prepared by the author with the express purpose of updating the training of those interested in becoming bakers. The revisions made in the course of study were such that the basic skills and knowledges were related and directed toward the new developments which have greatly affected the baking industry in recent years. Technological advances are spelled out in terms of the daily, practical experiences of the baker.

The expected outcomes resulting from the use of this publication should reflect a further development of skill, greater understanding of production requirements and production problems, a more efficient use of raw materials, improved production, and greater variety of baked products. Because the publication is directed toward the training and education of bakers through a better understanding and application of trade techniques and processes, and toward the self-improvement of the experienced baker, it should make more valuable and meaningful the many services, materials, processes, and publications provided by the industry and those associated with the further growth of the industry.

Acknowledgment is given to the cooperation and assistance of Mr. Peter Schiulaz and Mr. Burton Abramowitz of the staff of the Baking Department of the Food & Maritime Trades High School in the revision and improvement of the sequence of material and the illustrations. The author also wishes to thank Mr. David Martin of the University of Bridgeport for drawing the illustrations.

The third edition contains four new chapters concerning specialized areas of bakery food production, as the retail baker and the larger commercial baker are diversifying their bakery products to meet the growing markets for specialized bakery foods. For example, the rapid growth of the "natural" bakery products market has created a new and expanding product development area within the baking industry. The chapter on "natural" breads and other bakery foods contains a complete variety of bakery products that are characteristic of the present market for these foods. The baker may expand his product li ne with the use of the formulas in this chapter. The chapter on dietetic baking enlarges for the baker the variety of products that may be made for consumers on limited sugar and sodium free salt diets. The chapter will enable the baker to make his own products or use the prepared mixes for the production of dietetic bakery foods.

There is always the need for special products that meet ethnic needs. Such is the case of the Jewish consumer who requests the baked food specialties for the Passover holiday. The chapter containing the formulas for the more popular of these products will provide the baker with a complete line of these products and how they are made. Still other specialized products are made with the use of sour cream and sour cream substitutes known as sour dressings. The chapter on sour cream baking introduces the baker to the more popular products made with either sour cream or the sour dressing made without dairy products.

WILLIAM J. SULTAN

April 1976

Related AVI Books

ENERGY MANAGEMENT IN FOODSERVICE
Unklesbay and Unklesbay
FOOD OILS AND THEIR USES, 2nd Edition
Weiss
FOOD PRODUCTS FORMULARY
VOL. 1, 2nd Edition MEATS, POULTRY, FISH AND
SHELLFISH
Long, Komarick, and Tressler
VOL. 2 CEREALS, BAKED GOODS, DAIRY AND EGG
PRODUCTS
Tressler and Sultan
VOL. 3 FRUIT, VEGETABLE AND NUT PRODUCTS
Tressler and Woodroof
VOL. 4 FABRICATED FOODS
Inglett and Inglett
MENU PLANNING, 3rd Edition
Eckstein
L.J. MINOR FOODSERVICE STANDARDS SERIES
VOL. 1 NUTRITIONAL STANDARDS
Minor
VOL. 2 SANITATION, SAFETY AND ENVIRONMENTAL
STANDARDS
Minor
VOL. 3 BASIC ACCOUNTING STANDARDS
Ninemeier and Schmidgall
VOL. 4 EMPLOYEE MANAGEMENT STANDARDS
McIntosh
VOL. 5 STANDARDS FOR FATS AND OILS
Lawson
THE PASTRY CHEF
Sultan
PRACTICAL BAKING MANUAL
Sultan
PRACTICAL MEAT CUTTING AND MERCHANDISING
VOL. 1 BEEF, 2nd Edition
Fabbricante and Sultan
VOL. 2 PORK, LAMB, AND VEAL
Fabbricante and Sultan
QUALITY CONTROL IN FOODSERVICE , Revised Edition
Thorner and Manning
SCHOOL FOODSERVICE, 3rd Edition
VanEgmond-Pannell

CHAPTER 1

Sugars and Their Use in Baking

CLASSIFICATION OF SUGARS

Sugars, and syrups containing large percentages of sugar, are a primary ingredient in the manufacture of bakery products. "Sucrose" refers to sugars or syrups made from sugar cane or sugar beet. The process of sugar manufacturing and the composition of sugar is clearly and thoroughly explained in pamphlets distributed by sugar producers.

From the baker's point of view, sugar is classified into two principal types: (1) Single or simple sugars (*monosaccharides*), such as glucose, dextrose, levulose, etc., are directly fermentable by yeast. This means that they do not have to be converted by yeast enzymes before they can serve as food for yeast. (2) Double or complex sugar (*disaccharides*), such as sucrose, maltose, etc., must be converted by the enzymatic action of yeast into simple sugars before they can serve as food for yeast.

Sucrose

Granulated Sugar.—Since sucrose or granulated sugar is the principal sugar used in bakery production, this chapter will be concerned chiefly with the several forms in which sucrose can be purchased. The more important of these are granulated and powdered sugar. These are classed as fine, superfine, regular, coarse, and as 6X, 4X, 2X (powdered sugar) which appear on the bag labels. It must be understood that there actually is no regulated standard for the control of the labeling of packaged sugar. Most retail bakers use "fine" granulated sugar because the crystals of sugar are such that they lend themselves to practically all uses. The powdered sugar is generally sufficiently fine to meet the baker's needs in preparing variety icings, fillings, etc. Basically, the measure of sweetness of any sugar or syrup is compared with the standard of pure, white, refined, granulated sugar, which is given the value of 100 per cent. All other sugars are either above or below that standard. For example, corn sugar or dextrose sugar may vary from 75 to 90 per cent of the sweetness of granulated sugar.

Confectionery Sugar.—Confectionery or powdered sugar contains approximately 3 per cent corn starch to retard lumping or crystallization. It is used primarily in icings and is also often a component of cake mixes in which part of the sugar is first blended with the flour and then added in the final stages of mixing. The fineness of this sugar lends itself to easier blending and is often used this way in angel cakes.

Yellow or Brown Sugar.—Brown or yellow sugars are those which contain some caramel (which affects the color), and mineral matter and moisture. Yellow sugar has been refined to the point where nearly all the caramel has been removed. Brown sugar on the other hand still contains more of the molasses and moisture, and has not been notably purified. These sugars are used in products where the flavor and color of the brown sugar are desired. For example, in the preparation of Struessel topping, this type of sugar is desirable because it adds to the color and flavor, and blends well with the cinnamon and other spices used. Brown or yellow sugars are also often used in making dark cookies and cakes. However, care should be taken in their use in light cakes or cakes of delicate blend.

Other Sugars Used in Baking

Corn Sugar or Dextrose.—Dextrose or corn sugar is made from corn starch. The process of manufacture involves the hydrolysis of corn starch with an acid, converting it first to dextrin and then dextrose. Dextrose is approximately 75 per cent as sweet as granulated sugar (sucrose) and bakers use it primarily for the making of yeast doughs. Since dextrose is directly fermentable by yeast, using it increases the rate of fermentation. Although corn syrup contains dextrose, it is a complex mixture and will be discussed in a later section.

Milk Sugar (Lactose).—Lactose is milk sugar; it is present in fresh and skimmed milk. Although the retail baker does not use lactose as a separate ingredient for addition to recipes, it should be remembered that the lactose in milk and milk products imparts additional flavor and sweetness to the product.

Malt Sugar (Maltose).—Malt sugar is present in the malt syrup used in bakery products and adds sweetness to the product. In most instances maltose is used in hard bread and rolls.

Invert Sugar.—Invert sugar is made by boiling sucrose with dilute acid or by passing sucrose through an ion exchange system. The result is a mixture of equal proportions of dextrose (glucose) and levulose (fructose) which is noticeably sweeter than sucrose. Invert sugar is used mainly for its ability to absorb moisture so that it helps keep baked goods moist longer.

Honey and Molasses.—Various types of honey and molasses, liquid and dried, are available, providing flavor, color and moisture to baked products.

USES OF SUGAR

Sugar serves the following purposes in the production of bakery products. It: (1) gives the necessary sweetness in cakes; (2) serves as a form of food for the yeast in fermentation; (3) is used in the preparation of a variety of icings for baked products; (4) assists in the creaming and whipping processes of mixing; (5) provides good grain and texture in the product; (6) aids in the retention of moisture and prolongs freshness; (7) promotes a good crust color; and (8) adds nutritional values to the product.

Different cakes and yeast-raised products contain varying amounts of sugar. For instance, the average wine-cake mix contains approximately 70 to 80 per cent sugar, based on the weight of the flour. In any given recipe, the ratio of the sugar to the weight of the flour will affect the method of blending the sugar with the other ingredients. If the amount of sugar is 100 per cent or less, based on the weight of the flour, the sugar is usually creamed with the fat or whipped entirely with eggs. This takes place in most creamed mixes. When the amount of sugar used is in excess of 100 per cent, as in the case of the high-ratio cakes (100 to 140 per cent sugar), a special method is required to blend the sugar with emulsified shortening. This method dissolves the sugar in the liquid when it is added with the flour. (See Chapter 29, Cake Mixing Methods.)

In the case of whipped mixes, such as sponge or angel cake, the sugar excess over 100 per cent is dissolved in the milk or water and then added alternately with the flour. This method insures complete solution of the sugar and avoids common crust problems (see p. 352). Since confectioner's sugar tends to lump, it consequently is difficult to dissolve. When confectionery sugar is added in the later stages of mixing, that sugar should be mixed and sifted with the flour rather than attempt to dissolve it in liquid.

Problems Arising in Use of Sugar in Production

Blending.—In the preparation of rich doughs, such as coffee cake, sweet yeast or Babka doughs, the sugar is either creamed with the fat (as in the creamed-cake mix) or is dissolved in the milk or water and then added to the sponge. Where a high percentage of sugar is used in doughs, and it is merely added to the sponge, there is a good chance that part of the sugar will not dissolve and will form large pockets of concentrated syrup. This may cause many dark spots on the crusts and the formation of large holes or pockets in baked products. Therefore, it is especially important to check the bottom of the mixing bowl to see whether there is sedimentation of sugar or syrup which has not been incorporated in the dough or mix.

Coarse Sugar.—Although most of the granulated sugar used in retail shops is of fine granular form, some is coarser and may present problems. This coarser sugar is very often the cause of spots on the crust of baked products, coarse grain, and poor volume.

A coarse sugar does not lend itself to proper creaming because its larger crystals do not dissolve as readily and tend to remain granular. This granular condition may still exist even after eggs are creamed into the mix, especially in sponge- or angel-cake mixes when the eggs and the sugar have not been warmed to about 100°F. It is particularly common in angel cakes in which the cool egg whites are used (65°F.). The sugar crystals are dissolved by the heat of the oven and those exposed on the surface caramelize and create spots. In the mix, they dissolve and form droplets of concentrated syrup. It should also be noted that these same crystals of coarser sugar act as an abrasive in the machine. They can remove the tin from the kettles and cause a gray discoloration in the product, and they may even be more abrasive if the shortening or fat used in the mix is cold.

However, there are times when coarse granulated sugar should be used. Large, or coarse, granulated sugars are well suited for making sugar-sprinkled cookies. In fact, the special large cubes of crystal sugar are recommended for sprinkling on cut-out cookies because there is less loss of sugar when they are baked and displayed. Coarse sugar may well be used in cooking fillings and preparing syrups for icings or wash. (Sugar which has hardened by overexposure to moist and varying temperatures can be used for cooking purposes.)

Sugar as Remainder.—Referring to the remainder of sugar in a recipe or mix, it must be remembered that sugar absorbs moisture and makes the batter less fluid. If sugar is added or subtracted from a mix, it is important to balance the moisture content as well as the leavening. For example, an increase in the amount of sugar used in a sponge-cake mix tends to tighten or stiffen the mix, and may result in a product with closer grain and less volume. This occurs because the added sugar forms a more concentrated syrup, having absorbed more of the moisture supplied by the liquids (eggs, water, milk), and tends to bind the mix. If this happens, note the larger cell structure. On the other hand, a leaner mix, deficient in sugar, will result in a product that has a pale crust color and tends to dry quickly. It may lose its freshness rapidly because there is a tendency to overbake for better crust color. Further, the product will lack the formation necessary to maintain that soft freshness desirable in cakes or sweet goods. Addition of moisture-retaining or hygroscopic agents will help off set this. It must be remembered that sugars (in liquid or paste form) such as commercial glucose, invert sugar or syrup, add additional moisture and sweetness to the mix. The matter of syrups will be discussed in the chapters on cake and sweet goods production.

CHAPTER 2

Shortenings and Their Uses

INTRODUCTION

The use of standard fats, oils, and other shortenings in bakery production is accepted by the baker as a matter of course. It is only when unusual problems arise in production that special investigations on their use are carried out. Very often, shortenings or other fats are blamed for faults they do not cause, perhaps due to ignorance of their composition, properties, and proper usage. For example, an inexperienced baker might use standard, hydrogenated, vegetable shortening in lieu of emulsified shortening, and blame the poor results on the shortening. The manufacture of shortening will not be considered in this chapter; only the types of shortenings and fats, their characteristics, general uses, and other factors will be discussed here.

Reasons for Use of Shortenings

Fats, oils, and shortening are used for several reasons. In bakery products they: (1) impart "shortness," richness, and tenderness to the product; (2) improve the eating qualities of products; (3) provide for aeration and resulting leavening of the product; (4) contribute to the flavor, particularly special fats such as butter or lard; (5) promote a desirable grain and texture; (6) provide for the development of flakiness in product (Danish and puff-pastry products); (7) lubricate the gluten in the development of yeast-raised doughs; and (8) act as emulsifiers for the holding of liquids.

The Dispersion of Fats in Doughs and Cake Mixes

Although shortenings and other fats and oils are blended and creamed into a dough or mix, they do not lose their identity or become unified with the other ingredients. Unlike sugar, eggs, milk, and flour which dissolve and are absorbed in the mixing process (and thereby lose their original identity), fat does not. Particles of fat, which may or may not contain air cells, are dispersed throughout the mix. Fats are not soluble in water and exist in either a "water-in-fat" emulsion or "air-in-fat" foam, if the mix is well creamed. These particles should be well distributed as they are largely responsible for the tenderness of the baked product. This is especially true of cake mixes.

5

TYPES AND CHARACTERISTICS

Classification

Fats and oils may be classified as liquid or solid, referring to their state or condition at room temperature (75° to 80°F.). These states may of course be changed by heating or cooking. Solid fats have varying melting points (from 93°F. for cocoa butter to 110°F. for some puff pastes). At the same time, lowering the temperature will eventually solidify normal oils. Fats which are neither solid nor liquid, but in a semi-fluid state, are known as "compounds." For example, a blend of fat and oil for the purpose of greasing pans, may be termed "compound."

Sources.—The fats and oils used in bakery products are either animal or vegetable. The cow's milk provides butter; hog fat, the source of lard; cottonseed, peanuts, soybeans, coconuts, cacao beans, and others are the sources of most vegetable fats. Rather than expand on each one, the brief outline chart below presents the various fats used in terms of source, color, odor and flavor, consistency, approximate fat content and general uses. Specifics regarding each of the fats will be discussed. For example, the conversion of vegetable oil into hydrogenated shortening, and the addition of other fatty substances to convert hydrogenated fat to an emulsified shortening will be considered.

CHART OF COMMON FATS USED IN BAKING

Type of Fat	Source	Color	Odor and Flavor	Consistency	Fat Content, %
Vegetable shortening	Vegetable oil	White	None	Solid	100
Butter	Animal (milk)	Yellow	Sweet and pleasant	Solid	80
Oil	Vegetable	Neutral to yellow	None to mild odor	Liquid	100
Lard	Animal (hog)	White	Mild odor	Solid	98
Margarine	Animal or vegetable	White to yellow	Neutral to milk butter flavor	Solid	80–85
Puff paste	Animal or vegetable	White	None to mild salt taste	Solid	80–85
Cocoa butter	Vegetable (cacao bean)	Cream to yellow	Sweet "chocolaty"	Solid	92

Hydrogenated Vegetable Shortenings

Shortening is made by converting purified oil, which has been heated, and injecting hydrogen gas while the oil is still hot. The amount of hydrogen gas injected controls the firmness of the shortening. In the case of emulsified shortening for high-ratio shortening, mono- and di-glycerides are added to the shortening for greater absorption and retention of moisture. While standard, hydrogenated shortening is well suited for creaming and can be used for most purposes, the emulsified shortening, in contrast, does not cream as well but it retains a higher percentage of sugar and liquid. Thus they should not be used interchangeably. That is, it is best not to use emulsified shortening for a creamed-type cake mix. Nor should regular hydrogenated shortening be used for a high-ratio-type cake mix. The results will not meet the desired standards if improper use is made of either one.

Vegetable Oils

Vegetable oils are used primarily in doughs. Rolls, bread, and hard-type products are often made with oil. Special cakes, such as honey cake, call for the use of oil because the batter contains a high percentage of liquid and is made with a flour with no gluten-forming properties. Very often hard fats are melted and then added in place of the oil.

Oils are purified in the refining process during which the fibrous material as well as foreign odors and colors are removed. Nevertheless the end products are not completely identical. While peanut and cottonseed oil are practically neutral in color, corn oil and soybean oil may have a light-yellow color. A mild flavor exists in soybean oil but may have little effect on product flavor when used in small quantities.

Butter

Butter is made from the fatty portion of milk. Its approximate fat content is 80 per cent. If shortening is substituted in a recipe calling for a large amount of butter, the amount of the shortening should be reduced (by approximately 15 per cent), and moisture increased (equal to 10 per cent of the weight of the butter). Special attention must be given to butter containing salt. Although sweet butter is used by most bakers, salted butter may also be used. However, its salt content (varying from 1 to 6 per cent) must be taken into account, and provision for this extra salt must be made in the recipe. This is doubly important in yeast-raised products, where excess salt will retard fermentation. Salt can be removed from butter by kneading the butter in cold water; this dissolves the salt.

Lard

Lard provides a pleasing flavor in certain doughs, particularly pie crust. For a mild flavor, a percentage of the fat content is replaced with lard.

Margarine

Margarine is made from vegetable or animal fat churned with milk or cream. It can also be made without animal fat and milk to meet specific dietary requirements. Cake type or baker's margarine is relatively soft and contains emulsifiers (usually mono and diglycerides) for superior creaming properties. Roll-in type margarine is firmer and has a waxy consistency, whereas puff paste type margarine is firmest of all and waxy. Each has a higher melting point than butter or regular table margarine. Like butter, margarine contains 80 per cent fat.

Cocoa Butter

Primarily cocoa butter is used in confectionery work. It is added to chocolates and chocolate icings and gives a finer shine or luster to the chocolate, as well as increasing the tenderness of the icing or chocolate.

SPECIAL CONSIDERATIONS IN THEIR USE

Temperature

As mentioned in the earlier section on cake-mixing methods, temperature is an important consideration in choosing the fats to be used. This is particularly true of vegetable shortenings. Low temperatures make the shortening very hard. Cold fat takes longer to cream and will make brittle emulsified fat which will not blend. A shop temperature of 75°F. is desirable for the fat.

Blending

Correct blending of fats is equally important, and is also affected by temperature. For example, when butter, shortening, and margarine are mixed for rolling in, hard butter will break into small pieces and will not blend evenly with the softer shortening. In this case, the butter should be worked until it is plastic and almost the same consistency as the shortening before blending with the other fats. A small amount of flour added to the machine will aid in keeping moisture in the butter. Hard pieces of butter tend to flake out in the dough when rolling. Often this is the cause of the greasiness in the product and the lack of flakiness or "kick" in the baking. This is particularly true of puff-pastry dough. In a rich, sweet dough this butter and vegetable shortening are often melted before being added. For example, a sponge is usually prepared for Babka dough and the melted fat is added after the sponge has risen. This is to prevent overmixing when the final dough is made.

In the mixing of leaner doughs, the fat or vegetable shortening acts as a lubricant in developing the gluten. For example, in pan bread, where 5 per cent or less fat is used, the fat is added after the flour and dough development takes place. The fat helps prevent the breakdown or tearing of the gluten during mixing. In richer doughs, such as bun dough, the fat is blended and creamed with the sugar. Adding the fat at the end, will make added mixing necessary to get thorough and complete distribution of the fat. Again, it must be remembered that this is a physical change and not a chemical change; the fat remains as fat in smaller particles and does not lose its identity.

Proper Amount

The amount of fat to use often presents a problem. Fats will accomplish the purposes listed at the beginning of this chapter only if used properly. Cakes that are dense, greasy, lack volume, or are lean, tough, and have poor keeping qualities, are the results of improper balance. The fault may not always be the recipe but may be caused by mixing methods or improper use of fat instead. A plain pound cake will have an equal proportion of fat to sugar and flour. As the liquid is increased, the flour is increased, the sugar increased, and the fat remains the same. There is a variation in the resulting grain, texture, and volume of the product. This factor will be developed further in the chapter on formula balance.

Ratio of Butter.—The practice of using all butter in creamed mixes has long been disputed. Experience has indicated that a 50 per cent blend of butter and standard hydrogenated shortening will result in better creaming capacity, with less chance of curdling in the creaming process. It should be remembered that butter contains approximately 15 per cent moisture, which tends to separate from the fatty solids. This is especially so upon the addition and creaming of the eggs or egg whites. In a 50 per cent blend, the flavor of butter is not lost and it is very difficult to distinguish the 100 per cent product from the blended one. The matter of cost versus quality is also one to be considered. In this case, too, the happy medium is the 50 per cent blend.

Handling and Storage

Fats and oils become rancid not as the result of harmful bacteria, but from the effects of light, heat, and air. One form of rancidity is due to oxidation. In its initial stages, this rancidity is not apparent, but as oxidation increases, the odor is noticeable and the color often changes. The use of rancid fats or oils is doubly wasteful. It wastes other good materials, for rancid fats have their taste and flavor throughout the baked product; the rancid odor will also result in the loss of business. Fats and oils should be stored in cool, dark, clean places, away from other ingredients that have strong flavors, since fats readily absorb the smell and odor of spices and other materials having strong, individual, characteristic odors. Perishable fats, such as butter, should be refrigerated. Enough for the day's production may be removed and allowed to soften somewhat. The necessary amount should then be scaled off and the remainder returned to the refrigerator.

Caution should be exercised in heating plastic containers to remove fats or shortening from them. Some plastics have a low melting point and placing a plastic container in the oven may cause the container to melt and blend with the fat. A mild temperature of about 100°F. is safe for melting fat away from the container.

CHAPTER 3

Eggs—Their Composition and Uses

INTRODUCTION

Eggs are a very important and costly ingredient of bakery products, especially of cakes and rich sweet doughs. In fact, they represent 50 per cent or more of the cost of the ingredients used in cake production. The purchase, storage, handling, and proper use of eggs are factors which must be thoroughly understood if products of high quality are to be produced at a pre-established cost.

Kinds of Eggs Available

Eggs are available in four forms: (1) fresh, (2) liquid, (3) frozen, and (4) dried. Eggs may be further classified into whole eggs, egg yolks, and egg whites. "Fresh egg" refers to the egg still in its shell. "Liquid egg" refers to eggs that have recently been broken, or separated from the shell and placed in cans; these are usually preserved by freezing. Various blended egg products are available under different trade names, many containing whole egg plus additional yolk.

Composition

The composition of eggs is shown in the following table:

AVERAGE COMPOSITION OF EGGS

	Whole Egg, %	Yolk, %	White, %
Moisture	73.0	50.0	86.0
Protein	14.0	17.0	12.0
Fat	12.0	31.0	0.2
Sugar (as glucose)	0.0	0.2	0.4
Ash	1.0	1.5	1.0

In calculating the amount of eggs to be used in a recipe or formula, one can assume that the whole egg is approximately 75 per cent moisture, the remainder being solids. This will be considered further with the matter of recipe balance in Chapter 29.

Yolk.—The yolk of the egg, the more solid part, contains most of the fatty material, in a finely emulsified state. The approximate amount of lecithin fat in the yolk is between 7 and 10 per cent of total fat content. Yolks are used for improved creaming, greater volume, etc. Although the yolk appears to be almost semi-solid, it contains almost 50 per cent water.

11

Whites.—Egg whites contain approximately 86 per cent moisture. The whites are either firm or fluid in nature. The whites close to the yolk are generally firm, while that portion closer to the shell is fluid. In general, whites are fibrous in nature, they tend to gel or hold together.

Quality of Eggs

While government standards indicate the grading of eggs in terms of the depth or thickness of the air pocket, movement of the yolk and its position with respect to the center of the egg, the firmness of the egg whites, the clarity of the yolk and white and the condition of the shell are other factors. Freshness is a most important factor in all types of egg.

"Candling" is used to determine the quality of the egg. In candling, the egg is held up to a light in a darkened room or position so the contents and condition of the egg may easily be seen. If the yolk is in the center the air pocket is small. If the yolk is held firmly by the white when the egg is turned and the shell is unbroken and clean, then the egg is of good quality. Smell or odor is not revealed readily unless the shell is broken. Bad odors are caused by bacteria or mold and may be present even if the shell is not broken. The shell is porous and moisture or washing will permit entry of bacteria and mold spores. Musty-smelling or hay eggs should not be used. Their odor becomes more intense with mixing and baking and is not removed by dilution with liquid or increase in recipe. Mixes that contain a musty egg should be thrown away. Frozen eggs of good quality are not likely to be musty. Spots in eggs are generally due to blood fragments in the ovary and are found as spots on the yolk or suspended in the whites. Such eggs are edible and may be used.

Sanitation.—Eggs are a fine medium for the development of bacteria and molds. Eggs of undesirable odor may be high in bacteria or molds. While some of these odors are volatile and disappear in baking some will remain and will give an off-taste and smell to the baked product if the odor is concentrated and strong. Frozen eggs should be refrigerated if they have defrosted and will be exposed to shop temperature for a lengthy time. Off-odors are indicative of a general deterioration and, usually, of bacterial action. Such eggs should not be used. Food poisoning can result from using liquid eggs held too long a time before use.

FROZEN AND DRIED EGGS

Frozen Eggs

Frozen eggs of good quality were once prepared only from spring-laid eggs. Now, farmers have learned how to get chickens to lay good quality eggs all year around. The eggs are candled, broken, strained, thoroughly mixed, and placed in cans. The eggs are quick frozen at −10° to −15°F. and may be stored for long periods at 0°F. or below without spoiling.

Frozen Yolks.—Frozen yolks generally contain 10 per cent sugar. The purpose of the sugar is to prevent the yolk from jelling and to avoid separation of the fat. Normally, when yolks are frozen and stored at 28°F., the moisture crystallizes and jelling takes place. Sugar, salt, and glycerin lower the freezing temperature and prevent lumping and jelling resulting from crystallization of the moisture. In addition, sugar aids in maintaining freshness after the eggs have been thawed for use.

Frozen Whites.—Egg whites contain approximately 11 to 14 per cent solids. If the percentage of solids is higher, this is an indication that the whites are old, due to a loss of moisture in storage. Quick freezing is an aid to the return of whites to their original state when thawed. Some egg whites are sold with small amounts of whipping aids, such as tri-ethyl citrate.

Storage.—If the large shop has freezer capacity, frozen eggs may be stored for about two months at 0°F. Frozen eggs usually have a temperature of 15°F. or lower when delivered. The eggs defrost very slowly at ordinary refrigerator temperature (36° to 42°F.).

Thawing Frozen Eggs.—There are two methods of properly defrosting eggs. The eggs may be thawed slowly in the refrigerator or they may be placed in defrosting tanks where the running water maintains a temperature of 50° to 60°F. where the eggs defrost in 5 or 6 hr. In the small shop, the eggs may be placed in a sink and cool water allowed to run around the can. The water level should not reach the cover. The best method is the defrosting tank because it keeps the eggs at a more uniform temperature. Defrosted eggs must be stirred well before using. This is especially necessary to get uniformity in whole eggs and egg yolks.

Eggs should not be defrosted in hot water, as the eggs close to the surface of the can are practically coddled or cooked. The congealed egg, which results, will not blend into the mix and breaks up into small pieces which are seen as small yellow spots in the baked product and look like foreign matter. In addition, a congealed egg has lost its emulsifying power. If, in an emergency, eggs must be defrosted quickly, place the cans in warm water and stir the eggs constantly to prevent exposure to heat for a long period. Frozen eggs that have been thawed should not be refrozen.

Dried Eggs

The manufacture of dried eggs became important in the Western Hemisphere during World War II. Prior to that period, Chinese dried eggs were imported principally in the form of dried yolks. These were used in egg doughs for challah and hard-roll doughs. Although dried eggs are used to some extent in retail shops, they are principally used in prepared cake mixes.

Dried eggs are perfectly satisfactory in any type of baked product if they are of good quality. Albumen (egg white) is often used in the preparation of meringue powders and may serve as a stabilizer. These preparations will whip immediately and reconstitute quickly when blended with sugar during the whipping. Good-quality dried whites may function better than liquid whites.

Reconstitution.—Since eggs are dried by spraying into a heated chamber (160° to 170°F.), the moisture is almost completely removed. In order for the eggs to re-absorb the moisture, the eggs must be allowed to stand for the periods stated below for complete absorption. These eggs should be stirred periodically to avoid lumping.

If dried eggs are used, the following methods of reconstitution should be employed:

Whole Dried Eggs.—Use one part dried eggs and three parts water. Blend well and allow to stand one hr. before using.

Dried Yolks.—Mix one part dried yolks and two and one-half parts water. Mix well and allow to stand one hr. before using.

Dried Albumen (Whites).—Mix one part dried albumen and eight parts water. Blend well and allow to stand 3 hr. before using.

USES

Purposes in Recipe

Eggs serve the following major purposes:

Leavening.—The foam from whipped or beaten eggs entraps air bubbles which expand when heat is applied. In the mix, they improve creaming, increase the number of air cells formed and coat these cells with a fat which permits further expansion of the air cells. In baking, the air cells expand further and the partial evaporation of moisture, in the form of steam, increases leavening. When whipped, as for sponge cakes, the foam formed by the eggs affects the leavening.

Color.—The yolk of the egg provides the desirable yellow color which gives the cake a rich appearance.

Flavor.—Eggs have an odor which some people consider desirable in the baked product.

Richness.—Because of the fat and other solids of the eggs the product has additional fat and tastes sweeter. Eggs also provide shortness in the mix, enabling the mix to be handled easily.

Freshness and Nutritive Value.—As a food eggs have great nutritional value. Because they contain moisture (75 per cent for whole eggs) and natural ability to bind and retain moisture, they retard staling. This is especially true of products made with additional yolks.

Proper Use of Eggs

The factors of temperature and its effect on eggs, the addition of yolks to eggs, the use of sugar yolks and recipe balance, and the reduction of eggs in a recipe require further study.

Temperature.—As mentioned previously, temperature does have an effect on the creaming and whipping properties of eggs. Cold eggs, when used in creamed mixes, will chill the shortening of fat being creamed, making a longer mixing period necessary for proper creaming. This happens when eggs are added too rapidly and there is a separation of fat in water emulsion. Use cool eggs in warm or hot weather to keep the temperature of the mix within the 70° to 80°F. range. In cold weather, it is best to have the eggs at shop temperature. The addition of yolks to cold eggs will help to avoid curdling.

Use of Sugar Yolks.—When using sugar yolks in which the sugar is above the usual 10 per cent, allowance should be made for the extra sugar and lesser amount of liquid. If this is not done, the mix will be thicker and bake with a deep color and loss of volume. This practice also helps to produce a closer grain and moist texture. For example, if 1 lb. of eggs is replaced by 1 lb. of sugar yolks containing 20 per cent sugar, then the sugar in the mix should be reduced 20 per cent of 1 lb. or approximately $3^1/_4$ oz. of sugar. In addition, since the yolks contain 8 oz. of moisture instead of 12 oz., an additional 4 oz. of water or milk should be added.

Recipe Balance.—When eggs are reduced in a mix, allowance must be made for the loss of liquid and the leavening supplied by eggs. For example, if 1 lb. of eggs is removed from a mix it means that 12 oz. of moisture have been removed. This must be replaced by water. An increase in leavening, baking powder, or baking soda will also be necessary to replace the leavening power of the eggs. Since 1 lb. of eggs will moisten and leaven 1 lb. of flour (approximately) the additional moisture will have to be leavened by an extra $1^1/_4$ to $1^1/_2$ oz. of baking powder. Of course, it must be understood that the removal of eggs reduces the quality, shortness, and richness of the mix. The eggs which are removed may be replaced with a syrup (glucose 5 to 10 per cent) and a lecithinized fat.

Frozen eggs may be used for all bakery products. However, in the preparation of custards, special care must be taken in mixing the eggs with the milk or other liquid to prevent the formation of yellow spots in the cooked filling.   It is suggested that shell eggs be used for custards and also for egg wash for easier mixing and spreading.

Use of Dried Eggs in Doughs.—It is best to have the eggs dissolved and reconstituted before use.   Bakers who mix the dried eggs directly into the dough will find that the dough stiffens during fermentation.   This is because dried eggs absorb moisture from the dough during fermentation.   Solution also allows even distribution without the formation of yellow specks in the baked product.

CHAPTER 4

Wheat and Flour

INTRODUCTION

Flour is the basic ingredient in the production of bakery goods. There are various types, mill brands, and qualities of flour. Many bakers will use only a specific mill brand on the basis of its past performance in producing satisfactory products, but this practice can lead to production problems because of the lack of understanding of the many factors involved in the milling, composition, blending, and proper usage of the basic flours used in retail shops. Moreover, it is not possible for a mill to maintain the exact quality of a flour brand from year to year because of variations in the characteristics of the wheat with each crop.

While characteristics and types of flour will be covered in brief here, the most important factors of weak and strong flours will be covered in the section on fermentation and the production of bread and rolls. (See Chapter 11, Basic Operations in Bread Making.) An analysis and presentation of the different types of wheat, the milling of wheat, and the composition of the various flours are presented in tabular form, followed by a discussion of the extraction or separation of flour in the milling process.

Classification of Wheat

Wheat may be classified as follows: (1) Hard Red Spring, (2) Durum, (3) Hard Red Winter, (4) Soft Red Winter, and (5) White wheat. Durum wheat is never used for flour for bakery products. The terms "winter" and "spring" refer to the seasons in which the wheats are planted. Thus, winter wheat is grown in relatively warm climates and spring wheat is planted in colder climates. The terms "hard" and "soft" refer to the consistency of the kernel and the flour. Each type is useful for restricted purposes. Hard flours are used for bread and rolls and special sweet yeast products requiring a stronger flour. Soft flours are used for more delicate products, such as cakes, pastries, and cookies.

Grain or Kernel of Wheat

The diagram of a cross section of a wheat kernel and its component parts will be of aid in obtaining a better insight and understanding of flour. The beard is composed of hair sprouts which are removed in the milling. Bran is the hard outer portion of the berry and has several layers that serve to protect the fine starch particles in the endosperm. The bran is removed in the milling process.

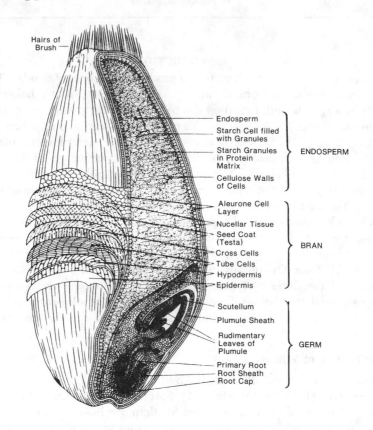

Hairs of Brush

Endosperm
Starch Cell filled with Granules
Starch Granules in Protein Matrix
Cellulose Walls of Cells
} ENDOSPERM

Aleurone Cell Layer
Nucellar Tissue
Seed Coat (Testa)
Cross Cells
Tube Cells
Hypodermis
Epidermis
} BRAN

Scutellum
Plumule Sheath
Rudimentary Leaves of Plumule
Primary Root
Root Sheath
Root Cap
} GERM

Courtesy of Northern Research and Development Division U.S. Dept. Agr.

VIEW OF WHEAT KERNEL BISECTED LONGITUDINALLY

Endosperm.—The endosperm contains the various fine starch particles and gluten-forming proteins. Germ is the fatty portion of the wheat berry and serves as its seed portion. The germ is removed in the milling process.

The Milling of Wheat into Flour

Before wheat is milled it is washed, cleaned, and tempered. The tempering of wheat involves moistening the wheat under controlled conditions so that it has a standard moisture content. Tempering enables easier removal of the bran and flaking out of germ particles. Of course, this should be carried out under sanitary conditions.

Wheat is sent through corrugated rollers which crack the wheat. The flour which is removed is called break flour. The bran particles are set aside. The middlings flour is then sent through smooth rollers where additional germ portions are flaked out. This is done several times to remove fatty portions and bran particles. These shorts are normally used for special foods and animal feed. The remaining flour, after impurities have been removed, is called straight. The flour is known as 100

THE MILLING OF WHEAT INTO FLOUR

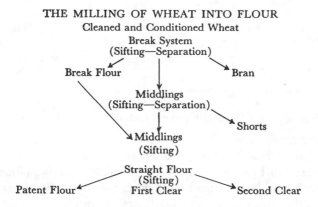

per cent extraction flour. The patent flour, or best portion of the flour, is removed. This may vary from 25 to 75 per cent extraction depending upon the nature and specifications of the flour desired. A long separation patent may be 65 to 90 per cent. A short separation patent may be of 25 to 40 per cent extraction. The clear flour remains after the patent flour is removed. In a short patent flour there will normally be several grades of clear. These grades are extracted in the same manner by grinding and sifting. In sifting, varying meshes of screen (silk or metal) extract the finer and coarser particles. Generally, the finer portions of the flour are closer to the center of the endosperm and contain gluten of high quality. The coarser particles are closer to the bran and generally add a darker color to the flour. This coarseness is particularly noticeable in the clear flour used for rye bread when it is compared with the fine starch particles of patent bread flour.

Clear flour contains more protein than patent, but this does not indicate that its gluten components are of a better quality. Generally, it is inferior; its quality depends on the quality of the wheat. Wheat may be identical in composition but there is a variation in the quality of the many types of wheat milled even if they are all spring wheat or winter wheat. There are many varieties of each of the general classes and the quality of the flour from them may be very different. A particular type of wheat will also vary in composition and quality from one year to the next or during several years. The climate, amount of rainfall, and temperature affect the composition.

The table below presents the average composition of flour. Variations exist in flours of the same classifications (e.g., hard or soft).

	Average Wheat, %	Average Patent, %	Average Cake or Pastry, %
Moisture	14.5	12 to 13	12 to 13
Protein	11 to 14	11 to 13	7 to 9.5
Carbohydrates (starch, sugar, dextrins)	69 to 72	74 to 76	75 to 77
Fat	2	1 to 1.5	1 to 1.5
Mineral matter (ash)	1.8	0.5	0.4

Other Types of Flour Used in General Baking

Whole-wheat flour is milled by grinding and sifting the entire wheat berry after the wheat has been cleaned and processed. This flour has a short storage life because of its larger percentage of fat (found in the germ) which tends to become rancid during storage. Rye flour is milled from rye in the same manner as other flours. Pumpernickel flour is milled from the whole rye berry after cleaning and processing. Bran flour is flour which has had extra bran flakes added to it. Gluten flour is that which has had a good portion of the starch removed. Its composition is about 47 per cent protein and 53 per cent carbohydrate.

Components of Flour

Gluten.—The mixture of wheat proteins which forms the tough, rubbery, elastic substance when flour is mixed with water or liquids containing water is called gluten. It exists in dry protein form in flour. Gluten is composed of approximately equal proportions of glutenin and gliadin. Glutenin gives the dough strength to hold leavening gases and determines the structure of the baked product. Gliadin gives elastic or stretching properties to gluten.

Enzymes.—The enzymes of flour are principally diastase and protease. Under proper conditions diastase acts upon some of the starch, liquifies it, and converts it into malt sugar. This is very important for the fermentation of lean doughs in which little or no sugar or syrup is used. Protease converts a portion of the proteins in doughs into a soluble form which adds to the elasticity of the gluten by mellowing and softening it.

Bleaching of Flour

A flour which has just been milled is known as green flour. It contains a relatively high moisture content (15 per cent is the maximum allowed under government standards) and may be slightly yellowish in color due to the xanthophyll and other carotenoid pigments present. Flour will age naturally if allowed to stand in proper storage for a period of 8 to 12 weeks. Oxidation gradually bleaches the pigments and oxidizes the proteins. Bleaching flour with chlorine dioxide or similar compounds matures and ages the flour in a short time. Chlorine is added to cake flours. It has a softening effect on the gluten and bleaches out the color. Bromates may be added to bread flours to help improve the grain and texture of the end product, but they have no effect on the bleaching of the carotenoid pigments present in the flour.

Properties and Characteristics

Absorption.—This characteristic refers to the ability of the flour to absorb and retain moisture from the mixing of the dough to the final baking of the product. This ability to absorb is dependent upon the amount and the quality of the protein, which will vary in different flours. Absorption of moisture will vary from 54 to 65 per cent based upon the weight of the flour and the way the flour is to be used.

Flour should be stored in a light ventilated room at a temperature of about 75° to 80°F. Improper storing will cause the flour to "sweat" and will result in an inferior baked product. Sweating refers to the absorption of additional moisture during storage causing a loss in absorption.

Strength.—The ability of the flour to produce products of large volume and well "piled" loaves is related to flour strength. "Piling" refers to an even smooth grain and fine texture. A large volume with a coarse uneven grain may indicate that the flour is not of high quality.

Flour Blends.—Prior to milling, various wheats may be blended in order to produce a flour of specific quality. Blending is also done by the baker in the shop in order to get a flour of desired characteristics. For example, a high-gluten flour may be blended with a weaker flour for the production of pan bread. A high-gluten flour may be used alone in the production of hard-type rolls. (Cake production and flour will be discussed later.)

Sifting of Flour.—Sifting the flour serves a double purpose—it removes any foreign matter and eliminates any lumps in the flour.

It is important to eliminate lumps by sifting. If they are not eliminated, there is a possibility of poor mixing or overmixing to remove the lumps. Aeration resulting from sifting insures proper moistening of the flour in the mixing procedure.

Identification of Flour.—Flour can be identified by color, feel, and sometimes smell. For example, a patent bread flour will be creamy in color, dry to the touch, will not pack when squeezed, and dusts easily on the bench. Cake flour is whiter in color, packs easily, lumps when squeezed, and lumps when dusted. Rye flour is grayish in color, lumps easily, and has a slight characteristic odor. While labeled storage bins are advisable, the baker should be able to detect an error in storage or dumping of the flour in the wrong bins. These characteristics will enable the detection of mislabeled or misrepresented flours.

CAKE FLOUR AND OTHER FLOURS USED IN CAKE AND PASTRY PRODUCTS

Cake flour is milled from a soft winter wheat; however there are variations in the qualities of soft winter wheat. Pastry flours, which are not of the same quality as cake flour, may be mistakenly used as cake flour with poor results. Cake flour has a lower amount of protein and forms soft-yielding gluten when mixed into the dough or cake mixes. This avoids toughness in the mix and in the product. However, the gluten must be of such quality that it will have the strength to form the structure of the cake. The protein content of this flour varies from 7 to 9 per cent. Absorption in cake flour refers to its ability to carry moisture and to retain moisture in the baked product. Gluten is not the most important factor of flour in cake production. There must be just enough to hold the cake together through the formation of a delicate and stable structure. The nature and quality of the flour needed depends upon the nature of the cakes. For example, a cake flour of 7 per cent protein and fine starch and gluten components is sufficient for angel cake, since the egg whites supply additional protein and structure for the cake. While the average shop stocks only one or two fine cake flours, perhaps a little too high in protein, this problem can be overcome by the adding of corn starch to the flour to increase its carbohydrate content and lessen the percentage of protein. The blending and adjusting of cake flour is a matter of judgment. For heavier cakes, such as plain pound cake or wine cake, a protein content of 8.5 to 9.5 per cent is advisable. The richness of the mix and the desired volume, grain, and texture make a stronger cake flour necessary. For high-ratio cakes, a protein content of 7.5 to 8.5 per cent is best. Here again, the average retail shop would do well to purchase a good-quality cake flour and adjust it as needed. For example, by adding 20 per cent bread flour to cake flour, the baker can adjust his basic cake flour for use in pound cakes (this percentage is increased for fruit pound cakes).

Chlorine is the standard bleaching agent used for cake flours, and causes a slight decrease in the pH of the flour, bringing it from about 5.6 to about 5.3. This means increased acidity. This decrease in pH aids in the mellowing of the flour. Bleaching also acts on starch particles in some poorly understood manner to make them more soluble. However, with a knowledge and understanding of the uses of flour and its composition, it should be possible to make the necessary adjustments with regard to flour. If in doubt about the purchase of a new brand, test a small batch of the flour in the exact procedure you will be using it before ordering the flour in large quantities.

PROBLEMS RESULTING FROM THE USE OF FLOUR

Toughness in baked goods is not always caused by the flour and may be due to improper mixing or lack of sifting. In cakes that have large percentages of liquid, the flour should be added alternately with the milk to avoid lumping and overmixing. In making cookies, a slight over-mixing in folding in the flour will cause toughness.

In rich doughs, such as Babka or Danish, a strong flour should be used. Most recipes will call for the use of 80 per cent high-gluten flour and 20 per cent cake or pastry flour. A short-patent bread flour may be used alone. This type of flour is necessary to support the active fermentation and the weight of the increased amounts of fat and sugar used in the dough. In puff-pastry dough, high-gluten flour is required to support the high percentage of fat rolled into the dough and to enable the dough to withstand the rolling-in process. For strudel doughs, a high-gluten flour is necessary to allow for the extreme stretching of the dough to maximum thinness. Pastry flour, rather than cake flour, is used for pie crusts. This flour is higher in protein and is able to sustain the high percentage of fat without becoming too tough and overly short—the point where the baked crust crumbles easily. A "developed" gluten, caused by overmixing, may make a strong batter or dough and a tough cake.

If an unsatisfactory product results from using a new flour, it is possible to adjust the new flour by blending it with a stronger flour or soften it by adding corn starch. However, this is at best a poor expedient and indicates the importance of the baking test for quality and proper use. There is no hard and fast rule for choosing any flour except sound judgment based on use together with a knowledge and understanding of flour characteristics. Purchase good-quality first and make substitutions or blends afterwards. Weak or poor-quality flour cannot be strengthened by adding another weak or poor quality flour to it, but a strong flour may be softened by blending a weaker flour with it.

CHAPTER 5

Milk and Its Uses in Baking

INTRODUCTION

In other than hard-type breads and rolls, milk is the basic means of supplying liquid to the dough or cake mix. While the retail shop may use a limited variety of milk and milk products, their proper use is an important factor and difficulties arise from ignorance of milk and its properties. For example, the solution of baking powder in fresh milk causes the milk to sour and curdle.

Milk, insofar as the baker is concerned, is defined as the lacteal secretion obtained by milking a cow 15 days before and not sooner than 5 days after calving. Milk, freshly obtained and not homogenized, will form a cream line on the surface if allowed to stand for a few hours. This is because the fat particles in milk have a lower specific gravity (0.92 to 0.94), or, in other words they are lighter than water. If milk is left standing at room temperature (e.g., 70°F.) for several hours it turns sour and curdles. This is the result of a lactic acid fermentation which increases the acidity of the milk. It changes from a normal pH (acidity) of 6.6 to a pH of 4.6. The curd (milk solids) and whey (liquid) separate. When cream is churned, clumps of fat are formed and the original fat in water changes to water-in-fat emulsion (butter). The liquid which remains is known as buttermilk.

A brief definition and explanation of the processing of the various types of milk and milk components follows, together with a table on the composition of the various types of milk.

Types of Milk

Homogenized.—Milk that has been forced through very small openings at high pressure to reduce the size of the fat particles is known as homogenized milk. With this process there is no visible sign of cream separation in the milk.

Pasteurized.—This term refers to milk that has been heated to 140°F. for 30 minutes and then quickly cooled to 50°F. or lower. Or, it may be milk that has been heated to 160°F. by a continuous high temperature-short time process and then rapidly cooled.

Whey.—The product that remains after removing most of the casein (protein) and butterfat from milk (as for example, in the process of making cheese) is whey.

Evaporated.—This term describes milk that is heated until part of the moisture is evaporated, the concentrated product is then homogenized.

Condensed.—This term also describes milk that is heated to allow part of the water to evaporate; but then 40 to 55 per cent sugar may be added to act as a preservative.   This milk may be classified as condensed or sweetened-condensed depending upon the percentage of sugar added.

Dried or Milk Powder.—Dried milk is the product from which almost all the moisture has been removed by heating the milk and spreading it on heated rollers or spraying it into a heated chamber.   It should not contain more than 5 per cent moisture.   The milk powder may be either whole dried milk which contains all the milk solids and fat, or the skim dried milk, which contains the solids without the fat.

COMPOSITION OF THE VARIOUS TYPES OF MILK

Type	Water, %	Butter Fat, %	Protein, %	Milk Sugar (Lactose), %	Mineral, %	Sucrose, %
Whole	88	$3^1/_2$	$3^1/_4$	$4^1/_2$	$^3/_4$	0
Dried whole	$1^1/_2$	$27^1/_2$	27	38	6	0
Evaporated whole	72	8	$7^1/_4$	$10^1/_2$	$1^3/_4$	0
Sweetened, condensed whole	31	8	$7^3/_4$	$10^1/_2$	$1^3/_4$	41
Liquid skim	91	Trace	$3^1/_2$	$4^3/_4$	$^3/_4$	...
Dried skim	$2^1/_2$	$1^1/_2$	36	$51^1/_2$	8	...
Evaporated skim	72	Trace	11	$14^1/_2$	$2^1/_2$	...
Sweetened condensed skim	29	Trace	11	$14^1/_2$	$2^1/_2$	43

Substituting One Milk for Another

When dried milk is to be substituted in place of fresh milk, it is very important to specify "high-heat" milk solids when ordering the product. Ordinary dried milk, or fresh milk that has not been scalded, causes a breakdown of gluten which results in sticky doughs and baked products with low volume and coarse crumb.   Condensed and evaporated milks have been heat-treated to an extent sufficient to eliminate the destructive factor.

When substituting milk powder for whole milk use 1 lb. whole milk powder and $7^1/_2$ lb. water for each gallon of milk.

When substituting skim milk powder for skimmed milk use 12 oz. skim milk powder and 7 lb. 12 oz. water for each gallon.

When substituting skim milk powder for 1 gal. whole milk add 12 oz. skim milk to $7^1/_2$ lb. water and add $4^1/_2$ oz. butter to the mix.   In other words, for every quart of skim milk used to replace whole milk 1 oz. fat (approximately) should be added to the mix.

When using evaporated milk or condensed milk refer to Table for contents and make the necessary changes. For example, an approximate method for using evaporated milk to replace whole milk is to add an equal volume of water to evaporated milk. This will practically reduce the amount of solids and fat by one-half. In the case of sweetened condensed milk, the amount of sugar content must be known and the necessary revisions made in the recipe. Milk processors will supply chart on conversion on request.

STORAGE AND CARE OF MILK

Fresh whole or skim milk should be kept under refrigeration when not in use. As mentioned on page 24, lactic acid fermentation takes place rather quickly at room temperature and milk is soured.

Evaporated milk is packed in sealed cans and storage presents no problem. However, care should be taken to use the cans in rotation of shipment and particular attention paid to swollen or blown cans. Such cans indicate fermentation and spoilage and should not be used.

Condensed milk is usually packed in cans or large containers. Once the large container is open it should be stored in a cool place and covered. Although the sugar acts as a preservative, condensed milk will spoil in a few weeks. Heat and light will speed up spoilage. It is also important to stir this milk before using because the sugar tends to crystallize along the sides and settle to the bottom of the container.

Milk powder, skim or whole, should be stored in a cool dry place, well covered. Since this form of milk contains so little moisture it tends to absorb moisture from the air. Skim milk powder stores better than whole milk powder because it contains little fat and will not turn rancid as quickly. Milk powder that hardens or lumps should be pulverized and sifted, and then be allowed to soak in cool water for complete solution before using. Do not expect the mixing machine to do this during mixing. It may break the lumps into smaller pieces, but they will not dissolve in the mix. When heat is applied in baking, these pieces become hard and pebbly and result in an unacceptable product.

USES OF MILK

When milk is used in doughs, it increases the absorptive qualities of the dough. Bread doughs made with milk should be slacker since the dough stiffens with fermentation. This is particularly important when the doughs are made with high-gluten flour. The casein in the milk tends to strengthen the absorptive and water retention properties of the dough. This also means that the rounded pieces must be relaxed longer or given a slightly longer preliminary proofing period. When using a softer type of flour milk tends to firm the dough. This is valuable in making soft or sweet doughs in which milk is used. The general rule is, if 6 per cent milk (based on the weight of the flour) is used in doughs, the amount of water in the dough should be increased by 6 per cent. This is especially true in the case of doughs made with strong flour. Milk, because of its strengthening effect, will also increase the fermentation tolerance of the dough. This means that the dough will not age as quickly. This condition is primarily due to the fact that milk reduces the acidity (pH) of doughs. This will be explained further in the chapter on fermentation (Chapter 6).

Milk gives richness to cakes because of its fat content as well as its natural sugar content (lactose). It also gives the cakes better bloom and crust color than cakes made without milk. In addition, milk aids creaming and the incorporation of more and larger air cells because it absorbs part of the moisture supplied by the eggs and prevents curdling during creaming. In addition, the emulsified butterfat present in powdered milk solids aids creaming and improves cell structure. This also produces better texture in the baked product and helps to maintain its keeping qualities.

Dried Milk

When adding dried milk to lean doughs, rich doughs, or cake mixes, it is not necessary to dissolve the milk in water. For lean doughs, such as milk bread or pan bread, the milk powder may be added with the flour and the dough then developed. The milk will be dissolved and spread throughout the dough during the development stage. For rich doughs and cake mixes, dried milk powder may be creamed in with the sugar and shortening.

In the preparation of custards and fillings in which milk powder is used, it is best to place the milk powder and sugar in cool water and stir until dissolved. Although hot water may speed up boiling, it causes the casein in the milk powder to congeal; the powder often forms small hard pieces which remain in the custard. If this happens, custard or filling is strained through a cheese cloth to remove the small lumps.

Sour Milk and Buttermilk

When sour milk or buttermilk is used in yeast-raised doughs the acidity of the dough is increased. This generally requires a shorter fermentation and makeup period. This is especially noticeable if sour milk or sour cream is used in the sponge for Babka.

When sour cream or buttermilk is used in cakes, especially in cakes containing cocoa and chocolate, the acidity is increased, and must be neutralized by the use of bicarbonate of soda. The soda will neutralize the acidity as well as assist in the leavening of the mix. The adjustment to make when sour milk is used instead of sweet milk in a cake mix is: for every quart of buttermilk used, add an additional $1/2$ oz. bicarbonate of soda and reduce the amount of baking powder by 1 oz. The action of the bicarbonate of soda on the acid in the milk will be the equivalent of the 1 oz. baking powder.

Common Faults and Problems in Use

Spots and "Scorched" or "Burned" Taste in Custards.—This is generally due to carelessness. When milk is placed on the stove to boil it requires stirring. Too often, after the milk powder is dissolved, the milk is allowed to come to a boil without stirring. The heat of the kettle caramelizes some of the lactose or milk sugar and causes it to burn. When the milk is stirred when adding the egg-starch solution, the caramelized skin along the bottom and sides of the kettle is scraped off by the wire beater. The pieces are then stirred throughout the custard. In addition, scorched milk has a bad taste.

Curdles and Fat Lumps in the Mix.—The temperature of the milk is important. When the milk is very cold (below 50°F.) it tends to congeal and the particles of fat separate out. Such milk should be added in small quantities before the flour is added and the remainder added after the flour is drawn into the mix.

Heavy Cream Curdling.—Milk when added to heavy cream for whipping should be cold. If the temperature of the cream is raised by warm milk, the friction of the machine, and temperature of the shop, this may cause the butterfat in the cream to clump into larger fat particles and may result in separation. This is very much the same effect as in the churning of milk into butter. The cream and the milk should both be very cold.

Acid Souring.—If the milk has been standing at shop temperature for some time, or has been out of the refrigerator a number of times, it may be on the verge of souring. The addition of any acid (cream of tartar, lemon juice, or other acids) in even a small amount may cause curdling. This condition holds true for powdered milk that has been prepared with water and left to stand.

Custard Souring.—Custards are made from a milk base. If left exposed for some time, they will sour very much the same as milk will. It must be noted that this is much more dangerous, for the coliform count may be high and may result in poisoning. It is not possible to make a lemon-flavored custard by adding lemon juice and flavor to regular custard, as the juice of the lemon is acid and will sour the custard.

CHAPTER 6

Yeast

NATURE AND GROWTH

Yeast makes possible many of the products made by bakers in both large and small shops. Yeast is a one-celled microorganism of the fungus type. By enzyme action, it converts certain fermentable sugars and some of the starch present in the dough into carbon dioxide gas and alcohol, and provides desirable and controlled fermentation. Since so many standard products (bread, rolls, and many varieties of sweet goods) are produced from fermented doughs it is necessary to know and understand the composition of yeast, its function in doughs, how it should be handled, and to be aware of the problems that arise in the shop.

The nature of yeast and fermentation were discovered by Louis Pasteur in 1859. Although history indicates that the early Greeks used fermented pieces of dough to cause freshly made doughs to ferment, this type of fermentation was not always controlled. Modern commercial production of yeast began with Pasteur. He developed the method of producing a pure culture by growing a large quantity of yeast from a single cell in a sterile medium that carefully excluded all other organisms. The original yeast cell is selected from a variety and strain best adapted to the purpose for which it is to be used, such as baking, brewing, wine-making, etc.

Purpose of Fermentation

Yeast fermentations are carried out for two purposes.

1. To convert sucrose (cane or beet sugar) or simpler sugars such as invert sugars (dextrose or levulose) into alcohol and carbon dioxide. This is done in the absence of air. Pure culture seed yeast is added to the dilute sugar and nutrient solution and the fermentation is continued until the conversion is substantially complete. The carbon dioxide is utilized if desired and the alcohol is recovered by distillation. The yeast grows and multiplies very slowly until a limiting concentration of alcohol in the fermentation vat is reached which inhibits further yeast growth. For alcohol production, this concentration is usually 12 to 14 per cent. The original concentration of sugar is limited so that by the time the action stops practically all of the sugar has disappeared.

2. When the objective is to produce yeast rather than alcohol, entirely different conditions are maintained. The yeast is grown under aeration. In this case, little carbon dioxide and alcohol are formed and what little

29

is formed is carried away by the vigorous current of air which bubbles up through the growing medium which may be contained in vats as large as 100,000 gal. or more in a commercial operation.

Conditions for Growing Yeast

The ideal conditions for yeast growth are: (1) plenty of water; (2) the right temperature; (3) as high a concentration of dissolved oxygen as possible (from the aeration); (4) a low but constantly maintained concentration of carbohydrate (sugar) and other nutrients such as nitrogen, phosphorus, and potassium as well as several trace elements; and (5) a hydrogen ion concentration maintained at about 3.5 to 4.0 by the addition of alkaline or acid nutrients containing nitrogen such as ammonia or ammonium sulfate is needed for proper fermentation.

The temperature is maintained at around 85° to 90°F., the chemical reactions are controlled by temperature and heating or cooling are applied as needed. The proper food concentration is maintained by starting with a low concentration of nutrients, adding a substantially pure culture of seed yeast, and then adding more nutrients continually at just the right rate to keep pace with the yeast growth.

In a batch operation, which is the type most commonly used, the original seed yeast is multiplied about 12 to 14 times during one run, which may take about 10 to 12 hr. The limiting factor for growth is the yeast concentration in the fermentation vat which at the end may reach 5 to 8 per cent. At higher concentrations, the growth slows down probably due to inability to cause oxygen from the aerating air to dissolve fast enough in the medium. In other words, the yeast at this stage would, if possible, consume dissolved oxygen faster than it can be supplied. When water is saturated with air at 86°F., only 0.53 per cent pure oxygen by volume is present (0.53 ml. oxygen per 100 ml. water). This is equivalent to 0.0008 per cent by weight (0.0008 gm. oxygen per 100 gm. of water).

When the operation is complete, the dilute yeast suspension from the fermentation vat is concentrated somewhat by cream-type centrifugal separators and then filtered in a cloth-lined filter press.

Budding.—Under favorable conditions of growth yeast cells multiply rapidly through a process known as "budding." Each cell develops to its full size, which is about 8 μ or about three ten-thousandths of an inch (about 3,000 cells placed together in a straight line would occupy 1 in.). Then it puts forth a bud which soon attains the size of the parent cell. It may then break off or form a chain or cluster by further division. Billions of cells are grown in each vat every hour in yeast plants. The process is closely controlled so that the product is of uniform activity, i.e., leavening power.

Composition of Yeast

The moisture content of yeast refers to the natural content of moisture present at the end of the manufacturing process. The other components are naturally present in the yeast as well. Yeast may vary in its outward appearance and yet may be of good quality. In general, fresh yeast will be gray to light yellow-brown in color, feel springy to the touch, break easily and sharply, and will have a yeasty odor. Although fresh yeast may be delivered regularly in transit, its storage and condition upon receipt are important. A rotation system should be maintained in the refrigerator and the older yeast used first. It has been found that both fresh moist yeast and dry yeast

AVERAGE COMPOSITION OF YEAST, PER CENT

Proteins	14.0
Carbohydrates	10.0
Fat	0.5
Mineral matter	2.3
Moisture	68 to 73
Enzymes and vitamins are present	

maintain activity best when stored at 32° to 34°F. Excessive aging of the yeast results in a loss in potency. Yeast may become moldy. If this condition develops, it must be discarded.

It is important to use yeast of uniformly high quality since its cost is small compared with that of the other ingredients. It is penny-wise and pound-foolish to take chances with cheaper and poorer quality yeasts. This will be discussed further under some of the problems in sweet yeast goods production.

PROPER HANDLING OF YEAST

The yeast to be used should be made into a slurry with cool water, or, in the case of active dry yeast, with lukewarm water (108° to 120°F.). The water should not be hot because yeast is killed at a temperature of 120°F. and higher. It is delicate and should be handled with care. It should be completely suspended in water for thorough distribution in the dough. There are still some who crumble the yeast directly into the dough. This results in uneven fermentation and a waste of yeast. Complete suspension means thorough distribution and proper fermentation.

Salt should not be added to the yeast slurry nor be allowed to come in direct contact with the yeast. If too much salt is used in a dough, it ferments very slowly. It is best to add the yeast suspension at the same time the flour is added to the dough. The flour acts as a buffer. This procedure is used for straight doughs.

In mixing a sponge dough, such as Babka, the yeast suspension is added with part of the flour and water and the sponge is set. Since there is little or no salt in sponge dough, fermentation proceeds rapidly.

The matter of how much yeast to use in sweet doughs is determined by a number of factors. Time in production is important. To ferment quickly, the amount of yeast may be increased. A no-time dough may be used in emergency. This means that the dough has such a large percentage of yeast that it can be taken to the bench for makeup a few minutes after it is mixed. In this case the chances are that the finished product will be yeasty in flavor and have the characteristics of a young dough. In sweet goods production, this may be true of the first units made up but will not be as noticeable in the units made up last.

Weather is another factor in the retail shop. In warm moist weather, yeast will be more active in doughs. The same amount of yeast may be used but the water or milk used in the sweet dough should be cooler. Lowering the temperature of the liquid will slow down the action of the yeast for a while. During the summer months ice water and even water containing small pieces of ice may be used in mixing. This slows the initial action but the rate of fermentation increases as the shop temperatures and humidity increase the temperature of the dough.

The richness or leanness of the dough is still another important factor. More yeast is used per quart of dough in a rich coffee cake dough than in a bun dough. This is necessary because the high amount of sugar retards the action of the yeast, as does an excessive concentration of any soluble material. A bun dough has a lesser amount of sugar and, therefore, causes less inhibition; the doughs rise more easily and require a lesser amount of yeast per quart. In bread doughs a still smaller amount is required to raise the dough.

THE ACTION OF YEAST IN DOUGHS

The fermentation or rising of the dough and its conditioning, which results from fermentation, are all due to the active enzymes present in the yeast. Enzymes are substances which cause changes to take place without being changed themselves. They may be termed organic catalysts. The principal enzymes present in yeast and their function in fermenting doughs are:

1. Invertase. Granulated sugar is sucrose (p. 1) and is not directly fermentable by yeast. This enzyme changes sucrose to an invert sugar

which is directly fermentable by yeast. This sugar is inverted much more rapidly than it can be used by the yeast.

2. Maltase. This enzyme changes the malt sugar, or maltose (p. 2), present in malt syrup and the traces of malt sugar present in flour and other ingredients into dextrose. Dextrose is directly fermentable by yeast.

3. Zymase. This is a name applied to the complex of many enzymes that act upon the invert sugar and dextrose and convert them into carbon dioxide gas, which causes the dough to rise and expand, and alcohol. Much of the alcohol is evaporated during baking.

Normal baker's yeast does not hydrolyze proteins. However, if the yeast is old or damaged, some proteolytic enzymes may be released which attack the gluten of the flour and lower the quality of the bread.

The changes that take place in the dough as a result of the enzymatic action start slowly but their activity increases as fermentation progresses. A heavy, sticky mass of dough gradually changes into a light, extensible, dry-feeling dough. The matter of softness of the dough is dependent upon its nature. Bread doughs vary considerably from richer, sweet doughs. In all doughs, the expansion and conditioning of the gluten, the entrapment of carbon dioxide gas, and the chemical changes that take place as a result of fermentation are due to yeast activity. Care and caution must be taken in the preparation of the yeast suspension and its use.

ACTIVE DRY YEAST

Active dry yeast is made the same way as regular fresh yeast, with one major exception. After the filtration process, which separates the freshly grown yeast from the spent fluid or food, the yeast is passed through a drier at controlled temperature (95° to 104°F.) and a carefully regulated drying speed to avoid destruction of the yeast cells and the moisture is reduced to approximately 8 per cent. Drying makes the yeast dormant (passively inactive) but does not destroy activity. Dry yeast should be rehydrated in lukewarm water (110°F.) for about 10 min. before using. The amount of water to use should be about four times the weight of the yeast to allow for complete hydration. Hot water will kill the yeast or greatly slow its action. When using dry yeast, it is advisable to use approximately 50 per cent of the weight of the fresh yeast. Dry yeast should be stored in a cool dry place with the container or package closed.

CHAPTER 7

Salt, Flavors, and Spices

The question is often asked, "Why is it that the product made with the best-quality ingredients often does not taste as good as the one made from a less expensive mix or dough?" The answer, assuming that the mixing and finishing are within trade standards, lies in the fact that there is not as much eye or "smell" appeal in the best-quality products. In fact, they should not be called best quality if salt, flavors, and/or spices were used improperly or not used at all. Although these ingredients are used in small amounts when compared with the basic ingredients, they are actually the "life" of the product. This chapter will try to explain their importance.

Flavors and spices add flavor, aroma, and color. The desire for specific baked products is influenced by the appearance of the product and its odor. The smell of freshly baked bread, rolls, Danish pastry, and other products is stimulating. However, the strong odor of some flavors is unappealing. For example, vanillin and maple flavor should be used carefully. Too much sugar color darkens pumpernickel undesirably. The appearance and odor in these cases detract from sales appeal. A knowledge of the proper use of flavors is important.

SALT

The salt used by the baker is purified table or cooking salt used for the preparation of food. While salt may be obtained from salt mines, seas, and salt lakes, most of our salt comes from salt beds. The salt is extracted in a highly-concentrated liquid form and is then purified and crystallized. Fine table salt is the principal salt used in baking. Except for coarse or crystal salt, which is used on salt sticks, pretzels, and similar products, this discussion will be confined to fine salt.

Purposes of Salt

Salt serves many purposes in bakery products. It (1) has a flavor which makes other foods taste good; (2) accentuates the flavor of other ingredients, i.e., the sweetness of sugar is emphasized by the contrasting taste of salt; (3) removes the flatness or lack of flavor in other foods or materials; (4) helps to control, in yeast-raised doughs, the action of the yeast and thereby controls the rate of fermentation (see Chapter 6, Yeast); (5) has a strengthening effect on the gluten of a dough; (6) modifies the crust color of yeast-raised products; and (7) aids in preventing the formation and growth of undesirable bacteria in yeast-raised doughs.

Fermentation problems and lack of flavor of some products may be due to the improper handling of salt. For example, suspending yeast in water to which salt has been added retards the action of the yeast.

In cakes and even in icings a definite amount of salt is required. The amount will vary with the type of cake. For example, a sponge-type cake will require less than a creamed-type of cake if the weight of the sugar in both mixes is the same because sponge cakes have little or no fat.

Unfortunately, many bakers still use guesswork in the addition of salt. The required amount should be weighed accurately and variations avoided. In yeast-raised doughs the usual amount is 1 oz. for each quart of water or milk used in the dough made for the item. In larger operations, the amount of salt is controlled exactly. When adding salt to cake mixes it is best to cream or whip the salt in with the sugar and/or shortening. This results in complete solution and distribution. Do not use moist salt that is lumpy for it may not be evenly distributed and will cause poor results.

SPICES AND SEEDS

Spices and seeds are aromatic vegetable products usually available in a finely ground state. They may come from the bark of trees, the seeds of vegetables or fruits, or the roots of various plants. A booklet or list can be obtained from the processors explaining the source, manufacture, and characteristics of the various spices and seasonings used in bakery products.

Spices

Spices contribute importantly to the taste and smell of the product and help to improve the quality. The most commonly used spices and seeds in baking are: cinnamon, mace, nutmeg, caraway, anise, allspice, poppy seed, coriander, ginger, cloves, and fennel. Not all of these are used in many retail shops. The amount used should be measured exactly as the matter of $1/_4$ oz. one way or another has a definite effect upon the baked product. For instance, $1/_4$ oz. cloves may give a product a pungent distasteful odor. However, the wise use of spices will improve many products; further, they add variety. It is important to weigh them carefully.

Seeds

Seeds such as poppy seeds and caraway, although not used to a large extent in cakes or cookies, should be applied carefully to certain kinds of bread and rolls. Large amounts of poppy seeds are often seen on the tops of rolls. Excessive amounts may be caused by a fast proof and sweating of the dough causing too wet a surface, so that whole clusters of seeds adhere to the dough surface. Clusters of caraway seeds may be observed within the bread; there may be large holes around these clusters.

Clusters of caraway seeds may be observed within the bread; there may be large holes around these clusters.

Storage

The aromas of ground spices are very volatile. That is, they lose their effective odor or flavoring when left exposed to the air for long periods. Consequently, they should be stored in sealed containers in a cool atmosphere when not in use. Whole beans or unground seeds have a longer storage life. These should also be stored in sealed containers since the moisture in the air has a pronounced deteriorating effect upon them.

FLAVORS

Pure and Imitation

Flavor extracts are solutions of the flavors in ethyl alcohol or some other solvent. The base of these flavors is the extracted essential oils of the fruit or bean, or imitation of the same. Many fruit flavors are derived from the natural oils found in the surface part, e.g., the exterior of the rind of the lemon or orange. Some are extracted from the fruit pulp. These fruit flavors are often supplemented by artificial flavor and coloring. The label of a container states whether a flavor is pure or imitation. The contents are controlled by the close supervision by the Food and Drug Administration. As a rule imitations are much cheaper than pure flavors.

The matter of purity and cost is important. Since most flavors are volatile—usually a considerable portion of the essence is lost in baking—it is important to use purer types of flavor. For example, the use of fresh lemon or orange rind (the outer surface) is retained better than artificial or imitation flavors. As a rule, the essential natural oils are better retained than others. Vanilla flavor is highly volatile. Even the use of the fresh bean, while far superior to liquid imitation flavors, loses much aroma. However, an increased amount of imitation flavors to replace a lesser amount of pure flavor is not wise. The addition of synthetic substitutes to support the natural flavors is helpful. The mixture of vanillin with vanilla has been beneficial. These synthetics do not bake out as rapidly and do enhance the flavor.

Vanillin.—Care should be taken in the use of the synthetics. A good policy to follow with vanillin powder is to blend one part with two parts of confectioner's sugar (1 lb. of vanillin and 2 lb. confectioner's sugar). It is also advisable to incorporate $1/2$ lb. corn starch to prevent lumping from the absorption of moisture. Use $1/2$ oz. of this preparation for each ounce of vanilla. Use a good quality vanilla flavor and add some of the vanillin preparation to it.

Storage

Liquid flavors should be stored in amber bottles and kept closed when not in use to avoid loss of flavor strength. Flavors are sensitive to light and may lose their strength if stored in the light. Since most of the loss of flavor takes place in baking through evaporation and vaporization, it has been found advisable to add the flavor to the fat in the creaming process. Flavors are better absorbed and distributed in this manner and don't vaporize as easily. It has also been found that if baked cakes are placed in compartments, such as humidors, with the flavoring at the bottom of the compartment, they absorb the desired flavor. However, this process is not feasible in the average retail shop.

Proper Amount and Use

Emulsions can be produced from aromatic oils by emulsification with a solution of a stabilizing agent (usually vegetable gum). Emulsions are more concentrated than extracts and should be used carefully. A general rule that may be applied is to use one-half the amount of emulsion as compared to the amount of extract. In the making of foam-type cakes such as sponge or angel cake, care should be used in the addition of emulsions. The oils present will cause the foam to fall back if beaten with the eggs or egg whites. The emulsion should be added or folded in lightly just before the flour is added.

Do not use too much flavor. An excessive amount of flavor is worse than no flavor at all. The odor is overpowering and is not conducive to repeat sales. Special care should be taken in the use of flavor-color preparations. These are found in the orange, lemon, cherry, strawberry, and maple flavors. Excessive use also means excessive color. In other words, an orange cake may be too orange in color as well as being over-flavored. This is especially important in the flavoring and coloring of icings. For example, a buttercream or fondant icing readily takes on color and retains flavor. There is little loss by vaporization for there is no baking in this case. Note must be made of the use of special butter synthetics. These are good for promoting a butter flavor but should be used with discretion. Follow the directions on the label for use and reduce the amount if it is too strong. If butter is used in your products use a lesser amount of the flavor.

When cooking custards and fillings of the custard variety, add the flavoring after the custard or filling has been cooked. In fact, if the custard is to be Frenched add the flavor at the time the buttercream is added. This will eliminate loss of flavor in hot filling.

When adding flavor-color preparations to fruit fillings such as cherry or strawberry these flavors should be added after the filling has been cooked and cooled somewhat. This will avoid loss of flavor through vaporization.

When blending flavors for cakes and icings it is important to have one flavor outstanding with the other flavors as supplements. For example, in orange cakes the use of a little lemon improves the flavor of the orange. In almond-flavored products the use of a little rum flavor will enhance the flavor of the almond. In chocolate cakes the flavor of the chocolate is basic and is supplemented with vanilla.

The preparation of cinnamon-sugar is often a hit and miss affair. Too many bakers simply mix the cinnamon with the sugar until the desired color is obtained without regard for the taste and flavor. Different cinnamons vary in color and strength. A Batavia or a Korintje is different in strength and character from a Saigon cinnamon. It is recommended that a blend of 1 oz. cinnamon for every $2^1/_2$ lb. sugar is sufficiently mild yet flavorful.

Careful and wise use of flavors and spices is recommended. Test all new varieties to find out how they work. Have others taste it for you and get their reactions. Above all, measure and weigh carefully rather than work by guessing and pouring from the bottle. This is particularly true in the case of icings, fillings, toppings, and whipped creams.

CHAPTER 8

Cocoa and Chocolate

Cocoa and chocolate are used very widely in the production and finishing of cakes, pastries, pies, and cookies. Not only do they provide for variety of product and special color and flavor in the product but they also supply body and bulk to the cake mix or icing. There are variations in cocoa as well as varieties of chocolate. Knowledge of these variations, the substitution of chocolate for cocoa and vice versa, and the understanding of possible causes for many problems that may arise from the use of cocoa and chocolate are essential to understanding their role in baking.

THE MANUFACTURE OF COCOA AND CHOCOLATE

The cacao bean of the cacao tree is the source of cocoa and chocolate. The cocoa pod, which looks something like an acorn squash, is cut from the tree and split open. The beans inside are picked, washed, dried, and the fibers removed before they are fermented and cured. Fermenting makes possible the easy removal of the pulp from the bean, which is essentially drying; curing removes the bitter taste and imparts aroma, taste, flavor, and color.

The beans are then shipped to the processor where they are roasted for further improvement in the taste and flavor. The hulls are broken off and discarded while the nibs are crushed and reduced to a thick mass called chocolate liquor. This liquor contains all of the contents of the cleaned cacao bean: cocoa butter, carbohydrates, and proteins. In the manufacture of cocoa, cocoa butter is pressed out by means of hydraulic presses. The pressed cake is then pulverized into a fine cocoa powder. Since the cocoa butter that is removed is neutral in flavor its removal increases the strength of the flavor of the cocoa to about 1.7 times as that of chocolate. The cocoa butter helps to carry or hold the flavor, and cocoa in which most of the cocoa butter has been removed tends to lose its flavor quickly.

In the manufacture of sweet chocolate additional sugar and/or dextrose is added. This usually amounts to about an equal weight of the chocolate liquor. For milk chocolate not less than 12 per cent milk solids are added. The following table will illustrate the approximate contents of cocoa and chocolate. Allowance should be made for the sugar when using sweet chocolate.

	Cocoa Butter or Fat, %	Carbo- hydrates, %	Protein and Ash, %	Sugar, %
Chocolate liquor	52	30	15	. . .
Cocoa	20–25	40–45	20–25	. . .
Sweet chocolate	25	25	. . .	50

Dutch-Process Cocoa

Dutch-process cocoa is a modified form of cocoa. That is, the cacao beans are treated with an alkali. A solution of the alkali (usually sodium bicarbonate) is added to the partially roasted beans and the excess water is evaporated off. The beans are then treated as for the manufacture of natural cocoa. The purpose of Dutching cocoa is to darken the color, modify the flavor, and improve the colloidal properties of the natural cocoa. This process also reduces the natural acidity of the cocoa because the alkali neutralizes some of the acidity. Dutching not only darkens the color, but also makes the cocoa less bitter and results in better solubility. Dutching has an important effect on the pH or acidity of the cocoa. This will be presented in tabular form after its importance has been explained.

Test to Distinguish Between Cocoas

Take 1 oz. of the sample, or unknown cocoa, and stir it into about 8 oz. of cool water. Compare this cocoa with a similar solution of natural cocoa of known source. If the color of the sample cocoa solution is much darker than the natural cocoa you will know that it is Dutched cocoa. Colors vary also due to the kind of cocoa beans and the degree of the roast. To double check, stir 1 oz. of each type of cocoa and 1 tsp. baking soda into about 8 oz. warm water. You will notice that the natural cocoa solution will foam and turn darker. The Dutched cocoa will not foam and may turn somewhat darker. This will allow you to tell one cocoa from another and be able to make the necessary adjustments to the recipe.

A color test may also be used. Since Dutched cocoa is made darker by an alkali, if you add a teaspoon of acid (cream of tartar) to a solution of Dutched cocoa the color will turn lighter. If the acid is added to a solution of natural cocoa there will be little change in color. Leavening agents have a notable effect upon the color, aroma, and flavor of a baked chocolate cake. Following is a pH table of cocoa.

pH	Acid		Neutral		Alkaline		
4	5	6	7	8	9	10
		(Dutched Cocoa)				
	Natural Cocoa		Light	Medium	Heavy		Excess Soda

From the above scale it can be seen that natural cocoa has a lower pH or greater acidity and requires the use of more baking soda as the leavening in the mix than does Dutched cocoa. The Dutched-process cocoa is not as strong or concentrated (pH is approximately 6–8.8). This cocoa requires less baking soda for leavening and more baking powder. The type of cocoa used should be known in order to make adjustments in the leavening depending on the nature of the cake. To repeat, natural cocoas require more soda and Dutched require less. You should also know whether the Dutched cocoa is heavy or light. When substituting more soda for baking powder reduce the amount of baking powder by 1 oz. for each $1/2$ oz. soda used. The acid in the natural cocoa will provide the leavening. When increasing the baking powder for a heavy Dutched-process cocoa add 1 oz. baking powder for each $1/2$ oz. baking soda removed. If the cakes are mahogany or reddish-brown it is a sure indication that too much soda was used. The cake will also have a baking soda or soapy taste. Adjust the type and quantity of soda used in the mix. If the cakes are light brown or cinnamon colored then they require an increase in the amount of baking soda. Make the changes or adjustments gradually by increasing or decreasing in one-half portions until desirable results are achieved.

Substituting Cocoa for Chocolate or Chocolate for Cocoa

Cocoa for Chocolate.—When 1 lb. of chocolate paste manufactured from the cacao bean is subjected to hydraulic pressing in order to make cocoa, approximately 6 oz. of cocoa butter are pressed off. The cocoa contains approximately 8 oz. of solids and 2 oz. cocoa butter. Cocoa butter has about one-half the shortening power of regular shortening. The removed cocoa butter can be replaced with 3 oz. regular shortening. The rule or guide to follow when substituting cocoa for chocolate is: Use five-eighths of the weight of the chocolate as cocoa plus shortening equal to one-half the difference between the weight of the cocoa and the weight of the chocolate to be replaced.

Example (using cocoa to replace 24 oz. of chocolate liquor):

$$5/8 \times 24 = 15 \text{ oz. cocoa}$$

24 oz. chocolate
—15 oz. cocoa
9 oz. difference
$1/2 \times 9 = 4^1/2$ oz. shortening

Answer: 15 oz. cocoa and $4^1/2$ oz. shortening are required to replace 24 oz. chocolate liquor.

If you are replacing sweet chocolate divide the weight of the chocolate (which is half sugar) by one-half to get the weight to be replaced by cocoa. The other half is to be replaced by an equal weight of sugar.

Chocolate for Cocoa.—The rule is: Multiply the weight of the cocoa by eight-fifths to get the weight of the chocolate. Reduce the amount of shortening used in the mix by one-half the difference in weight between the chocolate and cocoa.

Example (using chocolate to replace 15 oz. of cocoa):

$$^8/_5 \times 15 = 24 \text{ oz. chocolate liquor}$$

       24 oz. chocolate
      —15 oz. cocoa
       9 oz. cocoa butter to be replaced by reducing the shortening used in the mix by $4^1/_2$ oz.

This rule applies to natural cocoa. If you are replacing a Dutched cocoa with chocolate liquor increase the amount of soda by $1/_2$ oz. for each pound of Dutched cocoa replaced and reduce the amount of baking powder by 1 oz.

MIXING

When adding cocoa to a yellow or white mix allowances must be made for the absorption properties of cocoa. During roasting the cocoa is made more absorbent. The rule that may be used is: reduce the weight of the flour in the mix 6 oz. for each pound of cocoa used. This will eliminate binding and toughness. When making a yellow cake chocolate it is best to add melted chocolate for it contains more cocoa butter and will prevent extreme toughness. In addition 3 oz. of milk and $1/_4$ oz. of soda should be added to the mix for each pound of melted chocolate added. If cocoa is added to the mix it is best to dissolve the cocoa in milk with some additional sugar and melted fat and then add to the mix. Of course there must also be an increase in the amount of leavening depending upon the type and amount of cocoa used.

When adding cocoa to cake mixes it is best to cream or blend the cocoa in with the sugar and shortening when making creamed or blended cake mixes. For chocolate sponge or angel cake it is best to sift the cocoa with the flour and then fold into the mix in the last stage of mixing. When adding cocoa to custards and other cooked fillings it is best to dissolve the cocoa in part of the milk or water with the thickening agent (starch) before adding to the boiling milk or water. Allowances must be made for the absorption properties of the cocoa. A reduction in the amount of starch is necessary.

When adding chocolate to a mix it is best to have the chocolate melted and then added to the creaming sugar and shortening or to the first stage of a blended mix. Very often the chocolate is added to the mix with cool water or milk in the last stages and this causes the chocolate to lump. This is due to the lower temperature which causes the chocolate to solidify, and it is distributed in small lump form in the mix which causes unequal color in the baked product. When chocolate is folded into the mix in the final stage it should be poured around and over the mix and then folded gently a few times. The best example is in the marbling of Wonder cakes or marbled cheese cakes.

Chocolate reacts quickly to extreme changes in temperature. Its color and flavor are affected. For example, it is not uncommon to see chocolate placed in direct contact with intense heat to melt it quickly. This causes scorching and a burned taste. It also causes the chocolate to firm or harden in the scorched parts. The inexperienced baker tends to add milk to soften the chocolate and the chocolate becomes even firmer. This is due to the quick absorption of the liquid by the starch and still further firming results. The addition of oil or melted fat may help to soften the chocolate. Chocolate which has been heated to a high temperature or chilled very quickly tends to turn gray. This is due to the fact that the cocoa butter melts quickly and separates by floating to the surface. When cooled the grayish color appears. This does not harm the taste of the chocolate but does result in a poor appearance. Chocolate should be melted in a double boiler of warm water. For quick solution scrape the bar of chocolate into fine shavings or cut into small pieces. A common practice is to place the chocolate near the heat of the oven. This causes chocolate to melt and harden time and again as the heat intensity changes, and accounts for the discoloration as well as the lumping that takes place.

Flavoring Chocolate Cakes and Icings

Chocolate, as mentioned previously, has a characteristic taste and flavor. It is a dominant flavor and should not be overshadowed by the addition of large amounts of other flavors. Vanilla is an excellent supplement and a small amount of a good grade should be used. Almond and rum in small quantities will add to the flavor and give a variety of chocolate flavors. They must not be used to the point where the flavor of the chocolate is lost or a conflict in flavor exists. There are also chocolate flavor supplements which will strengthen the natural flavor of the chocolate and these should be used carefully.

CHAPTER 9

Chemical Leavening Agents

The purpose of chemical leavening agents is to aerate a cake mix or dough, thereby making the resulting product light and porous. This action is a supplement to other factors, which will be considered, that results in good volume, tenderness, and consumer-appeal. Although the experienced baker takes for granted the quality of the leavening, this chapter will indicate the values of understanding the composition, action, and proper uses of the various chemical leavenings used in daily bakeshop production.

BAKING POWDER

Baking powders are mixtures of chemicals varying in nature and composition which react in the presence of moisture and heat to release a gas. The amount of gas, the speed of the reaction in the release of gas, and the effect upon the product require careful study. Baking powders may be classified as follows: (1) single action which release gas quickly upon contact with moisture and require quick handling of the product in which it is used; (2) slow acting which release very little gas at low temperature and require heat for the release of gas; and (3) multiple action which release a small amount of gas at low temperature and require oven temperature for full reaction. This is the most widely used baking powder.

Composition

According to U. S. Government standards, "Baking powder is a chemical leavening agent composed of acid-reacting materials and bicarbonate of soda, with or without starch or flour. It yields not less than 12 per cent of available carbon dioxide gas." The acid reacting materials in baking powders are: (1) tartaric acid or its salts, (2) acid salts of phosphoric acid, (3) compounds of aluminum, or (4) any combination of the foregoing.

Single-acting powders are composed of tartaric acids or cream of tartar. Slow-acting powders are composed of phosphates (e.g., mono-calcium phosphate) which are not soluble at low temperatures. These types are not often used by bakers. Double-action powders are composed of (S.A.S.) sodium aluminum sulfate or sodium acid pyrophosphate and the mono-calcium phosphates. This makes a partial solution and minor release of gas at low temperature with a maximum release of gas at oven temperature. The purpose of the starch filler is to stabilize the baking powder by keeping the acid salts from contacting the bicarbonate of soda and it prevents reaction if moisture should get into the baking powder. Protection against moisture is quite limited and the baker should not carelessly expose baking powder to the atmosphere for any considerable time. The starch filler also acts as a means of standardizing the strength of the baking powder. For example, the average baking powder contains from 23 to 30 per cent corn starch. It should not be assumed, as is commonly done, that a proper balance of 60 per cent acid and 35 per cent soda with the addition of the remainder in the form of corn starch makes a proper baking powder recipe since each of the baking acids has a different strength.

The Action of Baking Powder

This is best explained in flow chart form.

FLOW CHART INDICATING THE ACTION OF BAKING POWDER

Baking powder composed of	Placed in the oven which provides the necessary heat
Bicarbonate of soda and acid-reacting materials	For the complete reaction of the bicarbonate of soda with the acid salts
mixed into	This produces the final maximum amount of carbon dioxide which assists in raising the product containing the residual baking powder salts
Cake mix or dough which contains the aqueous liquid	
Causing the solution and reaction of the bicarbonate of soda and the acid salts	The finished leavened and baked product is stiffened so that it is able to support itself after cooling
Resulting in partial release of carbon dioxide gas (CO_2)	

CARBONATES

Soda

Baking soda reacts much the same as baking powder except that the necessary acid must be provided by the ingredients used in the mix. For example, honey, molasses, cocoa, and other slightly acidic materials provide some of the necessary acid required by the bicarbonate of soda for reaction and release of carbon dioxide gas. The baker must be careful and understand that the action of baking soda is rapid and similar to the action of single-action baking powder. Mixes or doughs leavened with bicarbonate of soda must be handled without much delay for the release of the gases may be almost complete before placing the product into the oven. Delay will cause a loss in volume. Use of any substantial

amount of soda without added acid results in an alkaline reaction in the
baked product and may cause yellowing of normally white crumb and
undesirable odors and flavors.

Ammonium Bicarbonate

Ammonium bicarbonate reacts very rapidly in the presence of moisture
and heat, and so it is used in special products such as cookies, eclair and cream
puff shells, drop cakes, and Jewish Kichel. Its action is similar to that of bicarbonate of soda and products leavened by it should be handled without
delay and baked as quickly as possible.

ACTION OF CHEMICAL LEAVENING AGENTS

Chemical leavening agents, such as baking powder, are not the only
means of leavening products. The creaming of shortening with other
ingredients, the whipping of eggs, or blending of mixes or doughs are
equally important. Let us examine what actually happens in the mixing
and baking process. During the mixing stages air cells are formed and
trapped. These increase in number as mixing or whipping continues up
to a certain point. When the product is placed in the oven the chemical
leavening releases gas (CO_2). This gas is largely absorbed into the air
cells created during mixing causing these cells to expand. This results
in the desired volume, grain, and texture of the product.

Although mixing methods will be discussed in another chapter (Chapter
27), it will be noted that recipes indicate that a lesser amount of baking
powder or other chemical leavening is required in mixes that are creamed
or whipped than in those which are blended. This also applies to cakes
that have a larger percentage of eggs. For example, less leavening is
used in Wonder cake mix than in a high-ratio mix. This indicates that
the amount of eggs and the method of mixing have a distinct bearing
upon the amount of leavening. The amount of leavening may vary from
less than 1 per cent to as much as 7 per cent, based upon the weight of
the flour.

Because chemical leavening agents are alkaline (bicarbonate of soda)
and/or acidic (e.g., cream of tartar) in nature, they have a definite effect
upon specific products. For example, chocolate cakes very often use
both baking powder and baking soda. This is to produce a desirable
product in terms of color, taste, and eating qualities. Briefly, cocoa and
chocolate contain, naturally, an excess of acidity. To counteract this, to
keep the pH at a desirable level, and at the same time gain the desired
volume baking soda is used in conjunction with baking powder. The
soda, which is alkaline, neutralizes part of the acidity and provides a

darker chocolate color (p. 40). An examination of chocolate cake products will illustrate this point.

In Yeast Doughs

Baking powder is often used in conjunction with yeast doughs. For example, special doughnut mixes such as World's Fair doughnuts use both yeast and baking powder. This is to provide a more cake-like doughnut than is obtained with the use of yeast alone. Such doughs are made up and fried or baked after a short resting period of approximately $1/2$ hr. The normal fermentation period of yeast doughs is avoided. The acid action of baking powder over a lengthy period tends to weaken the gluten and results in an adverse effect upon the grain and texture of the baked product. Such mixes are refrigerated and retarded if not used quickly.

The amount of leavening required, as mentioned above, is largely dependent upon the nature of the recipe and type of product. Judgment must be employed. One fallacy must be rectified: more baking powder does not necessarily mean more volume. If eggs are replaced naturally the recipe must be balanced and more leavening used. It must be understood that open-grain, crumbly texture, cakes falling during baking, and other faults can be caused by excessive baking powder. By the same token, small volume, dense structure, shrinkage, and other faults may be attributed to the lack of leavening.

Chemical Leavening and Mixing Time

Although the various methods of mixing will be discussed in more detail in another section it is important to note that an increase in leavening will not make up for a decrease in mixing time. For example, it takes time (controlled by other conditions such as shop temperature, materials, etc.) to cream or whip a mix. Improperly mixed batters, resulting in a loss in the amount of aeration normally achieved, cannot be balanced by an increase in baking powder. Density, channels and holes, and lack of volume are some of the resulting characteristics present in the product, if this is done. At the same time mixing machines are often left running in second or high speed because bench or oven work prevents proper attention to mixing. Overmixing means a loss of aeration and cannot be replaced by the chemical leavening.

Chemical Leavening and Freezing and Retardation

Little or no leavening activity occurs in frozen, unbaked mixes or doughs. A state of suspended animation exists in the case of yeast or combinations of yeast and chemically leavened mixes. Under normal refrigeration (35° to

40° F.) a small amount of gas release takes place during the initial stages of refrigeration. At the same time, if the unbaked mix has been chilled throughout action of the chemical leavening ceases. The common question, "How long can unbaked mixes be kept under normal refrigeration without losing the effect of the leavening?" may be answered by stating that at a temperature of 38° F., 48 hr. would be the safe limit. In the frozen state different products react differently. In the most favorable cases moderately good results may be obtained after a storage period between three months to one year. However, the batters should be properly covered and wrapped when placed in the freezer. Moisture loss through sublimation must be prevented during long storage periods by tight wrapping in moisture-proof sheets or sheeting.

Frozen or normally retarded mixes should be defrosted or returned to shop temperature before baking. The ingredients, such as fats, eggs, and the liquid, are in a frozen or crystalline state; and placing frozen or chilled mixes immediately into the oven causes rapid melting of the external parts of the mix and a reaction of the chemical leavening in the melted parts. The released gas is not completely absorbed by the aerated cells in a frozen or chilled state. Unless these cells can absorb and expand at a rate which will enable them to absorb the released gases a loss in volume will result. Further refrigerating practices are discussed in a special section on freezing and retardation (Chapter 10).

STORAGE OF CHEMICAL LEAVENINGS

While it is true that the can of baking powder must be opened frequently during the work day and that constant removal of the cover of the can may be a nuisance, chemical leavening agents should always be tightly covered when not in use. Aside from the possible loss due to spillage, there is always the presence of moisture in the shop. Despite the fact that the starch filler acts as separator there is a limit to the amount of moisture the starch may absorb. A heavy flow of steam from the oven, at the time of baking hard rolls or bread, may saturate the surface of the exposed leavening and cause a loss in gassing power. This is especially true of the very volatile ammonium bicarbonate and of bicarbonate of soda which do not contain a starch filler.

CHAPTER 10

The Staling of Bakery Products

Why baked products stale and how they stale have been questions which have long been under careful study and research. While scientific progress has been made and experiment and testing of bakery products have indicated cause and effect of staling, no definite theory that completely explains staling has been determined. Staling is the greatest problem of the retail baker and is also a problem to larger producers of bakery products. Many measures have been taken by small and large producers to overcome the losses resulting from staling. This chapter will explain as simply as possible the cause, effect, and procedures recommended to reduce and control the rate of staling in bakery products.

Any baked product that has a soft, spongy body made possible by moisture is subject to staling. This fact applies to bread and roll products as well as cakes and sweet yeast dough products. Products containing more moisture tend to stale faster unless the moisture content can be kept at the same level as it was at the time the product was baked. The higher the moisture level maintained the slower the rate of staling.

BREAD AND HARD-TYPE PRODUCTS

With regard to bread and other hard-type bakery products there are two distinct areas of staling that are complete variance with each other and yet occur in the same product at the same time. The staling of the crust of the bread is different from that of the body or crumb of the bread. The crust is crisp and dry when freshly baked. As staling sets in it becomes moist and tough with a loss in flavor and taste. This is due to the transfer of moisture from the interior to the crust. The moisture is then spread throughout the crust, creating moistness and toughness. In moist, humid weather this toughness becomes worse because the crust will absorb moisture from the air. In fact, packaging bread often accelerates the rate of staling because the excess moisture in the crust cannot be evaporated.

Staling in the body or crumb may appear to be a drying effect. However, very little change in moisture content occurs in crumb staling. This phenomenon is due to a change in the physical nature of the starch molecules. The following experiment illustrates crumb staling. Baked units were placed under conditions which prevented moisture loss, and after 24 to 48 hr. staling was shown to have set in. However, the units that were tested were able to be freshened by heating again. It was also found that the bread units containing less than 30 per cent moisture could not be re-heated with good results. Further tests showed that staling was the result of the firming up of the starch gel formed in baking. This is called starch retrogradation. If it has not proceeded too far it can be reversed by heating. Of course, if the crumb is allowed to dry out, as by exposing slices of bread, a firming action also occurs and this may be indistinguishable from that caused by starch retrogradation. Staling may be unnoticed by the consumer and by many bakers. Staling begins as soon as baking is completed. Since freshness is commonly measured by softness the sense of touch indicates acceptable bread to the baker and to the consumer. This freshness or softness of the crumb is prolonged by packaging in moisture-proof paper wrappers. Wrapping does not delay the chemical staling that takes place but does prevent excessive loss. Packaging also helps to keep in the flavor of the bread.

Unwrapped bread dries and stales faster than wrapped bread. The crumb or body of the bread dries just below the crust of the bread in the first 24 hr. It is this dryness and resistance to the touch or feel that indicates staling. This is more pronounced in bread products made from lean doughs. They have an open grain structure and contain less moisture after baking. This is typical of French, Italian, Vienna, and other hard-type breads and rolls. This is another reason for careful production planning and the value of retarding and freezing doughs and made-up units.

In Sour Rye, Raisin, and Cinnamon Breads

Staling is not as rapid in sour rye bread, raisin, and cinnamon breads, and others made from richer doughs. Rye flour, because of its fine, absorbent, starch particles, tends to retain the moisture gel. Rye flour contains components which do not retrograde and hold water for long times. In addition, the close structure of the heavier types of rye and pumpernickel bread also retain moisture. Since all bread is not of the sour rye variety other factors may be considered to reduce the rate of staling.

To Reduce Staling

The use of milk powder helps to retain moisture and reduce the rate of starch retrogradation. Use of malt syrup helps retain moisture and delays staling. The use of limited amounts of soy flour (up to 5 per cent based on the total weight of the flour) is helpful in that it delays the separation of the gel of the starch in the body of the bread. An increase in fat content will help in retaining the tenderness of the loaf. High-gluten flours also aid in retaining moisture since they absorb more liquid during mixing. Doughs may be made slacker when using a high-gluten flour since they stiffen somewhat during fermentation. Proper fermentation is important in that doughs that are overfermented or allowed to develop a crust by exposure during fermentation will result in products that will stale faster. Staling is slowed by the presence of mono-glyceride emulsifiers.

CAKES AND SWEET YEAST GOODS

Since cakes and other sweet yeast goods have soft, spongy crumbs or interiors they do not stale as rapidly as bread and roll products made from lean doughs. Also, they do not have as large a proportion of starch to retrograde. Examination of the ingredient contents of these products indicates that they are rich in most of the moisture-retaining ingredients. The sugar is a tenderizer and forms a syrup when dissolved in the liquid of the mix. The large percentage of fat in cakes and sweet doughs increases the richness and naturally tends to absorb and hold the moisture. It also prevents starch retrogradation in the crumb of sweet yeast dough products. The egg yolks act as emulsifiers and allow added liquid in the recipe. The whole egg and egg white add additional moisture naturally and are balanced for their drying effect by the addition of added liquid.

Cakes and sweet yeast doughs have higher percentages of liquid in the form of milk or water. Many of these products are made with syrups added, such as molasses, corn syrup, invert syrup, and paste. These are hygroscopic agents and tend to retain moisture or absorb it from the air. Good examples of these are Jewish honey cake, molasses spice cake and holiday fruit cakes made with both honey and molasses.

The flours used in cakes and cookies are nearly always soft flours. This is particularly so in the production of high-ratio-type cakes. Notice the increased liquid, sugar, and fine cake flour in the recipes. The increased particles of fine quality supplied by the flour tend to absorb and retain moisture before and after baking. Examine the keeping qualities of high-ratio cakes and cakes made from the usual creaming method of mixing, such as wine cake. Cakes of close grain and rich in fat content stale at a slower rate than others. This is especially noticeable in pound cakes made on a pound for pound basis, as compared with other cakes made with more liquid in the form of milk. The fat maintains the richness and the close grain avoids rapid transfer of liquid in the chemical staling that takes place in all products.

In Cookies

The high percentage of fat and lesser amount of liquid in cookies make possible the longer shelf-life for cookies. You will note that short dough cookies or shortbread cookies keep longer than cookies which contain liquid in the form of milk and eggs. In fact, the shelf-life of rich cookies is more dependent upon the stability of the fat than the effect of staling. In contrast to the long shelf-life of cookies is the rapid drying and staling of straight sponge cake made with only the liquid of eggs.

To Retard Staling

The use of paper liners helps to retain freshness of cakes and other bakery products. It is advisable to bake as many products as possible in liners and containers. For example, a loaf cake baked in a liner will not be as exposed to staling as are the outside crusts of loaves baked directly in a pan and then removed after baking. As a test, bake some Babka loaves in paper liners and some in greased loaf pans. Those baked without liners will tend to stale or dry faster. This also applies to cupcakes. Large cakes which are cut and sold by weight dry quickly when exposed. While turnover or sale may be rapid, the exposed grain of the cake tends to lose moisture and consequently stales. These cakes should be covered or cut into portions and the sides encased in waxed paper or in a fine, thin wrap.

Role of Icings

Icings play an important part in the keeping qualities of cakes. A finished layer is completely encased by the icing and the bottom liner. The icing has much to do with freshness, depending upon the type of icing used. Flat icings do not have a lasting effect. In fact, icings which do not contain a small amount of fat and are not prepared properly will tend to absorb moisture from the cake. Such icings may peel from the sides of the cake after several hours. The best practice is to coat the sides and top of the cake to be iced with a flat or fondant icing with a thin coating of buttercream. The fat in the buttercream will prevent moisture absorption in addition to making the application of the icing a smoother and neater operation (see procedures for finishing layer cakes). Fudge and buttercream icings are both well-suited to the retention of moisture. The fat and sugar combination is more of a moisture barrier than is sugar and water and helps to prevent rapid staling.

RETARDING AND FREEZING IN RELATION TO STALING

Retarding and freezing have been mentioned in other sections related to the production of various types of bakery products. There is no question concerning the value of the retarder and freezer in controlling staling. The efficient use of these pieces of equipment depends upon the facilities of the bakeshop and the method of operation. There always seems to be a lack of space and equipment. However, the freezer and retarder must be used efficiently for maximum return in the control of staling.

While the common approach is to bake first and then freeze, this seems to be that of the sales approach of the large producers who do not deal directly with the consumer. The principal sales power of the retail baker is the aroma of freshly baked products and the appearance of freshly finished and decorated cakes. If the work schedule can be so arranged, periodic baking of the same products at intervals during the sales day is superior to the "take it out of the freezer approach" and selling products frozen. A warm, fresh pan of Danish pastry is superior in sales value to the frozen variety. A fresh, hot pie will sell faster than the frozen variety which the consumer defrosts and reheats if desired. The pie can be boxed in a special freezer box at the time of sale and then frozen by the consumer. The consumer is pleased to know that the pie was fresh when frozen. Prepared, sandwiched, and prime-coated layers can be kept in the freezer and finished when the production needs require them.

Freshly made-up units can be placed in the retarder for 24 hr. and baked the next day or as demand may warrant within the period. A week-end build up of made-up units of sweet yeast doughs (unbaked) may be stored in the freezer and then prepared for sale as needed. French pastries, cream and chocolate rolls, and other such products, should be made during the slack part of the week and stored in the freezer. Ice cream cakes and logs are the usual freezer items. A good sampling of the products available in your freezer, ready to be baked or finished, should be on display in the open-faced store freezer. An exposed retarder box with many of the whipped cream and other products should be present. This is an excellent sales promoter. It cannot be stressed too strongly that a fresh bake of variety bakery products is a sales-builder. Even the warm-up of frozen units that were frozen after a "just baked" state and known as "just done," is far better than the sale of the frozen product or frozen-defrosted product.

CHAPTER 11

Basic Operations in Bread Making

While the subject of yeast and its function in fermentation and conditioning doughs has been partially covered in previous chapters (see Chapter 6 especially), this chapter will review all the major steps and operations involved in the preparation and handling of yeast-raised doughs for bread and rolls. It is hoped that an understanding of the changes occurring during fermentation and the factors that affect fermentation will contribute to better and more consistent production of bread and rolls. Each of the operations will be treated in the sequence normally followed in production.

DOUGH MIXING

The principal objectives of mixing are: (1) thorough and complete distribution of the ingredients, and (2) maximum gluten development. Accuracy in scaling is necessary. This is especially true of salt, for salt has a direct effect upon the rate of fermentation, conditioning, and the taste of the product. Over- or under-scaling salt will lead to poor results. While the other dry ingredients, sugar and milk powder, should be scaled with care, a slight variation in their amounts will not have as bad an effect than one with salt. The principal areas of guesswork in the retail shop are the weighing or measuring of the water and the flour. True, a two- or three-pail dough would be difficult to measure to the ounce, but the 16- or 20-qt. pails should be properly filled. A variation of 2 or 3 qt. more or less will make the difference of a slack or stiff dough. In either case, added flour or water may mean the overmixing with harmful effect on the dough.

In the mixing of sponge doughs for bread and rolls, up to 50 to 75 per cent of the flour is used in preparing the sponge. The sponge is made with about 60 to 70 per cent of the water, depending upon the amount and type of the flour (stronger flours require softer sponges), malt (if used), part of the sugar, and added minerals or yeast food. Stiffer sponges require a longer fermentation period with better volume and gluten development. The sponge is covered and placed in a warm place to rise. In large plants a special fermentation room with controlled temperatures and humidity is used. Sponge time will vary with conditions: water temperature, amount of yeast, and temperature of the shop. It will vary from 3 to $4\frac{1}{2}$ hr. The test for sponge readiness is the point of maximum rise and fall. This will be noticed in the sponge trough. It

54

is common practice to allow the sponge to stand for about 20 min. after it starts to recede to allow maximum development of the sponge and the gluten. The sponge is then placed in the machine and the remaining dough ingredients are added and the dough mixed.

In the straight dough process the ingredients are mixed at one time. The dry ingredients are mixed with the liquid until thoroughly dissolved, the flour is drawn in and mixed until most of the liquid has been absorbed and the lumpy mass is formed. The yeast solution is added and the dough mixing is completed. Where a small percentage of fat is used in the dough the fat is added after the yeast is mixed in and the dough is allowed to develop. Where oil is used, as in a Kaiser roll dough, the oil is added at the beginning of mixing with the water. The length of mixing operation is very important. The time required for mixing is dependent upon the speed of the machine. A medium speed is best. The completion of mixing is generally noted by the "clean-up" stage. It is at that point the dough removes all dough particles from the sides of the machine and the dough is a smooth, elastic mass. The experienced baker can tell when the mixing is complete by the appearance and feel of the dough. The large plants have automatically controlled mixers. Stiff doughs reach the clean-up stage faster than slack doughs. The common fault in the retail shop is to allow for a little extra mixing; this results in the dough reaching the "let down" stage. At this point, the dough becomes slack, inelastic, and a tearing effect is noticed.

Most doughs are normally taken from the mixer at a temperature of 78° to 80°F. Variations due to weather conditions or production schedule will necessitate higher or lower temperatures. The common problem in summer production in retail shops is doughs becoming old. That is they over-ferment. To prevent this shaved ice is usually added or the amount of yeast used is reduced. Ice water may be used to obtain a slow rate of fermentation. One pound of shaved ice will reduce the temperature of a 16-qt. pail of dough approximately 7° or 8°F. An exact formula may be used to determine the amount of ice to be used. Where ice is not used the water temperature may be figured by a simple formula as follows:

1. Multiply the desired dough temperature by 3:

$$78°F. \times 3 = 234°F.$$

2. Add the temperature of machine friction, flour, and shop:

Machine friction	36°F.
Flour temperature	70
Shop temperature	+80
	186°F.

3. Subtract this total (No. 2) from the total of dough temperature times three (No. 1):

$$234°F.$$
$$-186$$
$$48°F.$$

4. The result is the temperature of the water: 48°F.

FERMENTATION

The mixed dough is placed in a fermentation room in a large plant with a temperature of 80°F. and a humidity of 75 per cent. In the small shop it is placed in a dough trough with enough space to ferment, to prevent crust formation, and to avoid drafts. Yeast activity begins slowly and increases as fermentation proceeds (the action of the yeast enzymes has been explained in Chapter 6). The volume of the dough increases due to the carbon dioxide gas resulting from the yeast action: The gluten is conditioned and mellowed and becomes elastic as a result of the effect of the alcohol and the lower acidity. The gluten forms thin walls which retain the gas and it is able to withstand the pressure of fermentation. The dough matures until it reaches maximum spring and elasticity.

Punching

When the dough has risen it is tested for punching. The test employed in the retail shop is to insert the fingers to the knuckles into the dough in several places. If the finger marks close very slowly the dough is ready to be punched. The insertion of the complete arm will rupture gluten and cause the dough to fall and give the impression that the dough is ready for punching. Punching is best done by folding the ends and the sides of the dough from one side of the trough to the other. The purpose of punching is: (1) to keep the dough at an even temperature by actually turning the dough inside out; (2) release the carbon dioxide gas which will restrict fermentation if allowed to concentrate; (3) introduce fresh oxygen which produces vigorous fermentation; and (4) to mechanically develop the gluten. The first punch usually takes place after about 50 per cent of the fermentation period has passed. The dough is given the second punch after an additional 30 per cent has passed. The remaining 10 per cent is used for scaling time. The rate or speed of fermentation is controlled by many factors. Primarily yeast is the basic factor in speeding it up or slowing it down. Shop and water temperature are the next important factors in hastening or retarding fermentation.

The amount of yeast used to speed up or slow down fermentation may be calculated quite accurately and simply without guesswork. This formula may be used: the amount of yeast normally used multiplied by the fermentation time, divided by the new fermentation time, will give you the amount of yeast to obtain the desired product or:

$$\frac{\text{Original yeast} \times \text{fermentation time}}{\text{New fermentation time}} = \frac{\text{Amount of yeast required for new}}{\text{fermentation time}}$$

For example:

$$\frac{1.5 \text{ lb. yeast} \times 4 \text{ hr.}}{3 \text{ hr.}} = 2 \text{ lb. yeast}$$

SCALING

Scaling the dough should be done as quickly and accurately as possible. The dough continues to ferment during scaling and delay will cause over fermentation of the last unit scaled. Quick scaling will maintain an even fermentation throughout. For large dough lots the scaling period should take no longer than 15 min. In large plants using automatic dividers and scalers, slacker doughs are less subject than stiffer dough to gluten damage from the pressure required to force doughs into the pockets of the dividers. Allowances for loss in baking are made at the time of scaling. Approximately $1^1/_2$ to 2 oz. of dough are added for each 1 lb. loaf of baked bread. This accounts for a loss of about 12 or 13 per cent by evaporation during baking.

Rounding the Dough

When the dough is scaled, especially in a retail shop, the dough usually is in uneven, exposed pieces. There is a loss of gas. The pieces are in poor shape to be molded into various bread shapes. Rounding provides a skin around the dough to hold the gas in, eliminates the stickiness of the dough, and consequently less dusting flour is required at the time the dough is shaped into loaves.

INTERMEDIATE OR OVERHEAD PROOFING

This is a short resting period of about 8 to 12 min. in which the rounded pieces of dough are relaxed. Fermentation continues and the pieces become gassy and the gluten relaxed for ease in handling the dough. In large plants the rounded pieces are placed in overhead proofers which contain pockets and move at a controlled speed to the molder. In the retail shop the rounded pieces are placed in a cabinet proofer at a humidity of 75 per cent to prevent heavy crust formation, or they are placed in boxes squarely covering each other as they are stacked. It is important to avoid heavy crustation. The crust will remain in the unit and will cause a gummy streak in the baked product. At this point, rounded units may be retarded in the retail shops if the weather or production schedule so requires.

Molding

At this point the dough should be properly conditioned. The rested units lend themselves well to shaping. A minimum of dusting flour should be used. For hard-type products, such as Vienna bread, rye bread, Kaiser rolls, etc., rye flour is used as the dusting flour because of its softness. It does not cause toughening or drying of the pieces of dough. Too much dusting flour will cause separation of the rolled dough and lead to open seams. These seams open in baking and are the cause of "cripples." In large plants special dusting flours are used to eliminate sticking in the molder.

PANNING

The made-up units are placed in clean, greased bread pans or are placed in boxes containing white cornmeal or a blend of cornmeal and rye flour. In some cases, as for French bread, the molded units are placed on dusted bread peels before proofing. These peels are then attached to special poles for loading into the oven. This avoids handling proofed units. An important factor is that of placing the units in the pans or boxes with the seam down and in the center bottom of the bread. This will eliminate the possibility of opening during baking or proofing. With regard to the size of the bread pan, approximately 6 cu. in. of space are required for each ounce of dough. This may be ascertained by finding the cubic capacity of the pan and then determining the amount of dough best suited for the pan.

PROOFING

This is a very important part of the production of yeast-raised products. Errors, such as under- or over-proofing, cannot be rectified. The average temperature of the proofbox or proofing room is 95° to 98°F. with humidity of 80 to 85 per cent. While this is controlled in large plants it is difficult for accurate control in the retail shops. Most bread and rolls are proofed in the boxes in which they have been placed. Those with large proofboxes will roll the boxes into the steam box. Others cannot. The major problem is careful changing of the first boxes to the top and the last boxes to the bottom. This is necessary in order to load the fully proofed units into the oven first. In the steam box the major problem is the use of excess steam which may cause the outside of the units to proof faster than the interior. This causes open grain and texture on the outside of the baked unit and close grain on the inside. Forced steam will also cause the outside of the unit to tear while the unit is not fully proofed. Proof is usually tested by feel as well as appearance. When touched gently a unit that is fully proofed will fill out the dents slowly. Underproofed units can be given maximum proof. Rich dough units should be placed in the oven before complete proofing is reached. Otherwise, the richness of the dough exerts extra weight on the gluten and may cause a collapse in baking or caved-in sides.

BAKING

Baking changes the dough to an appetizing, digestible product. Hardtype products are generally baked with steam. The following changes take place in the dough during baking. A moist film covers the unit placed in the oven. This is due to either the steam injected into the oven or the wash applied to the product before placing it in the oven. "Oven spring" or the rapid rise of the unit during the first few minutes of baking is caused by: (1) the release of carbon dioxide gas; (2) the expansion of the gas in the cells created during the fermentation period; (3) the evaporation of the alcohol at 175°F.; and (4) the continued rapid activity of the yeast until it is destroyed at 140°F. The dough is softened at this stage and the unit should not be touched or it will collapse. The starch granules start to swell at 130°F. There is a transfer of moisture from the other ingredients to the starch granules. The granules swell and become fixed in the gluten network. Part of the moisture in the gluten is removed by the starch granules and the gluten is strengthened and becomes more viscous (soft and elastic). The support of the structure of the dough, at this time, is supplied by the gelatinized starch. The gel formation draws more moisture from the gluten and causes the gluten to dehydrate. Coagulation or setting of the gluten begins at 165°F. and continues until the product is baked.

The greatest pressures are exerted in the initial stages of baking. They are reduced as baking continues and the cells merge and the release of gas slows up. The interior temperature of the unit does not go beyond 212°F. because the evaporation of the moisture and alcohol prevents a further rise. The crust is formed by the exposed starch and sugar at the surface of the dough. The sugar and starch are dextrinized and form the crust color of the product. Where sugar is not used in a dough the starch dextrins provides the basis for crust color.

Baking time is determined by the size of the unit, the richness of the unit, crust color desired, and often by the weather. Large units require a longer baking time than small units. Leaner dough units require higher oven baking temperature and bake faster than units made from a rich dough. Hard-type bread and rolls require a well baked crust.

CHAPTER 12

Egg Bread, French and Italian Bread, Hard and Soft Rolls

Egg bread or challah, as it is known from its Jewish origin, is a variety bread of great popularity among people of all faiths. Made properly the challah is very tasty and very attractive.

French and Italian breads are bread specialties which should have greater sales in many retail bakeshops. These breads are generally made by bakeshops that specialize in their production. Many bakers purchase these breads and resell them; however greater sales and prestige accrue to the baker that makes and bakes them on the premises.

Hard and soft rolls are a "must" in the bakeshop. Every baker in every establishment that sells or serves food should be able to make an assortment of fresh variety rolls. This unit will stress the important factors or points related to the production of these breads and rolls.

EGG BREAD

Egg bread or challah is made from a dough which has a high percentage of eggs. The eggs provide for added richness, increased volume, better keeping qualities, as well as supply additional structure-building protein. They also cause the dough to dry out rapidly. Extra fat, in the form of vegetable oil, is added to the dough to overcome the drying. The amount of sugar used is larger than that for pan bread. The sugar is a tenderizer. If egg yolks containing sugar are used in the dough, the amount of sugar should be reduced. If the amount of eggs is high, e.g., 1 lb. for every quart of water used for the dough, the salt should be increased by $1/4$ oz. for each quart of dough. The flour must be of fine quality and have a high-gluten content. The flour must make a stiff dough without tearing and must be able to withstand shaping of the braided strands of dough. In addition, a strong gluten is necessary to maintain the shape of the challah during the proofing and baking stages.

The mixing time is shorter because the dough is stiff and develops quickly, therefore care should be used to avoid overdeveloping and tearing.

The dough is given a shorter fermentation period. The period between the first and second punch is shortened and the dough taken to the bench slightly on the young side. This is to provide the extra time required for the makeup of the bread without allowing the last units to become old.

Remember that it takes longer to braid these breads than to shape or mold the average loaf of pan bread.

It is often advisable to place some of the presses of dough in the retarder to prevent the dough from becoming old. This may be necessary when large doughs are made or the weather is warm and humid. If made-up units are to be retarded, the challah which has been placed in loaf pans should be retarded or frozen; in this form it is easier to store in the refrigerator as the pans can be stacked.

Examine the recipe and procedure for makeup of the challah (p. 78). A point is made of the fact that too many presses of dough should not be pressed out at once if there is not enough help to make up the egg bread before the units of dough ferment into each other. One of the common faults of braided egg breads lies in the fact that the strands are not shaped properly and evenly. Each strand should be molded so that all large air pockets are removed. This will avoid large holes in the baked bread. The strands should be of equal size and shape. Stretching one or several of the strands while braiding will cause a pulling effect upon the bread while it is proofing and baking, and consequently bread will have a poor shape. Be sure the strands are dusted with rye flour before braiding. This will keep the strands separate and distinct during proofing and baking and avoid "blindness" wherein the strands bake into each other.

Challah should be given three-fourths proof before baking. The challah is washed again before baking and very often has to be placed on peels to be baked on the hearth. More than three-fourths proof may cause the bread to fall back when handled or may cause the units to lose shape and volume. The challah is baked in a relatively cool oven because of its characteristic richness and the crispness. The temperature for baking 1 lb. loaves is about 340°F. Larger units require a lower temperature. Of course, egg dough rolls require higher temperature since they are small units. The challah should be tapped at the bottom before removing from the oven. There should be a hollow sound to insure proper bake. The color should be light brown to a darker shade. Some bakers prefer a darker crust color.

FRENCH AND ITALIAN BREADS

French and Italian breads are made from a lean dough. They are similar doughs except for the fact that French bread dough has a small amount of malt or sugar added. Some Italian breads also contain malt. The flour used for these breads must have a high-gluten content to withstand the strong fermentation, large proof and strong "oven spring" in the first stages of baking. The dough for these breads is well developed in mixing and high-speed mixers are advisable. These breads lend themselves well to automatic scaling, rounding, and shaping.

The baker would do well to make separate doughs for each of these bread varieties rather than follow the procedure for making one dough for hard rolls and taking pieces for dough for some of the French- and Italian-shaped breads. These breads do not have the same airy, open, light grain and texture with the hard, crisp crust resulting from a lean dough. A Vienna dough for Kaiser rolls is much too rich. Refer to the recipe for the French and Italian breads for proper procedures to follow in handling the made-up units before baking. Wash the loaves before cutting. Cut them just before peeling into the oven. Very often the breads are placed on dusted peels as soon as made up and placed in the steam box to proof. Be sure there is enough cornmeal on the peels so that peeling into the oven after proofing, washing and cutting is easy and the breads do not stick to the peels.

These breads must be baked to a dry, crisp state. Avoid baking them in a flashy oven or one in which the temperature is too high. Allow the steam to enter the oven for a few minutes before loading. Allow the moist steam to continue until the loaves have had full spring and start to take on a light crust color.

The heavier, close-grained Italian loaves are made from a stiffer dough which is given a shorter proofing period. This accounts for the close grain and texture of the loaf. A small percentage (not over 15 per cent) of whole-wheat and bran flour are added to Italian bread doughs for variety. The bran gives a light brown coloring throughout and offers a nut-like flavor to the loaf. These breads are handled in the same way as the other Italian loaves. They may be given a shorter proof. Made-up units that are not baked may be placed in the retarder for several hours and baked as needed. Cover them to prevent crust formation. It is best to freeze a slightly underbaked loaf as soon as it is removed from the oven and cooled to shop temperature. The loaves can be defrosted and then placed in a steam-filled oven for a few minutes to restore full crispness and crust color to the loaf.

HARD ROLLS

Hard-type rolls such as club rolls, onion rolls, salt sticks, crescents, and Kaiser rolls are very popular. Of all of these, the Kaiser roll is the most popular. The dough for these rolls varies with the individual bakeshop. In fact, the doughs vary from the lean dough used for water rolls to the richer doughs containing eggs, malt, and oil used for Kaiser rolls. Less sugar is needed if malt syrup is used in the dough (see recipe p. 82). The addition of egg yolks to the dough will increase the volume and improve the crispness and keeping qualities of the roll. On the other hand, the water roll is made from a lean dough and bakes with a harder crust that is thicker than the rolls made from a Vienna dough for Kaiser rolls. For quality, the retail baker would do well to make his rolls from a richer dough. The flour used should be of excellent quality and high-gluten content to withstand full dough development, vigorous fermentation bench tolerance, full proof and good oven spring. Refer to the recipe and procedure for makeup of each of the various types of rolls. Stress is placed upon the variation and use of machines to make Kaiser rolls. The Kaiser-roll shaping machine makes the rolls with straight cuts and little overlapping of the cuts. The cuts are also perfectly equal. In addition, the machine requires a finer dusting flour than the rye flour used for the hand-made rolls. This often results in some blindness of the cuts in the roll. The hand-made rolls are uneven. However, the overlapping folds, the separation of the folds during baking, and the rose-like appearance may aid sales. The hand-made rolls require a stiffer dough than those made by machine. Large pockets or blisters are eliminated in the hand-made roll. There are decided advantages in both methods for production and often rolls made from both methods are made in the same shop.

These rolls have a firm, crisp crust. The are baked in hot—but not flashy—ovens at about 430°F. The steam injected into the oven reduces the temperature somewhat and also provides the full volume and crisp crust. The steam allows major expansion of the cuts in the Kaiser rolls or cuts placed in the club rolls. Blindness in Kaiser and other hard-type rolls is generally due to crust formation on the rolls before baking and the lack of steam during baking. Allowing the rolls to stand on the bench after makeup when they should be placed into boxes or on pans is the most common cause for crust formation prior to baking. Making rolls without the use of rye flour will have a drying effect on the crust and result in blindness. Care should be taken in proofing Kaiser rolls and other hard-type rolls which have to be peeled into the oven and baked on the hearth. The rolls should be given slightly less than full proof because they have to be picked up and placed on the cornmeal-dusted peels. Full proof may cause them to fall back. Full proof may also cause the rolls to stick to the boxes which contain either poppy seeds to prevent sticking (and for garnish) or to the canvas cloths used for the unseeded rolls.

SOFT ROLLS

Soft rolls are made from a richer type of dough. The dough usually contains more sugar and fat than hard-type rolls. The amount of eggs may be increased; however, the use of eggs in this dough is optional. Soft rolls made in the larger plants are generally made from doughs which do not contain eggs. However, the quality baker will use eggs for his rolls. A medium-hard type of flour is normally used for these rolls. Many bakers will use a short-patent flour which is not as strong in gluten content. The baked rolls are sweeter, softer, and have a finer grain and texture. Refer to the recipe for soft rolls for the procedure to follow in their makeup.

These rolls are given a little less than the maximum proof. They are baked in pans and generally are spaced so that the baked rolls touch slightly or fully after baking. This is the case for frankfurter and hamburger rolls. Other types, such as clover-leaf and butter-flake rolls, are baked in muffin tins after being given full proof. These rolls are given a quick bake with a mild amount of steam in the oven. The steam produces a thin crust and rapid crust-color formation. Rolls such as Parker House are often baked without steam but are brushed with milk or melted fat before baking and oftentimes brushed again with melted butter after baking.

Soft rolls are well-suited to retarding and freezing and the baker should make a good use of these practices in production. Retarding takes a refrigerator temperature of 35°F. to hold the rolls for a 24 hr. period without baking. The period may be prolonged with a slight reduction in temperature. The rolls may be wrapped for the freezer and frozen before baking thus providing a steady supply. Frozen units can be transfered to the retarder in advance and then returned to shop temperature for proofing and baking. Freshly baked rolls will insure consumer satisfaction and, consequently, greater sales.

CHAPTER 13

Rye Bread Varieties

A good loaf of rye bread is a lead item for increasing sales of other bakery products. In fact, there are specialty bakers who produce only rye bread varieties which are sold to smaller bakeshops that concentrate on other bakery products. However, "on premises" baking of the rye breads and rolls gives a distinct advantage to the retail bakeshop and the baker in a restaurant and hotel. Consistency of quality and appearance are the important factors and the practices and problems of production will be presented in this unit.

Rye bread and rolls are made from a dough which is lean and contains the basic ingredients of yeast-raised doughs. It is composed of common or clear flour, rye flour, salt, water, and yeast. The flavor of the bread may also be enhanced by using caraway seeds. Rye breads vary from the sweet rye bread containing some sugar and molasses to the dark rye and pumpernickel breads. Since sweet rye bread is made by a method similar to the process for making white pan bread, emphasis will be placed on the methods of making the sour rye bread varieties.

RYE FLOUR

The sour dough prepared with the rye flour is the principal source of rye bread flavor and variety. An understanding of the types of rye flour and their characteristics is necessary for the baker. Before describing each type of rye flour it should be understood that the proteins present in rye flour do not provide the type of gluten in the dough supplied by patent bread flour. The types of rye flour are: (1) White rye flour which is milled from the center of the rye wheat berry and is largely composed of fine starch particles. This flour is low in protein content and is used for light rye bread. (2) Medium rye flour is a straight flour. It is composed of all of the flour after the bran and shell have been removed. It contains about 1 per cent ash, is light gray in color, and is used mostly for the production of sour rye bread varieties. (3) Dark rye flour is similar to or may be compared with clear flour milled from regular wheat in that it is the flour which remains after some of the finer starch particles have been removed. It contains about 2 per cent ash and up to 16 per cent protein. It has small particles of bran in it and is used for the dark, heavier types of rye bread. (4) Rye meal or pumpernickel flour is made by grinding the entire rye berry. It is coarse, dark, and used for pumpernickel bread and rolls.

Since the proteins of rye flour do not provide the equivalent of wheat gluten ,there is an extra burden for the wheat gluten to carry. This is in addition to the support of fermentation and dough development. It is important, therefore, that the clear or common flour be of good quality and strong enough to carry the loaf. The average sour rye bread dough contains about 35 to 40 per cent flour which is present in the sour dough used as the base for the sour rye bread dough.

Cream or light rye flour is used for the sour dough preparation. Excessive use of dark rye flour or pumpernickel flour should be avoided because the bran particles will have a rupturing or breaking effect upon the gluten of the dough. Rye flour, because of its higher acidity and dextrins, lends itself well to fermentation. This fact means that a slightly lesser amount of yeast is used in the dough.

Since the sour-dough sponge or base is made without salt, the amount of salt added to the dough must be increased to compensate for the water used to make the sour dough. An average of $1^1/_2$ oz. salt is used for every 1 qt. water used to make the final dough. The extra $1/_2$ oz. meets the needs of the sour dough added.

SOUR STARTER

The production of "sours" for sour rye bread production is a continuous process. That is, a small portion of the sour dough which is fully developed and is used in the rye bread dough is removed. This small portion is used as the base or building block for developing a new sour dough. Some shops use a sour culture which comes in a dry form and contains lactic and acetic acids. It is these acids which are largely responsible for the fermentation and flavor development in sour dough. However, these cultures do not produce quite the same effect and characteristics of the sour rye bread made with a normally fermented, sour dough using rye flour.

Where there is no base upon which to build a sour dough, a sour-dough starter is made by suspending a small piece of yeast in the water used to make the sour dough. To this a quartered onion is added to promote acidity and flavor. The onion is removed as the starter is mixed for the beginning of the sour dough. Refer to the recipe for sour development in the making of sour rye bread (p. 101). Note that the water is increased in the preparation of the various stages of the sour dough. This is controlled by the amount of bread required. In other words, the baker governs the amount of sour dough to be prepared by the production requirements.

As in all fermented doughs control of the rate of fermentation of the sour dough is important. Since yeast is not the basic control the temperature of the water is the controlling factor. Cool water is best. Chilled or iced water is often used in warm weather to slow down or control the rate of fermentation. The practice of putting ice into the sour is not advisable since it melts and the water tends to separate the sour dough as well as form a paste at the bottom of the trough. The temperature for sour dough development is 73° to 76°F.

Doughs made without the regular sour dough base use either a sour dough culture or the addition of 1 to $1^1/_2$ oz. table vinegar for each quart of dough. The culture is dissolved in part of the water and allowed to stand for a while before mixing with other ingredients. These doughs are mixed as straight doughs and go through the regular stages of fermentation as a pan bread dough. While these doughs have the acidity they do not have the natural taste and flavor of the rye bread made with a regular sour dough base.

SOUR RYE BREAD MANUFACTURE

Mixing

Sour rye bread doughs are not mixed as long as regular doughs. The greater the amount of sour used the less mixing should be done. In addition, a slower mixing speed should be used to avoid high friction and tearing of the gluten. A mild clean-up stage is evident when the dough is completely mixed. Note that the dough will stick slightly to the sides of the mixing machine and yet tend to pull away cleanly. The dough feels smooth and developed.

Makeup

While the procedure for makeup of the bread is listed with the recipe, it is important that you remember that the dough is given a short resting period on the bench before scaling into desired units. If the batch of dough is large, or one dough is followed by another, the scaling should begin at once. The time lapse between the scaling and rounding the first units and the last units will be enough to permit proper conditioning of the rounded units. At this point, molded or shaped rye breads or rolls may be covered and placed in the retarder for later proofing and baking. While most of these breads are frozen after baking and then given a quick re-heat in a steam-filled oven before they are sold, the unbaked units may also be wrapped and then frozen.

Proofing

The proofing of sour rye bread units is one that requires care and understanding. The more acidity used in the dough, the less proof is required. Remember that the sour dough has been fermented. Over-proofing will result in large, porous grain, crumbly texture, and blister formation. It may also mean collapse of the proofed units while they are being handled for loading into the oven. The boxes into which the breads are placed should be rotated or changed so that the bottom box becomes the top box. This means that the breads shaped first are the first to be washed, stippled, or cut before going into the oven. The units are washed first and then stippled or docked. Washing after stippling or cutting makes a dull cut or blindness in the cut. Cutting of the bread takes place just before the bread is loaded into the oven.

Baking

The baking and peeling of the bread are very important. Rye bread should be baked in a hot oven (425° to 440°F.). The oven heat should be mellowed. That is, the heat should not be raw and flashy as with a freshly drawn oven but solidly distributed evenly over the top and bottom. Bread baked in a flashy oven has a dark crust formation and the crust is usually blistered. In addition the loaf is soft and soggy.

Steam is injected into the oven for a few minutes before baking. The bread is peeled into the oven and the steam settles on the surface or crust of the bread. This allows for expansion of the crust without tearing, breaking, or shredding during the rapid rise of the bread during the first few minutes of baking. After the bread has expanded fully and has taken on a light crust color the bread is then shifted in the oven to insure a thorough bake. This places the units in contact with fresh oven heat. In the more modern ovens this procedure is not necessary, since the heat is evenly distributed.

Pumpernickel.—Pumpernickel breads require a slightly lower oven temperature because they get crust color faster than the regular sour rye bread. Heavy rye breads (more sour used) require a slower bake for a thorough bake which will avoid sogginess and flattening of the loaves. In humid weather rye breads require a slightly longer bake to avoid the sogginess due to absorption of moisture from the air.

Pumpernickel bread doughs are handled and made much the same as sour rye bread dough. Pumpernickel flour (10 to 15 per cent) and sugar color are added to the dough to give it the characteristics of a darker bread with a bran-like taste and flavor. It is important to dissolve the sugar color in part of the water to avoid streaking the dough and the baked bread. The heavy type of pumpernickel bread is often baked in loaf pans (two or three rounded pieces to a pan). These are washed or brushed with water and dusted with bran flour before they are peeled into the oven. The pan contains the bread and provides a loaf shape.

The heavier types of pumpernickel tend to spread somewhat and flatten during baking. The pan shape also makes greater variety.

Steam.—The preparation of steam for the oven is important. A moist steam with tiny droplets of water are used to bake hard-type bread and rolls. The steam allows a better crust, bloom, and volume. The boiler is allowed to reach 5 to 10 lb. of pressure before the steam is allowed to enter the oven. A lesser amount may result in too little steam and some free water. This would hurt or cripple the loaves. Excessive boiler pressures (above 15 lb. per sq. in. steam pressure) means that the steam in the boiler is no longer moist and wet but dry steam which, if injected into the oven for bread, will cause a blistering and tearing effect on the crust of the bread. It is always best to allow the steam to drain first to remove excess water before allowing the steam to enter the oven. All safety practices and precautions should be followed in the preparation and use of steam for baking.

CHAPTER 14

Recipes for Bread and Rolls

HAMBURGER AND FRANKFURTER ROLLS

These rolls are in the category of the soft roll variety, and are to be made from a soft roll dough which is different from other doughs used for white pan bread and hard-type rolls. There are variations in recipes for soft rolls depending upon the production standards of the baker.

Soft Rolls (1 qt.)   **Yield:** 9 doz. rolls

Ingredients	Lb.	Oz.	Mixing procedure
Sugar	..	6	Scale ingredients carefully. Blend well to a
Salt	..	1	smooth paste
Milk powder	..	2	
Shortening	..	5	
Eggs	..	4	Add eggs and blend well
Water	1	8	Add and stir slightly
Yeast	..	3	Dissolve yeast and set aside
Water	..	8	
Bread flour	3	6	Sift and add the flour. Stir the flour slightly. Add the yeast solution and develop to a smooth dough

Procedures to Follow

Conditioning the Dough

1. Place the dough in a well-covered bowl or trough in a warm, moist place. Large plants use controlled fermentation rooms. The small shop will leave the dough in a covered trough or in a steam box with very little steam. This will cause the yeast to become active and the dough will rise.
2. Test the dough for punching readiness (the dough will fall back when the fingers are inserted).
3. Punch the dough by folding the ends over each other and pressing down to allow the carbon dioxide gas to escape.
4. Cover the dough and allow to rise once again. Place the dough on the bench and scale into presses of dough of specified weight.

71

5. Round up the presses of dough into round balls, cover with a cloth or place in a covered bread box. Allow the rounded units to relax for 10 to 15 min. This is known as the preliminary proofing stage.

6. Place the dough in the press machine or dough divider and cut into small units (36 pieces).

Makeup of Hamburger Rolls (Figs. 1 and 2)

1. Separate the units by dusting very lightly with flour. Place to one side.

2. Take one unit in the palm of each hand. Press down gently and move the hands in a circular motion. The right hand moves clockwise and the left counterclockwise. Keep the units enclosed in the palm of the hand until round. If the units stick to the bench dip the palm of the hand into some dusting flour (bread flour) and round the unit until smooth.

FIG. 1. ROUNDED AND PROOFED HAM-
BURGER ROLL

FIG. 2. HAMBURGER ROLL BAKED

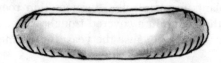

FIG. 3. FRANKFURTER ROLL BAKED

Makeup of Frankfurter Rolls (Fig. 3)

1. Round the units as for hamburger rolls. Allow to rest for a few minutes.

2. Take one unit in each hand and roll out to about 6 in. in length. **It is important that the units be of equal thickness.** Both hands may have to be used on each roll until experience is gained.

Proofing and Baking

1. Place the rolls on pans, spaced about 2 in. apart to allow room for proofing and expansion during baking. Larger plants have special machines which round and shape the rolls. Special pans are also used to maintain the shape of the rolls.
2. Place the rolls in the steam or proof box and allow them to rise. For full proof, the rolls will feel soft and when touched gently with a finger the indentation made will come back slowly Ability to test for proof will be gained by experience. The steam or proof box should be maintained at a temperature approximating 95°F. and a humidity of 90 per cent. The oven temperature should be approximately 410°F. Fill the oven with a small amount of wet steam before loading. Allow the steam to continue for the first 5 min. of baking when the rolls expand most rapidly. This is known as oven spring. Continue to bake the rolls until light brown. The total baking time is about 15 to 20 min., depending upon the evenness of the heat distribution in the oven.

Note: The rolls will touch and stick to each other after baking. This is as it should be, and indicates that the rolls have full volume; the closeness of the rolls will maintain the freshness and softness characteristic of soft rolls.

TWISTED SOFT ROLLS
Single-Knot Roll, Double-Knot Roll, Figure "8" Roll

As mentioned in the previous section on hamburger and frankfurter rolls, soft-roll dough offers the baker an opportunity to make a variety of soft rolls. This section will enlarge upon the variety by explaining the manner in which single-knot, double-knot, and figure "8" rolls are made.

Procedures to Follow (Figs. 4–7)

1. Be sure the dough is properly fermented. Scale the presses of dough carefully, round them up, rest them, and divide in the dough divider.
2. Separate the pieces of dough from one another and sprinkle lightly with dusting flour (bread flour).
3. Roll each piece of dough into strips about 6 in. long for single-knot rolls and 7–8 in. long for double-knot and figure "8" rolls. Do not use too much dusting flour. It is important that each strip be tightly rolled and of even thickness throughout the entire length of the **strip** (no points).

4. When twisting the strips avoid stretching the dough. If the dough is too short in length roll the strips longer. Allow the strips of dough to relax for a few minutes after they have been rolled out before twisting the rolls.

5. Line the twisted rolls up on a clean portion of the bench as you make them. Flatten them slightly and wash with egg-wash or melted fat and then place on pans about 2 in. apart. Usually a press of rolls will fit on a pan.

6. Give the rolls $^3/_4$ proof and wash a second time if desired.

7. Bake at 400° to 410°F. until golden brown (about 15 min.).

Fig. 4. Pull One End of the Rolled-Out Strip Through the Hole

Fig. 5. The Single-Knot Roll

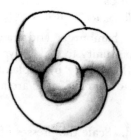

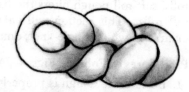

Fig. 6. The Double-Knot Roll

Fig. 7. The Figure "8" Roll

WHITE PAN BREAD AND WHITE MOUNTAIN BREAD

White pan bread is the most popular type of bread made in the United States. It is made from a fermented dough which follows the same principles and techniques of fermentation as rolls made from yeast-raised doughs. The operations involved in making the bread are similar to those used for sweet rolls and hard-type rolls.

White Pan Bread (1 qt.)   **Yield:** 6 1-lb. loaves

Ingredients	Lb.	Oz.	Mixing procedure
Sugar	..	3	Scale carefully. Dissolve ingredients in the
Salt	..	1	water. The temperature of the water helps
Milk powder	..	2	considerably in the rate of fermentation
Water	1	8	
Yeast	..	3	Dissolve the yeast and set aside
Water	..	8	
Bread flour (pat.)	3	6	Sift, add the flour, stir until absorbed, add the yeast and mix to a dough
Shortening	..	2	Add the shortening and develop the dough until smooth. (The dough pulls away from the sides of the kettle when it is developed)

Procedures to Follow (Figs. 8–19)

1. Place the dough, which has been covered, in warm, moist place to ferment.
2. Allow the dough to rise; punch, allow to rise again and punch again if necessary; allow dough to relax and then take to the bench.

    Approximate Fermentation Time Periods: first punch—1 hr. and 30 min. of fermentation; second punch—45 min. after first punch.

    Test for Punching: The dough starts to fall back when two or three fingers are inserted into the dough.
3. Scale the dough into desired weights (18 oz. dough for each 1-lb. loaf of bread; 2 oz. are lost in evaporation and in baking). Round the scaled units, cover and allow to relax about 10 to 15 min.
4. Make up the bread by molding the relaxed units into the desired shape.
5. Place the molded units into bread pans which have been cleaned and greased.
6. Allow the bread to get full proof (when touched gently with the finger the dough springs back slowly to the touch and the pan is almost full).
7. The bread is baked at 410° to 415°F. Mild steam is injected into oven before the bread is loaded. The steam is injected until the bread has risen well and then stopped rising, and the outer, top crust starts to show a pale golden color. At this point the steam is stopped and the bread baked until golden brown (average baking time for

1 lb. loaf of bread is about 35 to 40 min.). Baked bread sounds hollow when tapped with the fingers. The baked bread is removed from the pans immediately to avoid sweat.

White Mountain bread is made either in round or loaf form. The shaped units are given $^3/_4$ proof and sliced through the top with a sharp knife or blade about $^1/_2$ in. deep. The loaf shape is cut through top center. The round shape may be cut across the center or across the sides. After the top is washed with water and dusted lightly with cake flour it is baked as regular white pan bread.

FIG. 8.   SCALED, ROUNDED, AND RE-
LAXED UNIT OF DOUGH

FIG. 9.   FLATTEN TO ELIMINATE GAS
AND LARGE AIR POCKETS

FIG. 10.   FOLD ONE END OF THE
DOUGH TO THE CENTER

FIG. 11.   FOLD THE OPPOSITE END
OVER THE FIRST FOLD

FIG. 12.   ROLL UP SNUGLY AND SEAL
THE EDGE TIGHTLY.   BE SURE THE
SEAM IS CLOSED AND AT THE BOTTOM
CENTER

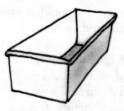

FIG. 13.   CLEANED AND GREASED
BREAD PAN

FIG. 14. MOLDED UNIT OF DOUGH PLACED IN THE PAN

FIG. 15. THREE-QUARTER ($^3/_4$) PROOF

FIG. 16. FULL PROOF

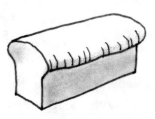

FIG. 17. BAKED LOAF

FIG. 18. FOR WHITE MOUNTAIN BREAD, WASH WITH WATER, MAKE CUT IN CENTER AND DUST WITH CAKE FLOUR

FIG. 19. ROUND-TYPE WHITE MOUNTAIN BREAD WITH CUTS IN CENTER

EGG ROLLS
Snail-Shaped Rolls, Owl-Eye Rolls, Cross Rolls, Three-Twist Rolls

Egg rolls are made from an egg bread dough which is used for twisted egg breads as well as challah. You will note from the recipe that it is rich in egg content, stiffer than the previously mentioned yeast-raised doughs, but requires the same fermentation procedures.

Egg Bread (1 qt.)   **Yield:** 3 press or 9 doz.

Ingredients	Lb.	Oz.	Mixing procedure
Sugar	..	6	Stir well to dissolve the dry ingredients
Salt	..	1¹/₄	
Oil	..	4	
Eggs (yolks)	..	12	
Water	1	8	
Yeast	..	3–4	Dissolve yeast and set aside
Water	..	8	
Bread flour	4	8	Sift, add, and stir lightly. Add the yeast and develop well

Procedures to Follow (Figs. 20–25)

1. Allow the dough to ferment as for pan bread. Be sure to punch on time (the shop temperature, water temperature, amount of yeast, fermentation room or trough are factors which control the rate of fermentation). Allow the dough to rise a second time and take to the bench. This dough is not punched twice, especially if it is a large dough, because the dough still ferments during the period of makeup. Punching a second time might cause the last pieces of dough to become old. In extremely warm weather the scaled presses of dough may be retarded to prevent the final units from becoming old.

2. Scale the fermented dough into desired presses (weight determined by the size of the roll) and allow the presses to relax.

3. After 10 to 15 min., press out the presses of dough and separate the pieces by dusting lightly with rye flour. (Rye flour is used instead of bread flour to prevent the pieces of dough from forming a heavy crust.) The flour helps to keep the twists of the strands of dough apart so that when the roll is baked, the shape and direction of the twists in the roll are clear and distinct.

4. When making the rolls, remember that the strips must be tight and rolled out into uniform shape and length. A loose or open strip will

Fig. 20. Roll Out Straight Strip of Dough with Palms of the Hands

Fig. 21. Taper Strip Gently at Each End

Fig. 22. Snail Roll. Tuck the End Under the Roll

Fig. 23. Owl-Eye Roll

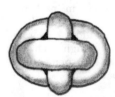

Fig. 24. Cross Roll. Use the Figure "8" Roll Which is Folded in Half and the Pinched Ends Placed Under the Roll

Fig. 25. Braiding the Three-Twist Roll

result in an uneven roll with poor shape. It is best to round or fold each piece of dough before rolling into a strip.

5. The strips for the *owl-eye* and *cross rolls* should be straight and without points at the end. If the dough sticks while rolling use a small amount of rye flour to dust the bench. Since this is a stiff dough very little dusting flour is needed.

6. Strips for the *snail* and *three-twist rolls* are shaped so that the ends are tapered from the center. The taper should be gradual and even. This controls the final shape of the roll.

7. Place the twisted rolls on a paper-lined or greased pan about 2 in. apart. These rolls can take full proof and have a lot of oven spring

during baking. Wash the rolls after makeup and again when they have $^3/_4$ proof. The rolls may be sprinkled with poppy or sesame seeds after they have been washed a second time. Bake at 390° to 400°F.

PULLMAN BREAD, SPLIT-TOP BREAD, AND ROUND SPLIT BREAD

Pullman bread is similar to the average white pan bread except that it is baked in a pan which is enclosed on all four sides. It is a square-shaped bread pan with a sliding top. It is larger than the average 1-lb. loaf pan. The size varies from a 2- to 3-lb. loaf. Pullman breads are primarily used for sandwich making and toast in restaurants and other eating establishments. The dough used for this type of bread and for the split-top variety is made by the sponge-dough method. The following recipe may be used for the Pullman and split-top loaves if a straight dough is not desirable.

Pullman Bread—   **Yield:** 8 1$^1/_2$-lb. loaves
    Sponge Method (2 qt.)

Ingredients	Lb.	Oz.	Mixing procedure
			Sponge Dough
Sugar	..	2	Dissolve the yeast in part of the water.
Malt	..	2	Dissolve the sugar and malt with the re-
Yeast	..	6	maining water. Add the flour and yeast and
Water	3	..	mix to a smooth dough. This is the sponge
Bread flour	4	..	dough. Allow the sponge to rise until it starts to fall back
			Final Dough
Sugar	..	2	Dissolve the sugar, salt, and milk powder in
Milk powder	..	4	the water. Add to the sponge and mix well
Salt	..	2	to break up the sponge. Add the flour and
Bread flour	2	10	stir in to a dough. Add the shortening and
Water	1	..	develop the dough
Shortening	..	4	

Procedures to Follow (Figs. 26–29)

1. Be sure the sponge dough starts to fall back before making the final dough. The sponge is the first part of the fermentation for the final dough. The sponge is a dough of soft consistency.
2. Allow the final dough to rise once and then take to the bench for makeup.
3. Scale the dough into units weighing 2 lb. 4 oz. for the 2-lb. loaf or 3 lb. 6 oz. for the 3-lb. loaf. Remember that for every pound loaf of

baked bread 2 oz. are lost in the baking process due to evaporation of part of the liquid.

4. The Pullman pans should be clean and greased lightly. The rounded units may relax during this period (15 min.).

5. The loaves may be shaped or molded as for pan bread. It is best to twist the dough (divide the units into two pieces and roll out each piece into a straight strip). Twist the two pieces together in the form of a braid and then seal the ends. Place in the pan for proofing. Twisting the dough makes for greater support of the gluten structure and prevents the sides of the bread from collapsing during baking and while cooling.

6. Place the top cover on the pan and leave it partially open so that the amount of proof may be observed. Give the units a little more than $3/4$ proof and close the top of the pan. Bake at 415°F. Allow the bread to bake with the top completely closed for $1/2$ hr. and then check to see whether the bread is coloring. The cover should be removed so that the bread may bake through evenly and allow the accumulated steam in the pan to escape. The top should slide off without sticking to the dough. If the top sticks slightly allow the bread to bake for a few more minutes (slightly open) and then remove the top. Return to the oven for complete baking.

FIG. 26. PULLMAN BREAD PAN. TOP OF PAN IS GREASED AS IS REST OF THE PAN

FIG. 27. LOAF OF BAKED PULLMAN BREAD

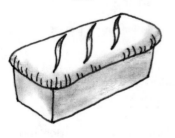

FIG. 28. SPLIT-TOP BREAD

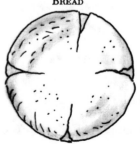

FIG. 29. ROUND SPLIT-TOP BREAD

Note: If malt is not available, use 2 oz. sugar to replace the malt.

For the split-top loaf bread, make up as for pan bread. Give the bread $^3/_4$ proof, wash the top lightly with water and make a cut with a sharp bread knife about $^1/_2$ in. deep across the length of the top of the bread. This cut will spring open when the bread is baking. Bake as for pan bread.

For the round split top, round up the units and place four to six on a clean, lightly greased sheet pan. Space them so that they have room for proofing and baking. Allow the units to get $^3/_4$ proof and then make four cuts at four sides of the dough about $^1/_2$ in. deep. Two cuts may be made across the top center of the units for variety. Bake the pan split top and the round split top at 415°F. with a mild amount of steam in the oven for the first 10 min. of baking or until the crust starts to take on color.

KAISER (VIENNA) ROLLS

Kaiser rolls, or Vienna rolls as they are often called, are the most popular hard-type rolls. In the past, they were shaped by hand; machines are now available to make them but hand-shaping is still the only method of production in many retail shops. The hand-shaped roll has a home-made appearance and more sales appeal than die-cut rolls. The hand-shaped roll lends itself to better spring and separation of the individual sections of the roll. Skill and speed in making these rolls are developed by application and practice. This section gives the recipe and procedure for making Kaiser rolls.

Kaiser Rolls (Vienna Dough)   **Yield:** 9 doz. or 4 lb. 4 oz. press

Ingredients	Lb.	Oz.	Mixing procedure
Sugar	..	6	Mix the dry ingredients with the eggs and
Malt	..	2	water. Stir well to dissolve
Salt	..	2	
Eggs	..	6	
Oil	..	6	
Water	3	..	
Yeast	..	6	Make yeast solution and set aside
Water (lukewarm)	1	..	
Bread flour	8	..	Sift, add the flour, stir slightly, add the yeast
(high-gluten)			solution and develop to a smooth dough

Procedures to Follow (Figs. 30–35)

1. Place the dough in a proper place to ferment (fermentation room or dough trough). Cover the dough to prevent crust formation as for all yeast doughs.

2. Allow the dough to rise well (time depends upon amount of yeast and fermentation conditions) and punch. Allow to rise again and take to the bench.

3. Scale the dough into presses (weight of presses will vary from 3 to 5 lb. depending upon the size of the roll and quality of the dough). Round up the presses and allow to relax 15 min.

4. Press out the dough and separate the pieces by dusting them lightly with rye flour. Rye flour used in makeup will prevent running together of the sections of the roll and avoid "blindness."

5. Flatten each piece of dough slightly into a round or partially round shape. Place the thumb of the left hand in the center of the piece of dough. With the forefinger of the left hand pick up about a section equal to one-fifth the dough and fold that portion slightly over the thumb. With the outside of the palm of the right hand hit the dough up against the side of the thumb. Pick up the second section and follow the same procedure. The fifth or final section of the dough is given a slight twist with the thumb and forefinger of the right hand and the section is pushed into the gap made by removing the left thumb from the center of the roll. The final edge must be pushed into the center so that it is firmly impressed. This will prevent separation in the proofing and baking. The entire procedure may be viewed as the assembling of spokes in a wheel. (See Figs. on pages 84 and 85).

6. After the roll is formed place it face down on a clean portion of the bench. When a full press is made up, the rolls are picked up and placed in a roll box that is covered with a clean canvas roll cloth or a box which has been sprinkled with poppy seeds, face down. Be sure there are enough poppy seeds to prevent sticking while the rolls are proofing.

7. Allow the rolls to get slightly more than $3/4$ proof (avoid maximum proof) and prepare for baking.

8. The rolls are baked at 425°F. with a generous amount of steam in the oven. Allow the steam to enter the oven about 2 min. before peeling in the rolls.

9. Dust the roll peel with cornmeal and pick the rolls up gently and turn them face up (with the fold facing up) on the peel. Allow sufficient space on the peel for each roll to expand in the baking process.

10. Place the peel into the oven, being careful to avoid the steam that comes out when the oven door is opened, and stop the peel. With a quick snap of the wrists and jerk of the arms the rolls are removed from the peel and are now on the hearth of the oven where the peel was. Practice is necessary to develop the skill in peeling hard-type rolls baked on the hearth.

11. Allow the steam to enter the oven until the rolls start to take on a light-brown crust color. Stop the steam and bake the rolls until crisp and dry. Be careful of underbaking, for the rolls will feel very soft and soggy, which is not characteristic of a Kaiser roll.

12. Remove the rolls with a roll peel by slightly tilting the peel upward and sliding the peel under the baked rolls. When the rolls are on the peel lower the peel to a level position and draw the rolls out. Deposit them in roll baskets.

Note: These rolls may be baked on sheet pans dusted with cornmeal, although they do not have the same bloom and oven spring when baked on pans. An equal amount of sugar may be substituted for malt if malt is not available. An increase in the amount of eggs will yield greater volume and a crisper roll crust.

FRENCH BREAD AND FRENCH OVAL ROLLS

French bread and rolls are quite popular, hard-type bakery products. While they are specialized to a degree, in that certain plants produce this type of bread and rolls for the restaurant and hotel trade, many small retail bakeshops have developed the demand for this type of bread and rolls by virtue of the quality and freshness of the product. It is the handling of the dough and makeup and baking of the bread and rolls which are important. The dough is simple to prepare.

French Bread (2 qt.)   **Yield:** 18–20 10-oz. loaves or 12 doz. rolls

Ingredients	Lb.	Oz.	Mixing procedure
Sugar	..	2	Blend the ingredients together to dissolve
Salt	..	2	
Malt	..	2	
Oil	..	2	
Water	3	..	
Yeast	..	6	Dissolve the yeast and set aside
Water	1	..	
Bread flour	7	..	Sift, add, stir slightly, add the yeast solution
(high-gluten)			and develop well to a smooth dough

FIG. 30.   FLATTEN PIECE OF DOUGH

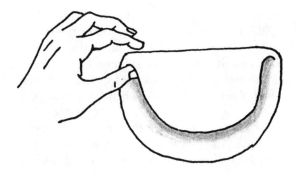

FIG. 31. PLACE THUMB IN CENTER OF DOUGH AND FOLD OVER A SMALL SECTION

FIG. 32. MAKE A CREASE IN THE FOLD BY HITTING THE DOUGH WITH THE SIDE OF THE HAND

FIG. 33. REPEAT THE FOLDS FOUR TIMES AND TUCK THE FIFTH FOLD INTO THE SPACE OCCUPIED BY THE THUMB

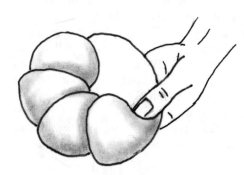

FIG. 34. FINISHED KAISER ROLL

FIG. 35. TURN THE ROLL UPSIDE DOWN IN A ROLL BOX LINED WITH A CANVAS CLOTH OR LINED WITH POPPY SEEDS

Procedures to Follow for French Bread (Figs. 36 and 37)

1. A high-gluten bread flour is necessary for this dough. The baked bread and rolls should have large volume. The interior of the baked loaf should be open-grained and the cell structure larger than that of regular white pan bread. This is due to the fullness of the proof given prior to baking and the strong-gluten capacity to withstand such proof. Be sure the dough is smooth and elastic when taken from the mixing machine.

2. Allow the dough to rise well. Test for punching and punch when ready. Give the dough a second rise and punch again. Allow the dough to relax for 10 to 15 min. after the second punch and take to the bench.

3. Scale the dough into units weighing approximately 12 oz. to 1 lb. The size of the bread is determined by the special requirements of the shop. Naturally, longer and larger breads require more dough. Round up the scaled dough units, cover and allow to relax for about 15 min.

4. Mold or shape the bread by flattening the dough and thus removing the gas. Fold the dough over and roll in with the thumbs and palms until a tight strand that is slightly tapered is formed. Seal the edges tightly to form a closed seam. This is important to prevent opening during proofing and baking.

5. Place the units in bread or roll boxes which have been dusted with cornmeal. They may also be placed on canvas cloths.

6. Give the units $3/4$ proof, wash the tops lightly with water, and make diagonal cuts across the top spaced about 4 in. apart. Allow the units to reach full proof before baking. By using the high-gluten flour the bread units should be able to withstand full proof (before being placed on peels and peeled into the oven.)

7. Set the oven at 430°F. and allow steam to enter 3 or 4 min. before peeling the bread into the oven. Lift the bread up gently with both hands and place on a peel dusted with cornmeal.

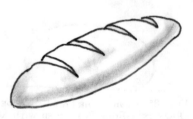

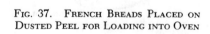

FIG. 36. FRENCH BREAD THAT IS PROOFED, WASHED, AND CUT

FIG. 37. FRENCH BREADS PLACED ON DUSTED PEEL FOR LOADING INTO OVEN

8. Place the loaded peel in the oven, raise it gently so that a slight incline is formed and with a quick jerk the length of the peel, the bread is removed from the peel onto the hearth of the oven.
9. Allow the steam to continue in the oven until the top crust of the bread starts to develop a light-brown crust color. Shut off the steam and allow to bake until the crust is golden brown and crisp.
10. The bread is considered baked when the top or bottom of the loaf is tapped with the knuckles and a hollow sound results.
11. Remove from the oven and stack in baskets in a vertical position.

Note: The bread must be spaced about 2 in. apart on the peel so that there is sufficient room for the bread to spring or rise in the oven during baking. This is also done when placing the units in the bread box to proof.

Makeup of French Oval Rolls (Fig. 38)

1. Scale the fermented dough into presses weighing about 3 lb.
2. Round up the presses and allow them to relax for about 10 min.
3. Press out the dough and shape into an oval or finger shape. This is done by first rounding the pieces as for hamburger rolls and then rolling forward and backward with the palm of the hand so that the ends are tapered evenly. Do not make sharp points.
4. Place the rolls on pans or in boxes on a canvas cloth. Allow the rolls to get $3/4$ proof, slice across the top of the roll diagonally. Make the cut for the bread and rolls about $1/4$ in. deep.
5. Allow the rolls to get full proof and bake at 425°F. with steam in the oven during most of the baking.

Note: The steam in the oven makes greater volume and a crispy hard crust. This is due to the fact that the moisture of the steam prevents the crust from drying too quickly and cracking or bursting during the first stage of baking. The crust is thus thin yet dry and crackly when the bread or rolls are cut or broken after baking. It is best to bake the rolls as well as the bread on the hearth.

FIG. 38. FRENCH ROLL PROOFED AND CUT

ITALIAN BREAD, ROLLS, AND BREAD STICKS

Italian bread is similar, in many respects, to French bread. The similarity exists in the nature of the dough (both are lean), handling of the dough, and the appearance of the baked product. Italian bread may be made in a variety of shapes and some of the breads vary in their texture and grain. For example, some breads are close-grained and somewhat heavier than others. Some have a thicker and crisper crust than others. The recipe which follows is one that is very popular and is used for the production of lighter Italian bread, rolls, and bread sticks.

Italian Bread—Straight Dough (2 qt.)

Yield: 18 10-oz. loaves or 12 doz. rolls

Ingredients	Lb.	Oz.	Mixing procedure
Salt	. .	2	Blend well to dissolve the salt
Malt	. .	1	
Water	3	. .	
Yeast	. .	4	Dissolve the yeast and set aside
Water	1	. .	
Bread flour (high-gluten)	6	12	Add, stir slightly, add the yeast solution and develop well

Procedures to Follow for Italian Bread (Figs. 39–42)

1. The rate of production will determine the temperature of the water and the amount of yeast to be used. These doughs (Italian and French bread) are lean and should be kept cool. However, the amount of yeast may be increased to speed fermentation. This is a better approach than using warm water. Care must be taken not to allow the dough to get old.
2. The dough should rise well and be punched. Allow to rise again and take to the bench.
3. Scale the dough into units of desired weights. The weight and size are determined by production requirements of the shop.
4. Round the scaled units and allow them to relax for about 10 to 15 min. for final conditioning of the dough. This is the preliminary proofing stage.
5. When molding or shaping the bread, flatten each of the units with the palms of the hands and fold over the dough as though you were forming three layers. Place the palms of the hands on the dough and press and roll. This will tighten the dough and remove further air pockets. Shape into a long oval or tapered strip. Seal the edges carefully. The ends of the bread should have a slight taper. This is similar to the French bread variety. The units may also be shaped in round form and baked that way. Other types may be made by rolling out a tight strand of even thickness to about 1 in. in diameter.

The strand is then formed into a "U" shape and the two strands braided over each other to form a horseshoe twist.

6. Place the shaped units in boxes lined with canvas cloths and give $3/4$ proof. The top of the bread may then be washed very lightly with water. The tops are then cut as follows; the long loaves may be cut with diagonal cuts about 3 in. apart and about $1/2$ in. deep. The long breads may also be cut straight down the center starting and ending about 1 in. from either end. The round breads may be cut across the tops from end to end. The twisted breads are not cut. The tops of the loaves may be sprinkled with sesame seeds after washing and cutting.

FIG. 39. BAKED ITALIAN LOAF OF BREAD

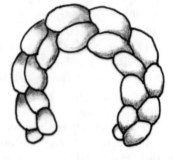

FIG. 40. THREE-TWIST BRAIDED AND HORN-SHAPED ITALIAN BREAD

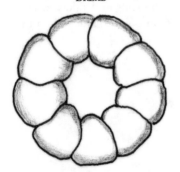

FIG. 41. RING-SHAPED ITALIAN BREAD

FIG. 42. ROUND-SHAPED ITALIAN BREAD WITH EDGES CUT

7. Allow the bread to get almost complete, full proof. The oven temperature should be set at 420°F. Inject steam in the oven a few minutes before loading. Bake the bread on the hearth. That is, place the units on peels dusted with cornmeal and peel onto the hearth. Allow the steam to continue into the oven until the crust takes on a light color. Shut off the steam and allow the bread to

bake to a light golden brown. Remember that this bread must have a hard crust and a golden brown color. The bread should sound hollow when tapped before removal from the oven. If the top heat is too strong, open the damper or open the oven door and allow the bread to bake properly without too strong a top heat.

Makeup of Italian Rolls (Fig. 43)

1. Scale the fermented dough into presses. The size of the roll desired will determine the weight of the press. It may vary from 3 to 4 lb.
2. Round up the presses and allow to relax. Press out the pieces and separate with a little rye flour. (Bread flour will cause a crust to form.) Shape the rolls as for the oval French rolls.
3. A club roll or straight roll may be made. The fermented dough is scaled into pieces weighing 1 to $1^1/_2$ lb. and rounded. The units are allowed to relax and then flattened and shaped into a long even strip about the length of a sheet pan or a roll box. The strands are then placed on the pan or box, which has a canvas cloth or is dusted with cornmeal. The long strand is allowed to rise to about half proof and the strand is then cut with a bun divider or roll cutter into equal sizes. The average roll weighs from 1 to $1^1/_4$ oz. when baked. The rolls are then given $^3/_4$ proof and cut down to center from one end to the other. The rolls are given almost full proof and then baked on the hearth. The oven temperature is approximately 415°F. Steam is injected into the oven before peeling in the rolls and allowed to continue until the rolls have started to take on color. The rolls must be baked to a crisp condition.

Fig. 43. Italian Roll

Makeup of Italian Bread Sticks

1. Scale the fermented dough into presses weighing about 3 lb. each. Round up the presses and allow them to relax for 10 min. Press out.
2. Separate the units and then roll each strip out about 6 in. Cut each strip in half. This will yield 72 pieces from each press of dough.
3. Roll each strip out about 6 in. in length. The strip of dough should

be even and about $1/4$ in. in diameter. Place each strip on a clean, greased or paper-lined pan. The strips may also be placed on pans dusted with cornmeal.

4. Give the strips about $3/4$ proof and bake as you would the Italian rolls.

Note: These sticks bake rapidly. Bake to a light, golden brown color of the crust and remove from the oven. The sticks are to be crisp and remain crisp. The sticks may be garnished with sesame seeds or with coarse salt (lightly). Be sure to allow space between the sticks when they are placed on the pans for proof. The sticks are not to be allowed to bake into each other. The entire outside crust of the sticks are to brown.

If longer, thicker sticks are required do not cut the pieces of dough in half. Roll out to about 9 in. in length and about $3/8$ in. thick. Judgment is necessary to meet specific production requirements.

PARKER HOUSE, CLOVER-LEAF, AND BUTTER-FLAKE ROLLS

These rolls require more handling and thus take more time to produce but they have the advantage of variety, a basic necessity for the baker who produces a complete line of bakery products. These rolls are different in shape and some have added butter or fat which make them richer and tastier. In addition, these rolls retard very nicely and may be baked as needed. They are made from a properly fermented and conditioned soft roll dough used for hamburger rolls.

Procedures to Follow for Parker House Rolls (Figs. 44–49)

1. Scale the conditioned dough into presses weighing about 3 lb. A lesser weight may be used for a smaller and more delicate roll.
2. Allow the presses to relax for about 10 min. and press out. Round up the units and place on a lightly dusted portion of the bench.
3. Allow the units to relax until soft. Where a number of presses are made the first units are relaxed by the time the last ones are rounded.
4. Take about 6 rounded units and place them in a straight line on a flour-dusted portion of the bench. Using a small rolling pin roll the centers of the units about two-thirds of the way toward each end. Note that the edges of each unit will have become thicker and the center is about $1/8$ in. thick. Wash the centers with melted butter or fat.
5. Fold one edge over to the other so that the thick ends overlap each other with the top one being slightly in back of the bottom one. The back or thin portion of the roll may be pressed with the palm of the hand to make it thinner and force more dough to the front.

FIG. 44.   PIECE OF DOUGH FROM THE
PRESSED-OUT UNIT OF DOUGH

FIG.   45.   ROUNDED-UP   UNIT   OF
DOUGH

FIG. 46.   ROLL OUT THE RELAXED
PIECE OF DOUGH WITH A THIN ROLL-
ING PIN

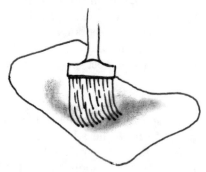

FIG. 47.   CENTER OF DOUGH WASHED
WITH MELTED BUTTER OR FAT

FIG. 48.   END FOLDED OVER END

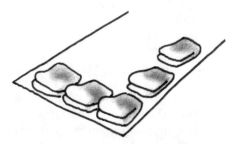

FIG. 49.   ROLLS PLACED ON SHEET
PAN

6. Place the units on a paper-lined or greased bun pan close together
   (six down and about eight or nine across).
7. Give the units ³/₄ proof and brush the tops with melted fat or butter.
   Bake the rolls at 400°F. until a golden, dull brown. Wash the rolls
   again with melted butter immediately after they are removed from

the oven. They may also be left unwashed. When made correctly, these rolls can be opened as a pocket, because the centers were brushed with melted fat.

Note: If these rolls are to be retarded for later baking, place them in the refrigerator as soon as made up and brushed with melted fat.

Makeup for Clover-Leaf Rolls (Figs. 49A, 50–53)

1. Scale the dough into presses weighing about 3 lb. The size of the muffin tin will determine the weight. A smaller than normal cupcake pan may mean that the presses may weigh 2 lb.
2. Round up the presses, relax for 15 min. and press out. Roll each unit into a strip about 3 in. long and of even thickness. Divide each of these strips into three equal parts.

FIG. 49A. PIECE OF DOUGH FROM THE PRESSED-OUT UNIT OF DOUGH

FIG. 50. ROLLED-OUT STRIP OF DOUGH CUT INTO THREE PARTS

FIG. 51. ROUNDED-UP PIECES OF DOUGH

FIG. 52. PIECES OF DOUGH PLACED IN MUFFIN PANS

FIG. 53. BAKED CLOVER-LEAF ROLL

3. Round up each of the divided parts into three round balls. Place the dough balls together (the three from each strip) and place in clean, greased muffin tins.

4. Allow the units to rise until $^3/_4$ proof. Wash the tops with melted fat. Egg-wash may also be used.

5. Allow the units to get full proof (reach the top of the muffin tin) and bake at 400°F. until golden brown. Remove from the tins while the rolls are still mildly warm.

Makeup of Butter-Flake Rolls (Figs. 54–57)

1. Scale the dough into units weighing about 4 lb. and shape each into a long rectangular shape. Allow the units to relax for about 15 min. until soft. They may also be retarded in this shape for later makeup.

2. Roll out the dough long and about 12 in. wide. Brush the top surface of the dough well with melted fat or butter.

3. Starting from the top, fold the top edge over so that a layer of dough $1^1/_2$ in. is formed. Continue folding (about five or six folds are made to the edge). The dough is now formed into a flat strip about $1^1/_2$ in. thick. Level the strip so that it is of even thickness throughout.

4. Cut pieces about $1^1/_2$ in. wide. Turn each cut piece face up with the separated layers exposed on the surface. With a scraper, cut into

FIG. 54. ROLLED-OUT DOUGH WASHED WITH BUTTER OR MELTED FAT

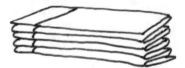

FIG. 55. DOUGH FOLDED INTO LAYERS AND CUT INTO SLICES

FIG. 56. SLICES OF DOUGH PLACED IN MUFFIN TINS

FIG. 57. BAKED BUTTER-FLAKE ROLL

each strip about five times $1/4$ in. apart. Place each of the strip cuts (units) in a greased muffin tin with the uncut side down. This will allow the cuts to spread as layers during proof and spread and flake during baking. Give the units $3/4$ proof and bake at 400°F. until golden brown. Remove the rolls from the tins while still warm. It is also advisable to wash the tops of the rolls with melted butter as soon as they come from the oven.

CLUB ROLLS AND WATER ROLLS

Club and water rolls are two of many hard-type roll varieties. These rolls are quite popular and are necessary items on the baker's daily production list of hard rolls. The mechanics of production are simple and follow procedures similar to those used in the manufacture of other hard rolls. It must be remembered that the term "hard" indicates that the baked product has a firm, crisp crust. The dough used for these rolls is the one used for Kaiser rolls (Vienna dough).

Procedures to Follow for Club Rolls (Figs. 58–61)

1. Scale the fermented Vienna dough into units weighing approximately 18 oz. They may be scaled more or less depending upon the size of the roll desired. Round up the units and allow them to relax about 10 min.
2. Roll out the dough into a straight, even strip about 1 in. in diameter. Allow the strip to relax when partially rolled and then roll to the

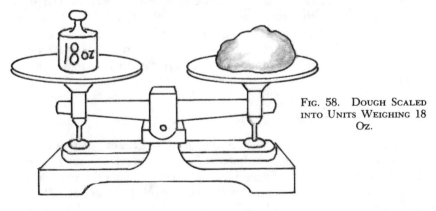

FIG. 58. DOUGH SCALED INTO UNITS WEIGHING 18 OZ.

FIG. 59. ROLL DOUGH INTO A STRAIGHT, EVEN STRIP ABOUT 1 ◄ IN. THICK

desired length and thickness. This will prevent shrinkage of the dough.

3. Place the rolled strips in roll boxes or pans which have been dusted with cornmeal. Allow the strips to rise to about half proof.

4. Divide the strips into rolls about 3–4 in. long (larger for rolls to be used for sandwiches). Allow the rolls to get about $^3/_4$ proof and cut across the tops in a diagonal line. These cuts should be about $^1/_4$ in. deep. The rolls may also be cut lengthwise across the top or left uncut.

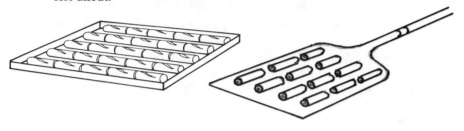

FIG. 60. PLACE STRIPS IN CORNMEAL-DUSTED ROLL BOX. WHEN HALF PROOF, CUT INTO 4 IN. STRIPS. ALLOW ROLLS TO GET $^3/_4$ PROOF AND CUT ACROSS THE TOP

FIG. 61. PROOFED ROLLS ARE PLACED ON CORNMEAL-DUSTED PEELS TO BE PEELED ONTO THE HEARTH OF THE OVEN

5. The proofed rolls are then placed on peels dusted with cornmeal and spaced about 2 in. apart. They are to be peeled onto the hearth of the oven after it has been filled with moist steam. The oven temperature is the same as for Kaiser rolls (420°F.). Allow the steam to continue until the rolls have taken on a light crust color. Bake the rolls until they are golden brown and crisp (about 20 min.).

Larger units require a longer baking period than do smaller dinner rolls).

Makeup for Water Rolls (Figs. 62–68)

1. Scale the conditioned Vienna dough into presses weighing from 3–4 lb. Round up the presses and allow them to relax about 10 min.

2. Press out the units and round up the pieces. Place the units in roll boxes which have been lined with a duck cloth (canvas) or roll cloth.

3. Allow the units to reach half proof and remove from the box, two or four at a time. Line up the units on a lightly dusted portion of the bench and press the centers down with a narrow rolling pin. This will create a butterfly effect. Return the pressed units to the box with

the crease in the center of the roll facing down. Allow about 2 in. of space between rolls. When the line of rolls (about 8 rolls) has been returned, push the duck cloth up against the sides of the rolls to form a cloth wall. This will prevent the water rolls from spreading while getting full proof. When filled, the roll boxes should contain about 8 rows of rolls with duck cloth walls. (See Figs. on p. 98.)

4. Bake these rolls by placing them on cornmeal-dusted peels with the crease side now facing up. Peel into the oven that has been filled with steam and bake as the club rolls.

Note: Be careful when lifting both club and water rolls from the boxes to avoid making indentations. It is best to give them slightly more than $^3/_4$ proof rather than the maximum full proof. This permits handling with ease and avoids damage due to falling back or collapse of the fully proofed rolls.

SWEET RYE BREAD AND ROLLS

The basic difference between sweet rye rolls and sweet rye bread is size. The recipe used for the two products is the same except for a slight decrease in flour when making rolls. Although not as popular as a standard roll, the sweet rye roll finds flavor with many customers. There are three types of rye flour available: light, medium and dark; the amount can be increased or decreased, depending on how heavy the bread or rolls desired. Ground caraway seeds can be added to the dough for flavor.

Sweet Rye Dough (2 qt.) Yield: 10 1-lb. loaves

Ingredients	Lb.	Oz.	Mixing procedure
Water	1	..	Break yeast into small particles. Dissolve in
Yeast	..	4	water. Place to one side
Salt	..	$2^1/_2$	Place ingredients in the machine. Stir
Sugar	..	1	slightly to dissolve and distribute the in-
Molasses	..	2	gredients
Shortening	..	2	
Water	3	..	
Rye flour	1	8	Sift and add the flour. Stir slightly, add the
Bread or clear flour	4	12	yeast solution and then develop the dough until smooth. Do not develop the dough as long as a pan bread dough

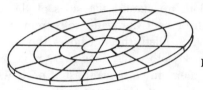

FIG. 62.   PRESS OUT THE UNITS OF
DOUGH INTO 36 EQUAL PIECES

FIG. 63.   ROUND UP THE PIECES OF
PRESSED OUT DOUGH

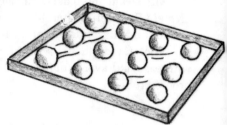

FIG. 64.   PLACE THE UNITS IN DUCK-
CLOTH-LINED ROLL BOXES AND GIVE
HALF PROOF

FIG. 65.   PRESS THE CENTERS OF THE
DOUGH   DOWN   WITH   A   NARROW
ROLLING PIN

FIG. 66.   FORCED-UP SIDES OF THE
ROLL

FIG. 67.   PLACE THE UNITS IN DUCK
CLOTH-LINED ROLL BOX FACE DOWN.
PUSH   CLOTH   AGAINST   THE   SIDES
TO   KEEP   ROLL   FROM   SPREADING
TOO MUCH

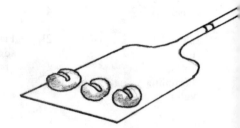

FIG. 68.   PLACE ROLLS FACE UP ON
CORNMEAL-DUSTED PEEL

Procedures to Follow for Sweet Rye Bread (Figs. 69–71C)

1. Fermentation time: one rise, punch, and allow to rest about 20 to 30 min.
2. Scale dough off at 18 oz.
3. Round up pieces and allow to rest in a bread box dusted with rye flour.
4. Cover and allow to rest for about 15 min. before making up.
5. Shape breads about 10 in. in length and seal the ends. The bread resembles a pan bread.

FIG. 69. SCALE DOUGH 1 LB. 2 OZ. AND ROUND UP

FIG. 70. RELAXED DOUGH

FIG. 71. FLATTEN DOUGH

FIG. 71A. FLATTEN TO ELIMINATE GAS AND LARGE AIR POCKETS

FIG. 71B. FOLD ONE END OF THE DOUGH TO THE CENTER

FIG. 71C. FOLD THE OPPOSITE END OVER THE FIRST FOLD

6. Place the bread 3–4 in. apart, in a bread box which has been dusted with cornmeal or put 12 loaves in each box.
7. Allow bread to proof in the proof box or on bench if desired until almost double in size. Test to see if proofed by squeezing the sides slightly. If finger marks remain and the bread has about doubled in size, the bread is considered ready to be baked. Swab the oven hearth.
8. Check the steam pressure. Allow the steam to flow into the oven, which should have a temperature of 400° to 425°F.
9. With a sharp Vienna knife, cut the bread lightly on top four or five times across the loaf. Do not cut deeper than about $1/4$ in. Some bakers prefer to cut bread on a peel.
10. After cutting the bread, wash it lightly with water.
11. Carefully place the bread on the peel 3 in. apart and insert in oven taking care to maintain spacing.
12. Allow bread to bake until a light color appears on the bread. Shut off the steam, open the door and damper for 5 min., then close both and bake until the bread has an even brown color.
13. Test to see if baked by rapping the bottom of the bread sharply with the knuckles of the hand. The bread should be crisp.

Makeup for Sweet Rye Rolls

1. Scale off the dough in 3 lb. pieces.
2. Round up, then place in bread box lightly dusted with flour.
3. Allow to rest for about 15 min.
4. Prepare dough for divider by rolling it out to the proper size.
5. Brush with oil, then cut with divider. Place the divided pieces on the bench.
6. Shape into pointed rolls in the following manner: begin by rounding a unit of dough in each hand using a circular motion, as you would when making hamburger rolls; apply slight pressure and cup your hand while moving back and forth on the bench so that the units take form and become pointed; avoid the use of flour if possible.
7. Place shaped units in even rows on lightly greased pans.
8. Place pans in proof box and allow $3/4$ proof.
9. With the aid of a Vienna knife cut each roll down the center.
10. Wash lightly and evenly with water. Sprinkle some with caraway seeds; leave some plain.
11. When doubled in size, peel into a steam-filled oven with a temperature of 400–425°F.
12. When half-baked, shut off steam, open door and damper for about 2 min. Then finish baking with door and damper closed.

SOUR RYE BREAD AND ROLLS

The term "sour," as it refers to rye bread indicates that this product has a higher pH, or higher degree of acidity, than other types of yeast-raised breads. In this instance, the sour is created with rye flour as the only flour and follows a prescribed procedure for natural sour development during successive stages of fermentation.

In order to prepare a sour dough for sour rye bread, there must be a sour starter from which to begin. The sour starter is then refreshed with additional flour and water during several additional stages of fermentation to form the fermented sour dough used in the sour rye bread formula.

A. Sour Starter

Ingredients	Lb.	Oz.	Mixing procedure
Yeast (variable)	..	6	Dissolve the yeast in cool water
Water	1	8	
Rye flour	2	..	Add the rye flour and mix to a smooth paste.
One onion, quartered			Distribute the onion pieces within the dough
(medium)			or paste that is formed

Procedures to Follow

Place the starter in a wooden pail or rust-proof container. Cover lightly so that air may enter and permit introduction of various bacteria, as well as yeasts, from the surrounding atmosphere. Allow to stand in a cool place for 24 hr. for formation of extra acidity during the concentrated and lengthy fermentation period. The onion gives additional acidity and flavor to the basic sour starter.

B. The Development of Fermented Sour Dough for Use in Sour Rye Bread

The sour starter is developed into a fully fermented and conditioned sour which serves the same purpose in rye bread as does the sponge for regular yeast-raised breads made by the sponge method. The difference lies in the fact that rye flour, the only flour used in sour dough, has no gluten-forming proteins. This is important to remember, for allowances must be made in the type of flour used when making the final dough.

First Sour Buildup

For every quart of water used in making or building the sour, $2^1/_2$ lb. rye flour are used. This is added to the sour starter after the starter has fermented and the onion sections have been removed. The first sour is allowed to ferment until it starts to fall back (about 3 hr. under normal shop conditions). The amount of water used in each of the sour development stages depends upon the amount of finished bread needed in the production schedule.

Second or Half Sour Buildup

As much as 4–6 qt. water may be used for the half sour. Remember to add $2^{1}/_{2}$ lb. of rye flour for each quart of water. The half sour is covered with rye flour and covered with a cloth or bench top or trough top (unless in a controlled fermentation room) and allowed to rise until it starts to fall back.

Third or Final Sour Buildup

Judgment must be used in determining the quantity of sour needed. This will be the determining factor in adding enough water to make the final sour. Since most sour rye bread (Jewish variety) contains 35 to 40 per cent rye sour it is simple to determine the amount of sour needed. As much as one pail (20 qt.) of water or more may be added to make the final sour. The usual amount of flour ($2^{1}/_{2}$ lb. rye flour per quart) is mixed in. The final sour is covered with rye flour and allowed to ferment (about 3 hr.) during the fermentation period. Remember to save enough sour dough to act as the base or starter from which to develop another sour for the next batch of sour rye or pumpernickel bread.

C. Sour Rye Bread (4 qt.)   Yield: 30 1-lb. loaves

Ingredients	Lb.	Oz.	Mixing procedure
Yeast (approximately)	..	6–8	Dissolve the yeast and set aside
Water	2	..	
Fermented sour dough	10	..	Dissolve salt, add sour, and break up sour by mixing
Salt	..	8	
Water	6	..	
Clear flour	16	..	Add flour and mix to a smooth dough. Be careful not to overmix

Procedures to Follow (Figs. 72–76)

1. Remove the dough from the machine and place on bench dusted with rye flour.
2. Scale the units of dough (18 oz. dough for each loaf of baked bread to weigh 1 lb.).

3. Round up the units and place in a bread box dusted with rye flour or on the bench, and cover with a box or canvas cloth. This will prevent crustation during the relaxing or preliminary proofing period.

4. Allow the units of dough to relax for about 20 min. (In large doughs, the first units scaled and rounded will have rested 20 min. by the time the last units are scaled and rounded.)

Fig. 72. Stretch Dough

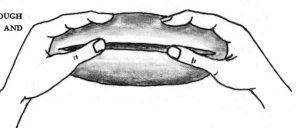

Fig. 73. Fold in Half

Fig. 74. Fold Dough Half-Way Back and Flatten Again

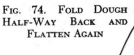

Fig. 75. Tuck Dough Under and Roll with Thumb and Heel of Palm

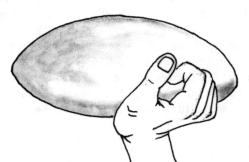

Fig. 76. Seal Bottom of the Bread by Pressing Firmly with Heel of the Palm. Seal Is Placed on the Bottom Center of the Bread

5. Shape the breads in either straight-sandwich form, as a pan bread, or in oval Vienna shape. If caraway seeds are added, the unit of dough is placed on some caraway seeds on the bench and are thus distributed into the bread while it is being shaped. When shaping the bread, use rye flour for dusting. Use only enough to keep the units of dough from sticking. Use a pressure of the thumbs and palms of the hands to press and roll the dough in. The pressure should be such that the dough is bunched toward the center and gradually tapered to the ends. The ends should not be rolled to extreme, sharp points.

6. Place the made-up breads in bread boxes well-dusted with rye flour and cornmeal. Leave 2–3 in. of space between each bread for proofing room. Cover each box with another box after each box is filled. After all breads are made up, change the boxes so that the last or top box becomes the bottom box of a new stack and the original bottom box now becomes the top box. The boxes should be placed on a dolly evenly and closed. The boxes may be stacked that way until the bread is proofed. The boxes may be placed in the steam box under low steam pressure. This will speed up the proofing. The bread should be given $3/4$ proof and prepared for baking. If the stacked boxes of bread are proofing rapidly then swing the boxes in opposite directions so that the corners of the boxes are open and the air allowed to circulate. This will slow the rate of proofing.

7. Be sure the oven is hot (440° to 450°F.).

8. Allow the steam to enter the oven for 2 or 3 min. before peeling in the bread.

9. The proofed bread should be washed lightly with water and stippled or cut. The sandwich loaves are cut across the top four or more times depending on the size of the loaf. The cuts should be about $1/4$ in. deep. When stippling use a pointed stick or dowel about $1/4$ in. in diameter. The size of the oval-shaped or plain round rye will determine the number of stipples. Place the stipples at even distances apart.

10. Be careful of the steam coming out of the oven when peeling. Peel the bread into the oven, being careful to allow sufficient space on the cornmeal-dusted peel between units of proofed dough. Be careful not to peel the units too close to each other when getting them into the oven.

11. After all the bread has been peeled into the oven, allow the steam to run for an additional 5 min. until all the bread (especially the last loaves peeled in) has had full oven spring and a slight crust color appears. Open the damper and door (if American or Patent hearth-type oven is used) to allow the steam to go out of the oven.

12. In the large straight hearth ovens, shift the bread in the oven to insure a better-baked bottom. When using the newer rotary ovens, the heat may be evenly distributed and shifting may not be necessary.

13. Allow the bread to bake through slowly on the open damper for about 20 min. (larger units require more time) and then close the damper to allow formation of desired crust color and completion of baking.

14. Wash the bread very lightly with water or a boiled solution of starch and water (1 oz. starch boiled in 1 qt. water) immediately upon drawing the bread out to the oven door. This will give a shine or gloss to the crust.

15. Stack the bread carefully to prevent breaking or shredding the crust.

Note: If a heavier type of sour rye is desired, the sour added may be increased to 12 lb. Increase the amount of salt to 9 oz. While 4 qt. water are used in the above recipe, you will note that 8 oz. salt is used. The extra salt is used for the fermented sour dough which is made without salt. This is the same as for a regular sponge.

While a strong clear or common flour is used to make the dough and to support the sour made with rye flour, care must be used in mixing. Overmixing will cause the gluten in the clear flour to tear, and the resulting bread will not have the proper volume and will tend to tear in makeup and in baking.

Sour rye rolls are made from the same dough as sour rye bread. In most cases the dough is scaled into presses weighing from 3 to 5 lb. The rolls are rounded and shaped into oval shape. The rolls are given $^3/_4$ proof and baked with steam in the oven.

BRAIDED EGG BREAD, FOUR-, FIVE- AND SIX-TWIST BREADS

A properly shaped and baked egg bread is an asset to the variety of a bakeshop. This unit concerns itself with the braiding of these breads. Refer to the recipe for egg bread dough (p. 78) and check the procedures for the mixing of the dough, the conditioning of the dough, and the preparation of the scaled dough for makeup into egg bread.

Procedures to Follow for Braided Egg Breads

1. The dough should be almost completely conditioned. That is, allow the dough to rise well after the first punch and take to the bench.

2. Scale the dough into the desired weight for the presses of dough. Allow the presses of dough to relax 10 to 15 min. before pressing out.

3. Separate the pieces of dough and shape into ovals, as for finger rolls. Use very little rye flour. In fact, some bakers prefer to wipe a small part of the bench with a little oil and shape the pieces of dough.

4. Roll out the pieces of dough into strands that are even in shape. Each strand should be tapered so that the center is thicker and the ends thin. Avoid sharp points at the ends of the strips of dough.

5. Line up the strips, dust them with rye flour lightly, and proceed to braid them. Keep the strands snug but don't pull them tight.

6. The braided breads are then placed on pans dusted with cornmeal or placed in bread boxes that are dusted with cornmeal. They are egg-washed before being panned or placed in bread boxes.

7. Allow the breads to get $3/4$ proof and egg-wash a second time. Poppy seeds may be sprinkled lightly over the tops of the bread at this time.

8. The egg breads are generally baked directly on the hearth at a temperature of 350°F. until brown and crisp. Avoid a hot or flashy oven.

Procedures to Follow for Braiding Four-, Five- and Six-Twist Breads (Figs. 77 and 78)

1. Odd-numbered breads using three or five strips of dough require that you start by lining up the strands and separating them in the center.

2. Even-numbered braids (four or six strips) require that you line up the strands and seal the edges at the top. You then braid from the top down.

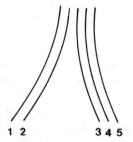

FIG. 77. FOUR STRIPS OF DOUGH FOR THE FOUR-TWIST BREAD. START BRAIDING FROM THE TOP

FIG. 78. FIVE STRIPS OF DOUGH FOR FIVE-TWIST BREAD. SEPARATE THE STRIPS IN THE CENTER AND START THE BRAID WITH No. 5 AND THEN No. 1

PUMPERNICKEL BREAD AND ROLLS

Pumpernickel bread is similar to sour rye bread except for the fact that it has a darker color (due to the pumpernickel flour, sugar color which may be added and the soaked stale bread which is still added in some retail bakeshops). A sour dough must be used as it is for sour rye bread. The nature of the pumpernickel flour (coarse or fine) also determines the character of the bread. Very often, the top of the bread is sprinkled with onions for variety. Pumpernickel rolls are made from the same dough and are similar in shape and variety as the rye rolls made from sour rye dough.

Pumpernickel Bread (4 qt.)   **Yield:** 28–30 1-lb. loaves

Ingredients	Lb.	Oz.	Mixing procedure
Salt	..	10	Break up the sour dough in the water and
Fermented sour dough	8–10	..	dissolve the salt. Add sugar color and mix until blended
Sugar color (as desired for color)			
Water	6	..	
Water	2	..	Dissolve the yeast and set aside
Yeast (variable)	..	10	
Pumpernickel flour	2	..	Sift and add the flour, stir lightly, add the
Clear or common flour	15	..	yeast solution and develop the dough

Procedures to Follow for Pumpernickel Bread (Figs. 79 and 80)

1. Place the dough on a rye-floured part of the bench and scale into desired weight for the bread (1 lb. 2 oz. dough for each 1 lb. baked loaf).
2. Round up the scaled units, cover to prevent crust formation and allow to relax or condition for 15 min.

FIG. 79. OVAL-SHAPED PUMPER-NICKEL BREAD   FIG. 80. ROUND-SHAPED PUMPER-NICKEL BREAD

3. Shape the loaves in round, sandwich type, or Vienna shape loaves. Caraway seeds may be used in the makeup of the bread during the shaping. Dip the rounded piece of dough into caraway seeds and mold the seeds with dough as the bread is being shaped.

4. Place the shaped units in bread boxes that are dusted with rye flour and cornmeal (white) and space about 4 in. apart. The space allows for proofing of the units.

5. Allow the bread to get $^3/_4$ (no more) proof and wash lightly with water and stipple three or four times for the round or Vienna shaped loaves. The sandwich loaves may be stippled or sliced with a knife. The cut should be about $^1/_2$ in. deep. It is at this point that the onions may be placed on top of the bread. The top of the bread may also be smeared with a soft mix of sour dough thinned with water.

6. Set the oven temperature at 425°F. and allow moist steam to enter the oven for 4 to 5 min. before loading the oven.

7. Load the bread into the oven with a peel which has been dusted with cornmeal. Be careful when lifting and placing the bread on the peel to avoid knocking the proofed bread down or causing irregular shape.

8. Allow the steam to continue into the oven after all the bread is loaded and until the bread has fully risen (oven spring). About 10 to 15 min. after loading, shut off the steam and allow the bread to bake until the crust is firm and the bread sounds hollow when tapped (about 1 hr. for each 1 lb. loaf). Larger breads take longer to bake.

9. It may be necessary to shift the bread after it has been in the oven for about $^1/_2$ hr. in order to insure a better bottom. This is necessary if the bottom heat of the oven is not strong.

10. Wash the bread lightly with water or starch glaze (2 qt. of water boiled with a solution of $1^1/_2$ oz. of corn starch) as soon as the bread is removed from the oven. This will maintain a shine or luster on the top crust of the bread. *Caution:* Wash lightly to avoid sogginess of crust.

Makeup for Pumpernickel Rolls

1. Scale out the dough into desired presses (weight determined by the size of the rolls).

2. Round up the dough into presses and allow the dough to relax about 15 min.

3. Press out the dough in the divider and shape into round, oval, or twisted shapes.

4. Place on flour-dusted pans or greased pans and allow to get $^3/_4$ proof. These rolls may be washed with water and garnished with onions for variety.

5. Bake at 425°F. with steam in the oven for the first 10 min. of baking.
6. Wash the rolls with water or starch glaze immediately after removal from the oven.

Note: Do not over-develop the dough until it starts to tear. This dough requires less mixing time than other doughs made without sour dough. Be sure the sour dough is fully developed and is the final sour or full sour. The more sour used the heavier and tastier the bread. Less mixing is also necessary to avoid tearing when more sour is used.

HEAVY SOUR RYE BREAD (CORN BREAD)

This bread is distinguished from regular sour rye bread in that it is heavier by volume and closer grained, requires more sour dough, and is often taken from a bread box and shaped by hand. The units also require a longer period of baking. Many of the specialty shops buy this bread because it requires special skill and knowledge in makeup. However, if the baker can make regular sour rye bread he can also make heavy rye or corn bread. It is a good business builder and provides variety.

Heavy Sour Rye Bread

Yield: Approximately thirty (30) 1 lb. loaves if made like sour rye. If taken and shaped by hand, baked loaves are cut and slices sold by weight.

Ingredients	Lb.	Oz.	Mixing procedure
Yeast	..	8	Dissolve the yeast and set aside. More yeast may be used if desired
Water	2	..	
Fermented sour dough	16	..	Dissolve salt, add sour and mix well to distribute sour dough
Salt	..	10	
Water	6	..	
Clear flour (approx.)	16	..	Add flour and mix in at slow speed until smooth to the touch. The dough will also be soft and sticky as compared to regular sour rye bread dough

Procedures to Follow

1. Place the dough in a bread box which has been moistened with water.
2. Allow the dough to relax in the box for about 20 min.

    Note: The oven should be ready to receive the bread at this point (temp. 430°F.), and the steam ready for injection 3 min. before the bread is loaded or peeled into the oven.

3. Dip hands in cool water and with the fingers and palms of both hands grasp a portion of the dough and remove by closing the fingers. The weight of the dough removed is only a matter of judgment. This is not too important because the baked bread is weighed and then sold by the pound. However, practice will make the amounts removed accurate to a reasonable degree. The unit of dough is then shaped in the palms of the hand by rounding as though you were rounding up a piece of dough in your hand. The wetness of the hands and the dough should keep the dough from sticking.

4. The peel is held by another baker or oven man. It is a small peel, to hold one loaf of bread. The peel is dusted well with rye flour and the bread is peeled into the steam-filled oven. Allow the steam to continue until the bread has had full oven spring and takes on a light crust color. The damper and doors are opened when the bread is thoroughly baked. A 2-lb. loaf of bread will take about 1 hr. to bake. Larger breads take longer.

5. For ease in handling the dough and makeup the dough is made stiffer by increasing the common flour so that the dough is almost as stiff as regular sour rye bread dough. The units are then scaled, rounded, relaxed, and rounded again. The units are placed in a bread box dusted with rye flour and are given about $3/4$ proof. A little less proof is advised for doughs using more sour.

Note: The units are not stippled if they are made by hand and peeled into the oven from the box. They may be stippled if they are made like sour rye bread.

WHEAT BREAD

Wheat bread is a popular type of bread and has special dietary appeal as well as variety appeal. This bread varies from the 100 per cent whole-wheat type to the various types containing lesser percentages of whole-wheat flour. The matter of percentage is determined by the amount of whole-wheat flour used. Thus, if all whole-wheat flour is used, the bread may be sold as 100 per cent whole-wheat bread. This type of whole-wheat bread will contain larger bran flakes and give the bread a coarser grain with a more nut-like taste and flavor. This has special sales appeal. The bakeshop demands will determine the type of bread made.

Whole-Wheat Bread (2 qt.)   **Yield:** 10 1-lb. loaves

Ingredients	Lb.	Oz.	Mixing procedure
Sugar	..	8	Scale carefully. Mix ingredients well to
Salt	..	2	dissolve
Milk powder	..	4	
Molasses	..	3	
Water	3	..	
Yeast	..	6	Dissolve yeast and set aside
Water (warm)	1	..	
Whole-wheat flour	3	3	Sift the flour. Do not remove bran flakes.
Bread flour (patent)	3	4	Add to above and stir slightly. Add yeast
Shortening	..	4	solution and mix until flour is absorbed and
			dough formed. Add the shortening and de-
			velop to a smooth dough

Procedures to Follow

1. This dough requires a shorter development period in the final stages of mixing. As soon as the dough works smoothly away from the sides of the kettle and balls up it may be considered properly developed.
2. This dough should be slightly softer than pan bread dough. It stiffens slightly during fermentation because the bran of the whole-wheat flour will absorb additional moisture during fermentation.
3. This dough should be given a slightly shorter fermentation period than pan bread. Allow the dough to rise, punch, and allow to rise again. Do not punch twice. The gluten in this dough is not as strong as that in white bread, and over-fermentation will cause tearing of the gluten with a loss in volume.
4. Scale the rounded units (1 lb. $2^1/_2$ oz. for each 1 lb. loaf). Round up and let rest 15 min. Shape the units as for pan bread. Use only enough dusting flour to prevent the dough from sticking or tearing during makeup.
5. Place the units in clean, lightly greased, loaf pans with the seam at the bottom.
6. Give the bread $^3/_4$ proof before baking. The bread may be washed with water and the top sprinkled with bran flour for variety.
7. Bake at 420°F. Allow a small amount of steam to enter the oven before loading the bread and continue the steam until the oven spring has been completed and the crust starts to show signs of color.
8. Bake this bread slightly longer than white bread (about 40 min. for each 1 lb. loaf). The molasses will tend to keep the loaf soft.

Note: A dark or blackstrap molasses is best used for color and taste. If 100 per cent whole-wheat flour is used, 3 lb. whole-wheat flour is used for each quart of water used in the dough. Remember, the dough stiffens as it ferments.

RAISIN BREAD

This bread will vary in the amount and nature of the ingredients used from one bakeshop to another. The variations may exist in the amount of raisins used per quart of dough, eggs, shortening, and shape of the bread. Naturally, the richer the bread the more expensive it is. It is good practice to make a better loaf of this variety bread to build and maintain sales. Of equal importance is the manner in which the bread is finished. Since it is a sweeter and richer bread the use of syrup and icing is important. By law, raisin bread must contain 50 per cent or more raisins, based on weight of flour.

Raisin Bread (2 qt.) **Yield:** 12 to 13 loaves

Ingredients	Lb.	Oz.	Mixing procedure
Sugar	..	12	Blend the ingredients to a smooth paste
Salt	..	2	
Milk powder	..	6	
Shortening	..	8	
Eggs	..	12	Add the eggs in two stages and blend well
Water	3	..	Add the water and stir slightly
Yeast	..	8	Dissolve the yeast and set aside
Water	1	..	
Bread flour (patent)	7	..	Sift, add the flour and mix slightly. Add the yeast solution and mix until almost developed
Raisins (moist)	3	8	Add the raisins and develop. Do not overmix at this stage

Procedures to Follow

1. Soak the raisins for about 15 min. in lukewarm water and then drain off the water. This will enable the raisins to regain their moisture. Very dry or hard raisins should be soaked longer to regain moisture.
2. Add the raisins in the final stages of mixing. This stage is to distribute the raisins throughout the dough. Overmixing will cause the soft raisins to mash and this will cause streaking (gray) of the dough.
3. Allow the dough to ferment as for white pan bread. One punch is enough.

4. Scale the units (1 lb. 4 oz. dough for the regular 1-lb. white bread pans). The raisins add weight, not volume, to the dough.
5. Makeup the bread as you would pan bread. Scale, round, rest, and makeup the units.
6. Place the units in properly cleaned and greased bread pans. Give the bread $3/4$ proof and wash the tops lightly with egg-wash.
7. Bake the breads at 400°F., with a mild amount of slow steam in the oven. Mild steam is necessary to avoid excessive blistering of the egg-washed crust. Bake these breads slightly longer than pan bread (about 40 min. for each 1 lb. 2 oz. loaf).
8. Remove the loaves from the pans as soon as baked and wash the top crust of the bread with hot, light syrup wash. Allow the breads to cool until slightly warm and ice the tops of the bread with a warm simple icing.

Note: These breads may be made in round shape and baked on a bun pan. Four loaves are generally placed on each pan. The round loaves may be cut on the sides when they reach $3/4$ proof. Diced, mixed fruit may be added to the dough for specialty breads during certain holiday seasons. This will add to bread variety.

VIENNA BREAD

Vienna bread is similar, in many respects, to French and Italian breads. The difference lies in the richness of the dough and the slight variation in the shape of the loaf. The dough is also similar to that used for hard-type rolls such as Kaiser rolls. The important factors are the shape and the crispness of the crust. The crust is crisp but not as thick as that of Italian bread.

Vienna Bread (2 qt.)   **Yield:** 15 to 18 loaves

Ingredients	Lb.	Oz.	Mixing procedure
Sugar	..	3	Stir the ingredients well to dissolve
Salt	..	2	
Malt	..	2	
Oil	..	4	
Eggs	..	4	
Water	3	..	
Yeast	..	6	Dissolve the yeast and set aside
Water (warm)	1	..	
Bread flour (patent)	7	8	Sift, add the flour and stir slightly. Add the yeast solution and develop well to a smooth dough

Procedures to Follow (Fig. 81)

1. Allow the dough to rise well and test for punching. The dough should be ready to fall back at the touch before punching. Punch well and allow the dough to rise well once again. If necessary, punch a second time and allow to rise again (15 min.). This dough must be properly conditioned but not allowed to become old as a result of over-fermentation.

Fig. 81.   VIENNA BREAD

2. Scale the dough into desired units (12 to 14 oz. is the usual weight). Round up the units and allow them to rest for 15 min.
3. The units are then shaped with a tapered effect similar to longer and narrower rye bread shape. The ends are not altogether pointed.
4. Place the made-up units in bread or roll boxes that are dusted with cornmeal (white).
5. Allow the breads to get $^3/_4$ proof, wash lightly with water and make about four cuts with a sharp knife about $^1/_2$ in. deep. These cuts will spread during baking and give the desired appearance to the baked loaf.
6. Bake the bread at 410°F. Allow the oven to fill with a good supply of steam before peeling in the loaves. The units are placed on bread peels dusted with cornmeal and peeled onto the hearth of the oven. Allow the steam to continue in the oven until the bread starts to form a crust color. Allow the steam to escape and bake the breads until they are golden brown and very crisp (about 35 min. for 12 oz. loaf).

Note: A strong, high-gluten flour is best suited for this type of bread.

CINNAMON BREAD

Cinnamon bread is one of a number of variety breads that is very popular. It lends itself well to variety in finish and in merchandising, which builds sales and provides greater variety in food service. Of equal importance, is the fact that cinnamon bread may be made from any of a number of doughs used for other products. Let us examine this bread and the manner in which it may be produced.

Procedures to Follow

1. Soft roll dough, sweet yeast dough, and pan bread dough may be used for making cinnamon bread. You will note that each of these doughs varies in richness and the resulting bread will vary with the dough. Generally, when the bread is made from sweet yeast dough smaller units or breads are made because they are more expensive.

2. Scale the fermented dough from which the bread is to be made into the desired weights. Round the units slightly and shape into an oblong form. Allow the units to rest for about 10 to 15 min. during this preliminary proofing stage.

3. Roll out the units into oblong shape about $1/4$ in. thick. Larger units made from soft roll or pan bread dough may be rolled slightly thicker. The units are then brushed with water and sprinkled liberally with cinnamon sugar. Be careful not to over-sprinkle the sugar. It may tend to run when dissolved and cause the baked loaf to stick to the pans. Roll up the unit into a pan bread shape and seal the edge. Place the bread, with closed seam facing down, into a greased bread pan or loaf pan. Allow the bread to rise to about $3/4$ proof and stipple slightly. The stippling is not necessary for breads made from a richer dough.

4. Brush the top of the bread with melted fat and bake at 385° to 390°F. for bread made from pan bread or soft roll dough. A small amount of wet steam may be used for this bread. Bake until mildly crisp and brown.

5. Remove the bread from the pan upon removal from the oven. This will reduce the possibility of bread sticking to the pan.

6. The top of the loaf is then brushed with melted fat and dipped into cinnamon sugar. This is done after the bread has cooled somewhat but is still warm. Some bakers prefer to stripe the top of the bread with simple icing or fondant icing.

7. When using a richer dough, such as bun dough or coffee cake dough, the units are generally brushed with melted fat and butter on the inside and sprinkled with cinnamon sugar. The units are then given $3/4$ proof and baked in a cooler oven (355° to 365°F.). After baking the units are allowed to cool until warm. They are then brushed with melted butter and dipped in cinnamon sugar. These loaves may also be iced with a fondant icing if not dipped in cinnamon sugar.

Note: A fine-grade cinnamon is recommended for these loaves. The blend of cinnamon and sugar may be a little stronger to emphasize the cinnamon effect and flavor.

DATE-NUT BREAD

Date-nut bread is one of a number of specialty bread varieties. While it is not as popular as others it has special sales appeal if made properly. The addition of dates and nuts and the fact that it is yeast-raised lends special flavor and appearance to the loaf.

Date-Nut Bread (2 qt.)   **Yield:**   12 loaves or 17 round units

Ingredients	Lb.	Oz.	Mixing procedure
Sugar	..	12	Blend all ingredients in this stage to a
Salt	..	2	smooth paste
Milk powder	..	6	
Shortening	..	8	
Water	3	..	Add the water and stir
Yeast	..	8	Dissolve the yeast and set aside
Water	1	..	
Bread flour	6	4	Sift, add the flour, stir slightly and add the
Chopped dates	1	4	yeast solution. Develop the dough until al-
Toasted chopped nuts	1	8	most smooth. Add the dates and nuts and blend in. Do not overmix at this stage

Procedures to Follow

1. The amounts of dates and nuts may be increased. This will make the dough richer and costlier. The volume by weight will be smaller.
2. Eggs may be added to the dough (8 oz. yolks) and this will require the addition of 8 oz. of flour to the recipe.
3. The dates and nuts are to be added after the dough is about completely developed. The dates will smear and discolor the dough if mixed into the dough beyond the point of distribution of the dates and nuts.
4. Allow the dough to rise well, punch, allow to rise again and take to the bench.
5. Scale the dough into desired units. If the shape of the bread is to be round, scale into 14 oz. pieces and place six breads on a sheet pan. If made into loaf form, the units should be scaled 1 lb. 4 oz. for the normal 1 lb. pan bread loaf size. Allowance must be made for the dates and nuts which add extra weight but do not increase volume.
6. Place the molded units on a clean, greased sheet pan or in greased loaf pans.

7. Give the units $^3/_4$ proof, egg-wash, allow to gain almost full proof, and bake at 385°F. A small amount of steam may be used in the first stages of baking. This will prevent splitting of the top crust.

8. The bread is baked about 40 min. for each 1 lb. loaf. The units may be washed with syrup immediately after baking and iced with simple icing when they are mildly warm.

BOSTON BROWN BREAD

Boston brown bread is a specialty bread that is not of the yeast-raised variety. It is made as a specialty item in plants that produce this type of product because of the special pans and baking or steaming procedures required. Of course, it may be made in the average bakeshop and sold on special occasions or as a special lead item. It is of the quick bread variety.

Boston Brown Bread   **Yield:** 8 loaves

Ingredients	Lb.	Oz.	Mixing procedure
Sugar	..	4	Blend all ingredients until smooth and the
Milk powder	..	8	milk powder and soda are dissolved.
Salt	..	1	
Melted shortening or oil	..	4	
Water	4	..	
Baking soda	..	$1^1/_2$	
Molasses	1	12	
Raisins	1	..	Add the raisins and cornmeal and stir in well
Cornmeal	1	..	
Rye flour	1	..	Sift the flour and baking powder, add and
Bread flour	1	..	mix to a smooth batter. The mix should be
Whole-wheat flour	1	..	often medium thick consistency and in a
Baking powder	..	$1^1/_4$	pourable state

Procedures to Follow

1. A dark and strong-flavored molasses should be used for color and taste.

2. Use special corrugated pans for the bread. Be sure the pans are clean and well-greased to prevent the baked bread from sticking.

3. The size of the pan will determine the size or weight of the mix. It is safe to fill the bottom half of the pan until almost three-fourths full. If made properly, the mix will rise in baking and fill the entire pan.

4. Fill all pans equally. Close the top over the filled bottom and seal with the overlapping catch. This is important to prevent the mix from running during the baking and steaming periods.

5. Place the closed pans in deep pans (similar to roasting pans) that have been filled with hot water to the level just beneath the closed seal of the bread pans. Too much water may cause seepage into the pans if they are not seal-proof.

6. Place these pans in the oven at 350°F. The baking time will vary from 2–3 hr. depending upon the size of the pan. Add additional water to the pans when the water runs low due to evaporation. Actually this is a steaming or cooking rather than dry-baking process.

7. Be careful when opening the top seal of the pan to test the bread for proper bake. Allow the steam to escape when opening the pan slightly. Test for bake by pressing gently in the center. It should feel spongy to the touch and spring back when pressed slightly. Allow the bread to cool slightly and turn the pan over on a clean pan to remove. Do not allow the pan to rest on the pan which will hold the baked loaves. This may flatten or break the loaves. Hold the pan in the air about 1 in. above the holding tray or pan.

GLUTEN (DIETETIC) BREAD

Gluten (dietetic) bread derives its name from the fact that it is made from flour which has had most of the starch removed. This is done by a washing process wherein the starch is washed out and the gluten particles remain. This flour is much more expensive than regular flour and is processed by companies specializing in this type of flour. It must be recognized that this flour absorbs and holds more water or other liquid than does regular flour, and the baker should be aware that the dough will stiffen even after it is mixed.

Gluten Bread (100 per cent gluten flour)   **Yield:** 9 to 10 loaves

Ingredients	Lb.	Oz.	Mixing procedure
Salt	..	$2^1/_4$	Stir well to dissolve the milk powder and
Milk powder	..	2	salt
Water	3	..	
Yeast	..	5	Dissolve the yeast and set aside
Water	1	..	
Gluten flour	5	..	Add the flour, stir slightly, add the yeast solution and mix to a dough
Shortening	..	4	Add the shortening and develop well until smooth

Procedures to Follow

1. The dough will feel smooth, slack, or soft and springy, when first mixed.
2. Allow the dough to rise, punch, and allow to rise again. Note the stiffening of the dough as it ferments.
3. Scale the units, 15 oz., for each normal 1 lb. pan of white bread.
4. Shape the dough as for pan bread and place in clean, greased pans.
5. Allow the dough to rise well; it will feel very gassy. Bake at 410°F. with or without a small amount of steam. The steam may cause some slight blistering on the top crust of the loaf.
6. Bake the loaf well until it feels hollow when tapped. Remove from pans immediately after baking.

LOW SODIUM BREAD

Yield: Approximately 16 loaves. Variable-Depending upon weight of each loaf.

Ingredients	Lb.	Oz.	Mixing procedure
Sugar	..	9	Dissolve the sugar and salt substitute in the
Salt substitute (Sodium free salt)	..	3	water
Water	4		
Yeast (variable)	..	9	Dissolve the yeast and set aside
Water	2		
Bread flour (Hard Winter 12–13% protein)	10	4	Sift and add the bread flour. Mix slightly and add the yeast solution. Mix to a dough formation and add the shortening. Develop to
Shortening		4	a smooth dough

Procedures to Follow

1. Dough temperature: 77–79°F.
2. Dough conditioning: Allow the dough to rise well (approximately 1½ hrs) Punch and relax for about ½ hr and take to the bench or scaler rounder. Preliminary proofing: 15 min.
3. This dough will tend to relax more rapidly because it is slightly softer than the average white pan bread and the sodium free salts will allow for a more rapid activity of the yeast.
4. Give the panned loaves approximately ¾ proof and then wash and cut the tops of the loaves, if desired. The loaves may be left plain and given slightly more proof before baking. It is advisable to bake these loaves with a mild steam injection into the oven and at a temperature of 400°F.

EGG BREAD
Section-Type, Oval-Shaped, and Snail-Shaped Breads

Most egg breads (challah) are usually made by braiding three, four, five, or six strands of egg dough into one bread. There are types which are common in many bakeshops such as the pan or section type. On special occasions, the oval- and snail-shape (Rudisch) egg breads are made.

Refer to the recipe for egg bread for dough preparation (p. 78). The dough should be properly fermented and handled as for egg breads of the twisted or braided variety. The following procedures are to be employed in the making of the types below:

Procedures to Follow for Section Egg Bread (Figs. 82 and 83)

1. Scale the conditioned dough into presses weighing about 5 lb. Round the presses and allow to relax for about 15 min.
2. Press out the dough into 36 pieces and round up the pieces. After all pieces have been rounded and dusted lightly with rye flour (to prevent sticking and excessive crust formation), shape each piece as you would for a short, thick, frankfurter roll.
3. The size of the pan, the richness of the dough, and the quality of the product will determine the number of pieces to be used. For example, using a rich dough (1 lb. eggs per quart) six pieces of dough are sufficient for the average pan holding 1 lb. of baked white bread. Place the six pieces together (side by side) and dust lightly with rye flour. This will prevent the sections from baking blind (the sections will not overrun each other and have a distinct line of separation showing after baking).
4. Place the sections in the bread pans which have been cleaned and lightly greased. Flatten the sections of dough lightly. Egg-wash lightly and allow the bread to get $^3/_4$ proof. Egg-wash again and sprinkle with poppy seeds if so desired.
5. Bake at 360°F. until the top has a golden brown color and a hollow sound is heard when the top crust is tapped. The bottom of the

FIG. 82.   SECTION EGG BREAD

FIG. 83.   SIX-TWIST EGG BREAD

bread should be checked for proper bake before removing from the oven. The average 12 to 14 oz. challah takes about 35 to 40 min. to bake. Remove the breads from the pans immediately after baking to avoid sweating.

Note: The units of dough may be scaled out separately for each pan loaf. Round up the scaled units and allow to relax. Divide the unit into six or more equal sections and proceed.

Makeup of Oval-Shaped Egg Bread (Fig. 84)

1. Scale the fermented dough into units weighing 14 oz. to 1 lb. They may be increased in weight if desired. Round the units and allow them to rest for about 15 min.
2. Shape the units as you would a Vienna bread, keeping the shape just slightly tapered toward the end. The unit is almost straight across the top. Be sure the seam at the bottom is sealed tightly.

FIG. 84. OVAL-SHAPED EGG BREAD WITH THIN STRIP OF DOUGH ACROSS THE TOP

3. A small piece of dough weighing about $1^1/_2$ oz. is to be rolled out into a narrow strip. Allow the strip to relax and stretch again to prevent tearing. Wash the top of the egg bread with egg-wash and place the strip of dough across the top center from end to end. Be sure to press the ends of the strip firmly into the edges of the loaf. Wash the top strip with egg-wash.
4. Place the units on clean pans which have been dusted with cornmeal. Allow the breads to get a little more than $^3/_4$ proof and bake at 360°F. This is desirable for it makes for better challah appearance.

Makeup of Snail-Shaped Egg Bread (Rudisch) (Fig. 85)

1. Scale the fermented dough into desired weights. The same weights are used for the oval shape. Special occasions call for larger units.
2. This type of challah generally contains raisins. The raisins may be added to each unit at the time the pieces of dough are scaled and rounded. Allow the rounded units to relax for 15 min.
3. Roll out the unit into a long, tapered strip (thick in the center and tapered at the ends). Twist the strip into a snail shape as you would for snail Danish. Be sure the center is tight and the edge of the dough is sealed tightly at the completion of the snail.

FIG. 85. SNAIL-SHAPED
EGG BREAD (RUDISCH)

4. Place the challah on a clean pan that is dusted with cornmeal. Egg-wash and allow the units to get slightly more than $3/4$ proof. Egg-wash again and bake at 360°F. Be sure to bake out well and that the crust is crisp.

SALT STICKS, CRESCENT ROLLS, AND ONION ROLLS

At the time hard rolls (Kaiser rolls, water rolls, etc.) were introduced it was mentioned that there are a great variety of hard-type rolls. The baker has learned that the greater the variety of rolls the greater the sales potential. This also holds true for the baker employed in a hotel or other establishment where food is served. Variety is important and essential. This unit will explain and show the procedures for making salt sticks, crescents and onion rolls.

Vienna dough, the same dough that is used for Kaiser rolls, is used for the preparation of these three types of rolls.

Procedures to Follow for Salt Sticks (Fig. 86)

1. Scale the fermented and conditioned dough into presses. The weight of the press will vary, according to need, from 4 lb. in the average bakeshop to 2 lb. for small rolls in hotels and restaurants.

FIG. 86. SALT
STICK

2. Allow the presses to relax for about 10 min. and press out. Separate the pieces by dusting lightly with rye flour. Round up the pieces lightly. They may be left in round or oval shape. Cover the units and allow them to relax for about 10 min.
3. Line up the units of relaxed dough, about four abreast, and roll out with a thin rolling pin (one used for pies) to about $1/4$ in. thick and line up on the bench. Be sure to dust the rolled pieces with rye flour to prevent sticking while rolling and relaxing. After all the units have been rolled out, start to shape the salt sticks beginning with units which were rolled first.

4. Begin by stretching the piece of dough slightly. Roll the top part in the right hand while stretching slightly with the left. Continue to roll and stretch slightly until the entire length of the dough is now rolled up. The right hand, which has been rolling the dough in the palm, is also applying mild pressure to the dough. This causes the unit to expand and the rolls of dough show as the unit is rolled up. The palm of the hand and fingers should keep the unit centered. The center of the unit or roll is thicker in the center and tapers evenly to each side. The end of the unit of dough is given a final stretch and the end is pressed against the roll to seal it. Place the end of the roll so that it is in the center and face down to the bench.

5. With practice, it is possible to make rolls the same length and with an equal number of turns. These turns of dough provide the layered effect of a horn-like roll. Line up the rolls on the bench until all are made up. Brush the top of the rolls with water after they have been flattened slightly. Sprinkle the tops lightly with caraway seed and coarse salt being careful not to over-salt the rolls. They are then placed in roll boxes sprinkled with cornmeal or placed on pans which have been lightly greased or lined with parchment paper.

6. Give the rolls almost full proof before baking. If the rolls are in a roll box give the rolls a little more than $3/4$ proof. This makes it possible to lift the rolls and place them on a cornmeal-dusted peel for placing in the oven. Allow the oven to fill with moist steam before loading. The temperature should be about 425°F. Load the oven and allow the steam to continue until the rolls take on a slight color. The steam may then be shut off. Bake the rolls until golden brown and the crust is dry and crisp. Remember, this is a hard-type roll.

7. If the rolls are not to be baked with steam, wash the rolls with egg-wash before sprinkling with caraway seeds and coarse salt. It is also advisable to enrich the dough with more eggs for this type of roll.

Makeup of Crescent Rolls (Fig. 87)

1. Roll the pressed out units longer, wider, and thinner. Be sure to use rye flour for rolling purposes to prevent sticking of the overlapping units of dough which have been lined up.

2. Make up the same way as salt sticks by stretching and rolling. The pressure of the palm is slightly harder. This will cause the roll to stretch out further while being rolled and the roll will be longer. The number of rolls is also greater than that of salt sticks.

3. Line up the rolls on the bench, flatten slightly, wash with water and sprinkle with poppy seeds. These rolls may also be left plain.

4. Proof as you would salt sticks and bake in the same manner.

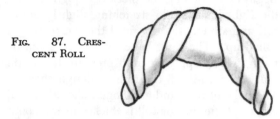

FIG. 87. CRES-
CENT ROLL

Note: When placing these rolls in roll boxes or pans be sure that you shape them so that they have a half-moon or crescent shape. Be sure that they stay in that shape when lifting and placing on the peel to be loaded into the oven. Roll appearance is important.

Makeup of Onion Rolls

1. Peeled fresh onions which have been chopped fine and mixed with salt and oil may be used. However, this takes time and exposes other delicate cakes and pastries to the strong odor of fresh onions. Most bakers use dried onions which are packed in cans weighing about 2 lb. These occupy less space and the odor is not as strong.

2. Soak these dried onions in enough cool water to cover them. Allow the flakes to soak several hours to absorb the moisture. Remove excess water from the onions and mix with approximately 1 oz. salt, 4 oz. oil, and 2 oz. poppy seeds. Keep the onions covered when not in use.

3. Scale the presses of dough, round up and allow them to relax. Press out and round up the units, and then place them on a lightly dusted part of the bench or in a box with cornmeal. Cover the units and allow to rest.

4. Roll the rounded and relaxed units gently with a rolling pin. Now dip the units into the onions and roll again so that the onions stick to the dough. Be sure that the onion dip faces the bench and not the rolling pin. This permits rolling the units without sticking. If the units stick brush the area of the bench where you are rolling them with a little oil.

5. Place the units in roll boxes dusted with cornmeal or on pans which are parchment-paper-lined or dusted with cornmeal. Allow the rolls to get $3/4$ proof and then stipple by pressing two fingers into the center of the roll. If the rolls are taken from the box, do this before they are placed on the peel. Bake the same as salt sticks and crescent rolls. These rolls take less time to bake because they are thinner. However, they must receive a crisp bake.

CHEESE BREAD

Cheese breads will vary in taste and texture in accordance with the type and nature of the cheese used. For example, a hard Cheddar cheese will provide a stronger cheese flavor than will a softer, grated American-type cheese. An increased amount of cheese will also have a decided effect upon the bread. It will also tend to soften the loaf and make for a closer grain. The nature of the bread is determined by the requirements of the bakeshop and the consumer.

Cheese Bread (2 qt.)   **Yield:** 10 loaves

Ingredients	Lb.	Oz.	Mixing procedure
Sugar	..	6	Mix all ingredients with the water to dissolve
Salt	..	2	
Malt	..	2	
Milk powder	..	4	
Water	3	..	
Yeast	..	6	Dissolve the yeast and set aside
Water (lukewarm)	1	..	
Bread flour	6	6	Sift, add the flour and stir slightly. Add the
Shortening	..	4	shortening and develop
Dehydrated cheese	..	10	Add the cheese and finish development of
or grated hard			the dough
cheese			

Procedures to Follow

1. Be sure the cheese is added before the dough is fully developed. If the dough is fully developed, the cheese will be hard to incorporate and the cheese may be smeared. The result will be excessive discoloration of the dough.
2. Allow the dough to rise well, punch, and allow to rise again.
3. Scale the units as for regular pan bread. A slight decrease in volume will be noticed in the baked bread due to the added weight of the cheese. Adjustment should be made if a larger loaf is desired.
4. Make up the bread as for pan bread and place in greased bread pans.
5. Give the units $3/4$ proof and bake with a mild amount of steam in the oven. Bake the units a little longer (extra 5 min.) than white pan bread to avoid slight sogginess caused by the melted cheese.

Note: It is best to keep this dough slightly on the young side. Full or slight over-fermentation will increase the acidity of the dough beyond the desired point. The cheese increases the pH (acidity) of the dough.

BAGELS AND BIALYS

These specialty items are usually made in bakeshops that are especially geared to making these products. However, understanding and experience makes it possible for the baker, in most shops where these products are not available, to make his own. It is also common knowledge that bakers specialize in just these areas. For example there are labor organizations whose membership is composed of bagel bakers and bialy bakers. This indicates that a special skill and knowledge are required. The following recipes and procedures will provide the necessary information for the baker to make these products.

The experienced and skilled bagel baker will not press out the dough. He normally cuts strips right from the dough and rolls these strips into narrower strips about $1/2$ in. in diameter and tears off the strip when he has circled the strip around the palm of his hand. This requires practice and judgment for controlling the size and shape. This is a faster process but should only be tried after experience with the first method.

In baking bagels, the specialist bagel baker places boiled bagels on boards (for the rotating or revolving oven) which are covered with canvas cloths. These boards are slightly shorter than the depth of the oven shelf. The boards and bagels are placed in the oven. When the bagels start to take on color the boards are given a quick twist and the bagels are turned over on the hearth and the boards are ready to be used again. The canvas on the boards is moistened with water before the bagels are placed on them.

Bagel varieties are made by sprinkling coarse salt and poppy seeds on top of bagels before they are put in the oven. Others are sprinkled with onions (using the same preparation for onions as for onion rye bread).

Water Bagels (2 qt.)   **Yield:**   18 doz. (6 press of $3^{1}/_{2}$ lb. each)

Ingredients	Lb.	Oz.	Mixing procedure
Salt	. .	4	Mix together to dissolve and blend the in-
Malt	. .	14	gredients
Water	4	. .	
Yeast	. .	6	Dissolve the yeast and set aside
Water	2	. .	
High-gluten flour	13	8	Sift, add, stir slightly and add the yeast solution. Develop to a smooth dough

Procedures to Follow (Figs. 88–91)

1. A high-gluten patent flour must be used to make the dough in order to maintain the structure and consistency of the dough and to avoid slackening or softening of the dough during the fermentation and makeup of the bagels.
2. Develop the dough in low speed, for this is a stiff dough and develops friction in the developing stage. The dough must be stiff and smooth.
3. Allow the dough to relax for about 1 hr. in a warm place and keep the dough covered to prevent crustation. The dough must feel slightly gassy before taking to the bench for makeup.
4. Place the conditioned dough on the bench and scale into presses weighing about 3 lb. 4 oz. to 3 lb. 8 oz. Allow the presses to relax before pressing out. Avoid using dusting flour or oil when pressing out. The dough is stiff and should require no flour. The use of oil will cause the ends of the bagel to open in the cooking and baking.

FIG. 88.   SEALING THE ENDS OF THE BAGEL IN THE PALM OF THE HAND

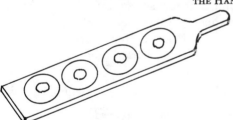

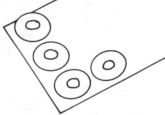

FIG. 89.   BAGELS PLACED ON BOARDS SLIGHTLY SHORTER THAN THE DEPTH OF THE OVEN SHELF

FIG. 90.   BAGELS (EGG AND PUMPERNICKEL VARIETY) PLACED ON PANS TO BE BAKED

FIG. 91.   BAKED BAGEL

5. The presses are separated without the use of flour. Roll each strip into an even strip long enough to go completely around the palm of the hand. Overlap the ends of the strip about $^1/_2$ in. and roll forward and backward with the palm of the hand to seal the edges together. Be careful to have the ends sealed properly and the thickness the same throughout.

6. Place the bagels in a roll box lined with a canvas cloth. Allow them to relax until about half proof.

7. To boil bagels prepare a mixture of 4 gal. water and $^1/_3$ qt. malt and bring to a boil. Turn the gas down until the liquid simmers. Deposit the half-proofed bagels into the water. Note that the bagels sink and then start to rise after about 30 sec. When the bagels float on the surface remove them from the liquid with a large skimmer and place on pans about 1 in. apart. Bake in a hot oven 450° to 460°F. When the tops of the bagels get a light brown color turn the bagels over for complete baking. This will also keep the bagels in a rounded shape without the sharp flatness of baking on one side. Remove from the oven when brown and shiny. The shine is provided by the syrup in the cooking and the partial cooking of the top surface of the dough.

Egg Bagels

Egg bagels, while similar in shape to water bagels, are completely different in composition and in the texture of the baked product. There are two methods of preparing this type of bagel for baking. The usual method is to allow them to proof and bake like an egg roll. These bagels may also be prepared in the same manner as water bagels by boiling before baking. Both methods will be explained following the recipe. Properly made, these bagels will add to the variety of specialized products.

Egg Bagels (2 qt.)   **Yield:** 16 doz.

Ingredients	Lb.	Oz.	Mixing procedure
Sugar	..	12	Mix all the ingredients well to dissolve the
Salt	..	$2^1/_2$	sugar and salt
Eggs (part yolks)	1	..	
Oil	..	12	
Water	3	..	
Yeast	..	6	Dissolve the yeast and set aside
Water	1	..	
High-gluten flour	11	..	Sift, add the flour, mix lightly, add the yeast, and develop to a smooth dough

Procedures to Follow

1. This is a stiff dough and should be developed in slow speed. A high-gluten flour is necessary to prevent slackening of the dough during fermentation.
2. Allow the dough to rise well, punch, and allow to relax about 15 min. before taking to the bench for makeup.
3. Scale the dough into presses weighing about 3 lb. 6 oz. If you have sufficient skill and experience cut pieces from the dough and roll out into strips and make up as for water bagel.
4. Allow the presses of dough to relax a few minutes before pressing out or dividing. Do not use oil to press out or dust flour. The dough is stiff enough to be divided without either.
5. Make up the bagel as you did for water bagels. Place on paper-lined pans about 1 in. apart and egg-wash. If the bagels are to be cooked place the bagels on canvas cloths in a roll box. Allow them to get half proof and boil as for water bagels.
6. If the bagels are not cooked, allow them to get $3/4$ proof and egg-wash again. Sprinkle the tops of the bagels with poppy seed and bake at 400°F. Note that the oven temperature is less than for water bagels since the dough is rich in sugar, eggs, and oil, and will develop a crust color much faster. If baked in a hot oven, the bagels will color too rapidly and will be soggy and soft after they are baked.
7. If these bagels are boiled be sure to turn them after the tops have taken on a mild brown color to prevent excessive flattening of the bottoms and maintain a round contour.

Pumpernickel Bagels

Pumpernickel bagels are specialized bread and roll items that are quite popular in many retail bakeshops. In fact, those shops not making this item will find a ready market for them if they are made properly and merchandised warm and fresh. These bagels are not cooked before baking and lend themselves well to retarding and baking as needed. Do not confuse these bagels with pumpernickel bread. The dough is quite different and the method of handling is also different.

Pumpernickel Bagels (2 qt.)   **Yield:** 13 doz.

Ingredients	Lb.	Oz.	Mixing procedure
Sugar	..	10	Mix all ingredients together until thoroughly
Salt	..	2$\frac{1}{2}$	dissolved and the sour is broken up. The
Milk powder	..	6	color may be checked at this time to see if
Oil	..	8	more color is required
Fermented sour (optional)	1	..	
Water	3	..	
Sugar color (enough to color° the dough)			
Yeast	..	6	Dissolve the yeast and set aside
Water	1	..	
Common or patent flour	8	8	Add and mix slightly. Add the yeast and develop until smooth
Pumpernickel flour	..	12	

° Amount depends on strength of sugar color.

Procedures to Follow

1. The dough should be stiff and developed in slow speed. Keep the dough cool by using cool water. A warm dough may cause too rapid fermentation and aging, which will cause tearing.
2. The amount of pumpernickel flour may be varied. An excess of pumpernickel flour will cause tearing in makeup and baking.
3. Allow the dough to rise once and take to the bench. Do not punch.
4. Scale the dough into presses weighing approximately 3 lb. 8 oz. The size will vary depending upon the bakeshop. Allow the presses to relax about 10 min. and press out with very little flour. Do not use oil.
5. Make up the bagels as you would water bagels. Do not use flour in the makeup for this will prevent proper sealing of the ends. It may be necessary to moisten the bench with a little water to prevent the strips from sliding while they are being rolled.
6. Dip each bagel in prepared onion mix (the same mix used for onion rye and pumpernickel bread) and place on paper-lined pans about 1 in. apart.
7. Allow the bagels to get $\frac{3}{4}$ proof, or slightly less, and bake in a hot oven (450°F.) until brown. Avoid overbaking. Be careful not to dump the bagels together while hot as this will cause the onions to fall off.

Bialy Rolls

These rolls are considered special bakery products and the trend is to have special bakeshops which make this product only. However, this does not mean that the normal retail or larger bakeshop cannot make them. The equipment and materials are those which are present in most bakeshops. There is a large market for these rolls and consumer demand is growing. Of course, the quality and freshness of the product are important factors.

Bialy Rolls (3 qt.)   Yield: 13 doz.

Ingredients	Lb.	Oz.	Mixing procedure
Sugar	..	4	Dissolve the sugar and salt in the water
Salt	..	3	
Water	4	..	
Yeast	..	8	Dissolve the yeast and set aside
Water	2	..	
Bread flour (high-gluten)	9	9	Sift, add the flour, stir slightly, add the yeast, and develop the dough well

Procedures to Follow (Fig. 92)

1. A high-gluten flour must be used so that the rolls may be given full proof and be able to stand up under handling in the final stages without falling back. It will also make for good rise (oven spring) during the early stages of baking. Develop the dough well.

Fig. 92. Cross-Section of a Bialy Roll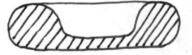

2. Allow the dough to rise well, punch, and allow to rise again.
3. Take the dough to the bench and scale into presses weighing from 3 lb. 8 oz. to 4 lb. The size of the roll is determined by the bakeshop or other establishment where the rolls are sold or served.
4. Allow the presses to relax and press out. Round up the units as for hamburger rolls and place in a roll box dusted with bread flour. Do not use excessive amounts of flour for dusting.

5. Allow the rolls to get $^3/_4$ proof. Pick up each unit and with the thumbs of both hands press into the center of the rounded unit so that the center of the dough is depressed and the sides are still risen. The unit now looks like a round filled bun without the filling. Place the units back in the box about 1 in. apart.

6. Dot each roll in the center with onions. Use the same preparation of reconstituted dried onions to which a small amount of oil, salt, and poppy seeds have been added. Allow the rolls to get almost full proof.

7. Bake the rolls in a hot oven 450°F. The rolls should be placed on a roll peel and peeled onto the hearth of the oven. The rolls may also be placed on clean dry pans and baked on the pans. The flour on the bottom of the roll will keep the dough and baked roll from sticking. These rolls are baked *without* steam in the oven. Bake the rolls until they are light brown and remove from the oven.

8. *Garlic biayls* may be made by the addition of garlic salt to the onions on top of the rolls.

   Note: Avoid the use of excessive flour. Excess at the bottom of the rolls will burn during baking.

Onion Boards and Breads

Onion boards and breads are also made from the same dough.

Procedures to Follow (Figs. 93 and 94)

1. Scale units into 4 to 6 oz. pieces and round up. Allow the units to relax until gassy and soft.

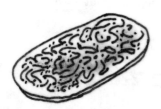

FIG. 93.   ONION BOARD MADE FROM
A BIALY DOUGH

FIG. 94.   ONION BREAD MADE FROM
A BIALY DOUGH

2. Roll out each unit with a small rolling pin until almost $1/8$ in. thick. They are usually made in oval rather than round shape. If the units do not roll easily and spring back allow the partially rolled units to relax and roll again to the desired thickness. Place the units on lightly greased pans and press the units gently to the pan so that the dough sticks and shrinkage is prevented. Dock or stipple the units, wash with a little water, and sprinkle the entire top of the dough with the onion preparation. Give the boards about half proof and bake in a hot oven (425°F.) until brown and crisp.

3. Onion breads are made by scaling 8 oz. units of dough and rounding up. Allow the units to relax and then dip into onions and work into Vienna bread shape. Give these units $3/4$ proof and garnish with onion mix. Bake at 420°F. until brown and crisp.

CHAPTER 15

Proper Handling of Sweet Yeast Dough

Sweet yeast doughs fall into various categories. They may be classified as the straight dough (bun dough or coffee cake dough), sponge dough (Babka), roll-in (Danish), or the re-mix dough (frozen dough or dough used for Babka rum cakes). A thorough understanding of dough richness, roll-in procedures, proofing, retarding, freezing, and baking is necessary. This chapter is concerned with the popular, daily doughs such as Danish pastry dough, coffee cake and Babka, frozen dough, and bun dough.

DANISH PASTRY

While Danish dough is leavened by yeast, the volume, flakiness, and general characteristics of Danish products are influenced by proper handling. For example, a fermented bun dough which has had 2 oz. of fat per pound of dough rolled in will not produce as good a product as one made from a regularly prepared Danish dough containing $2^1/_2$ to 3 lb. of butter or margarine for each quart of dough. The amount of yeast used in both doughs may be the same but the results vary.

Danish dough has the major portion of the fat rolled in. While the original dough is mixed in the same manner as most yeast doughs with more eggs and sugar per quart of dough than bun dough, the fat is prepared in advance (roll-in fat) and then rolled into the dough. The amount and type of fat are important factors. Butter is expensive but makes products of high quality. A blend of butter and margarine, in equal proportions, is a good roll-in preparation. Hydrogenated vegetable shortening may be used to good advantage but the flavor of the product is not nearly as good as one containing butter.

The roll-in blend should have a consistency stiffer than the dough. Hard or frozen fat tends to tear the dough during rolling and often flakes into large pieces which are not distributed evenly. A soft roll-in fat tends to run out of the sides of the dough and causes sticking to the bench and rolling pin. This requires more dusting flour and fatty lumps which do not roll into the dough evenly will form.

The question of how many rolls and turns to give a dough has always been a subject of disagreement. Some bakers insist on three rolls, others four. The flakiness and volume of Danish, as well as its rich tenderness, are the result of yeast activity in conditioning and proofing the dough

134

and the made-up units. The formation of layers of fat and dough in the roll-in process also requires careful treatment. Experience indicates that four rolls of four turns each produce excellent results.

After the initial layer of fat has been spread over the dough, the dough may be rolled twice in succession. Since the flour contains a strong gluten, the dough must be relaxed for the next two rolls. This relaxation should take place in the refrigerator to maintain firmness of the fat. After four proper rolls many layers of fat and dough have been formed. These layers, and the effect of fermentation due to yeast activity, provide lightness, volume, and flakiness of the baked product.

Too much rolling will make the layers of fat and dough so thin that layers will blend into one mass as though they were mixed together in the mixing machine. Improper use of the rolling pin will break down the layers rather than form them. It will distribute the fat unevenly, causing difficulty in making up the units and running out of the fat during baking. In general, such abuse will not create flakiness and volume in the baked product.

The rolled-in Danish dough is usually refrigerated from 12 to 24 hr. before makeup. This period is sometimes extended to 36 hr. in retarders that are lower in temperature (34°F.). During this period the yeast is still active and the dough goes through a slow fermentation and conditioning. Care must be used in adjusting refrigerator temperature. The yeast becomes inactive when the dough reaches 32°F. throughout. On the other hand, a refrigerator that is opened frequently will cause the dough to ferment faster. In addition larger units of dough (2 qt. or more) will ferment faster because it takes longer for the cold to penetrate them. Such large doughs must be checked to prevent them from over-fermenting and becoming old.

Crustation of the dough and made-up units is quite common. This is indicated in the rolling of the dough where the crust flakes out into hard pieces. This crust formation does not bake properly and tends to remain in gummy formation, as structural lines, because the moisture has been removed. When the crust is part of the surface of the unit, as in twisted Danish rings, they bake with an off-color or streaks. This condition will be avoided by greasing or oiling the dough as well as covering the dough before refrigerating. Made-up units should be egg-washed or brushed with melted fat before retarding to help prevent some of the crust formation. Covering with polyethylene sheeting will be of special help in the blower type of refrigerator. Sufficient space should be provided for proper circulation of cold air.

Freezing of Danish doughs or made-up units requires care. Freezer temperature should be 0° to −10°F. A lower temperature will make possible more rapid freezing. The doughs and units should be brushed with melted fat and wrapped in polyethylene before freezing to prevent crust and frost formation on the units and dough. Defrosting of doughs and made-up units should take place slowly. This is especially important in the retail shops where forced air defrosting is lacking. It is suggested that defrosting be done gradually by placing the doughs or units into the retarder for 24 hr. before makeup or proofing.

Poor volume, running out of the fat during baking, raw interiors after baking, and flattening of the baked products are the result of forced defrosting in the retail shops. This is caused by placing the frozen units in a warm place (steam box) which causes the fat near the surface to melt but leaves the interior still in a frozen or chilled condition. The stickiness of the outside surface leads the inexperienced baker to believe the units have full proof and require immediate baking. Defrosting at shop temperature is best in the smaller bakeshops without mechanical defrosting equipment.

The freezing and/or retarding of baked units require care and judgment. It is suggested that production be estimated and excess for future sales be frozen. If pre-baked units are frozen they should be baked with a light crust color and given a quicker bake to retain as much moisture as possible without collapse of the unit. The baked units should be allowed to cool to room temperature and then wrapped and quick frozen. This procedure will avoid shrinkage and formation of moisture crystals. Frozen baked units should be allowed to return to 65° to 70°F. and then placed in a warm oven for about 3 min. This will provide for additional crust color as well as providing for a freshly baked product. The Danish units should then be washed with hot syrup wash and glazed. This method of freezing and reheating will cause a slight loss in moisture but does not cause rapid staling. The richness of the fat maintains freshness and provides freshly baked products that do not have frozen-defrosted appearance.

The proofing of Danish and other rich types of sweet yeast dough products is a very important factor. The problems of units tearing during baking, flatness and spreading, greasiness and loss of volume may be the result of improper proofing. While controlled proof box conditions may be very difficult to maintain in the average retail shop, a slow, even proof is necessary. Too often the temperature of the proof box is above 100°F. and the humidity at a point where sweating and condensation form droplets of water on the proofing units. This undesirable condition causes the outside of the unit to tear while the inside of the units have just begun to relax and proof. Since the fat rolled into the dough is in a layer form and near the surface, as well as in the center of the unit, the surface fat melts and tends to run out of the unit in the proofing stage.

Units that require a topping, such as cocoanut or fruit topping, should be removed at half proof and the topping applied. Units with full proof have an extended gluten and the application of topping at this stage of proof often causes the unit to collapse because the gluten cannot support the weight of the applied topping. The topped, half-proofed units should be returned to the proof box until they have three-fourths proof. This stage of proof is recommended for Danish and other rich dough units which have heavy toppings. The eggs, egg yolks, the added fat, and the layers of fat and dough provide extra "kick" and volume of the Danish units baked at three-fourths proof. A fully proofed unit of Danish or other rich-type dough may collapse and spread in baking because the extended gluten cannot support the richness of the dough.

Products made from rich doughs require care in baking. Smaller units require higher baking temperatures than larger units. For example, miniature Danish pastries are baked faster than a coffee ring. Baking them at the same temperature may either cause the smaller units to be overbaked if the temperature is too low, or the rings to be raw or underbaked if the temperature is too high. The added fat and sugar in the doughs require a slower bake. A quick bake at higher temperatures (as for buns) will cause a quick color formation of the crust with an unbaked condition in the center. This will cause Danish units to flatten and be gummy in the center. In addition, a hot oven (425°F. or more) will cause burning of the tops, bottoms, or both.

Hot syrup wash should be applied to the Danish products while they are hot. This will avoid stickiness when the units are cool. The syrup wash should be boiled for about 3 min. before removal from the fire. The addition of glucose or corn syrup will help to prevent crystallization of the syrup upon cooling and flaking on the washed product. The incorporation of apricot coating will provide more body to the syrup and a better taste and luster to the washed products. If the units are to be iced, the icing should be applied to the baked product while it is warm, not hot. The icing should be warmed to about 110°F. before applying. The application of cool, diluted icing causes running and stickiness of the icing of the cool product.

COFFEE CAKE AND BABKA

Coffee cake and Babka are made from rich doughs that are not rolled in. These doughs are rich in fat, sugar, and eggs. Because of the added richness, these doughs are made by the sponge dough method. The sponge enables the yeast to multiply quickly and develop a fermented dough base. The use of a straight dough method will require longer fermentation in order for the yeast to be able to carry and raise the dough despite its extra richness. To allow for this bakers often add extra yeast and the product may have a yeasty taste and flavor. In the straight dough method, the sugar, shortening, salt, and eggs are creamed together. In sponge dough mixing the fat is melted and drawn into the final dough after the flour is added and the dough partially developed.

Doughs made with the sponge method should be allowed to rise once and taken to the bench. Time must be allowed for makeup of the units. Remember that the dough units continue to ferment and the last pieces made from a large lot of dough may become old. It is suggested that units be scaled and some of the units placed in the refrigerator to prevent aging during the prolonged makeup.

The scaling of the units of dough is very important. The contents of the dough and the volume of the dough units (under controlled conditions) must be known. Over- and under-scaling is often the cause of too little or too much volume. This is especially true of the popular aluminum foil pans in which products are baked. If the dough is rich in eggs and other ingredients providing for volume, necessary scaling allowances must be made. While leaner doughs may withstand greater proof, they may not give the same volume in baking as do the richer dough units.

Fillings must be used carefully. Heavy fillings, such as almond filling, should be applied with care. Excessive amounts make the units heavy and also cause loss of volume. They may also be the cause of large holes in units made in loaf form. The weight of the filling may not be supported by the gluten after proofing and during baking and separation of layers; the creation of large holes results. Fillings that are strong in flavor (cinnamon, chocolate, and others) may overshadow the natural, excellent flavor of the butter and other ingredients.

Toppings applied to Babka and products made from Babka dough should be put on the units when they are almost three-fourths proofed. For example, Struessel topping when put on freshly made Babka is spread thin before the unit is proofed. Sugar placed on units before proofing may melt in the steam box and create a sticky syrup and burning of the crust during baking.

Baking, retarding, and freezing of Babka dough units are much the same as for Danish pastry. However, it is easier to freeze units in aluminum foil pans and eliminate much of the crust formation. However, they must also be wrapped and covered to prevent crustation and crystallization. Toppings should not be placed on frozen units until they are defrosted and ready for proofing. Frozen Struessel topping may become pasty in the proofing stage if put on units and frozen. Jellies or toppings rich in sugar may tend to run in the proof box and make an unsightly baked product.

BUN DOUGH

Bun dough is a leaner dough. While there are many recipes for this dough they are basically alike in terms of the ingredients used and the mixing procedure. Most buns, since they are leaner, can take a greater proofing period and a higher oven temperature. The principles of washing and finishing are the same as for Danish units. In fact, the application of the icing is very important to the appearance and the taste of the product. The added sweetness of the icing is important. While buns are usually retarded many are often frozen. The same principles of freezing apply to buns as they do for other sweet yeast goods. It is important to place the units to be retarded or frozen in the retarder or freezer as soon as they are made up. Fermentation takes place until the units are completely frozen or retarder temperature has been reached. For large pieces of dough, it is best to scale them into 4 lb. pieces shaped into rolling condition before retarding or freezing.

FROZEN DOUGH

Frozen dough is made from a piece of fermented Babka or rich bun dough as a base. Additional sugar, fat, eggs, yeast, and/or baking powder added with the additional flour required. This dough is allowed to relax and then made up or placed in the retarder for later use. The made-up units require the same attention as do Danish units. Since these units are not given proof to the same degree as Danish or coffee cake because of the added leavening of the yeast and baking powder, they are allowed to relax to soften the gluten and gain about half proof before baking.

When freezing or retarding these units they are washed with melted butter or other fat combination before refrigerating or freezing. This prevents the formation of a crust. Defrosting frozen units require the same procedures as used for Danish pastry. Because of its added richness, frozen dough retards very well. The chilling or freezing of the added fat and eggs assures better keeping qualities.

CHAPTER 16

Recipes for Sweet Yeast Dough Products

CRUMB BUNS AND CINNAMON STICK BUNS

Buns are generally made from a yeast-raised sweet dough. The dough is sweeter and richer than the dough used for soft rolls. Its richness will vary from one bakeshop to another, depending on the quality of the buns desired and the standards of the bakeshop. Naturally, a richer dough will result in a better bun of better keeping qualities. The following recipe may be termed as an average in terms of standards and quality.

Bun Dough (Sweet Yeast Dough) 1 qt.)

Yield: 9 doz (1$^{1}/_{4}$ oz. each)

Ingredients	Lb.	Oz.	Mixing procedure
Sugar	..	12	Blend the ingredients to a smooth paste
Milk powder	..	4	
Salt	..	1	
Shortening	..	12	
Mace	..	$^{1}/_{4}$	
Eggs	..	8	Add the eggs and blend in well
Yeast	..	4	Dissolve the yeast and set aside
Water	..	8	
Water	1	8	Add the water and stir in
Cake flour	1	..	Sift, add the flour, stir slightly and add the yeast solution. Develop the dough until smooth
Bread flour	3	..	

Procedures to Follow for Crumb Buns (Figs. 95 and 96)

1. The temperature of the water will help in controlling the rate of fermentation.
2. The dough, as in the case of all yeast doughs, must be well developed.
3. Place the dough in a warm, moist place and allow to rise well. Test for punching and punch when ready. Allow the dough to relax for 20 min. and take to the bench for makeup.

4. You will note that this dough is not punched twice and the dough is taken on the young side. This is done because the dough will continue to ferment while the buns are being made. This will prevent the buns from becoming old. If large amount of buns are made some scaled units are refrigerated.

5. Scaled presses of bun dough or made-up buns may be placed in the retarder for later baking or baking the following day. (A press of dough is a rounded, scaled dough unit which is divided into 36 equal pieces in a dough dividing or press machine.)

6. Scale the fermented bun dough into presses of desired weight (approximately 2 lb. 12 oz. to 3 lb.) and round up.

7. Allow the presses to relax for 10 to 15 min. and press out.

8. Separate the pieces and then stretch each piece to about 4 in. in length and about 2 in. wide. The pieces of dough may be rolled out lightly with a rolling pin to the desired size.

9. Place each unit on a clean, paper-lined pan so that they touch. The average sheet pan should hold the units about eight down and seven across.

10. Flatten the units lightly with the palms of the hands or a small rolling pin.

11. Wash the tops of the buns with water, milk, or egg-wash and sprinkle with Struessel topping so that the buns are well covered.

12. Allow the buns to get $^3/_4$ proof and bake at 400°F. until the crumbs are golden brown and the buns spring back to the touch.

13. Allow the buns to cool and dust lightly with powdered sugar.

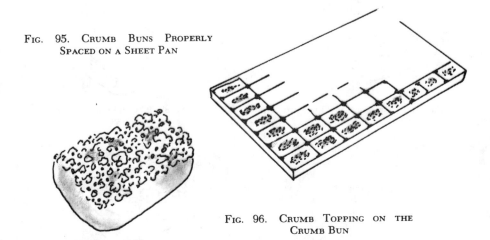

FIG. 95. CRUMB BUNS PROPERLY SPACED ON A SHEET PAN

FIG. 96. CRUMB TOPPING ON THE CRUMB BUN

Struessel or Crumb Topping

Ingredients	Lb.	Oz.	Mixing procedure
Sugar (granulated)	1	..	Blend well until soft and smooth
Brown sugar	1	..	
Salt	..	$1/2$	
Shortening	2	..	
Vanilla	..	$1/2$	
Cinnamon	..	$1/4$	
Cake flour	2	..	Sift, add and rub together with the palms of
Bread flour	2	..	the hands until small lumps are formed

Note: No liquid (water, eggs, or milk) is used in this mix. If it were the protein in the flour would form a gluten structure. If the topping is too dry a little oil or melted fat is added. If the topping is too moist a little bread flour is added.

Makeup of Cinnamon Stick Buns (Figs. 97–100)

1. Scale the fermented dough into desired presses as for crumb buns.

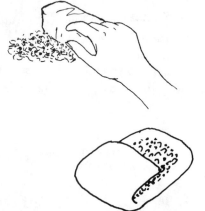

Fig. 97. Piece of Dough Being Dipped in Crumb Filling

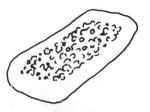

Fig. 98. Crumbs Sticking to the Dough

Fig. 99. Fold Over One Side

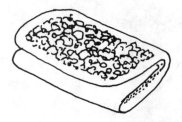

Fig. 100. Fold Over Second Side and Have the Edge at the Bottom of the Bun

2. Round the presses and allow them to relax.
3. While relaxing prepare crumb topping by mixing crumbs with melted fat or oil to make them slightly moist. Add cinnamon sugar to further sweeten the crumbs.
4. Dip each piece of dough into the crumbs which have been spread in a neat pile on the bench. Flatten the piece of dough and fold over twice while in the crumbs so that the dough has the shape of a frank-furter or finger roll. The cake crumbs are now on the inside as well as the outside of the bun.
5. Place these buns on a paper-lined pan so that they will touch when they are flattened slightly. Place them nine in the width and six in the length of the pan. Flatten slightly with the palms of the hand.
6. Give these buns almost full proof (they will spring back slowly when touched). Sprinkle the buns lightly with cinnamon sugar and bake at 400°F. Remove from the oven when the center buns spring back lightly to the touch.
7. These buns may be dusted with powdered sugar when cool or left plain.

Note: If cake crumbs are used, little or no fat is needed to moisten for these crumbs are rich in fat content. In addition, cake crumbs require less sugar than crumbs made from buns or rolls.

CINNAMON BUNS AND BUTTERFLY BUNS

Both of these buns are made from the same fermented bun dough used for making crumb buns and cinnamon stick buns. Stress should be placed upon the proper size and shape of the buns. Uniformity is of great importance. This is especially so in the small bakeshops. These buns are not divided mechanically on the dough divider. They are divided by hand. However, large plants have special dividers for these buns.

Procedures to Follow for Cinnamon Buns (Figs. 101–105)

1. Scale the fermented bun dough into pieces weighing 3 or 4 lb. Shape the pieces into rectangular shape so that the top and sides of the dough are smooth.
2. Cover the units and allow the dough to relax about 15 min. This will enable you to roll the dough without the dough shrinking.
3. Roll out the dough in a rectangular shape about $1/4$ in. thick.
4. Brush the top of the dough with oil or melted fat. Another type of smear, such as almond-crumb filling, may be used.
5. Sprinkle the top of the oil or fat with raisins, cake crumbs, and cinnamon sugar and roll the filling gently with the rolling pin.

6. Starting at the top of the dough fold about 1 in. of the dough over. With the thumbs and palms of the hands roll up the dough into a tight roll and seal the edge of the dough tightly.

7. Fold the roll over so that the seam is at the bottom center. Stretch or shrink the roll of dough so that it is of even thickness ($2^1/_2$ in. in diameter.

8. Brush the top of the roll of dough with oil or melted fat. Cut equal pieces or slices of dough with a scraper. Each unit should weigh about $1^1/_4$ to $1^1/_2$ oz. Scale the first few buns and then cut accordingly for equal size.

9. Place the buns on a sheet pan that has been greased or lined with paper. The buns are placed so that they touch each other when flattened slightly (about six down and nine across on a regular sheet pan).

Fig. 101. Roll Out the Dough $^1/_4$ In. Thick

Fig. 102. Brush Dough with Oil or Melted Fat and Sprinkle with Raisins, Cake Crumbs, and Cinnamon Sugar

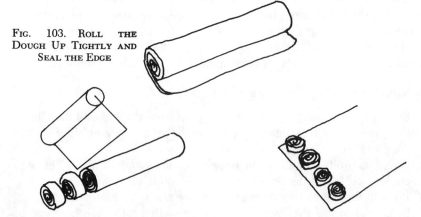

Fig. 103. Roll the Dough Up Tightly and Seal the Edge

Fig. 104. Brush the Top of the Roll with Oil or Melted Fat and Cut into Even Pieces with a Scraper

Fig. 105. Place on Pans Six Down and Nine Across (More if Buns Weigh Less), Flatten Lightly, and Wash with Egg-Wash

10. Flatten the units slightly, egg-wash, proof to almost full proof, and bake at 385° to 390°F.
11. Bake until golden brown and the center buns spring back to the touch. Wash the buns with simple syrup wash as soon as removed from the oven. Allow the buns to cool and then ice with simple icing.

Makeup of Butterfly Buns (Figs. 106–111)

1. Scale the fermented bun dough into the same weights as for cinnamon buns and allow to relax. These pieces are longer and narrower than cinnamon buns.

FIG. 106. ROLL OUT ¼ IN. THICK IN LONG, NARROW SHAPE

FIG. 107. WASH AND SPRINKLE AS FOR CINNAMON BUNS

FIG. 108. ROLL UP TIGHTLY AND SEAL

FIG. 109. CUT IN EQUAL PIECES

FIG. 110. PRESS DOWN IN CENTER WITH A THIN ROLLING PIN

FIG. 111. PLACE ON GREASED OR PARCHMENT-PAPER-LINED PANS AND EGG-WASH

2. Roll out the dough about $1/4$ in. thick, 6 in. wide, and as long as the amount of dough permits, keeping in mind the $1/4$ in. thickness. Be sure the edges of the dough are squared off so that roll is of even thickness when it is filled and rolled.

3. The filling for these buns is the same as for cinnamon buns.

4. Roll up the dough tightly and seal the edges. The roll of dough should be about 2 in. in diameter.

5. Cut the roll into slices weighing about $1^1/4$ to $1^1/2$ oz.

6. With a small rolling pin (about $1/2$ in. in diameter) press down in center of each piece of dough. This will cause the layers of dough to flange or spread out in the form of wings.

7. Place the units on sheet pans that are paper-lined about 1 in. apart. Egg-wash and give $3/4$ proof. Egg-wash again very lightly and bake at 385°F.

8. Wash with syrup as soon as removed from the oven. Allow the buns to cool until warm and ice with simple icing.

Cinnamon Sugar

Ingredients	Lb.	Oz.	Mixing procedure
Granulated sugar	3	..	Blend the cinnamon and sugar together until
Cinnamon	..	1	uniformly blended

Note: The color and strength of cinnamon sugar depend upon the color and quality of the cinnamon. The above recipe is based upon the use of a fine-quality cinnamon. The addition of more cinnamon will darken the blend and make the flavor of cinnamon more pronounced. Be careful to avoid using too much cinnamon, which will give a sharp taste.

Syrup Wash

Ingredients	Lb.	Oz.	Mixing procedure
Granulated sugar	5	..	Place in a kettle and stir well to dissolve the
Glucose or corn syrup	..	8	sugar. Bring the syrup to a boil and allow to boil well for about 2 min. Remove from
Water	4	..	fire and use while warm

Note: Apricot coating may be added and boiled with the syrup. This will darken the syrup to an amber color and also thicken it slightly. The syrup should be heated before using. This makes a better shine and quicker drying of the syrup on the baked product. The heat of the product also helps the syrup to dry. As much as 1 lb. coating may be cooked with the above recipe. The syrup must be covered when not in use. The wash brush should be removed from the syrup. In addition, slices of orange and lemon may be boiled in with the syrup for better flavor.

Simple Icing

Ingredients	Lb.	Oz.	Mixing procedure
Confectionery sugar	5	..	Sift the sugar. Mix with the liquid ingredi-
Hot water (approx.)	1	..	ents to medium stiff paste. Place in a
Glucose or corn	..	2	double boiler and warm to 110°F.
syrup			
Vanilla	..	$1/2$	

Note: Apply the icing while warm. If the icing is too soft add more confectionery sugar. If the icing is too stiff after it has been warmed, add a little simple syrup (wash) to thin it down. Scrape the sides of the icing pot (inside and out) and cover the icing with a thin film of water to prevent crust formation. Cover the icing when not in use.

ROUND CHEESE- AND FRUIT-FILLED BUNS AND OPEN POCKET BUNS

Buns filled with a variety of fillings offer a better display and variety. This is especially important for breakfast sales and to meet the requirements of restaurants, hotels, and institutions. The greater the variety, good taste, and uniformity of the product the greater the status of the baker. Bun dough used for cinnamon and other buns is used for these products.

Procedures to Follow for Round Filled Buns (Figs. 112 and 113)

1. Scale the conditioned (fermented) bun dough into 3 lb. presses (a smaller or larger size may be used) and round up. Allow the presses of dough to relax for about 15 min.
2. Press out or divide each press into 36 equal pieces. Separate the pieces and dust lightly with bread flour to prevent sticking.
3. Round up the units and place on a pan that is greased or lined with parchment paper. Space the units about 2 in. apart to allow for spread in proofing and baking.
4. Allow the units to relax until about half proof. With the fingers or with a rounded object about $1^1/2$ in. in diameter, press the center of each unit down in the center. This will cause a depression in the center and cause the sides of the dough to rise up. It now looks like a saucer.

5. Egg-wash each unit and place about $1/2$ to $3/4$ oz. cheese filling, fruit filling, jelly, orange or lemon filling in the center. Be careful not to put too much filling in the center for it may run over during baking or proofing. Place an equal amount in the center of each. The filling is to be dropped out as for cupcakes.

6. Allow the buns to rise to $3/4$ proof and bake at 390° to 400°F. Bake to golden brown. Avoid a cool oven. This will cause the filling to run before the bun is properly baked and has desirable color.

7. Wash the buns very gently with simple syrup immediately upon removal from the oven. Avoid smearing the filling.

8. Allow the buns to cool until warm and then ice with simple icing by dipping the fingers or an icing brush into the warm icing and striping the buns across the top so that they have a lattice-like appearance.

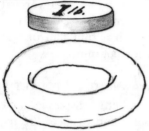

FIG. 112. FLATTEN CENTER OF PROOFED BUN WITH A 1 LB. WEIGHT OR SIMILAR OBJECT

FIG. 113. EGG-WASH BUNS AND FILL CENTERS

Makeup of Open Pocket Buns (Figs. 114 and 115)

1. Press out the presses of dough as for round filled buns.

2. Take four to six pieces of dough and place them alongside each other on a flour-dusted part of the bench. Be sure they are lined up straight. With a small rolling pin roll the pieces gently to about 4 in. long and about 2 in. wide. Place these pieces alongside each other on a clean portion of the bench in straight rows. Remove excess flour from the top of the units of dough.

3. Drop about $1/2$ to $3/4$ oz. cheese or other filling in the center of each unit.

4. Fold the end of one side over the filling. Then fold the other end completely over to the other side of the first side of the first fold of dough and press the end down into the dough with the thumb. Be sure it is sealed.

5. Line up the buns on the bench as you make them up. Egg-wash and give $^3/_4$ proof. Egg-wash lightly once again and bake at 400°F.
6. Wash the buns with simple syrup immediately upon removal from the oven. Ice while slightly warm by striping the icing across the top.

FIG. 114. ROLL PRESSED-OUT PIECES OF DOUGH INTO OBLONGS OR SQUARES. DEPOSIT FILLING IN CENTER

FIG. 115. FOLD END OF ONE SIDE OVER THE FILLING. FOLD OTHER END OVER AND SEAL

Cheese Filling

This type of filling is made with baker's cheese, made from partially skimmed milk with most of the moisture removed in the final pressing process. The moisture which remains is further bound up with the use of absorbing or binding ingredients such as starch, tapioca flour, and other binding properties. This cheese often varies in consistency. That is, the amount of liquid added to the mix will vary because of the variation in the abiilty of the cheese to absorb liquid (eggs and milk). A good-quality baker's cheese will be richer in milk solids and butterfat similar to a good-quality cottage cheese. The cheese filling should be of medium stiff consistency so that it can be handled easily and dropped out after it has been refrigerated.

The recipe is given on the following page.

Cheese Filling

Ingredients	Lb.	Oz.	Mixing procedure
Baker's cheese	5	..	Scale carefully. Mix all the ingredients to a
Sugar	1	6	smooth consistency
Salt	..	1	
Milk powder	..	4	
Shortening (soft)	1	..	
Bread flour	..	8	
Eggs	1	..	Add the eggs in three stages and blend in
Vanilla	..	1	Add the water gradually until desired con-
Cold water	1	..	sistency. Add more, if necessary
(variable)			
Raisins	1	..	Fold in the raisins

Note: Raisins are optional. They may be used or may be left out entirely. This filling must be kept covered and refrigerated when not in use. Add the water or milk gradually. As mentioned above cheeses vary in their ability to absorb and hold liquid. More liquid should be added to a good-quality cheese in order to reach the medium stiff consistency. Judgment is very important.

TWIST BUNS

These buns add to the variety which the baker can make and add to the sales display of the bakeshop. These variations may also be improved upon by varying the nature of their filling and topping.

Procedures to Follow (Figs. 116–120)

1. Scale the conditioned bun dough into 3 or 4 lb. pieces and shape into a narrow, rectangular form. Allow these units to relax about 10 min.
2. Roll out the dough on a clean, flour-dusted bench so that the dough is about $1/4$ in. thick and about 6 in. wide. Be sure the dough is of even thickness throughout.
3. The dough may now be filled with any of the following:
    a. Washed with melted fat and sprinkled with cake crumbs and cinnamon sugar;
    b. Smeared with almond filling and covered with cake crumbs and cinnamon sugar; or
    c. Smeared lightly with jam or jelly and then sprinkled with cake crumbs and cinnamon sugar.
4. Roll the cake crumbs in lightly with the rolling pin. Roll in the width.

5. Fold the dough towards you in three equal layers. There are now two layers of filling and three layers of dough. It is like a double-decker sandwich.

6. Flatten slightly by rolling the top of the dough gently with the rolling pin. This time roll the dough in the length. Adjust the dough for equal width and thickness.

7. With a scraper or pastry wheel knife cut the dough into strips about 1 in. wide. The pieces of dough should now be about 1 in. wide and 4 in. long.

8. Pick up each unit of dough by the ends and twist gently about three turns. This will cause a spiral effect. Place these twists on a clean portion of the bench and flatten slightly.

9. Wash the tops of the twist buns with egg-wash and sprinkle with Struessel topping, sliced nuts, ground nuts, cinnamon sugar, or leave plain.

FIG. 116. ROLLED-OUT DOUGH WITH FILLING APPLIED

FIG. 117. FOLDED DOUGH

FIG. 118. FLATTEN LIGHTLY WITH THE ROLLING PIN

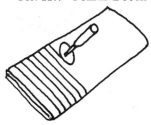

FIG. 119. CUT STRIPS WITH PASTRY WHEEL

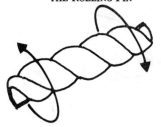

FIG. 120. TWIST IN DIRECTION OF THE ARROWS

10. Place on parchment-paper-lined bun pans six or seven down and five or six across. The units should have about $^3/_4$ in. of space between them. The ends should be about $^1/_2$ in. apart. After the buns are proofed and baked they will touch.
11. Allow the buns to get $^3/_4$ proof and bake at 390°F. Plain-topped buns should be washed with warm syrup on removal from the oven. These are striped with simple icing when slightly warm. Buns that have a topping may be left plain or dusted with confectionery sugar when cool.

HORSESHOE-SHAPED BUNS

When making these buns follow the same procedure for rolling and filling as for twist buns. When you have cut the buns into 1 in. slices do the following:

Procedures to Follow (Figs. 121–124)

1. Wash the tops of the sliced units with egg-wash. Use the wash lightly and avoid dripping of excess egg-wash between the buns. This will cause stickiness and difficulty in handling.
2. Sprinkle the tops of the washed slices with Struessel topping, sliced or ground nuts, and cinnamon sugar.

FIG. 121. ROLLED, FILLED, AND CUT PIECES OF DOUGH

FIG. 122. CUT IN THE CENTER MADE WITH A BENCH SCRAPER OR KNIFE

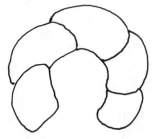

FIG. 123. TWISTED AND PLACED IN HORSESHOE SHAPE

FIG. 124. HORSESHOE BUN WITH SCRAPER CUTS

3. Take each unit and face it lengthwise in front of you. With the edge of the scraper, make five cuts about $1/2$ in. apart and cutting about one-third of the way into the unit. The small cut is about one-third in. deep and cuts all the way through the unit.
4. Give each unit a slight bend so that a half-moon or crescent shape is formed. Place on a paper-lined bun pan and space about 1 in. apart. You will note that the cuts made are now spread apart and the bun has a scalloped edge.
5. Give the buns $3/4$ proof (they will spring back lightly to the gentle touch) and bake at 390°F.
6. When the buns have cooled dust lightly with confectionery sugar.

BOW-TIE COCOANUT BUNS

Roll out and fill these buns as you did horseshoe buns except that the dough should be narrower and longer. After the dough has been filled roll in the length with a little more pressure so that the units are thinner (about $3/8$ in. thick). Thereafter, follow this procedure for makeup of the buns:

Procedures to Follow (Figs. 125 and 126)

1. Cut the dough into slices about $1^1/2$ in. wide. Each of the buns should weigh about $1^1/2$ to $1^3/4$ oz. each.
2. Pick up each unit and twist once in the center. This will form a bow-tie effect. Place the units on paper-lined pans spacing them about 1 in. apart.
3. Egg-wash the units lightly and allow them to get half proof.

FIG. 125. SLICE OF FILLED DOUGH CUT FROM THE DOUGH

FIG. 126. TWIST IN CENTER TO FORM THE BOW-TIE

4. Egg-wash lightly again and sprinkle the tops of the buns with cocoanut.
   Note: While the fine-shred, macaroon-type cocoanut may be used it is best to sprinkle the tops with medium-shred, medium-sweet cocoanut.
5. Return the units to the proof box and allow the buns to get $3/4$ proof.

6. Bake at 390°F. until golden brown. Be careful not to overbake and avoid too strong a top heat in the oven. Such heat will brown or burn the cocoanut topping.

7. Wash the buns lightly with warm syrup as soon as they are baked. Allow the buns to cool until mildly warm and then stripe with simple icing.

DANISH PASTRY

The principal factors in making assorted Danish pastry units are size, shape, and uniformity. Size is determined by the weight. Shape depends upon skill and judgment in makeup. Uniformity is a combination of both size and shape, as well as the manner in which the units are proofed, baked, and finished after they have been made up.

Danish Pastry Dough

Yield: 10–12 doz.—
$1^1/_4$–$1^1/_2$ oz. units

Ingredients	Lb.	Oz.	Mixing procedure
Yeast (variable)	..	4	Dissolve the yeast in the water and place to one side
Water	1	..	
Sugar	1	..	Blend the ingredients well to a smooth, soft paste
Salt	..	1	
Milk powder	..	4	
Shortening	..	8	
Cardamom or coffee cake flavor	..	$1/_8$	
Eggs (part yolks)	1	..	Add in two stages and blend well after each addition of eggs
Water	1	..	Add and stir in
Vanilla	..	1	
Patent flour	4	..	Sift, add, and stir slightly. Add the yeast solution and develop to a smooth dough. Place dough on a well-dusted bench
Roll-in fat, butter or margarine	1	..	Work the butter or margarine until a firm, plastic consistency. Blend with the shortening and place on bench
Shortening	1	..	
Total weight	11	$1^1/_8$	

Procedures to Follow (Figs. 127–130)

1. The dough should be folded into a rectangular shape with a smooth surface.
2. Allow dough to relax 5 to 10 min. and roll out into a rectangular shape about $1/2$ in. thick.
3. Distribute small pieces of the roll-in fat over two-thirds of the dough. Be sure the pieces of fat are small and evenly distributed.
4. Fold the uncovered third of the dough over one-third of the fat-covered portion of the dough. Remove the excess flour from the top of the dough and fold the remaining fat-covered third over the dough. Thus, three layers of dough and two layers of fat are formed.

FIG. 127. ROLL DOUGH TO RECTANG-ULAR SHAPE

FIG. 128. COVER TWO-THIRDS OF THE DOUGH WITH ROLL-IN FAT AND BUTTER PREPARATION

FIG. 129. FOLD THE DOUGH WITHOUT FAT OVER HALF OF THE FAT-COVERED PART

FIG. 130. FOLD THE REMAINING THIRD DOUGH ON TOP

5. Move the dough to one side and re-spread the dusting flour. Dust additional flour if necessary. Place the dough in the long position for rolling.
6. Roll the dough out carefully and evenly into a rectangular shape about $1/2$ in. thick. Be sure to check the bench for sufficient flour to prevent the dough from sticking while rolling.
7. Brush the excess flour from the top of the dough and fold the dough into four even sections.
8. Allow the dough to rest 15 min. and roll out a second time. This is to be repeated until the dough has been rolled four times.

9. It is best to refrigerate the dough between rolls. This keeps the fat firm.

10. After the fourth roll remove the excess flour and brush the top of the dough lightly with melted shortening or oil. Cover the dough and refrigerate. It is best to allow the dough to remain refrigerated for 12 to 24 hr. before making up into Danish units.

CHEESE POCKETS

Procedures to Follow (Figs. 130A and 130B)

1. Roll out the conditioned Danish dough into a rectangular shape about $1/4$ in. thick or slightly thinner. Check the dusting flour to prevent the dough from sticking. Remove excess flour from the top after the dough has been rolled.

2. Mark off 3 or 4 in. squares with the dough divider or pastry wheel. Cut one line of squares and weigh the units for correct weight. Allow $1/2$ oz. of filling weight for the total weight. For example, if the pocket is to weigh $1^1/2$ oz. the dough square should weigh 1 oz. If the units are to weigh $2^1/2$ oz. the dough square should weigh $1^3/4$ oz. and the filling $3/4$ oz. Judgment and care are important.

3. Wet the hands in water and drop out the filling in the center of the square of dough after the entire dough has been cut into squares.

4. To make the pocket grasp the diagonal corners of the square of dough and stretch them slightly. Fold one corner over the filling toward the opposite diagonal corner. Fold one corner over the filling toward the first. Do the same with the remaining two corners of dough. If the square of dough is not perfectly square stretch the narrow side with the hands to shape it as close to square as possible.

5. Place the units in a line and close together on a clean portion of the bench. When all units are made up flatten gently and wash with egg-wash.

6. Place the units on pans with sufficient room between each for proofing and growth during baking. Judgment is important.

7. Give the pockets half proof, wash again with egg-wash, and garnish the top with nuts or other garnish. Give slow proof until $3/4$ proof is reached.

8. Bake at 400°F. Wash immediately after baking with syrup wash.

OPEN PRUNE POCKETS

Open prune pockets are made the same way as closed pockets are except that only two corners of the square are folded over. This results in two open sides and a diamond shape.

Procedures to Follow (Figs. 130A and 130B)

1. In addition to prune filling, cheese and fruit fillings may be used. Fruit fillings should be slightly thicker in consistency to avoid running out of the pocket during proof and baking. Cake crumbs may be deposited in the center of the dough square and the filling dropped on top of the crumbs. The crumbs act as a binder.

2. Be careful to drop the filling in the center. This makes sealing the diagonal ends easier and the job cleaner.

3. The edges of the dough squares may be moistened with egg-wash before depositing the filling. This will make a better seal and avoid opening of the pocket during proof and baking.

4. Wash the made-up units lightly with egg-wash. Avoid washing the filling for this will discolor the filling and make an egg crust on the filling.

5. Be careful when applying the syrup wash after baking to avoid spreading the filling.

DANISH SNECKS

Procedures to Follow (Figs. 130C, 130D, 130E, and 130F)

1. Roll out the conditioned Danish dough into a rectangular shape about $1/4$ in. thick. The size and weight of the desired units will determine the length and width of the dough. Larger units require greater width so that the units will be larger when rolled up after the dough is filled.

2. Remove excess flour and wash the dough with egg-wash, melted fat, or smear with almond filling or other type of filling.

3. Sprinkle the wash or filling with cake crumbs, chopped nuts, and cinnamon sugar. Roll the filling in lightly with the rolling pin.

4. Roll the dough up tightly as for cinnamon buns. Do not seal the edge.

5. Cut into slices with a scraper or knife. Weigh the first few slices to check the weight. Add a piece of scrap dough if too small. Place the scrap under the sneck when placing on the pan.

6. Draw the loose edge around the sneck and tuck it under when placing it on the pan. Allow sufficient space for proofing and growth during baking.

7. Wash with egg-wash or dip the sneck in sugar before panning. Proof and bake as you would Danish pockets. Sugared snecks are not washed with syrup after baking.

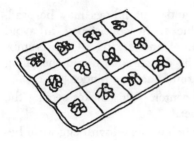

FIG. 130A. ROLL OUT DOUGH INTO SQUARES. DEPOSIT FILLING IN THE CENTER

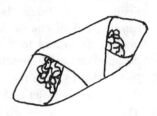

FIG. 130B. FOLD END OF ONE SIDE OVER THE FILLING. FOLD OTHER END OVER AND SEAL

FIG. 130C. ROLL OUT THE DOUGH ¼ IN. THICK

FIG. 130D. BRUSH DOUGH WITH OIL OR MELTED FAT AND SPRINKLE WITH RAISINS, CAKE CRUMBS, AND CINNAMON SUGAR

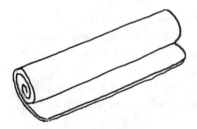

FIG. 130E. ROLL THE DOUGH UP TIGHTLY AND SEAL THE EDGE

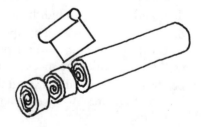

FIG. 130F. BRUSH THE TOP OF THE ROLL WITH OIL OR MELTED FAT AND CUT INTO EVEN PIECES WITH A SCRAPER

DANISH PASTRY HORNS

Danish pastry horns are made in two different shapes—the crescent or half-moon shape, and the straight or salt-stick shape. The filling for these horns may vary from an almond spread to jam, prune, or spread cheese filling.

Procedures to Follow (Figs. 131–138)

1. Roll out the conditioned Danish dough into a rectangular shape about $1/4$ in. thick. Remember to have the dough of even thickness throughout.
2. Remove the excess flour and wash the top of the dough with egg-wash, melted butter or margarine, or smear with almond.
3. Sprinkle the top of the filling with cake crumbs, ground nuts, and cinnamon sugar. Roll the filling in lightly with the rolling pin.
4. With the pastry wheel cut 6 in. strips across horizontally. Cut these strips into triangle shapes with a 3 in. base at the bottom. Roll up the base tightly to the point. Be sure the point is at the bottom of the horn. Place the horns on a clean portion of the bench in a straight line, flatten gently with the palms of the hands, and wash with egg-wash. Place on parchment-paper-lined pans allowing sufficient room for expansion in proof and baking.
5. Give the horns $3/4$ proof, egg-wash again, and sprinkle with nuts. Bake at 400°F. Be sure the bottoms are properly baked. Wash with syrup immediately after baking. For *crescent-shaped horns,* roll out and fill as above. Cut 5-in. strips across and cut into triangles 4 in. wide at the base. With the pastry wheel or scraper, make a 1-in. cut at the center of the base of each triangle. Spread the center cuts apart and roll up tightly to the point of the triangle. Be sure the point is under the horn. Form the two ends of the horn into a crescent or half-moon shape and place on the pan. The points may be pinched together to prevent spreading apart during proofing and baking. Proof, egg-wash, and bake as the plain horn.
(See Figs. page 160.)

DANISH PASTRY TWISTS

Danish pastry may be made into an assortment of twists with a variety of toppings and fillings. Basically, the strips are assembled in the same manner but are twisted into different shapes. The various twists are the snail, eyeglass, figure "8," and the three-strand loop. Diagrams of the different varieties will illustrate the manner in which they are to be twisted.

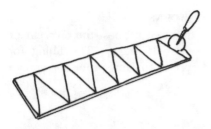

FIG. 131. ROLL DOUGH INTO REC-
TANGULAR SHAPE, APPLY FILLING, AND
CUT IN TRIANGLES

FIG. 132. ROLL THE BASE OF THE
TRIANGLE TOWARD THE POINT. KEEP
ROLL TIGHT

FIG. 133. FINISHED PLAIN, DANISH
HORN

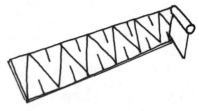

FIG. 134. FOR CRESCENT HORNS,
MAKE A SMALL CUT AT THE BASE OF
THE TRIANGLE

FIG. 135. SPREAD THE CENTER CUTS
APART

FIG. 136. ROLL TOWARD THE POINT
SPREADING AND TAPERING AS YOU
ROLL

FIG. 137. ROLLED-UP HORN IN
STRAIGHT SHAPE

FIG. 138. ENDS TURNED TO FORM
THE CRESCENT SHAPE

Procedures to Follow (Figs. 139–145)

1. Roll out the dough into an even oblong shape about $1/8$ in. thick. Remove excess flour from the top of the dough. Square the sides of the dough.
2. Brush the top of the dough with egg-wash, melted fat, or almond filling.
3. Sprinkle half of the dough (horizontally) with filling of cake crumbs, nuts, and cinnamon sugar.
4. Fold the top half (unfilled) over the bottom half (filled) and roll over the dough gently with the rolling pin.
5. For a unit weighing approximately $1^1/2$ oz. the strips should be cut $1/2$ in. wide and 7 in. long. Cut the dough with the pastry wheel into horizontal strips 7 in. wide. Cut each of these horizontal strips into thin strips $1/2$ in. wide. If the units are to be $2^1/2$ oz., the strips should be $3/4$ in. wide and about 8 in. long.
6. Roll out each strip about 10 in. long and form the twists as shown in the diagrams. Be sure to twist the ends to round the strip.
7. Place the twists on parchment-paper-lined pans, allowing sufficient room for expansion in proof and baking. Wash with egg-wash and give half proof.
8. Wash the proofed units with egg-wash and deposit the filling on each carefully. The custard or jam filling should be applied with a pastry bag for evenness and cleanliness. The filled centers of snail twists may be dropped out by hand. Allow the filled units to get $3/4$ proof and bake at 400°F. Wash carefully and gently with syrup immediately after baking. Be careful to avoid spreading the topping.

DANISH PASTRY STICKS

While Danish pastry sticks provide variety they are especially useful for using up the scrap dough which remains after other Danish units are made up. The scrap dough is not seen nor is it noticed or tasted when the pastry is eaten.

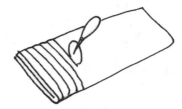

FIG. 139. SMEAR HALF THE ROLLED-OUT DOUGH WITH ALMOND FILLING AND EGG-WASH THE OTHER HALF

FIG. 140. FOLD IN HALF AND CUT IN $1^1/2$ OZ. STRIPS

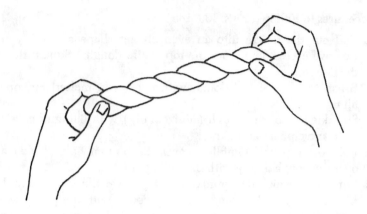

FIG. 141.   TWIST THE STRIP

FIG. 142.   MAKE UP INTO SNAILS BY
CURLING

FIG. 143.   SNAIL SHAPE

FIG. 144.   FIGURE "8" DANISH

FIG. 145.   EYE-GLASS DANISH

Procedures to Follow for Danish Pastry Sticks (Figs. 146–148)

1. Roll out the Danish dough about $1/2$ in. thick. Spread the scrap Danish dough evenly over the surface of the dough and press in gently with the fingers. Roll out the dough into an oblong about $1/4$ in. thick.

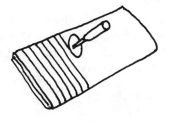

FIG. 146. CUT STRIPS WITH PASTRY WHEEL

FIG. 147. ROLL STRIP TO $1/4$ IN. THICK AND THEN ROLL AT AN ANGLE TO 4 OR 5 IN. IN LENGTH

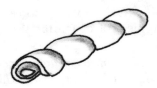

FIG. 148. DANISH PASTRY STICK COMPLETED

2. Remove the excess flour and wash the top of the dough with melted fat, egg-wash, almond filling, or other spread. The filling is then covered with chopped nuts, cake crumbs, and cinnamon sugar. Melted sweet chocolate may also be smeared on top of the almond filling for variety.

3. With the pastry wheel cut the dough into long strips about $1\frac{1}{2}$ or $1\frac{1}{4}$ in. wide. Be sure the filling has been rolled in well to prevent it from falling off when the dough is cut and the sticks rolled up.

4. Start by rolling the stick base until it is about $1/2$ in. in circumference. Then turn the started stick to a 45° angle, roll 4 or 5 in. long and seal it to the end of the stick. Be sure the stick is tightly rolled and of even thickness.

5. Line the sticks on the bench in even rows. When all sticks are made up it is wise to cut off the ends of extra-long sticks with the pastry wheel to insure evenness of size.

6. Wash the sticks with egg-wash twice. Sprinkle tops with sliced nuts. Proof and bake as other Danish units.

Note: Leftover scraps of dough may be added to the beginning of each stick and rolled in.

DANISH MINIATURES

Danish miniatures are a popular item and are made daily in most bakeshops. They are made much the same as the other, larger Danish units are made except that they are smaller. Each of these units weighs $1/4$ oz. They are sold by the pound very much as fancy cookies are sold.

Procedures to Follow

1. The dough should be rolled out about $1/8$ in. thick. Be sure the dough is of even thickness.

2. If a number of varieties are to be made such as open prune pockets, closed cheese pockets, small horns (Rugelach), snecks, etc., from one piece of dough, it is best to section off the rolled-out dough before cutting. This will allow you to spread the filling for some units and allow a clean piece of dough for almond-filled, or other type of filled, units.

3. In the making of *filled, open or closed, pockets* allow the dough to relax after it has been rolled out. This will prevent shrinkage when you cut out the small squares about $1^1/2$ in. square. Deposit the cheese or prune filling with a pastry bag and plain tube. It is cleaner and faster to do it this way. Be sure to seal the ends of the pockets well to prevent opening. Appearance is very important.

4. In the makeup of small horns, snecks, and others be sure to cut the dough evenly so that each of the units is the same size. Add a small piece of scrap dough to units that are small and remove a small piece of the dough if the units are slightly large. Evenness of size will be noticed in the baking and the merchandising.

5. Wash the made-up units and place on paper-lined pans. Allow about $1/2$ in. of space between units. This space will be filled after the units are proofed and baked. Give the units half proof, wash again, and sprinkle with nuts or other topping. Allow the units to get no more than $3/4$ proof.

6. If miniatures have been frozen before baking, treat them as you would regular frozen Danish. The procedure is:

   a. Remove from freezer and allow the Danish to return to shop temperature before proofing.

b. It is best to place the frozen Danish under normal refrigeration a day in advance. This makes defrosting a more normal procedure and avoids excessive sweating in the defrost period.

c. All Danish, frozen or otherwise, should be given a slow proof.

d. Be sure to wash the Danish with egg-wash before and after proofing.

7. Bake at 400°F. until golden brown. Wash immediately with syrup wash as soon as the units are removed from the oven.

Note: Be careful of too much bottom heat in the oven. Bake on double pans if the bottom heat of the oven is too strong. Be careful not to overbake or dry out in a cool oven. Miniature Danish will dry out and become hard if overbaked. Since they are small they continue to firm or bake for the first 2 min. after they are removed from the oven. You will note that this is also true of small cookies.

DANISH RINGS

Danish rings are a daily production item in most retail bakeshops. When properly made they make a beautiful display and an attractive merchandising item. The difference between plain and filled rings lies only in the variety of fillings that are used, and it must be remembered that the plain ring is also a filled ring. The size and weight of the ring depends upon the nature of the bakeshop and its production requirements.

Procedures to Follow (Figs. 149–153)

1. Roll out the conditioned Danish dough into an oblong shape about 20 in. wide, 1/4 in. thick, and as long as the amount of dough used permits. Use bread flour for dusting the bench and the dough. Remove excess flour from the top of the dough after it has been rolled out.

2. The top surface of the dough may be brushed with melted butter or other melted fat before applying the filling. A melted fat is recommended in that it allows for separation of the twisted layers in forming the ring and greater volume in baking. Egg-wash or almond filling may also be used.

3. Sprinkle raisins, chopped nuts, cake crumbs, and cinnamon sugar over one-half the width of the rolled dough. Do not use an excess of filling for it will fall out when making or shaping the rings. Roll the filling over gently with a rolling pin.

4. Fold the top half of the dough over the filled half of the dough and roll it gently with the rolling pin. You now have two layers of dough and one layer of filling.

5. With a scraper or pastry wheel cut the units into the desired weight of the ring. Add scraps of dough or remove excess. Avoid excess scrap dough. With the scraper make two cuts into the scaled units about 1 in. from the top and bottom (extending all the way). Roll and twist the units and place to one side.

6. After all units have been rolled and twisted take the first one, which is now relaxed, and roll out about 2 ft. long and twist. Do not over-twist. Place the ends of the rolled unit together, seal with heel of the hand, place the flattened edge under the ring, and place on a paper-lined or greased pan. Shape the ring on the pan so that it maintains its shape. The number of rings placed on the pan depends upon the weight of the ring.

7. Wash the rings with egg-wash, give slow proof until the rings are $^3/_4$ proof, egg-wash again, and garnish with nuts and other topping.

8. Bake at 385° to 400°F., depending on the richness of the dough.

9. Wash with syrup wash immediately after removing from the oven. The rings may be iced when cool.

Fig. 149. Wash the Rolled-Out Dough and Smear Half with Filling

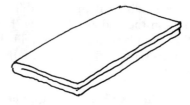

Fig. 150. Fold the Top Half Over the Filled Half

Fig. 151. Scale the Units and Make Cuts with a Scraper or Knife

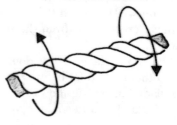

Fig. 152. Twisted Strand

Fig. 153. Sealing the Ends of the Ring

Procedures to Follow for Filled Rings (Figs. 154–161)

1. Filled rings that are twisted as above may have any filling, such as almond, prune, cheese, etc., smeared lightly on the dough to hold the rest of the crumbs and sugar. Follow the same procedure as for plain rings.

FIG. 154. CHEESE OR OTHER FILLING LAID EVENLY ACROSS THE DOUGH

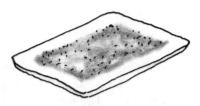

FIG. 155. ALMOND FILLING SMEARED ACROSS THE DOUGH

FIG. 156. ROLLED-UP DOUGH THAT HAS BEEN FILLED

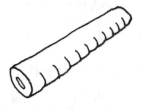

FIG. 157. ONE-INCH CUTS MADE IN ROLLED-UP DOUGH FOR HORNS

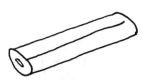

FIG. 158. ROLLED-UP DOUGH CUT THROUGH FOR ALMOND RING

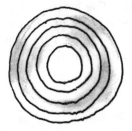

FIG. 159. ALMOND RING OPENED UP

FIG. 160. CUTS MADE IN THE STRIP WITH SCISSORS

FIG. 161. PALM LEAF STRIP

2. Rings that are filled with a greater amount of the above fillings are made by first scaling the desired units of dough in an oblong shape.

3. The units of dough are then rolled into square or oblong shapes and the filling is smeared on the dough or laid out in strip form on the dough. For example, almond filling is smeared on heavily over the entire dough. Cheese filling is laid out in strip form. Fruit filling is placed in a strip on a bed of cake crumbs.

4. Sealing and shaping of these rings varies. For example, rings may be rolled out in a square and then rolled up like a pan bread. The center is then cut through with a scraper and the ring opened up and placed on a pan. Other rings may be rolled up like a cinnamon roll for buns. The ends of the strips are sealed and the ring shaped and panned. The tops or edges of the ring may be cut with scissors into various designs.

5. Proof and bake these rings as plain rings except for the fact that filled rings require a slightly longer baking time to bake through properly.

Danish Cocoanut Ring (Figs. 162–164)

The Danish cocoanut ring is made the same way as plain rings except for the fact that the filled and scaled units of dough are cut into three even strips. These strips are then braided in three strands and the ends sealed. The braided ring is flatter and wider than the plain ring. This is necessary to support the cocoanut topping which is spread on the top of the ring after it has been given half proof. The topping should be evenly distributed over the center of the ring.

FIG. 162. SCALED DOUGH CUT IN THREE EQUAL STRIPS

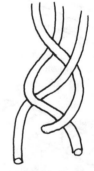

FIG. 163. BRAIDING THE THREE STRIPS

FIG. 164. BRAIDED STRIP
TO BE SHAPED INTO RING

Cocoanut Topping for Rings

Yield: Enough to garnish 28–30 rings

Ingredients	Lb.	Oz.
Macaroon cocoanut (unsweetened)	5	..
Sugar	2	12
Salt	..	$1/_4$
Melted fat	..	8
Eggs	1	..
Milk powder	..	3
Bread flour	..	6
Water	1	8
Vanilla	..	1

Mixing procedure

Mix all ingredients together to a smooth paste. If the mix becomes stiff after standing or storage, it is best to add some eggs (whites or whole) to soften it. This mix may also be mixed with a small amount of wine cake or yellow cake batter for lightness and greater spread

LARGE FILLED STICKS OR STONGEN
Cheese-, Prune-, Poppy Butter, and Fruit-Filled Sticks

Stongen or large sticks are made in most of the better bakeshops. These are often cut into slices and sold by weight or they may be cut to the customer's specification and then scaled. However, these stongen provide the baker with the opportunity of adding to his variety of sweet yeast goods products. There are several ways of preparing these large sticks and several types of dough may be used.

The dough generally used for sticks is that used for Babka (p. 174). This means that conditioned Babka dough is scaled into desired units weighing about 1 lb. 4 oz. to 1 lb. 8 oz. pieces. The dough is the base or structure for supporting the filling and should be large enough to form a stick the length of the sheet pan. If the stick is to be thick then the dough is as long as the width of the pan permits.

Procedures to Follow for Cheese-Filled Sticks (Figs. 165–169)

1. Roll the relaxed dough units about ¼ in. thick in a long, oblong shape about 5 in. wide. The edges of the dough should be even in thickness. Regular coffee cake dough, bun dough, frozen dough, or a combination of Babka and short dough (equal weights blended together) may be used for the stongen. Your judgment and consumer preference will determine the type of dough to use.

FIG. 165. ROLL OUT THE DOUGH INTO OBLONG SHAPE AND APPLY FILL-ING

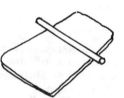

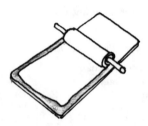

FIG. 166. ROLL FILLING IN WITH ROLLING PIN

FIG. 167. ROLLING THE DOUGH ON THE ROLLING PIN

FIG. 168. DOUGH ROLLED UP EVENLY AND SNUGLY

FIG. 169. SEAL THE ROLL AT THE BOTTOM

2. Use regular cheese filling or the richer cheese filling used for cheese strudel. Place a little bread flour on the bench and set cheese filling (about 3–4 lb.) on the flour. Roll the filling until it is almost as long as the dough.
3. Wash the dough with melted butter in the center and egg-wash the very edges. The center of the dough should be sprinkled with light-colored cake crumbs and toasted ground nuts.
4. Place the cheese strip on the crumb filling and be sure the filling is of even thickness.

5. To seal the filling fold one edge of the dough over to the other so that the egg-wash causes the ends to stick. Now fold the units over so that the seam is on the bottom center. Be sure the ends are sealed to prevent filling from running out.

6. Place the strip on a parchment-paper-lined pan and even out with the palms of the hands. Each pan may contain three such strips in the length and four or five in the width. The top of the strip may be cut with scissors, the cuts being about 2 in. in length and spaced about 3 in. apart. They may be closer if you wish.

7. The top of the stick may be washed with melted butter or egg-wash. The strip is then given $^3/_4$ proof and brushed again with butter or egg-wash. The top is then sprinkled with a variety of toppings such as Struessel (crumb) topping, ground nuts and sugar, sliced nuts, or it may be left plain.

8. Bake the stongen at 365° to 370°F. until it springs back firmly to the touch. Remember, the dough must be baked so that it is firm enough to retain its shape and support the filling. The average length strip takes about 40 min. to bake. Wider and thicker strips take longer.

9. The strips may be washed with syrup glaze upon removal from the oven, left plain, or iced lightly with fondant if the top is smooth and not garnished.

Note: Cheese strips may be filled with various fruits placed on top of the cheese: cherry, blueberry, and other fruit fillings may be used. Be sure the filling is slightly thicker than that used for pies to keep the filling from running too much. Be sure the edges are sealed well to prevent filling from running during baking. Bake fruit-filled cheese stongen a little longer than plain cheese-filled varieties.

Makeup of Prune-Filled Sticks

1. These are made by shaping the dough in the same manner as for the cheese-filled variety. The filling is softer and purchased in No. 10 cans or large pails. This filling is smeared on rather than rolled up as for cheese. The rolled-out dough is washed with butter or melted fat and then the prune filling is smeared on evenly. It is suggested that the dough be a trifle thicker than for cheese. It will be thinned by rolling after the filling is in.

2. The filling is sprinkled with nuts, cake crumbs, and cinnamon sugar and is rolled in gently with a pie rolling pin to insure adherence to the prune filling. The dough is then rolled up as it.would be for a cinnamon bun.

3. To finish the roll cuts may be made with a scraper about $1/2$ in. deep and spaced about 2 in. apart. This is done before the sealed edge is turned over. Now turn the roll over with sealed edge on the bottom center. The cuts will be exposed and serve as the finish.

4. The top is then egg-washed, given $3/4$ proof, egg-washed again, and the top sprinkled with nuts, sugar, or any other desired topping. Bake the same as you would the cheese stick.

Makeup for Poppy Butter (Mohn) Sticks

1. These are made the same way as prune sticks. Poppy butter is purchased in cans or in pails. Most bakers improve the prepared filling by softening it with simple syrup and adding toasted ground nuts, cake crumbs, and sugar to it. Some bakers use honey to soften the poppy butter rather than syrup. The honey will improve the taste and flavor. However, do not dilute or soften the poppy butter for the express purpose of using up excessive cake crumbs. This cheapens the product.

2. The dough is rolled out as for prune sticks and washed with melted butter and fat. Smear the poppy filling over the surface about $1/4$ in. thick. Sprinkle the top with chopped nuts, cake crumbs, and cinnamon sugar.

3. Roll up as you would a cinnamon bun roll and seal the edges. Place on a paper-lined pan with the seam at the bottom center.

4. Egg-wash and give $3/4$ proof. Wash again and sprinkle the top with nuts or leave plain. Bake poppy butter sticks as you would cheese sticks. Wash the tops with warm syrup or heated honey upon removal from the oven.

Note: Boil the honey and apply. This will allow the honey to dry and will also allow you to garnish the honey with chopped nuts while it is still hot.

Makeup of Fruit-Filled Sticks

1. These are another version of stongen. The filling used should be slightly thicker than pie filling to avoid too much spread and prevent running during baking.

2. Roll the dough a little thicker than for cheese sticks. Wash the edges of the dough with egg-wash. Sprinkle the center of the dough with cake crumbs. Place the fruit filling on the cake crumbs in an even row. Do not use an excess of fruit as this will make handling and shaping the stick difficult.

3. Fold the edges of dough over each other and seal. The egg-wash will seal it tightly. Fold over so that the seal is at the bottom center. Place on paper-lined pans.

4. Shape the sticks with the palms of the hand for even thickness. With scissors make cuts about 1 in. wide and spaced about 2 in. apart. This will provide a design as well as allow steam to escape during baking.
5. Allow the fruit sticks to get no more than $^3/_4$ proof before baking. Full proof will result in a flattened stick with a possibility of the dough tearing while baking. Bake the same as for cheese sticks. Wash with syrup upon removal from the oven. The strips may also be striped with warm fondant when they have cooled until mildly warm.

LARGE DANISH FILLED STICKS OR STONGEN

These large, filled sticks are made from scaled pieces of Danish dough weighing from $1^1/_2$ to 2 lb.

Procedures to Follow

1. Roll the dough into a long rectangular shape about $^1/_4$ in. thick and 6 in. wide.
2. For the soft filling such as almond, prune, poppy, etc., the smear is applied about $^1/_8$ in. thick. The crumbs, nuts, and cinnamon sugar are then sprinkled over the filling and gently rolled with the rolling pin.
3. Roll up the dough into a snug roll as you would a jelly roll.
4. Place the strips on paper-lined sheet pans and cut the tops with a scraper or scissors.
5. Egg-wash the top of the strip, give $^3/_4$ proof (with very little steam), wash again, and sprinkle the top with a garnish of nuts, sugar, or other desirable garnish. Bake at 375° to 380°F.
6. Units made with a soft type of filling such as cheese, fruit, etc., the dough is rolled out about $^1/_2$ in. thick and wide enough to cover the filling. The filling is then placed on a bed of cake crumbs or nuts to absorb the moisture in an even amount across the top of the dough. Be sure that the edges (1 in. from the top and bottom and from each end of the dough) are left clear. This is necessary in order to wash the edges and seal the strips.
7. Fold the top edge over the filling and seal with the bottom edge.
8. Cut the top of the strip with scissors at spaced intervals for design and to allow the steam created from the filling during baking to escape. These strips are proofed the same as the others and baked a little longer than the others. Underbaking will cause excessive flatness after baking.

BABKA

Babka is a very popular loaf-type cake that is made from a very rich, sweet dough. It is also commonly known as "coffee cake loaf" or "Grand-mother's loaf." The dough will vary in accordance with the recipe and the variations will have a distinct effect on the finished product. Naturally, the use of butter, eggs, yolks, and other enriching ingredients will determine the quality. Because of the richness of the dough a sponge-and-dough method of mixing is employed in preparing the dough.

Babka   Yield: 17–18 units

Ingredients	Lb.	Oz.	Mixing procedure
Water	2	..	Dissolve yeast in water. Mix flour in well.
Yeast (variable)	..	8	Allow to rise well and start to recede
Bread flour	2	..	
Sugar	1	6	Add all the ingredients, including eggs, and
Salt	..	$1^1/_4$	mix well to dissolve ingredients and break
Milk powder (add to sponge)	..	4	up the sponge
Vanilla	..	1	
Cardamom	..	$^1/_4$	
Orange and lemon (combined)	..	1	
Eggs (part yolks)	1	8	
Bread flour	3	..	Sift, add and mix until flour is absorbed
Melted butter	1	..	Add the melted fat in a steady stream and
Shortening or margarine	1	..	mix well until the fat is incorporated and the dough is smooth

Procedures to Follow

1. Allow the dough to rise well and take to bench for make-up for the Babkas.
2. Use warm water for the sponge dough. The sponge dough enables the yeast to develop rapidly and allows for a vigorous fermentation. This is done to enable the dough to ferment at a more rapid pace than if mixed in a straight dough method. The richness of the dough makes this necessary.
3. When mixing the final dough be sure the ingredients are well mixed with the fermented sponge. The temperature of the eggs should not be cold as this will slow down the fermentation.

4. The final dough should be allowed to rise well before taking to the bench for makeup. Avoid giving the dough a punching and second rise. This may cause the dough to become old during the makeup stage.

5. Scale the desired weights and form the units into oblong shape. Allow the units to relax before rolling out.

    Note: At this point, the scaled and rounded units are often placed in the retarder for makeup at a later time. Refrigerating the dough will firm the fat and make handling of the dough easier as this is a soft dough. Made-up units may also be placed in the retarder for later proofing and baking.

6. Roll out the units of dough into oblong shape about $1/4$ in. thick.

7. Wash with melted butter and smear with almond or other filling. Melted chocolate is often smeared on top of the almond smear for variety.

8. Sprinkle the top of the smear with chopped nuts, cake crumbs, cinnamon sugar and raisins, and dried fruits if desired. Roll the filling gently with the rolling pin.

9. Roll up the dough as for a cinnamon bun and seal the edge. Roll out the strip of dough as you would a coffee ring and twist as a cruller or shape into a large figure "8."

10. Place the units into form pans that have been lined with paper or well greased. Wash the top of the units with melted butter and give $3/4$ proof. Proofing should take place slowly. Avoid too much steam.

    Note: Babkas are form cakes and are made by placing the units into loaf pans or round layer pans. The size of the pan will determine the weight or amount of dough to scale for each of the units.

11. Sprinkle the proofed units with Struessel topping or garnish in any other desirable manner. Be careful to avoid too much Struessel or garnish.

12. Bake the units at 350° to 360°F. Units weighing about 1 lb. take about 45 to 50 min. to bake. Large units of equal height require a longer baking period. Smaller units or flat units require less baking time. It is important that the units be baked through properly. Bake on double pans if the bottom heat of the oven is too strong.

STOLLEN

Stollen is a fruit-filled specialty item made from Babka dough.

Procedures to Follow (Figs. 170–172)

1. At the time the melted fat is added to the final stage of dough preparation and the fat is almost completely incorporated, add 1 lb. cherries, 2 lb. raisins, and 1 lb. chopped nut meats (walnuts or pecans) to every quart of dough. Mix at low speed to incorporate and avoid crushing the fruit and discoloring the dough.
2. Scale the fermented dough into desired unit weights and round the units gently. Allow the units to relax.
3. Roll the units into oval shape about $1/2$ in. thick.
4. Wash the top of the dough with melted butter. Fold the top edge over until $1/4$ in. from the bottom edge. Press the back of the unit with the hand or rolling forcing most of the dough toward the folded edges. This is the same procedure used for making a Parker House roll.

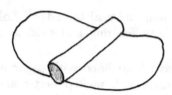

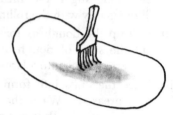

FIG. 170. ROLL RELAXED DOUGH TO AN OVAL SHAPE

FIG. 171. WASH CENTER WITH MELTED BUTTER

5. Place the units on paper-lined pans with sufficient space to proof and expand in baking.

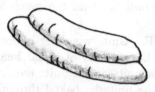

FIG. 172. FOLD ONE END OVER TO THE OTHER, FLATTEN AS FOR PARKER HOUSE ROLL, PROOF, AND BAKE. DUST WITH POWDERED SUGAR WHEN BAKED

6. Give the units slow proof and allow to reach $3/4$ proof. Wash the top with melted butter. Bake at 360°F.
7. The baked unit may be washed with melted butter immediately after baking and dipped in mild cinnamon sugar. The units may be dusted with confectionery sugar if not washed and dipped in sugar. The units should be cool before dusting with sugar.

RUSSIAN COFFEE CAKE

Russian coffee cake is made from Babka dough and is generally made in large pans similar to those used for large cheese cakes and Wonder cakes.

Procedures to Follow (Figs. 173–178)

1. For the regular large-size pan, scale pieces of dough approximately 6 to 8 lb. and form into a rectangular shape.

    Note: A very thin bottom Babka dough liner is advisable at the bottom of the pan.

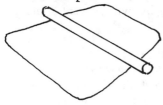

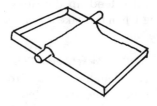

FIG. 173. ROLL OUT THE DOUGH FOR A BOTTOM

FIG. 174. LINE THE PAN WITH DOUGH

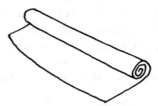

FIG. 175. ROLL DOUGH INTO A RECTANGULAR SHAPE

FIG. 176. ROLL UP THE DOUGH AS FOR SMALL SNECKS

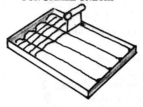

FIG. 177. PLACE STRIPS IN PAN

FIG. 178. FLATTEN STRIPS, CUT WITH SCRAPER, WASH, PROOF, AND BAKE

2. Wash the top of the dough with melted butter and apply the smears as you would in making the regular Babka cakes. Sprinkle with nuts, cinnamon sugar, and cake crumbs and roll in the filling lightly.
3. Start at the top of the dough and roll tightly into rolls about 1 in. in diameter as for miniature Danish snecks.

4. Roll the strips to even the thickness and twist lightly. Measure the length of the pan against the strips and cut the strips to the length or the width of the pan.
5. Place the strips in the pan about $1/2$ in. apart. When the pan is filled flatten the strips gently with the hands. Allow the strips to relax.
6. With a scraper, cut half way through the strips at about 1 in. intervals.
7. Allow the cake to proof until $3/4$ proofed. Wash the top with melted butter, and sprinkle with chopped nuts and cinnamon sugar.
8. Bake at 350°F.

Note: Be sure the sides of the pan are greased well if the paper liner does not extend up the sides of the pan. This will prevent sticking or tearing when the cake is removed.

FROZEN DOUGH PRODUCTS
Pockets, Fruit-Filled, Butter Horns, and Almond Snecks

Frozen dough is made from a basic sweet dough which has been fermented. The fermented dough serves as a base to which other enriching ingredients are added. The amount and nature of these ingredients will determine the quality of the dough and the resulting product. The term "frozen" is derived from the fact that this dough can be refrigerated for some length of time before makeup into units and the units that are made up can also be retarded or frozen. Recipes will vary, as mentioned above, and the following is an average recipe developed for a reasonably good product.

Frozen Dough   **Yield:** 12 doz. units of $1^1/_2$ oz. each

Ingredients	Lb.	Oz.	Mixing procedure
Fermented Babka or sweet yeast dough (bun)	4	..	Blend all ingredients in this stage to a smooth paste. Scrape down kettle for smoothness
Sugar	1	8	
Salt	..	$1/_2$	
Shortening or butter	2	..	
Baker's cheese (optional)	1	..	
Vanilla	..	$1/_2$	
Mace or cardamom	..	$1/_4$	
Eggs	1	4	Add the eggs in two stages and blend
Yeast	..	2	Dissolve yeast and add to above
Water	..	4	
Bread flour	2	2	Sift, add and mix to a smooth dough
Baking powder	..	$1^1/_2$	

Procedures to Follow

1. The dough should be of medium soft consistency. If the dough is stiff, add more eggs to soften. Water may be added but this will make the dough leaner and require an increase in baking powder.
2. Refrigerate the dough until firm. The dough may be frozen for lengthy periods.
3. For *pockets* roll the dough to about ¹/₄ in. thick and allow the dough to relax for a few minutes before cutting into squares. For *filled horns* or *snecks* melted fat or butter should be brushed on the dough before applying the almond or other filling. This will provide added richness.
4. The units indicated above are made up the same way as Danish units are made. However, since the dough is short, care should be taken in handling the units to prevent tearing the dough. This is especially important in the makeup of the pockets.
5. The made-up units should be washed with melted fat or butter. A combination of fats with butter is also suitable. The garnish applied to the tops of the units may be in the form of Struessel topping, ground nuts, or sugar.
6. The made-up units should be allowed to relax for about 1 hr. before baking. The proof box may be used to allow a mild action by the yeast. Where no yeast is added to the dough, a shorter rest period is sufficient.

Note: The baker's cheese adds further richness, taste, and flavor to the dough. If cream cheese is used the weight of the fat should be reduced 8 oz. for each 1 lb. cream cheese. If frozen dough is made without any additional yeast it will have a closer grain and for leavening depend primarily upon the baking powder and the leavening supplied by the yeast present in the basic sweet dough.

SEVEN SISTERS

Seven Sisters are made in round layer pans. The size of the pan will determine the weight of the unit of dough to be used. Normally, a 7-in. pan will require approximately 14 oz. Babka dough.

Procedures to Follow (Figs. 179–182)

1. Scale the unit of Babka dough. Remove 2 oz. of dough to be used as a bottom liner for the pan. Shape the dough into a rectangle and relax it.
2. Roll out the dough as for cinnamon buns, wash with melted butter, apply almond or other filling, sprinkle with chopped nuts, crumbs, and cinnamon sugar, and roll up into a tight roll.

3. Roll out the small piece of dough and cover the bottom of the layer pan which has been greased with melted fat or butter.
4. Divide the rolled-up and filled strip in seven equal pieces. Put the largest of the pieces in the center and the other six pieces around it. The pieces are to be placed cut side up as for cinnamon buns.
5. Egg-wash the unit and give ³/₄ proof. Egg-wash again and place a filling of orange, lemon, jam, or other topping on the unit. Bake at 360°F. Oven temperature may be reduced if the units are made from larger pieces of dough.

FIG. 179. FILL AND ROLL AS FOR CINNAMON BUNS

FIG. 180. CUT IN SEVEN PIECES

FIG. 181. PLACE IN A GREASED LAYER PAN, EGG-WASH, GIVE ³/₄ PROOF, GARNISH, AND BAKE

FIG. 182. FINISHED SEVEN SISTER

RUM CAKE

To prepare the dough for rum cake, you must begin with a properly fermented piece of Babka dough.

Procedures to Follow (Figs. 183–185)

1. Place the fermented dough in the machine after you have scaled it. For each pound of Babka dough, add 2 oz. eggs (yolks preferred) to the dough and mix until it is smooth and runny.
2. Place the dough into angel or Turk-head pans which have been cleaned and greased. Fill the pans about one-third full or slightly more.
3. Allow the units to proof until the pan is about two-thirds to three-fourths full.
4. Allow the units to bake at 350°F. until light brown and springy. Remove from pans and cool.

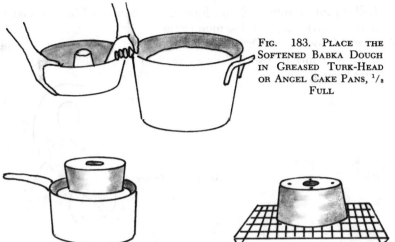

FIG. 183. PLACE THE SOFTENED BABKA DOUGH IN GREASED TURK-HEAD OR ANGEL CAKE PANS, $^{1}/_{3}$ FULL

FIG. 184. DIP BAKED CAKES IN HOT RUM SYRUP FOR A FEW SECONDS

FIG. 185. PLACE THE CAKES ON AN ICING SCREEN TO DRAIN

5. Dip the rum cakes into the hot syrup for a few seconds. Remove the cakes and place upon an icing screen to allow the excess syrup to run off. When cool, glaze the rum cakes by brushing with boiled apricot coating. When dry and cool, place a glazed cherry on four parts of the cake. The cherry may be flanked on each side by a wedge of citron.

Rum Syrup for Dipping

Ingredients	Lb.	Oz.	Mixing procedure
Water	4	..	Bring to a boil and boil for 2 min.
Sugar	6	..	
Glucose	1	..	
Rum		1 pt.	
or			Remove from fire and stir in the flavor or
Rum flavor		1	rum

FILLED BABKAS

Procedures to Follow (Figs. 186–188)

1. Scale the units in accordance with the pan size.
2. Roll out in rectangular shape and fill with almond, chocolate, lekvar, or other filling. Cover the filling with nuts, crumbs and cinnamon sugar.

3. Roll up into a tight roll and form into a figure "8" for the loaf pans or into a snail shape for the round pans.

4. Give $^3/_4$ proof, brush with melted butter, sprinkle with Struessel topping, allow to rise a little more, and bake 345° to 350°F. until light brown.

Fig. 186.   Start the Twist

Fig. 187.   Place Twisted Unit in the Loaf Pan

Fig. 188.   Shape the Babka Strip as for a Snail and Place in Round Pan

PECAN ROLLS

Each of the sweet yeast dough products add to the variety of products the baker can produce. Most of these are daily items that are retarded and baked as needed. Some, such as hot cross buns, are made during the Lenten period. Of great importance to the baker is the variation in the makeup and types of dough which may be used.

Pecan rolls are made from Danish dough or a coffee cake dough. The coffee cake dough, in this instance, is that which was used for the makeup of rich buns. Bun dough may be used but the best results are obtained from Danish pastry dough.

Procedures to Follow (Figs. 189–191)

1. Roll out the Danish or coffee cake dough $^1/_4$ in. thick and about 9 in. wide. The length is determined by the amount of dough being rolled and the length of the bench. The dough may be rolled out 18 in. wide and of the same thickness. This dough is then cut in half after it is filled

2. Remove the excess flour from the dough and brush the top with a thin film of melted butter or fat. Smear again with a thin coating of almond filling. Sprinkle the almond filling with broken pecan pieces, cake crumbs, and cinnamon sugar. Roll the filling in lightly with the rolling pin.

3. Roll up the dough into a tight round strip as for cinnamon buns or Danish snecks. The strip should be about 2 in. in diameter. Be sure the Danish strip is of even thickness throughout so that the cut pieces will be of equal weight. Cut the strip into slices approximately 1 in. thick and weighing about 2 oz. The units may be made smaller or larger by controlling the diameter of the roll and the size of the sliced unit.

4. Place the units face down on a sheet pan that has been filled with chopped pecan pieces and mixed with cinnamon sugar. Remove and place on a paper-lined sheet pan $1^{1}/_{2}$ in. apart. Give the units $^{3}/_{4}$ proof and bake at 400°F. Units may also be cut and placed directly on the sheet pan. The units are then egg-washed and given $^{3}/_{4}$ proof. The units are then egg-washed again and sprinkled with pecan halves. The units are baked at 400°F. and washed with warm syrup immediately after removal from the oven.

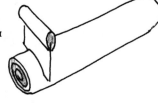

FIG. 189. ROLLED-UP, FILLED DOUGH IS CUT AS FOR CINNAMON BUNS

FIG. 190. PECAN ROLLS MADE IN SHEET PANS

FIG. 191. PECAN ROLLS MADE IN MUFFIN TINS

5. Pecan rolls may also be made up in muffin or cupcake tins. The tins may be greased or they may be lined with paper cupcake liners. In this case, the dough is rolled longer and narrower (6 in. wide). The rolled-up strip should be about $1^1/_2$ in. in diameter and the units cut thicker so that the weight is the same. Weight is determined by the size of the tin. The units are dipped in the nut-cinnamon preparation and placed in the tins. They may also be placed in the tins and given full proof, washed with egg, and sprinkled with nuts. Bake these units to 390°F. The lower temperature is necessary because the units are thicker and are confined to a pan. This requires a longer and slower bake to prevent falling back.

ORANGE-FILLED ROLLS

These rolls are made up from either Danish or coffee cake dough. Coffee cake dough is richer than the average bun dough and not as rich as Babka dough.

Coffee Cake Dough (1 qt.)   **Yield:** 9 doz.

Ingredients	Lb.	Oz.	Mixing procedure
Sugar	1	..	Blend all ingredients together to a smooth,
Salt	..	1	soft paste
Milk powder	..	4	
Butter and	1	..	
shortening			
Eggs	1	..	Add the eggs in two stages and blend in well
Yeast	..	5	Dissolve the yeast in the water and set aside
Water (lukewarm)	1	..	
Water	1	..	Add the water, flavor, and spice and stir
Vanilla	..	1	slightly
Cardamom	..	$^1/_4$	
Cake flour	1	..	Sift, add the flour, stir slightly, add the yeast
Bread flour	3	4	solution, and develop to a smooth dough

Procedures to Follow

1. Allow the dough to rise well, punch, allow to relax for about 15 min. and take to the bench.
2. Divide the dough into pieces weighing about 4 lb. and shape into long rectangular pieces as you would for cinnamon buns.

3. Roll out the relaxed dough or the Danish dough about $1/4$ in. thick and about 6 to 8 in. wide.
4. Smear the top of the dough with orange filling and sprinkle the top of the filling with light cake crumbs. Sponge or yellow-layer cake should be used. Avoid dark crumbs because this will discolor the appearance of the orange filling.
5. Roll up the dough as for cinnamon or pecan rolls and seal.
6. Cut the roll and deposit the units either on pans or in muffin tins. The tops of the rolls should be washed with egg and a circle of orange filling should be dressed out on top of each of the rolls after they have been proofed.
7. If the rolls are baked on sheet pans the rolls should be washed with warm, simple syrup and glazed lightly with orange-colored and flavored fondant or simple icing. Apply the icing while it is warm. These rolls may also be made with lemon filling and other filling preparations.

FRUIT-FILLED CUPS OR FRUIT ROLLS

A complete variety of these fruit cups or rolls may be made by using various types of fruits for the filling. Coffee cake dough is recommended as Danish dough is too rich in fat content and the fruit may tend to penetrate the dough and cause considerable sticking.

Procedures to Follow (Figs. 192–195)

1. Scale the conditioned dough into presses weighing approximately 3 lb.
2. Round up the presses and allow to relax for about 5 min. Press out the presses and separate with bread flour. Round up the units and relax for 10 min.
3. Roll out the pieces with a small rolling pin so that the units are about 4 in. around. Try to keep the units in circular form as for pies.
4. Place the rolled-out pieces in lines on a clean portion of the bench.
5. Deposit about 1 oz. of fruit filling in the center of each unit. Pick up the unit and squeeze the ends of the dough together so that a round, sealed ball with the fruit in the center is formed.
6. The units are then placed in greased muffin tins or tins which have been lined with cupcake liners. Tart pans may also be used. Be sure the sealed ends are placed at the bottom of the muffin tin or tart pan. The top should expose the smooth surface of the dough.
7. Snip the top of the units with a scissors. This will allow the steam formed during baking to escape and prevent seeping of the fruit on the bottom or sides which causes the rolls to stick.

8. Give units ³/₄ proof and egg-wash. Sprinkle the tops of the units with Struessel or crumb topping. Nuts, sugar, and or other toppings may be used to distinguish variations in fruit fillings. Give the units almost full proof (the tins are now full) and bake at 390°F. Bake until golden brown. Allow the units to cool until they are warm and then remove from the tins by tapping the muffin pan on the rack or bench and turning the tin over. Do not allow the entire tin to fall over completely for this may flatten the tops of the fruit-filled cups and spoil the appearance as well as reducing the volume.

9. The tops of the fruit cups may be dusted lightly with confectionery sugar when they are cool.

FIG. 192. ROLL OUT PIECE OF DOUGH
WITH SMALL ROLLING PIN

FIG. 193. ROLLED AND FILLED PIECES
OF DOUGH

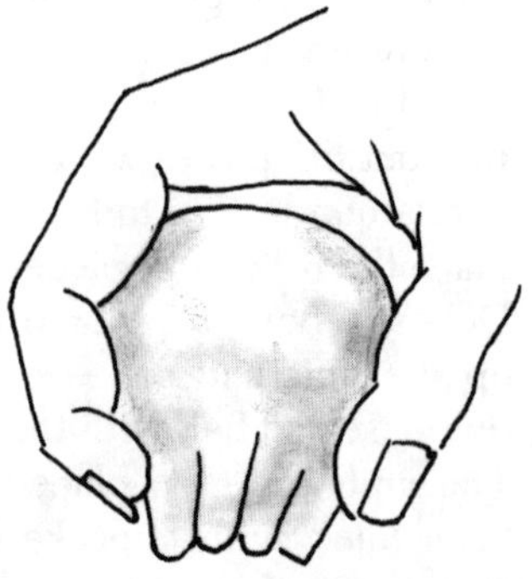

FIG. 194. SEALING THE MADE-UP
UNITS

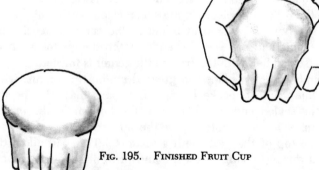

FIG. 195. FINISHED FRUIT CUP

HOT CROSS BUNS

These buns are best made from either a bun dough or coffee cake dough. The fruits are added to the dough in the final stages of mixing. To every quart of dough add the following:

Raisins, 2 lb.	Soak the raisins for about $1/2$ hr. and then
Mixed fruits, 2 lb.	remove the excess water. Do not allow the
Cherries	raisins to soak until they have completely
Citron	swelled and become very soft
Orange peel	

The raisins and mixed fruit are added to the dough in the last stages of dough development. Mix enough to distribute the fruit without mashing the fruit and discoloring the dough. Allow the dough to rise, punch, and relax for $1/2$ hr. before taking to the bench.

Procedures to Follow (Figs. 196 and 197)

1. Scale the dough into presses weighing about 3 lb. The size of the press depends upon the requirements of the shop and production.

2. Round up the presses and allow them to relax about 15 min.

3. Press out the dough and round up the units as you would for hamburger rolls. Place the units on sheet pans that have been greased or lined with parchment paper. Place the units six down and ten across. Be sure the units are lined up in straight lines.

4. Allow the units to relax for 5 min. and then flatten gently with the palms of the hands.

5. With a scraper make cuts about half way through the units. Be careful to make the cuts across the center of each unit. Do this in the length and in the width.

6. Wash the units with egg-wash, give $3/4$ proof, and egg-wash again. Give the units almost full proof and bake at 390°F. Bake until light brown. Test for bake by pressing gently the top of the center bun. If it springs back softly to the touch it is done.

7. Wash the buns as soon as removed from the oven with warm simple syrup. Allow the buns to cool until mildly warm.

8. Ice the buns by filling a paper cone with thick, warm, simple icing or fondant and bag out the icing in straight lines across the cuts made by the scraper.

Note: Large units may be made from the above dough. Scale into 12 oz. units and round up. Place six such units on a sheet pan and cut across the top after the units have relaxed. Follow the same procedure as for the buns. Bake at a cooler temperature (375°F.).

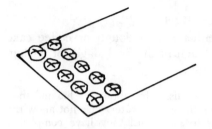

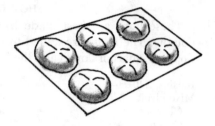

Fig. 196.   Hot Cross Buns in a   Fig. 197.   Six Large Units on a Pan
          Sheet Pan

BRIOCHE

Brioche is a sweet yeast dough product of French derivation.   It is different from the average sweet yeast dough product in that it is very rich in egg content and is baked to a crisp state rather than the usual softness characteristic of buns.   While brioche is not a common item the consumer demand is present when the product is made properly.

Brioche   **Yield:** 9 doz. (3 press)

Ingredients	Lb.	Oz.	Mixing procedure
Milk powder	..	4	Dissolve the milk powder in the water. Add
Cool water	2	..	the yeast and dissolve. Add the flour and
Yeast (optional)	..	8–12	mix to a smooth sponge dough. Allow
Bread flour	1	8	sponge to rise until it starts to fall slightly
Sugar	1	..	Add the sugar, salt and eggs and mix well
Salt	..	$1^1/_2$	to break up the sponge. The rind of two
Eggs (part yolks)	2	..	lemons may be used in place of the lemon
Lemon rind or flavor	..	$^1/_2$	flavor
Bread flour	4	4	Add the bread flour and mix smooth
Melted butter	..	8	Add the melted butter and fat in a steady
Melted shortening	..	8	stream and mix at second speed until the dough is smooth and works away from sides of kettle

Procedures to Follow (Figs. 198–201)

1. Note that a sponge dough is recommended for the fermentation base. This provides a more active fermentation to take care of the richness of the dough.
2. Allow the final dough to rise well and take to the bench for makeup.

3. Scale the dough into presses weighing about 4 lb. each. The size of the tart pans used will determine the size of the presses of dough.

4. Allow the presses of dough to relax 10 min. and press out the dough. (Each press of dough yields 36 units.)

5. Round up the pieces of dough as for a hamburger roll. With the outside of the palm of the hand press down at the side of the rounded unit and force a small portion of the dough out (about $1/4$ oz.) as a small round ball. Be careful not to break off this unit. It must be an attached ball or bulb. Roll slightly to make the groove separation distinct. For the beginner, it is advisable to detach a small piece of dough from each $1/4$ to $1/2$ oz.) before rounding. Then round the larger piece of dough and flatten it in the center. Round the small piece of dough and place it into the hollow after the larger piece has been egg-washed. The egg-wash will hold the small ball in place during the proofing stage.

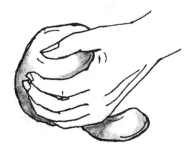

FIG. 198. ROUND PIECE OF DOUGH AS FOR HAMBURGER ROLLS, AND WITH SIDE OF HAND PRESS DOWN AND FORCE OUT A SMALL PORTION OF ROUND DOUGH

FIG. 199. DETACH A SMALL PIECE OF DOUGH FROM THE UNIT AND ROUND UP BOTH

FIG. 200. PLACE THE SMALLER UNIT ON THE LARGER UNIT AFTER IT HAS BEEN EGG-WASHED

FIG. 201. PLACE UNIT INTO GREASED TART PANS, GIVE $3/4$ PROOF, AND BAKE

6. Place the units into greased, scalloped tart pans with the small ball in the center and facing up. Wash the units with straight egg-wash.
7. Give the units about $^3/_4$ proof and then make three or four cuts with scissors at the sides of the unit. Be careful not to cut too deep. Wash the units with egg-wash again and give almost full proof.
8. Bake the units at 360°F. until deep brown and crisp. Do not burn or brown at a high oven temperature. The units weighing about 4 lb. per press take about 25 min. to bake. They must feel crisp.

CHAPTER 17

Factors Concerning Biscuits and Muffins

The baking and sale of biscuits and muffins should be a profitable part of the retail baker's business and can be made so, if it is not. Although they are often a breakfast item, biscuits and muffins can be an all-day sales item. The requirements are: good quality, care in production, variety, and freshly baked products. Practices and problems common to their production are considered in this chapter.

BISCUITS

Biscuits can be made from a variety of recipes. Those which presently give good results should be continued. They may even be improved with a better understanding of production practices. Basically, sugar, salt, milk, shortening, flour, and leavening are the ingredients used. To these may be added eggs, butter, and others for variety (variations are indicated in the recipes in the following chapter). These will improve quality and the baker must determine costs before revising his recipes. In addition eggs will improve the volume of the biscuits as well as the taste and flavor. Allowances must be made for reduction of the chemical leavening because of the natural leavening effect of the eggs.

Examine the recipe given for biscuits and note that the mixing procedure indicates complete development of the dough. This will result in a soft, cake-like interior. Other recipes, slightly richer in fat content, are mixed like a pie crust. The fat and flour are rubbed together and the dissolved sugar and salt are added with the liquid and folded in very gently. This makes a flaky type of biscuit. This type requires special care in handling because toughness in the dough is developed quickly. These biscuits also tend to lose some of their shape and bake somewhat flatter than others.

Combination doughs are often used for biscuits. This dough is leavened by yeast and baking powder. The recipes given for biscuits of this type are quite specific and excellent results are obtainable. It is important to allow the dough to relax for $1/2$ hr. before makeup, thus permitting the yeast to condition the dough. The time for conditioning and the yeast activity in the dough are controlled by the temperature of the water or milk used.

MUFFINS

It is not uncommon to find bakers in the retail shops using a single, basic mix for the production of all types of muffins. Cornmeal, whole-wheat flour, bran flour, and other ingredients are added to the basic mix. Additional milk or eggs may be added to this mix to soften it after the flour or other drying ingredients have been added. This means that the properly mixed basic mix, such as plain muffins, is now mixed again and this causes toughness. Improper balance often results and the muffins are characterized by a dense, close grain and poor volume. They may also have an open grain and large holes and tunnels. This is due to toughness and the added leavening forcing its way through the overmixed batter. It is much better practice to use a separate muffin mix for each type of muffin listed in the section on muffins and biscuits.

In the corn muffin mix the milk is added in two separate stages to allow the flour to absorb the first part of the liquid. If all the liquid is added at once the cornmeal tends to form into small lumps and mixing is prolonged with the possibility of toughness developing before all the lumps are removed. The stiffness of the batter, by withholding part of liquid, permits the cornmeal to be blended in easily and evenly. The mix will be very soft when first mixed but stiffens as it stands. Cornmeal does not readily absorb liquid because of its large, coarse, granular structure, and requires time for liquid absorption. This is also true of the whole-wheat muffin mix. The bran in the whole-wheat flour also requires time for complete absorption of liquid.

Corn syrup is added to the corn muffins and molasses to the whole-wheat muffins. Both syrups are moisture-retaining agents and produce better crust color and keeping qualities.

Muffins should be deposited evenly into either well-greased or paper-lined pans. For better appearance and improved volume greased tins are best. Paper liners tend to cause the mix to stick to the paper before the full leavening effect of the eggs and leavening agents is reached. This, in turn, leads to the formation of peaks on corn and whole-wheat muffins. Plain muffin varieties are best suited for paper liners.

The corn and whole-wheat muffins are leaner in fat and sugar content than are the plain muffins. They require a higher baking temperature and should be baked at 400°F. with a mild injection of steam in the oven during the first few minutes of baking. The steam prevents the rapid formation of a crust on the top of the muffin and allows an even expansion during the first stage of baking. Once the muffins have risen the steam is let out of the oven and the muffins are completely baked. This accounts for the slight rim around the edge of the corn and whole-wheat muffins and a smooth surface in the center. The steam also permits greater moisture retention and improved keeping qualities.

Muffins should be refrigerated or frozen to meet production requirements. Muffins under refrigeration return to shop temperature quickly and can be baked soon after removal from the refrigerator. Muffins can be frozen in the baked and unbaked state. The unbaked state will require the removal of muffin pans from use while they are in the freezer. Baked units should be baked just done and quick-frozen ($-10°F.$) as soon as they have returned to room temperature. They should be wrapped in a polyethylene freezer wrap to prevent frost formation. It is advisable to place the frozen muffins in muffin tins and reheat for 3 min. to complete the defrost and freshen the muffins. Special cartons may permit the consumer to reheat the muffins at home. Freshness and pleasing odor will increase sales.

CHAPTER 18

Recipes for Biscuits and Muffins

Biscuits are a very popular item prepared in bakeshops and other food establishments on a regular basis. Biscuits also vary in size, shape, filling, and in the type of recipe used. While they are simple to make, they require the care, the attention, and understanding necessary for producing a standard product.

Biscuits   **Yield:** 7 to 8 doz.

Ingredients	Lb.	Oz.	Mixing procedure
Sugar	..	8	Scale carefully. Blend all ingredients to a
Salt	..	$1/2$	smooth paste
Milk powder	..	4	
Shortening	..	8	
Eggs	..	4	Add the eggs and blend in well
Water	2	..	Add the water and stir in
Bread flour	2	8	Sift, add, and mix to a smooth dough
Cake flour	1	..	
Baking powder	..	3	

Procedures to Follow (Figs. 202 and 203)

1. Place the dough on a floured portion of the bench and form into a rectangle. Use bread flour for dusting the bench and rolling out the dough.
2. Allow the dough to relax 15 min. before rolling out.
3. Roll out the dough with a rolling pin about $3/8$ to $1/2$ in. thick. Be sure the dough is of even thickness and does not stick to the bench. Use your fingers to feel the thickness of the dough for evenness.
4. Allow the rolled-out dough to relax for 5 min. and cut out the biscuits with a cookie cutter or biscuit cutter. The size of the cutter will determine the size of the biscuit. When cutting out the biscuits, cut each biscuit as close to the next as is possible. This will prevent too much excess dough to be rolled over again. Remember that the more the dough is worked and rolled the more flour is absorbed and the tougher the dough becomes.

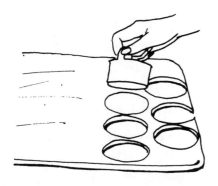

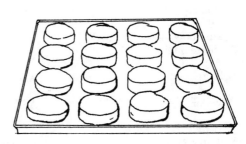

FIG. 202.   CUTTING OUT THE BISCUITS

FIG. 203.   SPACING THE BISCUITS ON
A PAN

5. Work the scrap dough into a square and allow to rest before rolling
   again.   It is advisable to cut scrap dough from the second roll into a
   square shape with a pastry wheel.   This will use up the dough and
   avoid excessive toughness by consistent rolling.
6. Place the cut out biscuits on greased or paper-lined pans about
   $1/2$ in. apart.
7. Wash the tops of the biscuits with egg-wash, milk, or melted fat.
8. Allow the biscuits to rest on the pan about 10 min. and bake at
   425° to 430°F. until light brown.   Do not overbake.

Note: A blend of cake and bread flours is used to avoid too tough a
dough.   The eggs may be increased and the baking powder decreased
for eggs have a natural leavening effect.   For each 4 oz. of eggs added,
add 2 oz. of bread flour or 3 oz. of cake flour to the mix.

Flaky-type biscuits require a different mixing method.   The flour and
shortening are rubbed together to small lumps.   The sugar, salt, and milk
are dissolved in the water and added last and the mix folded lightly.
This makes a sticky dough which requires refrigeration before rolling.
The baking powder is blended with the flour.

COMBINATION BISCUITS

The term "combination" with regard to biscuits refers to the use of a
chemical leavening agent (baking powder) and yeast (organic leavening
agent).   Thus, a combination of both leavenings will result in a biscuit
of lighter texture and grain with a variation in taste and appearance.
This biscuit dough lends itself well to the makeup of cinnamon biscuits
and muffin-type biscuits.

Combination Biscuits

Yield: 8 doz.

Ingredients	Lb.	Oz.	Mixing procedure
Sugar	..	10	Blend the ingredients in this stage to a
Salt	..	1	smooth paste
Milk powder	..	4	
Shortening	..	8	
Eggs	..	4	Add the eggs and blend well
Water	1	..	Add the water and stir slightly
Yeast	..	4	
Water (warm)	1	..	Dissolve the yeast and set aside
Cake flour	1	..	Sift the flours and baking powder, add, stir
Bread flour	2	10	slightly, add the yeast solution and develop
Baking powder	..	1	to a smooth dough

Procedures to Follow

1. Place the dough in a warm, moist place to rise. Keep the dough covered to prevent crust formation.
2. Allow the dough to rise once and place on the bench. Do not punch.
3. Form the dough into a rectangle and allow it to rest 10 min.
4. Roll out the dough as for baking powder biscuits and cut out the biscuits. The size depends upon the bakeshop requirements. The biscuits may also be cut out into small squares or triangular shapes. The dough which remains should be worked together and rolled out again and cut into squares. This will use up all the scrap dough.
5. Place the biscuits on lightly greased pans and allow the biscuits to rise until they feel soft and springy to the touch. Placing them in a proof box will speed fermentation after they are made up.
6. Wash the tops of the biscuits with egg-wash or melted fat and bake at 410°F.

CINNAMON BISCUITS AND MUFFIN BISCUITS

Procedures to Follow (Figs. 203A, 203B, 203C, 203D and 204)

1. Roll out the dough into a rectangle about $1/4$ in. thick as for cinnamon buns.
2. Brush the top of the dough with melted fat and sprinkle with raisins and cinnamon sugar. A light sprinkling of light cake crumbs may also be used. Roll up the filled dough and seal the edge well.

3. Brush the top of the rolled-up dough with melted fat and cut into slices about $^3/_4$ in. wide.
4. Place the slices on a paper-lined or greased pan face up and flatten. These pieces may also be placed in greased muffin tins.
5. Allow the biscuits to rise or get half proof, egg-wash, and bake at 400°F. Wash with syrup when removed from the oven. Ice with simple icing when the biscuits are mildly warm.

FIG. 203A. ROLL OUT THE DOUGH $^1/_4$ IN. THICK

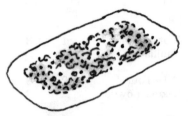

FIG. 203B. BRUSH DOUGH WITH OIL OR MELTED FAT AND SPRINKLE WITH RAISINS, CAKE CRUMBS AND CINNAMON SUGAR

FIG. 203C. ROLL THE DOUGH UP TIGHTLY AND SEAL THE EDGE

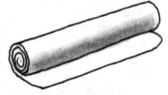

FIG. 203D. BRUSH THE TOP OF THE ROLL WITH OIL OR MELTED FAT AND CUT INTO EVEN PIECES WITH A SCRAPER

FIG. 204. CINNAMON BISCUITS

PLAIN AND RAISIN MUFFINS

Muffins are a regular breakfast item prepared in most retail bakeshops, hotels, and restaurants. A variety of muffins and biscuits, freshly baked, will add to the sales and prestige of the baker. Muffins vary in size and content. A basic recipe for plain muffins which may be varied by adding raisins, nuts, diced fruits, and fresh berries is given here.

Plain Muffins   Yield: 6 doz.

Ingredients	Lb.	Oz.	Mixing procedure
Sugar	1	8	Cream the ingredients in this stage until soft
Salt	..	$1/2$	and light
Milk powder	..	3	
Shortening	1	..	
Eggs	..	12	Add the eggs in two stages and cream well after each addition
Water	1	8	Stir in the water and flavor
Vanilla	..	$1/2$	
Cake flour	2	8	Sift, add and mix to a smooth batter
Baking powder	..	2	

Procedures to Follow (Fig. 205)

1. The muffin tins should be clean and greased with soft shortening blended with a small amount of neutral oil. This will make brushing of the greasing fat easier and will insure that the entire tin is greased. An ungreased part of the muffin tin will cause the muffin to stick and break when the muffin is removed from the tin. Do not use excess fat.

2. Deposit the mix or batter into the greased tins and fill half full. The mix is dropped in by hand. Pick up some of the mix in the palm of the right hand (if right-handed) and then place the thumb so that the forefinger is partially covered by the thumb. Close the fingers of the right hand slowly. This will force the mix in the palm to move to the small finger side in a ball form. Cut off the necessary amount of mix with the forefinger of the left hand and drop the mix in the muffin tin. Practice will enable you to increase the amount of mix picked up and increase the speed with which the mix is dropped out. Check each tin to be sure there is an equal amount in each. Remove or add mix so that each tin is half full.

3. Bake the muffins at 385°F. Average-sized muffins take about 15 min. to bake. When the muffins have risen and take on a golden color. Check for "doneness" or bake by pressing gently at the top of the baking muffin. If the muffin springs back gently to the touch it is baked.

4. Allow the muffins to cool until they are mildly warm, and remove from the pans by inverting the pan over a large, clean, sheet pan. If muffins stick slightly, as in the case of raisin muffins, tap the pan to release the sticking muffins.

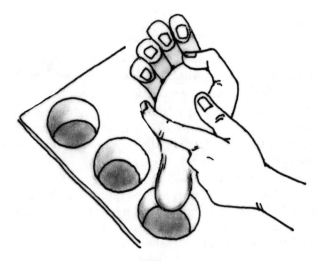

FIG. 205. DROPPING OUT MUFFIN BATTER

WHOLE-WHEAT MUFFINS

Variety muffins, such as whole-wheat muffins, are staple breakfast items and are often served at other meals as well. Variety muffins are made daily as their quality and freshness are the factors which determine consumer popularity. Bakers should prepare the batters, pan, and bake them as required. The manner of preparing and baking are standard for all varieties of muffins.

Whole-Wheat Muffins Yield: 6 doz.

Ingredients	Lb.	Oz.	Mixing procedure
Sugar	..	12	Cream these ingredients until soft and smooth
Salt	..	$1/2$	
Milk powder	..	4	
Shortening	..	12	
Molasses	..	4	
Cinnamon	..	$1/4$	
Eggs	..	12	Add the eggs in two stages and cream well after each addition
Water	2	..	Dissolve the soda in the water. Add alternately with the flour
Baking soda	..	$1/2$	
Bread flour	..	12	Sift the flour together. Do not remove the bran particles. Add alternately with the water. Mix until smooth
Cake flour	..	10 ·	
Whole-wheat flour	..	12	
Baking powder	..	$1^3/4$	

Procedures to Follow

1. The whole-wheat flour may be increased. This will make for a slightly heavier and closer grained muffin. The bread and cake flour may be entirely replaced with 1 lb. 4 oz. of whole-wheat flour.

2. A good-quality molasses is recommended for improved flavor.

3. The mix will feel soft when first mixed. It will tighten or stiffen as the mix stands. This is especially so when all whole-wheat flour is used. The bran in the flour does not absorb all the liquid it can until it has been standing for some time.

4. One pound of raisins may be added for variety. The raisins are added in the final stages of mixing. If the raisins are dry soak them for a few minutes and drain before adding to the mix. This will prevent the raisins from absorbing excess moisture in the mix and creating large holes in the muffin after baking.

5. Drop the muffin batter in clean, well-greased muffin tins. Fill half full. Bake at 400°F. To remove peaks and get a flat-ridged top insert a small amount of steam in the oven for the first few minutes of baking. Allow the steam to escape after the muffins have risen. Excess steam will cause peeling of the tops of the muffins. Muffins baked without steam will have a small, raised contour or top similar to a cupcake.

6. Allow the muffins to cool until mildly warm before removing from the tins. It is advisable to tap the tins before turning the tins over to remove the muffins.

Note: The muffin batter dropped in the tins may be refrigerated up to 48 hr. before baking.

BRAN MUFFINS

Bran Muffins   Yield: 6 doz.

Ingredients	Lb.	Oz.	Mixing procedure
Sugar	..	10	Blend all ingredients together until soft and
Salt	..	$1/2$	smooth
Milk powder	..	4	
Shortening	..	6	
Molasses ($1/4$ qt.)	..	12	
Eggs	..	4	Add the eggs and cream in well
Water	2	..	Dissolve the soda in the water and stir lightly
Baking soda	..	$3/4$	into the above
Bread flour	1	..	Sift the bread and cake flour. Add the bran
Cake flour	..	6	flour and baking powder and blend together.
Bran flour	..	10	Add to the above and mix smooth
Baking powder	..	$1/2$	
Raisins	..	8	Fold the raisins in during the final stages of mixing

Procedures to Follow

1. Use a good grade of dark molasses for color and improved taste.
2. Examine the bran carefully. Aged bran flour or that which has been stored for some time may have weevils.
3. You will note that the batter is soft when first mixed. It will thicken as it stands.
4. The raisins are folded in. Raisins which are dry should be soaked and drained before using.
5. Deposit the mix into clean, well-greased muffin tins. Fill half full.
6. The tops of the muffins may be sprinkled with bran before baking. Bake at 400°F. These muffins should be brown and feel springy to the touch before removing from the oven.
7. Remove from the pans while still warm. Tap the pans on the bench to free muffins which may be sticking before turning the muffin tins to remove the muffins.

CORN MUFFINS AND SOUTHERN CORN BREAD

Corn Muffins and Bread   **Yield:** 8 doz. 1 full sheet pan 16 x 24 in.

Ingredients	Lb.	Oz.	Mixing procedure
Sugar	1	..	Blend well until soft and light
Salt	..	$^3/_4$	
Milk powder	..	4	
Glucose or corn syrup	..	3	
Shortening	..	12	
Eggs	..	12	Add in two stages and cream well
Water	1	8	Add and stir slightly
Cornmeal	..	12	Sift, add, and mix smooth
Cake flour	2	6	
Baking powder	..	$2^1/_4$	
Water	..	12	Add and mix smooth

Procedures to Follow

1. Creaming the mix while adding the eggs will create more volume and a smoother grain and texture.
2. Note that the water is added in two stages. Adding the liquid at once will cause an excess and cause the cornmeal and flour to form lumps which float. This will make it necessary to mix excessively, and possibly toughen the mix, in order to remove these lumps. The water may be added alternately with the flour and cornmeal. You will note that the mix is soft when first mixed. It will tend to become thicker as it stands. This is due to the slow absorption of liquid by the cornmeal.
3. Deposit the mix in clean, well-greased muffin tins. Fill half full.
4. Bake at 410°F. It is advisable to have a small amount of steam in the oven until the muffins have risen. This makes a flat top and ridged edge. Muffins baked without steam have a tendency to peak in the center.
5. Muffins are considered baked when they have a golden-brown color and spring back lightly when touched gently in the center.
6. Allow the muffins to cool until mildly warm before removing from the tins. Tap the pan on the bench before removing to free muffins which may possibly stick.

7. For *southern corn bread* place the mix in sheet pans which have been greased and dusted with flour. The pans may also be lined with parchment paper and the sides of the pan greased. The corn bread is baked without steam in the oven. After baking, the corn bread is cut into small squares while still warm.

ENGLISH MUFFINS

English muffins are a specialized item and are not usually made in the average retail bakeshop but in plants especially equipped for their manufacture. However, it is possible and likely that English muffins will be made by the competent baker as a specialty.

English Muffins (2 qt.) **Yield:** 100 muffins of $1^1/_2$ oz. each

Ingredients	Lb.	Oz.	Mixing procedure
Salt	..	2	Dissolve the salt and milk powder in the
Milk powder	..	8	water
Water	3	..	
Yeast	..	4	Dissolve the yeast and set aside
Water (warm)	1	..	
Bread flour	4	8	Sift, add and mix slightly. Add the yeast solution and mix to a soft, smooth dough

Procedures to Follow

1. This dough, although quite soft, is made somewhat stiffer than that made in the plants equipped with depositors and rings for receiving the fermented soft batter. (Normally, about 2 lb. of flour is used per quart.)
2. Allow the dough to rise well and take to the bench. Use enough dusting flour to prevent sticking.
3. Scale the dough into presses weighing about 3 lb. or less. Round up and allow the presses to relax slightly.
4. Press out the dough with enough flour to prevent sticking. Round up each unit with very soft pressure to prevent sticking. It is advisable to dust the palms of the hands with bread flour before rounding.
5. Place the rounded units on pans or in roll boxes dusted with cornmeal.
6. Allow the units to receive about half proof.

7. The muffins are baked on a grill as you would pancakes. Heat the grill being sure that the grill is perfectly clean. Lift each of the units and place on the grill spaced about 1 in. apart. The fermented soft dough may also be spooned out on the griddle by ladling. In this fashion, the edge of the ladle is inserted into the top of the dough gently and a ladleful is placed on the griddle. Work from the top down to prevent collapsing the sponge. When depositing the batter, try to spoon or ladle the sponge dough into a round form when depositing.

8. The muffins will rise and brown at the bottom. Turn them gently with a spatula and brown the other side. The temperature of the grill is important in that too hot a surface will cause too rapid coloring and the collapse of the muffins after removal. Adjust the flame as you proceed.

Note: The dough is generally made softer and allowed to rise. The batter is then dropped into rings set on a pre-heated griddle. As the muffins rise and brown, the rings are then removed and the muffins turned to complete the baking process. This procedure is to be followed if the rings are available. The rings are filled about half full.

The above recipe is made stiffer to enable the sponge dough to be handled and the units rounded into shape for uniformity of size and shape without the use of muffin rings.

ORANGE MUFFINS

These muffins add to the variety of the muffin display produced by the baker and promote sales if they are made with skill and foresight. For example, the orange muffin may be used to excellent advantage in warm weather and at times when fresh oranges are cheap. However, the season does not limit their value as a variety item. They are especially valuable to the restaurant and hotel baker. While the recipe for plain muffins is advisable for use, with the addition of orange juice and the outside rind of the orange for flavor, some bakers prepare the muffins from a wine cake or high-ratio cake mix. The best mix or recipe is the one which builds sales and a satisfied consumer. The following recipe is similar to plain muffin mix but makes the necessary revisions to allow for the incorporation of orange juice.

Orange Muffins   **Yield:** 6 doz.

Ingredients	Lb.	Oz.	Mixing procedure
Sugar	1	8	Cream all ingredients until soft and smooth
Salt	..	$^1/_2$	
Milk powder	..	3	
Shortening	1	..	
Glucose or corn syrup	..	2	
Eggs (part yolks)	..	12	Add the eggs in three stages and cream
Orange juice (reconstituted)	..	12	Blend the juice, water and rind and stir in gently
Fresh juice may be used			
Water	..	12	
Rind of two oranges			
Vanilla	..	$^1/_2$	
Cake flour	2	8	Sift, add, and mix lightly until smooth
Baking powder	..	2	

Procedures to Follow

1. Care should be taken when preparing the fresh rind. It is only the very outside of the orange that contains the flavor and the oil of orange. The white, inner pulp is bitter and should not be used. Cover the fresh rind to prevent oxidation and turning brown. If this happens the rind will appear as dark specks in the mix.
2. Concentrated orange juice (frozen) may be used. Half the amount of such juice should be used. Make up the difference in liquid by adding additional water. The orange juice provides acidity and taste. The flavor is provided by the rind. Of course, a good-quality orange flavor may be substituted for the orange rind. This is to be mixed in with the water.
3. Deposit the mix in clean, greased muffin tins. Fill the tins half full and bake at 385°F. Be sure to fill the tins evenly for uniformity of size.
4. The tops of these muffins may be garnished with a piece of dried orange rind, which may be purchased as dried fruit.

CINNAMON BISCUIT MUFFINS

Biscuit muffins are made from the basic biscuit dough listed at the beginning of the biscuit-muffin recipe section.

Procedures to Follow

1. Roll out the prepared biscuit dough (which has been shaped in a rectangle and allowed to relax) approximately 8 in. wide, $1/4$ in. thick, and as long as the size of the dough will permit. Check for sufficient dusting flour to prevent the dough from sticking.
2. Brush the top of the dough with melted fat, butter, or oil. Sprinkle the top with raisins, cinnamon sugar, and cake crumbs if desired. Roll the filling gently with the rolling pin to assure sticking the filling to the dough.
3. Roll up into a tight roll as for cinnamon buns. Seal the edge well to prevent opening.
4. Cut the roll into slices weighing approximately $1^1/_2$ to 2 oz. Smaller muffin tins will require smaller units to be cut. This also means that the roll of filled dough must be thinner. The average muffin tin will require that the rolled-up dough be about 2 in. in diameter.
5. Place the sliced units into greased muffin tins and flatten gently.
6. Wash the tops of the muffins with melted fat or butter. Egg-wash may be used. If egg-wash is used, dab the egg-wash on with a small brush to avoid getting egg-wash on the sides of the tin. This will cause the muffins to stick and cause breakage when removed.
7. Bake the biscuit muffins at 410°F. until light brown and the muffins spring back to the touch.
8. Remove the muffins from the tins while they are warm. The muffins may be brushed with melted butter again and dipped in cinnamon sugar. They may also be finished by striping the tops of the muffins with simple icing. Be sure the icing has been warmed before application.

SCONES

Scones are English in source and the original recipes provide for a stiffer biscuit dough to which raisins have been added. The shape of the scones will be explained in the makeup. One lb. of raisins should be incorporated into the dough just before you complete mixing. If a stiffer dough is desired add approximately 4 oz. of cake flour to the dough mix.

Procedures to Follow for Old-Fashioned Round Shape (Fig. 206)

1. Scale the dough into 8 oz. pieces and round up. Allow the units to relax about 10 min.
2. Flatten the units with the palms of the hands or roll out with a rolling pin to a thickness of $1/_2$ in. Be sure the dough is of even thickness.

3. Place the round units on a greased or paper-lined pan and wash with egg-wash. Allow the wash to dry for a few minutes.
4. With a sharp bread knife (the type used for slicing the tops of various breads before baking) cut across the top of the units about $1/2$ in. deep. This will make for a cross-effect or the division of the units into four parts.
5. Bake the units at 410°F. until golden brown. These units may be sold or served as they are or each of the four sections may be separated by cutting or breaking off. After baking, the cuts made with the knife will show a white contrast of the interior against the brown top caused by the egg-wash and the baking.

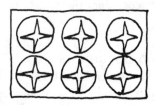

FIG. 206. OLD-FASH-
IONED, ROUND-SHAPED
SCONES

Makeup for Individual Quick Method (Fig. 207; see also Figs. 134–138)

1. Roll out the relaxed dough into a rectangular shape about $1/2$ in. thick.
2. With a pastry wheel cut strips 3 to 4 in. wide in a lengthwise manner. These strips are then cut into triangular shapes as you would for the shaping of butter horns or Danish horns.
3. Egg-wash the units after they have been cut and are still on the bench.
4. Place on a greased or paper-lined pan about 1 in. apart.
5. Bake at 410°F. until golden brown.

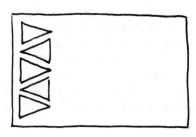

FIG. 207. TRIANGULAR
SCONES ON A PAN

CHAPTER 19

Factors Concerning Doughnuts and Crullers

In recent years there has been a sudden growth of doughnut shops that mass produce a variety of doughnuts and crullers. This business was formerly that of the retail or local baker. The bakeshop, with its great variety of bakery products, is still the best outlet for the sale of fried products. Still, these products are but a small part of the sales volume. The reasons for this are many. Principally, it is one of neglect, lack of understanding, and the "low" position of the doughnut in the daily production schedule. This chapter considers the causes of common defects in doughnuts.

YEAST-RAISED DOUGHNUTS

This type of doughnut is made from a special yeast dough. Many shapes and varieties can be made from this dough. The dough is made with the basic ingredients present in most sweet yeast doughs. The mixing method is the same as for bun dough. However, it is not advisable to use a sweet yeast dough commonly used for rich-type buns and other sweet yeast good varieties for the production of doughnuts. This is one of the basic faults and causes of poor doughnuts. A dough for this type of doughnut should be lean. Refer to the recipe for yeast-raised doughnuts (p. 213) and compare it with a sweet yeast dough for buns (p. 140). Note that there are lesser amounts of sugar, shortening, and eggs in the doughnut dough. The decrease in richness is necessary for a stronger structure to keep the shape of the doughnuts during and after frying. In addition, a lean dough can withstand a longer fermentation and greater proof.

The dough should be given a full rise and then taken to the bench. Fermentation continues during the makeup of the doughnuts. In a large batch of dough it may be that the last doughnuts made may become over-fermented or "old." These fry with the characteristics of an old dough; the units are pale, take longer to fry, and are greasy because of the lengthy frying. For larger production requirements, the scaled and rounded units may be placed in the retarder and made up directly from the retarder.

For jelly-filled or cream-filled doughnuts the pressed-out pieces may be left in the square or rectangular shape and proofed. This will speed up production. For improved appearance and consistency in size and shape the units of dough are rounded and then proofed. This practice takes longer but the results are well worth it.

Ring doughnuts are cut out of a rolled-out piece of dough. The doughnut dough must be rolled out to an even thickness and allowed to relax before the doughnuts are cut out. Cutting doughnuts from a dough that is not relaxed causes the ring doughnuts to shrink. This results in a smaller and thicker doughnut. If there is enough bench space two or three pieces may be rolled out and the first piece cut out after the third is rolled. This practice allows the baker to meet the production needs of ring doughnuts and allows him to round and scale the scrap dough into presses for others that may be made from the scaled and pressed out scrap dough, after ring doughnuts are made.

The proofing and frying of yeast-raised doughnuts depends upon the production requirements and the frying equipment in the bakeshop. With regard to equipment, most small shops have the usual one or two frying kettles (20 to 24 in. in diameter). The number of doughnuts that can be fried at one frying depends upon the size of the kettle and the desired weight of the doughnuts. It takes about $2^1/_2$ min. to fry a batch of doughnuts in the frying kettle.

The time per batch is important for the proofing and frying of large quantities of doughnuts. Since doughnuts should not be given more than three quarter proof, it is advisable to retard some of the doughnuts. This is especially important during the warm seasons. Lifting doughnuts which have more than the required proof and placing them on the frying screens will leave fingermarks and very often cause the doughnuts to collapse. This results in loss of volume, poor shape, and poor appearance. Retarding doughnuts also permits frying as needed.

CAKE-TYPE DOUGHNUTS AND CRULLERS

Cake-type doughnuts and crullers are usually made from prepared mixes. These mixes are soft and require automatic dropping machines. The machines vary from the large dropper of several dozen at once to the small, hand-cranked, single-doughnut dropper. The droppers are swung over the hot fat and the doughnuts are dropped directly into the fat. There are many compact frying units that are automated and it is suggested that the retail baker invest in an economical, yet efficient, frying unit.

The type of doughnut closest to the cake-type doughnut made by the retail baker without automatic equipment is that made from a hand-rolled dough. The doughnuts are cut, relaxed for a few minutes, and then fried. The cake-type doughnut is leavened by baking powder. In the whole-wheat types baking soda is added with the baking powder.

Very often the retail baker will add a small piece of fermented sweet yeast dough in the mixing of the dough. This dough is often called a Yankee cruller dough and has the advantage of being retarded and fried as needed. The doughnuts should be allowed to relax and return to room temperature before frying. This will allow maximum expansion during frying and makes it possible to shape other varieties from this dough.

A combination doughnut is one that is leavened by yeast and baking powder (see recipe for World's Fair doughnuts). This is an excellent dough for variety doughnuts. However, this dough is not used for the jelly-filled doughnuts. The structure is too close and delicate to fry completely and thoroughly and yet support the filling. The units made from this dough are given a short proofing period until about half proof and then fried. The baking powder will supply additional gassing power for complete leavening.

PREPARATION OF THE FRYING FAT

This is a very important factor and may be the cause of poor doughnut sales. To begin the frying fat should have the following characteristics: (1) it should be neutral in flavor (2) it should congeal after frying to avoid greasiness in the finished product, and (3) it should be stable for an extended period without breaking down or cracking. A hydrogenated shortening made from a vegetable oil is recommended. There are special frying fats or shortenings produced. These fats are pre-conditioned to avoid the dark, rapid crust color of the first doughnuts fried in regular shortening. This is known as a "pre-quality." These fats also have a higher smoke point and can withstand longer frying periods without breaking down or cracking.

The frying equipment must be clean. All sediment must be removed by straining the fat after cooking. Wait until the fat has cooled until it is only warm before straining. Don't strain hot fat. The sediment must also be removed from the bottom and sides of the frying kettle. Unclean fat and dirty frying equipment are the major causes of poor-tasting and spotty doughnuts. Fresh fat should be added to strained fat and the fat left ready for the next frying. This is a good production habit to be practiced for frying.

The amount of frying fat to place in the kettle is an important factor. Too little fat will make it difficult to turn the doughnuts as well as permit overheating the fat. Too much fat will take longer to heat and is also wasteful. The average depth of the fat should be 5 to 6 in. The fat is heated to about 380° to 385°F. for frying. A frying thermometer clipped to the side of the kettle will insure accuracy. Many bakers test the fat by dropping a few drops of water into the fat, noting the resulting crackling sound. If the crackling takes place immediately the fat is considered ready. A few doughnuts are fried to test fat readiness. This is better than waiting for the fat to smoke and then adding fresh fat to reduce the temperature. Automatic equipment may be used to control frying temperature of the fat and may also have a feed system to maintain the fat level.

If doughnuts are not automatically dropped into the hot fat they are lifted by hand, placed on a grate, and then lowered into the fat. The practice of dropping doughnuts directly into the fat two at a time should be avoided. Not only are accidents likely but it makes an uneven crust color. In the case of yeast-raised doughnuts, placing a smaller grate over the doughnuts after they have been fried on one side and turned, will make an even circular break in the crust color between the doughnut sides. It will also prevent the doughnuts from turning over during the frying process.

Doughnuts should be quickly and smoothly turned with a smooth, round stick which is slightly pointed at the end. To turn them gently, press the point of the stick against the side and the doughnut will turn. Blisters that may form in yeast-raised doughnuts should be punctured as soon as they form. If allowed to crust, these blisters will peel when the doughnuts cool. Doughnuts should be allowed to drain for a few seconds and then placed on brown paper to permit absorption of excess fat. Hot doughnuts should be handled gently and not stacked. They lose their shape if mishandled when hot.

FILLING AND FINISHING OF DOUGHNUTS

The finishing of doughnuts requires care and attention. The practice of dusting warm doughnuts with confectionery sugar, filling jelly doughnuts while hot, icing doughnuts with cool or thin icing, rolling doughnuts in confectionery sugar while warm, are all practices which must be avoided. Many poor doughnuts result from these practices.

Jelly doughnuts should be filled when cool. The jelly nozzle of the pump should be sharp and straight to avoid making large holes in doughnuts which permit part of the jelly to run out. An equal amount of jelly should be inserted into the center of the doughnut and not near the edge.

Doughnut glaze or icing should be warm for use. This will permit quick, even drying. A stabilizier may be used to maintain dryness. Avoid a hot icing dip. The doughnut will absorb some of the icing glaze and the icing will dry and peel when the doughnuts and icing cool. The confectionery sugar for rolling doughnuts for covering should contain as much as 15 to 20 per cent corn starch to prevent absorption of the sugar and pastiness. The coating should be even and dry.

Doughnuts that are to be iced with a simple icing or fondant should not be greasy. Greasiness causes the icing to peel off and makes icing difficult. When applying fudge icing the fudge should be medium soft and slightly warm. The doughnuts may be chilled slightly to make handling easier. When filling the doughnuts with custard or whipped cream the doughnuts should be chilled. This not only preserves the keeping quality of the filling but also makes handling easier. Doughnuts filled with cream or custard should be refrigerated immediately after they are filled and finished.

CHAPTER 20

Recipes for Doughnuts and Crullers

RING AND JELLY-FILLED DOUGHNUTS

Yeast-raised doughnuts are a very popular production item in most bakeshops. In fact, there are specially designed shops that produce this type of doughnut only. The knowledge and skill associated with their manufacture is of great importance to the baker, and very often they may determine his success. Since you are familiar with yeast-raised doughs (pan bread, bun dough, etc.), the preparation of the dough is simple. Note that the recipe that follows is not quite as rich as the dough used for buns. This is due to the fact that the doughnuts must be proofed, picked up, and placed on frying grates and finished while warm or cold. This means that the doughnuts must be able to withstand considerable handling without losing their shape.

Yeast-Raised Doughnuts (1 qt.) **Yield:** 8 doz. of $1^1/_2$ oz. each

Ingredients	Lb.	Oz.	Mixing procedure
Sugar	..	8	Blend ingredients together until smooth
Salt	..	1	
Milk powder	..	3	
Shortening	..	6	
Eggs	..	6	Add in two stages and blend well
Water	1	8	Add and stir in
Vanilla	..	1	
Mace	..	$^1/_4$	
Yeast (variable)	..	4	Dissolve and set aside
Water	..	8	
Bread flour	3	8	Sift, add, stir slightly, add the yeast solution and develop the dough

Procedures to Follow (Figs. 208 and 209)

1. Place the dough in a warm, humid place and allow to rise until ready to be punched.
2. Place the dough on the bench and scale into presses for the jelly-type, cruller-type doughnuts and round up as for rolls. For the ring doughnuts scale larger pieces of dough (up to 6 lb.) and form into rectangular shape. Allow the presses or larger units to relax for about 15 min.

Note: The reason for not punching the dough and allowing it to rise is to prevent the dough from getting old. Fermentation and conditioning of the dough takes place during the time spent to make up the doughnuts.

3. To make *jelly-filled doughnuts*, press out the large units and separate the pieces of dough as they are. The pieces may also be rounded up as for hamburger rolls. Allow the units to reach $3/4$ proof before placing on the frying screens to be put in the frying fat.

4. When making *ring doughnuts*, roll out the large pieces of dough evenly to about $3/8$ to $1/2$ in. thick. (Place the units jelly or ring doughnuts on flour-dusted pans or canvas cloths.) Cut out the doughnuts with a doughnut cutter. Cut as closely as possible to avoid excess scrap. The scrap is to be molded into a rectangular shape and allowed to relax before rolling again. It is wise when making both types of doughnuts to make the ring type first and then scaling the scrap dough with some of the fresh dough into presses. Ring doughnuts are also given $3/4$ proof before frying.

5. Most doughnuts are fried in clean fat or oil which has been heated to 380° to 385°F. Cleanliness of the frying fat is vital to the success of the finished product. The frying kettle should be clean and the fat must be strained if the fat has been used before. The temperature of the fat should be taken by means of a frying thermometer which is clamped to the inside of the frying kettle. Large plants have larger automatic equipment which controls the temperature. If a thermometer is not available drop a doughnut into the fat when you estimate it to be hot enough. If the doughnut turns a golden brown after about 1 min., then the fat is hot enough.

6. The units are then placed on the frying screen, about 24 units to a 20 in. diameter screen, and placed gently in the fat. The units will float because they are proofed and lightened by the carbon dioxide gas. Check to see if the doughnuts have browned (about 1 min.) and then turn carefully with a thin, round stick about 18 to 24 in. long. Allow the other side to fry and carefully lift the screen out of the fat. Pause for a few seconds to allow the excess fat to drip into the frying pot and then carefully dump the doughnuts on brown paper to absorb the excess fat.

7. *Jelly-filled doughnuts* should be allowed to cool before filling. The jelly should be worked smooth and softened with a little water or simple syrup if too stiff. Fill the jelly machine about half full and fill the doughnuts with an equal amount of jelly in each doughnut.

8. *Ring doughnuts* may be rolled in cinnamon sugar while they are warm. If the doughnuts are glazed dip them while warm into a thinned simple icing and place on an icing grate for the excess to run off. Be careful to avoid too much icing. The glaze should be thin.

Fig. 208.   Jelly Doughnut   Fig. 209.   Ring Doughnut

BOW-TIE, TWIST, AND CAKE-TYPE CRULLERS

Cruller-type doughnuts, and other shapes made from a cruller dough, provide a greater variety of fried products. Recently, many specialized doughnut shops have been established which employ bakers who make only fried doughnuts and crullers of various types. The average retail shop and large plant can and should produce doughnuts and crullers which can compete with the special shops and create customer demand for these products. The baker with diverse ability and knowledge profits.

While similarity exists in all doughnuts, since they are fried in deep fat, there is a distinct difference in the characteristics between the yeast-raised and cruller-type doughnut. The cruller is principally leavened chemically and requires no fermentation period or proofing. The following recipe provides the production of various crullers in the retail shop. Since the automatic equipment of the large shop is not available in the small shop the recipe is somewhat stiffer than that of the cake-type dough-nut mix which is dropped into the hot fat by machine. It is also stiffer than the prepared doughnut mixes used in larger plants.

Crullers   **Yield:** 9 doz. (3 press)

Ingredients	Lb.	Oz.	Mixing procedure
Sugar	..	14	Blend all ingredients together to a smooth
Salt	..	1	paste
Milk powder	..	4	
Shortening	..	7	
Vanilla	..	$1/_2$	
Lemon flavor	..	$1/_2$	
Mace	..	$1/_4$	
Fermented bun dough (op.)	..	8	
Eggs	..	8	Add the eggs and blend well
Water	2	..	Add the water and stir slightly
Cake flour	1	8	Sift, add, and mix to a smooth dough
Bread flour	2	8	
Baking powder	..	3	

Procedures to Follow:

1. Place the dough on a flour-dusted portion of the work bench. Fold the dough over to form a smooth surface.
2. Scale the dough into presses weighing approximately 3 lb. Round up the presses and allow them to relax for a few minutes. Roll out the press until it is the size of the pan for the press machine.
3. Press out the pieces. Use dusting flour or oil to prevent sticking. Separate the pieces and dust them with a little bread flour.
4. Fry the doughnuts at a temperature of 380° to 385°F. as you did for yeast-raised doughnuts. Be sure the frying fat is clean. Check the temperature of the frying fat as for the yeast-raised doughnuts.
5. The round doughnuts may be dipped in soft simple icing and placed on an icing grate to drain and dry; follow the same procedure as you did for the yeast-raised variety. Doughnuts may also be dipped in cinnamon sugar or the confectionery and starch preparation for further variety. The bow-tie and twist crullers may be left plain, dusted with confectionery sugar when cool, or rolled in cinnamon sugar (3 lb. of granulated sugar and $1^1/_2$ oz. of cinnamon which are blended well).
6. If a variety of crullers and doughnuts are made from one dough it is best to cut out the doughnuts from the first roll of the dough. This will then avoid toughness due to remixing of the scrap dough. The scrap dough can then be scaled and made up into presses for the bow-tie and twist crullers.

Makeup of Bow-tie Crullers (Fig. 210)

1. Pick up each piece and make a small hole in the exact center of the unit by pushing a finger through.
2. Take one end of the dough and push it through the hole and draw it back to its original position. This will cause a bow-tie effect. Do not stretch the units after the end has been pulled through. The unit should be about $1/2$ in. thick.

FIG. 210. BOW-TIE CRULLER

Makeup of Twist Crullers (Fig. 211)

1. Scale and round up the presses the same as for the bow-tie crullers.
2. Press out and separate the pieces by dusting lightly with bread flour.
3. Roll out each unit about 7 to 8 in. long. Be sure the strip is of even thickness throughout. Unevenness will make a poor shape.
4. Place the palm of each hand over each end and roll them gently in opposite directions. This will cause the dough to twist. Seal the ends of the strip without allowing it to unravel. Lift the sealed ends in the air and the strip will turn into a strip about 4 in. long with about four twisted folds. If there are not enough folds, twist the unit by hand.
5. Place the units on a lightly dusted pan (use bread flour for dusting) or on a flour-dusted canvas cloth. Allow the units to relax for about 20 min. before frying.

FIG. 211. TWIST CRUL-
LER

Makeup of Cake-type Crullers (Doughnut Shape) (Fig. 211A)

1. Place the mixed dough on a flour-dusted bench and fold over to form a rectangular shape with a smooth top. Let the dough relax 10 min.
2. Roll out the unit until it is about $3/8$ in. thick. Be sure the dough is of even thickness throughout. Be sure to roll up the dough on the rolling pin when it is partially rolled. This will enable you to check whether more dusting flour is needed to prevent the dough from sticking to the bench.

3. Using a doughnut cutter, cut out the doughnuts and place them on a flour-dusted pan or canvas cloth. When cutting, cut the doughnuts as close to each other as is possible to avoid too much scrap dough.
4. Gather the scrap dough together and scrape into a smooth rectangle. Allow the dough to relax and roll out again. Cut out the doughnuts. Gather the scrap again and repeat the performance. This time roll the dough about $1/2$ in. thick and cut out. It should be thicker because the scrap dough is now slightly tougher.
5. Place the doughnuts on floured pans or canvas cloths and allow to relax for about 20 min. before frying.

Fig. 211A.   Ring
Doughnut

CAKE-TYPE DOUGHNUTS

The majority of cake doughnuts are produced from prepared mixes and with the use of automatic frying equipment. The batters are soft in consistency and are dropped directly in the heated frying fat. The smaller shops (retail), generally do not have much equipment and the cake-type doughnuts must be made from doughs which can be rolled on the bench, cut out with a doughnut cutter, and then deposited by hand into the frying fat. This means that the doughs are stiffer than the batters for automatic frying.

Cake-type doughnuts are chemically leavened and are made up as soon as the dough has relaxed.

Plain Cake Doughnuts   **Yield:**   8 doz. of $1^1/_2$ oz. units

Ingredients	Lb.	Oz.	Mixing procedure
Sugar	1	..	Blend well until smooth and soft
Salt	..	$1/_2$	
Milk powder	..	4	
Shortening	..	8	
Nutmeg	..	$1/_4$	
Eggs	..	10	Add in two stages and blend well
Water	2	..	Add and stir in
Vanilla	..	1	
Cake flour	2	4	Sift, add, and mix to a smooth dough
Bread flour	2	..	
Baking powder	..	3	

Chocolate Cake Doughnuts

Yield: 8 doz. of $1^{1}/_{2}$ oz. units

Ingredients	Lb.	Oz.	Mixing procedure
Sugar	1	2	Blend well until smooth and soft
Salt	..	$^{1}/_{2}$	
Milk powder	..	4	
Shortening	..	8	
Vanilla	..	1	
Chocolate flavor	..	$^{1}/_{4}$	
Eggs	..	10	Add in two stages and blend well
Water	2	..	Add and stir in
Baking soda	..	$^{1}/_{2}$	
Cake flour	2	..	Sift, add, and mix to a smooth dough
Bread flour	1	14	
Cocoa	..	5	
Baking powder	..	2	

Procedures to Follow for Both Plain Cake and Chocolate Cake Doughnuts

1. Place the dough on a flour bench and form into an oblong. Rest 15 min.
2. Roll out the dough about $^{3}/_{8}$ in. thick. Be sure of even thickness.
3. Cut out the doughnuts with the cutter. Cut as close as possible to avoid excess scrap dough. Scrap dough becomes tougher each time it is rolled. Allow the worked scrap dough to relax before rolling and cutting again.
4. Place the doughnuts on a floured (lightly dusted) pan and allow to relax 15 min. before frying.
5. Fry in heated frying fat at 380° to 385°F. Test the fat before frying. These doughnuts require about 1 min. frying time on each side. The doughnuts dropped in first should be the first ones to be turned in order to maintain an even color.
6. Allow the doughnuts to drain before placing on a pan for finishing. They may be dumped gently on brown paper to absorb excess fat.
7. To finish doughnuts, those that are to be rolled in cinnamon sugar or glazed may be rolled in the sugar or dipped in the glaze while still warm. Those that are to be rolled in confectionery sugar and starch (80 per cent confectionery sugar and 20 per cent corn starch) or iced fudge-type icings are to be cool before finishing.

Note: Special care should be taken when frying the chocolate doughnuts. Color cannot be distinguished and they may not be fried enough or may be fried too much.

WORLD'S FAIR (COMBINATION) DOUGHNUTS

These doughnuts are leavened by a dual leavening process. Both baking powder and yeast are used. While this is not a new method the combination leavening does provide a doughnut that is light and quite easy to handle in the makeup, frying, and finishing. The dual leavening method has been used for years in the making of crullers. You will find that many of these older recipes call for the use of 1 lb. of fermented bun or sweet roll dough as a base. The fermented dough allowed for greater elasticity because of its conditioned gluten. It also provides the leavening from the active yeast in the dough.

World's Fair Doughnuts　　　　　　　　　　　　　　**Yield:** 9 doz. (3 press)

Ingredients	Lb.	Oz.	Mixing procedure
Sugar	..	4	Blend all ingredients to a smooth paste
Salt	..	1	
Milk powder	..	4	
Shortening	..	12	
Vanilla	..	1	
Eggs	..	8	Add the eggs and blend well
Water	1	8	Add the water and stir in
Yeast	..	2–4	Dissolve the yeast and set aside
Water (warm)	..	8	
Cake flour	1	8	Sift, add, stir slightly. Add the yeast solu-
Bread flour	2	8	tion, and mix to a smooth dough. The
Baking powder	..	1	dough should be developed

Procedures to Follow

1. Place the dough on a floured bench, cover, and allow to relax and partially ferment for about 30 min.
2. Roll out the dough evenly about $1/4$ in. thick, removing large gas pockets.
3. Cut the doughnuts and place on a flour-dusted cloth or pan.
4. Allow the doughnuts to rise approximately half proof before frying.
5. It is best to use the scrap dough after the doughnuts have been cut out for presses of dough for other types of doughnuts. For example, the scrap may be rounded into presses weighing 2 lb. 12 oz. and used for making twisted and other types of doughnuts. These are also given half proof before frying.

6. Fry the doughnuts at a temperature of 380° to 385°F. Do not over-load the frying screen for these doughnuts rise and spread con-siderably. Overloading will cause difficulty in turning the dough-nuts and make for uneven color.
7. Remove the doughnuts when fried properly and drain on brown paper or allow to drip drain on a drain pan.
8. The doughnuts may be finished by rolling in cinnamon sugar when cool. They may be dipped in warm fondant icing while warm and allowed to drain. This will make an icing-type glaze. They may also be dusted with confectionery sugar when cool. While jelly-filled doughnuts may be made from this dough it is best to use regular dough for jelly doughnuts. This doughnut is too tender and may not hold its shape for the jelly variety.

WHOLE-WHEAT DOUGHNUTS

The variety of doughnuts is enhanced by a well-made whole-wheat doughnut. Variations in both the recipe and the manner in which the doughnuts are made are quite common. The nut-like taste and dark color of whole wheat are the important consumer factors to be considered. The nut-like taste is based upon the percentage of whole-wheat flour used and the fine bran particles in the flour itself.

Whole-Wheat Doughnuts Yield: 7 doz. of $1^1/_4$ oz. units

Ingredients	Lb.	Oz.	Mixing procedure
Sugar	..	10	Mix all ingredients together to a smooth
Salt	..	$1/_2$	paste
Milk powder	..	4	
Shortening	..	5	
Cinnamon	..	$1/_8$	
Mace	..	$1/_8$	
Molasses	..	4	
Baking soda	..	$1/_4$	
Eggs	..	8	Add eggs in two stages and blend in well
Water (cool)	2	..	Add the water and stir in
Whole-wheat flour	1	6	Sift and add. Be sure to include the bran
Cake flour	..	12	particles. Mix to a smooth dough
Bread flour	..	12	
Baking powder	..	$2^1/_2$	

Procedures to Follow

1. Place the dough on a floured bench and form into a rectangle.

2. Allow the dough to relax for 10 min. and roll out gently about $^3/_8$ in. thick. Be sure the dough is of even thickness.
3. Cut out doughnuts with a cutter and place on a floured cloth or pan. Allow the doughnuts to relax for 10 min. before frying.
4. Cut the doughnuts as close together as possible to eliminate excessive scrap dough. Form the scrap into a square with as little kneading as possible. Allow the dough to relax and roll out again. This may be continued until all the scrap is used up. It must be remembered that the more the dough is kneaded and rolled, the tougher it becomes. It is best to let the small amount of scrap dough leftover be mixed into another batch.
5. Fry the doughnuts at 380°F. Be careful of excessive temperature for this will cause the doughnuts to color too rapidly. Turn the doughnuts when they have a nut-brown color and fry on the other side.
6. Remove and dump the doughnuts from the frying grate carefully. These doughnuts are more delicate than the usual doughnut made from yeast-raised dough. Allow the doughnuts to drain before finishing.
7. The most popular method of finishing these doughnuts is to allow them to cool until slightly warm. They are then rolled in a confectionery sugar and corn starch mixture (75 per cent sugar and 25 per cent corn starch).
8. The doughnuts may also be rolled in cinnamon sugar while warm.

FRENCH CRULLERS

French crullers are made from an eclair or cream puff mix (p. 284). The important factors are the thickness of the mix, preparation of the frying papers, and frying procedure.

Procedures to Follow (Figs. 212–215)

1. The mix is slightly stiffer than that used for cream puff shells.
2. It is better to use baking powder as the leavening agent than ammonium carbonate. In this case, $^1/_2$ oz. of baking powder will replace $^1/_4$ oz. of ammonium carbonate.
3. Grease heavy brown paper or flexible cardboards with plastic shortening (shortening that has been softened slightly by warming). Be sure the paper is well greased all over, otherwise the crullers will not come off when the paper is placed in the hot fat.
4. Bag out the French crullers in even-sized circles with a star or French tube. Do not allow the circles to touch each other when bagging out.

5. Be sure one corner of the paper has a free edge about 2 in. square.
6. Grasp the paper by the free edge and place the paper gently into the hot fat (375°F.) holding the corner up. Be careful of your fingers and hand. Avoid splashing. When all the crullers are released, remove the paper and allow the excess fat to run off into the kettle.

Fig. 212.   Filling the Pastry Bag

Fig. 213.   Divide the Pastry Bag in Half

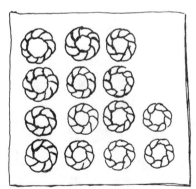

Fig. 214.   Spacing French Crullers Evenly on Greased, Heavy Paper

Fig. 215.   Dipping into the Hot Fat

7. You will note that the fat is slightly cooler (375°F.) than for dough-nuts: This is to allow the French cruller to color slowly. When the crust is golden brown, turn the crullers and fry the other side. It is advisable to fry the original side (with the creases of the tube) a second time for about 1 min. This will insure proper frying and prevent the crullers from shrinking or collapsing after they are re-moved from the fat.

8. The doughnuts are usually dipped in warm fondant icing after they have cooled. Place the iced doughnuts on a grate so that the excess icing may run off and be used again.

CHAPTER 21

Pie Crusts and Short Doughs

Pies, tarts, fruit cakes, and similar products are among the most popular desserts, but they are not selling well in many retail shops. This may be due to competition from the larger producer. However, greater care, attention, and understanding of the techniques of pie making should result in better pies with increased sales. This introductory chapter to the entire area of pies and fruit cake variety will consider the factors involved in the preparation of pie doughs and short doughs, and variations in their composition and use. The common problems related to these doughs will also be discussed.

PIE CRUSTS

Pie crusts are classified into three major types: (1) the mealy; (2) the medium flaky, which is the most common; and (3) the long-flake variety. They are basically alike in terms of the ingredients used. However, they vary in the method and degree of mixing the flour and shortening and in the amount of water or other liquids added to the dough. The mealy will absorb less water than either of the flaky varieties. This is due to the fact that the flour and shortening are blended to a degree where the flour is almost completely enveloped with shortening and there is less exposed flour to absorb the water.

Basic Ingredients Used in Pie Crust

Flour for pie crust should not be high nor very low in gluten as are most cake flours. The high-gluten flours tend to absorb water quickly and gluten develops rapidly causing toughness. Cake flours do not absorb and retain water as quickly and often result in pasty, sticky doughs. A pastry flour, usually milled from a soft winter wheat, is best suited for pie crust. In many retail shops a blend of flours is made to meet the requirements of pastry flour. In this case, a high-gluten flour may be used when blended with not more than 20 per cent corn starch or rice flour to produce the desired characteristics. A blend of 60 per cent cake flour and 40 per cent bread flour will also result in good flour for pie crust doughs. The necessity of sifting flours before use in the doughs should be noted again. The soft pastry flour or cake flour blend is lumpy. These lumps may not absorb the water readily and this may lead to overmixing in the attempt to get rid of the lumps. The result is a tough dough because of gluten development.

Shortening or fat used for pie crust should be plastic and have a good range in melting point. While lard is an excellent fat meeting these requirements, it imparts a flavor that may not be acceptable. Further, lard is variable in quality and characteristics. Vegetable shortening (hydrogenated) is the most common fat used. At normal shop temperature it mixes well to make excellent pie crust. It is plastic, has good temperature range without softening too quickly, and has no flavor. If butter is used to improve taste and flavor, it is suggested that about 30 to 40 per cent butter be blended with shortening and chilled before use in making the dough. Of course, the cost is higher and the flavor of the butter may be lost or overshadowed by the fruit fillings and spices.

Cold water should be used for pie crust. In warm weather, ice water is recommended. This keeps the fat particles or lumps in firm or hardened state and prevents dispersion or blending to a pasty, soft dough. As previously mentioned, the amount of water used (about 25 to 30 per cent based on the weight of the flour) varies with the type of dough and the method of mixing. Mealy doughs require less than the flaky variety. This is because more flour is exposed and not covered with fat in the flaky dough.

Salt is used to accentuate the flavor of the crust. It also emphasizes the flavor of other ingredients used. It serves as contrast in emphasizing the sweetness, taste, and flavor of the various fillings used for pies. From $1/4$ to $1/2$ oz. of salt should be used for each pound of flour in the dough. The salt should be dissolved in the water to insure complete distribution. If it is blended with flour, it may not be thoroughly distributed throughout the dough.

Milk in powder form should be dissolved in the water. When added with the flour, it may cause the dough to stiffen up after mixing due to the fact that absorption takes place after mixing. Milk adds richness and gives a better color to the crust. Up to 2 to 3 per cent of dry milk may be used. If pies are to be stored for some time a minimum of milk should be used, otherwise soggy bottoms may result if the weather is warm.

Sugar, dextrose, and corn syrup add color and sweetness to the crust. However, they tend to absorb moisture and cause sogginess in the crust if the pies are stored. Where pie turnover is good and production is controlled, 2 per cent or slightly more is recommended for pie crusts.

MIXING OF THE PIE CRUST DOUGH

This is a two-step procedure. The sifted flour and fat are mixed together. If the fat particles are in small lump form the popular medium-flake dough is formed. Flour and shortening are blended to a paste to obtain mealy crust. A cold solution of salt, milk powder, and sugar are added. This is the most important part of dough preparation. The dough is mixed lightly until the liquid is absorbed by the flour. At this point most pie crusts are lumpy and somewhat sticky. The water should be measured carefully and in accordance with the type of flour used. Very often, extra water is added to the dough that appears stiff or shows signs of dry flour. At times, extra flour is added to doughs that appear sticky and soft. This is dangerous in that it often leads to overmixing the dough with gluten development and toughness as the result. Careful scaling and measuring are necessary. Actually, the amount of water or liquid used is the most important factor in the mixing of pie crusts.

In the mixing of long-flake pie crust, the fat particles are left in large lumps when rubbed with the flour. After the water has been added, this lumpy, sticky dough is placed on the bench in about 10 to 15 lb. pieces and given three rolls of three turns each. The rolling results in thin flakiness of the fat and the resulting flakiness of the crust. This dough is quite tender and is best used for smaller pies and turnovers.

Freshly mixed pie crust doughs should be placed in a cool place of 60°F. or less to rest for a period of 4 to 24 hr. The dough is usually stored in the refrigerator in smaller shops. This is important for the conditioning of the dough. The gluten of the dough is mellowed by the action of the enzymes present in the flour and permits full absorption of moisture by the flour. This resting or conditioning period helps to eliminate toughness, shrinkage, and later soaking of the crust by the filling.

As mentioned above, the most common fault in the making of pie crust is overmixing. This will be indicated in a consideration of some of the common faults. It is also advisable to sift pastry flour and use it for dusting. A floured cloth will make rolling easier with this flour and helps to eliminate the toughness of scrap dough that results from the use of strong patent flour for rolling.

Crust for Soft-Filled Pies

This dough is made quite differently from fruit pie crusts. In this instance, a soft custard-like filling is placed on a raw piece of dough and the usual problem of rawness and sogginess exists. The dough should not be rich in fat content and must be mixed and handled differently. The method employed is one of blending the flour, shortening, salt, and sugar, if used, to a smooth paste. Warm water is then added and the dough is well mixed. The leanness of the dough and the warm water make rapid drying or crust formation on the pie bottom after the dough is rolled and placed in pie pans.

The Use of Scrap Pie Crust Dough

Since scrap pie crust has been worked or rolled at least once, it has absorbed additional flour and the gluten in the dough has become toughened. The scraps should be accumulated and pressed together gently rather than rounded, and used again for the bottoms of pies. Scrap dough that has been used more than twice should be re-worked into doughs after additional sugar, shortening, and baking powder have been added. The sugar, increased shortening, and baking powder make a different type of dough that has shortness rather than flakiness.

SHORT DOUGH

Short Doughs for Fruit Cakes, Tarts, Cake Bottoms, Etc.

A short dough is a form of cookie dough used for many purposes in the retail shops. In the making of this dough the procedure varies from that used in making pie crust in that large percentages of sugar and eggs are added with a variation in the method of mixing. The sugar, salt, shortening, corn syrup or glucose, and milk powder are blended well.

The eggs are blended in carefully to avoid curdling, the water slowly stirred in, and the flour and baking powder lightly folded in. The dough is rough and sticky but this is eliminated in the working of the dough on the floured cloth before rolling. This is a stock dough which may be kept for a long time under refrigeration. When used for large fruit cake bottoms, the cake bottoms are pre-baked before the filling is added. For smaller, 6 to 8 in. layers or tarts, the dough is placed into pans and the filling put in without baking.

The most important factor in the making and handling of this dough is the careful addition of the flour. The flour used for this dough should be a blend of a high-gluten or short-patent flour with cake flour. A soft pastry flour will tend to make the dough too short for ease in handling since this dough has to be rolled up on the rolling pin and then placed in the pans. Overmixing or the use of a straight high-gluten flour will make the dough tough.

Pie Crust and Short Dough Blends

It is not uncommon to find bakers using a blend of pie crust and short dough for special pie shells and cream rolls. The blend is usually that of 50 per cent short dough and 50 per cent pie crust dough. These doughs are blended together until smooth, chocolate or cocoa may be added for variety and used for the making of special crusts and chocolate cream rolls. The scrap from this dough becomes tough after considerable use and care should be taken in the rolling of the dough to avoid excess scrap.

PIE CRUST FAULTS AND THEIR COMMON CAUSES

Toughness: Too strong a flour used; overmixing; too much rolling; use of excess scrap dough; dough too stiff

Shrinkage: Use of scrap; dough tough or overmixed; dough not relaxed

Lack of flakiness: Fat blended too much with flour; overmixed dough; use of scrap

Dough falls apart when handled: Dough too rich in fat; flour too weak; fat in too large lumps; improper handling

CHAPTER 22

Fruit Pies and Pie Baking

The best of pie crusts cannot cover up for a poor pie filling. The finest quality fruits, in whatever form or manner they may be packed, must be properly handled and prepared to result in a fine quality filling that will make repeated sales. The appearance, taste, and "flow" of the filling are the result of the method of preparation and understanding of the factors involved in the handling of various fruits for fillings. This chapter treats the preparation of fruit fillings, pie makeup, pie making, and some of the common pie faults and possible causes.

TYPES OF FRUIT AND THEIR PREPARATION FOR FILLINGS

Canned Fruits

Canned fruits come in various types of pack. The solid pack contains little or no water other than the natural moisture of the drained fruit. The water pack contains added water or juice of the fruit which has been given a quick boil and packed in the water in which it was boiled. These types are common in sour-pitted cherries, blueberries, huckleberries, etc. The cost of the weight of the added water must be considered when determining fruit costs.

There are variations in syrup-packed fruits and these must be given consideration. Fruits may be packed in light, medium, or heavy syrup. The consistency of the syrup generally indicates the degree of sweetening. The added sweetening must be taken into consideration if this type of pack is to be used for pie filling. In most cases, the syrup-packed fruits are of better quality and are mostly used for finishing the tops of open fruit pies or cakes rather than for pie filling because of their high cost.

In the preparation of canned fruits for pie fillings the fruit is drained or separated from the water or juice. The fruit should not be cooked because fruit falls apart and loses its appearance when cooked. Part, or all, of the sugar is boiled with the water or juice. The starch or other thickener in solution is added and the filling heated until it gels and is clear. The remaining sugar is then added and heated until dissolved. Fruit, color, and flavor are then stirred into the gel.

Frozen Fruits

These fruits are generally prepared from fresh fruit which may be packed as picked, or panboiled and packed in the cans with a small amount of the liquid added with sugar. They are usually packed in 30-lb. cans and may contain color and flavor in addition to the sugar added. Frozen fruits should be defrosted very much the same as frozen eggs are defrosted. For quick defrosting, the fruit may be heated to 180°F. with a little water to defrost. This method requires constant stirring to prevent scorching and complete defrosting. The frozen fruit is drained from the juice or water and the same procedure is followed in cooking as for canned fruits. Special attention must be given to the contents of the can to allow for the added sugar, color, and flavor. The fruit should be completely defrosted before it is added to the cooked gel. If the fruit has not been completely thawed it will bleed and cause a separation of the filling when cooled.

Fresh Fruits

While these fruits are generally used for the finishing of the pies or cakes they may be a good buy in season for fillings. The fruit should be firm and ripe. When fruits are bruised and beginning to turn they should be prepared for fillings immediately to prevent complete spoilage. In preparing the filling, part of the fruit, usually one-third, is cooked with the water and sugar to provide for color, taste, and flavor in the prepared gel. The remainder of the fresh fruit is gently stirred into the cooked gel to prevent the fruit from mashing and losing its appearance.

The matter of how much water and sugar to use in preparing the cooked gel is important. It is advisable to use 65 to 70% water based upon the weight of the fresh fruit. In other words for every 3 lb. of berries approximately 2 lb. of water should be used. A larger percentage of water will make the filling cheaper and will not have the quality it should. Very often, fresh fruits are blended into fillings made with canned fruits to improve the appearance, taste, and quality of the filling. The amount of sugar to use in the gel depends upon the type and natural sweetness of the fruit. Judgment and taste should be used.

Dried Fruits

Dehydrated apples, prunes, apricots, etc., are often used in the preparation of fruit fillings. Since these fruits have had almost all the natural moisture removed they should be soaked in water to restore the water or moisture. It is often advisable to give the dried fruit a quick boil and allow the fruit to remain in the boiled water. The fruit is then drained and the water in which the fruit was soaked or boiled used for the water for the cooked gel. In the case of dried apples they should be soaked for several hours and then slowly boiled until most of the water has been evaporated or absorbed by the fruit. Boiling and soaking allows replacement of moisture as well as plumping and softening the fruit. Dried fruits are mixed with fresh or canned fruits for the final filling. They are also used in combination with other fruits such as apricot-prune, peach-apricot, etc.

THICKENERS FOR PIE FILLINGS

Specially processed corn starch is the most common fruit filling thickener that is used. Other types are tapioca, potato starch, rice starch, the various vegetable gums such as agar-agar, alginate, tragacanth, and gum arabic. The gums are expensive and are often used in conjunction with the starches. The purpose of the thickeners are: (1) to gelatinize quickly in cooking and thicken the filling, (2) to produce a good gloss or sheen in the filling, (3) to offset the action of fruit acids, (4) to maintain fruit color and flavor, and (5) to maintain the consistency of the cooked gel when cool.

Starch gelatinizes at 155° to 170°F. The starch particles absorb moisture and swell, thereby gelling. Addition of sugar to the water or juice before the starch solution is added often results in a filling of thin consistency, dull color, and a cereal taste. This is especially so when the starch is increased. If the water or juice is gelled without sugar it forms a very thick or firm gel and it becomes difficult to add the sugar and fruit.

In the cooking of fillings approximately $3^1/_2$ lb. of sugar should be cooked with the water and juice for 1 lb. of starch used to thicken the gel. The rest of the sugar is added and heated after the gel has been formed. This will help to avoid thin consistencies because the starch has been able to absorb and retain to its maximum the milder syrup solution. Make allowances for the sugar which may have been added to fresh-frozen and canned fruits packed in syrup.

Approximately 3 to 4 oz. of starch are used to gel 1 qt. of water or juice. The higher the acidity of the fruit and juice, the more thickener is generally required to thicken and hold the gel. In the case of fruits such as sour cherries, pineapples, and some varieties of berries, which are high in natural acidity, care should be employed in the amount of starch used. Very often a thick, gummy filling results. Fruit acids and sugar tend to tenderize the gel and should not be overly thickened. The use of tapioca flour with the corn starch (3 oz. starch and 1 oz. tapioca flour) leads to a satisfactory gel without the use of excessive starch.

The higher the fruit content the less starch is required. This means that less water or juice is being used and a lesser amount of gel is necessary. After the filling is cooked, it should be allowed to cool in a cool place and sheltered from dust. Immediate refrigeration is not recommended in that cooling does not take place at an even rate. Quick chilling of hot fruit fillings often leads to shrinkage and cracking of the filling. Fillings stored at refrigerator temperatures for a long period (3 or 4 days) tend to lose their clarity and separate. The starch tends to return to its former state, and color and moisture retention is decreased. As mentioned previously, the use of tapioca flour with the starch is recommended.

If potato starch is used greater quantities are required because its gelling properties are not as great as those of corn starch. Potato starch is used in conjunction with other starches for the formation of a tender gel. Rice starch is very sensitive to direct heat and is not generally used in the preparation of fruit fillings. It is used to better effect in the preparation of soft-filled pies. This will be discussed further in the preparation of these pies.

Vegetable gums are usually used with corn starch and other starches. When used alone, they tend to create a thick, gummy, dull finish in the filling. They provide a fibrous elasticity (gluten-like) when used with starches and help to prevent cracking or bleeding. The gums are blended with the sugar and then dissolved in the water or juice.

The newly developed, pre-gelatinized starches are added with the sugar to the water and juice. They thicken the filling in the presence of sugar and water without heating. This is due to the fact that the starch has been pre-cooked and does not require heat to enable it to absorb water and gelatinize. There are several kinds of this starch and they vary in absorption properties. For best results in their use, follow the instructions of the manufacturer.

PIE PRODUCTION

Practices and Procedures

1. The crust for the pies should be chilled for easier handling and to avoid stickiness and flaking out of the soft fat.
2. A flour-dusted cloth (canvas) will make rolling the dough easier and avoid the use of excessive flour. Excess dusting flour tends to toughen the scrap dough that is trimmed off the sides of the pie.
3. It is advisable to scale the pieces of dough for the bottoms and tops of the pies. This will avoid using excess dough, with resulting extra scrap dough, or thin bottoms which have to be stretched to

cover the pie tin. Shrinkage of the crust is avoided by placing it into the tin without stretching or tearing the crust.

4. The rolled pie crust should be of even thickness.
5. The rim of the pie bottom should be washed with water before filling.
6. Care is necessary in filling the pies. Equal weight of the pies and allowance for fruit expansion during baking must be kept in mind.
7. Pie fillings of berry and high-acid fruits should not fill the pie to the brim. This leads to leakage of the filling during baking because of expansion of the filling. Filling that is smeared on the rim of the bottom crust prevents proper sealing of the top crust to the bottom. This is often the cause of filling running out in baking.
8. The top crust should be thinner than the bottom.
9. The top crust should be stippled or holes made to allow the steam from the heated fruit to escape during baking. Restrained steam will cause the top of the pie to crack or cause the fruit to run out of the sides.
10. The edges of the pie must be properly sealed and the excess dough removed.

Finishing.—The tops of the pies may be finished in any desired fashion. The most common is the egg-washed pie top. This should be applied evenly before the pie is baked. It is advisable to dilute the eggs to avoid a very dark crust color. Lattice-type pies should have the strips washed on the bench before placing on the pie. This will avoid washing and smearing the filling in the pie with the wash brush. Pies are very often washed with milk or melted fat for a home-made effect. Melted butter will increase the expense but will improve the taste. Struessel topping should be mealy and cool when placed on the pie. Struessel placed on warm filling will become pasty. Warm or hot fruit should not be used to make pies. They will soften the crust and cause the filling to seep through even before the pie is baked.

Baking Pies

Pies should be baked at a temperature of 450°F. (hot oven). A hot oven is necessary to bake and color the crust of the pie and to avoid boiling of the fruit filling. A lower temperature will delay crust color formation and the fruit will reach boiling or bubbling temperature. This is the major cause of fruit filling that runs out of the pies. An even, strong bottom heat is important. This will cause an even bake of the bottom crust in conjunction with the baking of the top crust. It must be remembered that the moisture in the filling makes it difficult to bake the bottom crust thoroughly. An improper or weak bottom heat will cause the pie bottom to be raw or soggy. It is advisable to shift the pies in the oven when they are half-baked to allow the bottoms to come in contact with fresh heat. This insures a proper bake.

The color of the top crust, while important to eye appeal, is not the only determining factor of pie doneness. A sure indicator that the bottom crust is baked is that the pie will move when the tin is gently shaken. Many bakers line the bottom crust with cake crumbs before putting the filling into the pie. This allows absorption of moisture in the filling and allows for a more thorough bake of the pie bottoms.

Freezing of Pies

Pies are best frozen in an unbaked state. They should be covered or wrapped with polyethylene before placing in the freezer at $-10°$ to $-20°$F. Quick-freezing will permit the pies to remain in a frozen state for several months without loss of quality. Frozen pies should have frost or crystallization removed before baking and should be placed in the oven while still frozen. It must be remembered that the heat of the oven will thaw the filling which has already been cooked. The crust, being comparatively thin, will defrost quickly in the oven and bake properly without resulting gumminess and sogginess. Frozen pies should be shifted in the oven to insure thorough baking of the bottom.

Pies that are baked and then frozen tend to have crust shrinkage if not wrapped properly. In many cases, crystallization of the filling may cause running when the pie is defrosted. In most cases, pies that are to be frozen should have the fillings thickened with the use of a blend of tapioca flour and starches previously mentioned. The tapioca flour will help to prevent weeping or separation of the filling.

COMMON PIE FAULTS AND POSSIBLE CAUSES

Raw or soggy bottoms: Oven too cool, insufficient bottom heat, pie bottom dough too rich, bottom rolled too thin, filling too thin and filling used while warm or hot.

Blisters on the pie crust: Crust not stippled or docked and too much egg-wash.

Filling runs out during baking: Pies filled too much, pies not sealed properly, oven too cool, pies not docked, too much sugar in the filling, and filling too thin.

Shrinkage of the crust: Oven too cool, crust was tough before makeup of the pies, use of scrap dough for the top of the pie, and too much rolling or handling of the dough.

CHAPTER 23

Soft-Filled Pies

It appears that soft-filled pies, particularly the baked, custard variety, are not quite as popular as they should be. This is probably due to inconsistency of production. The most. common fault is the pasty, raw bottom crust of the pie. A second is the curdling or separation of the pie filling which causes "weeping." The principal cause of the faults is the thickener used.

Corn starch, the most common thickener used, tends to settle to the bottom of the pie and creates the thick paste or sediment at the bottom; as a result the filling is not properly gelled. There are several substitutes for corn starch. As mentioned previously in Chapter 22, Fruit Pies and Pie Baking, the use of precooked or pregelatinized starch will help to overcome this condition. This starch binds the water or milk and sugar. The filling will have more body when the pies are filled and separation will be avoided. Other substitutes are egg-white stabilizer ($1/4$ oz. per quart of filling) or tapioca flour ($3/4$–1 oz. per quart of milk). These should be blended with the sugar and then dissolved in the milk.

Another factor which troubles many bakers is the unevenness or blistering of the crust of the pie. The crust refers to the top surface of the baked filling. This is generally caused by too much whipping of the eggs and sugar which causes a foam or froth to form. The foam rises to the surface and, since it contains sugar and air cells, blisters are formed by the trapped air cells and the crust darkens quickly in spots caused by the exposed sugar.

Overbaking the pie is another cause of a watery condition in the pie. The pie should be baked at 410° to 425°F. and should be removed before blisters start to appear on the surface. As soon as the filling feels gelled (touch it with your finger) the pies should be removed from the oven.

The pie shells should be filled as soon as they are placed in the oven. They are filled half full for the first few minutes of baking and then are completely filled. Care should be taken to avoid crust formation that is thick or heavy after the pie has been filled half way. The nutmeg on custard pies should be sprinkled lightly over the top of the filling after the pie has been filled to the top. This will avoid the settling of the nutmeg to the bottom and causing a mottled appearance.

236

When making cocoanut custard pies, long- or medium-shred, unsweetened cocoanut should be used. Fine-shred or macaroon cocoanut tends to float to the surface and the cocoanut is not distributed evenly throughout the pie.

Cheese pies are very popular and can be made in a number of ways for greater variety. Cheese pie is actually a cheese-type custard filling baked in a pie shell. The filling should be smooth, close-grained and should not have the porous structure of a light cheese cake made with a large percentage of whipped egg whites. Pies made with excessive whipped egg whites folded into the cheese mix tend to settle after baking and the top crust of the pie is generally split and has a shrunken appearance.

Since baker's cheese will vary in consistency and its ability to absorb and hold milk, judgment should be employed in determining the amount of milk the cheese can absorb and hold without curdling. The final cheese filling should have a soft consistency and pour like a thick gravy. The pies should be baked in a hot oven (425°F.) and should be removed as soon as the center of the pie has gelled. The baked pie firms while it is cooling. You will note that the pie rises in a solid-top form without cracking or very little cracking. The top will settle smoothly after baking to its original position. These pies are often glazed or finished with a fruit filling on top. The pie shell may also be filled with fruit filling at the bottom of the center of the pie before the filling is added.

Pumpkin pie has large sales appeal, especially during the holiday season. The common problems of pumpkin pie are similar to those of custard pie. There is also the added problem of syrup formation on the top of the pie after baking. Basically, it must be remembered that pumpkin requires time to absorb liquid. The mixing of all the ingredients at once and the immediate filling and baking of the pie does not provide time for the pumpkin to absorb liquid and starch or other thickener to bind the ingredients. The binding and absorption take place unevenly and incompletely in the initial stages of baking and separation occurs as a result.

The filling should be allowed to stand for at least 1 hr. after preparation. The eggs are then whipped slightly and mixed into the initial mix (see the recipe p. 275). This avoids coagulation of the eggs during the resting period and permits the eggs to bind and provide body for the filling during baking. The mix should be stirred well before the pies are filled. This will pick up any settled starch or other thickener. A precooked starch thickener and tapioca flour will help considerably in avoiding weeping and permit a more rapid filling of the pies without the usual wait. However, you must permit the pumpkin to absorb. Many bakers leave the filling refrigerated for several hours and then stir it and fill the pies. There is a tendency to overspice pies. Spices should be used with discretion especially since bland pies sell better.

Cooked custard and chiffon pies are different from the soft-filled variety. When making these pies the shells are baked before the cooked filling is poured into them. While the regular pie crust used for fruit-filled pies may be used for the pie shells many bakers use a separate dough. A blend of equal amounts of pie crust dough and short dough used for fruit cake bottoms makes a good shell dough. The dough is placed on the back of the pie tin, stippled to avoid the formation of blisters during baking, and baked. To eliminate the mild bumpiness caused by air cells the dough is covered with another pie tin and baked. This will result in a shell with a smooth surface. The baked shells should not be thick and should be baked to a crisp state. Sogginess of the shell is often due to improper baking, and hot filling will also make the shell soggy. Care should be used in docking or stippling the shells before baking. Large holes will expand or become larger during baking. This allows the hot filling to run through the shell, causing sticking to the pie tin.

For regular vanilla or chocolate custard pies the usual baker's custard is used. Prepared pudding fillings, in powder form, are commonly used. Be particularly careful to follow the instructions of these prepared pudding recipes. When preparing chocolate filling, allowances must be made for the absorption properties of the cocoa. A reduction in the amount of starch or other thickener should be made. The hot fillings or puddings should be poured into the baked shells immediately after cooking. This produces a smooth finish on the top of the pie filling.

In the preparation of chiffons beaten egg whites and sugar are folded into the hot custard or pudding; this creates a lighter or chiffon effect. Chiffon pies should also be placed into the shells immediately after they are completed. This will avoid the lumpiness or unevenness that results when allowing the filling to cool and then the pie shell is filled.

In the preparation of fruit chiffon pies, such as lemon, orange, etc., the taste and flavor of the filling is important. The rind of the fresh fruit (lemon or orange), which contain the essential flavoring oils, should be folded into the filling when it is cooked. The juice of the fruit provides the tart taste as well as supplying part of the liquid. The use of concentrated, frozen juices is advisable. They should be reconstituted as directed and then carefully measured in accordance with the recipe. Special note should be made of the fact that milk should not be used in conjunction with fruit juices in the preparation of the fillings. The milk will curdle and the taste, appearance, and texture of the fillings will be that of a curdled custard or pudding.

Fruit custard or chiffon fillings require more thickening than do the regular custards made with milk. This is due to the effect of the acids upon starch and is the cause of synaeresis (separation). When adding fat or butter to any of the custard preparations it is advisable to stir in the fat after the filling has been cooked. When added at the beginning the fat melts and fat globules remain on the surface. The fat particles may not be cooked in thoroughly. The flavor of the butter is retained best when the butter is stirred in last.

In the preparation of the Bavarian-type fillings, such as in the making of Nesselrode pie, the filling is basically the same as a normal custard at the start. The addition of whipped whites is used to provide a chiffon base. After the filling has cooled whipped cream is folded into the filling and then the filling is deposited into the baked pie shells. There are variations in preparation. A simple, rich custard (use of butter and egg yolks for richness) is prepared with the use of gelatin to supplement the corn starch thickener. The gelatin provides a softer bind which makes the final incorporation of the whipped cream easier. In this filling, care should be taken not to add the whipped cream when the filling is warm. Further, the cream should be folded in gently and the filled pies kept under refrigeration. The addition of fruits, nuts, and flavors (rum, vanilla) should be made at the time the cream is folded in. Folding in or adding the fruit and nuts separately will cause overmixing and possible breakdown of the chiffon effect.

CHAPTER 24

Puff Pastry

Puff pastry is produced daily in most retail bakeshops. The basic units serve as the source for the finishing of many custards, whipped cream, cream toppings, and fruit-filled pastries. These are delicate, flaky, and tender products that bring good customers and repeat sales. There are a number of fundamental procedures which should be followed in the preparation and handling of the dough. These must be understood and practiced if consistently good results are to be obtained.

METHODS OF PREPARING PUFF PASTRY DOUGH

The Roll-In or French Method

In this method 1 to 2 oz. of fat are rubbed in with the flour, water added, and the dough well developed. The dough is put on the bench and pastry fat distributed over two-thirds of the dough and rolled. The dough is allowed to relax between rolls to allow the gluten to relax and make rolling easier. This is an important factor which will be considered later in the chapter. During the resting period the dough is placed in the refrigerator to keep the fat firm and prevent running out during rolling. Approximately 500 to 1500 layers of fat and dough are thus formed. The blending in of the 1 to 2 oz. of fat in the mixing of the dough before the fat is rolled in serves to lubricate the gluten in the development of the dough. This addition is advisable but not necessary. Some bakers may add up to 1 lb. of eggs to the dough and eliminate the fat. The yolk of the egg serves as a lubricant and the whites of the eggs contribute to the volume and dry flakiness of the baked product. However, they are not the only cause of flakiness in the baked product.

The Scottish Method

The Scottish method is one in which all the fat is broken into lumps and coated with the flour as in the preparation of flaky pie crust. Water and eggs (if used) are added and the flour absorbs the water to form a lumpy, moist dough. The dough is placed on the bench and rolled in. While many bakers prefer this method there is little decided advantage of one method over the other. The French method effects more even distribution of the fat without excessive use of dusting flour. The Scottish method often requires the use of a great deal of dusting flour in the first stages of rolling which may lead to greater absorption of flour and possible toughness of the dough.

Ingredients

In addition to the above ingredients used in the dough preparation cream of tartar, vinegar, or lemon juice is often added to the water in the making of the dough. The use of any of these acids has no direct bearing on the leavening or flakiness of the product but they relax the gluten of the dough by increasing its acidity and make the rolling of the dough easier and quicker. Excellent puff pastry products may be obtained without their use. Salt is often added to the dough in small amounts and improves the flavor of the product. However, in this instance, there is no definite need for its use as there is in the case of yeast-raised products.

The flour used in the preparation of puff pastry should be of the patent bread flour variety with good quality gluten. This is important in that a strong flour is necessary to support the large percentage of fat (approximately 100 per cent based on the weight of the flour) as well as to withstand the repeated rolling to form the layers of fat and dough. A weak or short patent flour does not have sufficient gluten strength and tends to break down and cause the formation of a paste rather than layers of fat and dough.

The fat used in the preparation of puff pastry dough should be firm and plastic and one that is stiffer than the dough. It should contain some moisture as does soft butter and margarine and specially prepared puff paste blends. Usually a combination of a puff paste blend and shortening, and/or butter is used. While it may, upon being blended, be softer than the dough it is firmed by refrigeration. This firming makes it easier to roll as well as eliminates the possibility of running out of the fat and resulting stickiness. Harder fats such as oleo-stearin and others containing an animal fat base have higher melting points (above 100°F.). Blending such a fat with vegetable shortening, butter, or margarine tends to mellow the hardness and eliminate the greasy taste or feeling when eating the product. The salt content of the fat must be taken into consideration. Eliminate the salt from the dough if using salted butter or salt-containing fats.

The rolling-in procedure is important to the formation of the many layers of fat and dough. The fat may be distributed over two-thirds of the dough or placed in one piece over one-half of the dough before rolling. It is advisable to seal the edges of the dough before starting to roll. The rolling pin should be used firmly and evenly to spread the fat evenly. The dough should be allowed to relax for at least 10 min. after the second roll as well as the third roll. Refrigerate the dough to keep the fat firm. Since hard lumps tend to flake and often tear, the fat should be of uniformly soft consistency during rolling. These tears and large flakes may not roll in evenly and are often the cause of poor, uneven greasy products. After the final roll the dough should be placed in the refrigerator. A crust may form if the dough is not oiled and covered. The crust may cause hard, gummy streaks that do not rise in baking. This is especially important for doughs that are refrigerated for long periods.

MAKEUP OF PUFF PASTRY PRODUCTS

Under normal conditions the dough should be removed from the refrigerator at least $1/2$ hr. before makeup. This will make rolling easier. Slamming the rolling pin down on the dough to soften it will rupture the layers of fat and dough and the resultant product will not have the normal flaky spring. Allow the dough to relax if it is hard to roll. Properly made puff paste dough should have a good "spring" and most units are made from doughs that have been rolled $1/8$ in. thick. However, certain products such as patty shells, creamsticks, and fruit baskets require slightly thicker doughs. Napoleon sheets are rolled thinner. Units that are folded such as turnovers require thinner doughs. Thickness does not make up for lack of spring. If the dough is made poorly it only produces raw, gummy products. The dough must be rolled so that it is of even thickness throughout, if even product size is to be obtained.

A sharp instrument should be used to cut the rolled-out dough. A pastry wheel is fine for thinly rolled doughs but a sharp bladed instrument should be used for thicker pieces. For example, cream-filled sticks should be cut sharply (they are about $1/4$ in. thick) so that the layers of fat and dough are not forced down together. It is also advisable to turn the cut pieces upside down so that the down cut faces up and maximum spring is obtained in baking. Scrap pieces of puff pastry should be folded between layers of leftover dough and then rolled out. These pieces or scraps should not be bunched together and placed on top of the dough in a lump. They should be spread thinly and distributed. A worked-over piece of scrap will be tough and will not have the desired flakiness and spring. Scrap should be used in rolling out thin pieces such as Napoleons and filled units as pastry horns.

Made-up puff pastry units should be allowed to relax $1/2$ to 1 hr. before baking. This procedure permits the gluten in the dough to relax completely. This factor will be explained in the leavening of puff pastry. Feeling the dough with your finger will indicate whether the dough is relaxed. A relaxed unit will hold the mark or depression made by the finger and be soft to the touch. Larger units, such as Napoleons and fruit strips, require a longer period of rest before baking. Units that are to be egg-washed should be washed twice. Wash once as soon as made up and again before baking. This gives a desirable crust color. This is recommended because there is no sugar in the dough to provide caramelization for brown crust formation. Some bakers will dust pastry units with confectionery sugar to obtain a desirable crust color. This requires even dusting of all units and may leave sugar on the pans or paper which will caramelize during baking and may cause sticking as well as burned edges and bottoms of the units.

THE LEAVENING OF PUFF PASTRY

The question is often asked, "What makes puff pastry units rise or spring in the oven?" This may be answered by analysis of the materials used and the method of dough preparation. The flour, as previously mentioned, must be of a strong gluten quality. The dough must be well developed in the French method for a complete gluten development. In the Scottish method the gluten development is dependent upon the rolling-in process. The French method has an advantage in this respect as the fat rolled in prevents tearing of the developed gluten. The water used to form the dough plays an important part as it provides moisture in the dough which later partially evaporates in the form of steam in the baking process.

As previously indicated, the fat used in the roll-in is very important. Stress was placed upon fats that contain moisture. Ordinary shortening contains little or no moisture and is not satisfactory for use in the making of flaky puff pastry. Of course, flakiness is obtained in some other products such as pie crust but the degree and the type of flakiness are not the same as that of the puff pastry. The moisture in the fat is converted into steam when the heat of the oven penetrates the dough.

The actual leavening begins as soon as the temperature of the oven penetrates the puff pastry units. The steam released by the moisture in the layers of dough and the moisture of the layers of fat begin to push up. The hundreds of layers of fat and dough all puff up producing the laminated flakiness in the product. The gluten in the relaxed units expands with the pressure of the steam and holds the steam in. The flaky expansion takes place until the gluten is set or firmed by the heat of the oven. The structure remains firm and the flaky characteristics of the product are developed. The temperature of the oven is very important. An oven temperature of 400° to 415°F. is necessary. A cool oven temperature will not cause the necessary rate of moisture evaporation and the gluten will dry and resist expansion. This will result in poor volume and a heavy product. A very hot oven will create an outside crust which binds the unit and prevents expansion. Instead, there is a cracking of the unit caused by the pressure of the expanding steam of the layers of fat and dough. The gluten can no longer expand and the resulting product is small in volume and greasy. The purpose of stippling or making of small holes in the units of puff pastry is to provide a passage for some of the steam to evaporate out of the unit and avoid the formation of large pockets or blisters. This is especially important in the making of Napoleon sheets and other large units. In fruit-filled units that are sealed, such as turnovers, the puncture or cut allows the exit of the steam created by the heated fruit. Large holes should be avoided in that they spread and may cause cracking or breaking of the baked units when handled.

RETARDING AND FREEZING

Unbaked Units

Unbaked units should be placed on parchment-paper-lined pans and re-frigerated. Washing with egg-wash or melted fat will help to prevent excess crustation on the units. The crust formation on the sides often causes poor volume. Since puff pastry is not leavened by yeast, it may be refrigerated for 4 to 7 days at a temperature of 34° to 38°F. However, the degree of acidity increases slowly and there is a weakening of the gluten with an increase of the acidity. A sour odor in the dough with over-age and loss in volume in baking may also result.

When freezing unbaked units it is best to cover the units with a polyethylene or freezer wrap to prevent crust formation. Units that are frozen, or dough that is frozen, may be kept at 0°F. for extended periods. Retarded and frozen units must be allowed to return slowly to shop temperature in the retail shop before baking. Rapid reduction to shop temperature may cause the fat near the surface to melt with the resulting greasiness and lack of volume during baking.

Baked Units

Baked units to be frozen should be baked lightly and not glazed or iced when made in the retail shop. The frozen units should be wrapped in a special wrap to prevent excess crystallization and gumminess in the product. Care should be taken to wrap the units to be frozen when cool. When warm, products tend to shrink considerably when subjected to freezing temperature. Frozen baked units should be thawed first and then returned to the hot oven (425° to 435°F.) for about 3 min. to improve color and to restore the dry flakiness to the product. The units are then syrup-washed and iced. The rich fat content of the product will prevent excessive drying or staling which normally takes place in products made from lean doughs. This insures a freshness of the baked product and the removal of the frozen appearance.

COMMON FAULTS AND THEIR CAUSES

Shrinkage: Dough tough—rolled too much; not relaxed before baking; and hot oven.

Fat runs out during baking: Fat not rolled in properly; weak flour dough rolled too much; hot, or cool oven; and dough over-aged.

No lift—poor volume: Improper rolling in of fat; dough or units not relaxed; improper fat used; and cool or hot oven.

Blisters and flaking: Units not stippled and edges of dough not washed.

Fruit or filling runs out: Units not stippled; edges of dough not washed and sealed properly; and cool oven (*Note:* it is common practice to fold or shape the units, bake them, and then fill them when almost cool).

Toughness: Dough over-worked and too much scrap dough used.

COMMON VARIETY OF PRODUCTS MADE FROM PUFF PASTRY

Napoleons	Filled pockets	Fruit baskets
Cream rolls	Stars or pin wheels	Pastry horns
Pastry cream fingers	Fruit-filled sticks	Horseshoes
Turnovers	Fruit boats	Patty shells
Fruit squares	Palm leaves	Miniatures
	Pastry pretzels	

CHAPTER 25

Factors Concerning Cream Puffs and Eclairs

The cream puff mix is a very useful paste that lends itself well to the preparation of a variety of pastry products. In addition to cream puff and eclair shells, swans, and other decorative shapes for the garnish of pastries, soup nuts, and French crullers can be made from the same basic mix. Consistency in the daily production of these items without variation in standards from one day to the next is important. Variations may be overcome with a better understanding of the materials and processes involved in the production of cream puffs, eclairs, and related products.

CREAM PUFF MIX

The first part of the cream puff mix is a cooked and emulsified blend of water, fat, salt, and flour. The second part is composed of eggs, water, or milk with a leavening agent. While the recipe is simple the procedure must be followed carefully to insure good results. Carelessness will lead to poor products. For example, at the start, water, fat, and salt are brought to a rolling boil. At this point, the fat is completely dispersed in the boiling liquid. If the fat remains in small lumps or is in a film on top of the water, the emulsion formed when the flour is added is not complete and the mix tends to separate. Many bakers prefer to use oil instead of fat because a liquid is easily dispersed. Continued boiling to dissolve hard fat will cause evaporation of some of the water and the mix will be stiffer after the flour is added.

The sifted flour is added in a quick, steady stream and stirred well until the flour is completely absorbed and gelatinized. At this point, the mix is smooth and pulls away from the sides of the kettle. The mix is then placed in a mixing machine and cooled to about 140°F. before the eggs are added. The eggs are added slowly and each addition is absorbed fully before the next addition is made. The water or milk and leavening are added last and the paste mixed until smooth.

Although the eggs supply most of the moisture and leavening after the paste has been prepared or cooked, milk or water is often used to soften the mix further. Milk will provide additional crust color because it contains milk sugar. It will also make a smooth crust in the baked shell. The shell will also be thinner if milk is used.

When milk or water is added additional leavening must be used in order to obtain full volume. A fast-acting leavening must be used so that

246

the liberation of carbon dioxide takes place rapidly before the crust of the shell is completely formed and dried by the heat of the oven. Ammonium bicarbonate acts rapidly and consequently is the leavening usually used. It should be dissolved in part of the water or milk and added to the mix in the last stage of mixing. A common fault, that of a greenish tinge on the inside of the shell, is caused by the excessive use of ammonium bicarbonate. This is due to its reaction with the eggs and the steam released during baking. A combination of ammonium bicarbonate and baking powder is recommended in equal parts. Approximately $1/2$ oz. of this leavening blend is suggested for each pound of water or milk added to the mix. When the mix is softened by the use of eggs only (without water or milk), no chemical leavening is needed.

The actual leavening or raising of the shells takes place in this sequence: the heat of the oven penetrates the units bagged out on the pans, the eggs in the mix naturally start to expand, the chemical leavening releases gas, part of the moisture in the mix is formed into steam and rises, and the combination of all these actions causes expansion of the shell.

The eggs supply proteins, which, in addition to the flour which has been precooked and contains a strong gluten content, form the expanding structure and holds the gas in producing leavening. The expansion continues until the gas and moisture evaporation is controlled by the "set" of the baked shell. The cracks in the shell crust and the thickness of the crust depends upon the amount and rate of leavening. Additional moisture in the form of milk or water will make a thinner shell in that the extra moisture prevents the shell from drying and setting too quickly. A thick paste will result in smaller volume and a thicker shell. This produces many strands of gluten and protein inside the shell and makes the filling and handling of the shells more difficult.

MAKEUP AND BAKING

The mix should be bagged out as soon as it is ready. Crust formation sets in quickly if the mix is permitted to stand for some time. If this happens, the crusted mix will be the cause of excessive cracking in baking. To correct this condition, the mix should be remixed lightly with some eggs, water, or milk to remove the crust.

The units should be bagged out on clean pans (without grease) or on parchment-paper-lined pans. The problem of sticking to the pans after baking and tearing upon removal are overcome with the use of parchment paper. Grease on the pans will cause the units to spread and bake flat. Before baking it is good practice to flatten slightly the points on top of cream puff units. This is done by dipping the fingers into eggs or milk and patting the points gently. This makes a smoother shell after baking and prevents crust formation before baking. It also provides a shine or luster on the tops of the shells.

The shells should be baked at 425° to 430°F. until crisp. In addition to having a light, golden color the shells should feel "crackly" or almost brittle before removing from the oven. Shells that are removed too soon will shrink and flatten because the shell structure has not been firmed or set sufficiently and the trapped steam or moisture causes shrinkage and collapse. Overbaking due to cool oven temperature and the lack of a desirable crust color will also cause shrinkage due to the excessive evaporation of moisture. This will also make the shells very brittle. These shells will crack and fall apart when they are filled or finished.

Storage

Baked shells, if not used the same day, should be covered and stored in the refrigerator. Exposed shells dry quickly and become hard to use. Shells should not be exposed to the high humidity of a refrigerator without being covered as they absorb moisture and this will cause dampness and shrinkage. Covering the shells will also prevent the absorption of foreign odors. Since the fillings used (custard and cream) are so bland they must be free from odors absorbed in the refrigerator.

Cream puffs and eclairs must be made from pure ingredients under sanitary conditions. Custard and cream-filled shells must be refrigerated as soon as they are finished. Their bacteria and perhaps the coliform count increases rapidly at room temperature. The shells should not be filled with custard or cream when they are warm. This will not only cause souring and curdling but will be dangerous to the consumer. By the same token, warm custard should not be placed into chilled shells. This will cause sogginess of the shell.

Finishing

The finish of the shells with icing is important. An even smooth finish is desirable. Very often, the tops of eclair shells are rough and uneven. It is advisable to ice the smooth bottoms of these shells. When dry the bottoms are then cut off, the shells filled with cream, and the smoothly-iced tops replaced. The fondant or flat icing used for icing should be slightly thicker than usual in order to cover large cracks in the shells of cream puffs. A thin icing will leave cracks exposed and the icing will have an uneven appearance.

CHAPTER 26

Recipes for Pies and Pastry

APPLE PIE—DUTCH APPLE PIE

Pies are a great American dessert, and apple pie is the most popular of all. With experience, you will find that pies vary in size, quality, nature of the fruit filling, and the finish of the pie. Quality of pies is important. The quality is influenced by the richness of the pie crust, the percentage of fruit in the filling, the manner in which the pies are made, and appearance of the baked pie. The recipes for the pie crust and pie filling which follow are of average quality but make an excellent pie if handled with skill and understanding.

Pie Crust

Yield: 15 8-in. pies (top and bottom crusts)

Ingredients	Lb.	Oz.	Mixing procedure
Cake flour	3	..	Sift the flour together. Add the shortening
Bread (patent) flour	2	..	and rub together into small pieces or lumps.
Shortening	2	8	Do not mix to a paste
Milk powder (op.)	..	2	
Salt	..	1¹/₂	Dissolve the sugar and salt in the water.
Sugar	..	3	Add to the above and fold over lightly until
Water (cold)	2	8	the flour is absorbed. The dough should be lumpy and sticky

Notes on Pie Crust

1. All pastry flour may be used to replace the bread and cake flour. Reduce the amount of water by 4 oz. if pastry flour is used.

2. The shortening may be replaced with the use of neutral lard.

3. Overmixing of the dough will cause gluten development and toughness of the dough.

4. Place the dough on a floured pan and shape into a rectangle. Refrigerate the dough before using. This will prevent the fat from sticking and make rolling the dough easier.

Apple Filling (1 No. 10 Can of   **Yield:** 9 8-in. pies
    Apples)

Ingredients	Lb.	Oz.	Mixing procedure
Water	1	8	Bring the sugar and water to a boil
Sugar	..	8	
Corn starch	..	3	Dissolve the starch and add to the above
Water (cool)	..	8	and stir well to a boil
Sugar	..	12	Add the sugar and bring to a boil
1 No. 10 can of apples			Remove from the fire and add the apples and
Cinnamon	..	$^1/_4$	cinnamon. Stir in gently
Lemon°	..	..	

° Rind of one lemon and a few drops of lemon juice (concentrate) may be added.

Notes on Apple Filling

1. Remove the filling from the cooking kettle as soon as the filling is prepared. Place it in a clean sheet pan or pot and allow to cool. When cool, cover the filling and refrigerate.
2. Stir the filling before using to eliminate possible lumps caused by starch that had not been mixed in properly.
3. For Dutch apple filling add 12 oz. to 1 lb. raisins to the apple filling.

Procedures to Follow (Figs. 216–221)

1. With a scraper cut long strips of dough from the chilled pie crust (about 2 or 3 in. wide). Roll the strips lightly with the palms of the hand to form into a circle.
2. Divide the dough into equal pieces weighing about 7 to 8 oz. for an 8-in. pie. These will be used for the bottoms of the pies. Leftover pie crust dough that has not been overworked may be used for the bottoms.
3. On a floured cloth, which will prevent excessive use of flour and stickiness of the dough when rolling, roll out the pieces of dough about $^1/_8$ in. thick and in a circular form. The dough should be rolled slightly larger than the top of the pie tin so that the dough can cover the bottom and sloping sides of the tin.
   Note: Pie tins should be prepared in advance. These are to be clean and greased lightly. Tinfoil pans need not be greased since the pies remain in the pans after baking and are sold in the pans.

4. Fold the rolled out bottom dough in half and pick up gently and place the dough over half of the pie tin. Lift up the folded half of dough and cover the other half of the tin. Be sure that the dough covers the entire rim of the pie tin. Pat the dough gently to remove air pockets.

5. Fill the pie with the apple filling so that the filling is slightly below the rim of the pie. Be sure the filling has been stirred to insure even distribution of the fruit.

6. The rim or edge of the pie should be washed with water. This is best done before the filling is placed in the pie. Egg-wash may be used for better adhesion of the top and bottom crusts.

7. Roll out fresh pie crust (do not use old dough or tough dough for the tops of the pies) into round strips. Cut into equal pieces weighing from 4 to 5 oz. Keep the pieces in round shape to make rolling easier.

8. Roll out these pieces slightly thinner than the bottom crust pieces. Remove the excess flour. Be sure the dough is of the proper size and shape so that the entire top of the pie will be covered.

9. Make a small hole in the top crust or cut small gashes in the center of the crust before placing the top crust on the pie. Fold the dough in half and place on top of the pie as you did the bottom crust.

10. With the thumb and forefinger seal the edges of the pie so that a slight ridge of dough is formed on the rim of the pie.

11. Place the dough on a 4 or 8 lb. weight and with the palms of the hands press the rim of the pie tin so that the excess crust is removed. The excess crust is gathered together and gently folded into and used for the bottom crusts of pies to be made again later on.

12. The pies may be washed with milk, melted fat or butter, or egg-wash. Pies washed with egg-wash will have a shiny crust when baked. Pies washed with melted fat or milk will have a dull, home-baked finish.

13. The pies are to be baked in a hot oven of 425° to 440°F. It is advisable to shift the pies carefully after they have been in the oven for about 15 min. This will insure a well-baked bottom. Pies are considered baked when the pie is shaken and the pie bottom moves freely in the tin. Avoid cool oven temperatures for this will cause the fruit to boil over and will result in a poor crust color.

14. For *Dutch apple pies*, in place of the top crust the pie is covered with Struessel or crumb topping. The crumb topping is usually dusted with confectionery sugar when the pie is cool. (See Figs. on page 252.)

FIG. 216. TINFOIL OR METAL PIE TIN
THAT HAS BEEN GREASED

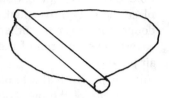

FIG. 217. ROLLED-OUT DOUGH FOR
THE BOTTOM CRUST OF THE PIE

FIG. 218. WASH THE OUTSIDE EDGE
OF THE BOTTOM CRUST

FIG. 219. FILLING DEPOSITED IN PIE

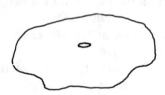

FIG. 220. TOP CRUST ROLLED OUT
AND HOLE MADE IN THE CENTER

FIG. 221. PIE IS WASHED BEFORE
BAKING

PINEAPPLE PIE, CHERRY PIE, AND BLUEBERRY PIE

Pies made with these fillings are very attractive and very tasty when handled with care, understanding, and skill. They are basically made the same way as the apple pie, using the same type of pie crust. There are some small changes in the method of finishing the tops of these pies. The following are recipes for the preparation of the fruit filling using No. 10 cans of unsweetened fruit packed in water or the natural juices.

Pineapple Pie Filling Yield: 8–9 8-in pies
  (No. 10 Can)

Ingredients	Lb.	Oz.	Mixing procedure
Juice and water	2	..	Drain the juice from the fruit. If less than
Sugar	1	12	2 lb. add water to make 2 lb. Bring to a boil
Corn starch	..	4$^1/_2$	Dissolve starch and add in a steady stream
Juice or water	..	8	stirring briskly. Boil again
Drained pineapple of 1 No. 10 can			Add the sugar and boil stirring well. Remove from fire and add fruit and color (add
Yellow color, 3 or 4 drops			color if necessary). Stir gently to distribute
Sugar	1	..	fruit

Notes on Pineapple Filling

1. Be sure to drain the fruit well by placing the contents of the can into a fine collander or sieve and gently pressing the fruit to remove all the juice. Generally, 2 lb. of juice may be obtained in this manner.
2. If there is less than 2 lb. of juice add water to meet the requirements of the recipe.
3. Grades of crushed pineapple vary. Variations will exist in color, amount of natural sugar present, and coarseness of the cut.
4. If fruit packed in syrup is used the amount of sugar used should be reduced. For light syrup reduce the weight of the sugar by 12 oz. If heavy syrup is used reduce the sugar by 1 lb.
5. Color is added only to bring out the natural color of pineapple. Be careful not to use an excessive amount. This will make an unnatural appearance.
6. Allow filling to cool before using. Keep covered and refrigerated.

Cherry Pie Filling (No. 10 Can)

Ingredients	Lb.	Oz.	Mixing procedure
Drained juice and water	2	..	Bring the juice, water (if necessary), and sugar to a boil
Sugar	1	..	
Corn starch	..	5	Add the dissolved starch solution in a steady
Juice or water	..	8	stream and boil
Sugar	1	..	Add the sugar, stir in well, and boil
Drained cherries of 1 No. 10 can			Remove from fire, add the cherries, and color
Red color, a few drops			and stir in gently

Notes on Cherry Filling

1. Pie cherries are usually packed in water and are pitted. They have a light red color and require the addition of a few drops of red color for better appearance. Be careful when using the color.
2. Stir the cherries in gently to prevent breaking or mashing the fruit.
3. Cool the filling before using. Keep covered and refrigerated when not in use.

Blueberry (Huckleberry)   Yield: 10 8-in. pies
    Pie Filling

Ingredients	Lb.	Oz.	Mixing procedure
Water or juice	2	..	Bring the juice and water (if necessary) to
Sugar	..	12	a boil
Corn starch	..	$4^1/_2$	Add the starch solution in a steady stream
Water or juice	..	8	and bring to a boil
Sugar	1	..	Add the sugar and boil again
Drained fruit	..	..	Remove from fire and add the fruit and
Cinnamon (pinch)	..	..	cinnamon. Stir gently to distribute the fruit

Notes on Blueberry Filling

1. Allow the fruit to drain without pressing the berries. Add water to make up the necessary liquid.
2. Stir the drained fruit in gently to prevent crushing the berries.
3. A pinch of cinnamon is equal to $1/_{16}$ oz.
4. Allow the filling to cool before using.

Procedures to Follow for Pineapple, Cherry, and Blueberry Pies
(Fig. 222)

1. Roll out the bottom crust for the pie as you would for apple pies.
2. It is advisable to sprinkle the bottom of the pie crust with some light cake crumbs (sponge or yellow cake crumbs are best). This will help to absorb excess liquid of the filling while baking and insure a well-baked bottom crust.
3. Wash the edge or rim of the bottom crust with water or egg-wash before filling the pies.
4. Fill these pies three-fourths full. Because of the acidity of the filling and the higher percentage of sugar in the filling these fillings expand more than apple filling during baking. This will prevent running out of the fruit during baking.

5. A regular pie crust top may be used or a lattice effect may be used. The lattice effect is obtained by rolling out a piece of pie crust dough into a rectangular shape about $1/8$ in. thick. Cut strips with a pastry wheel about $1/2$ in. wide. Wash the strips with egg-wash. Lay the strips gently across the top of the pie and snip off the ends at the rim of the pie. Do not stretch the strips of dough. Be sure the strips are equally spaced and are criss-crossed.

6. Bake the pies at a temperature of 425° to 435°F.

7. These pies may also be covered with Streussel topping and baked without the use of a pie crust top. These pies are dusted with confectionery sugar when cool.

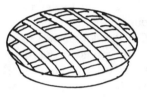

Fig. 222. Lattice-Top Pie

PIE CRUST TURNOVERS

Turnovers vary according to the nature of the dough used and the type of fruit filling used. One of the old-fashioned types of turnover is that which is made from pie crust dough. In the making of pies there is always some scrap dough left over. This will accumulate and dough may be re-worked and made into a dough which is very suitable for turnovers. Of course, fresh pie crust dough may be used for turnovers.

Scrap Pie Crust   **Yield:** 150 turnovers

Ingredients	Lb.	Oz.	Mixing procedure
Scrap pie crust dough	10	. .	Place all ingredients in this stage in the machine and mix until the dough is blended smooth with the other ingredients
Sugar	1	. .	
Salt	. .	1	
Milk powder	. .	4	
Shortening	1	. .	
Cold water (approx.)	1	. .	
Bread flour	. .	12	Sift the flour and baking powder, and add
Cake flour	. .	8	and mix to a smooth dough
Baking powder	. .	$1^1/_2$	

Procedures to Follow (Figs. 223–226)

1. You will note that the amount of water is approximated. More water may be necessary if the dough scraps are tough and the dough is

lean. Remove darkly stained scraps of dough that have been discolored with blueberry or other dark fruit filling.

2. Form the dough into rectangular shape and chill before using. The dough may be divided into smaller units if the bench is not large enough.

3. Roll out the dough about $1/_8$ in. thick. Check to see if sufficient flour is under the dough when the dough is partially rolled out. This will prevent sticking when the dough is rolled to the desired thickness. Be sure the dough is of even thickness throughout. Thick or thin spots will make uneven sizes.

4. Cut the rough edges of the rolled out dough with a pastry wheel. Use the cut pieces to be rolled in with the next dough to be rolled out.

5. Cut the dough into squares about 4 in. Mark the dough first. A divider should be used for accuracy. Cut the squares with a pastry wheel after you have marked off the size of the squares.

6. Wash the edges of the squares lightly with egg-wash or water. This will help to seal the edges when the dough is folded.

7. Deposit the fruit filling in the center of each of the squares. An equal amount should be deposited in each square. An excess amount of fruit filling will make it difficult to fold and seal the squares. It will also result in the fruit running out during baking. Filling that is too soft should not be used for it will run too much before the turnover can be sealed. Light-colored cake crumbs may be deposited on the square of dough (in the center) and the fruit placed on top of the crumbs. Crumbs may also be mixed in with the fruit filling to thicken or bind it.

8. Fold one corner of the square diagonally across to the opposite corner and seal the edges. This will form the triangular shape.

9. Place the turnovers on a paper-lined or greased pan in clusters of four. The four points of each turnover face each other. Cut the top of the turnover with a scissors or a knife and wash the top of the turnover with egg-wash. These turnovers may be left plain and baked as such.

10. Bake at 400° to 410°F. Wash with syrup upon removal from the oven. Ice the tops with simple icing when the turnovers are slightly warm.

11. Turnovers may also be washed with water or milk and then dipped in coarse granulated sugar. These turnovers are left plain after baking. Care should be used in baking these turnovers to prevent strong color or caramelization due to strong oven heat or excessive top heat.

12. Turnovers baked plain or washed with melted fat or milk before baking are generally dusted lightly with confectionery sugar after they have been baked and allowed to cool.

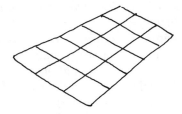

FIG. 223. ROLLED-OUT DOUGH CUT INTO EVEN-SIZED SQUARES

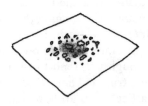

FIG. 224. CAKE CRUMBS IN CENTER OF THE SQUARE

FIG. 225. FRUIT FILLING IN CENTER ON TOP OF THE CRUMBS

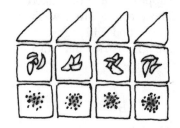

FIG. 226. MAKEUP OF THE TURN-OVERS

LATTICE-TYPE PIES

Pies are generally considered the most popular American dessert. Within the area of pies the varieties and methods of makeup are great. One of the popular varieties is the lattice-type pie. The term "lattice" refers to a lace-like or criss-cross effect. This finish permits the fruit to be seen. The procedure for making the lattice effect is simple but it does require care to achieve uniformity of strips of dough and placement of the strips.

Procedures to Follow (Figs. 227 and 228)

1. After the pies have been filled, a piece of pie crust dough is rolled out about $1/8$ in. thick, and into a rectangular shape.
2. Cut the rolled-out dough into strips about $1/2$ in. wide and long enough to cover the center diameter of the pie. At this point the strips are washed with egg-wash or milk.

3. Place the strips across the pies about 1 in. apart (they may be spaced closer if desired). Be sure to space them evenly. Press the edge of the strip against the edge of the pie to remove the excess. Place other strips across the others at a 45° angle. This will cause diamond-shaped spaces and a lattice effect. Remove the excess dough by trimming the outside rim of the pie.

Note: Use fresh dough only for the strips. Dough which has been rolled before and is now scrap dough is tough. The strips made with this dough will tend to shrink and pull away from the sides after the pie edge is trimmed or during baking. This will spoil the effect of the pie.

Lattice pies are generally made with softer fruit fillings such as pineapple, cherry, blueberry, etc. The pies should not be filled to the very brim or edge. This type filling expands in baking and will run over the sides and may cover the strips partially. This will detract from the appearance of the baked pies.

The pies are often washed with syrup after baking if the strips have been washed with eggs. Strips washed with milk or melted fat are left plain. The strips may also be washed and dipped into granulated sugar before they are placed on the pie.

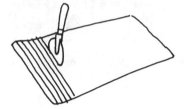

FIG. 227. CUTTING STRIPS FOR LAT-
TICE-TOP PIES

FIG. 228. LATTICE-TOP PIE

SHORT-DOUGH FRUIT CAKES

A short dough is a form of cookie dough. It is used for cookies as well as the bottoms and sides of fruit cakes and other types of cakes which require support because of the nature of the filling or cake mix. Short dough fruit cakes, both the cobbler and small layer variety, are very popular. This unit will concentrate on the small layer variety.

Short Dough for Fruit Cakes   Yield: 16–18 6-in. fruit cakes

Ingredients	Lb.	Oz.	Mixing procedure
Sugar	3	..	Blend well until soft and smooth
Salt	..	1	
Milk powder	..	2	
Glucose or corn	..	3	
syrup			
Shortening	3	..	
Eggs	1	..	Add the eggs in two stages and blend in well
Water	1	..	Stir in the water and vanilla
Vanilla	..	1	
Cake flour	3	..	Sift, add the flour and baking powder. Fold
Bread flour	3	..	or mix lightly until the flour is absorbed. Do
Baking powder	..	$1/2$	not overmix.

Notes on Short Dough

1. The mix does not have to be creamed to a very light stage. Blending well is sufficient.
2. Be sure the flours are blended by sifting to remove lumps.
3. The flour is mixed in slow speed. Be sure to scrape the bottom of the kettle as well as the sides to be sure all the ingredients and liquid are blended. The dough has a rough uneven texture and appearance. It is smoothed by gently working on a floured cloth when it is used.
4. It is best to refrigerate the dough to keep it firm. The dough should be removed from the refrigerator about $1/2$ hr. before using to make it easier to handle. When the dough is very cold it becomes brittle in handling and may require extra working on the bench to make it pliable. This may tend to toughen it by overworking and the absorption of dusting flour.

Procedures to Follow (Figs. 229–231)

1. Shape a large piece of short dough into a round strip about 4 in. in diameter. This will make cutting equal pieces for each cake easier. Cut pieces as you would cinnamon buns. The size of the pan will determine the weight of the dough to use. A 6-in. layer about $1^1/4$ in. high will require 6–7 oz. of short dough.
2. On a floured cloth roll out the short dough about $1/8$ in. thick. Roll the dough with a pie pin and roll into a circular shape. The dough should be large enough to cover the bottom and sides of the pan. The pan must be clean and greased evenly.

3. Roll up the dough on the rolling pin. Place the edge of the dough slightly below the edge of the pan. Now unroll the dough so that the dough covers the sides as well as the bottom of the entire pan. Press the sides of the dough against the sides of the pan. Be sure the entire side of the pan is covered. Trim the excess dough.

4. The excess dough may be used to patch parts of the sides which are not covered. Simply press some of the trimmed dough against the sides of the pan so that the exposed pan is covered. Check the bottom of the pan for even thickness of the dough. Thin spots should be filled in with a patch of the excess dough trimmed from the sides. If this is not done the fruit may run through in baking and the cake may fall apart when removed from the pan.

5. Fill the pans about three-fourths full with the softer fruit fillings. The pans may be filled almost to the top if apple filling is used.

6. The tops of the fruit cakes may be covered completely with a thin top of short dough or they may be finished with a lattice effect as you would for lattice-top pies. Fruit cakes that are completely covered with dough are usually egg-washed twice and striped across with a fork. This will make a criss-cross design when the cakes are baked.

7. Bake the fruit cakes at 400°F. Do not bake in a cool oven for the filling may boil over before the dough is baked. The cakes are baked directly on the hearth of the oven or oven shelf. This will insure a properly baked bottom. Lattice-topped pies are washed with simple syrup as soon as they are removed from the oven. They may also be washed, after they have cooled and have been removed from the tins, with hot apricot coating.

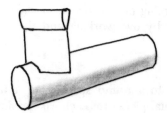

FIG. 229. CUTTING PIECES OF SHORT DOUGH

FIG. 230. ROLL UP DOUGH ON ROLLING PIN AND UNROLL INTO PAN

FIG. 231. COVER WITH A THIN SHORT DOUGH TOP AND TRIM EDGES

8. Remove the cakes from the pans when they have cooled. Turn the cake on a cake circle and then place another cake circle on the bottom and turn over. This method will prevent breakage.

Note: Large fruit cakes require a baked bottom. The sides of the pan are then covered with dough by rolling the short dough into long $1/2$ in. strips and then pressing the strips of dough around the pan. The excess is removed and the large cake filled. The top is placed on the cake by rolling out the short dough the size of the pan, rolling the dough up on a large, thin rolling pin and then unrolling on the top of the cake.

CRUMB-TOPPED PIES AND CAKES

Struessel topping (p. 142) is generally used as the topping for these cakes. The Struessel should not be sandy or fine. It is best to have the topping on the moist side and then running the topping through a coarse sieve. This will cause small lumps to form. These lumps create a desirable effect and appearance. Chill the topping after sifting to prevent a pasty effect when sprinkling the tops of the pies. The topping is dusted with confectionery sugar after the cakes and pies have been baked and cooled.

Procedures to Follow (Fig. 232)

1. The Struessel topping is placed on the pies and fruit cakes after the filling has been deposited in the dough-lined pie tins or cake pans. Be sure the entire top of the cake is covered and the fruit filling does not show through.
2. These cakes are removed from the pans when they are cool. Use the same method of turning the cakes out on layer-cake liners applied to the top and then to the bottom of the cake when turned over. This will prevent the topping from falling off the top of the cake.
3. Pies topped with Struessel are left in the tins if the tin-foil type of pie tin is used.

Fig.   232. CRUMB-
TOPPED FRUIT CAKE

PUFF PASTRY

Puff-pastry dough is a very versatile dough. It is used by the baker to make a complete variety of puff-pastry products suited to all seasons. Many staple products made daily in most bakeshops (turnovers, etc.) and many of the cream-filled and topped products made from special shells are prepared from this dough. Proper preparation of puff-pastry dough is of great importance. Without a properly made dough puff-pastry products cannot meet standards. The recipe for the dough and the manner of preparation should result in a dough which will meet requirements for all puff-pastry products. Puff-pastry dough may be prepared in two ways: the French method or the Scottish method. The French method is used in this recipe.

Puff Pastry   Yield: 100 turnovers, baskets, or
                                                                dumplings

Ingredients	Lb.	Oz.	Mixing procedure
Bread flour	4	..	Blend the flour, salt, and cream of tartar and
Cream of tartar	..	1	blend with the shortening
Salt	..	$1/_2$	
Shortening	..	4	
Eggs	..	4	Stir the water and eggs together. Add to
Cold water	2	4	the above and develop well to a smooth dough

Roll-in Fat (keep separate from the above)

Puff paste	2	8	Blend the fats together until smooth. Do
Margarine	1	..	not cream. Refrigerate until the fat is firm (not hard)

Procedures to Follow (Fig. 232A, 232B, 232C, and 232D)

1. Cream of tartar is an acid and its purpose is to mellow the gluten and allow the dough to relax quickly so that rolling of the dough is easier. The juice of two lemons or 4 oz. of table vinegar may be used in its place.

2. Place the developed dough on the bench and form into a smooth, rectangular shape. Relax the dough for a few minutes and roll out into a rectangular shape about $1/_2$ in. thick. Be sure to use enough dusting flour (bread flour) to prevent the dough from sticking to the bench.

3. Spread or dot the roll-in fat which has been firmed in the refrigerator over two-thirds of the dough as you would for Danish dough. You may also roll the dough a little thicker and smaller and place the fat on half the dough.

4. If the fat is over two-thirds of the dough fold the portion without fat over one-third of the fat-covered dough. Fold the remaining dough over the other and you now have three layers of dough and two layers of fat. If one-half the dough is covered with fat place the uncovered portion over the half that has the fat, and seal the ends to prevent the fat from seeping through when rolling.

5. Dust the bench well with flour and roll the dough out into a rectangular shape about $1/2$ in. thick. Check to see if you have enough flour while rolling. This is done by rolling half the dough up on the rolling pin and respreading the flour or adding additional flour. Do the same with the other side. Use enough flour on the top of the dough to keep the rolling pin from sticking. After rolling out the dough to an even thickness throughout remove the excess flour from the top of the dough with a brush. Fold the dough over into four sections so that four layers of dough are formed.

6. Allow the dough to relax for about 10 min. and roll a second time.

7. Place the dough in the refrigerator after the second roll to relax. This will chill the dough and the fat and make rolling easier and prevent stickiness caused by the running of soft fat.

FIG. 232A. ROLL DOUGH TO RECTANGULAR SHAPE

FIG. 232B. COVER $2/3$ THE DOUGH WITH ROLL-IN FAT AND BUTTER PREPARATION

FIG. 232C. FOLD THE DOUGH WITHOUT FAT OVER HALF THE FAT-COVERED PART

FIG. 232D. FOLD THE REMAINING $1/3$ DOUGH ON TOP

8. Roll a third and fourth time, rolling evenly and checking the flour. After the fourth roll place the dough on a dusted pan and remove the excess flour. Brush the top of the dough lightly with oil or melted fat. This will prevent a crust formation on the dough. It is also advisable to cover the dough with a cloth or piece of parchment paper. Allow the dough to remain in the refrigerator for at least 12 to 24 hr. before using. This will enable the gluten to relax and the dough to mellow before using.

APPLE TURNOVERS

Procedures to Follow (Figs. 233, 233A, 233B)

1. Cut a piece of dough from the larger conditioned unit and place on a flour-dusted portion of the bench. Sprinkle the top of the dough lightly with flour so that the rolling pin will not stick.
2. Roll out the dough into a rectangular shape about $1/8$ in. thick. Be sure the dough is of equal thickness throughout. Remove excess flour.
3. Mark off the dough into 4 in. squares (larger or smaller, depending upon production requirements). Cut out the squares with a pastry wheel. Be sure to cut the squares in uniform size and shape.
4. Brush the edges of the squares lightly with water or egg-wash. This will cause the folded edges of the turnover to stick when the turnover is sealed.
5. Deposit the apple filling in the center of the square. The apple filling may be made up of cooked apple pie filling to which some light crumbs may have been added to keep the filling from running if it is too soft. Chopped, canned, or fresh frozen apples may be used as filling. Cinnamon sugar may be mixed with the apples before depositing on the dough squares or the cinnamon sugar may be deposited on the apples after they have been placed on the dough. Cake crumbs may be placed on the dough center before the apple filling is placed on the dough. This will prevent sogginess if the filling is too soft or syrupy.
6. Fold one end of the square diagonally over to the other side. Be sure the edges line up evenly and then seal by pressing the edges with the fingers.
7. Place the turnovers on a paper-lined pan and space about 1 in. apart in clusters of four. Egg-wash the turnovers and allow them to relax for about 1 hr. before baking. The turnovers may be placed in the refrigerator or freezer at this time for future baking. Stipple the center.

8. Wash the turnovers a second time with egg-wash before baking. This will make a golden brown crust when baked. Bake at 390° to 400°F. until the turnovers are flaky, crisp, and golden brown. Wash with simple syrup as soon as removed from the oven. Allow the turnovers to cool until slightly warm and ice with warm, simple icing.

Note: Turnovers are often made in some bakeshops by folding the cut squares of dough into the triangular shape without the filling. The units are stippled and allowed to rest without washing. They are then baked to a crisp, light brown condition. The baked units are then spread apart slightly by lifting the top edge of the turnover shell and the fruit filling then deposited into the turnover shell. The turnover is then dusted with confectionery sugar before displaying.

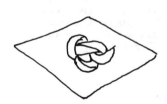

FIG. 233. ROLL OUT DOUGH AND CUT IN 4 IN. SQUARES

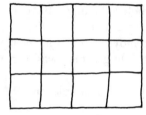

FIG. 233A. FRUIT FILLING IN CENTER ON TOP OF THE CRUMBS

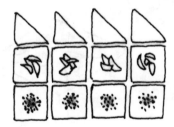

FIG. 233B. MAKEUP OF THE TURN-OVERS

FRUIT BASKETS

Procedures to Follow (Fig. 234)

1. Roll out the conditioned puff-pastry dough slightly thicker (about $1/4$ in. thick) than you did for apple turnovers.

2. Cut into even squares about 4 in. square. Be sure the dough is of uniformly even thickness and size. Size is determined by the production requirements of the shop.

3. Place the squares of dough on a parchment-paper-lined pan. Depress the center of the dough with 1 lb. weight or some device about 2 in. in diameter. This depressed space will be used to deposit the fruit filling.
4. Deposit the fruit filling in the depressed space. Be sure it is centered and do not use too much. If the filling is too thin blend with some cake crumbs. It is best to have the fruit filling a little thicker than usual to prevent excessive running during baking.
5. Roll out a piece of the dough about $1/8$ in. thick and in rectangular shape. Cut into strips about 5 in. long and about $1/2$ in. wide. The strips may be egg-washed before placing on the fruit squares.
6. Place two strips of the dough diagonally across the fruit square. Do not stretch the strips. This may cause them to tear during baking.
7. Allow the units to rest about $1/2$ to 1 hr. before baking. Bake at 390° to 400°F. The units are to be light brown and crisp.
8. Wash the units with syrup as soon as removed from the oven. Be careful to avoid smearing the hot fruit filling when washing with simple syrup.
9. When the units are almost cool stripe the tops with simple icing.

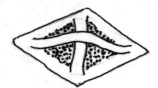

Fig. 234. Depress Center of Dough, Deposit Filling, and Place Two Strips of Dough Diagonally across the Fruit Square

APPLE DUMPLINGS

Use a hard type of apple when making the dumpling. Avoid the soft, eating variety. The size of the apple will determine the size of the dough squares to be cut. It is advisable to taste the apple to determine sweetness, tartness, or flatness of the apple. This will help you determine the amount of cinnamon sugar to add. The apples must be peeled and cored. The baker orders fresh peeled, cored, and treated apples in advance. This saves time and labor. It also insures uniformity of size.

Procedures to Follow (Figs. 235 and 236)

1. Roll out the puff-pastry dough as for apple turnovers. The dough may be rolled slightly thinner. Divide the dough into squares that are large enough to cover the entire apple when the corners are drawn up over the apple. Test by cutting one square and covering the apple.

2. Cut the dough into the squares and wash the edges lightly with egg-wash or water. Place a little cake crumbs in the center of the square of dough.

3. Set the apple on the crumbs with the flattest side down. Fill the hole, made when the core of the apple is removed, with cinnamon sugar. Fill the hole completely if the apple is flat-tasting or is very tart.

4. Fold each corner of the dough over the top of the apple and stretch the ends a bit to thin the dough. You now have the ends covering each other. Seal the edges of the dough together so that the entire apple is covered with dough. It is advisable to cut a small round disc of dough about $1^{1}/_{2}$ in. in diameter and place it over the sealed ends at the top. Egg-wash the top of the dumpling before placing the round seal on top. This will keep the ends from separating and is also decorative.

5. Bake the dumpling at about 400°F. until golden brown. Bake on parchment-paper-lined pans. Wash the dumplings lightly with syrup upon removal from the oven. Allow the dumplings to cool and stripe with simple icing. Avoid overbaking for this will cause the dumpling to settle or flatten. Soft apples will also do the same.

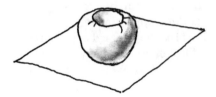

Fig. 235. Place Pared, Cored Apples on Each Square, and Fill Center with Cinnamon Sugar

Fig. 236. Fold Sides over the Top of the Apple and Seal with a Small Disc of Dough

NAPOLEONS

Napoleons are very popular pastries and provide further variety in bakeshop displays and in other food establishments. Basically, the pastry sheets made from puff-pastry dough serve as the structure for Napoleons. The filling, generally, is made from baker's custard. The custard itself may also be varied. The toppings or finish of the Napoleons may also vary. You then see that while Napoleons are considered as a single pastry item there are various methods of finishing them.

Baker's Custard Filling (2 qt.)   Yield: 1 Napoleon of three sheets

Ingredients	Lb.	Oz.	Mixing procedure
Sugar	1	. .	Place the ingredients into the cooking kettle
Salt	. .	$1/4$	and stir well to dissolve the milk powder and
Milk powder	. .	8	sugar. Place on fire and stir while heating.
Water (cool)	3	. .	Allow the mix to boil
Water (cool)	1	. .	Dissolve the starch in the water
Corn starch	. .	6	
Eggs	1	. .	Whip the eggs slightly and add to the starch. Add in a slow, steady stream to the boiling milk and stir constantly until the custard boils and thickens
Butter	. .	5	Remove from the fire and stir in the butter
Vanilla	. .	1	and vanilla

Pour the custard into clean, wet sheet pans and spread the custard evenly (one pan is enough for 2 qt.). Sprinkle the top of the custard lightly with granulated sugar to prevent a crust from forming and allow the custard to cool. Do not place the custard into the refrigerator while it is hot.

Note: The custard, when chilled, is mixed smooth before using. It may also be lightened or Frenched by adding approximately 3 lb. of buttercream icing to the smooth custard. Mix the custard and buttercream in medium speed to prevent a curdling effect. The custard may also be chiffoned (Bavarian style) by adding 1 qt. of whipped cream or topping to the smooth custard. Fold the whipped cream in lightly.

Procedures to Follow for Napoleons (Figs. 237–240)

1. For the average sheet pan approximately $2^1/_2$ lb. of puff-pastry dough is required. For best results fresh dough (without scrap) is suggested. However, clean scrap dough may be added. This is done by placing the scrap dough in between the layers of the puff-pastry dough. Stretch the scrap dough to avoid tough lumps of dough, shrinkage, and discoloration during baking.

2. The sheet pans should be clean and the edges of the pan moistened lightly with water. The dough will stick to the water and keep the dough from shrinking too much.

3. Roll the dough out evenly to about $1/_8$ to $1/_{16}$ in. thickness. Be sure it is of even thickness throughout. This will avoid burning in one

spot and rawness in another. Roll the dough slightly longer and wider than the pan to allow for some shrinkage while the dough is resting. Roll up the dough on a rolling pin and then unroll it on the pan.

4. Stipple the dough with a roller docker or with the point of a knife or bench scraper. Space the stipples about 1 in. apart. Spacing them too far apart will cause the formation of large blisters when baking. These blisters break when the sheets are handled and the entire sheet may fall apart. Do not make large holes, for these spread and also cause breakage. Prepare three such sheets of dough for each Napoleon sheet. Where a thick filling is used (French custard or custard and whipped cream), two sheets may be enough.

5. Allow the sheets to relax for about an hour and bake at 380°F. until golden brown and crisp. Allow the sheets to cool before using.

6. Level off the baked sheets by slicing thick ends down to even size. Save these pieces of the baked Napoleon sheet. They may be used for garnish.

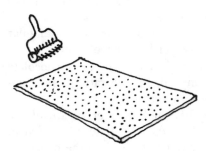

FIG. 237. ROLLED-OUT AND STIPPLED SHEET OF PASTRY DOUGH

FIG. 238. SHEETS PUT TOGETHER AND ICED

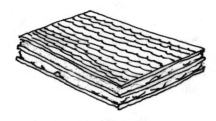

FIG. 239. FINISHED SHEET

FIG. 240. FINISHED NAPOLEON SLICE

7. Turn one sheet over on a clean pan with the flat bottom up. Spread the custard filling about $1/4$ to $1/2$ in. thickness evenly over the sheet. Place the second sheet over the custard filling with the flat bottom facing up. Cover the sheet with custard filling again. Place the third sheet on top of the second filling with the flat side up. Place a clean sheet pan on top of the Napoleon and press down with some firmness so that the sheets and custard filling stick together. Do not force the custard out of the sides. It is advisable to chill the Napoleons before finishing. This makes finishing and cutting easier.

The Napoleons may be finished in the following manner:

1. Spread a thin coating of custard across the top sheet. Chop the pieces of the ends into fine pieces and sprinkle over the top of the custard filling so that the entire area is covered with pastry crumbs. Cut the Napoleons into desired portions and then dust with confectionery sugar.
2. The top may be iced with warm fondant icing and then striped with chocolate icing in a paper cone. Be sure the chocolate stripes are put on evenly. Draw a knife edge through the chocolate stripes while the icing is still soft and not set. This will create a marbled effect. Allow the icing to dry and then cut into squares or rectangular shapes. Dip the knife blade into hot water for a smooth cut.
3. The top of the Napoleons may be finished by covering with chocolate fudge icing and combing with a fine edged decorating comb immediately after the fudge has been evenly spread.
4. The French custard may be made with melted sweet chocolate added. This will make further variety. Be sure the chocolate is blended in evenly. Some melted butter or fat may be stirred into the chocolate before adding to the custard. This will prevent the chocolate from lumping.

PATTY SHELLS

Procedures to Follow (Figs. 241–243)

1. Roll out a piece of puff-pastry dough about $1/8$ in. thick. Remove the excess flour. Using a plain-edged cookie cutter (size depending upon needs) cut out as many discs as required or the dough permits. As the units are picked up, turn them over before placing on a paper-lined pan.
2. Roll out another piece of dough to the same thickness and cut out an equal number of discs. Cut the center out of these discs with a 1 in. round cookie cutter.

3. Egg-wash the discs that are on the pan and place those with the holes directly over them. Be sure to turn the rings over when placing on the others. Wash the top rings with egg-wash and allow the patty shells to rest for about 1 hr. before baking.

4. Bake at 390°F. until crisp.

5. Patty shell may also be made by rolling the dough $1/4$ in. thick and stippling the dough. The discs are then cut out as follows: A small cookie cutter is then pressed partially through the center of the disc. After baking, the centers are then scooped out to make the hollow. The shells are often used by bakers for pastries filled with variety fruit fillings. They are also used by caterers for the preparation of hot delicacies.

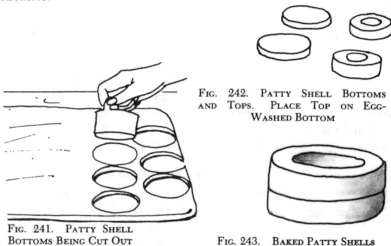

FIG. 242. PATTY SHELL BOTTOMS
AND TOPS. PLACE TOP ON EGG-
WASHED BOTTOM

FIG. 241. PATTY SHELL
BOTTOMS BEING CUT OUT

FIG. 243. BAKED PATTY SHELLS

SOFT-FILLED PIES

Soft-filled pies are those which are filled with an uncooked custard-type filling and baked. It is during the baking process that both the crust and the filling are baked and the filling thickened or firmed. These are popular pies and careful handling and understanding of the techniques in their making will ensure success in their production.

The crust for the soft-filled pie must be leaner than the regular short or flaky type of pie crust because it must stand up under rolling, shaping of the raised edge, and support the filling without becoming soggy or raw.

The filling for these pies is jelled or thickened during baking. The thickening agent may be corn starch, precooked starch or tapioca flour, or the natural thickening properties of eggs. Therefore, you will find a number of different recipes used for soft-filled pies. When a large percentage of eggs is used, and the pie therefore more costly, a lesser amount of thickening, or none at all will be used. Variations must be made to suit the requirements of production standards.

Crust for Soft-Filled Pies

Yield: Approx. 18 8-in. shells

Ingredients	Lb.	Oz.	Mixing procedure
Cake flour or pastry flour	5	..	Sift the dry ingredients together. Add shortening and blend well to a smooth paste
Sugar	..	3	
Salt	..	$1^1/_4$	
Milk powder	..	2	
Shortening	1	12	
Water (warm)	2	..	Add the water and mix well to a smooth paste

Note: You will note that the ingredients are mixed well and the dough is developed until smooth. This is different from that of the regular pie crust. It is necessary to avoid pieces or lumps of fat which melt and make the breaking of the shell edge or holes resulting from the melting of the fat which allows the filling to run out.

Procedures to Follow for Pie Shells (Figs. 244 and 245)

1. Scale the dough into units large enough to cover the pie plate (5 oz. for a 6-in. pie). Form the pieces of dough into round shape.
2. Roll out the dough in round form large enough in diameter to cover the tin. Make allowance for the sides of the pie plate.
3. Place the dough into the tin and be sure the entire tin is covered.
4. Take a piece of dough in round form and dip it into bread flour. Pat this dough against the bottom of the crust therefore thinning the bottom crust and forcing the excess against the sides of the tin. Be careful not to make the bottom crust too thin or cause a hole to form.
5. With the fingers press the dough on the sides of the tin forcing the excess dough to the top of the rim. This excess dough will serve as the raised rim of the pie.
6. With the fingers, press this excess dough together, thus raising the dough about $1/_2$ in. above the rim of the pie plate. The edge is then scalloped by pressing the dough between the fingers about 1 in. apart.

Note: Some shops use special machines and machine dies to form these shells mechanically.

7. Allow the shells to rest for several hours to form a crust. The warm water used in the dough aids in crust formation. It is this crust formation which helps to prevent the filling from seeping through the crust during the filling and baking periods.

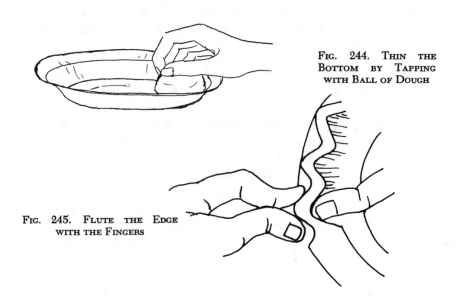

FIG. 244. THIN THE BOTTOM BY TAPPING WITH BALL OF DOUGH

FIG. 245. FLUTE THE EDGE WITH THE FINGERS

Custard Pie Filling   Yield: 6–8 8-in. pies

Ingredients	Lb.	Oz.	Mixing procedure
Sugar	1	4	Blend the dry ingredients together
Salt	..	$1/4$	
Milk powder	..	8	
Corn starch	..	$1^1/_2$	
Pre-cooked starch	..	$1/_2$	
Eggs	1	4	Stir the eggs well to get them well-mixed and mix into above
Water	4	..	Add the water and vanilla and stir in well
Vanilla	..	1	
Melted butter (optional)	..	3	Allow the custard filling to stand before filling the pies ($1/_2$ hr.). The melted fat is stirred into the custard before the pies are filled

Notes on Custard Pie (Fig. 246)

1. Be sure to mix the custard filling well before filling the pies. This enables you to mix the starch and/or sugar into the liquid if they have settled to the bottom. Avoid whipping too much air into the custard. This is the cause of blisters and uneven crust color in baking.

2. Fill the pies half full and place into the oven. Allow 5 min. before filling the pies to the point just below the edge of the brim. This double fill will ensure a better bake and eliminate curdling or separation. If pre-cooked starch or tapioca flour is used the pies can be filled to the top immediately and placed in the oven. The pre-cooked starch will bind the custard slightly before filling the pies (during the $1/2$-hr. absorption period) and will prevent bleeding or curdling.

3. Custard pies should be baked at 425°F. Shift the pies gently if the heat of the oven is uneven. Pies are considered baked if they feel slightly jelled or firm in the center. Touch them gently in the center to test the consistency of the custard.

4. For *cocoanut custard pie* sprinkle the bottom of the crust with unsweetened shredded cocoanut. Avoid using the sweetened variety for they tend to darken before the pie is baked.

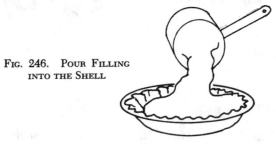

FIG. 246. POUR FILLING
INTO THE SHELL

Pumpkin Pie Filling

While pumpkin pie filling may be made from fresh pumpkin the recipe that follows is based upon canned pumpkin. The principles applied to the preparation of custard pie apply to pumpkin pie.

Pumpkin Pie Filling

Yield: 12–14 8-in. pies

Ingredients	Lb.	Oz.	Mixing procedure
Sugar	1	8	Blend the dry ingredients together
Brown sugar	..	8	
Salt	..	$1/2$	
Milk powder	..	12	
Cinnamon	..	$1/2$	
Bread flour	..	5	
Nutmeg	..	$1/4$	
Eggs	1	8	Add the eggs and stir well
Corn syrup or glucose	1	..	Add and blend in well
Pumpkin (one No. 10 can)			
Water	6	..	Add in three stages and blend in well

Notes on Pumpkin Pie

1. Allow the filling to rest at least $1/2$ hr. before filling the pies. Be sure to stir the filling well before filling the pies.
2. Fill and bake the pumpkin pies as you would the custard pies.
3. Bread flour is used in place of starch because it has greater binding properties. Starch or precooked tapioca flour may be used instead.
4. If the proportion of eggs are increased less thickening agents are used.

Cheese Pie Filling

This is a custard type of filling in which baker's cheese is used. You will find recipe variations in which a blend of cream cheese is used. You will find that some recipes call for the addition of whipped whites and sugar. This makes a chiffon effect. The following recipe is for a straight cheese-custard type of filling.

Cheese Filling   Yield: 12 8-in. pies

Ingredients	Lb.	Oz.	Mixing procedure
Sugar	2	..	Blend together to a smooth paste
Salt	..	1	
Milk powder	..	12	
Shortening	..	8	
Baker's cheese	5	..	Mix the cheese and flour together. Add to
Cake flour	..	8	the above and blend in
Eggs	..	12	Add the eggs and blend in well
Cold water	2–3°	..	Add the water in four stages and blend well
Vanilla	..	1	after each addition. The filling should have the consistency of a thick gravy and pour easily

° Variable.

Notes on Cheese Pie

1. For pineapple or other fruit-filled cheese pie place the fruit filling in the bottom of the pie and then pour the cheese filling on top.
2. Bake at 425°F. until the edge has a brown ring-like crust and the center of the pie feels jelled.
3. This pie will rise in the oven and recede to its original height when cool.

PIE SHELLS FOR CREAM, CUSTARD, AND CHIFFON PIES

The custard-cream and chiffon custard pies referred to are those in which the custard filling is cooked and then immediately poured into prebaked pie shells. Points will be presented regarding the preparation of the pie shells as well as the preparation of the fillings. Toppings for these pies will also be considered in this unit.

Pre-baked Pie Shells

The pie crust dough used for the production of fruit-filled pies (p. 249) is suitable for making these shells. It is recommended that a pie dough is extra-rich in fat content be made leaner to avoid a crust that is too tender and will crumble easily when handled or when the filling is poured into the shell. A pie crust dough containing 50 per cent fat (based on the weight of the flour) is best suited.

Procedures to Follow for Pie Shells (Figs. 247–250)

1. Scale the chilled pie dough into equal units (5 oz. for a 6-in. pie tin) and form into round shape. Be careful not to over-handle to avoid toughening the dough. It is best to cut a thick strip from the dough and roll it gently into a strip about 3 to 4 in. in diameter. Cut into pieces of 2 in. thickness an scale. Add or subtract a piece of dough if necessary. Once you get the correct weight the other pieces may be cut by estimating size and shape.

2. Roll the dough on a floured cloth if possible (this prevents sticking and the use of excess dusting flour) to the size of the pie tin. Make allowances of about $1\frac{1}{2}$ in. for the sides of the tin. It is important to have the dough of equal thickness (about $\frac{1}{8}$ in.) to prevent burning in baking and breakage after baking.

3. Fold the rolled-out dough in half, pick up, and place over half of the tin. Uncover the other half and cover the rest of the tin.

4. Place the tin on a No. 10 can and press the sides of the dough to the tin. Cut the excess crust away from the edge of the pie tin.

5. Stipple or puncture the crust on the top and sides with a sharp point. Remember that the pie tin is inverted before putting the crust on it. Actually, the bottom of the tin is now the top.

6. Bake the shells at 400°F. until a brown crust is formed. Check the inside of the shell to see if it is baked through. If the oven has a weak bottom or the oven is flashy the partially baked shells may be taken from the outside of the tin and placed on the inside, like a regular pie, and the outside exposed to the oven heat for proper bake.

7. Allow the shells to cool before removing from the backs of the tins.

8. It is also customary to cover the stippled crust with another pie tin. Thus the dough is sandwiched between two pie tins. This prevents the formation of large blisters during baking and insures more even crusts and less shrinkage.

FIG. 247. PLACE DOUGH ON THE
BACK OF THE PIE TIN

FIG. 248. COVER WITH ANOTHER PIE
TIN

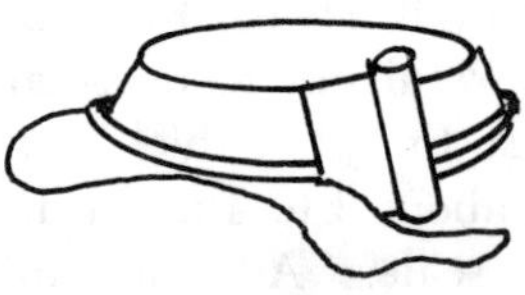

FIG. 249. TRIM EXCESS DOUGH

FIG. 250. TOP PIE TIN REMOVED TO
STIPPLE THE DOUGH

LEMON MERINGUE PIE

Lemon Pie Filling (2 qt.)   **Yield:** Filling for 7–8 8-in. pies

Ingredients	Lb.	Oz.	Mixing procedure
Sugar	1	8	Dissolve the sugar and salt in water and
Salt	..	1/4	lemon juice. Bring to a boil
Water	3	..	
Juice of 6 Lemons	..	8	
Corn starch	..	7	Dissolve the starch in the cool water. Whip
Water	1	..	in the eggs and rind. Add a small amount of
Rind of 2 lemons			the boiling syrup and stir in. Pour all into
Eggs	1	..	the boiling syrup in a steady stream stirring
Butter or shortening	..	4	constantly. Bring to a boil and thicken. Remove from the fire. Add fat and stir in well

Procedures to Follow (Figs. 251 and 252)

1. The cooked lemon is poured into the baked shells as soon as the butter or fat is dissolved and distributed evenly through the filling. Use a dipper or ladle to prevent scalding.
2. If powdered lemon or lemon crystals is used follow the recipe on the can put there by the manufacturer. If the filling is too thin add some stabilizer (precooked starch) to it at the time the eggs are added.

3. If frozen lemon juice is used be sure to dilute the juice according to directions if it is of the concentrated variety.

4. The rind of the lemon refers to the yellow outside only and not to the white pulp. The yellow part of the rind contains the natural oil of lemon and is used for flavor. If no lemon rind is used add 1 oz. of good lemon flavor to the custard filling after it is removed from the fire.

5. If prepared lemon filling is used place the filling in the shells and even the top of the filled shell.

6. The filling must be cool before placing the meringue on top.

FIG. 251. PLACE BAKED SHELL INTO PIE TIN

FIG. 252. POUR CUSTARD FILLING IN BAKED PIE SHELL

Meringue Topping

Yield: To cover 10–12 8-in. pies

Ingredients	Lb.	Oz.	Mixing procedure
Egg whites (cool)	2	..	Place the whites in a clean mix-bowl (no fat). Whip to froth. Add the blended sugar and stabilizer in a steady stream to the whipping whites. Whip to a dry peak
Salt (pinch)	..	..	
Sugar	2	..	
Precooked starch or stabilizer	..	1	

Procedures to Follow for Topping

1. Be careful not to overwhip. You will note that the whites whip to a wet or shiny peak. Whip a few moments longer and the peaks start to take on a dull appearance.

2. Apply the meringue topping to the cool lemon-filled pie shells. This may be done with a pastry bag and tube or with a bowl knife. The top of the meringue may be dusted with confectionery sugar if a darker and quicker-coloring meringue topping is desired.

3. Bake the meringue pies at 385° to 400°F. until the meringue has an even brown crust. Be careful not to bake the meringue at a very high temperature or in a flashy oven. This will cause the meringue to brown quickly and the meringue will shrink after baking. Use fresh egg whites.

CHOCOLATE CREAM PIE

This pie is composed from a chocolate custard, similar to a chocolate pudding, which is cooked and poured hot into prebaked pie shells then cooled and later topped with whipped cream or whipped topping. You will find various recipes for chocolate pie filling and a number of pre-pared powders to be used in cooking the chocolate filling. Some recipes will contain eggs. Eggs are not essential in the preparation of this filling for the thickening or binding effect of the eggs may be replaced by the use of corn starch or precooked starch or tapioca flour.

Chocolate Pie Filling   **Yield:** Filling for 12–14 8-in. pies

Ingredients	Lb.	Oz.	Mixing procedure
Water (cool)	7	. .	Stir well to dissolve the sugar and milk
Sugar	2	4	powder. Place on fire and boil. Stir well to
Salt	. .	$^1/_4$	avoid scorching
Milk powder	. .	7	
Water (cool)	2	. .	Dissolve cocoa and starch in water. Add
Cocoa	. .	7	some of hot liquid to starch solution and stir.
Corn starch	. .	9	Pour in steady stream into boiling syrup and stir constantly until thick
Vanilla	. .	2	Remove from fire and add vanilla and fat.
Butter or shortening	. .	6	Stir well

Pour the hot filling immediately into pre-baked shells

Procedures to follow

1. Use a natural dark cocoa. The use of a dutched cocoa will not provide the dark chocolate color.
2. In all custard-type fillings where milk powder is used the milk powder should be dissolved in cool water to avoid lumping and hardening of the casein in the milk. Once formed, it cannot be removed without straining the custard filling.
3. The use of hot liquid (a small amount) added to the dissolved starch and eggs (if eggs are used with the starch as in regular custard) brings the temperature of the starch solution up and the starch particles expand before they are put into the boiling syrup. This causes a quicker thickening effect and there is less chance of lumping and scorching. It also allows liquefying of the fat in the yolk, better distribution of the egg in the starch solution, and quicker jelling of the custard. This also avoids lumping of the finished custard.

4. Be sure the melted butter or shortening is completely mixed into the custard before filling the shells. This will prevent separation.

5. Whipped cream, whipped topping, or a combination of both may be used to finish the chocolate cream pies. Whip the cream or topping to a moist peak. Do not overwhip. This will cause the cream to weep or bleed during the bagging out of the cream with a pastry bag and tube and while the cream is on the pie. Be sure the filling is cold before applying the cream topping. These pies should be refrigerated before applying the topping and after they are finished.

BANANA CREAM PIE

This pie is made very much the same way as chocolate cream and lemon meringue pies. It requires you to prepare a custard filling which is poured into the prebaked pie shells immediately after the filling is cooked. The use of the bananas is but one of the means by which this type of pie may be finished for variety. Other fruits, such as fresh strawberries, pineapple, etc., may also be used.

Custard Filling   Yield: Filling for 6–7 8-in. pies

Ingredients	Lb.	Oz.	Mixing procedure
Sugar	1	..	Dissolve the dry ingredients in the water.
Salt	..	$1/2$	Stir well and bring to a boil
Milk powder	..	8	
Water (cool)	3	..	
Eggs	1	..	Dissolve the starch in the water. Stir the
Corn starch	..	6	eggs in well. Add a little of the hot milk to
Water (cool)	1	..	the starch-egg solution and stir
Butter or shortening	..	6	Pour into the boiling milk in a steady stream.
Vanilla	..	1	Stir constantly and boil. Remove from fire and stir in the butter and vanilla

Procedures to Follow (Figs. 253–255)

1. Pour the custard into prebaked shells immediately after cooking. As with chocolate custard be careful to prevent scorching during cooking and when pouring the custard into the shells.

2. Allow the custard to chill before finishing the pie.

3. When ready to finish the pies peel bananas and cut them in half. If the bananas are large and thick cut them in half and cut the slices into quarters.

4. Dip the sliced bananas into lemon juice or a mild solution of citric acid. This will prevent oxidation and discoloration.

5. Place the bananas lengthwise across the top of the chilled custard and press them in slightly.

6. Cover the top of the pie with whipped cream or whipped topping, or a combination of both whipped together.

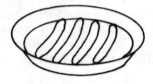

Fig. 253. Bananas Are Placed in the Custard, Evenly Spaced

7. Slice or cut the pie so that the cut banana shows clearly through. To remove the smear that may be caused by the cutting edge of the knife dip the knife in warm water before cutting or dip a bowl knife in water and slide it gently over the sliced edge of the pie to remove the smear. Place a piece of waxed paper across the cut portion of the pie to prevent slight spreading and oxidation of the cut banana.

Fig. 254. Cross-Section of Banana Cream Pie

8. The bananas may also be cut into slices and spread across the custard filling before the cream is bagged out. The top of the pie may be garnished with flat, thin slices of banana dipped in lemon juice or citric acid solution.

Fig. 255. Finished Banana Cream Pie

Note: As mentioned above, various fruits may be used. Crushed pineapple (cooked) may be spread across the custard filling before the cream topping is applied or fresh strawberries may be used.

LEMON CHIFFON PIE

Chiffon pies are those in which the fillings are made light and airy by the addition of whipped egg whites and sugar. The whipped whites are incorporated into the cooked filling immediately after the filling has been removed from the fire. The more whipped white added the lighter the filling will be. However, when a lighter pie is made the chiffon must be supported by a stabilizer or binder. The binder, in the form of egg-white stabilizer, precooked tapioca flour, or dissolved gelatin, is added to the whites and whipped in. The chiffon will then maintain its lightness without falling back.

Lemon Chiffon Pie Filling

Yield: 8–9 8-in. pies

Ingredients	Lb.	Oz.	Mixing procedure
Water	3	. .	Dissolve sugar and salt. Bring to a boil
Sugar	1	2	
Salt	. .	$1/4$	
Lemon juice	. .	8	
Rind of two lemons			
Water	1	. .	Dissolve starch and stabilizer in water. Stir
Corn starch	. .	6	yolks in well. Add some of the hot liquid
Egg yolks	. .	8	and stir in. Add to the boiling liquid in a
Stabilizer	. .	$1/2$	steady stream. Stir well and boil
(Tapioca flour)			
Butter	. .	3	Remove from fire and stir in
Egg whites	1	4	Whip whites and sugar to a wet peak. This
Sugar	. .	12	should be ready before the filling is cooked. Fold in gently but thoroughly

Procedures to Follow

1. Remove the hot filling from the fire and fold the whites gently into the hot filling with a wire whip. Be careful to fold in evenly and gently. Overmixing at this point will cause a loss in structure and volume of the chiffon. Undermixing will leave parts of the egg whites exposed and this will make a coarse, uneven structure and appearance.

    Note: If the egg whites are increased, a stabilizer should be whipped into the egg whites.

2. Place in prebaked pie shells immediately.

    Note: Refer to lemon pie filling for the use of concentrated frozen lemon juice or the use of lemon powders (p. 278).

3. Avoid using prepared, cold lemon fillings. The egg whites will not blend easily and the albumen in the egg whites will not coagulate. Neither will the stabilizer jell properly. This will lead to poor volume and weeping due to the separation of the egg whites from the filling.

4. These pies may be sprinkled with light, toasted cake crumbs. They may also be finished with toasted, long-shred cocoanut. Whipped cream may also be used to garnish the tops of the pies.

ECLAIRS AND CREAM PUFFS

The most important part of making eclairs and cream puffs is the knowledge and skill involved in the preparation of the shells, which are made from a paste or emulsion of fat, water, and flour. The paste is further emulsified by the addition of eggs to the cooked paste. Water and leavening may also be added if the amount of eggs used is not enough to soften the paste to the desired consistency. The recipe and procedure below should be carefully followed.

Eclair and Cream Puff Paste   Yield: 100 eclair or cream puff shells

Ingredients	Lb.	Oz.	Mixing procedure
Water	2	..	Bring the water and fat to a rolling boil.
Salt	..	1/4	Be sure the fat is completely dissolved
Shortening or oil	1	..	
Bread flour	1	5	Add the flour and stir briskly to a smooth paste. Remove from fire and cool to about 150°F.
Eggs	2	..	Place in the machine and add the eggs slowly. Blend well after each addition of eggs
Milk or water	..	8–12	Dissolve the leavening in the milk (part of it) and add. The amount of milk will vary
Ammonium carbonate	..	1/4	

Procedures to Follow (Figs. 255A and 255B)

1. Be sure the fat and water are boiling strongly before adding the flour.
2. Stir constantly after the flour is added and until the paste is removed from the fire. Do not overcook the paste. The paste is done when it tends to ball up and works away from the side of the kettle.
3. Place the paste in the mixing machine and run at slow speed until the temperature of the paste has been reduced to about 150°F. Placing the eggs in the very hot paste tends to cook the eggs.
4. The eggs are to be added in small amounts to the machine and each addition must be allowed to be absorbed into the paste before the next. This further increases the emulsifying properties of the mix. Be sure to scrape the sides of the kettle for uniformity of the paste.

5. The paste for eclairs should be soft to the point where it is almost ready to spread and yet retains its shape when bagged out. If the paste is too stiff additional egg may be added. In this case the milk or water and leavening are left out.

6. Dissolve the ammonium carbonate in part of the milk and add that part to the paste after all the eggs have been mixed in. Do not add all the milk at once. The paste may become too soft and cannot be thickened without spoiling the mix.

7. Cream puffs and eclairs are bagged out with a plain tube. The eggs create great leavening action and the puffs, when made correctly, rise to three or four times their original size. They are best bagged out on paper-lined pans.

8. Bake at 410° to 425°F. until the shells are crisp. Tap them gently for crispness. If they sound hollow and feel crisp they are baked.

9. Allow the shells to cool before filling. The shells may be boxed and stored in a cool place or refrigerator for use the following day. Refrigerating empty shells for lengthy periods of time causes them to absorb moisture and often shrinkage takes place.

10. The most popular filling for these shells is the plain custard which has been cooked and chilled. The recipe for this has been provided previously in the unit on banana cream pie. Be sure the custard is cool or chilled before filling the shells.

11. Be sure the jelly or doughnut filling machine has been washed and rinsed before placing the custard in the pump. If the custard filling is too stiff it should be placed on the machine and worked smooth. An equal amount of buttercream may be added to the custard to soften or "French" it. It is known as French custard.

12. Fill the shells with enough custard so that it may be tasted as soon as the consumer bites into it. Do not fill the shells so that the shells burst. Be sure to fill the eclair shells evenly.

13. The shells are then dipped into fondant icing so that the top surface is covered. Generally, half of the top surface of the shell is covered. The flavor of the icing or fondant is optional. The most popular icing is chocolate. After the icing has dried the tops may be decorated with a striped design with a paper cone with a small hole. The same icing or contrasting-colored icing may be used.

14. If pistachio nuts or other ground nuts or crunch are applied to the icing they must be applied while the icing is still soft and moist. This will cause them to stick to the icing.

15. Very often cream puffs are dusted with confectionery sugar rather than iced. This is especially so in the case of the miniature puffs.

16. When finishing cream puff or eclair shells with whipped cream or topping the shells are first dipped in the icing and the icing allowed to dry. The shells are then cut with a sharp knife through the center. The bottom half of the shell is then filled with cream with a pastry bag. Fruit fillings may be put in the shell first and then covered with cream. The top is then replaced and may also be garnished with cream and nuts.

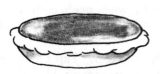

FIG. 255A. CREAM-FILLED ECLAIR   FIG. 255B. CREAM-FILLED CREAM PUFF

Note: All finished eclairs and cream puffs should be refrigerated as soon as they are finished. Custards and creams are easily contaminated and spoil if left at room temperature for a number of hours.

Specialties made with ice cream are also made with these shells. The shells are sliced in half and then filled with a slightly softened ice cream. It is best to use a round flat scoop for the cream puffs. There are the finger-shaped scoops made for ice cream to be placed in eclair shells. The tops are then replaced and the filled shells are placed in the freezer.

FRENCH CRULLERS

Dry or baked French crullers are made from the same mix or paste as eclairs and cream puffs. The same recipe is used except for the fact the paste is slightly stiffer in consistency so that ridges made by the star tube are clear and distinct after the crullers are baked.

Procedures to Follow

1. Bag out the mix with pastry bag and star tube. Be sure that the ring is even and round. Release the pressure on the bag when you have completed the circle. This will leave a slight excess of mix overlapping the closed end of the circle. It is important to have the ring of even thickness all the way around. This will give you an evenly shaped ring after baking and will avoid an uneven bake. Allow about 1-in. space between each ring. Use clean pans or pans lined with parchment paper.

2. Bake the French crullers at 410° to 425°F. Tap them to be sure they are crisp.
3. Allow the French crullers to cool and then dip them in warm fondant or fudge-type icing. The color and flavor of the icing may vary.
4. The shells may also be cut in half and filled with whipped cream, topping, or French custard, the top replaced and dusted with confectionery sugar.

SOUP NUTS

Soup nuts are made from the same paste as eclairs and cream puffs with the difference that the paste is made a bit softer and it is advisable to use whole, fresh eggs to thin the paste. This makes a lighter soup nut with a greater crispness. The shell crust is also thinner than that of the cream puff shell. The salt may be increased slightly and a pinch of finely ground pepper may be added to the mix.

Procedures to Follow

1. The paste is bagged out with a pastry bag and small plain tube.
2. The nuts are bagged out on clean pans or paper-lined pans in small dots slightly smaller than a dime. The skill involved is difficult and speed will come with practice. It is advisable to fill the bag only half full. This will make tilting the bag and controlling the flow of the soft mix easier.
3. It is important to have the soup nuts in a uniform size. This will prevent burning and uneveness of color.
4. Bake the soup nuts 400°F. and keep them a light, golden color if possible.

PALM LEAVES

Palm leaves made from puff-pastry dough are also commonly known as "pig's ears." While they are a little more time-consuming in the makeup and baking they add to variety. When made in miniature form palm leaves are often sold as a variety with other cookies.

Procedures to Follow (Figs. 256–258)

1. Sprinkle a clean, dry portion of the bench with granulated sugar. Do not use confectionery or fine berry sugar for they are readily absorbed by the dough and may cause sticking and lumping of sugar.
2. Roll the conditioned puff-pastry dough into an oblong form using the sugar to dust the top as well as the bottom of the dough in place

of the flour. For regular size units the dough should be about $^1/_4$ in. thick. For miniature leaves the dough should be about $^1/_{16}$ in. thick. Sprinkle additional sugar over the top surface of the dough if the dough feels sticky or tacky.

3. Make a slight impression in the form of a line running lengthwise through the center of the rolled dough. This is to be used as a guide. Fold each end of the dough three times toward the center. You now have three folds or layers of dough side by side. Fold one side over the top of the other and you now have six layers of dough held together by one side of the rolled dough. Be sure the strip is of even thickness.

4. Slice into pieces $^1/_2$ in. thick with a knife or sharp-edged scraper.

5. Place the pieces on a greased pan with the flat side up. In other words each piece is a cross section of the six-layered strip with three layers on each side of the top fold of dough. Space the units about 2 in. apart to allow for spreading during baking. The bottom folds of each unit may be spread apart slightly to prevent the units from turning over during baking.

6. Bake at approximately 400°F. after the units have been allowed to relax for about 30 min.

7. When the bottoms of the units have turned a golden brown, turn the units over with a bowl knife and return to the oven for a few minutes. This will allow better caramelization of the sugar and result in a better gloss and appearance. Be careful not to burn your fingers.

8. Wash the units with syrup wash immediately upon removal from the oven. The tops of the units may be sprinkled lightly with pistachio nuts as soon as they are glazed with hot syrup wash.

FIG. 256. FOLD BOTH ENDS TO CENTER

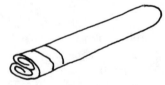

FIG. 257. FOLD ONE SIDE OVER THE OTHER

FIG. 258. TOP VIEW OF CUT SLICE OF PALM LEAF

PIN WHEELS

Pin wheels or stars made from puff-pastry dough vary according to shape and the kind of fruit and other fillings used. The matter of careful cutting and shaping of the dough is of great importance. Uniformity of size is equally important.

Procedures to Follow (Figs. 259–261)

1. Roll out the conditioned puff-pastry dough into an oblong shape about $1/8$ in. thick.
2. Cut the dough into squares of 4–5 in. The size may vary with production policy, but all pieces should be of equal size.
3. Starting from the corner of each square make a diagonal cut to about 1 in. from the center. There should be four cuts in each square of dough with a circle of 1 to $1^1/_2$ in. in the center of the square of dough that is not cut. This may be done with a pastry wheel without moving any of the squares of dough.
4. Grasp the right side of the cut edge corner, fold the point into the center of the square, and press the point in gently.
5. Repeat this until all four corner points are pressed into the center. This will form a pinwheel or star effect.
6. Place the stars on a greased or paper-lined pan and press the centers of the stars down to form a hollow effect. Do not press too hard for this will tear the dough and expose the pan or paper.

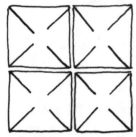

FIG. 259. ROLL OUT DOUGH EVENLY AND CUT WITH PASTRY WHEEL

FIG. 260. FOLD ALTERNATE POINTS TO THE CENTER AND PRESS DOWN GENTLY TO MAKE THE BORDER

FIG. 261. FINISHED PIN WHEEL

7. Egg-wash the units and allow to rest 20 min. Fill the center of each star with fruit filling and bake at 400°F. The stars may be washed and dipped into sugar before panning. Struessel or nuts may also be used for variety.

8. If the stars are to be filled after baking be sure the centers are pressed down very well to prevent formation of peaked or high centers. If this does happen depress the baked centers while they are hot and then fill with the desired filling. If pinwheels are to be dusted with confectionery sugar dust them before applying the filling.

SUGAR PRETZELS

Sugar pretzels made from puff-pastry dough are an attractive variety product. These may be made combining puff-pastry dough with chocolate short dough for contrast. Sugar pretzels may also be made in miniature form for variety and sold as cookies. The use of different jams, jellies, and other fillings will add further variety.

Procedures to Follow (Figs. 262–265)

1. Roll the puff-pastry dough into an oblong shape about 12 in. wide and about $1/4$ in. thick. Be sure the dough is of even thickness.

2. Remove the excess flour and spread the entire piece of dough with jam, jelly, or other filling. Sprinkle half of the dough (lengthwise) with cake crumbs, ground nuts, and cinnamon sugar. Fold the top half of the dough over the bottom half and roll the dough gently with the rolling pin to be sure the filling sticks to the jam or jelly.

FIG. 262.   ROLL AND CUT DOUGH INTO STRIPS

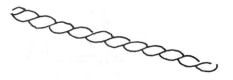

FIG. 263.   TWIST THE STRIPS

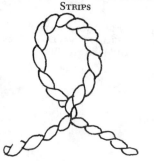

FIG. 264.   TWIST STRIPS

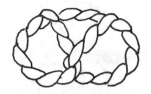

FIG. 265.   SHAPE INTO PRETZEL

3. Cut the long strip of dough with the sandwiched filling into strips about $1/2$ in. wide. Be sure the strips are of even size and weight.
4. Twist each of the strips as you would when making snails.
5. Grasp each end of the strip and cross one end over the other. Now press each of the crossed ends into the strip of dough.
6. Dip the shaped pretzels into a pan with granulated sugar and place on a greased or parchment-paper-lined pan.
7. Allow the units to rest for $1/2$ hr. and bake at 385°F. until crisp. Do not wash or ice the pretzels.

If Chocolate Short Dough is Used as a Filler (Fig. 266)

1. Roll the puff-pastry dough out in oblong shape about $1/8$ in. thick.
2. Spread a thin film of jelly or jam over the surface of the dough.
3. Roll the short dough out about $1/4$ in. thick into an oblong shape half as wide as the puff-pastry dough but of the same length.
4. Roll the short dough on a small rolling pin and then unroll on top of the lower half of the puff-pastry dough.
5. Fold the top half of the puff-pastry dough over the bottom and this will give you three layers of dough (two layers puff pastry and one short dough).
6. Make pretzels as above.

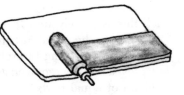

Fig. 266. Chocolate Cookie Dough Placed on Puff-Pastry Dough as a Filling

CREAM ROLL

Cream roll shells made from puff-pastry dough are very popular and profitable items, though they are time-consuming in makeup and require special attention. Cream rolls are also made from a blend of equal parts of pie crust dough and short dough, but the procedures described below are based on puff-pastry dough.

Procedures to Follow for Cream Roll Shells (Figs. 267 and 268)

1. The cream roll sticks should be clean and well-greased.
2. Roll out the dough into an oblong form about $1/8$ in. thick.
3. Cut the dough into strips about 1 in. wide.
4. Wash the tops of the cut strips with egg-wash.
5. Hold the stick (metal tube) at the wide end and grasp the strip of dough so that the floured or bottom part of the strip is placed on

the greased part of the stick. Make one complete turn so that the egg-washed part of the strip covers the first circle of dough. Continue to wind the dough about the stick at a 45° angle so that a spiral effect is formed. Break off and seal the spiral of dough $1/2$ to 1 in. from the top of the stick.

6. Dip the top of the dough into granulated sugar and place on a greased or parchment-paper-lined pan. Be sure the sugar faces up.

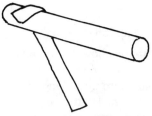

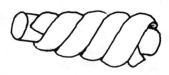

FIG. 267. ROLL STRIP OF DOUGH ON TUBE WITH WASHED SIDE UP

FIG. 268. ROLLED-UP CREAM ROLL

7. Bake at 385°F. The shells are considered baked when they feel light and crisp. Remove one of the shells from the stick to test the bake of the inside of the cream roll.

8. While the rolls are still mildly warm remove from sticks by tapping the narrow end of the cream roll stick on the bench. If the rolls stick this is largely due to the fact that excess egg-wash was used and stuck to the metal. It might also be due to excess sugar or unclean sticks. Heating the rolls if they stick may help to loosen them and they should be removed at once while hot.

9. A blend of equal parts of pie crust dough and short dough may be used for cream rolls. Cocoa or fudge base may be added for chocolate cream rolls. The dough is mixed well and rolled out about $1/4$ in. thick. The dough is then cut into oblong sections about 5 to 6 in. long and 3 in. wide. The metal sticks are rolled around the dough. Before sealing egg-wash the edge of the dough and remove the excess dough. The sticks may be egg-washed and dipped into chopped nuts before baking or baked plain and iced after baking.

10. When filling the rolls with whipped cream or topping filling, fill half of the roll from each end. This will ensure that the entire roll is filled. Make a slight spiral effect on each end with a pastry bag and tube. The ends may also be dipped in toasted ground nuts, sprinkles, or cake crumbs. Neatness in finishing is most important.

CREAM CHEESE PRODUCTS—*Rugelach, Pockets, and Snecks*

Cream cheese dough, as the name implies, is made with cream cheese with added fat (butter) and flour as the basic ingredients. Of course small amounts of sugar, salt, and flavor are added. This is a rich dough with the characteristics of a combination of a rich cookie dough and a pastry dough. While the recipe appears simple special care must be used in preparing the dough and handling the dough during makeup.

Cream Cheese Dough Yield°

Ingredients	Lb.	Oz.	Mixing procedure
Cream cheese	3	..	Blend the cream cheese until it is medium
Butter or margarine	3	..	hard and plastic. Do the same with the butter. Blend the two together
Salt	..	1	Add and blend into the cheese and fat
Confectionery sugar	..	10	
Vanilla	..	1	
Bread flour	3	..	Add the flour in a slow speed and blend to a smooth dough

° Made up into miniatures and sold by weight rather than unit.

Procedures to Follow

1. Place the dough on the bench and form into a rectangle. Allow the dough to rest 10 to 15 min.
2. Roll out the dough three times and give a four-fold turn and refrigerate. Allow the dough to relax between rolls. Cover the dough after the final roll and refrigerate overnight or for several hours. This will allow the dough to condition itself.
3. The units—Rugelach, horns, snecks, or small pockets—are made up the same way as miniature Danish are made. Roll out the dough 1/8 in. thick.
4. For *Rugelach* and *snecks* wash the rolled-out dough with melted butter, sprinkle with raisins, chopped nuts, cake crumbs, and cinnamon sugar. Roll the filling lightly with a rolling pin using gentle pressure.
5. For the *horns* cut into triangles about 3 in. long and 1 in. wide and roll up. Line the horns up neatly on the bench and then flatten gently with the palms of the hands. Wash the tops of the horns with melted butter and sprinkle with chopped nuts.
6. For *snecks* roll and fill the dough the same as for horns. Roll into tight rolls about 1 in. in diameter. Cut into slices about 1/4 in. wide and place on pans spaced about 1/2 in. apart. Wash the tops with melted butter and sprinkle with nuts and sugar.

7. For *pockets* roll out the dough as for the above and cut into squares, with the pastry wheel, about $1^{1}/_{2}$ in. square. Fill the squares with cheese filling, prune filling, or jam. Fold over once so that you have a diamond shape. Line up the open pockets, flatten slightly, and wash with melted butter. Sprinkle the tops of the pockets with ground nuts.

8. It is important to allow the madeup cream cheese units to relax at least $^{1}/_{2}$ hr. before baking. Bake at 350°F. until light brown and crisp.

HOMINTASHEN (TRIANGULAR COOKIES)

Homintashen are triangular cookies made principally from a short dough or cookie dough. They are also made from a rich sweet yeast dough at special holiday times of the year. The filling used in these cookies may vary from prune (the most popular) to poppy filling or a filling made of jam, ground nuts, cake crumbs and spices. Short dough used for cake bottoms or short dough used for short-bread cookies may also be used. The recipe for cake bottoms using short dough is reproduced.

Short Dough (Cake Bottoms and Cookies)

Yield: 225 $2^{1}/_{2}$–3-in. cookie bottoms

Ingredients	Lb.	Oz.	Mixing procedure
Sugar	3	..	Blend all ingredients until soft and smooth. Do not cream until light
Salt	..	$^{3}/_{4}$	
Milk powder	..	2	
Shortening	3	..	
Glucose	..	4	
Eggs	1	..	Add the eggs in two stages and blend in very well
Water	1	..	Add and stir in lightly
Vanilla	..	1	
Cake flour	3	..	Sift, add, and fold in lightly until the flour is absorbed. The dough should appear sticky. It is worked smooth on the bench
Bread flour	3	..	
Baking powder	..	$^{1}/_{2}$	

Procedures to Follow (Figs. 269–270)

1. Place the dough on a pan or container and chill before using.
2. Before rolling out the chilled dough place the dough on a floured canvas or cloth and work mildly until the dough is smooth. Do not

overwork; it will toughen the dough. Scrap dough or leftover short dough may be worked in with the fresh dough for cake bottoms.

3. Roll out the cookie dough about $1/8$ in. thick. Cut out round circles with a cookie cutter. The size of the cutter is determined by the size and cost of the Homintash. Remove excess dough from between the circles of dough.

4. Place the filling in the center of the cookie. Do not use too much filling because this will make it difficult to shape and close the edges of the dough.

5. The Homintash is shaped by squeezing the edges of the dough into a triangular shape. Try to have each seam of the triangle of equal size so that the shape is uniform.

6. Place the cookies on paper-lined pans. They may be egg-washed or left plain. Bake the cookies at 385°F.

FIG. 269. CIRCLE OF COOKIE DOUGH WITH PRUNE, POPPY, OR OTHER FILLING

FIG. 270. EDGES OF DOUGH PRESSED TOGETHER WITH FILLING SHOWING

FRUIT TARTS AND FRUIT CAKES

Fruit tarts and fruit cakes require a short dough, pie dough, or combination dough of pie crust and short dough. These doughs serve as the shell or support of the fruit and, in some cases, the top. The dough referred to for tarts and fruit cakes in this unit is the basic short dough used for the bottoms of cheese cakes and other rich cakes.

Procedures to Follow for Fruit Tarts (Figs. 271 and 272)

1. Be sure the tart pans, scalloped-edged or plain-edged, are clean. It is not necessary to grease them for the short dough is rich.

2. On a cloth dusted with patent flour roll out a piece of short dough about 2 ft. wide and 3 ft. long. Be sure the dough is about $1/4$ in. thick and of equal thickness.

3. Space the tart pans on the bench so that they are set neatly into rows about eight across and twelve long. Of course, the size of the tart pan will determine the amount you set up in the space indicated.

4. Dust the top of the rolled-out short dough lightly with patent flour. Place a thin rolling pin at the top of the dough and roll up the dough gently on the thin rolling pin. Be sure that you have about 1 in. of rolling pin free and clear on either end.

5. Lift the rolled up dough and unroll very gently over the tops of the tart pans so that the dough sinks slightly over the tops of the tarts. Where the dough does not cover roll out the scrap and some fresh dough and patch those tarts which have been partially covered or not covered at all.

6. With a ball of short dough about 2 in. in diameter (depending on the size of the tart pan) press each tart pan gently. Dust the ball of dough with bread flour so that it does not stick when the dough is depressed into the tart pans.

7. Roll over the tops of the tart pans with a rolling pin. Do this gently so that the short dough is cut. Remove each tart pan and trim the excess dough from the sides. You may also add a patch of dough to a part that has cracked and the pan exposed. Remove all excess dough.

8. Fill the tart pans with fruit filling that has already been prepared. Fill the pans about three-fourths full. Do not fill to the brim. Place the tart pans on a large sheet pan and bake at 400° to 415°F.

9. Allow the tarts to cool and remove by squeezing the sides of the tart pan gently and turning the tart over. Place the tarts in paper cupcake liners.

Note: Special aluminum foil tart pans are available. These may be filled about one-fourth full with yellow cake or sponge mix and baked. After baking, custard and fruit are added and the tarts finished by adding additional fruit such as bananas, peaches, and other fresh fruits, glazing the top with apricot coating and garnishing the edges with sponge cake crumbs or toasted nuts. These tarts remain in the pans.

FIG. 271. TART SHELL

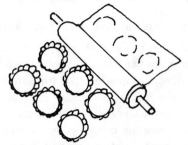

FIG. 272. PLACING ROLLED-OUT DOUGH ON SHELLS

Procedures to Follow for Fruit Cakes (Figs. 273–276)

1. Large-pan fruit cakes require baking the short dough bottom first.
2. The sides of the pan are then lined with short dough which has been rolled out on the bench into strips 1/2 in. round and pressed against the sides of the pan.
3. Fill the pans with fruit about three-fourths full (apple filling can be filled almost to the top). Cover the top by rolling out the short dough 1/4 in. thick, rolling up on the rolling pin, and then covering the fruit cake. Smaller fruit cakes that are made in layer pans, varying in size from 6 to 8 in., do not require that the bottom be baked first.
4. The entire pan (bottom and sides) is covered with short dough like a pie. Be sure that the dough is filled in around the bottom edges to avoid air pockets and that the dough is pressed against the sides of the pan.
5. Remove the excess dough by rolling over the edges with a thin rolling pin. The amount of filling varies with the type and purpose of the fruit cake. For example, cakes that are to have slices of fruit on top, such as sliced apples, require less filling. Cakes that are to be finished with fresh fruit or canned fruits such as strawberries or peaches also take less filling. The topping fruit requires space.
6. Cakes that are to be finished with whipped cream also take less filling. The tops of these cakes, large or small, may also be finished with a lattice effect, covered completely with short dough, stippled, and egg-washed, or they may be sprinkled with Struessel or crumb topping.
7. Bake these cakes at 400° to 415°F. Do not bake in a cool oven for the fruit filling will tend to run out and the color of the crust will be pale.

FIG. 273. TRIM EDGE WITH ROLLING PIN

FIG. 274. COVERED FRUIT CAKE

FIG. 275. LATTICE-TOP FRUIT CAKE

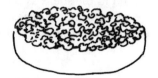

FIG. 276. STRUESSEL TOP

NESSELRODE PIE

This pie is a light, chiffon variety. There are two separate ways of preparing the filling for this pie; the Bavarian method and the egg-white chiffon method. In either method, the important factor to remember is careful use of diced, glazed fruits which have been mixed with rum flavor of excellent quality. There are special prepared mixes which can be used by merely following the instructions on the label. These come in powdered form with the rum-flavored fruits in a separate package.

Nesselrode Pie Filling   **Yield:** 12 8-in. pies
     (Chiffon Type) (3 qt.)

Ingredients	Lb.	Oz.	Mixing procedure
Sugar	1	4	Place on the fire and stir well to dissolve the
Salt	..	$1/4$	milk powder. Bring to a boil, stirring to pre-
Milk powder	..	12	vent scorching
Water (cool)	5	..	
Eggs (part yolks)	1	8	Whip the eggs slightly
Corn starch	..	9	Dissolve the starch and add to the whipped
Water	1	..	eggs. Add to the boiling milk in a steady stream and boil. Stir constantly
Butter	..	6	Remove from fire and stir in the butter until dissolved
Gelatine	..	1	Dissolve the gelatine and stir into the above
Water	..	12	
Egg whites	1	8	Whip to a wet peak
Sugar	..	8	
Mixed fruit	1	8	Add the fruit and the whites and fold in
Rum flavor	..	1	lightly with a wire whip until the whites are incorporated evenly. Pour into the baked pie shells

Notes on Filling (Fig. 277)

1. Have the baked pie shells ready for the filling. The filling must be placed in the shells as soon as prepared for this filling sets up quickly.
2. Be sure the egg whites are whipped to a soft peak. A firm peak will cause overmixing and loss of volume when trying to incorporate.

FIG. 277. NESSELRODE PIE

3. Allow the pies to cool and refrigerate. When cold, cover the tops of pies with whipped cream, whipped topping, or a blend of both. Sprinkle the top of the cream topping with shaved sweet chocolate or chocolate swirls.

Procedure for Bavarian-Type Filling

1. To every 3 qt. of regular baker's custard (p. 268) used for Napoleons, cream puffs, etc. which has been chilled, add $1^1/_2$ qt. heavy whipped cream. This will result in about 4 qt. whipped cream or topping.
2. Place the custard in the machine and mix smooth at low speed.
3. Place the whipped cream or topping and the mixed fruit and rum flavor in the machine and mix lightly with a wire whip until the cream and fruit are blended in.
4. Deposit the filling into the baked shells and top as the above.

BOSTON CREAM PIE

Boston cream pie is actually a light cake baked in a pie shell which is cooled after baking and filled with baker's custard, Frenched custard, or whipped cream. A filling or fruit may be used with the custard and pineapple or lemon filling is recommended.

Procedures to Follow for Frenched Custard (3 qt. custard base)

1. Place the chilled custard (3 qt. cooked) in the mixing machine and slowly whip until smooth. Three pounds of light, neutral butter-cream are added in three stages to the custard and whipped in carefully. Do not use high speed which might cause the custard to separate and curdle.
2. The same amount of custard may be mixed with 1 qt. cream that has been whipped and folded in. This is the Bavarian type of custard. Fold in gently to avoid separation.

Procedures to Follow for Boston Cream Pie (Fig. 278)

1. Chill the cakes baked in pie tins. A sponge cake mix of good quality is best suited for this type of cake since it is delicate in nature. Be sure to grease and dust the tin.
2. If the tops of the pie are to be iced it is best to ice them before slicing the cake. This makes it easier to handle the cake later on. Ice the tops with fondant icing or fudge icing. Allow the icing to dry and then gently cut through the center. Place the tops to one side.

3. If fruit or other filling is to be used fill the bottom parts lightly with the pineapple or lemon filling. With a pastry bag cover the bottom part about $1/2$ in. from the edge with the French or Bavarian custard. Pipe a neat border about $1/2$ in. high around the edge of the pie and place the iced top of the pie on top of the filling.

4. The top of the pie may be left plain and later dusted with confectionery sugar. These pies should be refrigerated.

FIG. 278.   BOSTON CREAM PIE

STRUDEL

Strudel is a very popular pastry but requires skill and know-how in the makeup of its various types. Strudel types add to product variety and are important items in retail bakeshops as well as restaurants and hotels. This unit provides the wherewithal to enable you to make the dough, prepare the fillings, and make and bake the strudel. The quality and variety of the strudel depends upon the quality and variations of the filling. Except for the puff-pastry type, the strudel dough used for the varieties indicated in this unit is the one given below.

Strudel Dough   **Yield:**   4 units for medium 4 × 6 table

Ingredients	Lb.	Oz.	Mixing procedure
Water	2	..	Dissolve the dry ingredients in the water and
Sugar	..	3	the oil and eggs
Salt	..	$1/2$	
Eggs	..	4	
Oil	..	6	
Bread flour (high-gluten)	3	4	Sift, add the flour, and develop well to a smooth dough

Procedures to Follow for Apple Strudel (Figs. 279–281)

1. Be sure the dough is well developed. Place the dough on a floured bench and divide into two or three parts, depending upon the size of the bench or table to be used for stretching or pulling the dough.

2. Shape the dough into oblongs with a smooth surface as for pan bread. Place the dough pieces in rectangular bread pans which have been well brushed with oil. A small amount of excess oil should

be left at the bottom of the pan. This will make removal of the relaxed dough easier. Brush the top of the dough with oil to prevent
crustation. A crust will cause tearing of the dough when it is pulled.
It will also cause thick streaks of dough if it does not tear.

3. The dough may be allowed to relax for 1 hr. at shop temperature or
placed in the refrigerator overnight. This dough may be refrigerated
for several days and used.

4. Cover the bench or table with a canvas cloth or other straight cloth
and dust the cloth with bread flour to prevent the dough from sticking.

5. Remove the dough with both hands and stretch between the hands
before allowing the dough to rest on the cloth. Starting from the
center of the dough grasp the opposite edges of the dough and
stretch the dough gently by lifting the edges of the dough slightly
and pulling toward the outside of the cloth. Remember to lift
gently and pull toward the outside of the cloth and toward the
extreme edges of the table. Allow the dough to relax a bit if it tends
to resist pulling or springs back too much after it is pulled. Keep
stretching the dough until the entire cloth and table is covered. At
this point the dough should be transparent. Sprinkle the top of the
dough with melted butter or oil. This will prevent excessive cracking
when the strudel is rolled.

   Note: The filling and other necessary materials should be ready so
   that the dough does not dry excessively.

6. In the making of apple and cheese strudel line the top 4 in. of the
dough with about $1/4$ in. of light cake crumbs. If the crumbs are
too dry a small amount of melted butter or oil should be rubbed
into them.

7. Canned, solid pack apples or fresh-cured apples may be used. A
blend of equal amounts of both types is often used. Place the apples
in a firm line about $1^1/_2$ to 2 in. thick across the top of the crumbs
sprinkled at the top of the stretched dough. Sprinkle the apples with
cinnamon sugar. The amount of sugar depends upon the taste of
the apples.

8. Sprinkle the remainder of the dough lightly with cake crumbs,
toasted chopped nuts, and raisins.

9. With a pastry wheel remove the thick edges of the dough at the sides
and top. The bottom edge is removed after the strudel is rolled up.

10. Fold over the top of the dough over the apples. Be careful not
to tear. Grasp the edges of the cloth with both hands and roll up
sections of the strudel as you would for jelly roll. About 2 in. from
the bottom tighten the roll by lifting gently and stretching the dough

by rolling the strudel. This will tighten the roll. If the dough is dry and tends to crack omit this step.

11. Even the thickness of the strudel roll by lifting and stretching or lifting and pushing together so that the thickness of the roll is equal throughout. Hold the roll between palms of the hand while doing this.

12. Allow the dough to relax and cut the strudel into desired slices or lengths. Place the strudel on a clean, well-oiled pan close together in even lines. Egg-wash the top of the strudel for a shiny crust. Wash the top of the strudel with melted butter or fat for a home-made effect.

13. Bake the strudel in a hot oven 425° to 435°F. until brown. Egg-washed strudel is then washed with hot syrup or boiled honey. Butter-washed strudel (very often used for cheese strudel) is allowed to cool and then dusted with confectionery sugar.

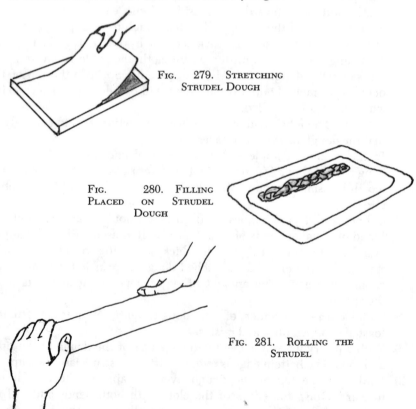

Fig.   279.   Stretching
Strudel Dough

Fig.   280.   Filling
Placed   on   Strudel
Dough

Fig. 281.   Rolling the
Strudel

Cheese Strudel Filling

Yield: 2 strips 2 in. thick and 6 ft. long

Ingredients	Lb.	Oz.	Mixing procedure
Baker's cheese	5	..	Blend the ingredients in this stage to a
Sugar	1	8	smooth consistency
Salt	..	1	
Cake flour	..	8	
Butter or shortening	..	8	
Eggs (half yolks)	1	8	Add the eggs in three stages and blend well
Raisins	..	12	Fold in the raisins and flavor
Vanilla or rind of two fresh lemons	..	1	

Procedures to Follow for Cheese Strudel (Fig. 282)

1. Prepare the dough and sprinkle with cake crumbs and chopped nuts as for apple strudel.
2. Roll the cheese in chopped nuts or flour on a separate part of the bench. Roll to about $1^1/_2$ in. in diameter. Place in strips on the cake crumbs. Dust the rest of the dough with crumbs and nuts.
3. Follow the same procedure for rolling up the strudel as for apple strudel.
4. Place the strudel in long strips (the width of the pan) and wash with melted butter. Oil the pan and bake as for apple strudel. Dust with confectionery sugar when cool.

Note: The strudel may be cut into individual slices before baking. This may allow some of the cheese to run slightly while baking. Common practice is to cut the strudel after it is baked and cooled with a sharp knife that is dipped in hot water between each slice. This makes a smooth slice effect. It may cause slight cracking but the dusted sugar will cover the mild cracks.

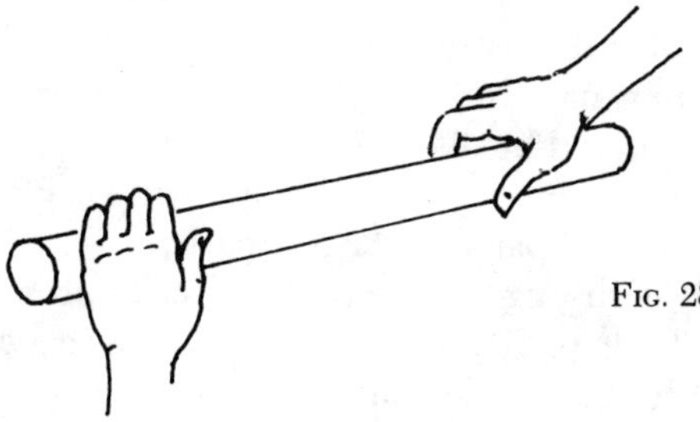

FIG. 282. ROLLING CHEESE FILLING

Fruit Strudel Filling

Yield: 10 thin strips of 1 in.
diameter

Ingredients	Lb.	Oz.	Mixing procedure
Raisins	10	..	Grind the dried fruit through a coarse
Glazed cherries	3	..	grinder. Grind the nuts last to remove any
Mixed diced fruit	2	..	fruit left in the grinder. A piece of stale
Orange peel	1	..	cake may be ground after the nuts
Walnuts or filberts	3	..	
Raspberry jam	2	..	Blend the jam with the ground fruit
Cake crumbs			Add sufficient cake crumbs to make the mix
(enough to stiffen mix)			medium stiff and easily handled

Other jams or jellies may be added for variety or to thin or stretch the fruit mix. Additional cake crumbs will take up softness or slack.

Procedures to Follow for Fruit Strudel

1. Stretch the strudel dough as for apple or cheese strudel.
2. Sprinkle the top of the dough with enough toasted ground nuts and cake crumbs to support the fruit filling.
3. Roll out the filling into strips 1 in. in diameter. Use ground nuts or cake crumbs to prevent the filling from sticking to the bench. Place the filling across the dough on top of the nuts and roll up so that at least three to four rolls of dough are formed from each piece of pulled dough.
4. Place the strips together and cut into small slices with a knife or bench scraper. Place in straight rows on an oiled pan, egg-wash, and bake at 400°F. Wash with syrup after baking. The strips may be egg-washed and sprinkled with nuts and sugar before baking. This will be the final finish and no syrup wash is used after baking.

Procedures to Follow for Puff-Pastry Strudel (Figs. 283 and 284)

1. Roll out a rectangular piece of puff-pastry dough into a rectangular shape about the width of a bun pan and as long as the size of the dough will allow. The dough should be about $1/8$ in. thick.
2. Cut the dough, after trimming the edges, into 4-in. wide strips. Place the strips on a paper-lined or greased pan about 2 in. apart.
3. Wash the edges of the strips with egg-wash. Sprinkle cake crumbs and/or nuts in the center of the strip. Place a row of apples or cheese on the crumbs as you would for strudel leaving the washed edges of the dough free and without crumbs or nuts on the edges.

4. Roll out a similar piece of puff-pastry dough into the same shape but slightly thinner than the dough used for the bottoms. Cut this dough into strips about 6 in. wide. Fold each strip in half so that it is now 3 in. wide and of the same length. With a bench scraper make cuts about 2 in. deep across the folded edge and space the cuts about $3/4$ in. apart. Open the folds to its original shape. Pick up each strip and place it evenly over each of the filled strips and seal the edges well. The egg-wash will keep the strips together. Remove the excess or uneven edges of dough with a scraper or pastry wheel.

5. Egg-wash the top and sprinkle with nuts and sugar. Bake at 400°F. until brown and crisp. Be careful not to underbake.

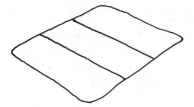

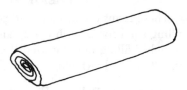

Fig. 283. Rolled Out and Cut Dough for Pastry Strudel Bottoms

Fig. 284. Filled Pastry Strudel

FRUIT-FILLED OBLONGS

Fruit-filled oblongs, cheese rolls, poppy horns, and miniatures add to puff-pastry variety and allow a wider display and greater consumer attraction. They are especially important to the baker during the warm months of the year, when they make excellent substitutes for perishable cream goods. The makeup and finish of these specialties may be varied.

Procedures to Follow

1. Roll out the conditioned puff-pastry dough and divide the dough the same way you did for the turnovers.

2. Wash the edges lightly with water or egg-wash and place the varied fruit filling in the center. The filling should be slightly thicker than for pies to allow ease in handling and prevent excessive running.

3. Fold the dough directly over the fruit to about $1/4$ in. from the edge of the square of dough and press down firmly. Fold the dough over so that the $1/4$-in. dough and seam of the pressed dough are in the center bottom of the folded oblong. Press the outside edges of the oblong with the outer side of the palm to seal the edges. Line the units up on a clean portion of the bench. Trim uneven edges off with a pastry wheel, knife, or scraper. This will make them all even in size. Stipple the centers of each unit.

4. The oblongs of pastry may be finished by washing the tops with egg-wash and dipping the tops in granulated sugar. The tops may be egg-washed and strips of puff-pastry dough about $1/4$ in. wide may be placed diagonally across as you would for a lattice-type effect. Two strips are sufficient. Egg-wash the strips after they have been placed on the oblong.

5. Place on parchment-paper-lined pans and rest for about $1/2$ hr. Bake at 400°F. to a golden brown color. Those dipped in sugar are left as is. Those that have been egg-washed and crossed with strips of dough are washed with simple syrup upon removal from the oven. They may also be striped across with simple icing when almost cool.

CHEESE ROLLS (OBLONG SHAPE)

These items are often called puff-pastry cheese strudel. Regular cheese filling used for Danish pastry and variety buns may be used as the filling. A richer filling may be used if desired by adding egg yolks and butter to the filling and reducing the amount of milk or water in the mix.

Procedures to Follow (Figs. 285–290)

1. Roll out the puff-pastry dough into a rectangular shape about $1/8$ in. thick. The dough should be thin to allow crispness and avoid a soggy interior after baking.

2. Cut the dough with a pastry wheel into long strips about 4 in. wide. Wash the edges of the strips of dough with water or egg-wash.

3. Sprinkle the center of the strips of dough with light cake crumbs and cinnamon sugar.

4. Dust a portion of the bench with bread flour and roll out the cheese filling in the flour to round strips about 1 in. in diameter. Lift portions of the cheese strips and place directly on the cake crumbs in the center of the strip of dough.

5. Fold over the dough so that the cheese filling is covered and press the edges of dough together to seal the dough ends. Fold over so that the sealed edge is at the bottom. Place each of the strips alongside each other and flatten slightly with palms of the hands.

FIG. 285. PASTRY DOUGH ROLLED INTO RECTANGULAR SHAPE

FIG. 286. ROLL OUT CHEESE FILLING 1 IN. IN DIAMETER

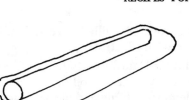

FIG. 287. PLACE CHEESE ON PASTRY
DOUGH

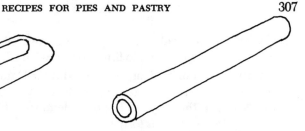

FIG. 288. ROLL UP AND SEAL THE
EDGE

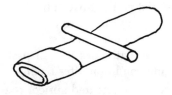

FIG. 289. MAKE DEPRESSIONS WITH
THIN ROLLING PIN AT 4 IN. SPACES
AND CUT THROUGH WITH PASTRY
WHEEL

FIG. 290. STIPPLE UNIT AND WASH
WITH BUTTER. TOP MAY BE
SPRINKLED WITH STREUSSEL OR OTHER
TOPPING

6. With a very thin rolling pin make depressions spaced about 4 in. apart. With a pastry wheel or knife cut through where the depression has been made. The depression made with the rolling pin will seal the edges of the units.

7. Stipple the units while on the bench and wash with melted butter. Bake at 400°F. until golden brown. The tops may also be garnished with sliced nuts or Struessel topping after they have been washed with the melted butter. These units are dusted lightly with confectionery sugar after they have been baked and cooled.

POPPY HORNS

Variety may be extended in the making of horns by using different fillings. For example, the poppy butter spread may be replaced with the use of raspberry jam, apricot jam, prune filling, and others.

Procedures to Follow (Figs. 291–294)

1. Roll out the puff-pastry dough into a rectangular shape about $1/8$ in. thick.

2. Spread half of the surface of the dough with poppy filling. Sprinkle the top of the filling with toasted, chopped nuts, cake crumbs, and cinnamon sugar. Any of the other fillings may be used and covered the same way.

3. Fold the uncovered part of the dough over the filled part and roll gently with a rolling pin to firm the sandwich effect.

4. Cut the dough into triangles as you did for Danish pastry horns. The size of the triangles is based upon the desired size. Roll up the units by starting at the base. It is advisable to stretch the end of the dough so that a tighter horn is formed.

5. Line up the horns on a clean portion of the bench. Flatten them slightly and trim off large ends so that all horns are equal. Wash the tops with egg-wash and place on paper-lined pans. Space about 2 in. apart to allow for spread during baking. Allow the horns to relax for about $1/2$ to 1 hr. and bake at 390°F. until brown and crisp. Horns require a longer baking period than do the flat types of puff-pastry products. This will avoid a raw or gummy condition after baking.

6. The horns may be washed with heated syrup and heated apricot coating, or hot honey which has been boiled. After the honey or apricot wash has been applied the horns may be sprinkled with ground filberts.

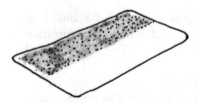

FIG. 291. ROLL DOUGH INTO RECTANGULAR SHAPE. SPREAD POPPY FILLING OR OTHER FILLING OVER HALF THE DOUGH

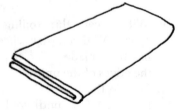

FIG. 292. FOLD FILLED DOUGH IN HALF

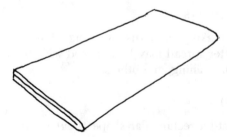

FIG. 293. ROLL OUT THE DOUGH GENTLY

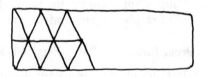

FIG. 294. CUT INTO TRIANGLES AND ROLL INTO HORNS AS FOR DANISH

PUFF-PASTRY MINIATURES

Miniatures made from puff-pastry dough will add to the variety of cookies and other small units sold by the pound. Common varieties are open pockets filled with cheese, prune filling, chopped apples, and other fillings; small pigs' ears; filled horns; turnovers; pretzels; and others. A sense of proportion and ingenuity is required. Remember the following factors when making these miniatures.

Procedures to Follow

1. The dough must be rolled thin and the sizes cut small. A miniature unit should weigh about $1/4$ oz.
2. It is important that all the miniatures of one variety be the same size.
3. Makeup of the units must be done with care for uniformity and appearance.
4. Miniatures are generally baked at 400°F. to a crisp state.

CHAPTER 27

Cake Mixing Methods

Many an excellent recipe has been condemned by bakers because the end product was poor. Ordinarily, little thought is given by the baker that he might have been wrong in how he handled the recipe. The recipe represents only the raw materials. Knowing how to mix them is another matter. This chapter presents the various methods of mixing, and illustrates the type of cake for which each method is used.

Proper mixing of cakes is supposed to accomplish the following purposes: (1) achieve a uniform and complete mixture of all the ingredients in the mix or recipe; (2) form and incorporate air cells, the amount depending upon the method of mixing suited to the recipe; and (3) develop a desirable grain and texture in the baked product.

THE SUGAR-SHORTENING OR CREAMING METHOD

In this method the sugar and shortening are blended together first and then creamed by additional mixing. During this stage small air cells are formed and then incorporated into the mix. The mix takes on added volume and becomes softer in consistency. The exact time for proper creaming at this stage is controlled by several factors, one of the most important of which is the temperature of the shortening or fat. Shortening or fat that is cold must first be brought to a temperature of 70°F. before the best creaming potential will be achieved. In other words, cold shortening is not sufficiently plastic to incorporate quickly and hold air cells. This applies to butter and margarine as well. Therefore, cold fats require a longer mixing time for maximum creaming. By the same token fats that are warm (above 75°F.) will not be able to hold as much air, nor give as much volume, because they are soft and cannot tolerate the friction of the machine and constant mixing. The temperature of the shop is another factor. Creaming takes place faster in warm weather than in cold weather. If the shop temperature is affected by seasonal temperatures then allowances must be made for mixing time. The speed of the mixing machine is another factor. Too often, young bakers allow the machine to turn at high speed and find the mix has not creamed properly. Not only does high speed create friction but it also tends to destroy or reduce the number of the air cells that are formed and incorporated during the early stages of mixing. The sugar and shortening are best creamed at medium or second speed until soft and light.

During the second stage the eggs are added in several portions. This does not mean that the eggs are added as soon as they are absorbed by the mix. Very often an inexperienced baker will have the mix curdle before all the eggs are incorporated. The egg contains the albumen or egg white and the yolk. It is the yolk of the egg that contains a fat which coats the surface of the cells formed in creaming and allows the cells to expand and hold the liquid added (egg whites, milk, etc.) without curdling.

Curdling is the result of having more liquid than the fat-coated cells have a capacity to retain. A creamed mix that has been carefully mixed and does not curdle has a water-in-fat solution. Cake mixes that curdle are those in which the water or liquid has been released by the cells and created a fat-in-water emulsion. Adding the eggs too quickly or adding all the other liquid (milk) at once will cause curdling. The addition of a small portion of the flour at the start of the mix will help to eliminate curdling in mixes with high-liquid content. Adding the flour alternately with the liquid when the mix is creamed will also eliminate the tendency to curdle.

THE BLENDING METHOD OF MIXING

This method is used primarily in the making of high-ratio type cakes. In this method, most of the ingredients, including the liquid, are placed at the machine at one time. The machine is allowed to run for 5 to 6 min. in medium speed until the ingredients are blended. The eggs and additional milk are then added and the mix is blended for another period of 4 to 5 min. In this type of mixing air cells are formed and incorporated but there are not as many cells nor do they become as large and extended as they do in the creaming method. It is important to get the ingredients blended properly and to have a smooth mix that is not curdled.

Curdling takes place as a result of improper mixing or the use of unsuitable ingredients. For example, in a high-ratio type mix a high-ratio shortening must be used. This is an emulsified or special fat. This fat enables the cells formed in mixing to hold the large percentage of moisture and sugar without curdling. A regular hydrogenated vegetable shortening will not serve the purpose in this instance. The temperature of the fat or other shortening is important, for example, hard or chilled fat must first be softened or made pliable by mixing before the other ingredients are blended into it. If this is not done the fat will break into brittle pieces which are not dispersed in the liquid of the mix. Because of this, blending does not take place properly. Where high percentages of sugar (140 per cent or more) are used it is best to dissolve the sugar in the liquid and then add it to the mix. This will eliminate the possibility of incomplete blending of the sugar and results in a more tender crust in the baked product.

THE WHIPPING METHOD

This method of mixing is used mostly in the preparation of sponge and angel cakes. It is also used in the whipping of egg whites for meringues, marshmallow-type icing, whipped cream, and chiffon products. Generally, most of the sugar is added to the eggs used in sponge cakes before beginning whipping. In whipping eggs air cells are formed and incorporated into the mix. In fact, in pure sponges these cells effect the entire leavening; no baking powder is used. The eggs and sugar are warmed to about 100°F. before whipping. This softens the egg yolk and allows quicker whipping and greater volume. The egg yolk contains lecithin which surrounds the cells in the foam. This permits a greater number of cells to be formed and the cells contain a larger amount of air. It has been found that an addition of 20 per cent yolks to the whole eggs will improve the foam formation during the whipping of the eggs. For some types of sponge cakes it is advisable to whip the yolks and part of the sugar, then the egg whites and remaining sugar are whipped and the two whipped products combined. This has the added advantage of producing maximum aeration of the foam formed in the whipping of the eggs.

Where large amounts of sugar are used compared to the amount of eggs, part of the sugar is dissolved in the added liquid (water or milk) and then folded in after the eggs have been whipped. For example, if the sugar is above 100 per cent part of it is added later.

In leaner-type sponge cakes, where lesser amounts of eggs are used, the added liquid (water or milk) is added after the eggs are almost completely whipped and the whipping completed. Water should be added in a steady stream while the machine is running and not added after the flour.

In the case of hot milk and butter sponge the milk and butter are heated to about 140°F. and added after the flour has been gently folded in. For the whipped-type cakes, the flour should be sifted and folded in gently, in stages. It is not advisable to add all the flour at once and then mix. Loss of aeration results from mixing too much at one time. This loss of aeration will have an adverse effect on the volume of the resulting product.

When whipping egg whites, as for angel cake, best results and maximum volume are obtained from the egg whites that are cool (60°F.). In this procedure, the whites are whipped slightly to a foam and then the sugar is added in a steady stream while the machine is running. Since a large percentage of sugar is used, not all the sugar is whipped into the whites. This is to prevent an extra load for the whites to carry in formation of the protein foam. Too much sugar prevents maximum aeration in whipping. The additional sugar is sifted with the flour and/or corn starch and then folded in gently.

Egg whites are usually whipped to a wet peak or a dry peak as the recipe requires. For example, when used in cakes such as angel cake or Wonder cake the whites are whipped to a wet peak. For meringue or marshmallow icing, the whites are usually whipped to a dry peak. A wet peak is usually determined by a shiny appearance of the egg white peaks.

Over-whipping or under-whipping are the most common problems in the whipping of eggs. The quality and condition of the eggs are important. A poor grade of eggs cannot be expected to result in maximum aeration. Storage eggs or poor quality egg whites will not result in maximum aeration. Deterioration is very often the cause of poor results. This leads to weakening of the protein in the whites and ability to aerate is lessened. Off-flavors may also result from the use of storage eggs.

Although most bakers whip eggs right from the can or after the eggs have been broken and separated from the shell, the temperature of the eggs has an effect upon the amount of time necessary for greatest aeration. As explained previously, the condition of the yolk and lecithin naturally present determine the speed of whipping. It is for this reason that eggs are warmed. This is doubly important when melted fat is added to the mix. A cool mix may cause the fat to solidify before it is fully mixed in.

The speed of the machine is an important factor. Best results have been obtained by running the machine in high speed until the eggs are about almost completely whipped and then slowing it to second speed for a maximum aeration. Loss in volume may be the result of the mixing at high speed in the final stages. Cells formed may be ruptured by high speed and volume reduced. If necessary, measure and weigh the whipped mix in a quart measure to determine maximum volume. The lower the weight of a quart of the aerated mix the greater the volume obtained.

THE COMBINATION METHOD OF MIXING (CREAMING AND WHIPPING)

Actually this is a combination of two methods. This is very often used in the making of old-fashioned pound cake. The flour and shortening are creamed until soft and light. The eggs and sugar are whipped as for sponge cake. The two are then gently combined by folding the whipped eggs and sugar into the creamed flour and shortening. The maximum aeration is the basic means of leavening; little, if any, other leavening is used. This method is also used in cakes such as Wonder cakes and cheese cakes.

In these types of cakes, care must be exercised in folding in the whites. Overmixing results in the formation of large holes in the cake and uneven grain. Overmixing results in a loss of volume. The whites should be whipped to a wet peak for they are more easily folded in in this condition. If in a dry-peak state, the whites tend to break up into pieces and they are difficult to fold in. This leads to excessive mixing with loss of volume and possible toughness in the mix and resulting product.

The problem of under- or over-mixing is always present. The inexperienced helper must be taught how to determine complete and thorough mixing no matter what the method of mixing may be.

CHAPTER 28

Icings and Toppings

The icing used and the finish of the baked product add to the sales appeal of baked goods. The ordinary bun and the elegant wedding cake both need icings which require special application. Attractiveness of the product, resulting from the icing or topping, are noted before tasting. In fact, a good icing skillfully applied aids in selling the product even if it is not made from expensive ingredients. By the same token the finest of products are often unsold because of improper or poorly applied icing. This chapter is a consideration of the important factors concerning icings and some of the problems common to their preparation and use.

Icings are sweet coverings or coatings in which sugar is the predominant ingredient. The materials used and the manner in which they are mixed determine the type of icing.

Powdered or confectioner's sugar is a highly refined sugar used primarily in the preparation of flat or simple icings, fudge icings, and buttercream icings. A straight method of mixing is used in making them, i.e., the sugar is not boiled before addition. This type of sugar makes smooth icing without the grit of coarser sugars.

Granulated sugar is used primarily in icings in which the sugar is made into a syrup by boiling with water before adding to the other ingredients used in the preparation of the icing. Fondant is an example of this type of icing. In making fondant, the sugar, water, glucose, or corn syrup and invert sugar are boiled to about 238° to 240°F., allowed to cool to 120°F., and then worked into a smooth icing. The fondant is used as is or may be used as a base for the preparation of other types of icings.

Fats

Neutral shortening, emulsified or hydrogenated, is the basic ingredient used in cream-type icings. They are neutral in taste and flavor and blend well with other ingredients in the mixing and flavoring of the icing. Each of these shortenings is used for different icings. The light cream icings (the fudge variety contains approximately 15 per cent fat) are generally made with emulsified shortening. The hydrogenated shortening is generally used for the preparation of buttercream icings (up to 40 per cent fat). Either may be used to provide softness and gloss in other icings.

Butter is used in richer and more expensive icings. High-score sweet butter should be used. In most cases butter is used in conjunction with shortening to reduce the cost as well as to get the maximum volume. Butter cannot be creamed to as great a volume as vegetable shortening.

Chocolate contains considerable fat and contributes to the richness and flavor of icings. This is particularly noticeable in buttercream icings and in fudge-type icings. The cocoa butter in the chocolate contributes to the gloss and keeping qualities of the icing. Cocoa butter and cocoanut fat are used specifically for this purpose in icings. When added to other icings, other than chocolate, they add to the "setting" properties of the icing because of their high melting point.

Other Ingredients

Non-fat or skimmed milk powder is best suited for use in light or rich buttercream icings. The milk powder absorbs moisture, provides body, and contributes to the taste and flavor of the icing. Fresh milk is not recommended because it is perishable. Icings that may be kept for several days, or be exposed to room temperature for some time, may spoil because of the fresh milk. When adding milk powder it is best to sift the milk powder with the sugar to avoid small, gritty lumps. These lumps, if formed, make it difficult to use the buttercream when bagging out with a fine pastry tube.

Water is used to dissolve the sugar in making icings. Water permits the boiling of sugar and syrups without burning the sugar. A large percentage of water is evaporated in the boiling of syrups to be used for icings. Water should not be used to thin the consistency of icings that are rich in fat (25 per cent or more) because it may curdle them. It is best to use a simple syrup for this purpose. Simple syrup is also best for thinning flat or fondant icings. The use of water, especially if the icing is cool, will cause the icing to run and remain sticky.

Eggs used as ingredients of icings must be fresh and free from all odors. Special attention must be given to the use of frozen eggs. If defrosted, frozen eggs with an undesirable odor are used, it will permeate the icing. This odor will become worse if the icing is permitted to stand. Fresh, shell eggs of good quality are recommended. Whole eggs, egg whites, and yolks increase the volume of creamed icings. They also contribute to the taste and flavor of the icing. They should be added slowly or gradually to creamed icings to prevent curdling and to assure maximum volume. It is advisable to use cooler eggs for icings than for cakes. This is especially important in warm weather. Egg whites are often whipped separately and then folded into a creamed icing. Egg whites are also used to improve the shine of flat-type icings.

Stabilizers of various types are used in icings. These may be vegetable gums, tapioca starch, pectin, wheat or corn starches. Their principal purpose is to absorb excess water or moisture by forming a gel. By thus holding the moisture they help to avoid the crystallization of sugar and help to eliminate a sticky condition in warm, humid weather. They are especially important in the packaging of iced products.

As mentioned previously, flavors are natural, processed, or artificial supplements. The natural flavors are those naturally present in the ingredients used (e.g., butter). The processed flavors are developed by the method of preparation, as in the boiling and mild caramelization of sugar for caramel. The added and artificial flavors are either the extracts of fruits or other flavors or those added by the use of cocoa or colorings. Flavors added to icings are not lost or lessened as those which are volatilized or weakened in the baking process. The flavor or flavor blend should not be strong to the degree that it overpowers or overshadows the natural and processed flavors. Colored flavors require special care in that flavor and color do not always give equal results. The color may be weak and the flavor strong, or vice versa.

Many bakers are hesitant when it comes to the use of salt in icings. Some do not use salt at all in icings. When small amounts are used they supplement and emphasize the taste and flavor of the other ingredients used. Sugar tastes sweeter when contrasted or highlighted with a small amount of salt. The flatness of creamed icings or whipped icings is removed with the use of a pinch of salt.

TYPES OF ICINGS AND THEIR PREPARATION

Icings may be classified into three major types: (1) flat icings, (2) fluffy or creamed icings, and (3) combination icings.

Flat icings are those made with confectioner's sugar, water, corn syrup, and flavor. A small amount of fat or oil may be added. A thick paste is made of all the ingredients and the icing warmed to about 110°F. A double-boiler arrangement should be used to avoid direct contact of the icing with the flame or heat. Overheating or direct heat are most often the cause for the loss of the gloss or shine of the icing when it cools. When the consistency of the icing thickens while working with it, it should be rewarmed to soften the consistency. The common error of adding water to cool icing to soften it causes running and stickiness. The addition of cocoa or chocolate to flat icings will thicken the icing and create a luster or shine if the icing is warmed properly. Simple syrup should be added if the cocoa stiffens the consistency. When through using this icing the sides of the icing pot should be scraped and covered with a thin film of water to prevent crust formation. These principles apply when using fondant icing.

Creamed icings are made with fat, confectioner's sugar, milk powder, eggs, water, salt, flavor, and perhaps a stabilizer. All or some of these ingredients may be used. Each recipe will vary. The procedure is to cream the dry ingredients (after they have been sifted) with the shortening and other fats. The eggs are added gradually and creamed in well. The water and flavor are blended in last. In the fudge type of creamed icing an emulsified fat is used and a blending, rather than creaming method, is used. While air cells are absorbed and retained in each, the creaming method makes a lighter icing in that more air cells are retained. Egg whites are usually whipped with part of the sugar and blended into the creamed fat. This gives added lightness. Very often the whites are warmed in a double boiler with fondant and then whipped before being added to the creamed fat. This added lightness makes this a French type of butter cream. It is recommended that a wire whip be used on the mixing machine for the blending of the whipped whites and fat which is creamed. This will reduce the loss of air cells and give complete blending.

When boiling the syrup to be added to whipped whites the syrup should be boiled to approximately 235° to 238°F. and then added to the whipping whites in a slow steady stream while the mixing machine is at medium speed. High speed tends to spread the syrup in threads around the machine kettle and sticking or "balling up" may result. High speed may be used to complete the whipping after all the syrup has been added. This is typical in making marshmallow icing.

The combination type of icing uses both a flat-type icing and the creamed type. For example, fondant may be warmed with egg whites to 110°F. and then whipped to a thick consistency. The fat and the remainder of the powdered sugar are creamed until light. The creamed fat and sugar are then added to the whipped whites and blended until smooth.

When adding cocoa to an icing it is best to sift and blend the cocoa with the powdered sugar. This makes easy the more complete dispersion of the cocoa without the formation of cocoa lumps. When adding chocolate to icing, the chocolate should be melted and added in liquid form for even distribution. The common problem of chocolate streaks or lumps is due to the addition of the chocolate in a semi-liquid state, causing it to solidify into small lumps or streaks before blending is complete. Chocolate liquor is suggested for addition to chocolate icings. It contains a greater percentage of cocoa and cocoa butter thus providing for better color and flavor. The use of sweet chocolate is expensive as well as the use of larger quantities to obtain the desired results.

Creamed icings should be stored in a cool place and covered to prevent crustation. Refrigeration of an icing causes hardening of the fat and requires considerable mixing to return it to its original state. This is time-consuming. Do not permit creamed icings, especially those made with part butter, to remain in a warm place for any length of time. Creamed icings tend to lose their smoothness when standing for some time. The icing seems to tear when used in that state. Such an icing should be placed in a warm water bath and mixed well until smooth. Do not overheat or melt most of the fat. This practice will also restore the shine to the icings as well as smoothness. If the creamed icing or fudge is too stiff the addition of small amounts of warm syrup will help to soften and smooth the consistency of the icing.

When adding fruit, nuts, and other varieties of toppings care should be used not to overmix the icing. In addition, berries should be blended in carefully to avoid breaking the skins and streaking the icing.

Leftover icings, without nuts or fruits, may be blended together and chocolate added. Chocolate will disguise or cover the variety of colors of other leftover icings. The chocolate will also predominate over most of the flavors of other leftover icings.

WHIPPED CREAM AND CREAM-TYPE TOPPINGS

Heavy cream contains approximately 40 per cent butterfat. The lighter creams will average about 18–20 per cent butterfat. Heavy cream is best suited for whipping. The cream should be aged by storing under refrigeration for 1 or 2 days at 33° to 35°F. Fresh, heavy cream does not whip as well and the butterfat tends to separate faster causing curdling of the cream or weeping while the cream is bagged out. Continued whipping will churn the cream into butter. The aged cream emulsifies and retains the liquid better. Cream stabilizers are used to form a froth in the first stage of whipping. With the use of cream stabilizers the amount of milk may be increased substantially. It is possible to add 50 per cent chilled milk to the volume of heavy cream (1 pt. of milk to each quart of cream). However, increased use of stabilizers may change the taste of the cream. Heavy cream should be whipped until it has body and retains its shape. Whipping at medium speed is advisable for the last stages of mixing. This will avoid the possibility of overwhipping. The cream is sweetened with confectioner's sugar (approximately 4 oz. per quart of heavy cream). A fine grade of vanilla is added in the final stage of whipping.

Whip-toppings are very popular and useful. When used in place of heavy cream one can detect a slight difference in taste, which is almost like the flavor given by the excessive use of stabilizer. However, because of their body, stabilizers and emulsifiers are useful for blending heavy cream with the topping. Greater shelf-life is assured. In addition, greater variety in the production of cream goods is made possible. For example, various fruit fillings and other soft fillings and toppings may be blended into these toppings without running. The stabilizers and emulsifiers increase the potential for maintaining the added moisture and the weight supplied by the fillings and toppings.

When boiling sugar for various icings a clean kettle should be used. The sugar should be dissolved and stirred periodically until the syrup starts to boil. Upon boiling the film should be removed from the top of the syrup. These are impurities present in the sugar and water and separate out when the syrup is boiled. The sides of the kettle should be brushed with a brush and water to dissolve any crystals. This is not necessary when the kettle is covered. The steam will wash the sides. The temperature of the syrup should be determined with a thermometer. The following temperatures indicate the stages of sugar boiling:

Syrup—220°F.	Blow—235°F.	Soft crack—280°F.
Thread—225°F.	Soft ball—245°F.	Hard crack—312°F.
Pearl—230°F.	Hard ball—255°F.	Caramel—350°F.

CHAPTER 29

Balancing Cake Recipes

Recipe or formula balance refers and applies to the proper combination of various ingredients used in cake baking to achieve a desirable baked product. Most bakers have developed a file of recipes which they use daily or as the need arises. Their recipes have been obtained from other bakers and other sources such as trade and labor publications. Excellent recipes have been published in these journals. Bakers are always trying to improve recipes. Some do it by trial and error. However, the trial and error method may be avoided, in large measure, by being able to balance a cake recipe before using it. It is equally important to be able to make changes in a recipe to reduce costs or improve the quality of the product. Knowledge of formula balance also gives the baker better insight for understanding special cake faults and their causes. This will enable him to correct these faults.

Each basic ingredient used in a recipe serves a special purpose in the cake. Each has a definite effect upon the cake and upon the other basic ingredients. Since they are interlocked and dependent upon each other, any changes in one of the basic ingredients will require a change in one or several of the others. It is noteworthy that the leavening, if any, will have to be changed, increased, reduced or eliminated entirely. The basic ingredients are classified in terms of their purpose and function in the cake. The following classifications have been made for the basic ingredients used in cake making:

Tougheners—These ingredients provide the structure and toughen or bind the cake. They are flour, milk solids, egg whites, and other binding ingredients.

Tenderizers—These ingredients provide shortness and softness in the cake. They are sugar, shortening, egg yolks, chocolate and other fat-containing ingredients.

Moisteners—They provide moisture and keeping quality. They are liquids such as, milk, water, eggs and syrups.

Driers—These absorb and retain moisture and provide the body of the cake. These are flour, milk solids and starches.

Flavorers—These ingredients provide natural flavors. They are cocoa, chocolate, butter, eggs, and other natural, flavor-bearing ingredients.

In balancing a cake recipe, it is necessary to balance the tougheners and tenderizers, the driers and the moisteners, so that a cake of desirable characteristics will result.

THE BALANCING OF POUND CAKES AND OTHER CREAMED CAKE MIXES

The original and first type of cake that was really acceptable in terms of the standards of the present was the cake made by mixing equal amounts of sugar, butter, eggs, and flour. This resulted in a form of pound cake. With time and experience, the methods of mixing these ingredients improved, resulting in a cake of better grain and texture. However, the desire for greater variation led to further experiments. The results of many years of research and experience led to the development of new methods of mixing, new processes and new materials for cake production. This also led to the development of a method of formula balance for pound cake. This same method applies to cakes made with the creaming method of mixing (discussed in the unit on cake mixing methods). The basic rules which follow apply to pound cake and will be compared with a recipe for wine cake. It must be understood that these and other rules for cake balance are not hard and fast but serve as guiding principles.

Rules for Balancing Pound Cakes and Creamed Cake Mixes

1. The weight of the sugar should equal the weight of the flour. In leaner cake mixes, the weight of the sugar will be less than the flour.
2. The weight of the shortening or fat should equal the weight of the eggs.
3. The combined weight of the eggs and milk should equal the weight of the sugar or the flour.

Let us examine the basic ingredients and their weights (in percentage form) in a pound cake and a wine cake and account for the variations and balance of the mix.

Pound Cake

Ingredient	Lb.	Oz.	%*
Sugar	1	..	100
Butter or fat	1	..	100
Eggs	1	..	100
Flour	1	..	100

Wine Cake

Ingredient	Lb.	Oz.	%[1]
Sugar	3	..	67
Shortening	2	..	45
Eggs	2	..	45
Milk	2	..	45
Flour	4	8	100
Baking powder	..	3	4

---

* The percentage of ingredients is based upon the weight of the flour being 100 per cent.

Note that the pound cake recipe is in accord with the rules. Let us examine the wine cake recipe.

The weight of the sugar is less than the weight of the flour. This indicates that the cake is less sweet and is lacking in tenderizing components. The weight of the shortening and eggs are equal and meet requirements. The eggs and milk (total weight) are in accord with rule No. 3. They exceed the weight of the sugar and almost equal the weight of the flour.

From the pound cake mix it can be seen that 1 lb. of eggs is enough to moisten the sugar and flour and also to leaven the mix. In the wine cake mix there are 2 lb. eggs that can moisten and leaven 2 lb. of sugar and 2 lb. flour. The remaining sugar and flour now require moistening and leavening. The addition of 2 lb. milk will moisten the extra sugar and flour not moistened by the eggs and also provide tenderizing needed because of the lack of sugar. However, the milk is not a natural leavening agent as eggs are and therefore the batter will require some other leavening or the cake will have very poor volume and very dense grain. In addition, a wine cake should have a more porous grain and structure than a pound cake. It should also have more volume by weight of the baked mix.

The rule for leavening milk or water in creamed-type cake recipes is: for 1 lb. liquid milk or water, 1 to $1^1/_2$ oz. baking powder are required. In this instance, $1^1/_2$ oz. baking powder is used for 1 lb. milk to obtain the desired characteristics of the cake. A lesser amount of baking powder would result in a closer grain and lesser volume.

Judgment is a very important factor. The nature of the flour used might require an additional change. For example, if a strong flour (one high in protein) were blended with the cake flour an additional amount of baking powder would be necessary to overcome the resistance of the stronger flour. If the recipe contained an acid-containing ingredient such as natural cocoa a further change in the type of leavening would be necessary. Baking soda would have to be substituted for part of the baking powder.

Rules Governing the Balancing of High-Ratio Type Cakes

1. The weight of the sugar should equal or exceed the weight of the flour.
2. The weight of the eggs should exceed the weight of the fat or shortening.
3. The weight of the liquid (eggs and milk) should equal or exceed the weight of the sugar.

An emulsified, high-ratio type of shortening must be used for these cakes. It is because of the emulsifying properties of this fat that extra sugar and milk may be used in the recipe. A fine grade of cake flour must be used to absorb and retain moisture as well as providing structure for the cake. The method of mixing is "blending." This method of mixing is fully explained in Chapter 27, Cake Mixing Methods.

In high-ratio yellow cakes the percentage of sugar may be as high as 150 per cent based on the weight of the flour. In chocolate cakes it may go as high as 165 per cent. Because of the extra sugar, additional liquid is necessary to dissolve the sugar and still provide enough liquid for the gelatinization of the starch in the flour. This accounts for the increase in the milk and eggs.

The eggs, in addition to supplying moisture, are also tougheners because of their protein content. They also supply emulsifying properties because of the lecithin and fat in the yolk of the egg. Therefore, a lesser amount of fat is used. This fat should not be much less than the eggs because it acts as a tenderizer and helps to eliminate toughness. When egg yolks are used a decrease in the amount of emulsified shortening is made because the yolks naturally contain lecithin.

For the third rule, the weight of the liquid should equal or exceed the weight of the sugar. As has been indicated the emulsified fat is able to carry the added liquid without curdling. It is a liquid in fat emulsion. This is also supported by a fine cake flour with fine starch particles to absorb and retain moisture. Any change in the amount of sugar must be followed with an adjustment in the amount of flour and liquid. Excessive use of sugar and liquid will result in a cake of dense grain and poor volume. The amount of leavening to be used in high-ratio cakes is usually based upon the weight of the flour. For each pound of flour in the recipe, approximately $3/4$ to 1 oz. of baking powder is used. This will vary with the amount and type of eggs used.

CHAPTER 30

Recipes for Cakes and Cake Specialties

CUPCAKES
Plain, Crumb-Topped, and Flat-Iced

An assortment of cupcakes makes a good display item in a bakeshop. Variety in cupcakes may be obtained by finishing with different icings and toppings. Many recipes may be used for cupcakes from the high-ratio-type mixes to the basic wine-cake mix. This unit is based upon use of the wine-cake mix.

Wine Cake   **Yield:** 12 doz. cupcakes

Ingredients	Lb.	Oz.	Mixing procedure
Sugar	3	..	Scale carefully. Cream these ingredients
Salt	..	1	until soft and light. Scrape the bottom and
Milk powder	..	4	sides of the kettle several times
Shortening	2	..	
Eggs	2	..	Add the eggs in four stages and cream well after each addition
Water	2	..	Add the water and flavors and stir in slightly
Vanilla	..	1	
Lemon flavor	..	$1/2$	
Cake flour	4	8	Sift the flour and baking powder. Mix until
Baking powder	..	3	the flour is absorbed and the mix is smooth

Procedures to Follow (Figs. 295 and 296)

1. Be sure the mix is creamed light. The volume and texture of the cupcake is dependent upon the creaming process, which adds one-third the leavening to the cupcakes.
2. Drop the mix into paper-lined muffin pans about half full. It is important to have equal amounts of mix in all pans. Drop the mix as you would for plain muffins.
3. For crumb-topped cupcakes sprinkle Struessel topping on top of the mix. A dab of jelly, jam, or soft fruit filling may be placed on top of the crumb topping for variety. The cupcakes may be left plain and sold as such.
4. Cupcakes to be iced are left plain and baked, then iced after baking.

5. Bake the cupcakes at 375°F. until they are golden brown and spring back gently to the touch. The average cake takes 15 min. to bake.

6. Remove the cupcakes from the pans when they are almost cool. Be careful not to dump one on top of the other.

7. Iced cupcakes finished with a flat icing are dipped in simple icing when they are cool. Be sure the icing is warmed to about 110°F. Fudge base or color may be added to white flat icing for variety. In the case of chocolate or fudge, simple syrup should be added to the icing while warming so that a proper consistency is reached. The icing should have the consistency of a thick gravy.

Fig. 295.   Dip the Top of the Cupcake in the Warm Icing

8. Dip the top of the cupcake into the warm icing so that only the top surface touches the icing. Lift the cupcakes and turn it so that the top is in a vertical position for a moment. This will allow excess icing to run off.

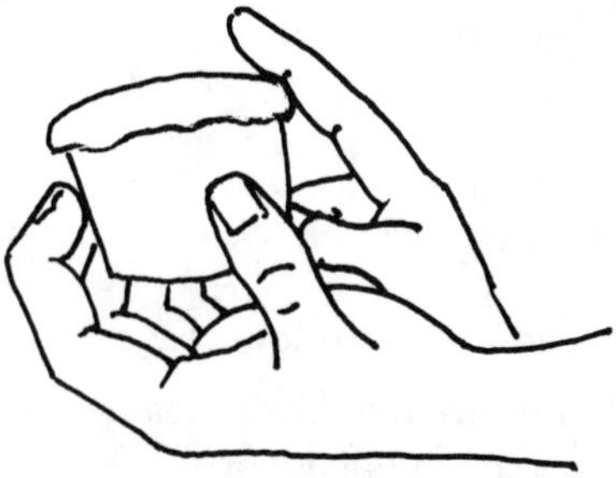

Fig. 296.   Wipe Off Excess Icing by Running Forefinger along Edge of the Cupcake

9. Run a forefinger along the edge of the cupcake. This makes a smooth edge and prevents the icing from running. If the icing is too thin or soft or the cupcake dipped too deep there will be too much icing on top and it will drip over the sides. This should be avoided. Allow the cupcakes to dry before displaying.

10. The icing pot should be scraped around the inside and outside to prevent the leftover icing from crusting and hardening.

DROP CAKES

Drop cakes, Metropolitans, and fudge-iced cupcakes are usually made from wine-cake mix used for cupcakes. This is especially applicable to the production of drop cakes and Metropolitans. Of course, cupcakes baked in paper liners may also be made from cake recipes following a high-ratio cake mix. The important factor is the fact that the wine-cake mix can be used for a large variety of cupcakes and other items in the line of small cake units.

Procedures to Follow (Figs. 297–299)

1. To the wine-cake mix starting with 3 lb. of sugar add 14 oz. additional cake flour. This means that if you have dropped out 6 doz. cupcakes and now have about one-half the mix left, you would add only 7 oz. of additional cake flour. The added flour will stiffen the mix a bit and prevent the units from spreading or running too much during baking. Be careful not to overmix when adding extra flour to an already prepared wine-cake mix. This will toughen the mix and cause it to peak too much.
2. Bag out or drop out the units on bun pans that have been greased and then dusted with bread flour. The excess flour should be brushed off lightly or the pan inverted and tapped to remove the excess flour. It is best to sprinkle the flour at one end and then tilt the pan to have the flour run over the entire greased surface. This will cause the flour to stick. Parchment-paper-lined pans may also be used.
3. Bag out or drop out (as for cupcakes) equal amounts of batter weighing about $1^1/_4$ oz. The units may be made larger. Space the units about four down and six across. Larger units should be spaced three down and six across. They should be spaced alternately so that the units will spread evenly in baking without touching each other. If the units bake into each other they will not have a completely round shape. This is to be avoided. The center of the unit should be higher. Paper-lined pans may be used.
4. Bake at 390°F. until light brown. The test for complete bake is to touch the center of the cake gently. If it springs back it is baked. Do not overbake.
5. Remove the pans from the oven and allow the units to cool until warm. Tap the pan gently on the bench to loosen the cakes. Turn the cakes over so that the smooth bottom is now the top and allow to cool.
6. When cool ice the top of the cakes with warm icing (fondant or simple icing). Begin by icing half of the drop cake with vanilla icing. Allow the icing to dry and then ice the other half with warm choco-

late icing. Apply the icing in one motion if possible by picking up enough icing with a bowl knife and starting at one end, smear directly across the center of the cake. Remove excess icing by running the edge of the bowl knife along the edge of the cake. Too little icing will cause a thin spread and possible pickup of cake crumbs. This will spoil the appearance. If the icing is applied in two or more applications lines will show and the top will not be smooth. The cake should be held in the left hand if you are right-handed, and the icing applied with the right hand holding the bowl knife. Avoid getting cake crumbs in the pot of icing.

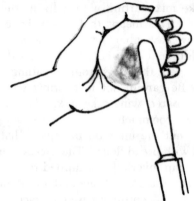

Fig. 297. Apply White Icing to Half the
Drop Cake

Fig. 298. Inverted Drop Cake   Fig. 299. Icing Applied to Drop
Cake

METROPOLITANS

The procedure for making Metropolitans is quite standard. However, the type of toppings and fillings (jelly, jam, buttercream) used may vary, making many varieties of the same item. The recipe for buttercream will be presented after the procedure for Metropolitans.

Procedures to Follow (Figs. 300–303)

1. A wine-cake or high-ratio type cake mix may be used. The more common mix used is the wine-cake mix.
2. Deposit the prepared mix into greased and dusted muffin tins. Fill

half full. Bake as for cupcakes. Remove from the tins while warm, not hot.

3. Turn the cakes over so that narrower bottom is now the top. If the cakes are quite warm dust the pan with cake crumbs to prevent the cakes from sticking while they are cooling. The sticking is due to condensation.

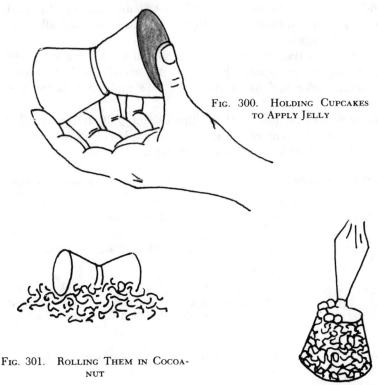

FIG. 300. HOLDING CUPCAKES
TO APPLY JELLY

FIG. 301. ROLLING THEM IN COCOA-
NUT

FIG. 302. USING THE PASTRY BAG TO
MAKE THE BORDER

FIG.   303. FINISHED
METROPOLITAN   WITH
JELLY CENTER

4. The sides of the cakes are to be smeared with a jelly or jam. Either are to be worked smooth to remove lumps and make application easy. If too stiff, a little water or simple syrup should be added to the jelly. The jelly may be applied with a small bowl knife. Clean hands and fingers may be used for smearing two cakes at a time. (Fig. 300).

5. Roll the smeared sides of the cake in fine or medium cocoanut, toasted ground nuts or macaroon crunch. Cake crumbs may also be used. Be sure there are no lumps in the toppings as these will not allow for complete coverage of the sides.

6. With a medium star, French or plain tube draw a complete, even circle of buttercream around the edge of the cake. The buttercream may vary in color and flavor from white to pink, strawberry, and chocolate.

7. Fill the center of the cake with a filling of jam, jelly, fudge, or other topping to suit the type of buttercream used. It is best and neatest to deposit the center filling with a pastry bag or paper bag.

Simple Buttercream Icing

Yield: To cover 3 doz. 6-in. layer cakes

Ingredients	Lb.	Oz.	Mixing procedure
Confectionery sugar	5	. .	Sift the sugar. Add the water and mix to
Hot water	. .	12	stiff paste. Add a little more water if too
Salt (pinch)	. .	. .	stiff
Shortening or butter	2	. .	Sift the milk powder and add with the
Emulsified	2	. .	shortening. Cream well until soft and light.
shortening			Scrape sides of kettle two or three times
Milk powder	. .	2	
Egg whites	. .	6	Add the whites and flavor and cream well
Vanilla	. .	1	
Water (optional)	. .	4	Add the water and mix smooth

Notes on Buttercream

1. This buttercream may be made without the use of egg whites or any form of egg. However, egg yolks may be substituted for egg whites.

2. Butter may be used in place of the regular shortening. Use the emulsified shortening for this contains a lecithin fat which enables the absorption and retention of the water to take place without curdling. Creaming is important to absorb air and make the buttercream light.

3. Warm or hot water may be used in the last stage of mixing in cool weather. Cold water is used in the summer or during hot temperatures.
4. Keep the buttercream covered and stored in a cool place when not in use.

FUDGE-ICED CUPCAKES

The fudge referred to in the title means any type of fudge icing. This type of icing has more body and is stiffer than the normal simple, flat icing. It is applied with a bowl knife and designs can be made on the cupcake or layer with the bowl knife. The designs will retain their shape and the fudge icing will dry with a soft crust formation. The fudge may vary from plain vanilla to strawberry, orange, lemon, or chocolate. A basic recipe for white fudge icing and one for chocolate fudge icing will be presented after the procedure for icing cupcakes is explained.

Procedures to Follow (Figs. 304–307)

1. The cupcakes should be cool before applying the icing. Delicate cupcakes (high-ratio) may be chilled before icing. This makes them easier to handle.
2. The fudge should be warm and in a semi-soft state similar to a buttercream. Do not apply cold fudge. Keep the fudge in a double boiler to prevent stiffening while working.
3. Hold the cupcake in the left hand. Dip the edge of the bowl knife (narrow blade) into the fudge and pick up enough fudge to cover the top of the cake about $1/4$ in. thick. Place the edge of the knife in the center of the iced cupcake after the top has been covered, and give the knife blade a flat twist. This will cause a spiral effect. Keep the knife slightly tilted so that the end of the knife is in the center of the cake.
4. The iced cupcake may be left plain or garnished with toasted, chopped nuts, toasted cocoanut, glazed cherries, or other topping.

FIG. 304. UNFINISHED CUPCAKE   FIG. 305. MAKING BOWL KNIFE DESIGN

FIG. 306. DESIGN MADE WITH PASTRY BAG AND TUBE

FIG. 307. FINISHED CUPCAKE

Plain Fudge Icing (White)

Yield: To ice 10 doz. cupcakes

Ingredients	Lb.	Oz.	Mixing procedure
Confectionery sugar	4	..	Sift the sugar. Blend with the shortening
Salt (pinch)	..	..	until smooth
Emulsified shortening	1	4	
Hot water	..	10	Add the water in two stages and blend well
Vanilla	..	1	until soft and smooth

Notes on Plain Fudge Icing

Apply the icing immediately. If the icing stiffens place in a double boiler and stir constantly until soft and smooth. Stir continuously. Various colors and flavor may be added for variety fudge icings.

Chocolate Fudge Icing

Yield: To ice 7 doz. cupcakes

Ingredients	Lb.	Oz.	Mixing procedure
Confectionery sugar	3	..	Sift the sugar. Blend all the ingredients
Salt (pinch)	..	..	with the water and mix smooth
Glucose or corn syrup	..	2	
Cocoa (natural)	..	4	
Hot water	..	8	
Melted shortening	..	4	Add the fat and flavor and mix smooth.
Vanilla	..	1	Warm in a double boiler if too stiff

Recipe to Follow when Using a Fudge Base

Ingredients	Lb.	Oz.	Mixing procedure
Fudge base	1	..	Sift sugar. Add fudge base and blend well
Confectionery sugar	3	..	with water and flavor. Warm in double
Hot water (approx.)	1	..	boiler if too stiff
Vanilla	..	$1/2$	

DUCHESS LOAF, RAISIN LOAF, AND CRUMB-TOPPED LOAF CAKES

Wine-cake mix has many uses in the bakeshop. In addition to the variety of cupcakes made, this mix lends itself very nicely to the production of variety loaf cakes. While the loaf cakes made from this mix should not replace pound cake and other loaf cakes made from high-ratio mixes, many bakers use wine cake for all loaf-type cakes. However, we will use this mix in this unit for the production of loaf cakes which lend themselves well to the mix and the type of loaf.

Loaf cake sizes vary from bakeshop to bakeshop and also in accordance with production requirements. Some shops only use the small loaf pans which will hold from 8 to 10 oz. of cake batter. Other shops use larger loaf pans if they are using the mix to make loaf cakes that look like pound cake or rich mixes similar to those used for pound cake. The following loaf cakes should be made in smaller or medium-sized loaf pans and the pans should be lined with pan liners that have been purchased to size or cut to size from parchment paper. This mix yields 18 to 20 12-oz. loaves.

Procedures to Follow for Duchess Loaf Cakes (Figs. 308–310)

1. Duchess loaf cakes are made from the wine-cake mix. The paper-lined pans are filled approximately half full or they are scaled accurately so that the pan is half full. This makes all other loaf pans equal in size by the scaling of the required amount of mix into each pan. The pan should be tapped gently to settle the mix.
2. In order to get the crack in the center of the baked loaf cake, dip one finger into oil and draw the finger across the center top of the cake mix after it is deposited in the pan.

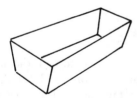

FIG. 308.   LOAF CAKE PAN

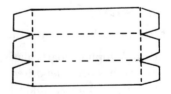

FIG. 309.   PAPER LINER FOR THE PAN, CREASED AND CUT

FIG. 310.   DUCHESS LOAF

3. Use enough oil to cover the indentation made (about $1/4$ in. deep). The oil tends to keep the cake batter separated in the center and this creates that cracked or split-top effect on the cake.
4. The loaf cake is allowed to cool before it is iced.
5. Ice the top with warm fondant or simple icing. One side of the top is generally iced with white or vanilla fondant and the other with chocolate icing. Neatness and evenness is important for a good appearance after the icing is applied.
6. The center should still show the split of the cake and the immediate sides are white and chocolate.

Procedures to Follow for Raisin Loaf Cake (Fig. 311)

1. Raisin loaf cake is made by folding in fresh raisins that have been dusted lightly with bread flour and then sifted to remove the excess flour.
2. The light coating of flour will help to prevent the raisins from sinking to the bottom. This may cause a gummy effect. A dried-out raisin will absorb moisture and may be the cause of large holes around the raisin due to loss of moisture. This will cause a crumbly grain and texture.
3. Fill the pan slightly more than half full in order to get a full loaf slightly higher than a loaf pan.

FIG. 311. RAISIN LOAF
CAKE

Procedures to Follow for Crumb-Topped Loaf Cake (Fig. 312)

1. Crumb-topped loaf cake is made by sprinkling the top of the mix after it has been deposited in the pans with Struessel or crumb topping. Some prefer to sprinkle lightly with crumb topping and add sliced nuts and sugar. The variations in topping are many and meet the needs of the bakeshop and the desires of the customers.

FIG. 312. PLAIN LOAF, CRUMB
TOPPED

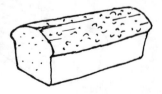

2. Loaf cakes are larger units and therefore require a longer baking period. The larger the loaf, the longer it takes to bake. Suggested temperature for wine-cake loaves is approximately 355° to 365°F. The cake is considered baked when it springs back to the touch when the center of the loaf cake is touched gently. The average 8 to 10 oz. loaf takes about 30 min. to bake. Richer cake mixes take longer to bake.

CHOCOLATE CUPCAKES, LOAF CAKES, AND BUTTERFLIES

Chocolate cakes are very popular. While there are many, many recipes and various methods of mixing these recipes, the baker must produce a desirable product to insure sales and consumer demand. This unit will treat one of the methods of mixing chocolate cakes and use a recipe which is proven in its excellent results. The mixing procedure and baking of these products are as important as the finishing. The mix may be used for all shapes of chocolate cakes—cupcakes, loaf, sheet, and layer cakes.

Chocolate Cake
(Creaming Method)

Yield: 7–8 doz. cupcakes or 14 10-oz. loaves

Ingredients	Lb.	Oz.	Mixing procedure
Sugar	2	..	Cream all the ingredients until soft, smooth, and light
Salt	..	$1/2$	
Milk powder	..	3	
Shortening	1	..	
Fudge base	..	8	
Eggs (part yolks)	1	8	Add the eggs in three stages and cream well after each stage
Water	1	8	Dissolve the soda in the water. Add vanilla and add to the mix alternately with the flour and baking powder. Mix smooth but do not overmix
Baking soda	..	1	
Vanilla	..	1	
Cake flour	2	..	
Baking powder	..	$1/2$	

Procedures to Follow (Figs. 312A and 313)

1. Cocoa may be substituted for the fudge base. If cocoa is used, substitute 5 oz. of cocoa and add 2 oz. of shortening to the mix. Use dark, natural cocoa. The cocoa should be blended with the flour.
   Note: The fudge base referred to is the unsweetened fudge base.
2. The use of egg yolks or egg yolk preparations is optional. Their use will provide greater creaming properties and result in better volume.
3. Melted bitter chocolate or chocolate liquor may be used in equal amount to replace the fudge base. The chocolate should be dissolved and added after the eggs have been creamed in.

4. For *cupcakes,* deposit the prepared mix into cupcake tins lined with paper. Fill them half full. Bake the cupcakes at 375°F. Cupcakes are considered baked when they spring back lightly to the touch. The sense of touch is important in this instance since crust color is not easily visible for the test for proper bake. Allow the cupcakes to cool before applying icing. These cupcakes may be iced with any icing. However, a chocolate fudge icing is best suited. The icing may be applied with a bowl knife or bagged out with a pastry bag and tube. The tops of the cupcakes may be garnished with chopped pistachio nuts or other nuts and dried fruits.

5. For *loaf cakes* line the loaf pans with paper liners. Ridged or fluted liners are best suited, for the mix bakes into the ridges and the paper liners do not separate easily from the cake after baking. Fill the loaf pans about half full and bake at 360°F. Larger units require lower baking temperatures. The loaves are baked when they spring back to the touch. Allow the loaves to rise and set (about 25 min.) before touching. Touching the cakes for doneness before they have set will leave marks or indentations on the top of the cake. They may also cause the cakes to fall.

6. Allow the loaf cakes to cool before finishing or icing. Finish them with chocolate fudge icing or other buttercream type icings. The loaves may be filled with white buttercream inserted into the loaf cake with a pastry bag and tube. To do this, insert the tube into the loaf cake from the top until tube is almost completely in the cake. Use a small plain or star tube for this. Squeeze the buttercream in. Space the insertions about 1 in. apart. The loaf cakes are then iced to cover the marks made by the tube.

FIG. 312A. FINISHED CUPCAKE

FIG. 313. CREAM BEING INSERTED INTO THE LOAF CAKE

Procedures to Follow for Butterflies (Figs. 314–318)

1. Make these cupcakes slightly higher by filling the tins a little more than half full. Bake a little longer because of the extra mix.
2. After the cupcakes have cooled cut the tops of the cupcakes at the point where the paper liner ends. Slice the tops carefully and evenly with a saw knife. Be careful.
3. Place the tops in a straight line on the bench or on a clean sheet pan. Cut through the center of each top thus dividing the top in half. Dust the halves lightly with confectionery sugar.
4. Bag a ring of white or other flavored and colored buttercream or whipped cream around the center top of the cut cupcake as you did for finishing a Metropolitan. Be sure the ring is about $1/2$ in. high so that the cut halves of the tops may be inserted and kept in position.
5. Place the two pieces of each of the cut tops into the ring of buttercream with the dusted, smooth side exposed. Tilt the halves so that they spread outwards as wings.

FIG. 314. CUPCAKE

FIG. 315. TOP CUT OFF THE CUPCAKE

FIG. 316. TOP OF CUPCAKE SPLIT IN HALF

FIG. 317. CREAM BAGGED ON TOP

FIG. 318. WINGS INSERTED IN THE CREAM FOR BUTTERFLY EFFECT

6. With a pastry bag and tube, bag out a drop design with the same type of icing or cream used to make the ring now supporting the wings. The design is to be placed at the base of the wings where they are inserted into the cream. The center of the butterfly may be garnished with a glazed cherry, chopped nuts, or a whole pecan or walnut.

Note: If whipped cream or cream topping is used, the finished butterflies are to be refrigerated immediately after makeup.

YELLOW LAYER CAKES

High-ratio type mixes vary, in many respects, from the usual creamed type mixes. Variations exist in the method of mixing, the greater percentage of sugar and liquid, the leavening (amount) used and in the general characteristics of the cake compared with these of the creamed-type. There are many recipes for different high-ratio cakes. The variations exist in the percentage of sugar used compared with the amount of flour. There are also variations in the percentage of eggs used in these mixes. These recipes do have one common factor—the shortening used is of the emulsified type. The following recipe is a 100 per cent sugar mix. That is, the weight of the sugar equals the weight of the flour. However, no matter what type of high-ratio mix he uses, sound judgment is of great importance to the baker in the mixing procedure.

Yellow Layer Cake   **Yield:** 18 6-in. layers

Ingredients	Lb.	Oz.	Mixing procedure
Sugar	3	..	Sift the dry ingredients. Blend all ingredients on medium speed for about 5 to 6 min. Scrape down the sides of the kettle and beater periodically
Salt	..	1	
Milk powder	..	4	
Emulsified shortening	1	4	
Cake flour	3	..	
Water	1	8	
Water	..	8	Add the water and blend for 3 min. at medium speed
Eggs (part yolks)	1	8	Add the eggs in two stages and blend for about 4 min. after each addition. Add the baking powder and flavor with the last of the eggs. Scrape the sides of the kettle
Baking powder	..	$2^1/_4$	
Vanilla	..	1	

Procedures to Follow

1. The mixing procedure, as it is specified, must be followed. It cannot be hurried. Increasing the speed of the machine will not make the proper absorption of air and formation of air cells. You will note that the air cells are not formed as they were for creamed mixes. The

mix should have a smooth, soft, semi-liquid appearance. Improper mixing will cause an uneven lumpiness and a very fluid or liquid appearance. This will result in a loss of volume and close grain.

2. Yolks will help to emulsify (retain the liquid and moisture) the mix. A curdled mix (fat-in-water) is the result of improper mixing.

3. The layer cake pans should be clean and greased and dusted with flour. Remove the excess flour by tapping the pan on the bench. Special, round paper liners, the size of the pan, are often used. This eliminates the need for dusting the pans with flour.

4. Fill the pans about one-third full. The mix is often scaled into each pan for uniformity of size. Deeper pans may be filled half full. These layers are higher and a single layer is sufficient to make one finished layer.

5. Bake the layers at 360°F. Bake to a golden brown color. Avoid overbaking. Use your sense of touch to test for baking.

6. Remove the cakes from the oven and allow to cool. Remove the layers from the pan while slightly warm. It is advisable to tap the pans to release any part of the cake which sticks, or may stick, before turning the layers out of the pan. Do not turn hot layers out on a pan. They sweat and stick to the pan or bench. This mix may also be used for cupcakes, sheet and loaf cakes.

Procedures to Follow for Filling and Icing (Figs. 319–323)

1. Determine the required height of the layer. Each bakeshop has a different specification.

2. Level the layers by removing any high peaks and loose top crust formation.

3. Cut the layers into equal parts with a saw knife. If the layers are thin, then it may be necessary to put two layers together. A high layer (about 2 to $2^1/_2$ in. high) may be cut into three sections and two fillings placed between the three layer sections.

4. Fill each layer with buttercream, jam, jelly, fudge, or any special combination according to the requirements of the job. Place an equal amount of filling between each layer. Set each of the layers on the filling evenly and press down gently so that the cake sticks to the filling. Be sure the layer is even all around before applying the outer icing or covering. Remove all cake crumbs from the top of the layer and the working area, as these may get into the icing (buttercream or fudge) and cause lumps.

5. Have the buttercream or fudge icing in a smooth state ready for use.

6. Place the layer cake on a thin cardboard liner that is slightly smaller or the same diameter as the cake. Do not use oversized liners. Place the cake in the exact center of the turntable. It is wise to place a wet cloth on top of the turntable to prevent the cake from moving or slipping while the icing is being applied.

Fig. 319. Cutting and Preparing Layers

Fig. 320. Filling the Layer

Fig. 321. Applying the Icing

Fig. 322. Combing the Sides

Fig. 323. Finished Layer

7. Place a sufficient amount of icing on the layer cake to cover the top and sides about $1/8$ to $1/4$ in. thick. Hold the bowl knife in an almost flat position with the blade slightly tilted up. Place the point or edge of the bowl knife in the center of the cake and spread the icing by turning the turntable slowly with the left hand while the right hand holds the knife in a steady position. Keep the pressure even. This will spread the icing evenly over the top of the layer cake. The excess icing will spread to the sides of the cake. Use this excess to place the thin coating over the sides by holding one edge of the bowl knife gently against the side of the layer cake and turning the turntable gently. Apply additional icing to the sides of the cake so that the entire surface of the side is covered with a coating of icing $1/4$ in. thick.

8. If the top of the cake is not altogether smooth, dip the bowl knife in warm water and place it on top of the layer gently. Spin the turntable and press gently with the bowl knife. This will even the top. If necessary, add more icing to the top and smooth the icing with the knife and turntable. The sides of the cake may be combed with a serrated edge. These special serrated combs are made of plastic or metal. Press the edge against the sides of the layer gently and spin the turntable. Keep the pressure even. If any bald spots appear where the layer cake shows through apply more icing and comb once again.

9. For a spiral design, after the cake is iced, place the tilted edge or point of a thin-bladed bowl knife about $1/4$ in. in from the outside of the layer. Place a light pressure on the knife and spin the turntable at the same time moving the knife point closer to the center. When the center is reached lift the knife from the cake. This will form a spiral effect.

10. Simple bowl knife designs may be made by moving the point edge of the knife across the top of the cake making a series of ridges across the top. Remember to keep the pressure of the knife, whether it is the long edge or the point, even. This controls the depth of the swirls or ridges made in the icing. Practice will increase the neatness and speed.

11. Place the iced cake on a larger cake liner with a doily. The garnish may then be applied to the top of the layer. The sides of the layers may also be garnished with toasted cake crumbs, light cake crumbs, toasted nuts, sliced almonds, chocolate sprinkles, and other toppings.

OLD-FASHIONED, MARBLE, FRUIT, AND HIGH-RATIO POUND CAKES

As the title indicates, there are many varieties of pound cake. They vary from the original, old-fashioned type to the special, dark holiday varieties. The term "pound" refers to the original recipe wherein equal portions (pound for pound) for the basic ingredients were mixed together to make pound cake. Later developments included pound cake made from high-ratio mixes. This led to the more commercialized types of pound cake. The raisin and other fruit-nut combinations require minor recipe changes and an understanding of the preparation and addition of the fruits and nuts to the recipe. The marble pound cake varieties are simply the addition of the chocolate, cocoa, fudge, or combination of either, to the mix.

Old-Fashioned Pound Cake   **Yield:** 12 1-lb. loaves

Ingredients	Lb.	Oz.	Mixing procedure
Shortening	1	8	Sift the flour. Add the fats and cream well
Butter	1	8	until soft and light. Scrape the sides of the
Cake flour	1	8	kettle to remove lumps
Bread flour	1	8	
Sugar	3	..	Whip the sugar, salt, and eggs until light (as
Salt	..	$^3/_4$	for sponge cake). Fold in the vanilla last.
Eggs	3	..	Fold the whipped sugar and eggs into the
Vanilla	..	1	creamed fat and flour

Procedures to Follow for Old-Fashioned Pound Cake (Fig. 324)

1. You will note that in this recipe all the basic ingredients are of equal weight (3 lb. of sugar, flour, eggs, and shortening and butter).

2. Since this is a two kettle method of mixing, each mixing procedure must be handled carefully. This means that maximum aeration must take place in the mixing procedures. You will note that there is no baking powder or other chemical leavening agent used. It is the air cells formed in the creaming and whipping methods which provide the leavening together with the natural leavening effect of the eggs.

3. It is best to add the whipped eggs in three stages to the creamed flour-fat. Fold in gently to avoid collapsing the cell structure. Be sure that the eggs and flour-fat are evenly blended to avoid an uneven grain, structure, and possible collapse during baking.

4. Deposit the mix into sheet pans that have been lined with paper for special sheet cakes. This mix is excellent for petits fours. The mix is also excellent for loaf cakes and layer cakes for special occasion cakes. Be sure that the loaf cake pans are lined with paper liners. Fill half full.

5. Bake the large loaf cake units at 345° to 350°F. Sheet cakes, which are thinner, are baked at 360°F.

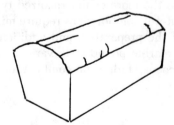

Fig. 324. Plain Pound Cake

Procedures to Follow for Marble Pound Cake (Fig. 325)

1. Add the following to one-third of the above mix: 4 oz. cocoa, 4 oz. water, and $1/4$ oz. baking soda.   Make a smooth paste and fold into one-third of the mix. Mix smooth.
2. Fill the loaf pan about one-quarter full with yellow mix. Spread a layer of the chocolate mix over the yellow and cover again with yellow. This will produce a marble effect.
3. The chocolate may be folded in a few turns into the entire yellow mix and deposited gently into the pans.

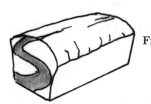

Fig.   325. Marbled Pound Cake

Procedure to Follow for Fruit Pound Cake (Fig. 326)

1. The amount of fruit added to a pound cake may vary from 25 to 50 per cent of the weight of the entire mix. In fact, some special fruit cakes may have a greater percentage of fruits and nuts added. The fruit used is the dried fruits (raisins, glazed cherries, diced mixed fruit, orange peel, and citron). Cooked or moist fruits are not to be used. In fact, glazed fruits that have an excess of syrup are to be washed before use. Allow the fruit to drain before using.
2. It is advisable to dust raisins and other fruits with bread flour before adding to the mix. The flour becomes an adherent and prevents the fruits from sinking to the bottom during the baking period.
3. Nuts may also be added with the fruit. However, the nuts need not be dusted with flour.
4. When adding fruit and nuts, care must be taken that they are not over-mixed with the batter. This may cause some of the fruits to be mashed. This, in turn, will detract from the appearance of the baked cake and will also cause discoloration of the batter. The nuts and fruits are folded in gently during the final stages of mixing.

Fig. 326. Fruit Pound Cake

High-Ratio Pound Cake   Yield: 10–11 loaves

Ingredients	Lb.	Oz.	Mixing procedure
Sugar	3	..	Blend all ingredients to a soft, smooth paste.
Salt	..	1	Scrape kettle often. Blend for about 7 min.
Milk powder	..	$2^1/_2$	at medium speed
Cake flour	3	..	
Emulsified shortening	1	12	
Water	1	2	
Eggs (part yolks)	1	12	Add the eggs in three stages and blend well after each addition
Flavor (vanilla, orange, lemon, mace)	..	1	Add the flavor and baking powder with the last of the eggs
Baking powder	..	$1/_2$	

Procedures to Follow for High-Ratio Pound Cake

1. While this is a high-ratio mix, it must be remembered that the blending process also permits the incorporation of air and the formation of small air cells. These cells are smaller than those created in the creaming method of mixing. The mix should be of medium soft consistency and feel smooth to the touch. Rapid mixing will cause lumping and a heavy, thin consistency.
2. Part of the mix may be made chocolate for a marbling effect. Use the same proportions to make the mix chocolate as you did for the old-fashioned pound cake. Baking soda leavens the cocoa and the thickened mix.
3. For fruit cake made from this high-ratio mix add approximately 2 lb. raisins in the final stage of mixing.
4. Bake the loaves at 345° to 350°F. Sheet cake and thin, small units may be baked at a slightly higher temperature.

CHOCOLATE LAYER CAKE

This unit will deal with the high-ratio type of chocolate cake mix. The procedure for mixing high-ratio cakes is the same for all cakes made with high-ratio shortening and whose recipes are balanced so that they are characteristically of this type. The value of the high-ratio mix lies in the fact that it has a longer shelf-life and can be handled easily when finished.

Chocolate Layer Cake **Yield:** 18 6-in. layers
  (High-Ratio)

Ingredients	Lb.	Oz.	Mixing procedure
Sugar	3	6	Blend these ingredients well in medium
Salt	..	1	speed for about 7 to 8 min. Scrape sides of
Milk powder	..	6	the kettle. The mix should be soft and
Cocoa (natural-dark)	..	9	smooth
Cake flour	3	..	
High-ratio shortening	1	4	
Water	2	..	
Water	1	..	Add the water in which the soda is dissolved
Baking soda	..	$1/_2$	and mix 5 min. at medium speed
Eggs	1	8	Add the eggs in three stages and blend in
Baking powder	..	2	well after each addition. Add the baking
Vanilla	..	1	powder and flavor with the last of the eggs. Blend well until soft and smooth. The mix should pour like a thick gravy

Procedures to Follow

1. Deposit the mix into layer cake pans which have been greased well and dusted with flour. It is advisable to use special paper disc liners that fit the bottom of the pan. The size of the layer will determine the weight of the mix to be used. On the average, layers are generally filled slightly more than one-third full.

2. This mix may also be used for cupcakes, sheet cakes, and loaf cakes.

3. Bake the layers at 365°F. They are considered baked when they spring back gently to the touch. Allow the layers to rise fully in the oven and a light crust appears before you attempt to test for baking. Cupcakes and sheet cakes take less time to bake as they are thinner. Loaf cakes take longer because of their size and thickness.

4. Remove the layers and other cakes made from this mix from the pans after the cakes have cooled until slightly warm. It is good practice to free the sides of the cakes from the pans with the knife edge before turning the layers out of the pans. This will avoid breakage due to sticking.

5. It is advisable to cool or chill the layers before finishing. This makes the layers easier to slice and fill without much crumbling. It is especially advisable to do so if the layers are to be finished with whipped cream or cream topping.

Note: Remember that a high-ratio mix requires sufficient mixing time in order to blend all ingredients well. This allows for partial incorporation of air cells. High-speed mixing is to be avoided. This unit will concentrate on the finishing of chocolate layers with marshmallow icing; the recipe and method employed for finishing are explained on the succeeding pages.

Marshmallow Icing   **Yield:** To ice 20–24 layers

Ingredients	Lb.	Oz.	Mixing procedure
Granulated sugar	6	..	Bring to boil stirring constantly. Boil to
Water	2	..	240°F. (soft ball stage)
Glucose	..	8	
Egg whites	2	..	Whip the whites and sugar to a wet peak.
Sugar	..	8	Add the hot syrup in a slow, steady stream
Vanilla	..	1	and whip until thick. Add the dissolved
Gelatin (powder)	..	1	gelatine and whip in
Cool water	..	4	

Notes on Marshmallow Icing

1. Be sure to stir the sugar and water to prevent the sugar from scorching at the bottom and sides of the kettle. A copper kettle is best suited for cooking syrups. Wash the sides with a moist brush to prevent sugar crystallization on the sides of the kettle.
2. For temperature accuracy, it is best to use a sugar thermometer (sucrometer). If none is available dip a spoon into the boiling syrup and place one drop or more into a cup filled with cold water. If the syrup then forms a soft ball when rolled between the fingers it is considered ready.
3. Time the whipping of the egg whites with the boiling of the syrup so that there is little delay. The whites should be whipped to a wet peak. A dry peak may cause difficulty in adding the syrup and possible collapse.
4. Be careful when pouring the syrup. It is advisable to use a pot or pitcher with a spout. While the whites are running at medium speed add the hot syrup in a steady stream until all the syrup has been added. The machine may then be run at high speed until the marshmallow is light and fluffy.
5. Be sure the gelatine is dissolved and in liquid form. Dissolve it just prior to the addition. Whip in medium speed after the gelatin is added. Scrape the sides of the kettle to be sure the gelatin is distributed. Use the icing while it is warm.

Note: There are many marshmallow preparations in powder or prepared form. These may be used to excellent advantage. Follow the instructions on the containers of the prepared marshmallow for preparation and use.

Procedures to Follow for Icing a Cake (Figs. 327–331)

1. A single layer about $2^1/_2$ in. high may be used. The layer may be cut into halves or thirds. Place a generous amount of marshmallow between the layers and press each layer gently. The marshmallow will cause the layers to stick.
2. The top and sides of the layer are iced generously. Use a bowl knife for quick application of the icing. The sides may be garnished with chocolate cake crumbs. The tops may be spread with sweet chocolate and a dual spread design made. The cakes may also be striped with melted chocolate or fudge icing. Long-shred cocoanut may be used for the top and sides.

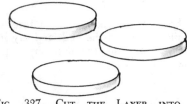

Fig. 327. Cut the Layer into Thirds

Fig. 328. Fill Layers with Marshmallow

Fig. 329. Cover Cake with Marshmallow, Use Bowl Knife for Top Design, and Garnish Sides with Chocolate Cake Crumbs

Fig. 330. The Cakes May Be Striped with Sweet Chocolate

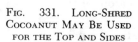

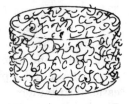

Fig. 331. Long-Shred Cocoanut May Be Used for the Top and Sides

3. The marshmallow may be colored by adding your choice of color (pink, green, and others) at the final stage of mixing. The batch of marshmallow may be separated into different parts and then colored. It is advisable to add some orange flavor to the pink and mint flavor to the green. Keep the color in a light, pastel shade.

SPONGE CAKE

Sponge cakes are those which are primarily leavened with eggs—whole eggs, egg yolks, egg whites, or a combination of two or all three types eggs mentioned. Singularly, the whipping method of mixing is used to mix the cake mix. There are many variations, both in the recipe and the method of handling the mix. The matter of quality and cost control must also be considered in the production of sponge cakes. The recipes presented in this unit are basic to the baker and variations in recipes can certainly be made.

Plain Sponge Cake for Layers   **Yield:** 18 6-in. layers

Ingredients	Lb.	Oz.	Mixing procedure
Sugar	2	..	Warm the eggs to room temperature or
Salt	..	$1/4$	slightly higher. Whip the eggs and dry in-
Glucose or corn	..	4	gredients (and glucose) to a light airy stage.
syrup			(The marks of the whip show)
Eggs	2	4	
Hot water	..	4	Add in a steady stream in second speed and whip in
Water	..	2	Fold in the water and flavor by hand
Flavor (lemon)	..	1	
Cake flour	2	2	Sift and fold in lightly by hand in a gently
Baking powder	..	$1/2$	folding over motion. Do not overmix

Procedures to Follow

1. Be sure the kettle and whip are clean and free from grease.
2. Frozen eggs should be defrosted carefully and then warmed. Warming the eggs provides speed in whipping and results in maximum volume.
3. The final stages of whipping should be done in second speed. This will allow for the maximum incorporation of air.
4. Be sure to check the bottom of the kettle to prevent settling of some of the sugar and glucose.
5. The hot water keeps the temperature of the mix warm and makes easier distribution within the mix.
6. The flavor is mixed with a small amount of water to dilute it. This makes easier distribution. The flavor, especially if it is an emulsion

with an oil or fat base should not be whipped in. It may cause the sponge to collapse. Fold in the flavor lightly.

7. Sifting the flour and baking powder will eliminate foreign particles and also remove lumps. It also aerates the flour and makes folding in easier. The flour is added in a steady stream while being folded in. Adding the flour all at once will cause the flour to settle to the bottom and make added mixing necessary to incorporate it and remove lumps. This will cause loss of some of the air cells and resulting heaviness.

8. Mix enough to have all the flour thoroughly distributed.

9. Deposit the mix gently into greased and flour-dusted layer pans. Fill the pans approximately half full.

10. Sponge cakes should be placed in the oven as soon as the pans are filled. Bake at 365° to 370°F.

Note: Where the recipe calls for 1 lb. 8 oz. eggs or even up to 2 lb. eggs for each pound of sugar, no water nor baking powder is required to moisten and leaven the mix. The eggs are sufficient.

HOT MILK AND BUTTER SPONGE CAKE

This type of sponge mix requires the use of heated milk and melted butter or fat. The fat used, if other than butter, may be margarine or shortening. Be careful of the salt content of the butter or fat you use. Allowances must be made in the recipe. The use of egg yolks in this recipe will allow greater volume and easier absorption of the milk and melted fat. It is important that both the milk and the melted fat be hot (165° to 175°F.). This will keep the eggs in a soft, runny state and make handling easier.

Hot Milk and Butter Sponge Cake

Yield: 16 6-in. layers

Ingredients	Lb.	Oz.	Mixing procedure
Sugar	1	12	Warm the eggs and whip with the sugar
Salt	..	$1/4$	until light and airy. The whip marks will
Whole eggs	1	..	show in creases made in the mix. Place the
Egg yolks	..	6	mix in a bowl
Cake flour	1	9	Sift and fold in gently
Baking powder	..	1	
Milk powder	..	$1^{1}/_{2}$	Place the water and milk powder on the fire
Water (cool)	..	12	and stir well. Add the butter and heat until
Butter or fat	..	6	butter is dissolved. Add vanilla and add to
Vanilla	..	1	the sponge mix in three stages and fold in gently after each addition. Be sure the mix is smooth

Procedures to Follow

1. Be sure the kettle and beater are clean and free from grease.
2. Complete the final stages of whipping in medium speed.
3. Large mixes should be poured into a mixing bowl. This makes folding in the flour easier and prevents overmixing and toughness.
4. Break the fat into small pieces to dissolve quickly in the hot milk, since large pieces of fat or butter may cause the milk to boil before the fat is dissolved.
5. Be careful when adding the hot milk and butter. It is best to pour each stage in from the side of the kettle and fold over gently from the center bottom of the bowl.
6. You will note that after all the milk and butter is folded in gently the mix is quite soft and runny. Be careful in depositing the mix into the layer pans or sheets.
7. Fill the pans approximately half full.
8. Bake as soon as the pans are filled. Bake at 375°F.

CHIFFON CAKES

Chiffon cakes are similar to sponge cakes in that similar methods are used in their production. In this instance, egg whites, rather than whole eggs and/or egg yolks, are whipped. Similarity to butter sponge cake is evident because of the use of fats in the form of neutral oil. Variations in chiffon cakes are made possible by the use of cocoa, flavors, extracts, and natural flavors of fruits and nuts.

Yellow Chiffon Cake   Yield: 32–36 6-in. layers

Ingredients	Lb.	Oz.	Mixing procedure
Sugar	3	..	Blend the dry ingredients together by sifting
Salt	..	1	
Cake flour	3	8	
Baking powder	..	$2^3/_4$	
Oil (neutral)	1	12	Add to the above in a steady stream and mix
Egg yolks	1	12	smooth. Continue to mix for about 2 min.
Water	2	..	Scrape sides of bowl
Water	..	10	Add and mix in until smooth. Scrape sides
Vanilla	..	1	of bowl
Lemon	..	1	
Egg whites	3	8	Whip whites to a soft peak. Add the sugar
Sugar	1	10	in a steady stream and whip to a firm wet
Cream of tartar	..	$1/_4$	peak. Fold the whipped whites into the blended egg mix

Procedures to Follow for Chiffon Cakes

1. Be sure the egg yolks are at room temperature.
2. Be sure to scrape the sides of the kettle or bowl when mixing the eggs to be sure there are no lumps of flour or sugar which have not been blended in.
3. The eggs, oil, and water should be added either gradually or in a slow, steady stream so that they are absorbed evenly and lumping is avoided.
4. Use a flat beater for the blending of the eggs and flour. Do not whip eggs, flour, sugar, and oil.
5. Egg whites should be cool and of good quality. Egg whites that are old and watery will not provide sufficient volume.
6. Be careful not to over-whip egg whites. A firm dry peak will make it difficult to fold egg whites into the egg blend.
7. When folding in whipped egg whites use the same overhand folding motion as is used for folding flour into sponge cake.
8. Be sure egg whites are completely folded in. Do not overmix.
9. Deposit the mix immediately into greased and dusted layer pans. Fill the pans half full.
10. Bake at 365°F.
11. Invert the cakes (leaving them in the pans) on dusted cloths as soon as they are removed from the oven.

Note: If whole eggs are used in place of egg yolks, reduce liquid (water content) by 3 to 4 oz. It is also advisable to increase the baking powder $^1/_4$ oz.

ANGEL FOOD CAKES

Angel food cakes are similar, in many respects, to sponge cakes. The similarity exists in the whipping of eggs (in this instance, egg whites), aeration or leavening resulting from whipped eggs, and in the sponge-like character of the grain and texture. There are variations in the production of angel food cakes which include the chocolate, fruit-flavored, and marbled varieties. Each one requires a slight change in the basic recipe.

Angel Food Cake   **Yield:** 12 6-in. cakes

Ingredients	Lb.	Oz.	Mixing procedure
Egg whites	2	..	Whip the egg whites to a froth
Sugar (fine)	1	..	Sift together and add in a steady stream
Cream of tartar	..	$1/_4$	while the machine is running. Whip to a
Salt	..	$1/_4$	wet, shiny peak
Vanilla	..	$1/_2$	Fold flavors in gently
Almond flavor	..	$1/_4$	
Cake flour	..	12	Sift together and fold in gently. Deposit in
Sugar (fine)	1	..	clean, moist pans. Bake at 350°F

Procedures to Follow

1. Use egg whites that are of good quality and not overaged. The body of the whites should be firm rather than watery.
2. Whip the whites to a froth before adding the sugar. This will allow easier absorption of the sugar and faster whipping.
3. Fine sugar allows easier solution and makes a finer grain and texture in the cake.
4. Whipping to a wet peak means that the whites have not been whipped to the extreme maximum of a dry peak, in which the whites stand up firmly and have a dry, dull appearance. In this stage, it is difficult to fold in the flour and sugar in the final stage of mixing. This causes overmixing and lack of volume.
5. The final stage of folding in the flour and sugar should be done gently as you would for sponge cake.
6. The mix is deposited in angel cake pans that have been cleaned and left slightly moist. The moistness permits the mix to adhere to the sides of the pan and prevents slipping or falling back during baking.
7. Fill the pans about two-thirds to three-fourths full.
8. Avoid overbaking. Turn the angel cakes upside down and allow to cool in the pans. This will prevent falling back and will make removal from the pans easier after the cakes have cooled.
9. When removing the cakes pull the top of the cake away from the sides of the pan gently and then tap the pan firmly on the bench. The cakes will come out leaving the crust formation attached to the pans. Soak pans immediately to make cleaning easier.
10. Angel cakes are best finished with a thin covering of fondant icing. The cakes may be filled or left plain before the icing is applied. Color and flavor of the icing is optional.
11. For *chocolate angel cake* add 4 oz. natural cocoa in the last stage and reduce the cake flour to 10 oz. instead of 12 oz.

WONDER CAKE

Wonder cake is a marble cake that combines the creaming and whipping methods of mixing. While most recipes are similar in structure and mixing procedure, they vary in the amount and type of chocolate used to make the marbled effect. In addition, there are other ingredients used in small quantities which will improve the taste and flavor of the cake.

Wonder Cake   Yield: 20–22 loaves or 1 large pan
(16×24×3½)

Ingredients	Lb.	Oz.	Mixing procedure
Almond or macaroon paste	..	8	Mix together to a smooth paste
Eggs	..	2	
Sugar	2	8	Add to the above and cream well. Scrape the sides and bottom of the kettle several times
Salt	..	$3/4$	
Milk powder	..	1	
Bread flour	..	8	
Butter and shortening	2	..	
Eggs	2	..	Add the eggs in four stages and cream well after each addition
Egg yolks	1	..	
Water	..	8	Stir in slightly
Vanilla	..	1	
Cake flour	2	12	Sift, add and mix in lightly until smooth
Baking powder	..	1	
Egg whites	2	..	Whip to wet peak and fold in lightly into the above
Sugar	..	8	
Sweet chocolate	2	..	Dissolve and pour over the mix. Stir through in three or four folds and deposit in pans. Bake at 360°F.

Procedures to Follow

1. It is important to work the almond or macaroon paste smooth to avoid lumps within the mix and the baked cake.
2. Creaming is important. Leavening is largely dependent upon the air incorporated in creaming, and in whipping the whites.
3. Be careful in dissolving the sweet chocolate. Do this in a double boiler or by placing the chocolate in a warm place long before the mix is made. Do not place the chocolate in the oven or over a direct flame to melt. This will cause scorching and binding of the chocolate into a solid with a bitter taste and flavor.

4. Be careful in marbling the mix. A few strokes is enough. Further marbling takes place when the mix is deposited into the pans. Scoop the mix in the palm of the hand and deposit it gently. This will prevent excessive spread of the chocolate and complete discoloration of the mix into a chocolate type cake. Thick stripes of chocolate are quite desirable. This is a characteristic of wonder cake.
5. Paper-lined loaf pans or large baking pans may be used. Some bakers prefer to stripe the top of the cake with sweet chocolate before baking.

JELLY ROLL AND CHOCOLATE ROLL

Jelly rolls and chocolate rolls are made from a sponge cake mix. While high-ratio and other mixes may be used, they do not lend themselves to easy handling and light texture as do the sponge mixes. Sponge recipes for these rolls may vary from the extreme use of 2 lb. of eggs for each pound of sugar to the minimum of 12 oz. to each pound of sugar used in the sponge mix.

Jelly Roll

For regular jelly roll, use regular sponge cake mix with this variation: increase the amount of water whipped into the eggs from 4 to 6 oz.

Procedures to Follow

1. Be sure the sponge is whipped properly, as for sponge cake, and all the flour folded in gently.
2. Divide the mix (2 lb. of sugar mix) into three pans which have been greased well and dusted with flour. If a paper liner is used grease the paper.
3. Spread the mix evenly and quickly over the pan with a large bowl knife. Try to do this without too much manipulation and in long even strokes. Too much spreading with the knife will cause toughness. Evenness of the mix on the pan is important to avoid an uneven bake.
4. Bake the sheets immediately at 400° to 415°F. Do not overbake for this will cause drying and cracking when the cake is rolled.
5. Turn the rolls over on a dusted cloth leaving the pans on the cake. This will prevent loss of moisture during cooling.
6. When the cake is cool, spread with jam or jelly and roll up into a snug roll leaving the edge of the roll at the center-bottom.
7. The rolls may be finished with jam or jelly and cocoanut or with some other filling and topping. The rolls may be dusted with confectionery sugar after they have been cut.

Chocolate Roll (Swiss Roll)   **Yield:** 2 rolls

Ingredients	Lb.	Oz.	Mixing procedure
Sugar	1	2	Whip well to a peak
Salt	..	$1/4$	
Glucose or corn syrup	..	2	
Eggs	1	..	
Water (cool)	..	7	Dissolve soda and sugar in the water. Fold
Sugar	..	2	into the above lightly
Baking soda	..	$3/8$	
Vanilla	..	1	
Cake flour	..	13	Sift together and fold into above gently
Cocoa	..	3	

Procedures to Follow

1. Deposit mix in 2 pans that have been greased and dusted or lined with greased paper liner.
2. Bake at 415°F. until just done.
3. Handle as for jelly roll. When cool, roll up the roll in cloth or paper unfilled. Fill with assorted buttercream or whipped cream and roll up again. Finish as desired.

WHITE LAYER CAKE

While recipes for this type of cake will vary in sugar content, the mixing procedure for the high-ratio cake is constant. In the case of white layer cake, egg whites are substituted for whole eggs. This means that this cake is not quite as rich since the properties of egg yolk present in whole eggs is lacking. However, white cake usually has a high percentage of sugar when compared with other types of high-ratio cakes.

White Layer Cake (High-Ratio)   **Yield:** 15 6-in. layers

Ingredients	Lb.	Oz.	Mixing procedure
Sugar	3	..	Sift the dry ingredients together. Add the
Salt	..	$^3/_4$	water and mix to a smooth paste (approxi-
Milk powder	..	4	mately 5 min. in medium speed). Scrape
(skim)			sides of kettle and mixing arm
Cake flour	2	12	
High-ratio	1	4	
shortening			
Water	1	..	
Water	..	12	Add and mix to a smooth paste (3 min.)
Egg whites	1	14	Add the egg whites in three stages and blend
Baking powder	..	$2^1/_2$	in well after each addition. Scrape sides of
Vanilla	..	1	kettle. Add the baking powder and flavor
Almond flavor	..	$^1/_2$	with the last of the egg whites and blend
			well

Notes on White Layer Cake

1. The egg whites should be fresh and free from off-odors.
2. Egg whites at room temperature, or slightly cooler, are best. Cold, or icy whites, will delay the blending stages of mixing.
3. Baking temperature for the cake (sheet and layer cakes) is 350° to 360°F.
4. Be careful not to overbake the cakes. This will cause shrinkage and cracking, especially noticeable in sheet cakes.
5. Larger units, such as loaf cakes and deeper layer cakes, should be baked at 350°F.
6. To reduce the pH (acidity) due to the alkaline effect of the egg whites, $^1/_4$ oz. cream of tartar may be added. This will also have a softening effect on the structure of the cake.

BROWNIES

The brownie considered in this unit is a cake variety and should not be confused with the chewy, cookie variety. Cake Brownies are rich in fat and eggs. Very often the brownie is not iced but cut into slices after it is baked and cooled. The leaner type of Brownie is usually iced with a chocolate fudge icing after baking. This unit will provide two types of brownie recipes for use.

Brownies (Leaner Type)   **Yield:** 1 large sheet cake

Ingredients	Lb.	Oz.	Mixing procedure
Sugar	2	8	Cream well until light. Scrape sides of kettle and beater
Salt	..	$1/2$	
Milk powder (skim)	..	3	
Shortening	2	..	
Fudge base	..	14	
Eggs	1	8	Add the eggs in four stages and cream well after each addition
Water (cool)	1	8	Dissolve the baking soda in the water and stir in slightly
Vanilla	..	1	
Baking soda	..	$1/4$	
Cake flour	2	4	Sift, add, and mix until the flour is absorbed
Baking powder	..	$1/4$	
Walnuts (pieces)	1	8	Add the nuts and mix until smooth

Brownies (Richer Type)   **Yield:** 1 large sheet cake

Ingredients	Lb.	Oz.	Mixing procedure
Sugar	2	8	Cream well until light and soft. Scrape sides of kettle and beater
Salt	..	$1/2$	
Shortening	2	..	
Fudge base	..	14	
Eggs	2	8	Add the eggs in four stages and cream well. Add the vanilla with the last of the eggs
Vanilla	..	1	
Cake flour	1	..	Sift the flour, add, and mix until the flour is absorbed
Bread flour	1	..	
Walnuts or pecans	1	8	Add the nuts and mix until smooth

Procedures to Follow

1. Deposit the mix in a regular-sized sheet pan that has been lined with parchment paper and whose sides have been greased lightly.
2. Bake at 360°F. Be careful not to overbake.
3. The rich type of brownie may be egg-washed before baking. This will provide a shiny crust. The lean type should be iced with fudge icing.
4. If fudge base is not available substitute 9 oz. natural cocoa and 3 oz. shortening. The cocoa is to be blended and added with the flour. The shortening is to be added to regular amount of fat used and creamed in the first stage of mixing.
5. Do not dust the nuts with flour before adding to the mix.

SPICE CAKE

Spice cakes, when made and finished properly, have great value to the baker. They provide variety in production, economy in cost of production, and make provision for the use of cake crumbs. (The use of cake crumbs will be explained in the notes.) It must also be indicated that there are recipes which make no provision for the use of these crumbs. This recipe allows for their use.

Spice Cake

Yield: 2 sheet cakes or 9–10 doz. cupcakes

Ingredients	Lb.	Oz.	Mixing procedure
Brown sugar	1	. .	Cream the ingredients well. Scrape sides of kettle and beater
Salt	. .	$1/_2$	
Milk powder	. .	5	
Shortening	1	. .	
Ginger	. .	$1/_4$	
Allspice	. .	$1/_4$	
Cinnamon	. .	$1/_4$	
Eggs	. .	8	Add in two stages and cream well
Molasses (approx. $1/_2$ qt.)	1	8	Add and stir in lightly
Water (variable)	2	4	
Baking soda	. .	$1^1/_2$	Dissolve the soda in the water, add and stir in slightly
Cake crumbs	1	8	
Cake flour	2	6	Add and stir in well
			Sift, add, and mix smooth

Notes on Spice Cake

1. While the brown sugar imparts flavor and taste granulated sugar may be substituted.
2. Blackstrap or dark-grade molasses should be used. It contributed to the color, taste, and flavor of the cake. It is also more economical.
3. The crumbs used should be of the cake or sweet dough variety. Dry crumbs made from lean bread or roll products will tend to absorb more moisture and cause the cake to dry and crack after baking. It will also require that more water or milk be added to the mix. Very rich cake crumbs will require less water or milk. Care should be used in avoiding lumps or caked-up crumbs. These will produce an uneven texture and grain in the baked cake.
4. Once the recipe is mixed it should not be allowed to stand too long without panning and baking. The strength of the leavening (baking soda) is weakened in that the soda reacts with the acid in the molasses upon contact. An extensive waiting period before baking may cause the loss of volume.
5. This recipe may be used for cupcakes, sheet cakes, and loaves. Spice cupcakes or sheet cakes should be iced with fudge or fondant type icings. The color and flavor of the icing is optional.
6. Bake at 375° to 380°F. Larger units should be baked at slightly lower oven temperatures.

DEVIL'S FOOD CAKE

Devil's food cake is not very different from chocolate cake. In fact, many bakers use the same recipe for both. The difference between the two is the fact that the devil's food cake is slightly reddish in color, has a more open grain, and is somewhat leaner in fat content. The color and grain are caused primarily by the use of baking soda as the principal leavening agent. This has a tendency to react with the cocoa imparting a reddish tone to the color. The rapid action of the soda also causes a more open cellular structure.

Devil's Food Cake (High-Ratio)

Yield: 2 large sheets or 16–18 6-in. layers

Ingredients	Lb.	Oz.	Mixing procedure
Sugar	3	6	Blend well to a smooth mix. Medium speed
Salt	..	1	for 5 min. Scrape kettle and beater
Milk powder (skim)	..	5	
Cocoa (natural)	..	9	
Cake flour	3	..	
Emulsified shortening	1	4	
Water (cool)	2	..	
Water	1	..	Dissolve the soda in water and add. Blend
Baking soda	..	$3/_4$	for 3 min.
Eggs	1	8	Add the eggs in three stages. Scrape kettle
Baking powder	..	$1^1/_2$	after each addition. Add the baking powder
Vanilla	..	1	and vanilla with the last of the eggs. Blend well 5 min.

Notes on Devil's Food Cake

1. Bake at 355° to 360°F.
2. This mix can be used for cupcakes, loaves, layers, and sheet cakes.

Devil's Food Cake (Creamed Method)

Yield: 20–22 6-in. layers, 3 sheet cakes or 18 doz. cupcakes

Ingredients	Lb.	Oz.	Mixing procedure
Sugar	4	..	Cream well until soft and light. Scrape
Salt	..	1	sides of kettle and beater
Milk powder (skim)	..	6	
Shortening	2	..	
Fudge base°	1	..	
Eggs	3	..	Add the eggs in four stages and cream well after each addition
Water	3	..	Dissolve the soda in the water. Add the
Baking soda	..	2	water alternately with the sifted flour and
Vanilla	..	1	baking powder. Scrape the kettle and
Cake flour	4	..	beater several times to insure complete and
Baking powder	..	1	smooth mixing. Blend well until smooth

° If fudge base is not available, use 10 oz. cocoa and 3 oz. shortening.

CHEESE CAKES

Cheese cakes made in large or small layer pans are a popular item and are included daily in the production lists of retail bakeshops. While most cheese cakes are made from special baker's cheese, the richer and more expensive types are made with cream cheese, whole or mixed with baker's cheese. While cream cheese is rich in butterfat content, baker's cheese has almost no fat since it is made from soured skim milk. Baker's cheese will also vary in its capacity to absorb liquid (milk). Judgment must be used by the baker in determining the amount of milk to add. Basically, the cheese mix should have the consistency of a thick gravy before the whipped egg whites are added.

Cheese Cake (Heavy Type— German)   **Yield:** 1 large sheet pan

Ingredients	Lb.	Oz.	Mixing procedure
Sugar	2	6	Cream well until soft and smooth
Salt	..	$^3/_4$	
Milk powder	..	6	
Shortening	1	8	
Baker's cheese	5	..	Blend cheese and flour. Add to the above
Bread flour	..	9	in three stages and blend in well
Eggs	2	..	Add eggs in four stages and blend in
Vanilla	..	1	Add flavors and water. Water is added
Lemon	..	$^1/_2$	gradually until a thick gravy consistency is
Cold water	2–3	..	reached. The amount will vary with the cheese

Procedures to Follow

1. Scraping the sides of the machine kettle is important in order to get a smooth mix. This should be done often.
2. Blending the flour and cheese increases the capacity of the cheese to absorb liquid and prevents small lump formation of separating cheese.
3. It is best to have eggs and water on the cold side. This increases the absorption capacity of the cheese mix.
4. Once the cheese has been added to the mix, it is best to run the machine on slow speed. When adding the final portions of water run the machine at slow speed. This will help to prevent curdling.
5. A baked bottom made of short dough is best suited to support the cheese mix. The baked bottom may be smeared with pineapple or other fruit before depositing the cheese mix.

6. The sides of the deep pan should be greased before filling with the mix. This will prevent the cheese mix from sticking and allow it to settle evenly after baking.

7. The cheese cake should be baked at 400°F. The cheese cake is considered baked when it feels springy when touched in the center. Remember that cheese cake is more like a custard than a cake and feels the same as a baked custard in a pie.

8. Allow the cheese cake to settle and cool in the pan before removing from the pan.

Note: A baked bottom is required.

Cheese Cake (Medium-Type) **Yield:** Large pan
　　(Baked Bottom)

Ingredients	Lb.	Oz.	Mixing procedure
Sugar	2	..	Cream until soft and smooth
Salt	..	1	
Milk powder	..	5	
Shortening	1	8	
Baker's cheese	5	..	Blend together and add to the above in three
Bread flour	..	8	stages. Blend well
Eggs	2	..	Add in four stages and blend well
Vanilla	..	1	Add slowly and blend in well. Scrape sides
Lemon	..	1/2	and bottom of kettle
Cold water	2	..	
(approx.)			
Egg whites	1	8	Whip in clean kettle. Whip whites to a
Sugar	..	8	froth and gradually add sugar. Whip to a
			soft peak and fold gently into the cheese mix

Procedures to Follow

1. The egg whites are to be fresh and cool for whipping. Be sure bowl and beater are clean and free from grease.

2. Whip whites to a wet peak (when picked up on a finger the whites will tend to fall over slightly and have a shiny appearance). Over-whipping the whites will cause them to separate into small lumps and will make it necessary to overmix in order to fold the whites into the cheese mix. This will cause loss of volume and large holes.

3. Bake at 385°F. If the sides of the cheese cake are higher than the top of the pan, be sure that the sides are pushed into the pan while the cheese cake is hot (after baking) so that the cake settles evenly.

French Cheese Cake   **Yield:** Large pan
   (Baked Bottom)

Ingredients	Lb.	Oz.	Mixing procedure
Sugar	1	6	Cream until soft and smooth
Salt	..	1	
Milk powder	..	5	
Shortening	1	8	
Baker's cheese	5	..	Blend together and add to the above in three
Bread flour	..	10	stages. Blend well
Eggs (part yolks)	2	..	Add in four stages and blend well
Vanilla	..	1	Add slowly and blend in well. Scrape sides
Lemon	..	$1/2$	and bottom of kettle
Cold water	1		
(approx.)			
Egg whites	3	..	Whip in clean kettle. Whip whites to a
Sugar	1	..	froth and gradually add sugar. Whip to a
			soft peak and fold gently into the cheese mix

Procedures to Follow

1. Bake at 340° to 355°F. This type of cheese cake requires a lower temperature and slower bake so that the egg whites will have an opportunity to set properly during baking and avoid too much settling after baking.
2. This cake should feel firmer than other cheese cakes before removing from the oven.

NUT CAKE, COCOANUT CAKE, MALIBU CAKE, AND FRENCH COFFEE CAKE

These cakes, except for the Malibu, are usually made in large form pans or in regular sheet pans. They are usually cut into slab form and sold by weight. They may also be cut into single servings for dessert purposes in hotel or restaurant service. As in the case of most cakes, recipes will vary in terms of the amount and quality of the basic ingredients used. In some instances, these cakes will require a short-dough bottom as the base to support them. This is especially true of the nut and cocoanut cakes. Malibu cake is generally baked in loaf or oval pans. French coffee cake is usually baked in a deep, large pan. It is also baked in loaf or round layer cake pans. Neither Malibu nor French coffee cake requires a bottom to support it.

Nut Cake (Single Sheet°) **Yield:** Large sheet (18 × 26 in.)

Ingredients	Lb.	Oz.	Mixing procedure
Sugar	2	. .	Work the macaroon paste smooth with about
Salt	. .	$^3/_4$	2 oz. of the eggs. Add the other ingredients
Milk powder	. .	2	and cream until soft and light
Macaroon paste	. .	6	
Shortening	2	. .	
Glucose	. .	4	
Eggs	2	. .	Add the eggs in four stages and cream
Water	. .	8	Add the water and flavor and stir in
Almond flavor	. .	$^1/_2$	
Toasted ground nuts	1	12	Blend the dry ingredients, add, and mix
Dry cake crumbs	1	12	smooth
Cake flour	. .	8	
Baking powder	. .	$^1/_4$	
Egg whites	1	. .	Whip the whites and sugar to a soft peak.
Sugar	. .	6	Fold in gently into above

° Bottom required for single sheet.

Procedures to Follow

1. If the above recipe is used for one sheet a lightly baked short dough bottom should be used as the base. The bottom may be smeared with jam or jelly before the mix is placed in the pan. It is best to use a deep pan. If the regular sheet pan is used line the sides of the pan with cardboard.
2. Bake the cake at 350° to 355°F. When cool, the cake may be dusted with powdered sugar or the top smeared with jam and sprinkled with toasted, ground nuts.
3. If the recipe is to be used for two sheets, it is advisable to make one and one-half times the above recipe for two full sheet pans. Place the mix on paper-lined pans and be sure the sides of the pan are greased.
4. Bake as above and when the sheets are cool, sandwich both sheets by using a raspberry or apricot jam as a filling. The tops of the sheets may be finished as above.

Caution: If a raw cashew nuts are used, be sure to toast them before grinding them. A blend of filberts and cashews is excellent. The cake crumbs used should be dry and made from cakes that are reasonably rich in content.

Cocoanut Cake (One Sheet*)   **Yield:** Large sheet (18 × 26)

Ingredients	Lb.	Oz.	Mixing procedure
Sugar	1	11	Cream all ingredients until soft and smooth
Salt	..	1/2	
Milk powder	..	2	
Glazed cherries	..	6	
Dried mixed fruit	..	6	
Shortening	1	11	
Eggs	1	4	Add eggs in four stages and cream well
Water	1	..	Add water and flavor and stir in
Vanilla	..	1	
Orange flavor	..	1/2	
Macaroon cocoanut	2	10	Blend cocoanut, flour and baking powder,
Cake flour	..	8	add and mix smooth
Bread flour	..	8	
Baking powder	..	1/4	
Egg whites	1	..	Whip to a wet peak and fold in gently into
Sugar	..	4	the above

* Baked bottom required.

Notes on Cocoanut Cake

1. Be sure the cocoanut is unsweetened and fine. Sweetened cocoanut is not to be used, as it will burn, make the cake too sweet, settle during baking, and will not absorb the liquid as well as the unsweetened variety. Do not use coarse or long-shred cocoanut.
2. The bottom may be smeared with apricot or orange jam before the mix is placed into the pan. Be sure to line the sides of the pan with cardboard if you are not using a deep pan.
3. Your attention is called to the need for a baked bottom (short dough) to prevent sogginess that would result from an unbaked dough bottom.

Malibu Cake Yield: 18–19 12-oz. loaf cakes

Ingredients	Lb.	Oz.	Mixing procedure
Sugar	3	8	Blend all the ingredients in this stage until
Salt	..	3/4	soft and smooth (about 5 min. medium
Emulsified shortening	2	8	speed)
Milk powder	..	3	
Cake flour	3	8	
Water	1	8	
Eggs (half yolks)	3	..	Add the eggs in four stages and blend well
Vanilla	..	1	after each addition. When adding the last
Lemon flavor	..	1/2	stage of the eggs, add the flavors and baking
Orange flavor	..	1/4	powder and blend for 4 min. on medium
Baking powder	..	2	speed

Procedures to Follow

1. Deposit the mix into loaf cake, oval, angel cake or Turk-head pans which have been lined with paper liners.
2. Bake at 350° to 360°F. Larger units require a lower temperature.
3. Malibu cakes may be left plain or they may be iced with a delicate form of icing. If iced, fondant icing is recommended.

French Coffee Cake Yield: 1 large or 16–18 small loaf cakes

Ingredients	Lb.	Oz.	Mixing procedure
Sugar	3	..	Mix the almond paste smooth with a small
Salt	..	3/4	portion of the eggs. Cream all ingredients
Milk powder	..	2	until soft and light
Almond paste	..	8	
Shortening	2	..	
Bread flour	..	4	
Eggs	3	..	Add in four stages and cream well
Water	1	..	Add and stir in slightly
Vanilla	..	1	
Cake flour	3	..	Sift, add, and mix smooth
Baking powder	..	1	

Procedures to Follow

1. The almond paste may be left out. If this is done add 4 oz. cake flour to the mix.
2. Butter or margarine may be substituted for part of the shortening.

3. This mix will fill one large deep pan. The sides of the pan should be greased. The bottom of the pan should be paper lined. The mix may also be deposited in smaller sized pans—round or loaf form.
4. Part of the mix may be mixed with chocolate and the chocolate smeared into the center for a marbled or filled effect. The pan may also be filled with half the mix, cinnamon sugar may be sprinkled on top as a filling and the remainder of the mix placed on top of the cinnamon sugar. Melted sweet chocolate may also be striped lightly through the mix before depositing in pans.
5. The top of the mix should be sprinkled with either Struessel topping or ground or sliced nuts and cinnamon sugar.
6. Bake at 350°F.

FRENCH PASTRY
Square-Shaped, Triangular-Shaped, Diamond-Shaped, Rectangular-Shaped

French pastries are individual units of different shapes that have been cut from large sheets of cake. The sheets of cake are layered with various fillings and creams and the cakes themselves may also be varied. For example, high-ratio sheet cakes—yellow, chocolate, etc.—sponge or chiffon sheets may be used. In addition, there may be two or more layers used to prepare the sheet which is to be cut into various shapes.

The figures given will illustrate the various methods of preparing the sheets and cutting of the individual pieces. Various icings and methods of finishing may be employed. Important factors are neatness of work, careful use of icings, blending of colors and final appearance.

Procedures to Follow (Figs. 332–339A)

1. Prepare the sheet cakes so that they are of even thickness. Use care in spreading the cake mix evenly over the sheet pan. The baked sheets should be approximately $1/2$ to $3/4$ in. thick.
2. Since the layered sheets should not be more than 2 in. high (allowance must be made for additional height in finishing), estimate the number of sheets to be used by the type and amount of filling to be used to put the sheets together so that they stick.
3. It is best to place the bottom sheet on a cake board that has been sprinkled with fine cake crumbs or ground nuts. This will prevent sticking.
4. The fillings used may be a light buttercream, a combination of buttercream and jelly or jam, fudge icing, or a combination of several icings where more than two sheets are used.
5. If yellow and chocolate or other sheets are used be sure to alternate the layers.

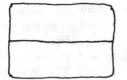

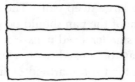

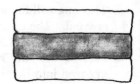

FIG. 332. TWO SHEETS WITH ONE FILLING OF JAM OR BUTTERCREAM

FIG. 333. THREE SHEETS WITH TWO FILLINGS

FIG. 334. TWO SHEETS WITH ONE HEAVY FILLING OF CHOCOLATE OR RUM FILLING

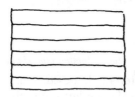

FIG. 335.   FIVE, SIX, OR SEVEN SHEETS (THIN) WITH THIN FILLING BETWEEN LAYERS

FIG. 336. PASTRIES COVERED WITH BUTTERCREAM ON THE SIDES AND GARNISHED WITH TOASTED GROUND NUTS OR CHOCOLATE SPRINKLES. DECORATED WITH BUTTERCREAM AND JAM ON TOP

FONDANT-ICED FRENCH PASTRY SQUARES WITH DESIGNS MADE WITH FONDANT

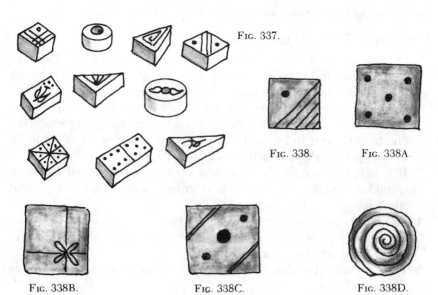

FIG. 337.

FIG. 338.

FIG. 338A.

FIG. 338B.

FIG. 338C.

FIG. 338D.

ROUND SHAPES WITH SIDES ICED WITH BUTTERCREAM AND GARNISHED WITH GROUND NUTS OR CHOCOLATE SPRINKLES. TOPS FINISHED WITH COLORED BUTTERCREAM AND JAM OR OTHER FILLING

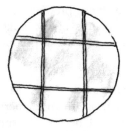

Fig. 339.   Fig. 339A.

6. The filling should be spread evenly so that the sheets are all level. Where sheets are uneven, build up the low sides with additional fillings.

7. When the sheets are put together, press down firmly by placing a sheet pan on top and pressing down with the palms of the hands. In addition, when the sheets are refrigerated, weights may be evenly spaced on top of the covering sheet pan so that the sheets are firmly stuck together.

8. When cutting the chilled sheets, it is best to use a sharp knife and have a container of hot water handy to dip the knife before each cut. This will allow for a smooth, even cut, and prevent smearing of filling. Frozen sheets should be allowed to thaw before cutting. This will avoid undue labor and accidents.

9. Each of the cut units should be iced on the sides first. Since the top and bottom of the unit does not have any icing it will enable you to hold each unit in your fingers and ice the sides easily. The topping is applied to the sides as soon as the buttercream or fudge is applied. The toppings may vary from finely ground cake crumbs of various shapes to toasted ground nuts or chocolate strips.

10. The tops of the pastries are then decorated. The important factors are neatness of design, proper color blend, and careful use of garnish.

11. The units may also be covered with warm fondant. These units are placed on icing grates and the fondant poured over the top and sides as you would for petits fours. The units may also be dipped into the warm fondant and then placed on grates to allow the excess icing to run off.

WHIPPED CREAM AND WHIPPED TOPPING VARIETIES
Short Cakes, Mushroom Cups, Cream Topped Pies, Cream Rolls,
Filled Eclairs, and Cream Puffs

Because of modern store refrigeration and freezing facilities, cream products can be sold all year. Naturally, more of these products are sold during the cooler months. They are the eye-catchers of the bakeshop and require thought, planning, ingenuity, and variation in their production.

Preparation of the Whipped Cream

Cream for whipping is usually the heavy variety and contains as much as 40 per cent butterfat. Light cream contains from 18 to 20 per cent butterfat. When using light cream, a stabilizer must be used to support the cream during whipping and after the cream is bagged out on the various products. Heavy cream requires no stabilizer, although many bakers use a small percentage ($1/4$ oz. per quart of cream) to insure the shelf-life of the products and keep the cream from running or weeping after bagging out.

Procedures to Follow for Whipping of Cream

1. Cream (heavy or light) should be at least 24 hr. old. Slight aging makes a better whip.
2. Cream should be very cold (avoid freezing) and the kettle and beater used should be clean and chilled.
3. Cream should be whipped in a cool part of the bakeshop and should be whipped in second speed (third speed on a four-speed machine).
4. Sugar (about 4 oz. confectionery sugar per quart) and stabilizer should be sifted or blended together and added when the cream starts to life (slight marks of the whip are seen in the cream).
5. Chilled milk (fresh whole milk), about 8 oz. per quart of heavy cream, is added in the final stages of whipping. Add the milk in a slow steady stream so that it is easily blended.
6. Vanilla flavor is added last. Use the best quality of vanilla ($1/4$ oz. per quart).
7. Whip the cream to a medium wet peak. Avoid overwhipping. This will cause separation and conversion to butter. It leads to weeping while bagging out.
8. Leftover whipped cream must be stored in the refrigerator.

Procedures to Follow for Whipped Toppings (Figs. 340–348)

1. Toppings should be refrigerated and chilled at all times. Avoid freezing. If frozen, blend with topping that is not frozen and whip as usual.
2. Toppings contain sugar and flavor. They also contain stabilizers.

3. Toppings should be whipped to a medium wet peak. Avoid over-whipping (stiff peak). Toppings firm up after they are bagged out. The addition of extra stabilizer may cause a stiff, tearing effect when bagging out.

4. If topping and light or heavy cream are blended, whip the topping to a soft peak and then pour the cream into the topping in a steady stream while the machine is whipping at medium speed. Add extra sugar and flavor for the amount of cream added. Refer to the preparation of whipped cream. Many bakers use an equal amount of topping and cream; some use all topping.

5. Most toppings can absorb and hold many varieties of cooked fruits, jellies, jams, and fillings (orange and lemon). These are added in the final stages of whipping. Fruited toppings should be applied with a bowl knife or large plain tube. A small tube (French or star) will clog because of the fruit.

6. The sketches which follow (Figs. 340–348) will show how the above varieties are prepared.

FIG. 340. FINISHED STRAWBERRY, OR OTHER FRUIT, SHORT CAKE

FIG. 341. MUSHROOM (CREAM - FILLED) CUPCAKE

FIG. 342. BUTTERFLY (CREAM-FILLED) CUPCAKE

FIG. 343. CREAM-TOPPED FRUIT PIE

FIG. 344. CREAM-TOPPED CUSTARD PIE

FIG. 345. CREAM ROLL FILLED WITH WHIPPED CREAM

FIG. 346. CREAM-FILLED ECLAIR

FIG. 347. CREAM-FILLED CREAM PUFF

FIG. 348. CREAM-FILLED ROLL

SEVEN LAYER CAKE

Seven layer is a form of French pastry. It is a popular pastry item and has large sales potential when made properly. It may be made with regular or chocolate sponge. The following recipe is quite standard in most bakeshops. The glucose added to the mix will maintain the moisture of the mix and prolong shelf-life.

Seven Layer Cake   **Yield:** 7 thin sheets

Ingredients	Lb.	Oz.	Mixing procedure
Eggs (half yolks)	6	..	Warm the eggs to about 100°F. in a double
Sugar	3	..	boiler. Add the rest of the ingredients and
Salt	..	1	whip until light, airy, and thick
Glucose or corn syrup	..	4	
Cake flour	3	2	Sift and fold in the flour lightly by hand. Avoid overmixing

Procedures to Follow (Fig. 349)

1. Prepare seven sheet pans. Grease the sides and edges and line the pans with parchment paper.
2. Divide the whipped mix equally into the seven pans. Level the mix evenly with a bowl knife. Be sure the mix is evenly distributed to avoid thin parts which brown or burn during baking. Use the bowl knife sparingly to avoid toughening the mix while spreading.
3. Bake the sheets at 400°F. until very light brown. Do not overbake.
4. Allow the sheets to cool and put together with chocolate buttercream. It is best to cover the sheets with a sheet pan and place some weights on the cake while it is refrigerated. This will insure sticking together of all layers. Chilling the cake provides easier cutting and smoother finish of the cut strips.
5. Cut the cake into strips about 3 in. wide (smaller if desired) and place the strips on an icing grate (three to a grate, spaced several inches apart).

Fig. 349. Seven Layer Cake

6. Ice the top and sides of the cake strips with chocolate fudge icing or melted sweet chocolate. The sides and top of the strips are usually combed before the icing or chocolate sets. Be sure the chocolate is not overheated. It should be slightly warmer than body temperature.
7. The top of the seven layer strips may be garnished with chopped pistachio nuts or other garnish if desired. Cut the strips into desired size. Use a sharp knife that is dipped into hot water after each cut. This will make a smooth finish and avoid smearing the fudge or chocolate.
8. For *chocolate seven layer cake,* add 6 oz. cocoa to the mix and reduce the amount of flour to 2 lb. 12 oz. Be sure to sift the cocoa and flour together. Use natural cocoa.

MINIATURE CAKE ROLLS

These are small cake rolls and are classified as a type of French pastry. Their diameter is seldom over 2 in. and often less than that. They are filled with various colored buttercream and very often the cream may be filled with toasted nuts. There are two basic sponge mixes which are used for these rolls. Since the rolls are thin, the recipe for seven layer cake or chiffon cake may be used for the yellow type of roll. A chocolate sponge recipe will be listed to provide the chocolate variety.

Chocolate Roll   Yield: 4 rolls

Ingredients	Lb.	Oz.	Mixing procedure
Sugar	2	4	Warm the eggs to 100°F. Add the rest of
Salt	..	$1/2$	the ingredients and whip until thick. Re-
Glucose or corn syrup	..	4	move from the machine
Eggs (part yolks)	2	..	
Water	1	..	Dissolve the dry ingredients in the water.
Sugar	..	4	Add the flavor and fold lightly into the
Baking soda	..	$3/4$	whipped eggs
Vanilla	..	1	
Cake flour	1	12	Sift the flour and cocoa and fold lightly into
Cocoa	..	6	the above

Procedures to Follow (Figs. 350 and 351)

1. Prepare four sheet pans by greasing the sides and lining with paper.
2. Divide the mix into four equal parts on each of the pans. Spread evenly over the entire surface of the pan with a bowl knife. Do this as quickly and evenly as possible to prevent setting and tearing of the mix. The eggs tend to set and the mix tears when spread if left to stand too long.
3. Bake immediately in a hot oven 410°F. Bake until just done. The cake continues to dry or bake for the first minute or two after it is removed from the oven. Overbaking will cause cracking.
4. Allow the sheets to cool and fill with various colored buttercream icings. The buttercream may be mixed with toasted nuts or glazed fruits, and may also have various flavors from mocha to rum, and others suited to the type of buttercream used. Spread the buttercream evenly over the cake so that the roll is of even thickness.
5. Roll up the roll tightly in paper and chill.
6. The rolls are generally finished with sweet chocolate, fudge icing, or the same buttercream used for the filling. The sides and top of the roll are usually combed and garnished as desired.
7. Slice the rolls while they are chilled by dipping a sharp knife into hot water after each cut. This will make a smooth cut without smearing the icing or coating. The size of the cuts depend upon the place or serving. The slices are usually made on a diagonal angle or bias.

Fig.   350.   Buttercream-Filled
Miniature Cake Roll

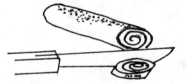

Fig. 351.   Miniature Cake Roll
Cut at an Angle

SPONGE AND HONEY CAKES
Almond Sponge, Nut Sponge, Royal Fruit Sponge, and Honey Cakes

These special sponge and honey cakes are prepared for certain holidays and special occasions. Many retail shops prepare these cakes at regular periods during the week as a part of the production schedule. Normally, they are prepared for weekend sales. These cakes are usually made in loaf form. Many bakeshops prepare them in large pans and merchandise them by the pound or slice. The important factors regarding their production are whipping of the eggs and combining of the other ingredients which are not usually used in making regular sponge cake.

Almond Sponge Cake

Yield: 11 loaves of 12 oz. or 1 large pan

Ingredients	Lb.	Oz.	Mixing procedure
Almond or macaroon paste	1	8	Add the eggs gradually to the almond paste and mix smooth
Eggs	1	..	
Sugar	2	..	Warm the eggs slightly and whip until light.
Salt	..	$1/2$	Add the almond filling gradually. Machine
Eggs (half yolks)	2	..	to run in second and whip light
Cake flour	1	12	Remove from machine and fold in the flour lightly by hand

Procedures to Follow

1. The almond filling should be worked in the machine with a flat beater. The mix should be smooth and free from lumps. Add the eggs gradually to the almond paste to avoid lumps. Scrape down the sides of the machine.

2. When adding the soft, smooth almond filling after the eggs and sugar are whipped, the machine should run in second speed until all the almond filling is incorporated. Full speed will cause the mix to lose air. Continue to whip in second speed until the mix is thick and light. The marks of the wire whip should be distinct and hold like a soft meringue.

3. Sift the flour and fold in lightly with an overhand motion. Be sure your hand goes down to the bottom of the kettle and around the sides to incorporate all the flour and avoid lumps. Mixing must be done lightly and gently at this point to avoid loss of air and toughness resulting from overmixing.

4. Deposit the mix gently into loaf pans and fill slightly more than half full.

5. A large, deep pan about the size of a sheet pan may be used for the entire mix given above.

6. Bake at 350°F. for the smaller loaf pans and 340°F. for the large pan. The cakes are considered baked when they are gently touched in the center and they spring back to the touch. If the oven has a strong bottom heat, bake the cakes on double pans.

7. The mix may also be deposited in layer pans lined with special paper liners. These layers are dusted with confectionery sugar when cool.

Nut Sponge Cake   **Yield:** 10 loaves or 1 large pan

Ingredients	Lb.	Oz.	Mixing procedure
Almond or macaroon paste	..	12	Blend together to a smooth paste. Remove all lumps
Eggs	..	12	
Sugar	2	..	Warm the eggs slightly and whip with the
Salt	..	$1/4$	sugar and salt until light. Add the almond
Eggs (half yolks)	2	4	filling slowly in second speed. Whip until thick in second speed.
Toasted ground nuts	1	..	Sift the flour and blend the nuts with the
Cake flour	1	12	flour. Fold into the above lightly by hand

Notes on Nut Sponge Cake

1. Toasted filberts or cashews are recommended. They add a special flavor and nut-like appearance to the baked cake.
2. Bake as you did the almond sponge cake.

Royal Fruit Sponge Cake   **Yield:** 18 loaves or 1 large pan

Ingredients	Lb.	Oz.	Mixing procedure
Sugar	2	..	Warm the yolks slightly and whip with the
Salt	..	$1/2$	sugar and salt until light. Place in a mixing
Egg yolks	3	..	bowl
Cake flour	2	..	Sift the flour. Break up the butter and chop
Bread flour	1	..	in with a scraper into the flour until fine
Hard butter or margarine	1	..	lumps of butter and flour are formed. Fold lightly into the above
Nut pieces	1	8	Fold the cherries and nuts lightly into the
Chopped glazed cherries or mixed fruit	1	8	above
Egg whites	2	..	Whip the whites to a froth. Add the sugar
Sugar	1	..	and whip to a soft peak. Fold lightly into the above by hand

Procedures to Follow

1. The butter or margarine must be hard so that small hard pieces are formed when chopped with the flour. Soft butter will form a paste. This is to be avoided for the paste will form an uneven texture and grain.

2. The egg whites are to be whipped to a soft peak for easy incorporation into the mix. A firm peak will cause the whites to break up into lumps and require more mixing to incorporate. This will cause loss of air and toughening of the mix.
3. It is advisable to dust the nuts and cherries with a bit of bread flour. This will absorb some of the syrup released in chopping the cherries and prevent nuts and fruits from sinking to the bottom of the cake.
4. Deposit into loaf pans or large pans and bake 355°F. Larger pans require a lower temperature.
5. The cakes made in loaf form are dusted lightly with confectionery sugar. Cakes in large pans are turned over and the bottom is now the top. This may be finished by dusting with confectionery sugar or smeared with jam and dusted with toasted chopped nuts.

Honey Cake   Yield: 11 1-lb. loaves

Ingredients	Lb.	Oz.	Mixing procedure
Sugar (brown preferred)	1	..	Place all the ingredients in this stage into a bowl or machine and blend well to dissolve all ingredients. Be sure the honey is blended in well
Salt	..	$1/4$	
Eggs	..	8	
Oil	..	8	
Honey (dark) (1 qt.)	3	..	
Cinnamon	..	$1/8$	
Cloves (good pinch)	..	$1/16$	
Allspice (good pinch)	..	$1/16$	
Water	1	..	Dissolve the soda in the water and mix into the above
Baking soda	..	1	
Nuts (walnuts or filberts)	1	..	Blend in the nuts and fruits
Mixed fruit or orange peel	1	..	
			Sift the flour, add, and mix well until smooth and the mix runs freely
Rye flour	3	..	

Procedures to Follow

1. Brown or dark honey is preferred for the stronger taste and darker appearance of the cake. The best type of honey is buckwheat. Clover honey is not advisable for it is too light in color and fine in flavor. If the honey is crystallized, place in a double boiler and heat until the crystals are dissolved before using.

2. Rye flour is used because it provides a fine, soft texture and added taste. The rye flour has no gluten-forming proteins and the mix can be mixed well without creating toughness in the cake.

3. Deposit into loaf pans that are lined with paper and fill a little less than half full. Larger pans should also be lined with paper.

4. Garnish the top of the cake with blanched almond halves neatly spaced.

5. Bake in a cool oven 325° to 335°F. It is advisable to bake honey cakes on a sheet pan or double pan. This will prevent burning of the bottom of the cake if the oven has a strong bottom heat.

6. The cakes are considered baked when touched very gently in the center and it springs back to the touch. Avoid moving the cake in the oven during baking. Its delicate structure will cause it to fall if the cake has not fully risen and the structure is set.

DARK FRUIT CAKE

Christmas Cake

This cake is a seasonal holiday specialty. You will find many recipes and variations for the product, although most of the recipes are similar in basic structure. Most are pound cake recipes that employ regular pound-for-pound mix and the creaming method of mixing. Other recipes may use more commercial, high-ratio type of pound cake. You will also find variations in the amount, type, and preparation of dried fruits used for the cake. The recipe and procedures which follow are those which are normally found in the preparation of dark fruit cake. These cakes are usually made and wrapped in advance of the holiday so that the busy production schedule is not burdened.

Dark Fruit Cake   Yield: 42 lb., the yield depending
                                                                on pan size

Ingredients	Lb.	Oz.	Mixing procedure
Macaroon or almond paste	1	8	Blend well to a smooth paste
Eggs	..	8	
Granulated sugar	3	..	Add to the above and cream light and soft.
Brown sugar	3	..	Scrape sides of kettle to remove lumps
Salt	..	$1^1/_2$	
Shortening	6	..	
Bread flour	1	..	
Eggs	6	..	Add the eggs in four or five stages and
Molasses (about $^1/_3$ qt.)	1	..	cream well after each addition. Cream until soft and light
Cinnamon	..	1	Add and stir in lightly
Cloves	..	$^1/_4$	
Nutmeg	..	$^1/_2$	
Bread flour	3	..	Sift, add and fold into the above until smooth
Cake flour	2	8	
Baking powder	..	$^1/_2$	
Nuts (walnuts, pecans, etc.)	3	..	Fold into the mix

Preparation of Fruit

Ingredients	Lb.	Mixing procedure
Raisins	15	Wash the glazed fruit in cool water to re-
Cherries (glazed)	10	move the excess syrup or sugar. Soak the
Pineapple (glaced)	4	fruit overnight in the following preparation:
Drid citron	3	honey $1^1/_2$ lb. ($^1/_2$ qt.) and syrup (hot)
Orange and lemon peel (glazed)	5	(1 qt.); 1 fifth of rum may be used in place of the syrup
Pitted dates and figs	5	

Procedures to Follow for Fruit Cake

1. It is advisable to drain any excess liquid from the fruit after the 24 hr.
   soaking period. This may occur if the sugar is not removed from the
   glazed fruits. The fruits are prepared in advance of the preparation
   of the mix. Fold the fruit into the cake mix gently but thoroughly for
   even distribution.

2. The batter is placed in parchment-paper-lined pans. Loaf cake pans are most popular. However, the angel or ring-type pans are also used. The size of the pan determines the weight of the batter. The pans are filled three-fourths full. The average flanged pan is filled about seven-eighths full.
3. Bake the cakes at 325° to 350°F. Small units require a higher baking temperature. Large units require a lower temperature. It is also advisable to have a low pressure moist steam in the oven during baking. If this is not possible pans of water placed in the oven will help to prevent the top crust from drying out.
4. Fruit cakes of this variety are usually finished after they have been baked and cooled. They are normally glazed and decorated with sliced almonds and dried, glazed fruit. They may be glazed and left plain. This will make a shiny and more attractive appearance.
5. To finish fruit cakes wash the top of the fruit cakes with boiled apricot coating. Apply nuts and fruits while the coating is still warm.

The following glaze may also be used:

Glucose 1 qt. (about 3 lb.)	Boil the water and glucose. Add the gum
Water 1 qt.	arabic and boil about 5 min. Apply while
Gum Arabic 1 oz.	hot

ICE CREAM CAKES, ROLLS, TARTS AND BAKED ALASKA

Ice cream cakes are a very popular item in many of the finer bakeshops, restaurants, and hotels. There are many varieties and the baker need only use his skill and imagination to prepare them. This unit will confine itself to the most popular of these specialties used for birthday and other special event cakes.

The quality and type of ice cream are important factors to be considered in the makeup of various cakes, rolls, and tarts. The French type of ice cream is easier to handle and is capable of being molded better than the leaner or commercial types of ice cream. The major point is the amount of butter or other fats present in the ice cream. The French type is richer in fat content. This means that there are less moisture crystals present and ice cream does not melt or soften as rapidly as other types containing a lesser amount of fat. This has an important bearing on the speed with which the ice cream is to be worked as well as where the ice cream products are to be made. The average retail bakeshop does not have a chill room especially set up for this sort of work. Neither does it have walk-in refrigerators to work in.

The ice cream should be in a frozen state and not permitted to soften on the outside if possible. Ice cream that is semi-hard results in a smeared flavor and color effect when various ice creams are blended in one cake.

An ice cream knife should be used to slice the ice cream. This is a knife that has handles at both ends similar to a large wood saw. This makes it possible for the baker to place pressure with both hands and arms to make slicing the ice cream easier. If using the single edge French knife dip the blade into hot water before cutting the ice cream. This will make cutting easier and make a clean, unsmeared cut. Above all, it is necessary to have the cakes ready before the ice cream is cut.

The best types of cakes to use for ice cream cakes and other varieties are those made from a sponge or high-ratio cake mix. The chiffon mixes are excellent. These cakes are tender and have a moist, even texture. This makes it possible for the cakes to absorb the soft or melting outside of the sliced ice cream without dripping on the sides of the cake. It is best to fill the layer cakes and rolls and then freeze these units before they are finished.

Preparation of Ice Cream Layers (Figs. 352 and 353)

1. A single layer about 2 in. in height is sufficient. The layer may be cut into two or three pieces. The three section layer will require two fillings of ice cream. This means more work but does make a more effective and appealing appearance.

2. Cut the ice cream (normally a $2^1/_2$ gal. round shape) in two pieces by cutting in half from the top down. Lay the halves on the sides and cut slices varying from 1 to $1/_2$ in. thick, depending upon the needs. These slices may then be cut in quarters by cutting along the length once again.

3. The slices are then placed into the layers and the uncovered parts of the layer are filled in by cutting small pieces to take care of the uncovered parts. An ice cream scoop or spoon (flat) should be used to level off the ice cream filling so that the layer is even when completed. If two layers of ice cream are used the flavors of ice cream may be varied.

4. After the layers have been filled, place a wax paper (heavy type) liner around the sides. This will keep the melted cream from running and keep the sides even. Place the layers in the freezer until frozen before finishing. The size of the layer will determine the size of the slices of the ice cream cut.

   Note: If a large amount of soft ice cream remains on the pan place the pan in the freezer and then scrape the ice cream off and use as a filler for blank layer spaces or for ice cream rolls. The ice cream should be cut on a large, clean, stainless steel bun pan.

5. After the ice cream layers have been frozen the sides and top of the layers are usually covered with whipped cream or topping. Be sure to have the cream whipped and all the necessary materials ready before finishing begins.

6. The cakes are to be placed in the display freezer immediately after each cake is finished.

7. For birthday cakes, cover all the layers with the cream and freeze. When you are ready to apply the decorations, remove the cakes (a few at a time) and apply the decoration quickly. Roses and other flowers should be made in advance and placed on the cake quickly. This will avoid softening of the cakes. Softening and re-freezing results in a loss of ice cream volume.

FIG. 352. LAYERS OF CAKE FILLED WITH ICE CREAM

FIG. 353. FINISHED ICE CREAM LAYER WITH WHIPPED CREAM TOPPING

Procedures to Follow for Ice Cream Rolls (Figs. 354–357)

1. A yellow or chocolate sponge roll should be used. This is similar to the cake mix used for jelly or chocolate Swiss roll. Chiffon mixes are excellent.

2. Lay the sheet out on a large sheet of wax paper. The sheet is then cut in half if it is thick enough and two ice cream rolls are made from the one sheet of cake. Thick rolls may be made for special cakes.

FIG. 354. ICE CREAM LOG READY FOR ROLLING IN CAKE

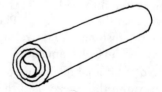

FIG. 355. ICE CREAM LOG FINISHED WITH WHIPPED CREAM

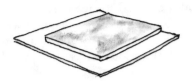

FIG. 356. LAYER OF ICE CREAM ON THIN SHEET OF CAKE READY FOR ROLLING UP

FIG. 357. ICE CREAM ROLL FINISHED WITH WHIPPED CREAM

3. Cut the ice cream brick or round $2^1/_2$ gal. container in half and then into $^1/_2$ in. strips. One inch strips of ice cream may be used for a thicker roll. Lay the ice cream out on the sheet leaving a 1 in. edge of cake at the top and bottom. This will enable you to fold the cake into the ice cream when you start the roll and allow 1 in. of cake at the edge to seal or cover the ice cream at the bottom. Be sure the ice cream is evenly distributed and of equal thickness so that the ice cream roll is even.

4. Roll up the ice cream roll in the wax paper. Be sure the paper is firmly around the roll for this will help to keep the round shape.

5. Place each roll in the freezer as soon as it is made up. If the ice cream softens, it will tend to flatten the roll.

6. Finish the roll after it has been frozen. Follow the same procedure for finishing as you would for ice cream layers.

Procedures to Follow for Ice Cream Tarts (Figs. 358 and 359)

1. Ice cream tarts are best made with pre-baked cake that has been baked in tinfoil cups.

2. The ice cream is then placed in the cup on top of the cake with an ice cream scoop. Two scoops of ice cream may be placed on top of each other and pressed into each other. This will make a full cup and provide variety of ice cream flavors.

3. Baked tart shells may also be used. These may be filled with a base of soft sherbet and ice cream then placed on top. A thin slice of cake may be placed at the bottom of the tart shell before filling with cream and/or sherbet to absorb any softness of the cream and prevent the shell from becoming soggy. Pre-baked shells should be placed in paper liners before putting in the freezer. When the tarts are completely frozen, garnish the tops with whipped cream or whipped topping and return to the freezer. It is best to finish the tarts with a charlotte effect.

4. Eclair and cream puff shells may also be used for ice cream and/or sherbet desserts. Cut the eclairs in half. Using a long-shaped special ice cream scoop fill the scoop with ice cream and place it into the bottom half of the shell. Two scoops of various ice creams may be used.

5. For cream puffs, cut the shells in half and fill with a regular round ice cream scoop.

6. Dip the scoop in warm water periodically. This will make it easier to scoop hard ice cream and prevent excessive smearing.

7. Place the tops on the shells and freeze. The tops of the eclairs or cream puffs are finished with a rosette or spiral, running dog effect made with whipped cream or whipped topping. Return the finished products to the freezer immediately after finishing.

FIG. 358.   ICE CREAM PLACED IN A   FIG. 359.   ICE CREAM TART FINISHED
            TART SHELL   WITH WHIPPED CREAM

Baked Alaska

This is a specialty item made in better hotels and restaurants. While its preparation is rather simple, browning of the meringue and speed of service of the dessert are important factors. This unit will explain the preparation of the dessert as well as suggest a procedure for service.

Procedures to Follow (Figs. 360–362)

1. Cut strips of sponge cake, high-ratio cake, or chiffon cake from a sheet that is about 1 in. thick. The strips should be about 3 to 4 in. wide. The width is determined by the requirements of the establishment. Place strips on a cake board so that they are firm. Place two strips on a board about 4 in. apart.

2. Full gallon squares of ice cream are recommended for this dessert because they are easy to cut and make easy placement. Cut each half the same way so that you now have quarters about $2^{1}/_{2}$ in. square. Place these cuts of ice cream evenly on the cake strips leaving about $^{1}/_{2}$ in. of space at either end.

3. Prepare the meringue topping in advance. This is the same topping that is used for lemon meringue pies. Bag the topping quickly, using a large star tube, along the sides of the cake and across the top. The top should be built up to a peak resembling the triangular roof of a bungalow.

4. Dust the top of the meringue with confectionery sugar and place immediately into a very hot oven (650°F. or better). The purpose of the intense heat is to brown the meringue without letting the heat penetrate the cake and soften the ice cream.

5. For quick results that are effective, it is best to place the covered strips under the broiler at low flame or medium (depending upon the distance of the cake to the flame). This will brown the top of the meringue and the heat will apply only to the top and outside surface of the cake. Confectionery sugar dusted on the meringue will cause quicker browning.

6. For serving Baked Alaska, it is advisable that the cake be cut, placed on dishes, and served as quickly as possible to avoid melting of the ice cream.

7. Dip a sharp French knife into water and make clean, quick strokes to cut the strips of dessert. Avoid a sawing motion. Make the cut with one stroke for each unit cut. You will note that you are cutting on a cake board and do not have to be concerned with cutting edge of the knife. The waiters or people serving the dessert should be present and ready to serve as soon as the dessert is placed on dishes.

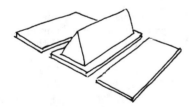

FIG. 360. CAKE SHEET CUT INTO THREE EQUAL STRIPS WITH ICE CREAM ON CENTER STRIP

FIG. 361. CAKE STRIPS PLACED AGAINST SIDES OF ICE CREAM TO FORM TRIANGLE OR "A" SHAPE

FIG. 362. MERINGUE TOPPING PLACED ON CAKE AND READY FOR QUICK BROWNING

8. Baked Alaska may be made up and placed in the freezer. The units or strips are taken from the freezer and placed under the broiler as the waiter comes in. In other words, it is best to prepare the dessert to order.

UPSIDE DOWN CAKE

This cake has the advantage of permitting the skilled baker to make a variety of upside down cakes from the same cake recipe. The varieties are made by simply changing the nature of the fruits and their arrangement, as well as of the glazing of the fruits after the cake is baked. Various cake recipes may be used. However, a cake with sufficient body must be used, because one of delicate structure will break or cause the fruit to fall out at the time the cake is removed from the pan.

Upside Down Cake   Yield: 18 6-in. cakes

Ingredients	Lb.	Oz.	Mixing procedure
Sugar	3	..	Cream all ingredients in this stage until soft
Salt	..	1	and light
Milk powder	..	4	
Glucose or corn syrup	..	4	
Shortening	2	..	
Eggs (part yolks)	2	..	Add the eggs in three stages and cream well after each addition
Water	2	..	Add the water alternately with the flour.
Vanilla	..	1	This will prevent curdling and lumping of
Lemon and orange flavor	..	$1/2$	the mix. Mix until the batter is smooth. Do not overmix
Cake flour	4	..	
Baking powder	..	2	

Note: This mix is similar to the wine-cake or French coffee cake mix. Mix the same as you would the other cake mixes. Proper creaming is important.

Pan Spread for Upside Down Cakes

Ingredients	Lb.	Oz.	Mixing procedure
Sugar	1	..	Cream the sugar and shortening. Mix the
Shortening	..	12	jelly or jam smooth and add in three stages
Jelly or jam	..	12	and cream in well

Procedures to Follow (Figs. 363–365)

1. Use individual 6 in. layer pans only. Do not use bracket-type pans. These are difficult to handle since the cakes have to be removed from the pans as soon as they are removed from the oven.

2. Grease the pans heavily (the metal should be completely covered) so that the cakes do not stick and there is sufficient spread to caramelize and glaze the cake during the baking process. A red-colored jelly is preferred because of the pleasant color of the baked crust.

3. Drain the fruit before using. Pineapple is the most popular variety. Cherries are used in conjunction with the fruit for added color and variety. Whole round slices of pineapple or sections may be used. Space them so that the cake has a pleasing appearance.

4. Bake the cakes at 375°F. The cake should be tested for proper bake by its color as well as the touch test. If it springs back lightly to the touch it is baked.

5. Turn the cakes over as soon as removed from the oven. Turn them on clean sheet pans which have been dusted with cake crumbs to prevent sticking. They may be turned immediately on cardboard cake liners.

6. Glaze the top of the cake with hot simple syrup to create a better shine and lustre to the fruit and cherries. A combination of heated apricot coating and syrup (in equal parts), to which a few drops of red color has been added, may be used. This will make a quick-drying shine.

7. Additional canned fruits may be added to the cake after baking and then these fruits glazed with heated syrup or apricot coating.

FIG. 363. PANS GREASED HEAVILY

FIG. 364. PLACE PINE-APPLE SLICES AND CHERRIES IN PAN

FIG. 365. AFTER CAKE IS BAKED AND TURNED, GLAZE WITH HOT SYRUP

BANANA CAKE

While banana cake is a specialty item, it has many advantages for the baker. It enables him to add to his variety as well as taking advantage of the use of fresh fruit. Bananas that are slightly overripe can be purchased at a cheaper price and are excellent for use in producing the cake. Avoid using bananas that have started to discolor in the interior. This cake is an excellent warm weather item and a good lead item.

Banana Cake   **Yield:** 18 6-in. 12 oz. layers

Ingredients	Lb.	Oz.	Mixing procedure
Ripe bananas	2	8	Blend the peeled bananas and flour to a
Cake flour	1	..	smooth paste
Brown sugar	2	..	Add these ingredients to the bananas and
Granulated sugar	1	..	blend well for 8 min. at medium speed.
Salt	..	1	Scrape the sides of the kettle and beater to
Milk powder	..	4	remove lumps
High-ratio shortening	1	6	
Eggs (part yolks)	1	8	Add the eggs in three stages. Blend well after each addition
Water	2	..	Dissolve the soda in the water, add the flavor
Baking soda	..	$1^1/_4$	and mix alternately with the sifted flour and
Vanilla	..	1	baking powder. Scrape the sides of the
Banana flavor or grated rind of banana	..	$^1/_2$	kettle after each addition. Mix in medium speed for about 6 min. Be sure the mix is smooth
Cake flour	2	..	
Baking powder	..	1	

Procedures to Follow

1. Be sure the mix is blended well in each stage. Avoid curdling by insufficient mixing.

2. Deposit the mix into layer cake pans which have been greased and dusted. It is advisable to use special cake liners for this is a delicate cake and will handle easier if baked in liners. The mix may also be baked in sheet pans and sheets put together with the special icing. The sheets may then be cut into oblongs or squares and sold in that fashion.

3. Bake the units at 365° to 370°F. until light brown and the cake springs back lightly to the touch.

4. Ice the cakes when they are cool. Use the icing fresh since this icing will develop a slight crust when standing. Use a bowl knife finish for a home-made effect. Round or long slices of banana may be placed on the cakes.

Banana Icing   **Yield:** To ice 18 layers

Ingredients	Lb.	Oz.	Mixing procedure
Confectionery sugar	3	..	Sift the dry ingredients together
Salt	..	$1/4$	
Milk powder	..	4	
Shortening (high-ratio)	1	..	Add the shortening and bananas. Mix until soft and light
Bananas	..	8	
Water	..	4	Add the water and flavor and blend in well
Banana flavor	..	$1/2$	
Vanilla	..	$1/2$	

CREAM CHEESE CAKE

Cream cheese cakes have become very popular. There are many variations in recipes used based on the cheese content. For example, there are cakes made with 100 per cent cream cheese, eggs, and light cream. These are rich and expensive. However, the consumer is willing to pay for a quality product and bakers are encouraged to make such products. There are recipes which call for a blend of baker's cheese and cream cheese. These are cheaper to produce and also require a different method of production. The blend recipes often call for the use of egg whites which are incorporated into the cheese mix. Either or both varieties have a place in the bakeshop and both should be made to meet consumer tastes. Recipes for both types are presented.

Cream Cheese Cake (100 Per Cent Cream Cheese)   **Yield:** 6–8 6-in. layers

Ingredients	Lb.	Oz.	Mixing procedure
Cream cheese	5	..	Blend in slow speed until smooth. Do not overmix
Sugar	1	4	
Salt	..	$1/2$	
Rind of two lemons or lemon flavor	..	$1/2$	
Whole eggs (fresh preferred)	2	..	Add in three stages and blend in. Scrape sides of kettle. Add slowly and blend in. Scrape sides of kettle
Light cream	..	8	

Note: Mix this batter at slow speed. It is only a matter of blending the ingredients to a smooth state and high speed will cause a separation.

Procedures to Follow (Figs. 366–370)

1. This cheese cake is baked in layer cake pans of various sizes (from 6 to 12 in. size). Prebake the bottoms (short dough). Grease the sides of the pan after the bottoms are baked and line the sides with short dough.

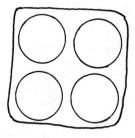

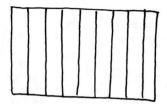

FIG. 366. CUT OUT AND PREBAKE BOTTOMS

FIG. 367. CUT OUT STRIPS OF SHORT DOUGH

FIG. 368. LINE SIDES OF PAN WITH SHORT DOUGH

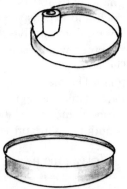

FIG. 369. REMOVE EXCESS DOUGH

FIG. 370. FILL THE PANS ALMOST FULL AND BAKE ON A SHEET PAN

2. Fill the pans with the cheese mix almost to the top. Bake at 450°F. until the cheese cake rises and the edge of the cake turns a light brown (about 20 min.). Remove from the oven and allow the cake to set or cool for about 15 min. Run a bowl knife around the edge of the cake about ¹/₂ in. deep. This will allow the cake to settle evenly. Return the cake to the oven at 350°F. for about 20 min. and bake

until the edge is browned and the center feels set or slightly firm. Allow the cakes to cool for about 2 hr. before turning out of the pans. The tops of the cakes may be covered with pineapple or cherry.

Cream Cheese Cake (50 Per Cent Cream Cheese)

Yield: 12 6-in. layers

Ingredients	Lb.	Oz.	Mixing procedure
Sugar	1	4	Cream these ingredients until soft and light
Salt	..	1	
Shortening (part butter)	..	12	
Milk powder	..	6	
Cream cheese	2	8	Blend the cheese and flour together and
Baker's cheese	2	8	blend into the above. Use slow speed
Bread flour	..	8	
Eggs (half yolks)	1	4	Add in three stages and blend in
Milk or water (approx.) (milk preferred)	2	..	Add the water or milk in three stages and blend in slowly
Vanilla	..	$1/2$	
Rind of two fresh lemons			
Egg whites	1	..	Whip to a wet peak and fold lightly into the
Sugar	..	8	cheese mix

Procedures to Follow

1. Prebake the bottoms for the layer pans. Grease the sides of the pan well and sprinkle the sides with cake crumbs. Tip the layer pan to remove the excess cake crumbs. Use light cake crumbs.
2. Fill the pans about seven-eighths full and bake on a sheet pan at 400°F.
3. Cheese cakes will rise and turn brown at the edges after about 20 min. of baking. Draw the pans with the cheese cakes to the oven door and draw a knife around the edge of the cheese cake about $1/2$ in. deep. This will release the cake from the pan and prevent cracking of the top.
4. Bake for 15 or 20 min. more until the cake feels set or springy to the touch. Fruit may be placed on the baked bottom before the cheese mix is placed in the pan.
5. The top of the cheese cake may be dusted with light crumbs and a small portion of cooked fruit filling placed in the center top of the cheese cake. The crumbs will hold the fruit in place and prevent it from sinking into the cake.

6. Allow the cakes to settle and cool before removing from the pans. The cakes are best removed by placing a liner on top of the cake and then inverting the pan. Another liner is then placed on the bottom part of the cake and the cake inverted again. This will prevent breakage.

EGG COOKIES (KICHEL)
Sugar Kichel, Bow-Ties, Steam Kichel, Small Bagged Kichel

Kichel are specialties made in many retail bakeshops. Originally, they were popular within certain ethnic groups but they have grown in popularity and spread to many bakeshops that cater to consumers of various nationalities. They have the advantage of being durable (long shelf-life). Each of the varieties requires a special makeup approach and procedure which should be watched carefully to insure good results.

Large Sugar Kichel and Bow-Ties

Yield: 3 doz. large or 250 small units

Ingredients	Lb.	Oz.	Mixing procedure
Sugar	..	4	Blend all the ingredients in this stage well to dissolve the dry ingredients
Salt	..	$1/2$	
Whole eggs	1	..	
Yolks	1	..	
Oil	..	8	
Rum flavor	..	$1/2$	
Bread flour	2	8	Add the flour and mix well to a smooth dough

Procedures to Follow for Sugar Kichel (Fig. 371)

1. Place the developed dough on a floured portion of the bench and allow to relax for a few minutes. Scale the dough into a press weighing about 5 lb. The size of the press determines the size of each unit. Smaller kichel will require presses weighing less than 5 lb. Allow the press to relax after it has been rounded. Press out and separate the 36 pieces.

   Note: Round up each of the units gently. The dough is not stiff and may require dusting flour for the rounding. Avoid the use of excess flour.

FIG. 371. PLACE SIX KICHEL ON A
SHEET PAN

2. Roll each of the rounded units, after they have relaxed, directly in granulated sugar. Pat the top of the dough with dusting flour if the rolling pin sticks. The units should be rolled about 6 in. in diameter. It is important that they be rolled evenly and of even thickness.

3. Place each of the rolled units on a cleaned, oiled pan with the sugar side facing up. It is customary to place six on a sheet pan.

4. Allow the units to relax for about $1/2$ hr., stipple with a fork, and bake at 375°F. until golden brown and crisp. Remove from the pans while they are mildly warm to prevent sticking.

Procedures to Follow for Bow-Ties (Figs. 372–374)

1. Use the same recipe as for the large sugar kichel. Place the dough on a floured portion of the bench and allow to relax for about 15 min. It is customary to place the dough in the refrigerator if the dough is to be used the following day. Brush the top of the dough with oil to avoid crust formation.

2. Place the dough on a sugared portion of the bench and dust the top of the dough with granulated sugar. Roll the dough out into a rectangular shape about $1/8$ to $1/4$ in. thick. Check to see if there is sufficient sugar on the bench to prevent the dough from sticking while rolling and makeup. Dust the top of the dough with sugar after rolling.

3. Cut the dough into small rectangles about $1^1/2$ in. long and $1/2$ in. wide.

4. Pick up each unit and give one twist to form a bow-tie effect. Place the units on an oiled pan about $1/2$ in. apart.

5. Allow the units to relax about $1/2$ hr. and bake at 350°F. until golden brown and crisp. Avoid high oven temperatures. This will cause the cookies to brown quickly and then collapse after baking.

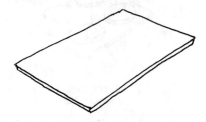

FIG. 372. ROLL DOUGH ON SUGAR TO A RECTANGULAR SHAPE

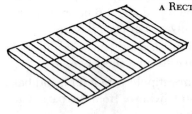

FIG. 373. CUT EQUAL OBLONGS WITH A PASTRY WHEEL

FIG. 374. TWIST TO A BOW-TIE SHAPE

Large Steam Egg Kichel   **Yield:** 36 large units

Ingredients	Lb.	Oz.	Mixing procedure
Sugar	..	2	Blend well to dissolve the dry ingredients.
Salt	..	$1/2$	Be sure to pulverize the ammonium bicarbonate before dissolving
Pepper (white) (Pinch)	..	..	
Eggs (fresh shell variety)	2	..	
Oil	..	8	
Ammonium bicarbonate	..	$1/4$	
Bread flour	1	14	Sift, add the flour and mix well to a smooth dough

Procedures to Follow

1. Place the dough on a floured portion of the bench and round up lightly.
2. Allow the dough to relax for a few minutes.
3. Press out the dough in divider. Be sure to use enough flour in the divider pan and on top of the dough to prevent the dough from sticking and make separation of the pressed out units easier.

4. Round up each of the units gently. This is a soft dough and may stick easily. It is advisable to use a flour-dusted cloth on which to round the units.

5. Allow the rounded units to relax for a few minutes and roll out into circles about $1/4$ in. thick. Place the rolled units into roll boxes that are dusted with cornmeal. Cover the boxes to prevent a crust formation.

6. Allow the units to rest from 1–2 hr. and then peel into a hot oven (425° to 435°F.) with a generous amount of steam. Allow the kichel to rise to a saucer or bowl shape and get a light brown color. Allow steam to escape and bake for about 10 min. until the kichel are crisp and of a light color.

7. Remove the kichel from the oven with a peel. Handle gently to avoid breaking. These kichel are crisp and mildly brittle.

Small Bagged Kichel

Yield: 300 small units

Ingredients	Lb.	Oz.	Mixing procedure
Bread flour	1	8	Mix all ingredients together and continue to
Sugar	..	4	mix until the oil shows signs of separating
Salt	..	$1/2$	from the mix. This takes about 12 min. on
Ammonium bicarbonate	..	$1/4$	second speed. Scrape sides of kettle
Oil	1	..	
Eggs (fresh preferred)	1	..	Add the eggs in very small portions until all of the eggs have been absorbed. Continue to mix until the mix tears short (about 15
Eggs	1	..	min.)

Procedures to Follow

1. Deposit the mix into a pastry bag with a medium size plain, pastry tube.

2. Deposit on clean pans that have been lightly oiled or greased. Bag out the size of a quarter-dollar. Using a tearing motion after the desired amount has come through the tube, touch the tube to the pan and twist or tear sharply away from the pan. It will take some practice to eliminate the stringy pull that results if this motion is not used. Space the kichel about 1 in. apart to allow spread during baking.

3. Bake the kichel at 410° to 415°F. The kichel will rise in the initial stages of baking and take the form of *mushroom caps.* Bake until light brown and crisp.

MARZIPAN FRUITS

Marzipan fruits are a specialty item. While they are primarily made during the holiday seasons they are also produced for added variety and display of the cookies and petits fours. True, it does require skill and patience to make them properly but they are valuable to the baker and the industry. Special attention must be paid to shaping and molding of the various fruits and the manner in which they are colored. Marzipan is ideal for the baker of artistic talent.

Marzipan   **Yield:** 60 1-oz fruits

Ingredients	Lb.	Oz.	Mixing procedure
Almond paste	2	..	Blend the almond paste smooth with the egg whites. Add the rest of the ingredients and mix to a smooth paste
Glucose or corn syrup	..	4	
Fondant	..	4	
Confectionery sugar	1	8	
Corn starch	..	1	
Egg whites	..	4	
Rum flavor	..	$1/_4$	

Note: If the marzipan is too soft, add additional sifted confectionery sugar. Corn starch may be added with the sugar. Keep the marzipan in a clean, dry container in a cool place. Cover with a damp cloth to prevent drying and crustation. Moisten the cloth from time to time.

Procedures to Follow (Figs. 375–382)

1. Modeling tools made of wood are of advantage in the molding of the various fruits. They make it possible to make the necessary indentations in the formation of the fruits.
2. Following is the syrup base recipe to which various colors are added for coloring the fruits.

Syrup Solution for Coloring

Ingredients	Lb.	Oz.	Mixing procedure
Sugar	1	..	Bring to a rolling boil and allow the syrup to cool
Glucose	1	..	
Water	1	8	
Alcohol (pure)°	..	4	Add the alcohol to the cool syrup

° The alcohol allows the syrup to dry quickly on the molded fruits.

3. The following procedures and colors are suggested for these fruits and vegetables:

Peaches: Shape the peaches from the marzipan. Color yellow with a faint touch of light red in the center sides of the peach. A small brown marzipan twig and chocolate leaf may be inserted after coloring.

FIG. 375. PEACH

Pears: Shape the pears. Color yellow with a trace of pink-red. Apply a stem and leaf as for the peaches.

FIG. 376. PEAR

Apples: Shape the apples; make the stems from chocolate marzipan; color light to dark red with a trace of yellow-green at the base and top.

FIG. 377. APPLE

Bananas: Shape the bananas. Color light to dark yellow. Draw fine lines of chocolate (cocoa and syrup) to indicate peel coloring. Place a brown stem at the base and at the top.

FIG. 378. BANANA

Potato: Shape in long, oval, and round form. Roll in light cocoa and starch mixed with confectionery sugar. They may also be painted light brown. Dark chocolate dots may be made for the eyes.

FIG. 379.   POTATO

Beans: Shape the beans. Be sure to show variations in thickness for the pods.

Green Peas: Color light to dark green.

FIG. 380.   GREEN PEAS
IN POD

Strawberries: Shape the strawberries. Make the puckered indentations with a toothpick or sharp instrument. Color red and roll in granulated sugar. Place the green marzipan stem at the top.

FIG. 381.   STRAWBERRY

Carrot: Yellow color with irregular taper to point. Green stalk-like stem.

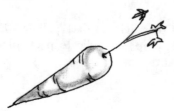

FIG. 382.   CARROT

Note: Use a liquid color (food color) for easy solution. Use small amounts of syrup to make various colors and color shades. Apply with a good, fine artist's brush. Wash the brush with water when changing colors except when shading one color into another.

PETITS FOURS

Petits fours are small delicately shaped and decorated cakes. They are usually prepared to order and are very often used in conjunction with other desserts. They make a beautiful dessert display and the skill and variety of decoration are important to the finished product. Neatness of icing and finish are the two major characteristics of a fine display.

Procedures to Follow (Figs 382A–382F)

1. A cake with a fine grain and texture (closely grained and smooth texture) is required. Generally, an old-fashioned pound cake mix is used. A malibu mix may also be used. Avoid grainy and soft cakes such as wine cake and sponge cakes. The cake must have body and be firm when chilled and cut. One thick sheet about $1^1/_2$ in. high or two thin sheets which have been sandwiched with a fine jam spread and of equal height should be used.
2. It is best to chill the sheet first before using. Cover the top of the sheet with a fine, thin coating of jam. Raspberry or apricot is advised.
3. Cover the top of the sheet with a thin layer of marzipan. Roll over the marzipan top with a rolling pin to insure that the marzipan sticks to the jelly. Use the recipe for marzipan.
4. With a sharp knife, cut the sheet into various shapes about 1 to $1^1/_2$ in. overall, no matter what the shape. The shapes may be square, oblong, round, diamond, etc.
5. Place the cut out shapes on an icing grate and space about 1 in. apart.
6. The petits fours are iced with fondant icing. Place a pot of such icing in a double boiler and warm to about 110°F. Use simple syrup to thin the fondant if it is too thick.
7. The petit fours may be iced by dipping the unit into the warm fondant and returning to the grate for the excess to run off. The units may be placed on a fork (stick at the bottom) and dipped and removed and placed on the grate. A pastry bag and plain tube (medium small) may be filled with the fondant and the fondant allowed to run out of the tube over each unit. Be sure the entire unit is covered so that there are no exposed sides of the cake. Avoid re-icing the unit as this will leave an uneven appearance. Allow the fondant to dry and carefully place the units on a clean pan.

   Note: Ice those units which are white first. Remove enough icing for the yellow, pink, and other pastel (light shades) colors in separate icing pots. When all petits fours are iced in pastel and white, combine all the leftover icings in the pots and on the pans which held the icing grates.

8. Add fudge base or bitter chocolate to the combined icings and warm for the units to be iced chocolate. Chocolate will disguise all other colors. Remove any cake crumbs from the icing.

9. A small dab of buttercream may be placed on units and a cherry or pecan inserted into the buttercream dab. These units are chilled to harden the buttercream before the fondant is poured over them.

10. The diagrams of various methods of decorating the petits fours will provide you with ideas for finishing. They are by no means complete. Your own ideas and reference books will provide you with others. Use fine lines for piping designs, pastel colors for buttercream or small flower designs, and piping jel for stems, leaves, and other designs. Do not overdecorate. Neatness and simplicity are important.

Fondant-Iced Petit Fours with Designs Made with Fondant

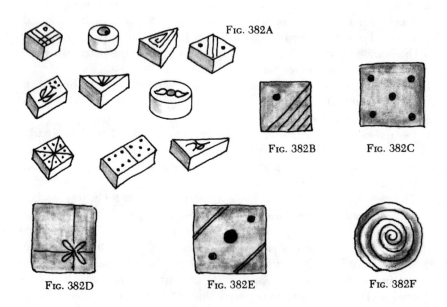

Fig. 382A

Fig. 382B

Fig. 382C

Fig. 382D

Fig. 382E

Fig. 382F

CHAPTER 31

Factors Concerning Cookies

A beautiful display of variety cookies, well finished, is always attractive to the customer and generally means increased sales. True, careless display of well-made cookies often detracts from the work of the baker. However, although some bakers use excellent ingredients some are careless and do not make products of high quality, often because of lack of understanding of the fundamental principles. This chapter will explain the basic principles and methods used in the production of variety cookies, after a brief review of the basic ingredients used in the production of cookies.

Basic Ingredients of Cookies

Sugar.—A coarse type of sugar in a creamed butter cookie mix will cause the cookies to spread too much and make them difficult to handle. In addition, there will be considerable breakage when these cookies have to be finished or dipped. On the other hand, the use of confectionery sugar alone, in the same type of mix, will not allow enough spread during baking. This will produce a close, dense grain and the possible separation of the fat from the mix when the cookies are being bagged out. This, in turn, will result in a measure of toughness and greasiness in the baked product. A fine-granulated sugar is normally best for the cookie mix unless the recipe specifies otherwise.

Fat.—Most cookies are rich in fat. The small butter cookie of the bagged-out variety may contain as much as 65 to 70 per cent fat based upon the weight of the flour. Richness is important in a cookie for taste, tenderness, and keeping qualities. The type of fat and the method of handling in the preparation of the mix is important. While a straight hydrogenated shortening may be used with good results, a better tasting product may be made if a mixture of butter and vegetable shortening is used.

Since the percentage of fat is high and must withstand considerable creaming a blend of butter and shortening, in equal amounts, is recommended. The butter should be cool but not so cold that it is brittle. The shortening will act as a support to prevent curdling in the later stages of creaming after most of the eggs have been creamed in. The natural flavor of the butter will impart its flavor to the neutral flavor of the shortening. In cookie doughs, such as short doughs or ice-box cookie doughs, the vegetable shortening will keep the dough in better working condition because of its higher melting point and plasticity.

401

Eggs.—Eggs are not only necessary in cookie making, but also impart natural flavor, taste, and keeping qualities. They also play an important part in the shape and structure of the cookie. For example, in making kisses and sponge zwieback, eggs are an ingredient of major importance. The condition of the eggs is as important as the way in which the eggs are handled. The odor, flavor, and temperature of the eggs must be considered. The slightest off-odor will have an undesirable effect on the flavor of the cookies.

In creaming mixes or the whipping of egg whites, the temperature of the eggs is important. Eggs at shop temperature cream in better and faster. Egg whites whip faster when cool. Egg whites are generally whipped to a wet peak rather than a dry peak when nuts, flour, and other ingredients have to be folded into the beaten whites. They blend in more easily and avoid overmixing without loss of volume.

Flour.—The flour supplies the structure and support in conjunction with eggs in cookie production. Since most cookie recipes are rich in fat a blend of various flours is often required. For example, in the bagged-out cookie, a butter cookie variety, a blend of cake and bread flour is used to support the fat and maintain the design of the baked cookies. A soft cake flour will allow too much spread and resulting loss of cookie design. Cake flour is often used with recipes that are made with egg whites. Wafers are commonly made with egg whites. Where egg yolks are used the additional fat in the yolk often requires the use of a strong flour. The sifting of flour blends is necessary to eliminate lumps which may cause overmixing when the flour is added, and also to aerate the flour and make its incorporation in the mix easier.

Mixing, Makeup, and Garnishing of Cookies

Improper mixing is the common cause of cookie toughness. Proper mixing or creaming before the addition of flour is necessary. Short doughs on the other hand, do not require creaming but a good blend of the sugar, fat, and eggs is necessary before the flour is added. In either case, the flour should be folded in gently to avoid development of the gluten. Gluten development in the mixing in of the flour makes the cookies tough. This condition may lead to difficulty in bagging out and running of the fat during the bagging-out process. In overmixed short doughs, the rolling of the dough becomes tougher; the dough stretches and pulls and is not short and tender. In the case of cookies made with whipped egg whites a dry peak will not permit easy absorption of the flour and cause toughness.

In the makeup of the cookies, evenness of size and pan spacing are the important factors. Most rich cookies are best if bagged out on parchment-paper-lined pans. This provides for cleanliness and prevents sticking.

Each of the cookies should be of the same size and the same design within the group. Uneven cookies do not make a good appearance. This problem is eliminated by the use of automatic equipment.

Where pans are greased for cookies, as in the making of some wafer types, it is important to have the pans greased evenly and with a minimum of fat. Excessive or careless greasing of pans causes too much spread. Lack of grease or ungreased spots will cause sticking and little spread.

Cookies that are to be garnished should be garnished as soon as they are deposited on the pans. If cookies are allowed to stand they form a crust, which prevents the garnish (nuts or fruits) from sticking properly to the cookie. This is generally the cause of nuts and other garnishes falling off the tops of cookies when they are displayed. Nuts, cherries, and other garnishes should be firmly set into the center of the cookie with the skin of the cherry or wrinkled surface of the nut uppermost. This is especially important when the cherry is divided into sections before garnishing, or the nuts are in broken pieces rather than full halves, and is the only decoration the cookie may have.

Baking

Cookies are small, flat units. They require a short baking period. Cookies that are low in sugar content (35 per cent or less based on the weight of the flour) require a higher baking temperature than those that are leaner in fat content and higher in sugar. However, the important factor is proper baking. Too often, freshly baked cookies are dry and overbaked to a point that makes them seem like stale cookies. A temperature of 385° to 400°F. is the average baking range. Cookies should be removed from the oven just as soon as they are done. The color of the top and bottom crust will indicate that point. The heat of the pan and the heat within the cookie itself continue to dry or bake the cookies during the first few minutes after the cookies are removed from the oven.

Cookies baked on parchment-paper-lined pans are not as subject to burned bottoms or burned edges as those baked directly on the pans. Special care should be taken in the baking of wafer-type cookies and those which are to be rolled and filled after baking (nuisettes). Overbaking will cause them to crack and break while they are being rolled. They should be rolled while slightly warm.

PRODUCTION FACTORS OF DIFFERENT TYPES OF COOKIES

The following points are listed as factors to be observed in the production of each of the following types of cookies:

Short Dough Cookies

1. Chill the dough before rolling the dough for makeup.
2. Roll the dough on a flour-dusted canvas cloth.
3. Do not use excessive amounts of dusting flour when rolling the dough.
4. Fold the scrap dough into the fresh dough after each rolling of the dough to avoid toughness from excessive scrap dough.
5. Roll the dough to an even thickness throughout.

Bagged-Out Cookies

1. Bag out evenly in size and shape.
2. Allow even space and enough space for cookies to spread in baking.
3. Garnish the cookies before they dry or develop a crust.
4. If jelly or jam is used for a garnish use a small amount.

Ice-Box Cookies

1. Chill the dough before making into various designs (checkerboard, etc.)
2. Avoid the use of too much color. Be sure it is blended in evenly.
3. Freeze the made-up cookies before slicing. Slice into even thickness with a sharp knife.
4. Allow cookies to return to shop temperature before baking.
5. Be careful of the top heat of the oven which may "brown out" the colors of the cookies.

Cocoanut Macaroons

1. Heat the mix in a double boiler to avoid scorching. Mix well to avoid scorching the mix and creating brown or burned spots.
2. Bag out the mix while warm. If the mix cools, re-heat it.
3. Apply the garnish before the macaroon dries.
4. Allow the macaroons to dry and form a crust before baking.
5. Bake the cookies on paper-lined pans.
6. For chocolate cocoanut macaroons, blend the cocoa with the sugar before adding it to the egg whites. When making chocolate macaroons, use additional egg whites to allow for the absorption of the cocoa.

Almond Macaroon Cookies

1. Blend the paste with a little egg white to remove lumps or dried pieces before adding the sugar.
2. Add the egg whites gradually and allow time for proper blending.
3. Moisten the canvas bag with cold water before filling with the mix.

4. Use parchment-paper-lined pans for bagging out the cookies.
5. Garnish the cookies before allowing the cookies to dry.
6. Allow the cookies to dry and form a crust before baking.
7. Plain macaroons should be allowed to dry overnight.
8. Do not overbake the cookies. A small percentage of corn syrup added to the mix (3 to 5 per cent based on the weight of the sugar) will help to keep the cookies fresh and soft for a longer period.
9. Wash the cookies with a hot glaze as soon as they are removed from the oven.

Decoration, Garnishing, and Icing

The coloring of cookies is an important factor. While some colors may be lost in baking, this generally is due to overbaking and partial caramelization of the sugar on the surface of the cookie. This dulls the color. Excessive coloring is another common fault. Deep colors are not attractive in cookies and they may also affect taste and flavor. Use a controlled amount of a fine grade of concentrated, approved food color. Avoid the use of combination colors and flavors. They tend to overshadow and dominate the natural flavor of the cookie ingredients. This is especially true of fruit-type color-flavor combinations.

The manner in which cookies are finished provide the greatest sales appeal. Aside from the natural taste and flavor of the ingredients the finish is very important. Such factors as "graying" chocolate dip, runny icing, smeared cookies, unevenly dipped cookies, filled cookies that fall apart, garnishes that fall off, and violently sharp colors used in icings are some of the faults. Detailed care is absolutely necessary. Equal care must be observed in displaying the cookies attractively.

A major portion of the finished cookies are dipped in, or decorated with, chocolate. Cookie dip is a fast-drying chocolate that has an emulsifier added to it with a lesser amount of the natural cocoa butter. Additional sugar (20 to 25 per cent) has been added for sweetening. It has the advantage of drying quickly with less chance of "graying" due to the lesser amount of cocoa butter. It is not equal in quality to natural, fine-grade sweet chocolate. In any event, all chocolate for dipping or garnishing should be dissolved in a double boiler with controlled heat which will not permit the chocolate to go beyond 100°F. Excessive or direct heat applied to chocolate is one of the reasons for "graying." Another cause is placing the freshly dipped cookies into the refrigerator to harden. The addition of a little melted cocoa butter will help to maintain the shine and luster of the chocolate.

Dipping should be done carefully for even and equal dip. The chocolate should be kept at an even temperature while dipping. When the chocolate cools the amount of dip thickens and increases on the cookie.

When fudge icing is used to dip or garnish cookies the fudge should be warm and easy to bag out. It should firm up when cool and remain tender on the inside. Fudge icings that dry quickly and crust too heavily should have melted fat added to them. Emulsified fat is best. If jam is not used for sandwiching cookies fudge is recommended. It is tasty and prevents separation of the cookies. A fine grade of jam should be used. Using a cheap grade of flavored jelly will cheapen an otherwise fine cookie. This is being penny-wise and pound-foolish.

The use of a nut garnish or fruit garnish on top of a dipped or bagged cookie should be done carefully. The whole or half cherry or nut should be placed neatly with the smooth or groved side up. Broken nut pieces or fruit pieces should not be used for they lack quality and appearance. Variety in the types of nuts and fruit pieces will increase the variety of assortment of the cookies.

CHAPTER 32

Recipes for Cookies

SUGAR COOKIES—CHOCOLATE SUGAR COOKIES

These cookies are the larger cut-out cookies that are popular in most bakeshops. The quality and appearance of the cookies are very important, and a moderately priced cookie is often an excellent sales leader and always attracts the youngsters. Of greatest importance in the production of these cookies is preparation of the dough and the method of makeup.

Sugar Cookies   Yield: 200 2-in. cookies

Ingredients	Lb.	Oz.	Mixing procedure
Sugar	2	..	Cream the ingredients in this stage to a soft
Salt	..	$1/2$	mix
Milk powder	..	2	
Shortening	1	8	
Glucose or corn syrup	..	2	
Eggs	..	8	Add the eggs in two stages and cream in
Water	..	12	Add the water and vanilla and stir in slightly
Vanilla	..	1	
Cake flour	4	..	Sift the flour and baking powder together,
Baking powder	..	2	add, and fold in lightly. Do not overmix

Procedures to Follow (Figs. 383–385)

1. The dough should be sticky and rough-looking. This will indicate that the flour has been mixed so that all the liquid is absorbed and the gluten in the flour is not developed. Overmixing causes toughness.
2. Chill the dough in the refrigerator before using.
3. Place the dough on a flour-dusted cloth and work gently into a smooth rectangular shape. Do not use too much flour in working the dough.
4. Dust the cloth with enough bread flour to prevent sticking and flatten the cookie dough slightly. Roll out gently with a rolling pin to about $1/4$ in. thick. Check the thickness of the dough with the fingers. A small rolling pin may be used to roll parts of the dough

which may be too thick. It is necessary to have the entire, rolled dough of even thickness to have uniform cookies. Check the dough, when rolling, to see that there is enough flour to prevent sticking. Excess flour is brushed off after the dough is rolled out.

5. Wash the top of the dough lightly with egg-wash, water, or milk and sprinkle the dough with granulated sugar. Cut out the cookies with various shaped cookie cutters which will yield cookies of equal weight. Round, heart, diamond, square, and other shapes may be made. The dough may be left unwashed and the cookies cut and dipped into a pan of sugar. The cookies may be garnished with jam or nuts before baking. Place on paper-lined pan.

6. Be careful to cut out the cookies as closely as possible to prevent an excessive amount of scrap dough. The scrap dough is worked over and rolled again. Bake the cookies at 385°F. until golden brown.

7. For *chocolate sugar cookies*, add 6 oz. cocoa and reduce the flour to 3 lb. 12 oz. Dissolve $1/4$ oz. baking soda in the water and reduce the baking powder to $1^1/_2$ oz.

FIG. 383. ROLL DOUGH TO $1/_4$ IN. THICKNESS ON FLOUR-DUSTED CLOTH

FIG. 384. CUT OUT THE COOKIES AS CLOSE AS POSSIBLE

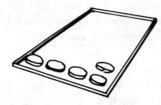

FIG. 385. PLACE ON PAPER-LINED SHEET PANS IN EVENLY SPACED ROWS

LEMON SNAPS, CHOCOLATE DROP COOKIES, AND COCOANUT COOKIES

Bagged cookies of the larger variety are an important asset to the showcase and the window when made properly. Variety and quality are the essence of their production. These cookies are merchandised by the unit or dozen rather than by the pound. There are many variations and different recipes. The following recipes have resulted in good cookies with good shelf-life.

Lemon-Snap Cookies   **Yield:** 12–14 doz. cookies

Ingredients	Lb.	Oz.	Mixing procedure
Sugar	1	8	Scale carefully and cream the ingredients
Salt	..	$1/2$	well
Milk powder	..	1	
Shortening	1	1	
Eggs	..	4	Add the eggs and cream well
Water	..	7	Add the liquid (water and flavor) and stir in
Lemon flavor	..	1	slightly
Rind of one lemon			
Cake flour	2	..	Sift, add, and mix smooth. Do not overmix
Baking powder	..	$1/2$	

Procedures to Follow (Figs. 386–391)

1. Be sure the mix is smooth. Fold the flour in lightly and avoid too much mixing. Overmixed batters will result in stiffness, difficulty in bagging out the mix, and cookies which do not spread and are tough.

2. Prepare the sheet pans by cleaning them and greasing lightly and evenly.

3. Fill a pastry bag with a large, plain tube with the mix and deposit the cookies about the size of a half dollar. Allow about $1^1/_2$-in. space between each cookie for spreading during baking.

4. The points on the bagged cookies are removed by dipping the fingers in milk or egg-wash and flattening the points. Avoid too much milk. The cookies should be flattened slightly. They will spread during baking.

5. Bake the cookies at 375°F. until light brown. Remove from the oven while still slightly soft. These cookies are thin and continue to bake and dry for the first few minutes after they are removed from the oven.

Fig. 386. Pastry Bag and Tube

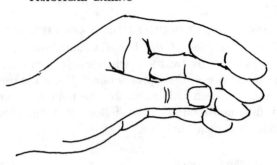

Fig. 387. Hold Hand in This Position

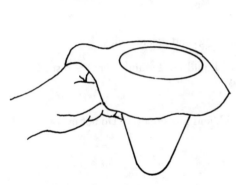

Fig. 388. Put Pastry Bag in Hand and Turn Down Edge About 6 In.

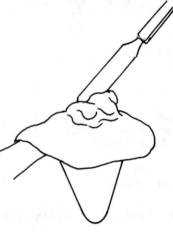

Fig. 389. Fill Pastry Bag with Batter using a Bowl Knife. Close the Hand Against the Knife and Withdraw the Bowl Knife

Fig. 390. Close Top of Filled Pastry Bag with Fingers

Fig. 391. Divide Bag in Half, Squeeze Out Small Amount of Batter to Release Any Air Pockets and Proceed to Bag Out Cookies

6. Allow the cookies to cool before removing from the pan or finishing the cookies. If the cookies stick to the pan silghtly, tap the pan on the bench and they will be released.

7. These cookies may be finished by placing a dot of lemon fondant icing in the center. Be sure the fondant has been warmed and the icing has a thicker consistency than that used for icing cupcakes. The icing will dry and the cookies will not stick to each other when displayed.

Chocolate Drop Cookies

Yield: 180–200 cookies

Ingredients	Lb.	Oz.	Mixing procedure
Sugar	1	8	Cream these ingredients well
Salt	..	$1/_2$	
Milk powder	..	2	
Shortening	1	5	
Eggs	1	..	Add the eggs in three stages and cream well after each addition
Water	..	8	Dissolve the baking soda in the water. Add
Baking soda	..	$1/_4$	the vanilla to the above. Stir slightly
Vanilla	..	1	
Cake flour	2	12	Sift the flour, cocoa, and baking powder to-
Cocoa	..	5	gether. Add to the above and mix lightly
Baking powder	..	1	until the mix is smooth. Do not overmix

Procedures to Follow

1. Sheet pans should be clean and lightly greased.
2. Fill the pastry bag using a plain or star tube with the mix.
3. Bag out the cookies in plain or star form, spacing them about $1\frac{1}{2}$ in. apart. The average size of the bagged cookie is about 2 in. in diameter.
4. Plain drops may be flattened slightly by moistening the fingers in water and flattening the point of the cookie slightly.
5. These cookies may be garnished with chopped nuts, chocolate sprinkles, or left plain and finished after baking.
6. Bake the cookies at 385°F. The cookies are considered baked when they feel almost firm in the center. Do not overbake.
7. Ungarnished cookies may be finished with a dot of chocolate fudge icing or chocolate fondant icing after they have cooled.

Macaroon Drop Cookies   **Yield:**   180 cookies

Ingredients	Lb.	Oz.	Mixing procedure
Sugar	1	12	Cream all the ingredients in this stage to-
Salt	..	$1/2$	gether
Milk powder	..	$1^1/2$	
Shortening	1	..	
Baking soda	..	$1/4$	
Eggs	..	6	Add the eggs in two stages and cream
Water	..	12	Add the water and vanilla and stir slightly
Vanilla	..	1	
Macaroon cocoanut	1	10	Add the cocoanut and stir in.
Cake flour	1	12	Sift, add, and mix smooth. Do not overmix
Baking powder	..	$1/4$	

Procedures to Follow

1. Bag out the cookies with a pastry bag and plain tube on lightly greased pans.
2. Flatten the cookie points, if any, by dipping the hands in milk and patting the point.
3. Bake at 375°F. until golden brown.

JUMBLE COOKIES—VANILLA AND CHOCOLATE

Jumble cookies are bagged cookies that are larger in size than the usual fancy cookies sold per pound. These cookies are sold by the unit or dozen. They are bagged out in many different sizes and shapes and are finished with various decorations. Very popular with children, they make a wonderful addition to the large-size cookie display. There are a number of recipes, from the very rich to the lean, which may be used. The following recipe meets the median in terms of cost, quality, and shelf-life. It has the added value of easy recipe conversion to make chocolate jumble cookies.

Jumble Cookies **Yield:** 200 cookies

Ingredients	Lb.	Oz.	Mixing procedure
Macaroon paste	..	8	Blend the eggs and macaroon paste until
Eggs	..	3	smooth
Sugar	1	8	Add these ingredients to the above and
Salt	..	$1/_2$	cream well until soft and light. Scrape the
Milk powder	..	2	sides of the kettle periodically
Glucose	..	2	
Shortening	1	5	
Eggs	1	..	Add the eggs in three stages and cream well after each addition
Water	..	8	Add and stir slightly
Vanilla	..	1	
Cake flour	3	3	Sift, add, and fold in lightly. Do not over-
Baking powder	..	$1^1/_2$	mix

Procedures to Follow (Figs. 392–395)

1. The mix is to be bagged out with a pastry bag and tube. A star or French tube of medium size should be used. The variation in tubes will allow variation in the appearance of the cookies.
2. Bag out the cookies on lightly greased sheet pans or on parchment-paper-lined pans. Space them about 1 to $1^1/_2$ in. apart to allow spreading.
   Note: Hold the tube directly above the pan when bagging out. Do not allow the tube to drag along the surface of the pan. Keep an even pressure on the bag to keep the shapes of the cookies uniform. Practice develops skill and speed. (See Figs. 386–391, p. 410.)
3. The cookies may be bagged out into star forms, rosettes, straight sticks, "S" shapes, heart shapes, and others. The illustrations will provide you with some of the more popular varieties.
4. Cookies may be garnished with glazed cherries, mixed fruit, or whole or chopped nuts before baking. Cookies may also be finished after baking by dipping into icing or dipping chocolate, or striping the cookies after they have cooled.
5. Bake the cookies at 385°F. until golden brown.
6. For *chocolate jumbles* make the following changes in the recipe:
   1. Add 5 oz. of dark, natural cocoa to the flour.
   2. Reduce the flour to 2 lb. 13 oz.
   3. Add $1/_4$ oz. baking soda which is dissolved in the water before adding to the mix.

Reduce the baking powder to $1^1/_4$ oz.

Note: The mix must be creamed well and the flour folded in gently to avoid toughness. It is advisable to mix the flour in by hand.

FIG. 392. ROSETTE JUMBLE

FIG. 393. "S" SHAPED JUMBLE

FIG. 394. BLACK AND WHITE JUMBLE

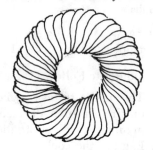

FIG. 395. RING-SHAPED JUMBLE

BUTTER COOKIES

The small, dainty, carefully finished type of cookie is the backbone of the baker's cookie display case. The variety is great. The important factors to be considered are: quality of the cookie mix (ingredients and balance), uniformity of size and shape, and the neatness with which the cookies are finished. Skill, understanding, and efficiency will be developed with practice and experience in making these cookies. The recipes presented are those which have been tested with satisfactory results.

French Butter Cookies   Yield: 6 pans of 60–70 cookies per pan

Ingredients	Lb.	Oz.	Mixing procedure
Almond paste	..	8	Blend the almond paste and whites to a
Egg whites	..	4	smooth paste
Sugar	1	..	Add these ingredients to the above and
Salt	..	1/2	cream well until soft and light. Scrape the
Butter	1	..	sides of the kettle often to avoid lumps
Shortening	1	..	
Egg whites	1	..	Add the egg whites in three stages and cream
Vanilla	..	1	in well after each addition
Cake flour	1	8	Sift the flour and fold into the above lightly.
Bread flour	1	8	Do not overmix

Procedures to Follow

1. Avoid overmixing. This will cause the batter to toughen and make bagging-out difficult. It will also result in a tough cookie.
2. The cookies are bagged out with pastry bag and medium-sized French tube. Bag the cookies on a parchment-paper-lined pan.
3. Bag the cookies into star shapes, pear shapes, stick shapes, and rosettes.
4. Space the cookies about 3/4 in. apart. Be sure they are of equal size and shape.
5. The star-shaped and rosette-shaped cookies may be garnished with a variety of toppings before baking. Nuts, cherries, diced fruits, etc., may be used. Be sure to press the topping or garnish into the cookie. This will prevent the garnish from falling off after baking.
6. Bake the cookies at 385° to 390°F. to a light, golden brown color. Don't overbake. The cookies continue to bake and dry after they are removed from the oven for the first few minutes.
7. The cookies may be garnished with sweet chocolate in drop or stripe form. They must be dipped partially into cookie dip and then into toasted ground nuts. The nuts may be colored green or ground pistachio nuts may be used. The tops of the round cookies may be garnished with a small fudge icing rosette and a whole or half nut placed on top.

Note: Whole eggs or egg yolks may be used in place of the egg whites for the above recipe. This will provide a yellow, rich color to the interior and exterior of the cookie. If yolks are used it is advisable to increase the egg content by 2 oz.

SANDWICH-TYPE COOKIES

The recipe for this mix lends itself well to the preparation of a great variety of cookies. The sandwich cookie implies that two cookies of similar shape are sandwiched together after baking and then finished. This indicates that a variety of fillings may be used for sandwiching and that many varieties may be obtained by the method of finishing. The cookie mix may be colored yellow, pink, green, etc., for still further variety.

Sandwich-Type Cookies   **Yield:** 6 pans of 70 cookies each

Ingredients	Lb.	Oz.	Mixing procedure
Sugar	1	8	Cream the ingredients in this stage until soft
Salt	..	$1/2$	and light. Scrape the sides of the kettle to
Butter	..	12	insure smoothness of the mix
Shortening	..	12	
Eggs	1	8	Add the eggs in four stages and cream in
Vanilla	..	1	well after each addition
Cake flour	2	4	Sift, add, and fold in until smooth

Procedures to Follow (Figs. 396–403)

1. It is important that the mix be creamed well until soft and light. The flour should be mixed lightly and the mix smooth without being tough. If the mix is to be colored add the color after the flour has been absorbed and not completely mixed smooth. The final mixing will allow the color to be distributed without overmixing and toughening the batter. Avoid excessive color. Use a good color concentrate to avoid fading of the color during baking.
2. Bag out the cookies with a pastry bag and medium-small, plain tube. Bag out on parchment-paper-lined pans. Space the cookies about $3/4$ in. apart to allow a mild spread in baking. Be sure the cookies are bagged out evenly in size and shape as they are to be sandwiched.
3. Bake the cookies at 380°F. until a light-brown edge appears at the edges of the cookie. The center of the cookie is yellow in appearance. The cookies will feel slightly spongy to the touch. Do not bake until crisp. The cookies continue to bake and dry after they are removed from the oven. Cookies which are colored will also show a slight crust at the edge. Feel the cookies to determine proper bake.
4. Allow the cookies to cool and turn over one-half of the cookies of similar size and shape. For example, turn only half of the round, button shapes, short stick shapes, half-moon shapes, and others.

5. Apricot, raspberry, and other fine-grade jams should be used to sandwich the cookies. It is advisable to work the jam smooth before using. Place the filling in a large, paper cone or pastry bag with a small, plain tube. Bag the jam filling over the center of the turned-up cookie. Use enough to make the cookies stick. Do not use excessive amounts which will cause the jam to run out of the sides when the cookies are sandwiched together. Place one cookie on top of the other evenly.

6. The cookies may be finished in the following manner:
   a. Striping with melted, sweet chocolate or cookie dip.
   b. Dipping about one-third of the sandwiched cookies into chocolate and tipping with toasted nuts, chocolate sprinkles, or pistachio nuts.
   c. Dipping both edges of the sticks into melted chocolate and tipping with toasted nuts, chocolate sprinkles, or pistachio nuts.
   d. Garnish the tops with fudge icing or French chocolate mix.

FIG. 396. SANDWICH-TYPE COOKIE BAGGED OUT WITH PLAIN TUBE

FIG. 397. TURN BAKED COOKIE AND FILL

FIG. 398. SANDWICH COOKIES TOGETHER

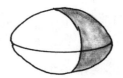

FIG. 399. DIP $^1/_3$ TO $^1/_2$ THE COOKIE INTO SWEET CHOCOLATE OR COOKIE DIP

FIG. 400. SHORT STICK-TYPE COOKIE BAGGED OUT WITH PLAIN TUBE

FIG. 401. TURN BAKED COOKIE AND FILL

FIG. 402. SANDWICH COOKIES

FIG. 403. DIP $^1/_4$ INTO SWEET CHOCOLATE OR COOKIE DIP

ICE-BOX COOKIES

There are many variations of cookies made from ice-box cookie dough which will enhance the cookie display when made in an attractive manner. There are also a variety of recipes used for ice-box cookies. Some recipes richer in fat content use a blend of granulated sugar and confectionery sugar, and often use egg whites in place of whole eggs or egg yolks. Each of the recipes may be excellent. The important factors are the method of preparing the dough and the makeup of the various ice-box cookies. The following recipe is practical and useful.

Ice-Box Cookies   **Yield:**   400–450 cookies or 6 full pans

Ingredients	Lb.	Oz.	Mixing procedure
Confectionery sugar	1	8	Cream together until soft and smooth
Salt	..	$1/2$	
Shortening	2	12	
Glucose or corn syrup	..	2	
Eggs	..	10	Add the eggs in two stages and blend in well.
Vanilla	..	1	Add vanilla last
Cake flour	2	4	Sift, add, and mix lightly until a smooth
Bread flour	2	4	dough is formed. Place the dough on a floured bench

Procedures to Follow

1. All or parts of this dough may be colored. Separate the amount of dough you wish to color from the rest of the dough. Add color in small amounts and blend in well until the entire dough is colored. Avoid excess color for this will make the color too deep and may create streaks of color throughout the dough. It is best to mix the light colors first and then mix the chocolate color last. Melted chocolate or fudge base is best used for making the dough chocolate. The addition of cocoa will cause toughness and cracking when the dough is handled for makeup.

2. Keep each colored piece of dough separate from the rest.

3. Refrigerate the dough before making up the cookies. Place the dough or made-up cookies on a floured cloth when refrigerating.

4. It is best to use a flour-dusted cloth for rolling the cookie dough for makeup.

5. While water may be used for making the different layers of dough stick together, egg whites or regular egg-wash have better adhesive qualities. Use only enough wash to cover the surface of the dough. Excess wash will cause sloppiness in makeup and separation of the different layers of dough during baking.

6. Before slicing the made-up rolls of dough or checkerboard shapes it is best to chill or semi-freeze the dough.

7. Use a sharp knife to cut the slices. Cut each slice of even thickness.

8. Place the cookies on parchment-paper-lined pans as soon as they are cut.

9. Allow the cut cookies to come to room temperature before baking.

10. Bake the cookies at 380°F. Do not overbake.

Procedures to Follow for Checkerboard (Figs. 404 and 405)

1. Divide the dough in half. Color both halves in contrasting colors. Any combination of two colors may be used. The most popular combination is natural or yellow and chocolate.

2. Remove a small piece of dough, about $1^1/_2$ lb. of each part if a large dough is made, and place to one side. These pieces of chilled dough will later serve as the wrap-around cover of the cookies.

3. Chill the dough and then divide each colored part in two pieces. You now have four pieces of dough (two of each color).

4. Roll each piece of dough on a floured cloth about $1/_4$ in. thick. Place the first piece (yellow or chocolate) on a cloth-covered pan. This may be done by rolling the dough up on a small rolling pin and then unrolling it on the pan. Avoid stretching the dough and thinning it.

5. Roll out the second piece of dough of the contrasting color. Egg-wash the first layer of dough on the pan and then unroll the second piece on top of the first piece. Repeat the procedure with the next two pieces. There will be four layers of contrasting dough about 1 in. high in a square or oblong shape. Square off the uneven edges and corners with your hands or a flat board. If the layers are too thick or too high roll the layers gently with a large rolling pin. This will reduce the height.

6. Chill the made-up strips of four layers until they are firm.

7. Roll out the pieces of dough removed from each color on a floured cloth to about $1/_{16}$ in. thick. Scrap dough may also be used for this purpose.

8. Slice the chilled layers into long slices about $1/4$ in. wide. Place each of the long slices on the rolled-out cover dough which has been egg-washed in advance. Egg-wash each slice of the four-layer dough before placing the next slice on top of it. Reverse each slice so that one edge of the layered slice contrasts with the other. Make four layers and wrap the thin layer of dough around it. Place the covered strips on a flour-dusted cloth and chill once again until firm.

9. Place each of the strips on the bench and slice with a sharp knife about $1/8$ in. thick. Place on pans about $1/2$ in. apart. Allow to return to room temperature and bake at 380°F. Do not overbake.

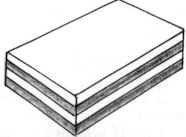

FIG. 404. ALTERNATE TWO YELLOW AND TWO CHOCOLATE LAYERS OF COOKIE DOUGH

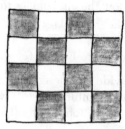

FIG. 405. FINISHED CHECKERBOARD STRIP READY FOR CUTTING

Procedures to Follow for Pinwheels (Fig. 406)

1. Two or three different color combinations may be used. If two are used roll out each of the colored doughs about $1/4$ in. thick. Wash the top of one color and then roll the other colored dough on top of it.

2. Roll up the two doughs as you would a cinnamon bun until about 1 in. in diameter. Cut the dough with a knife or rotary cutter. Roll up again into a similar roll. Continue until the entire dough has been rolled up.

3. Chill the rolls and then slice into $1/4$-in. slices. Place on pans $1/2$ in. apart. Bake at 380°F. Do not overbake.

FIG. 406. PINWHEEL COOKIE ROLL READY FOR CUTTING

Procedures to Follow for Bull's Eyes (Fig. 407)

1. Scale the colored doughs into 1-lb. units.
2. Take the scaled units of one color and roll out with the hands into a round strip about $1/2$ in. in diameter. Flatten the strip with the hands or roll gently with a rolling pin until $1/4$ in. thick and 2 in. wide.
3. Egg-wash these strips that have been flattened. Roll out the other colored units to the length of the flattened strips. Place these rolls in the center of the flattened units and roll the flattened and washed dough around the dough in the center.
4. Chill the strips and slice $1/4$ in. thick. Place on pans $1/2$ in. apart. Bake at 380°F. Do not overbake.

Fig. 407. Bull's-Eye Cookie Roll Ready for Cutting

Procedures to Follow for Spiral Cookies (Fig. 408)

1. Scale the colored dough into 1-lb. units.
2. Roll all the scaled units into round strips about $1/2$ in. in diameter.
3. Flatten each slightly and place one of each color alongside each other. Wash the tops of each lightly with egg-wash and twist the strands around each other in the form of a braided rope.
4. Roll the braided strips into a round roll about 1 in. in diameter. Place on pans and chill.
5. Slice after chilling into $1/4$ in. thickness. Place on pans $1/2$ in. apart. Bake at 380°F. Do not overbake.

Fig. 408. Spiral Cookie Roll Ready for Cutting

Walnut Ice-Box Cookies

This cookie will provide further variety in the ice-box cookie selection. Its shape, color, flavor, and nut content are the factors which make variation. Of course, the use of butter to replace part of the fat content, increasing the nut content, and the use of good flavoring will enhance the quality of the cookie.

Walnut Ice-Box Cookies   **Yield:** 300–325 cookies

Ingredients	Lb.	Oz.	Mixing procedure
Granulated sugar	1	..	Cream together until soft and light
Brown sugar	1	..	
Salt	..	$1/2$	
Shortening	1	..	
Baking soda	..	$1/4$	
Eggs	..	12	Add the eggs in two stages and cream in
Vanilla	..	$1/2$	Stir in the flavors
Walnut maple flavor	..	$1/2$	
Cake flour	2	6	Sift, add and mix lightly until the flour is absorbed
Chopped walnuts	..	12	Fold the nuts in gently until distributed

Procedures to Follow

1. Scale the dough into 1 lb. units. Use very little flour. If the dough feels a bit sticky, refrigerate and scale the units.
2. Roll the scaled dough units into rolls about 1 in. in diameter. Use a lightly floured cloth.
3. The rolls may then be rolled in granulated sugar or finely chopped nuts. The sugar or nuts will adhere to the outside of the roll.
4. Refrigerate the rolls until firm. A slight freeze is advisable to make slicing of the cookies from the roll easier and without loss of shape.
5. Slice the chilled roll into cookies about $1/4$ in. thick.
6. Place on parchment-paper-lined pans and space about $1/2$ in. apart.
7. Allow the cookies to return to room temperature and bake at 375° to 380°F. Be careful not to overbake.

Note: These cookies may also be made in square or rectangular shape. Roll the chilled dough into a rectangular shape about $1/2$ in. thick. Chill or partially freeze the dough. Cut strips of dough $1/2$ in. wide and slice each of the strips into $1/4$ in. apart. Allow to return to room temperature and bake as indicated above.

LADYFINGERS

Ladyfingers are delicate, cookie-type, sponge items that are very useful for decorating cakes and pastries as well as being sold as special bakery items. For example, ladyfingers may be placed around the sides of a whipped cream layer. They may be used for decorating oblong-shaped French pastries. They are also sold as a special cookie.

Ladyfingers Yield: 120 fingers

Ingredients	Lb.	Oz.	Mixing procedure
Sugar	1	8	Warm the eggs to room temperature. Whip
Salt	..	$1/_4$	with the sugar as for sponge cake
Glucose	..	2	
Eggs (part yolks)	1	8	
Flavor (lemon, orange, vanilla)	..	$1/_2$	Fold in gently
Bread flour or pastry flour°	1	8	Sift and fold in the flour by hand. Do not overmix

° If pastry flour or short-patent flour are used, increase the amount of flour to 1 lb. 10 oz.

Procedures to Follow

1. Place the mix in a canvas bag with a medium, plain tube.
2. Bag out the mix on paper-lined pans about 3 in. long (size may vary according to needs).
3. Dust the tops of the fingers with confectionery sugar as soon as they are bagged out. Do not permit the fingers to dry for the sugar will not stick. Shake the excess sugar from paper.
4. Bake the fingers at 400°F. Be careful not to overbake.
5. When cool, remove from the paper and put two fingers together as though forming a sandwich. If the fingers do not come off the paper easily moisten the back of the paper lightly with water. Allow the water to penetrate slightly and then remove the fingers. Water tends to melt the sugar that causes the fingers to stick.
6. Remember to bake these fingers lightly to avoid drying out and burning the sugar on top of the fingers.

SPONGE ZWIEBACK

These cookie-type delicacies are not difficult to make if handled with care and attention. Made properly, they add to the variety and attractiveness of any cookie display. A sponge method of mixing is employed. In addition, these cookies require double handling. The recipe and procedure follow.

Sponge Zwieback (Toasted   **Yield:** 9 strips or 250 slices
Sponge Mondel Bread)

Ingredients	Lb.	Oz.	Mixing procedure
Sugar	3	..	Mix the sugar, salt, macaroon paste and eggs
Salt	..	1	to a smooth paste
Macaroon or almond paste	1	..	
Eggs	..	8	
Eggs (part yolks)	3	8	Add the eggs and whip until thick as for
Vanilla	..	1	sponge cake. Fold in flavor gently
Almond flavor	..	$1/2$	
Bread flour	3	8	Sift and fold in the flour by hand
Filberts or walnuts	2	..	Add the nuts and cherries and fold in gently
Glazed cherries	1	..	

Procedures to Follow (Figs. 409–412)

1. Place the mix into a clean, canvas bag without any tube. The small end of the bag should be about 1 in. in diameter to allow the nuts and cherries to pass through.

2. Bag out the mix on paper-lined pans in strips about the length of the pan. Try to use even pressure so that the thickness of the strip is as even as possible. This will avoid burning during baking of thin parts of the strip.

3. Bake the strips as soon as they are bagged out. Do not permit the bagged strips to remain unbaked too long. The strips will spread after bagging. Bake at 400°F. Do not overbake.

4. Allow the strips to cool. Remove from the pans and cut into bars about $1/2$ in. wide. Be careful in slicing for safety and evenness of size.

5. Lay the cut slices on end and toast at a moderate temperature. (350°F.). Be careful to avoid overbaking. Check bottom heat of the oven. It may be necessary to turn the zwieback if the bottom or top heat of the oven is either too cool or too hot. An even, golden-brown color is very important for the appearance of these cookies.

Fig. 409. Bag Out the Sponge Zweibach Mix on Paper-Lined Pans

Fig. 410. The Baked Zweibach Strip

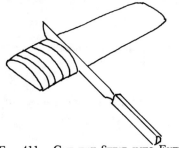

Fig. 411. Cut the Strip into Even Slices

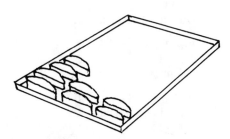

Fig. 412. Lay the Cut Slices on Their Sides and Bake Again to a Golden-Brown Color

MONDEL BREAD

Mondel bread is a bar-type of cookie which may be made in plain or marbled form. There are a number of variations in which these cookies may be made and the size and shape are determined by the demands of the bakeshop. They are very often made in a loaf form and sold as complete units. In either form, they are popular in special shops and provide greater variety.

Mondel Bread   **Yield:**   12 strips or 245 slices

Ingredients	Lb.	Oz.	Mixing procedure
Sugar	2	..	Cream all the ingredients to a smooth paste
Salt	..	1	
Macaroon paste	..	12	
Glucose	..	4	
Shortening	1	..	
Milk powder	..	2	
Eggs	..	4	
Eggs	..	12	Add the eggs in two stages and cream well
Water	1	..	Add the water and flavors and stir in
Vanilla	..	1	slightly
Orange and lemon	..	$1/2$	
Bread flour	2	..	Sift, add the flour, and mix smooth
Cake flour	2	..	
Baking powder	..	2	
Walnuts or filberts	1	..	Add the nuts and fruits and mix gently until
Glazed cherries and	1	..	distributed
mixed fruit			

Procedures to Follow (Figs. 413–415)

1. If a marbled effect is desired, remove half the mix and place on a floured portion of the bench. Add sufficient melted chocolate or fudge base to color the remaining half chocolate. If cocoa is used add 4 oz. cocoa, 2 oz. shortening, 4 oz. water, and $1/8$ oz. baking soda to the chocolate part of the mix.
2. Scale the white and chocolate parts into 1 lb. pieces. Combine one of each and roll into a long strip the length of a pan. Place on paper-lined or greased and flour-dusted pans. Shape the strip so that it is of even thickness and about 1 in. high. Flatten gently with the fingers.
3. The top of the strips may be washed lightly with egg-wash and then garnished with chopped nuts and sugar before baking.
4. The strips may be baked without a garnish and then coated with a chocolate or other colored fondant or fudge icing.
5. Bake the strips at 400°F.
6. Allow the strips to cool before slicing. Slice into strips in a diagonal fashion about $3/4$ in. wide.
7. One-pound loaves may be made out of this mix. The loaves may also be marbled by combining $1/2$ lb. of each color of the mix. Shape the loaves as you would a rye bread. Keep them short and thick. Wash the tops of the loaves with egg-wash and garnish with nuts and sugar.

FIG. 413. SCALE DOUGH TO DESIRED WEIGHT AND ADD FRUIT OR CHOCO-LATE FOR FRUIT OR MARBLED EFFECT

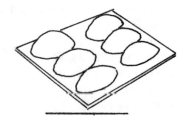

FIG. 414. PLACE SIX ON A PAN AND BAKE

FIG. 415. WASH AND GARNISH

FRUIT BARS

These bar-type cookies are made as a year-round sales item for variety. They are made especially during the holiday seasons. The use of molasses and fruits allows variety as well as good-keeping quality. There are variations of this recipe and variations in the use of nuts and fruits. The following recipe is of average cost and good quality.

Fruit Bars   **Yield:** 8 strips—160 slices

Ingredients	Lb.	Oz.	Mixing procedure
Brown sugar	2	. .	Cream the ingredients until soft
Salt	. .	1	
Shortening	1	4	
Cinnamon	. .	$1/4$	
Milk powder	. .	1	
Baking soda	. .	1	
Eggs	. .	12	Add the eggs in two stages and cream in
Molasses ($1/2$ qt.)	1	7	Add the molasses and blend well
Water	. .	8	Add the water and stir slightly
Raisins	2	. .	Stir in the fruit and nuts
Walnuts or cashews	1	. .	
Cake flour	4	6	Sift, add, and mix smooth

Procedures to Follow

1. Place the cookie mix on a floured portion of the bench.
2. Scale the pieces into 2-lb. units. They may be scaled smaller for smaller bar cookies.
3. Roll the scaled units into bars about 2 in. wide and 1 in. thick.
4. Place the strips on paper-lined or greased and flour-dusted pans.
5. Flatten the strips slightly.
6. Bake at 400°F.
7. Allow the strips to cool and ice the tops with any color of fondant icing.
8. Allow the icing to dry well and slice into bars about $1/2$ in. wide.

LINZER TARTS (MIRRORS), ALMOND TARTS, AND ALMOND HORNS

These items are specialty cookies. They are larger than the usual small cookie and are sold by the unit rather than by weight. They may also be made small in size and displayed with assorted French pastries. The Linzer tarts are made from short dough or shortbread cookie dough. When made small in size they may be sold as cookies or as petits fours.

Procedures to Follow for Linzer Tarts

1. Use the short dough normally used for cake bottoms or the regular, rich shortbread dough.
2. Roll out the dough on a floured cloth to $1/8$ in. thickness. Be sure the thickness of the dough is even throughout. Remove excess flour.
3. With a round cookie cutter (scalloped or plain edge) cut out the round bottoms and place on a pan. Cut an equal number of round cookies for the tops. Before placing the tops on the pan cut out the centers with a small-size cookie cutter, so that a 1- to $1^1/_2$-in. hole is made in the center.
4. Bake these cookies at 385°F. until light brown.
5. Turn the cookies used for the bottoms (without the holes in the center) over so that the bottom of the cookie faces up. This is important in order to sandwich the cookies.
6. With a paper cone, or by hand, place a large drop of good quality jam or jelly in the center of the cookie.
7. Place the top cookie (containing the hole in the center) directly over the bottom cookie so that the jam sandwiches the two cookies together and a small portion of the jam is forced slightly up through the center hole.
8. The top cookies may be dusted with confectionery sugar before sandwiching.

Almond Tarts

These tarts are similar, in many respects, to the procedure used in making fruit tarts. The variation is in the almond filling used. The following is a recipe for the almond tart filling.

Almond Tart Filling   **Yield:** 4 doz. tarts

Ingredients	Lb.	Oz.	Mixing procedure
Almond or macaroon paste (or a blend)	3	..	Blend the paste and whites to a smooth paste
Egg whites	..	8	
Sugar	3	8	Add the sugar, flour, and part of the whites
Cake flour	..	2	(8 oz.) and blend smooth. Add the rest of
Egg whites	1	..	the whites in two stages and blend smooth
Almond flavor	..	$1/2$	

Procedures to Follow (Figs. 416 and 417)

1. Prepare the tart pans as though you were making fruit tarts. Be sure the short dough covers the entire pan. A slight opening or crack will cause the filling to run out and the tart will stick.
2. Place a small dot of jelly or jam at the bottom of the tart. This is done with a paper cone. Do not place a large amount of jam in the tart.
3. Drop the filling into the tart tins as you would drop a cake mix into a cupcake pan. The tart pan should be almost, but not quite, full. Filling to the brim will cause the mix to run over during baking.

FIG. 416. ALMOND TART   FIG. 417. ALMOND TART WITH COOKIE DOUGH CROSS ON TOP

Note: The almond filling should have the consistency of a thick gravy. If the mix is too stiff add a little egg white to soften it.

4. The top of the tart may be covered with two strips of short dough crossed over each other. The strips of dough should be egg-washed before placing on top of the tart. If the top is left plain then moisten a wash brush, used for egg-wash or syrup, with water. Shake the

excess water from the brush. Snap the brush over the tarts so that a fine spray of water droplets will be deposited on the top of the filling. Be careful not to have too much water or large drops of water deposited on the filling. The fine droplets of water will cause a lace-like cracking to take place when the tarts are baked.

5. Bake the tarts at 370°F. until light brown and the tops feel hard. Underbaking will cause the tarts to shrink or collapse after baking. Remove from the pans when the tarts are cool.

Almond Horns

Almond horns are made from an almond paste mixture which is quite stiff and can be molded or shaped by hand. Several shapes may be made in addition to the horn shape. For example, a finger shape and round shape may be made.

Almond Horns   **Yield:** 7 doz.—$1^1/_4$ oz. each

Ingredients	Lb.	Oz.	Mixing procedure
Almond or macaroon paste or a blend of both	3	..	Blend to a smooth, stiff paste
Egg whites	..	6	
Sugar	1	8	Add the sugar and whites and blend well to
Egg whites (approx.)	..	6	a smooth paste

Procedures to Follow (Figs. 418–420)

1. Place the mix on a lightly floured portion of the bench to keep the mix from sticking. Place a mound of sliced or ground nuts on a clean part of the bench away from the flour; spread $^1/_2$ in. thick.
2. Moisten the hands in cool water from a pot near the almond filling. This will make ease in handling and avoid excessive sticking.
3. Remove pieces of the filling so that each weighs about $1^1/_2$ oz. (size will determine the weight). Round up each piece in the palms of the hand and place on top of the nuts.
4. Roll the pieces in the nuts and shape into a strip about 4 to 5 in. long and of equal thickness.
5. Place each strip on a greased and flour-dusted pan or on a paper-lined pan and shape into a horseshoe shape. The pieces may also be shaped into a finger shape or rounded and flattened slightly on the pan as a hamburger roll. The finger or round-shaped units are depressed slightly in the center and half a glazed cherry or jam deposited in the depression.

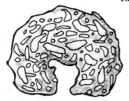

FIG. 418. ALMOND HORN

FIG. 419. ALMOND HORN MIX MADE INTO A FINGER SHAPE (JELLY OR CHERRY IN CENTER)

FIG. 420. ALMOND HORN MIX MADE INTO A ROUND SHAPE (JELLY OR CHERRY IN CENTER)

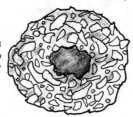

6. Allow the units to dry for about 2 hr. and bake at 375° to 385°F. Bake until golden brown and slightly soft. Do not overbake. Wash with warm or hot syrup as soon as the almond horns are removed from the oven. Wash gently to avoid damaging the horns.

NUT BARS

Nut bars are cookies which may be made in the larger pastry form or in the smaller form of a petit four. This cookie may also be cut so that it may be blended with other cookies for variety and sold by the pound. A number of factors enter into the preparation of nut bars which will effect the success and quality of the item. These will be explained in the procedure.

Nut Bars

Yield: 1 sheet—162 bars (9 × 18 slices)

Ingredients	Lb.	Oz.	Mixing procedure
Sugar	2	10	Combine all ingredients in a cooking kettle.
Egg whites	..	12	Place on fire, stir well during the cooking,
Toasted ground nuts	1	14	and boil for about 2 min.

Note: A prebaked short dough bottom must be prepared in advance.

Procedures to Follow

1. The short dough bottom must be baked lightly. These cookies are baked again and the bottom will burn or become too dark if baked strongly at the beginning. Line the baked bottom with a thin spread of jam.

2. Pour the hot mix into the prepared sheet pan (grease the sides of the pan) and level the batter with a bowl knife. This must be done before the cooked mix is cool.

3. Allow the cookies to dry overnight at room temperature.

4. Remove from the pan by warming the pan in the oven for a minute and then freeing the sides with a knife. Turn the sheet over on the back of a pan and then turn again on a cake board so that the cookie bottom is on the cake board.

5. Mark off the rectangular shapes—larger cookies are cut 1 by 3 in., small cookies are cut $1/2$ by $1^1/2$ in., and cut the shapes with a sharp knife. The knife blade should be dipped into hot water to make cutting easier. A straight edge or ruler should be used as a guide.

6. Place the cookies on a paper-lined sheet pan about 1 to $1^1/2$ in. apart. Bake at 370°F. until the cookies are light brown. You will note that the cookies spread slightly and cover the short dough during baking. Be careful not to overbake. If the cookies stick insert a bowl knife under the cookies to release them. In most cases the cookies will lift freely when they are cool.

Note: Ground cashew, hazel nuts, or filberts are best used. These must be toasted before using. Avoid the use of pecans or walnuts. These contain a large amount of fat and may cause excessive spread.

MACAROONS

Macaroons are a very popular type of cookie made in most bakeshops all year round, and especially for certain holidays. They must be made carefully and baked properly but they should not be a production problem if there is understanding of the procedures involved in their manufacture. The following recipes are standard, although there are many variations, and should provide excellent results.

French Macaroons   **Yield:** 5 pans (6 × 10)

Ingredients	Lb.	Oz.	Mixing procedure
Almond or macaroon paste	4	..	Place the dry ingredients in the machine and add one-quarter of the egg whites. Blend until smooth. Add the rest of the whites in three stages and blend well after each addition
Salt	..	$1/4$	
Granulated sugar	2	..	
Confectionery sugar	1	..	
Egg whites	1	6	

Note: The mix should be medium stiff so that the cookies will retain their shape when bagged out. Hold back about 2 oz. whites to be sure the mix is stiff enough. If too stiff add a little whites at a time until the desired consistency is reached.

Procedures to Follow (Figs. 421–425)

1. Pans for the cookies may be lined with parchment paper or the clean pans should be lightly greased and dusted with bread flour. Be sure to brush off the excess flour. Extra flour will cause the cookies to be pasty after baking and may also cause burning.

2. It is best to rinse the pastry bag with cold water and then wring out the excess water so that the bag is moist. This will prevent a sticky seepage of the mix through the bag that makes bagging out difficult.

3. Bag out the cookies into rosettes, pear shapes, finger shapes, heart shapes, and star shapes. Be sure the cookies are of equal size and height. Space the cookies about 1 in. apart. Space them alternately to allow enough room for the mild spreading during baking.

4. Garnish the cookies with half cherries, pieces of diced fruit, pecans, and/or other types of nuts and fruits as soon as the cookies are bagged out. Do not allow the cookies to develop a crust before garnishing. This will cause the nuts or fruits to fall out after baking.

FIG. 421. HEART-SHAPED FRENCH MACAROON

FIG. 422. PEAR-SHAPED FRENCH MACAROON

FIG. 423. WING-SHAPED FRENCH MACAROON

FIG. 424. DROP-SHAPE FRENCH MACAROON

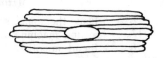

FIG. 425. BAR-SHAPED FRENCH MACAROON

5. Place the cookies on the rack and allow them to dry for several hours. This will cause a heavy crust to form. This crust is important because it causes the mild cracking on the baked cookie which is desirable. The crust also prevents excessive spread of the cookie during baking and keeps the moisture of the egg whites within the cookie. This extends the shelf-life of the cookie.

6. Bake the cookies at 375° to 380°F. until the cookies are light brown. Turn the pans if the oven heat is uneven. Wash the cookies with hot, simple syrup as soon as they are removed from the oven. Be careful to use the syrup brush lightly to avoid damage to the cookies.

Cocoanut Macaroons

Since there are many variations in recipes for cocoanut macaroons, each having specific values, two recipes will be provided. Each represents a standard method of macaroon preparation and each will also indicate variations in cost and quality of the product. The variations in preparing the mix will be indicated in the recipe. Makeup procedures are similar for both.

Cocoanut Macaroons (A)   **Yield:** 6 pans (8 × 10)

Ingredients	Lb.	Oz.	Mixing procedure
Sugar	4	..	Place all ingredients in this stage in a kettle and heat until quite warm. Stir to avoid scorching
Salt	..	$1/_2$	
Glucose (corn syrup)	..	6	
Egg whites	2	..	
Macaroon cocoanut	4	..	Blend the flour and cocoanut. Add, stir well constantly, and heat to approximately 150°F. Stir in the vanilla before removing from fire
Cake flour	..	4	
Vanilla	..	1	

Cocoanut Macaroons (B)   **Yield:** 7 pans (8 × 10)

Ingredients	Lb.	Oz.	Mixing procedure
Sugar	3	8	Place the sugar, salt, macaroon paste in the mixing machine and add $1/_4$ of the whites. Blend smooth. Add the rest of the whites in three stages and blend smooth. Place on fire and heat in a double boiler to 155°F. Add the cocoanut and stir in well. Remove from fire and stir in the confectionery sugar and vanilla
Salt	..	$1/_2$	
Macaroon paste	2	8	
Egg whites	2	..	
Macaroon cocoanut	3	..	
Confectionery sugar	1	8	
Vanilla	..	1	

Procedures to Follow (Fig. 426)

1. The pans may be lined with parchment paper or greased and dusted with flour. Remove the excess flour as for French macaroons.
2. Wash the bag in cold water and wring out well.
3. The macaroons may be bagged out with a plain tube or star tube.
4. The mix must be bagged out while very warm. If allowed to cool the mix will firm up and be difficult to bag out. Warm the mix in a double boiler if it becomes too cool. Do not add egg whites to soften it.
5. Space the cookies about 1 in. apart and bag out alternately.
6. Garnish the cookies, if they are to be garnished, with cherries or other diced fruits while the cookies are freshly bagged. Do not permit them to form a crust before garnishing.
7. Allow the macaroons to dry for about 2 hr. at shop temperature and bake at 380°F. until golden brown. Do not overbake. Cookies continue to bake or dry for 3 or 4 min. after they are removed from the oven.
8. For *chocolate French* or *cocoanut macaroons* add 4 oz. cocoa and 2 oz. egg whites to either mix in the last stage of preparation.

Note: To remove French or cocoanut macaroons that do not come off or lift up easily allow the cookies to cool and then turn the paper over so that the cookies face the pan. Moisten the paper lightly with cool water and turn the paper over again so that cookies face up. After 2 or 3 min. lift the macaroons from the paper. Cookies baked on greased and dusted pans should be allowed to cool and then loosened by tapping the pan on the bench. Use a bowl knife to lift those that stick.

FIG. 426. COCOANUT MACAROON

Chocolate Almond Macaroons

These macaroons are not to be mistaken for chocolate French or cocoanut macaroons. They are made with almond or macaroon paste and require a special mixing as well as drying procedure. The following recipe and procedure for makeup will show you how these cookies can be made with excellent results.

Chocolate Almond Macaroons

Yield: 5 pans (7 × 10)

Ingredients	Lb.	Oz.	Mixing procedure
Almond or macaroon paste	3	..	Mix these ingredients to a smooth paste
Sugar	3	..	
Salt	..	1/2	
Egg whites	..	8	
Egg whites	..	8	Add the whites and blend smooth
Confectionery sugar	1	..	Place in a double boiler and heat to 135°F. (very warm). Remove from fire and add sifted sugar and cocoa. Blend in well
Cocoa	..	6	

Procedures to Follow

1. Pans for the cookies may be lined with parchment paper or greased and dusted with flour. Remove the excess flour.

2. The pastry bag should be rinsed in cold water and wrung to a damp dry.

3. Use a small tube to bag out these cookies. You will note that the mix is quite soft and tends to run a bit.

4. Drop out the cookies about the size of a 25¢ piece and space them about 1 in. apart.

5. If the cookies have a slight peak (the mix may be a trifle stiff), moisten a cloth in cool water, wring out well, and place over the tops of the cookies. Run the palms of the hands lightly over the top of the cloth and this will eliminate the peaks.

6. These cookies should be allowed to dry overnight at shop temperature. This will cause a crust to form on the cookies. The crust will cause the desired cracked effect on the top of the cookie when it is baked.

7. The cookies are to be baked at 375°F. Bake them slightly on the tender side for they continue to dry for the first few minutes after they have been removed from the oven.

8. Allow the cookies to cool before removing from the pan. If the cookies stick slightly they should be turned on the paper and the back of the paper moistened as for cocoanut macaroons. They may also be lifted with a bowl knife.

Note: Be sure to stir the mix well while heating to prevent scorching if you are heating the mix over a direct flame.

ANISE DROPS

Anise drops are cookies made for special holidays. The name is derived from the anise flavor. The anise is ground and is quite strong. While special care must be given to preparation of the mix and makeup these cookies are not difficult to make.

Anise Drops   **Yield: 5 pans (7 × 10)**

Ingredients	Lb.	Oz.	Mixing procedure
Sugar	2	..	Whip the eggs, sugar, and salt as for sponge
Salt	..	$1/_4$	cake
Eggs (part yolks)	1	8	
Cake flour	1	..	Sift the flour and anise seed together and
Bread (patent) flour	1	..	fold in lightly by hand. Do not overmix
Ground anise seed	..	$1/_2$	

Procedures to Follow

1. Bag out the cookies with a pastry bag and small, plain tube.
2. The pans should be lined with parchment paper.
3. Bag out the cookies in drop form about the size of a 25¢ piece.
4. Space the cookies about $1^1/_2$ in. apart. The cookies will spread a bit on the pan.
5. Allow the cookies to dry overnight at shop or room temperature. This will cause a crust to form which causes the cracking to take place on the top of the cookies during baking.
6. Bake the cookies at 375°F. until light brown. The cookies will have a white crust-like effect and be slightly brown around the edges. They take about 12 min. to bake. It will take less if the bottom heat is strong. Be careful not to overbake since these cookies tend to dry after removal from the oven.
7. Allow the cookies to cool before removing from the pan. Tap the pan against the bench. This will free the cookies easily.

ORANGE, LEMON, AND NUT WAFER COOKIES

Wafer cookies are thin, flat cookies which may be garnished before baking or sandwiched and dipped after baking. It is understandable that there are many varieties of cookies which may be made from the various wafer cookie mixes. There are basic factors which require the careful consideration of the baker in order to produce a pleasing variety of wafer-type cookies. These will be indicated with each of the recipes for wafers as they apply.

Orange Wafers   **Yield:** 6 pans (5 × 9)

Ingredients	Lb.	Oz.	Mixing procedure
Sugar	1	..	Cream these ingredients until smooth and
Salt	..	$1/4$	soft
Shortening and butter	..	12	
Eggs	..	8	Add the eggs in two stages and cream in well
Light cream	..	4	Add the cream and stir in lightly
Rind of 2 oranges and 1 lemon			Stir in the fruit rind
Bread flour	1	..	Sift, add, and mix smooth

Procedures to Follow for Orange Wafers (Figs. 427–431)

1. The rind of the fresh fruit is best suited for flavoring these cookies. The flavor is more delicate and lasting than other types.
2. Bag out the cookies on very lightly greased pans or on parchment paper. Bag out the size of a quarter. They must be made smaller if they are sandwiched after baking. Space the cookies about 2 in. apart to allow spreading during baking.
3. Bake the cookies at 375° to 380°F. The cookies are to be baked to a delicate or just-done state. This holds for all wafer-type cookies. The orange wafers will have a light brown ring around the edge of the cookie and will be orange colored or yellow in the center. The cookies should then be removed from the oven. The cookies of the wafer type continue to bake or dry for the first few minutes after they are removed from the oven. Avoid overbaking.
4. Allow the cookies to cool and then finish in any of the following ways:

   a. Sandwich the cookies with a chocolate fudge icing and then dip into cookie dip or sweet chocolate about one-third of the way. This will provide a contrast of chocolate and orange colors. Orange and chocolate are an excellent flavor combination.

   b. Turn the cookies over so that the flat side or bottom becomes the top. Spread each cookie with melted chocolate and comb the top. They may be left as is or a pecan may be inserted into the chocolate. When the chocolate firms the nut will adhere.

   c. Leave the cookies on the pan as they are and then prepare a French chocolate mix. Bag a small rosette on the top of each of the cookies. The chocolate may be garnished with a pecan, walnut, or half cherry.

FIG. 427. WAFER COOKIE

FIG. 428. WAFER COOKIE TURNED OVER AND FILLED

FIG. 429. SANDWICHED WAFER COOKIE

FIG. 430. COMBED CHOCOLATE TOP

FIG. 431. SMALL ROS-
ETTE AND HALF CHERRY

Lemon Wafers

Yield: 6 pans (5 × 9)

Ingredients	Lb.	Oz.	Mixing procedure
Sugar	1	4	Blend well until soft and smooth
Salt	..	$1/4$	
Shortening and butter	1	..	
Egg whites	..	8	Add the whites in two stages and blend in well
Rind of 2 lemons			Stir the rind in lightly
Cake flour	1	6	Sift, add, and mix smooth

Procedures to Follow

1. You will note that this mix does not require creaming. It does require a good blending. This will mean that the cookies will not be overly porous and break easily after baking. They will have a close grain and submit to handling without breakage.
2. The cookies are bagged out on lightly greased or paper-lined pans. Space them about 2 in. apart to allow spreading during baking.
3. The cookies may be garnished with a pecan half before baking. Be sure to press the pecan firmly into the cookie. This will prevent the nut from falling out after baking.

4. If the cookies are baked without a top garnish they may be finished by sandwiching with a lemon or chocolate fudge. A fine apricot jam will also make a good filling. The cookies may then be striped with sweet chocolate or dipped in chocolate cookie dip.

5. Bake these cookies at 380°F. A slight, brown edge around the cookie will indicate that it is baked. Do not overbake.

Nut Wafers   **Yield:** 6 pans (7 × 10)

Ingredients	Lb.	Oz.	Mixing procedure
Sugar	1	..	Cream until soft and light
Salt	..	$1/2$	
Shortening	1	..	
Egg whites	..	8	Add in two stages and cream well after each
Almond flavor	..	$1/2$	addition
Toasted ground nuts	2	..	Blend the flour and nuts. Fold in lightly by
Bread flour	..	4	hand until smooth

Procedures to Follow

1. The nuts should be ground medium fine so that they can be bagged out without clogging the bag and tube. Toasting the nuts is very important. It brings out the flavor of the nut. The cookie bakes quickly and the nuts, if raw, do not toast in the baking process.

2. Bag out the cookies on lightly greased pans or paper-lined pans. Space about 2 in. apart to allow for spreading in baking. Bag the cookies out with a plain tube about the size of a quarter.

3. Bake the cookies at 350° to 360°F. A light brown edge will indicate that the cookie is baked.

4. Finish the cookies by sandwiching with jam, chocolate, or fudge. Stripe the tops of the cookies with chocolate or dip half-way in chocolate.

LACE COOKIES (FLORENTINES)

Lace cookies are similar to wafer cookies in that they are flat, spread considerably while baking, and have crispness. They are not similar in that they are porous (lace-like) and are generally made by pre-cooking the mix. There is also a cold process used. Both methods, and the recipes for each, are given. Both recipes provide good results.

FIG. 432. LACE COOKIE

FIG. 433. SANDWICHED AND STRIPED COOKIE (LACE-TYPE)

FIG. 434. LACE COOKIE DIPPED ONE-THIRD INTO CHOCOLATE

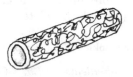

FIG. 435. ROLLED AND FILLED LACE-TYPE COOKIE

Lace Cookies (Cooked Process)   **Yield:** 10 pans (6 × 10)

Ingredients	Lb.	Oz.	Mixing procedure
Sugar	2	..	Bring all the ingredients in this stage to a boil. Stir constantly to prevent scorching
Salt	..	$1/2$	
Butter and shortening	1	8	
Honey	..	8	
Water	..	8	Add water and boil
Ground nuts (untoasted)	1	14	Add and reboil. Stir constantly to prevent scorching. Remove from fire after boiling and cool to 145°F.
Bread flour	..	11	
Cinnamon	..	$1/4$	

Procedures to Follow (Figs. 432–435)

1. Be careful when boiling to prevent burns and scorching of the mix. Stir constantly through the center and around the sides. The nuts need not be toasted because they are coated with honey and syrup. This develops the taste and flavor of the nuts.
2. Allow the mix to cool so that it may be placed in a pastry bag with a small, plain tube and handled without burning the hands. Do not allow the mix to become cool. It will stiffen and be difficult to bag out.
3. Bag out on lightly greased or paper-lined pans about the size of a penny. Allow about 2 in. space between each cookie to provide room for spreading during baking.

4. Bake at 350°F. until medium dark brown. The edge of the cookie will form a brown crust.
5. Allow the cookies to cool and sandwich with jam, fudge, or chocolate. The cookies are generally striped with sweet chocolate. They may also be partially dipped in sweet chocolate.
6. Each of the cookies may be rolled while warm to the form of a cigarette. The cigarettes are allowed to cool and set in shape before filling with chocolate fudge or sweet chocolate and cream (French chocolate).

Lace Cookies (Cold Process)   **Yield:**   8 pans (5 × 9)

Ingredients	Lb.	Oz.	Mixing procedure
Brown sugar	2	..	Cream the ingredients in this stage until soft
Salt	..	$1/_2$	and light
Shortening	..	11	
Glucose or corn	..	4	
syrup			
Cake flour	..	8	
Water	..	8	Add the water in two stages and cream
Cake flour	..	8	Sift the flour, blend with the nuts and cinna-
Toasted ground nuts	1	..	mon and fold in lightly until smooth
Cinnamon	..	$1/_4$	

Note: Bag out, as above, bake at 380°F., and finish as the above type.

CHOCOLATE LEAVES, RAINBOW COOKIES, MIRRORS, AND SHORTBREAD COOKIES

This assortment will add to the variety of the cookie display. While recipes and procedures are presented it is the care and neatness with which the cookies are produced that make the difference between an attractive and a slovenly appearance. It is important that the baker take special care in displaying the cookies and in their arrangement on the display pans.

Chocolate Leaves   **Yield:** 5 pans (5 × 7)

Ingredients	Lb.	Oz.	Mixing procedure
Almond or macaroon paste	1	8	Mix to a smooth paste
Egg whites	..	4	
Sugar	1	..	Add the ingredients to the above and mix
Salt	..	$1/4$	well until smooth
Butter or shortening	..	2	
Bread flour	..	6	
Egg whites	..	8	Add the whites in two stages and blend in well until smooth

Procedures to Follow (Figs. 436–439)

1. The mix must be of a soft consistency and yet not runny. It may be necessary to add a little egg white as the mix stands for it may bind or stiffen.
2. The pans for these cookies are to be greased and dusted with flour. It is best to deposit these cookies on parchment-paper-lined pans.
3. The cookies are deposited on the pans with the help of a stencil. Leaf stencils may be in mat form the size of a sheet pan or in two hand stencil form. For speed in production, the large mat is best. Place the stencil (mat or two hand form) on the pan. With a bowl knife deposit the mix on the stencil and spread evenly over the mat or the hand stencil so that each of the stencil spaces is filled in evenly. It is important to have each stencil space of even thickness. After the mix has been spread run the bowl knife over the top of the stencil mat and scrape the excess mix off. This is returned to the bowl.
4. Lift the mat or stencil form up carefully to avoid smearing the leaves. Scrape the excess off and return to the bowl. The underside of the mat or hand form must be kept clean or else it will stick to the paper or pan.
5. Allow the leaves to dry for about 1 hr. and bake at 375°F. until they are light brown. Do not overbake.
6. Allow the cookies to cool and then coat them with cookie dip or melted sweet chocolate. Be careful not to overheat the chocolate. Melt the chocolate in a double boiler at a low flame. Avoid getting water into the chocolate. This will cause it to bind. The chocolate is applied with a bowl knife. Leaf veins are made by holding the

bowl knife on edge and gently marking the chocolate with the edge at a 45° angle facing toward the base of the leaf. Allow the chocolate to dry at cool temperature (do not refrigerate) before stacking.

FIG. 436. BAKED LEAF COOKIE

FIG. 437. PREPARED CHOCOLATE FOR DIPPING OR COATING COOKIES

FIG. 438. COATED LEAF COOKIE READY TO BE COMBED

FIG. 439. FINISHED CHOCOLATE LEAF COOKIE

Rainbow Cookies

These cookies are very colorful and attractive. They are made by layering colored, baked sheet cakes into one sheet of four or five differently colored layers. The cookies are then cut smaller in size.

Rainbow Cookies   Yield: 4 sheets

Ingredients	Lb.	Oz.	Mixing procedure
Macaroon or almond paste	2	..	Mix the ingredients to a smooth paste
Eggs	..	8	
Sugar	2	..	Add these ingredients to the above and cream well until soft and light
Butter	1	..	
Shortening	1	..	
Salt	..	1	
Eggs	1	8	Add the eggs in three stages and cream well.
Vanilla	..	1	Add vanilla with the last stage of eggs
Cake flour	2	..	Sift, add, and fold in lightly until smooth

Procedures to Follow (Figs. 440 and 441)

1. Divide the mix into four equal parts by weighing $2^1/_2$ lb. of mix for each part.
2. Color each of the parts into a separate color—chocolate, red, yellow, and green. Be sure the color is added carefully and mixed in well to avoid uneven stripes. The color should be quite strong. Pastel shades fade during baking. Avoid excess coloring.
3. Deposit each colored part into a sheet pan lined with parchment paper. Level off evenly as you would for a jelly roll. Be sure it is even.
4. Bake the sheets at 375°F. Do not rely upon crust color for this is very misleading to tell when the sheets are baked. After 12 min., touch the sheet gently in the center. If it springs back lightly to the touch it is baked. Avoid overbaking. This will make the sheet brittle and the color will partially fade.
5. Allow the sheets to cool and sandwich them together with a good quality jam. Apricot jam is recommended. Be sure the jam is smooth. Use only enough jam to make the sheets stick to each other. Avoid excess jam. It will run after the cookies are cut. It may also cause the sheets to slide.
6. Place the sheets in the refrigerator with some weights on them. Be sure the sheets are covered with another sheet pan before applying the weights.
7. When chilled and firm remove from the refrigerator and coat one side with cookie coating or melted sweet chocolate. Comb the chocolate lightly. Allow the chocolate to dry well, place a sheet of parchment paper over it, and turn the entire sheet cake over. Ice this side with chocolate and comb. Allow the chocolate to dry well.
8. Cut the cookies into rectangular shapes about $1^1/_2$ in. long and $1/_2$ in. wide. If the knife blade sticks or pulls dip the knife into hot water for a smooth cut. These sheets may also be cut into various shapes and used for petits fours.

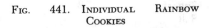

FIG. 440. COLORED SHEETS PUT TO-
GETHER AND TOPPED WITH SWEET
CHOCOLATE

FIG. 441. INDIVIDUAL RAINBOW
COOKIES

Mirror Cookies

The regular short dough used for cake bottoms may be used as the base for these cookies. However, if a better quality is preferred the following recipe for shortbread cookies may be used.

Short Dough or Shortbread   **Yield:** 18 doz. 3-in. cookies

Ingredients	Lb.	Oz.	Mixing procedure
Sugar	2	..	Cream these ingredients together until soft
Salt	..	1	and light
Shortening and butter	4	..	
Glucose or corn syrup	..	6	
Eggs	1	..	Add the eggs in two stages and cream in.
Vanilla	..	$1^1/_2$	Add the vanilla with the last stage
Cake flour	3	..	Sift, add, and fold in very lightly until the
Bread flour	3	..	flour is absorbed. Do not overmix

Procedures to Follow (Figs. 442–444)

1. Chill the short dough before using. Remove a part of the dough and work out smooth on a floured cloth. Roll out the dough to about $^1/_8$ in. thick.
2. With a round cookie cutter ($2^1/_2$–3 in. in diameter) cut out the circle cookies. Place these on a parchment-paper-lined sheet pan.
3. Bake the cookies at 400°F. until just lightly browned. Remove from the oven at that point. These cookie bases will be baked again.
4. Allow the cookies to cool and turn them over so that the bottom is now the top. You now have a smooth surface to work on.

Topping for Mirror Cookies   **Yield:** Top or circle 18 doz. cookies

Ingredients	Lb.	Oz.	Mixing procedure
Macaroon or almond paste	3	..	Mix to a smooth paste
Egg whites	..	8	
Sugar	2	4	Add to the above and mix smooth. Add the
Salt	..	$^1/_4$	whites in two stages
Egg whites	..	8	

5. The mix should be of medium-stiff consistency so that the design of the tube remains fixed and does not run.
6. Wet the pastry bag with cold water. Fill the bag with the mix and bag an even ring of the almond mix around the edge of the cookie bottom. Allow the almond ring to dry for about 1 hr. before baking.
7. Bake at 390°F. until the almond ring is golden brown.
8. Wash the almond ring on the cookie with hot syrup. Do this gently to avoid marring the shape of the ring. Allow the cookies to cool and fill the center with a good quality jam that has been worked smooth. The center may also be filled with sweet chocolate or colored fondant icing. The centers may also be garnished with nuts (pistachio) or other topping.
9. For small cookies cut the short dough bottoms with a cookie cutter about 1 in. in diameter. Fill and finish the same as larger units.

FIG. 442. CUT OUT BAKED COOKIE BOTTOM

FIG. 443. APPLYING THE ALMOND MIX TOPPING FOR MIRROR TARTS

FIG. 444. FINISHED MIRROR TART WITH JAM FILLING

Shortbread Cookies

These cookies may be cut in many different shapes. Variety is also provided by finishing these cookies in different ways.

Procedures to Follow (Figs. 445–452)

1. Roll out the short dough (the same dough used for the bottoms of the mirror cookies) a little less than $1/4$ in. thick. Be sure the dough is of even thickness for uniformity of the cookies.
2. The cookies may be cut into various shapes with various cookie cutters. For example, the bridge-type variety may be cut in hearts, diamonds, and others. The cookies may be cut out with a pastry wheel into rectangular and square shape. Various animal forms may be used if the cutters are small. Larger units may also be cut from the dough.

3. The cut-out cookies may be left plain and finished after baking, or the rolled-out dough garnished with various toppings such as ground nuts, sugar, chocolate sprinkles, and other garnishes before cookies are cut out. Avoid excessive scrap by cutting cookies too far apart. Dough may also be washed with a combination of eggs and egg yolks and striped across with a fork for a criss-cross effect. Let the wash on the dough dry before cutting out cookies.

4. These cookies are baked at 390°F. until golden brown. Plain cookies should have a slight yellow coloring in the center to show the proper doneness.

5. Allow plain cookies to cool before finishing. Then they may be dipped in cookie coating or melted sweet chocolate. Others may have a small circle of fudge in the center topped with a pecan (see below).

FIG. 445. CHOCOLATE DIPPED

FIG. 446. GROUND NUT TOPPING

FIG. 447. SUGAR TOPPED COOKIE

FIG. 448. CHOCOLATE SPRINKLE TOP

FIG. 449. FUDGE-PECAN TOPPED

FIG. 450. EGG-WASHED TOPPING

FIG. 451. CHOCOLATE CHIP TOP

FIG. 452. COOKIE WITH JAM CENTER

Chocolate Chip Cookies

Yield: 24 doz.

Ingredients	Lb.	Oz.	Mixing Procedure
Brown sugar	1	8	Cream these ingredients together until soft
Granulated sugar	1	8	and light
Salt	..	1	
Milk powder	..	3	
Shortening	2	..	
Eggs	1	8	Add eggs in three stages and cream in well after each addition
Water	..	8	Dissolve baking soda in water. Add flavor-
Baking soda	..	$1/2$	ing and stir into the above lightly
Vanilla	..	1	
Cake flour	3	..	Sift, add, and fold in
Chocolate chips	3	8	Fold into batter until smooth

Procedure to Follow

1. Bag out cookies with pastry bag and large plain tube. Place on parchment paper lined pans or lightly but evenly greased pans. Space about 1 in. apart to allow for spread during baking. Bake at 385°F.

SPICE DROPS, KISSES, MACAROON CUPS, AND NUISETTES

Spice Drops (*Pfefferneusse*)

Yield: 500 cookies

Ingredients	Lb.	Oz.	Mixing Procedure
Honey (1 qt.)	3	..	Place all the ingredients in this stage in
Brown sugar	..	8	mixing bowl and mix smooth
Eggs	..	4	
Oil	..	3	
Salt	..	1	
Cinnamon	..	1	
Allspice	..	$1/4$	
Ginger	..	$1/4$	
Cloves	..	$1/4$	
Water	..	12	Dissolve soda and ammonium bicarbonate
Baking soda	..	$1^1/2$	in water and add to the above. Stir well
Ammonium bicarbonate	..	$1/4$	
Bread Four	2	4	Sift, add, and mix to a smooth dough
Cake flour	2	4	

Procedures to Follow (Figs. 453 and 454)

1. A dark, buckwheat honey is suggested because of its darker and stronger color. If light, clover honey is used, it can be mixed with fine-grade molasses.

2. Spices are to be scaled carefully and not used carelessly. Over-spicing is far worse than under-spicing. Be sure that the spices you use come from a sealed can. Spices that have been exposed may have lost their flavor and aroma.

3. The ammonium bicarbonate is used for an immediate spreading as well as lifting effect. Be sure the leavening comes from a well-sealed can.

4. The finished dough should be of medium-stiff consistency. It is advisable to refrigerate the dough before using. This will make it easier to handle and prevent the use of excess flour.

5. Roll out the dough into strips about $1/4$ in. thick. Cut the strips into pieces about 1 in. long. Roll each piece into a ball and place on paper-lined pans. Space the cookies about 1 in. apart to allow spreading.

6. Bake the cookies at 360° to 370°F. until they feel springy to the touch. Do not overbake for they will become too hard.

7. Cool the baked cookies and place them into a large mixing bowl. Pour the hot syrup over the cookies and stir them gently so that all the cookies are coated with this syrup made up of: 1 lb. 8 oz. water and 6 lb. sugar. Boil to 240°F. (soft ball).

8. Remove the cookies with a ladle and place into a pan filled with confectionery sugar. Roll the cookies in the sugar until they are coated. The sugar may also be colored pink and green for variety.

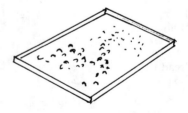

FIG. 453.   POUR HOT SYRUP OVER THE
SPICE DROPS

FIG. 454.   PLACE ON A PAN FILLED
WITH CONFECTIONERY SUGAR

Kisses

These cookies are made in various sizes and shapes. They may also be made into mushroom shapes, chicks, and other forms to garnish the tops of French pastries. Color may be added to the mix for further variety. Very often the tops of the kisses are dusted with colored sugar.

Kisses   **Yield:** 250 large cookies

Ingredients	Lb.	Oz.	Mixing procedure
Egg whites	2	..	Whip the whites to a wet peak. Add the
Granulated sugar	2	..	sugar in a slow, steady stream and whip to
Salt	..	$1/4$	firm peak. Add the vanilla in the final stage
Vanilla	..	$1/2$	
Granulated sugar	4	..	Fold in the sugar gently by adding slowly and folding over lightly. Do not overmix

Procedures to Follow (Figs. 455–458)

1. Use whites that are slightly aged but have not taken on an odor. The temperature of the egg whites should be about 55° to 60°F. for best results in whipping. Be sure the kettle and wire whip are free from grease. Any oily substance will cause the whites to fall back.
2. Be careful when adding the remaining sugar. Avoid overmixing.

FIG. 455. STAR TUBE AND PASTRY BAG FOR KISSES

FIG. 456. PLAIN TUBE AND PASTRY BAG FOR KISSES

FIG. 457. DROP-SHAPE KISSES COOKIE

FIG. 458. MUSHROOM-TYPE KISSES COOKIE

3. Bag out the mix with a pastry bag and star tube. For the piping of animals, mushrooms, etc., use a small plain tube. Bag the cookies on parchment-paper-lined pans.

4. If the cookies are to be garnished or dusted with colored sugar do so as soon as the cookies are bagged out. The garnish will not stick if a crust has formed.

5. Bake the cookies in a cool oven (300°F.). Actually, the cookies are slow-baked or dried in a cool oven to prevent the formation of a brown crust. The cookies are considered baked when they can be lifted from the pan without leaving an imprint in the cookie.

6. For *cocoanut kisses* add 1 lb. fine-shred, macaroon cocoanut to the mix. Reduce the sugar content by 8 oz. if this is done.

Macaroon Cups   Yield: 6–7 doz.

Ingredients	Lb.	Oz.	Mixing procedure
Egg whites	2	..	Whip the whites to a soft peak. Add the
Sugar	1	8	sugar and salt gradually and whip until al-
Salt	..	$1/4$	most dry
Vanilla	..	$1/2$	Fold in the vanilla flavor
Macaroon cocoanut	2	4	Blend the cocoanut, sugar, and flour to-
Sugar	2	..	gether and fold gently into the above. Do
Cake flour	..	2	not overmix

Notes on Macaroon Cups

1. Be sure to add the sugar in a slow, steady stream when adding to the whipping whites. Do not whip the whites and sugar to a dry peak. This will make it difficult to fold in the sugar and cocoanut. Fold very carefully so as to avoid loss of volume.

2. Drop the mix into paper-lined cupcake pans and bake at 370° to 375°F. until golden brown. Fill the pans three-quarters full. The air in the whipped whites will cause the leavening effect.

Nuisettes

While this type of cookie may be made from other recipes such as the Florentine lace cookie mix, the recipe given is one made from the use of almond or macaroon paste. It also requires a stencil. This special care will result in a smooth-finished cookie that genuinely looks like a cigarette. While it does require care and extra work it is well worth the effort. It adds to the variety of cookies by its appearance and finish.

Cigarette Cookie   **Yield:**   450 cookies

Ingredients	Lb.	Oz.		Mixing procedure
Almond paste	2	..		Soften the almond paste with a small amount
Confectionery sugar	3	..		of the egg whites. Mix smooth to eliminate
Salt	..	$1/4$		lumps. Add the rest of the ingredients and
Cake flour	..	8		mix smooth. Add the whites a little at a
Bread flour	..	8		time and mix well after each addition. Mix
Egg whites	1	8		until the mix is soft and smooth and can be
(variable)				smeared easily

Procedures to Follow (Figs. 459–464)

1. The mix must be soft and smooth. It should not run when placed on the pan.
2. A stencil of 2-in. squares is used as you would for chocolate leaves.
3. The pans should be greased lightly and evenly and then dusted with flour. Parchment-paper-lined pans may be used.
4. Place the stencil at one end of the pan and fill the spaces evenly. Lift the stencil quickly to avoid smearing the squares. Space the stencil so that the squares are about 1 in. apart.
5. It is important that you bake one pan at a time. Bake at 385°F. When the edge of the square shows a light touch of color remove from the oven. Do not overbake for they will dry and crack when rolled.
6. While the cookies are still quite warm, remove them from the pan one at a time and roll up in a thin rolling pin or stick $1/4$ in. in diameter. Wood is best for it does not conduct heat quickly. Remove from the stick and place on a clean pan. The rolled cookies will hold their shape. Of course, it is necessary to work quickly. Use a bowl knife to lift the warm cookies. If the pan becomes cool and the cookies crack return them to the oven for a few seconds to reheat and then roll.
7. Finish the cookies by filling with fudge icing or French chocolate. Fill them from both ends to be certain the cookie is filled completely.
8. Next, dip in chocolate on one side or end about $1/4$ in. deep and then dip in toasted, ground nuts. Both ends may be dipped if desired.

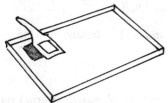

Fig. 459. Stencil the Cookie on a Paper-Lined Sheet Pan

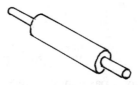

Fig. 460. Roll the Cookies on a Thin Rolling Pin or Stick

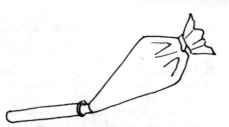

FIG. 461. FILL END OF COOKIE WITH
CHOCOLATE OR FUDGE

FIG. 462. DIP ONE END
INTO THE CHOCOLATE

FIG. 463. DIP CHOCOLATE END INTO
TOASTED GROUND NUTS

FIG. 464. FINISHED CIGARETTE
COOKIE

FRENCH BUTTER COOKIES, CHINESE COOKIES, AND HONEY NUTS

These specialty cookies have an important place in the cookie assortment of the retail bakeshop and restaurant. While the French butter cookie and Chinese cookie are always in stock, honey nuts are specialty items made at special holiday seasons.

French Butter Cookies   **Yield:** 15 pans (7 × 10)

Ingredients	Lb.	Oz.	Mixing procedure
Macaroon paste	4	..	Mix the ingredients to a smooth paste.
Sugar	2	..	Avoid lumps by carefully scraping the sides
Salt	..	1	of the kettle
Egg whites	..	8	
Butter	3	..	Add the butter and shortening and cream
Shortening	3	..	well until soft and light
Vanilla	..	1	
Egg whites	2	..	Add the whites in four stages and cream well after each addition
Bread flour	7	..	Sift, add, and fold in lightly by hand. Do not overmix

Procedures to Follow (Figs. 464A–464F)

1. Almond paste may be used in place of macaroon paste. Kernel paste is not advisable for this quality cookie.

2. The tenderness of the cookie lies in the richness of the mix. This means that creaming of the fat and sugar is important. It is also important to cream the egg whites carefully into the mix. The mix should have the appearance of a light buttercream before folding in the flour.

3. Be sure to sift the flour and fold it in carefully by hand. Avoid overmixing for this will cause toughness. As soon as the flour is blended in the mix will look rough. It will smooth out as you press the mix through the pastry bag and tube.

4. Bag the cookies out into the same shapes as you did for the regular bagged cookies (butter cookies); stars, rosettes, pear shapes, and others. Use a French tube of medium size. Space the cookies about $3/4$ in. apart. Bag out on parchment-paper-lined pans. Bake the cookies at 385° to a light color. The bottom edges of the cookies will show a light brown crust. Avoid overbaking.

5. The tops of the cookies may be garnished with glazed fruits, half cherries, nut pieces, jam, and sprinkles before baking.

6. Allow the cookies to cool before finishing with chocolate or fudge.

Fig. 464A. Heart-Shaped French Cookie

Fig. 464B. Pear-Shaped French Cookie

Fig. 464C. Wing-Shaped French Cookie

Fig. 464D. Drop-Shaped French Cookie

Fig. 464E. Bar-Shaped French Cookie

Fig. 464F. Cocoanut Cookie

Chinese Cookies

These cookies may be made with a good deal of variety. For example, part of the dough may be colored and contrasted as for ice-box cookies. The outside of the cookies may be rolled in nuts, sprinkles, and other toppings. In addition, the tops of the cookies may be finished with toppings and icings.

Chinese Cookies   **Yield:**   250 cookies

Ingredients	Lb.	Oz.	Mixing procedure
Sugar	3	8	Mix to incorporate and blend to a smooth
Salt	..	1	paste
Shortening	3	8	
Baking soda	..	$3/4$	
Eggs (whole)	..	12	Add the eggs and blend in
Cake flour	5	8	Sift the flour. Add the flavors and stir
Vanilla	..	1	lightly. Add the flour and fold in lightly to
Almond flavor	..	$1/2$	form a smooth dough

Procedures to Follow (Figs. 465–469)

1. Scale the dough into pieces weighing about 2 lb. each.
2. Parts of the dough may be colored and striped in with the dough for a striped effect. Avoid too much handling of the dough to prevent smearing.
3. Melted sweet chocolate may be striped into the dough for a marbled effect.
4. Roll the units into round strips about $1^1/2$ in. in diameter. The diameter of the strips is controlled by the size of the cookies desired.

FIG. 465. PART OF THE DOUGH MAY
BE COLORED AND MIXED IN

FIG. 466. ROLL UNITS INTO STRIPS
ON CHOCOLATE SPRINKLES

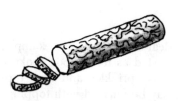

FIG. 467. WHEN CHILLED CUT INTO
$1/4$ IN. SLICES

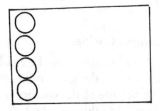

FIG. 468. SPACE COOKIES SO THAT
THEY DO NOT TOUCH WHEN BAKED

Fig. 469. Chinese Cookie Garnished with Chocolate Fudge in the Center

5. Roll the strips of dough in toasted chopped nuts, chocolate sprinkles, or colored sugar. Roll each of the strips in parchment paper to maintain the round shape.

6. Refrigerate until firm or even hard. Slice while chilled into slices about $1/4$ in. thick. Place the slices on parchment-paper-lined pans and space about 1 in. apart. Larger cookies will require a larger space to prevent touching while they are baking.

7. Bake the cookies at 360°F. They require a slower bake because of the richness of the fat content. The cookies are to be crisp at the edges. They will be tender because of the high percentage of fat.

8. Allow the cookies to cool before garnishing the centers with chocolate or fudge. A sliced almond or almond half may be placed in the center of the cookie before baking. Press the nut in firmly to prevent falling out after baking.

Honey Nuts (Taiglach)

These are specialty items and require skill and care in preparation. They make a colorful display at holiday seasons. They will also create consumer demand by their attractive appearance.

Honey Nuts			Yield: 36 8-oz. units or 12 doz. 2-oz. cups
Ingredients	*Lb.*	*Oz.*	*Mixing procedure*
Sugar	..	4	Blend these ingredients together until
Salt	..	1	smooth
Eggs (half yolks)	2	..	
Oil	..	8	
Rum flavor	..	1	
Bread flour	2	14	Sift, add, and mix well until the dough is smoothly developed

Procedures to Follow (Figs. 470–476)

1. Place the dough on a floured bench and form into a rectangle.

2. Cut strips from the dough and roll out into $1/4$-in. strips. Line up four or five strips and dust them liberally with bread flour. Cut the strips into $1/4$-in. pieces and dust with flour again. Spread the dough pieces so that they are covered with flour. Place the coated pieces in a coarse sieve and shake to remove excess flour. Place on a pan and spread the pieces apart. Do not allow the pieces to pile over each other.

3. Bake the pieces of dough in a cool oven—350°F. Give them a light, golden color and bake until crisp and firm.

4. Allow the units to cool and sift again to remove excess flour.

5. The honey is then boiled at a very slow flame to the hard ball stage (265°F.): 1 qt. honey, 1 lb. sugar, and a pinch of cloves are combined for this honey mixture. A drop of the boiling honey placed in cool water will form a hard ball that will crack when squeezed at cool temperatures. Stir the honey occasionally. Wash the sides of the kettle periodically to prevent crystallization.

6. When the honey has reached the proper stage remove from the fire and add the baked honey nuts, approximately 3 lb. glazed cherries and 5 lb. filberts. Stir gently with a wooden paddle. Be careful not to crush the cherries. You will note that the honey coats the nuts and fruits.

7. Allow the mix to cool slightly on a clean, lightly oiled part of the bench. The units may be scaled into 8-oz. pieces and shaped as loaves or rounded. Dip the base of these units into ground nuts to prevent sticking to the doilies. The units may be made up into small balls (about 1 or 2 oz.) and placed in cupcake liners.

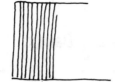

Fig. 470. Cut Honey Nut Dough into Strips

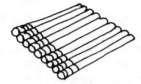

Fig. 471. Line Up the Cut and Rolled Strips and Cut in ¼ In. Units

Fig. 472. Place the Baked Units of Dough into a Coarse Sieve, Shake to Remove the Excess Flour

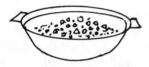

Fig. 473. Cook the Honey to the Proper Temperature and Add the Honey Nuts, Regular Nuts, and Fruits

Fig. 474. Allow the Mix to Cool on the Bench

Fig. 475. Scale into 8 Oz. Balls

Fig. 476. Place Smaller Units in Cupcake Liners

CHAPTER 33

Dietetic Baking

Dietetics, as it is presently applied to commercial baking, refers to the production of bakery products that meet special consumer dietary needs. For example, there are consumers who must be on sugar-free or limited sugar intake diets. There are others who must be on a salt-free or limited salt intake diet. Since a large number of consumers of bakery products are thus affected, the dietetic aspect of baking has grown considerably. This makes the consumption of bakery products possible for those who were restricted. Producers of sugar substitutes and bakery supplies manufacturers have developed a number of prepared mixes which the bakers use for the production of dietary or dietetic bakery products. The more enterprising retail and wholesale bakers who produce dietetic products have developed their own recipes or formulas. They purchase the sugar substitute and work from "scratch."

The fact that these "dietetic formulas" contain no sugar (only sugar substitutes) may make them acceptable for use by diabetics (they should check with their physicians), but does not necessarily qualify the products as "low caloric," as the formulas contain fairly normal quantities of shortening or butter, milk, eggs, etc.

Also, removing salt (sodium chloride) via replacement with a salt substitute does lower the sodium content some, but, in most cases, this may not be sufficient to qualify the baked products as "low-sodium." Sodium content is naturally present in relatively high quantities in milk, dough conditioners, eggs, and even flour. A truly hypertensive person (high blood pressure) may require low-sodium products rather than just salt-free products, and should check with his physician.

This chapter has been developed for bakers who produce their own products using only a sugar substitute as a sweetener and for bakers who wish to develop their own line of dietetic bakery products. Approved sugar substitutes that are used to replace the sweetness supplied by granulated sugar are primarily composed of saccharin, lactose, dextrose and minimal amounts of cream of tartar.

Most sugar substitutes, commonly called artificial or synthetic sweeteners, may be used as follows: *2 oz. of sugar substitute may be used to replace 1 lb. of granulated sugar.* For exactness, the baker may request a specification analysis from the purveyor or manufacturer of the sugar substitute for his own experimental development of sugar-free bakery products.

Dietetics in baking also includes bakery products made without the usual table salt (sodium chloride) content. These bakery products are for consumers who must be on a total or limited salt-free diet, more correctly called a low-sodium diet. The replacement for the usual, common salt (sodium chloride) are the special sodium-free salts produced especially for those consumers who are limited in their salt intake. These special salt preparations are used by bakers as they normally use salt presently in their formulas. There may be some difference in the taste of the finished product and bakers may make some adjustment as they experiment in product development. In some instances, bakers develop their formulas so that both the sugar-free and salt-free requirements are provided. It is also very likely that the supplier of the sugar substitute will also provide the sodium-free salt.

The formulas provided are those which have been developed and tested with the use of both the sugar substitute and sodium-free salt. The suggestions and comments that follow are facts which have been derived from the development of the formulas and the resulting products. The baker should have an understanding of the normal uses of granulated sugar in baking and what the elimination of sugar will do. This refers not only to the matter of taste or sweetness but also to the methods of production and the characteristics of the baked products. For example, the baker will find those cakes and similar products that require large volume, through creaming of sugar and shortening in the initial stages of mixing, are now limited in production because the sugar has been removed.

FACTORS TO BE CONSIDERED IN DIETETIC BAKERY PRODUCTS PRODUCTION

Yeast-Raised Products

Sugar is a source of food for yeast growth and activity in doughs. Part of the sugar is converted by enzymatic action into yeast food and thereby promotes a more active fermentation. (Refer to pages 32 and 33.) Thus, with sugar substitutes, this may require an increase in the amount of yeast used, particularly in sweet yeast doughs. Italian and French bread are almost sugar-free (the minimum amounts of sugar and malt may be removed) and these may be made with sodium-free salts, often without yeast adjustment.

Sugar helps in developing a deep and desirable crust color. Using sugar substitutes, the dough should be kept on the young side so that crust color formation may be achieved without overextensive baking periods which dry the product. Increased baking temperatures will also be necessary to develop the desirable crust color. The use of mild steam in the baking of hard-type yeast-raised products will also be helpful in the development of crust color.

The sodium-free salts, if used, may have to be increased slightly to regulate fermentation and provide an improved taste. Such doughs are generally allowed to rise only once and then are taken to the bench or machine for make-up.

Cakes and Cookies

In many cake and cookie batters, sugar is used to cream up shortening and other dry ingredients and thereby aid in the formation of air cells. These cells contribute to the leavening and cell structure of the product. Sugar is equally important in the whipping of eggs, and in cakes using the whipping method of mixing. The grain, texture, and prolonged freshness of the product are improved through the use of sugar.

To replace the sugar with a sugar substitute will necessitate changes in order to produce a desirable product. Use of increased eggs (yolks and egg whites), dry skim milk, shortening and butter is advisable. Methods of mixing may be revised to eliminate the usual creaming procedures. It must be noted that some creaming can take place with mixing of flour and shortening to incorporate air cells. The formulas that follow will indicate appropriate changes. These may be used as a basis for further development by the baker.

Baking of cakes and cookies containing sugar substitutes will require higher baking temperatures. This is necessary for the development of desirable crust color without extensive baking time which may dry out the products. Note is made of the fact that products tend to have a firm crust as soon as removed from the oven, but the crust then softens as it cools in most cakes and pastries.

Cake finishing is limited in view of the lack of suitable icings normally used in sugar-free cake production. Most cakes are usually finished with a nut topping, crumb topping made with leftover or stale dietetic products which have been ground and sifted, dusted with a blend of corn starch and sugar substitute, or decorated with a sugar-free fruit filling or jelly.

DIETETIC BREAD AND ROLLS

Ingredients	Lb.	Oz.	Mixing procedure
Yeast (variable)	..	6	Dissolve the yeast and set aside
Water	1	..	
Sugar substitute	..	1	Dissolve the dry ingredients
Salt*	..	2	Stir well to blend
Dry skim milk	..	4	
Eggs (yolks)	..	8	
Water	3	..	
Bread flour	7	..	Add and stir in. Add the yeast solution and mix to a dough
Shortening	..	6	Add the shortening and develop

* An equal amount of salt substitute may replace the regular salt.

Procedure for Dough Handling and Make Up

1. Keep the dough temperature cool (approximately 78°F.).
2. The dough should be kept on the slightly young side. Allow the dough to rise once, punch, and relax for 15 min. and make up.
3. Scale and round the units. Relax (intermediate proof) about 15 min. Dough presses for rolls should be treated as for bread.
4. Shape the bread and rolls as for regular pan bread and soft rolls.
5. Give the made-up units slightly more than ¾ proof. The units should spring back to the touch with some firmness.
6. Bake the bread with mild steam in the oven. Bake at 415° to 420°F. If the crust color is formed before the bread is completely baked, reduce the oven temperature. Rolls are to be baked in the same manner. Rolls that are egg-washed may be baked without steam.

DIETETIC WHEAT BREAD AND ROLLS

Ingredients	Lb.	Oz.	Mixing procedure
Yeast (variable)	..	8	Dissolve the yeast and set aside
Water	2	..	
Sugar substitute	..	1¼	Blend all ingredients to dissolve. Sugar color
Salt (or salt	..	2	will determine the darkness of the crumb of the
substitute)			baked loaf
Shortening	..	8	
Dry skim milk	..	4	
Water	2	..	
Sugar color or			
caramel color			
(optional) (as			
desired)			
Eggs (part yolks)	..	8	
Whole wheat flour	3	8	Sift and blend the flours
Bread flour	3	4	Add and stir in. Add the yeast and develop the dough

Procedure for Dough Handling and Make Up

1. Keep the dough at a cool temperature (approximately 78°F.).
2. Allow the dough to rise well, punch, and relax for 15 min. Take to the bench for makeup into bread and rolls.
3. For pan bread, scale the units 1 oz. more than for white pan bread. For

rolls, scale the dough presses approximately 3 lb. This is a suggested average. The size of the roll will determine the weight.

4. The bread and rolls should be given no more than ¾ proof. Bake at 410°F. with steam in the oven. Reduce the oven temperature if a desirable crust color is obtained before the bread is baked.

For raisin bread and rolls add 3 lb. 8 oz. of pre-soaked raisins in the final stages of mixing and developing the dough.

For 100% whole wheat bread and rolls use 6 lb. 8 oz. of whole wheat flour and eliminate the bread flour. This dough should be given a shorter fermentation period and a shorter proofing period. The whole wheat flour is not as strong in gluten content as the dough made with bread flour and whole wheat flour.

Refer to pages 111 and 112 for additional information regarding wheat bread and rolls.

DIETETIC EGG BREAD AND ROLLS

Ingredients	Lb.	Oz.	Mixing procedure
Yeast (variable)	..	8	Dissolve the yeast and set aside
Water	1	..	
Sugar substitute	..	1½	Blend these ingredients well to dissolve and
Salt (or salt	..	2½	distribute evenly
substitute)			
Egg yolks	1	..	
Vegetable oil	..	12	
Water	3	..	
Bread flour	9	..	Sift and add the flour. Mix slightly and add the yeast. Develop to a smooth dough

Procedure for Handling and Make Up

1. The dough temperature out of the machine should be approximately 76° to 78°F. The cool temperature will help control fermentation.
2. Allow the dough to rise and take to bench or machine for makeup. The bench time for makeup will be longer than for regular pan bread and the dough should be taken on the young side.
3. Units should be given no more than ¾ proof. The egg yolk content will help to expand the dough for greater volume.
4. Egg-wash the made-up units twice, once at the time of makeup or shaping. The other wash application should be made before the units are placed in the oven. The units may be garnished with poppy seeds or sesame seeds before baking.

Refer to pages 78–79 and 105–106 for additional information.

DIETETIC COFFEE CAKES AND BUNS

Ingredients	Lb.	Oz.	Mixing procedure
Sugar substitute	..	2½	Blend all ingradients together to a smooth
Salt (or salt substitute)	..	2	consistency
Dry skim milk	..	8	
Butter or margarine	1	..	
Shortening	..	8	
Eggs (part yolks)	2	..	Add in 3 stages and blend in
Water	2	..	Add and stir in
Vanilla	..	1	
Orange and lemon flavor	..	1	
Yeast (variable)	..	12	Dissolve the yeast and set aside
Water	2	..	
Bread flour	7	..	Sift and add. Stir in well and add the yeast.
Cake flour	1	8	Develop to a smooth dough

Procedure for Handling and Make Up

1. Allow the dough to rise well and take to the workbench for makeup. The dough should be slightly on the young side. This will allow for conditioning and aging while the units are being made up.
2. The size of the pans will determine the weight of the dough units when scaled. Allowance must also be made for fillings and variety toppings used.

Refer to pages 138 through 154 and 174–175 for additional information and for the makeup of a variety of products from this dough.

Crumb Filling

Leftover and stale cake and yeast-raised products that have been made with DIETETIC FORMULAS may be used for the crumbs. The stale products are ground and then sifted. The amount of cinnamon and sugar substitute will depend on the products that were ground. For example, if dry cakes, such as chiffon, were ground and sifted, then little or no sweetening is necessary. If plain rolls or white bread were used, then additional sweetener and cinnamon would be necessary. The following is an average blend for crumb filling for coffee cakes and buns:

Ingredients	Lb.	Oz.	Mixing procedure
Ground and sifted cake crumbs	3	..	Blend the ingredients together well by sifting several times
Sugar substitute	..	2	
Cinnamon	..	1	
Almond flavor (optional)	..	½	

If the crumb filling is dry, melted butter or shortening may be added and rubbed in. If the crumb filling is too moist, add additional dry crumbs (be sure to add additional sweetener). To use the crumb filling as a smear, add sufficient water to soften. It is advisable to smear the surface of the rolled out dough units with melted butter or margarine for added taste and flavor. This will also serve to hold the smear and crumb filling in place. For added richness and flavor variety, toasted ground nuts (cashews, pecan pieces, walnuts, hazelnuts, etc.) may be added with the crumb filling. This crumb filling may be used for special cakes and buns (cinnamon sticks, Russian coffee cake) by further moistening with melted butter or shortening.

To replace the usual syrup wash used for sweet rolls, Danish, etc., the following preparation is suggested:

Ingredients	Lb.	Oz.	Mixing procedure
Water	2	..	Boil the water. Sift the corn starch and sugar
Sugar substitute	..	2½	substitute to blend
Corn starch (Dissolve in 8 oz. water)	..	1½	Dissolve in the 8 oz. of COOL water
Juice and rind of 1 orange and 1 lemon	..	..	

Add in a steady stream to the boiling water stirring rapidly with a wire whip. Bring to a boil again and remove from fire. Squeeze the juice of the fruits into the wash and stir in the orange and lemon pulp. This glaze should be used on the baked products while hot. The glaze may be re-heated for later use.

To replace confectionery sugar usually used to dust baked products such as crumb buns, streussel topped cakes, and similar products, use the following preparation:

Ingredients	Lb.	Oz.	Mixing procedure
Corn starch	1	..	Sift together 4 or 5 times to blend evenly. Dust
Sugar substitute	..	1½	the baked product lightly

DIETETIC STREUSSEL TOPPING

Ingredients	Lb.	Oz.	Mixing procedure
Sugar substitute	..	3	Blend together to a smooth consistency
Salt (or salt substitute)	..	½	
Shortening	3	..	
Cinnamon	..	1½	
Cake flour	3	..	Sift together. Add and rub together to small
Bread flour	1	8	lumps

Add melted shortening if too dry. Add additional flour if too moist.

Baking Coffee Cakes and Sweet (sugar substitute) Rolls and Buns.—Crust formation on these products is not as rapid as it would normally be on similar products made with regular sugar and other natural sweetening ingredients. Thus, a higher baking temperature is required. For larger units, the baking temperature is approximately 400°F. The temperature is lowered when the crust color is satisfactory, and the product allowed to bake thoroughly if it is not completely baked. For smaller units, the baking temperature should be slightly higher (410°–415°F.). The baked products will have a rather firm crust when first removed. This crust will soften as the product cools. Products made with dietetic fruit fillings and toppings, may develop a satisfactory crust color faster. These products made with fruit fillings and toppings must be baked through properly in order for the internal structure to support the heavier type of filling and topping.

For Cream Cheese Dough.—Refer to pages 293–294. Substitute 1 oz. of sugar substitute for the 10 oz. of confectionery sugar called for in the formulary. Bake at a slightly higher temperature.

For Frozen Dough.—Refer to pages 139, 178–179. Follow the same formula but replace the sugar with 3 oz. of sugar substitute. Bake the made-up units at a slightly higher temperature.

DIETETIC CORN MUFFINS

Ingredients	Lb.	Oz.	Mixing procedure
Sugar substitute	..	2	Blend all dry ingredients together. Add the
Salt (or salt substitute)	..	½	shortening and mix to a smooth consistency
Dry skim milk	..	4	
Cake flour	..	12	
Bread flour	..	12	
Shortening	1	..	
Eggs	1	4	Add the eggs in 3 stages and cream well after each addition
Water	..	8	Add and stir in
Vanilla (optional)	..	½	
Corn meal (yellow)	1	..	Add and stir in
Water	..	8	Add and mix to a smooth batter
Baking powder	..	3	

Note: The water or milk may be increased slightly if necessary. This will allow for the increased absorption capacities of coarse corn meal. It will also make easier machine dropping.

Deposit the batter in greased muffin tins. Fill slightly more than half full. Bake at 400°F. with a small amount of steam in the oven. Muffins baked without steam will tend to crack and peak slightly. Remove the muffins from the pans while they are still warm.

DIETETIC BASIC MUFFINS

Ingredients	Lb.	Oz.	Mixing procedure
Sugar substitute	..	2½	Sift the dry ingredients together to blend
Salt (or salt substitute)	..	½	Add the shortening and cream to a soft, smooth consistency
Dry skim milk		3	
Cake flour	1	4	
Shortening	1	2	
Eggs	1	..	Add in 3 stages and cream in
Water	1	..	Stir in lightly
Vanilla	..	1	
Cake flour	1	4	Sift together, add, and mix to a smooth batter
Baking powder	..	2	

For Muffin Varieties

Raisin muffins: Add 1 lb. of pre-soaked and drained raisins to the batter during the final stages of mixing.

Nut Muffins: Add 1 lb. of chopped and lightly toasted nuts to the batter in the final stages of mixing.

Blueberry muffins: Fold 1 pint of washed blueberries into the batter by hand or use slow speed when mixing in the mixing machine. Avoid crushing the blueberries.

Fill the muffin tins (greased) ½ full. Bake at 395°F. These muffins will tend to crack slightly at the surface. This is due to the higher baking temperature required for crust color formation. Remove the muffins from the tins while they are still warm. This will avoid condensation at the bottom of the pan.

DIETETIC WHEAT MUFFINS

Ingredients	Lb.	Oz.	Mixing procedure
Sugar substitute	..	2	Sift the dry ingredients together to blend
Salt (or salt	..	½	well
substitute)			Add the shortening and cream to a soft, smooth
Dry skim milk	..	4	consistency
Cake flour	1	..	
Shortening	1	..	
Cinnamon	..	½	
Sugar color (optional) (Darken the color of the batter)			
Eggs	1	..	Add in 3 stages and cream
Water	1	8	Add and stir in
Bread flour	..	8	Sift the flour and baking powder. Add and mix
Whole wheat flour	..	12	smooth
Baking powder	..	2¼	
Raisins (optional) (Pre-soak and drain)	1	..	Add in the final stages of mixing

Deposit the batter in greased muffin pans. Fill slightly more than one-half full. Bake at 400°F. These muffins may be baked with a small amount of steam in the oven. This will tend to keep the top crust of the muffins even and eliminate cracking. The tops of the muffins may be sprinkled with bran flakes before baking for added variety. Remove the muffins from the pans while they are still warm.

DIETETIC CHIFFON CAKE

Ingredients	Lb.	Oz.	Mixing procedure
Cake flour	4	..	Sift the cake flour and dry ingredients together.
Sugar substitute	..	6	Add the oil and eggs and mix to a smooth blend.
Salt (or salt substitute)	..	1	Do not whip or aerate this part
Vanilla	..	1	
Lemon and orange flavor	..	1	
Baking powder	..	2	
Vegetable oil	2	..	
Egg yolks	2	..	
Water	1	..	Add and mix to a smooth consistency
Egg whites	3	8	Whip to a soft peak. Fold in gently and evenly
Cream of tartar	..	¼	into the above

Note: It is important to have the egg whites whipped to a soft peak. Since sugar is not added, the egg whites will whip up quickly. Fold the whipped whites gently into the batter. Be sure there are no egg white particles or lumps that are not folded in.

The batter should be deposited quickly into prepared layer pans or sheet pans. Pans should be lined with parchment paper. If paper is not used, the bottom of the pans should be greased and dusted with bread flour to prevent sticking.

Layer cakes should be baked at approximately 375°F. Sheet cakes that are to be used for special rolls filled with dietetic jelly or jam, are baked at approximately 400°F. Cakes are considered baked when they spring back firmly to the touch.

Upon removal from the oven, draw the sides of the layer cakes gently away from the sides of the pan to be sure the sides of the cake are not stuck to the pan. Turn the layer cakes over on parchment paper-lined pans. This will maintain the volume of the cake, prevent sagging in the center, and make removal from the pans easier. Jelly roll cakes in sheet pans may be allowed to remain in the pans until cool before removing, filling, and rolling.

CHIFFON CAKE SHEETS THAT ARE FILLED WITH DIETETIC FILLING

These sheets require a firmer body to support the fillings. Make the following changes in the formula:

1. Reduce the water from 1 lb. to 9 oz.
2. Reduce the egg whites from 3 lb. 8 oz. to 2 lb. 8 ozs.
3. Increase the egg yolks from 2 lb. to 2 lb. 8 oz.

The same mixing procedure should be followed. The batter will be thicker.

A dietetic short dough bottom (pre-baked) is necessary to support the dietetic fruits that are distributed over the thicker chiffon sheet. This will prevent the fruit filling from sticking to the bottom of the pan and will make removal and handling of the baked cake easier. Variety dietetic fruit fillings (pineapple, cherry, blueberry) may be dropped and spaced over the chiffon filling in the sheet pan. Sheet pans with higher sides will allow for a higher cake. Formulas for dietetic fruit fillings will be provided in the section devoted to dietetic fruit pies. The following formula for dietetic short dough is a stock dough which may be used for cake bottoms and dietetic short dough cookies.

DIETETIC SHORT DOUGH

Ingredients	Lb.	Oz.	Mixing procedure
Sugar substitute	..	7½	Sift the dry ingredients together to blend well.
Salt (or salt substitute)	..	1½	Dissolve in the eggs and water. Blend well
Dry skim milk	..	3	
Eggs (part yolks)	1	..	
Vanilla	..	1	
Lemon flavor	..	1	
Water	..	12	
Shortening	6	..	Add and mix to break up into small fat particles
Cake flour	4	8	Sift together, add, and mix to dough. Do not
Bread flour	4	8	overmix

The dough may be somewhat soft and sticky. Refrigerate before using to firm up the fat content. This will make the dough easier to handle. It is advisable to roll this dough on a flour-dusted cloth or send through the sheeter for dough bottoms and cookies. Stipple or puncture the dough for sheet cake bottoms before baking. This will avoid the formation of blisters or pockets. Bake the short dough bottom at 410°F. Do not overbake since the bottoms are returned to the oven to bake the cake. The baked cake bottom may also be smeared with a light covering of dietetic jam or jelly before filling the pan with the chiffon cake batter.

DIETETIC CHOCOLATE CHIFFON CAKE

Ingredients	Lb.	Oz.	Mixing procedure
Sugar substitute	..	6½	Sift all dry ingredients
Salt (or salt substitute)	..	1	Add the eggs and oil and mix to a smooth batter. Do not whip or aerate in excess
Cake flour	3	12	
Cocoa	..	12	
Baking powder	..	1½	
Baking soda	..	¾	
Vegetable oil	2	..	
Egg yolks	2	..	
Vanilla	..	1	
Orange flavor	..	½	
Water	1	4	Add and mix smooth
Egg whites	3	4	Whip the egg whites to a soft peak. Fold into
Cream of tartar	..	½	the above gently

Deposit the batter into prepared pans as quickly as possible. Layer cakes and thicker sheet cakes should be baked at 370°F. Thin sheets for rolls should be baked at 400°F. The cakes will have a firmness to the crust when baked. The crust will soften after the cakes have been turned over on parchment and allowed to cool. The layer cakes and sheet cakes may be finished with the use of a variety of dietetic fillings and toppings. The thinner sheet cakes may be used for special dietetic ice cream rolls. A dietetic custard may be used for the layer cakes.

DIETETIC CHEESE CAKE

Ingredients	Lb.	Oz.	Mixing procedure
Sugar substitute	..	4½	Blend together to a smooth consistency
Salt (or salt substitute)	..	1	
Skim milk powder	..	8	
Rind of 2 fresh lemons	..	..	
Shortening	1	6	
Bakers cheese	5	..	Blend together and then blend into the above
Bread flour	..	8	
Cornstarch	..	2	
Eggs (part yolks)	1	8	Add to the above in 3 stages and blend in well
Vanilla	..	1	
Sour cream	1	..	Add in 2 stages and blend in
Water (variable)	..	12	Add in 2 stages and blend in
Egg whites	2	..	Whip to a wet peak and fold into the above
Cream of tartar	..	¼	gently

Procedure for Handling and Baking

1. *For the large sheet pan type of medium cheese cake*
   Use a pre-baked bottom made from the dietetic short dough. The bottom may be lined with dietetic pineapple or other filling. Fill the pan of a deep (3½ in.) size almost to the top. The cheese cake may be garnished with crumbs and nuts. Bake at 390°F. The cake is considered baked if the center feels jelled and springs back lightly to the touch. Allow the cheese cake to settle and cool before removing from the pan. It is advisable to free the sides of the cake from the pan upon removal from the oven.

2. *For Small Cheese Cakes Baked in Layer Pans*
   The bottoms of the layer pans may be lined with a pre-baked dietetic short dough bottom. The bottoms of the pans may also be greased well and then lined with crumbs made from dietetic cakes. In either method the bottoms may have dietetic fruit filling deposited at the bottom before filling. Fill the layer pans almost to the top and place on a sheet pan containing a thin layer of water. Bake the cheese layers at 400°F. until the cakes have risen and have taken on a light brown crust color around the edge. The center of the cheese layers will spring back gently to the

touch when baked. It is advisable to trim the sides of the cakes to free them from the sides of the layer pan. This will allow the cakes to settle evenly.

Remove the cakes from the pans while still warm. The tops of the cakes may be garnished with dietetic pineapple filling.

DIETETIC PIZZA DOUGH

Ingredients	Lb.	Oz.	Mixing procedure
Yeast (variable)	..	8	Dissolve the yeast and set aside
Water	2	..	
Salt (or salt substitute)	..	4	Dissolve the salt in the water
Water	6	..	
Dough extender and conditioner (This is optional)	..	..	
High gluten bread flour	13	8	Add the flour and stir in lightly. Add the yeast and mix to a dough
Gluten flour (optional)	..	4	
Shortening	..	4	Add and develop to a smooth dough

Notes: A high gluten flour is important to pizza dough. Since the dough must be stretched or rolled very thin without tearing, it must have strength and extensibility. A dough conditioner and extender is helpful. The use of the small percentage of gluten flour also increases the strength of the gluten.

Allow the dough to rise well and then punch. Rest the dough about 30 min. and take to the bench or scaler-rounder. If the dough is to be used immediately, allow the rounded units to relax approximately 15 min. (preliminary proofing) and roll out or stretch by hand. The units may be sent through the sheeter before stretching. Units of dough (scaled according to the desired size) that are to be placed in the retarder or freezer, should be oiled lightly to avoid crustation.

DIETETIC PIE CRUST (COOKIE TYPE)

Ingredients	Lb.	Oz.	Mixing procedure
Pastry flour	5	..	Sift all dry ingredients to blend well. Add the
Sugar substitute	..	¼	shortening and mix until smooth
Salt (or salt substitute)	..	1½	
Dry skim milk	..	1	
Shortening	3	8	
Cold water	2	..	Add the water and eggs and mix to a smooth
Eggs	..	8	dough consistency. Do not overmix

This dough will be soft. Chill the dough before using

DIETETIC PIE CRUST

Ingredients	Lb.	Oz.	Mixing procedure
Pastry flour	5	..	Blend the dry ingredients together by sifting
Salt (or salt substitute)	..	1½	well
			Add the shortening and rub together or mix in
Sugar substitute	..	½	slow speed until small lumps are formed
Dry skim milk	..	2	
Shortening	3	12	
Water (cold)	2	..	Add the water and fold over lightly until the flour is absorbed. DO NOT OVERMIX

This dough will feel soft, sticky, and be lumpy. Refrigerate the dough for several hours to condition the dough and firm up the shortening in the dough. This will make handling the pie crust dough easier.

DIETETIC PIE SHELL DOUGH

(This dough is used for pre-baked pie shells and tart shells.)

Ingredients	Lb.	Oz.	Mixing procedure
Sugar substitute	..	4½	Sift the dry ingredients to blend well. Add the
Salt (or salt substitute)	..	3	shortening and mix to a smooth consistency
Dry skim milk		6	
Shortening	5		
Eggs	1	2	Add the eggs in 2 stages and blend in well
Water	1	12	Add the water and flavor and stir in
Vanilla	..	1	
Pastry flour	8	4	Sift and add the flour. Mix lightly to a smooth dough

Chill the dough before using.

DIETETIC PIE DOUGH FOR FRIED PIES

Pie crust for fried pies are leaner in fat content. They contain approximately 40% fat based on the weight of the flour. A leaner pie crust will contain the filling better and absorb less fat during frying.

Ingredients	Lb.	Oz.	Mixing procedure
Pastry flour	5	..	Sift the flour. Add the shortening and rub to-
Shortening	2	..	gether, or mix in slow speed to form small lumps
Salt (or salt substitute)	..	1½	Dissolve the salt in the water
Water (cold)	2	4	Add and mix lightly until the flour is absorbed

Chill the dough before using.

DIETETIC FRUIT FILLINGS

When replacing sugar with a sugar substitute in the cooking of dietetic fruit fillings, careful judgment will have to be made. When using canned fruits (number 10 cans), the type of fruit, degree of acidity, packing (water-based only), fresh fruits, and the use of fruit supplements (lemon powder or the juice of fresh lemons), flavorings, and related ingredients must be considered. While dietetic fruit fillings may be purchased in a ready to use form, it is advisable to produce your fillings for freshness and quality for the special fruit-filled products to be made. It may be necessary to make adjustments periodically because of the possible changes in the canned fruits used. This will require changes in the amount of sugar substitute used as well as in the amount of thickening agents used.

DIETETIC PINEAPPLE FILLING
1 Number 10 can of Crushed Pineapple

Ingredients	Lb.	Oz.	Cooking procedure
Drained juice and water	1	8	Drain the juice from the fruit. Add water if necessary to make up the required weight. Bring to a boil
Corn starch	..	4½	Dissolve the starch and sugar substitute in the
Sugar substitute	..	3	water. Add to the boiling juice in a slow, steady
Water or juice	..	8	stream stirring constantly. Boil until thick and
Juice of 1 lemon			clear

Remove from the fire, add the drained pineapple pulp and stir well. A few drops of yellow color may be added to enhance the color of the fruit filling. USE WHEN COOL.

DIETETIC APPLE FILLING
1 Number 10 Can of Apples

Ingredients	Lb.	Oz.	Mixing procedure
Water	1	8	Bring to a boil
Sugar substitute	..	2½	Dissolve the starch and sugar substitute in the
Cornstarch	..	3	water. Add to the boiling water in a steady
Water	..	8	stream stirring constantly. Bring to a clear boil
Cinnamon	..	¼	again. Remove from the fire and add the
Juice of 1 lemon (optional)			contents of the can of apples
			Add the cinnamon and the juice and stir in gently

Note: It is advisable to taste the apples and determine the amount of water pack in the apples. This will determine the amount of sugar substitute to be used and the amount of thickening to use. Allow the filling to cool before using.

DIETETIC CHERRY FILLING

1 Number 10 can of Cherries Packed in Water (Sour pitted)

Ingredients	Lb.	Oz.	Mixing or cooking procedure
Drained juice and water	2	..	Bring the juice and water to a boil
Sugar substitute (variable)	..	4	Dissolve the starch and sugar substitute in the water. Add to the above in a steady stream and
Corn starch	..	5	bring to a clear boil again
Water or juice	..	10	

Add the drained cherries and stir in gently. A few drops of red color and/or cherry flavor may be added to enhance the color and flavor. Use the filling when cool.

DIETETIC BLUEBERRY FILLING

1 Number 10 Can of Blueberries Packed In Water

Ingredients	Lb.	Oz.	Mixing or cooking procedure
Drained juice and water	2	..	Bring the juice and water to a boil
Sugar substitute	..	3½	Dissolve the sugar substitute and starch in the
Corn starch	..	4½	water. Add to the above in a steady stream and
Water or juice	..	10	bring to a clear boil again

Add the drained blueberries and a pinch of cinnamon and stir in gently. Use the filling when cool.

When using fresh blueberries replace the canned fruit with 3 pints of fresh blueberries. Be sure to wash the berries and remove stems that may remain. Cook one pint of the berries with the water (2 lb.) to provide the color and base for the filling. The berries will mash and become pulpy during cooking and the natural color of the fruit will provide the color to the filling. Stir in the fresh fruits carefully into the cooked filling base to avoid crushing the fruit or berries.

For further information on making and baking pies, refer to pages 249–261 in the text.

DIETETIC FRENCH COOKIES

These cookies may be bagged out into various shapes and sizes.

Ingredients	Lb.	Oz.	Mixing procedure
Cake flour	1	..	Sift the dry ingredients together to blend
Bread flour	2	..	well
Sugar substitute	..	4	Add the butter and shortening and cream well
Salt (or salt substitute)	..	1	until light
			Scrape sides of kettle often
Butter or margarine	3	..	
Shortening	3		
Egg whites	2	..	Add the egg whites and flavor in 4 stages and
Vanilla	..	1	cream in well after each addition
Almond flavor	..	1	
Bread flour	4	..	Sift the flour and baking powder. Add and fold
Baking powder	..	¼	in lightly. Do not overmix

Note: Folding in or mixing in the flour gently is important to avoid toughening of the mix through gluten development.

For chocolate cookies, add 8 oz. of cocoa and reduce the bread flour by 6 oz. Add ¼ oz. of baking soda instead of the baking powder. Refer to page 455 for a variety of designs which may be bagged out. Bake these cookies at 410°F. The cookies may be garnished with nuts or dietetic jam or jelly before baking. The cookies may be dipped and sandwiched with dietetic jelly and then dipped in toasted ground nuts after baking.

CHAPTER 34

Baking with Sour Cream

Sour cream has long been a basic ingredient in many of the bakery products and desserts prepared by pastry chefs, bakers, and homemakers. Because of its richness and slight acidity, sour cream imparts special taste, flavor, tang, smoother texture, and improved keeping qualities to the product. The use of sour cream extends from the yeast-raised coffee cakes to a complete variety of cakes, pastries, and cookies. While the cost of the bakery product made with sour cream may be increased, the resulting product provides a new variety that will attract consumers of quality awareness. The quality baker and pastry chef are aware of the uses and values of baking with sour cream. Bakers, in general, would do well to expand their product line by producing quality products that are made with the use of sour cream.

Sour cream is cream that has been "turned or soured" because of the fermenting action of bacteria. The production of sour cream is a carefully controlled process in that the degree of sourness or pH is dependant upon the bacteria count. Extreme variables in production will create variables in acidity or degree of sourness. It is important for the baker to know this since extreme acidity will have a decided impact upon the finished product. A good quality sour cream that is fresh and kept refrigerated will usually result in standard products. Aged sour cream that has a high bacteria count and excessive acidity will have a negative effect on finished product. Fresh sour cream may be replaced with simulated sour cream that is made from a vegetable oil base. Some are cultured and are subject to variables in bacteria count and acidity. Others are not cultured and have a more controlled or stable pH. Selection of a good quality sour dressing is important if it is to replace fresh sour cream.

FACTORS TO BE CONSIDERED WHEN BAKING WITH SOUR CREAM

In Yeast-Raised Doughs

Because of its low pH and its tendency to increase the acidity of the dough, sour cream is usually incorporated into the sponge dough. This will tend to speed up the rate of fermentation of the sponge. The distribution of the sour cream within the final dough is also more effective when incorporated with the sponge. Even if used in a straight dough method, the rate of fermentation will increase due to the softening effect of the lower pH upon the dough. Many bakers may increase the percentage of sugar slightly to compensate for the slight tang and acidity. Note is also made of the fact that sour cream

478

increases the richness of the dough by virtue of its butter fat content. Bakers may reduce the fat content of the dough as a result. However, the use of sour cream for enrichment and improved quality of the product should not be diluted by reducing the amount of other enriching ingredients.

In Chemically-Leavened Products (Cakes, Cookies, Pastries, etc.)

Because of the increased acidity in sour cream or simulated sour cream, many formulas will require the use of small percentages of baking soda to neutralize the acidity to a degree and to provide leavening as well. Cakes that also contain natural syrups such as honey or molasses, will have the usual amount of baking soda increased. The formulas provided are balanced to meet specific requirements for neutralization and leavening. Adjustment may have to be made by the baker or pastry chef in relation to the type and quality of the sour cream or simulated sour cream used.

SOUR CREAM COFFEE CAKE DOUGH

Ingredients	Lb.	Oz.	Mixing procedure
Sponge Dough			
Yeast (Variable)	..	8	Dissolve the yeast in the water
Water	2	..	
Sour cream	2	..	Blend the sugar and sour cream.
Sugar	..	4	Mix into the yeast solution. Add the flour and mix to a smooth dough. Allow the sponge to rise well and then settle slightly before mixing the final dough (approximately 2 hr)
Bread flour	3	8	
Mixing the Final Dough			
Sugar	1	8	Add to the fermented sponge and mix well to break up the sponge
Salt	..	1½	
Dry skim milk	..	6	
Eggs (part yolks)	2	..	
Flavors (variable)	..	1	
Bread flour (variable)	3	8	Add the flour and mix until the flour is absorbed and a dough is formed. Do not develop the dough
Melted butter	1	..	Add to the above and mix in slow speed until the melted fat is blended in. Develop the dough
Melted margarine or shortening	1	..	

Procedure for Handling the Dough

1. Allow the dough to rise until soft and gassy (about 45 min.). DO NOT PUNCH THE DOUGH. THIS DOUGH IS NOW FULLY CONDITIONED.
2. Refer to pages 169 to 182 for methods and products to be made from this dough.
3. Units should be given no more than ¾ proof before baking. Because of the added richness in the dough and the increase in pH, extending the proof may have a weakening effect on the structure and the products may tend to settle during baking. This will result in a loss of volume.
4. Loaf type cakes (babka or grandmother's loaf) should be baked at 350°F. Smaller units may be baked at higher temperatures. Filled units, such as stongen filled with cheese, prune filling, etc., will also require a lower baking temperature, depending on the size of the unit. When properly baked, larger units such as loaf cakes (babka) will spring back quite firmly to the touch.

SOUR CREAM FROZEN DOUGH

Ingredients	Lb.	Oz.	Mixing procedure
Bun dough or Coffee Cake dough that has been fermented	5	..	Blend well to break up the dough and mix to a smooth consistency
Sugar	1	8	
Salt	..	1	
Butter or margarine	1	12	
Baker's cheese	1	..	
Eggs (part yolks)	1	..	Add and blend in well
Sour cream	2 (1 qt.)	..	Add and stir in well
Vanilla	..	1	
Yeast (variable)	..	8	Dissolve the yeast and set aside
Water	..	12	
Bread flour (variable)	4	..	Sift the flour and baking powder. Add and stir slightly. Add the yeast and mix to a smooth dough. The dough should be of medium soft consistency
Baking powder	..	1½	

Procedure to Follow

1. Form the dough into a smooth, rectangular shape and place on a flour-dusted pan. It is advisable to refrigerate the dough for several hours. This will firm up the dough for easier handling during make up. It will also allow the dough to be conditioned by the slow action of the yeast.

2. A variety of units similar to Danish pastry may be made from this dough. Refer to pages 156 to 165 for Danish pastry varieties. Allow the made up units to relax until they have about one-half proof. They will feel slightly gassy to the touch.

3. Wash the units with melted butter or margarine and sprinkle with Streusel or other special topping. Bake at 385° to 390°F.

SOUR CREAM TOPPING OR FILLING

The following formula for a topping or filling has many uses. It may be used as a filling for the better quality babka loaves or coffee cakes. It may also be used as a filler for cake-type loaf cakes. As a topping, it is excellent for loaf cakes and yeast-raised coffee cake varieties.

Ingredients	Lb.	Oz.	Mixing procedure
Brown sugar	1	8	Blend all ingredients together lightly. Then rub together as for a Streusel topping. If the topping is too moist, add additional cake crumbs. If too dry, add some melted butter and margarine
Granulated sugar	1	8	
Sour cream	2	..	
Salt	..	¼	
Toasted, chopped nuts (walnuts, cashews, pecans)	1	..	
Chocolate chips or bits	1	..	
Cocoa	..	1	
Cinnamon	..	1	
Cake crumbs (variable)	1	8	

1. The topping or filling should have the crumbly appearance as for a regular crumb topping. It is important that the cocoa and cinnamon be well distributed for maximum distribution and flavor. The cake crumbs should be soft and slightly moist. A dry type of crumb will tend to absorb moisture and result in a drying effect. When used as a filling, it is advisable to smear the dough with a thin coating of melted butter or margarine before applying the filling. When used as a topping on yeast-raised products, it is advisable to brush the top of the dough with egg wash or melted butter before applying the topping. KEEP THE TOPPING REFRIGERATED WHEN NOT IN USE.

SOUR CREAM CAKE

Ingredients	Lb.	Oz.	Mixing procedure
Sugar	4	..	Cream together until soft and light
Salt	..	1	
Emulsified shortening	2	..	
Butter or margarine	2	..	
Eggs (part yolks)	4	..	Add in 4 stages and cream in well after each addition
Baking soda	..	¾	Add and stir in lightly
Vanilla	..	1	
Sour cream	4	..	
Cake flour	6	..	Sift together, add, and mix smooth. Be sure to scrape sides of kettle to eliminate lumps
Baking powder	..	1½	

The following cake varieties may be made from this basic mix.

1. Plain loaf cakes or sheets can be made as for plain pound cake.
2. For marble loaf cake, stripe the batter through with melted sweet chocolate or mix some of the batter with chocolate and stripe this through for a marbling effect.
3. For raisin loaf cake, dust the raisins lightly with bread flour. Remove the excess flour and fold the raisins into the batter.
4. For nut cake loaves, fold in toasted nuts, either large or chopped pieces may be used.
5. Apple-Marble squares may be made by striping the batter with chocolate and spreading into a sheet pan about ½ full. Sprinkle apple sections over the batter and then sprinkle with a sugar and nut topping before baking.
6. Blueberry and other fruit square varieties may be made by dropping the fruit in equal spaces over the top of the batter in the sheet pan. DO NOT SMEAR THE FRUIT.

Bake the loaf cakes at 350°F. Sheet cakes may be baked at 370°F.

SOUR CREAM DOUGHNUTS

Ingredients	Lb.	Oz.	Mixing procedure
Sugar	1	6	Blend to a smooth consistency
Salt	..	1	
Dry skim milk	..	6	
Shortening	..	8	
Eggs (part yolks)	1	..	Add in 2 stages and blend well
Sour cream	2 (1 qt.)	..	Add and stir in
Water	3	..	Add the water and flavors and stir in
Vanilla	..	1	
Orange flavor	..	½	
Lemon flavor	..	½	
Cake flour	4	..	Sift the flour and baking powder together. Add and mix to a smooth dough
Bread flour	4	..	
Baking powder	..	5	

Procedure for Making the Doughnuts

1. The dough should be medium soft. For machine dropping, add 8 ounces of eggs. This will soften the batter and also enrich the doughnut. It will also provide for a more cake-like doughnut.
2. The dough should be rolled out about ¼ inch thick and then cut into ring doughnuts. For bowtie, Longjohn, and twist doughnuts, scale the dough into desired presses and then divide on the dough divider.
3. Allow the made up doughnuts to relax for about 15 min. and then fry at a temperature of 380° to 385°F.
4. Refer to pages 208 through 218 for further information regarding the preparation of frying fat, shaping, and frying doughnut varieties.

SOUR CREAM APPLE CAKE

Ingredients	Lb.	Oz.	Mixing procedure
Granulated sugar	1	8	Blend all ingredients together to a smooth consistency
Brown sugar	1	8	
Salt	..	½	
Dry skim milk	..	2	
Emulsified shortening	1	4	
Chopped apples	1	8	
Cinnamon	..	½	
Cake flour	1	..	
Eggs (part yolks)	1	4	
Sour cream	2 (1 qt.)	..	Add the eggs in 3 stages and blend well after each addition.
Water	..	12	
Baking soda	..	½	Dissolve the baking soda in the water. Add and stir in gently. Add the flavor and sour cream and blend in. Sift the flour and baking powder together. Add and mix to smooth batter.
Vanilla	..	1	
Cake flour	2	4	
Baking powder	..	1½	

Procedure for Handling

1. Canned apples should be drained and then chopped. Apple sauce may be used instead of apples. If the apple sauce is watery, reduce the water content in the formula to 8 oz. instead of 12 oz. Deposit the batter in layer cake pans that are greased and lined with paper. The pans may also be greased and dusted with flour. Fill the pans slightly higher than half full.

2. The batter may be deposited in small size loaf pans and baked as loaf cakes. The batter may also be deposited in sheet pans and baked as sheet cakes. The cakes are baked at 365° to 375°F.

SOUR CREAM SPICE CAKE

This cake may be made with added cake crumbs or without the cake crumbs. There is the advantage of using stale cakes which have been ground, sifted and incorporated into the cake. The formula change for cakes made without crumbs is listed at the bottom of the formula.

Ingredients	Lb.	Oz.	Mixing procedure
Sugar	1	..	Cream together until soft and smooth
Salt	..	½	
Shortening	1	4	
Dry skim milk	..	4	
Eggs	1	..	Add in 3 stages and cream well after each addition
Molasses	1	14	Dissolve the baking soda in the water. Add to the above with the molasses and spices
Water	1	..	
Baking soda	..	1	
Cinnamon	..	½	Stir in slightly
Allspice	..	¼	
Cake flour	3	..	Sift the flour and baking powder. Add and mix smooth
Baking powder	..	1	
Sour cream	3	..	Add the sour cream and cake crumbs and mix smooth
Cake crumbs (sifted)	3	..	

Procedure for handling

1. If cake crumbs are not used, increase the cake flour from 3 lbs. to 5 lbs.
2. Deposit the batter in layer cake pans, loaf cake pans, or sheet pans.
3. Bake at 370° to 375°F. When cool, ice with various colored fondant icing or fudge type icings.

SOUR CREAM DOUGH-MINIATURES

These specialties are similar to those made with a cream cheese dough and those made from a rich Danish pastry dough.

Ingredients	Lb.	Oz.	Mixing procedure
Confectionery sugar	..	8	Sift all dry ingredients together. Add the butter and margarine and blend in lightly.
Salt	..	1	
Cake flour	3	..	
Bread flour	3	..	Add the sour cream and mix to a smooth dough
Butter	3	..	
Margarine	3	..	
Sour cream	4	..	

Procedure for Handling and Make Up

1. Place the dough on a flour bench and form into a rectangular shape. Allow the dough to relax 10 min and roll out as for Danish pastry. Give the dough one roll and fold into three layers. Refrigerate the dough overnight or for a few hours at least. This will chill the fat in the dough and also condition or relax the gluten in the dough. These factors will enable the dough to be rolled and made up easily.

2. Refer to pages 293 and 294 for procedures to follow in the make up and shaping of small horns (rugelach), open pocket miniatures, miniature snecks, and other varieties.

3. Allow the made up units to relax for at least 15 min. before baking. Bake the units at 380°F. The units should be baked until the crust is golden in color and has attained a mild crispness. The units may be brushed with melted butter and garnished with sugar and nuts before baking. The fillings used may vary.

SOUR CREAM CHOCOLATE CAKE

Ingredients	Lb.	Oz.	Mixing procedure
Sugar	3	4	Cream to a soft, smooth consistency
Salt	..	3/4	
Dry skim milk	..	4	
Shortening	1	8	
Fudge base or	..	12	
(Cocoa-8 oz. and shortening-2 oz.)			
Eggs (part yolks)	2	..	Add in 4 stages and cream well after each addition
Sour cream	2	..	Add and blend in lightly
Water	1	..	Dissolve the baking soda in the water. Add with the flavor and stir into the above
Baking soda	..	1¼	
Vanilla	..	1	
Cake flour	3	8	Sift together, add, and mix to a smooth batter
Baking Powder	..	1	

Procedure for Make Up

1. Deposit the batter into layer cake pans, sheet pans, loaf pans, or muffin pans. It is advisable to line the pans with parchment paper liners or cup cake liners.

2. Large units should be baked at 365° to 370°F. Smaller units should be baked at 385°F. Ice with sour cream fudge icing.

SOUR CREAM FUDGE ICING

Ingredients	Lb.	Oz.	Mixing procedure
Confectionery Sugar	8	..	Soften the fudge base. Combine all the ingredients and blend smooth. If too stiff or firm, add simple syrup. If too soft add additional confectionery sugar
Water (hot)	1	..	
Fudge base	2	12	
Sour Cream	1	..	
Vanilla	..	1	
Salt	..	¼	

SOUR CREAM SPRITZ COOKIES

Ingredients	Lb.	Oz.	Mixing procedure
Almond paste or macaroon paste	1	..	Mix together until smooth
Confectionery sugar	2	4	Scrape down to remove lumps
Salt	..	½	Cream well until soft and light
Egg yolks	..	8	
Butter or margarine	2	..	
Shortening	2	8	
Sour cream	2	..	Add and stir in slightly
Cake flour	1	8	Sift the flours. Add and fold in lightly. Do not overmix
Bread flour	3	..	

A variety of flavors and colors may be added to this batter to increase the variety and appearance. For example, a few drops of red color with added cherry or strawberry flavor (about 1 oz.) may be mixed into the batter.

A complete variety of spritz (bagged out) cookies may be made. The cookies should be bagged on parchment paper-lined pans or pans that have been greased and dusted with flour. The cookies may be garnished with fruits, nuts, jams or jellies, before baking. Other cookies may be baked and then dipped after baking in chocolate or fondant type icings. Still others may be sandwiched together after baking and striped with chocolate.

Bake these cookies at 400°F. The cookies will show a slight brown crust color around the edge when baked.

SOUR CREAM CHOCOLATE COOKIES

Ingredients	Lb.	Oz.	Mixing procedure
Almond paste (kernel paste or macaroon paste may be used)	1	..	Mix together to a smooth paste
Egg whites	..	4	
Sugar	2	8	Add to the above and cream well. Scrape sides of kettle to eliminate lumps
Salt	..	1	
Butter or margarine	1	..	
Shortening	1	..	
Fudge base	..	12	
Egg whites	..	12	Add in 3 stages and cream well after each addition
Sour cream	2 (1 qt.)	..	Add and stir in lightly
Vanilla	..	1	
Baking soda	..	1/4	
Cake flour	2	..	Sift the flours, add, and fold in lightly until the batter is smooth. DO NOT OVERMIX
Bread flour	2	8	

Procedure for Make Up

1. Bag out the cookies on parchment paper-lined pans. A star, French, or plain tube may be used. There will be slight spreading but the lines and shapes of the cookies will be maintained. Various shapes of spritz may be made as with other types of bagged cookies.
2. Bake the cookies at 390°F. When cool, the cookies may be finished by dipping, sandwiching and striping, or the cookies may be garnished with nuts and other toppings before baking.

SOUR CREAM SHORTBREAD COOKIES

Ingredients	Lb.	Oz.	Mixing procedure
Sugar	1	8	Blend together to a smooth consistency
Salt	..	1	
Dry skim milk	..	2	
Butter or margarine	2	..	
Shortening	2	..	
Eggs (part yolks)	1	..	Add in 2 stages and blend in well after each addition
Sour cream	2 (1 qt.)	..	Add the sour cream and stir
Water	..	10	Dissolve the soda in the water and stir in with the vanilla
Baking soda	..	¼	
Vanilla	..	1	
Cake flour	2	4	Sift the flours. Add and fold in gently. DO NOT OVERMIX
Bread flour	4	..	

Procedure for Make Up

1. It is advisable to chill the dough before using. This will make handling and rolling out of the dough easier.
2. Roll the dough out on a flour dusted cloth. This will avoid stickiness and the use of lesser amounts of dusting flour. It will also reduce the possibility of toughness due to overworking the dough.
3. Roll the dough out about ¼ inch in thickness. The top of the dough may be brushed lightly with egg wash and sprinkled with sugar, nuts, and a variety of other toppings. Plain cookies may be dipped in chocolate or fudge after baking. A variety of shapes and designs may be cut out. Bake at 390°F. until golden brown. Do not overbake. Cookies continue to bake and dry after removal from the oven.

CHEESE CAKES MADE WITH SOUR CREAM

Cream cheese, baker's cheese, cottage cheese, are all products of milk and cream. The process of manufacture will vary as will the enrichment values of each when used to make cheese cakes. Sour cream will act as an enrichment supplement to cheese cakes by virtue of its high butter fat content as well as the tangy taste and flavor important to cheese cakes. The formulas that follow will cover most types of cheese cakes. Each will contain varying amounts of sour cream, as well as cheese variables and egg content variations. Some cheese cakes will require pre-baked short dough bottoms and sides to support the cheese cake. The formula for the sour cream shortbread cookie may be used for these bottoms. Other types of cheese cakes will require that pans be lined with cake crumbs to serve as the holding factor or base for the cheese cake. This is particularly so in the case of the cheese cakes of quite light texture which are baked in layer cake pans.

Cheese cakes are actually similar to cheese type puddings or souffles. The method of baking will vary with each specific type. For example, cheese cakes whose pans are lined with cake crumbs are usually baked in double pans. The supporting sheet pan contains a small amount of water so that it has a steaming effect rather than a direct dry, baking effect. This will prevent the cake crumbs from scorching or burning because of direct contact with the oven shelf. Cheese cakes that are supported by baked cookie bottoms are usually baked directly on the hearth or shelf of the oven. The cookie crust serves as base with the moistness of the cheese cake batter preventing excessive drying or burning of the bottom crust. In addition, many bottoms are lined with a fruit filling before the cheese filling is placed into the pan. This tends to keep the crust tender and prevents excessive drying.

SOUR CREAM CHEESE CAKE—FIRM TYPE

Ingredients	Lb.	Oz.	Mixing procedure
Sugar	2	4	Blend well to a smooth consistency
Salt	..	1	
Dry skim milk	..	4	
Shortening	1	6	
Baker's cheese	5		Blend the cheese, flour and starch together. Add to the above and blend smooth
Bread flour	..	6	
Corn starch	..	4	
Eggs (part yolks)	1	8	Add in 3 stages and blend in
Sour cream	1	..	Add in 2 stages and blend in
Water (variable)*	2	..	Add the water in 3 stages and blend to a smooth consistency
Vanilla	..	1	

* The ability of the cheese to absorb and retain water or milk will vary with the type and quality of the cheese. The cheese batter should have the consistency of a smooth, thick gravy.

A large pan with a 3 to 4-in. side is required. The pan should have a pre-baked short dough bottom. The bottom may be covered with a thin base of fruit filling before pouring the cheese batter into the pan. Bake at 365°F. The cake may be considered baked when there is a mild springiness when the cake is touched gently. The cake will rise during baking and will settle again to its original volume after it is baked and has cooled. It is advisable to free the sides of the cake from the side of the pan as soon as the cake is removed from the oven. This will allow the sides of the cake to settle evenly.

FRENCH TYPE SOUR CREAM CHEESE CAKE

Ingredients	Lb.	Oz.	Mixing procedure
Sugar	1	8	Blend well to a smooth paste
Salt	..	1	
Dry skim milk	..	8	
Shortening	1	..	
Baker's cheese	5	..	Mix the cheese and flour together
Bread flour	..	12	Add to the above and blend smooth
Eggs (part yolks)	2	..	Add in 3 stages and blend in
Sour cream	1	8	Add to the above in 2 stages and blend smooth
Vanilla	..	1	
Grated rind of 2 lemons			
Water (variable)	1	..	Add in 2 stages and blend in
Egg whites	3	..	Whip to wet peak. Fold gently into the above
Sugar	1	6	

Procedure for Handling

1. Prepare a large deep pan with a pre-baked cookie dough bottom. The bottom of the pan may be lined with a thin covering of fruit.
2. Deposit the cheese batter into the pan.
3. Bake at 350°F. The cheese cake will rise approximately 1½ to 2 in. above the top of the sides of the pan if the pan is filled almost to the top with filling. It is advisable to move the cake gently and cut the sides of the cake along the sides of the pan. This will prevent the cake from sticking and the sides of the cake will rise evenly. This cake should take about 1 hr. and 30 min. to bake. The center will spring back to the touch when completely baked.
4. Remove carefully from the oven and allow the sides to settle evenly.

MEDIUM TYPE SOUR CREAM CHEESE CAKE

Ingredients	Lb.	Oz.	Mixing procedure
Sugar	1	12	Blend these ingredients to a smooth consistency
Salt	..	1	
Dry skim milk	..	4	
Shortening	1	..	
Bakers cheese	5	..	Blend the cheese and flour together and blend into the above
Bread flour	..	10	
Eggs (part yolks)	1	8	Add in 3 stages and blend in
Water (variable)	1	..	Add in 3 stages and blend in
Vanilla	..	1	
Grated lemon rind (2 lemons)			
Sour cream	2 (1 qt.)	..	Add and blend in
Egg whites	2	..	Whip to a wet peak and fold into the above
Sugar	1	..	

Procedure for Handling

1. If the cake is to be baked as one large cake, prepare a large pan with a pre-baked cookie bottom. The sides of the pan should be greased before depositing the cheese batter. The baked bottom may be covered with a fruit filling before depositing the batter. If the cakes are to be in layer cake form, the layer pans are to be well greased and then lined with cake crumbs. The bottom of the layer pan should have a heavier layer of crumbs to support the cheese cake. Chocolate cake crumbs may be used for contrast in color as well as taste and flavor.

2. Bake the large cake at 365°F. Small cakes are baked on double pans with water in the large supporting pan. Bake at 385°F.

SOUR CREAM-CREAM CHEESE CAKE

Ingredients	Lb.	Oz.	Mixing procedure
Cream cheese	7	8	Mix all ingredients in slow speed to a smooth consistency
Sugar	1	12	
Salt	..	1	
Bread flour	..	1	
Vanilla	..	1	
Rind of 2 lemons (optional)			
Egg yolks (Half whole eggs may be used)	1	8	Add in 3 stages and blend well after each addition
Sour cream	2 (1 qt.)		Add in 2 stages and blend in until smooth. Mix in slow speed

Procedure for Handling

1. These cheese cakes are usually baked in layer cake pans. The size of the pans may vary. Pre-baked bottoms of short dough are necessary. After the bottoms are baked, line the sides of the layer pans with a thin cover of short dough. Grease the sides of the pans, as the raw short dough may stick to the sides. The bottoms may be covered with a film of fruit filling before depositing the batter. Fill the pans almost to the very top.

2. Place the layers on a sheet pan and bake at 425°F. until the cheese cake has risen and a light brown crust color has formed around the edge of the cheese cake. At this point, the oven temperature is reduced to about 350°F. and the cake is slow baked until done. The cake will have a slight springy feel when touched in the center when it is completely baked. Avoid overbaking and cracking of the top crust of the cheese cake.

SOUR CREAM CHEESE PIE

Ingredients	Lb.	Oz.	Mixing procedure
Sugar	3	4	Blend together to a smooth consistency
Salt	..	1½	
Dry skim milk	..	3	
Shortening	1	12	
Bakers cheese	9	..	Blend the cheese and flour together. Add to the above and blend in
Bread flour	..	14	
Eggs	2	..	Add in 3 stages and blend in
Sour cream	2	..	Add and blend in. Use slow mixing speed
Vanilla	..	1	Add and mix smooth. The amount of water will depend upon the quality of the cheese. The batter should have a thick consistency so that it may be picked up without excessive running
Water (variable)	..	8	

Procedure for Handling

1. The pie pans should have prepared pie shell dough in them. A fruit filling may be deposited at the bottom of the pie shell before filling the pie. The pies should be filled almost to the very top. If the shell has a crimped edge, as for tart shells, and is higher than the pie pan edge, the filling should not extend beyond the crimped edge. It may break through during baking and spill.

2. Bake the pies at 425°F. The pies will rise slightly in the pan and will have a light brown crust color around the edge. The center of the pie will feel slightly firm to the touch when baked. After baking, the tops of the pies or the pie centers may be garnished with fruit fillings of various types.

SOUR CREAM CHEESE FILLING

This enriched cheese filling may be used for the filling of Danish pastry cheese varieties, cheese buns, cheese miniatures, cheese-filled puff pastry products, and cheese strudel.

Ingredients	Lb.	Oz.	Mixing procedure
Bakers cheese	5	..	Blend the cheese and flour together
Bread flour	..	10	
Sugar	1	12	Add to the above and mix in slow speed to blend together
Salt	..	1	
Dry skim milk	..	4	
Shortening	1	..	
Sour cream	1	8	
Eggs (part yolks)	1	..	Add in 2 stages and blend in
Vanilla	..	1	Add and blend in until smooth
Water (variable)	..	8	

The amount of water will depend upon the quality of the cheese and its ability to absorb liquid. It is advisable to refrigerate the freshly mixed filling. This will make handling easier.

CHAPTER 35

Passover Recipes

CAKES AND COOKIES THAT MEET DIETARY REQUIREMENTS

Many bakers have often found themselves in special situations or jobs which demanded observance of all dietary requirements in the preparation of supervised cakes and pastries for Passover. The following Passover recipes were prepared by the author in conjunction with the members of the Baking Department of the school. The recipes are basic and many varieties can be made from each. It will be up to the baker to be creative and imaginative in his work. Suggestions will be made with the recipes to help the baker.

Ingredients for Passover Products

Matzoh Flour and Matzoh Meal.—These are basic replacements for the regular flour varieties for normal baking. Both matzoh flour and matzoh meal are derived from the baked matzoh or unleavened bread. The meal is refined to several degrees of fineness. The flour variety is, of course, even more highly refined. These flours or meals are very dry, containing only traces of moisture as compared with the normal amount of moisture present in regular flour. Thus, they tend to absorb and retain more moisture. In addition, the absorption becomes even greater with time after the flour or meal has been added to the mix or batter. This is important to the baker in that prolonged periods in which cake batters or other batters containing matzoh flour or meal are allowed to stand will tend to increase binding and have a toughening effect on the product.

Matzoh flour is recommended for use in most of the recipes in that it does result in a softer texture and finer grain than does matzoh meal. There is also a greater control of consistency of the cake mix or cookie batters than there is with the use of the meal variety.

Potato Starch.—Potato starch is used in conjunction with matzoh flour or meal in many recipes. It is also used extensively in the preparation of fruit fillings and custards. The starch is a highly refined starch derived from the potato. Its particles are very fine and soft. While it has greater absorption qualities than regular cornstarch, in certain instances the baker must be familiar with its special characteristics. For example, potato starch, when used as the thickening agent for cooked fillings, must be stirred well and cooked longer. A short cooking period that does not allow for complete hydration

496

of the starch and maximum absorption of the liquid by the starch particles, will cause retrogradation. This means that the liquid absorbed will be held in a gel form for a short period before the starch releases the liquid and the gel effect is gone. Potato starch must be cooked well.

Because of its greater absorption capacity, the potato starch, when used for a thickening purpose in fillings, is used in lesser amounts than cornstarch. Thus, a baker using 3 oz. of cornstarch to thicken the filling base for a number ten can of apples, may use only 1½ to 2 oz. of potato starch. Follow the usual recipes for your approved fruit and custard fillings, but use from 50 to 75 per cent potato starch to replace the weight of the cornstarch usually used for these fillings.

Eggs.—Eggs are very basic and important to the recipes for Passover cakes and cookies. They supply the leavening in most part, the moisture for the cakes, the protein (albumen) for structure, and taste and flavor. In many cases, yolks are recommended for use in conjunction with whole eggs. The baker is advised to refer to Chapter 3 in the text to refresh his memory regarding the use and function of eggs in baking.

Chemical Leavening Agents.—These are used in small amounts, or not at all, in most Passover recipes. In fact, baking powder, until recently, was forbidden for Passover use. Only recently, has an approved baking powder been manufactured for this purpose. The baker would do well to check the baking powder for the approved stamp for Passover use. Baking soda is not restricted. However, it has limited use in most Passover recipes.

Canned Fruits.—Unless they have the approved stamp, canned fruits are restricted from Passover use. In many cases the approved canned fruits are packed in a light or medium syrup. The baker must make allowances for fruit fillings by adjusting the sugar content in the recipes. Fresh fruits are not restricted, but their use will require adjustment in the method of preparing the fruit fillings. The baker is advised to refer to Chapter 22 in the text for fruit filling recipes and adjustments to make when using frozen, fresh, and other fruit types.

Note: Glazed fruits, especially prepared to meet the dietary requirements for Passover use, make excellent supplements for cakes and cookies. You will find suggested uses in many of the recipes that follow. The syrup content of these fruits adds to the taste, flavor, and keeping qualities of the product.

Nuts.—Shelled nuts are permitted. The most popular varieties are hazelnut, walnut, pecan, butternut, and filbert. It is suggested that these nuts, when ground for special use, be ground with a coarse grinder to prevent loss of the natural fats and oils in the nuts. Toasting the nuts lightly before grinding will bring out the flavor. These nuts may be purchased in a shelled condition, in fancy halves or broken pieces. Sliced almonds or hazelnuts are also used extensively.

Baking Passover Cakes and Cookies

The baker must be aware of the composition of the ingredients used so that proper baking will result in products that meet the highest standards. Passover cakes and cookies are high in sugar and egg content. In addition to the sugar added as such to the recipe, there are sweeteners present in the various pastes (almond, macaroon, kernel) used. Frozen egg yolks usually contain approximately 10 per cent of their weight in sugar added to maintain the stability of the yolks. The sugar also acts as a preservative. In view of this fact, Passover cakes should be baked at a lower or cooler oven temperature. This will allow for a slower formation of crust color and avoid a dark or burned bottom crust. Thus the cake will be sufficiently baked before the crust is overly browned.

A slower bake will allow the structure of the cake to set properly before it is removed from the oven. The principal cause of cakes settling or falling back after baking is due to the weakness or incompletely baked condition of the structure of the cake. The baker should be aware of the fact that larger cakes take longer to bake. This may require the baker to place large, high cakes on double pans to bake to avoid a strong or burned bottom.

Passover cookies also require a comparatively cooler temperature than regular cookies, due to the higher percentage of sugar. In many cases, cookies such as macaroons and others made with almond paste, go through a drying period of several hours. This causes a crust formation on the cookie. The crust then cracks during baking and reduces spread during baking. The lower baking temperature promotes a desirable crust color and allows for maximum spread on the top surface of the cookie.

PASSOVER CAKES AND COOKIES

Passover Sponge Cake (for loaves, Sheets, Jelly Roll, etc.)

Ingredients	Lb.	Oz.	Mixing procedure
Sugar	8	..	Whip the eggs, sugar and salt until light and
Salt	..	1½	fluffy. (The eggs will whip faster if first
Eggs (part yolks may be used)	11	..	warmed in a double boiler)
Lemon flavor. (The rind of 4 to 5 lemons may be used in place of the flavor)	..	2	Fold the flavor gently into the whipped eggs
Potato starch	3	..	Sift the starch and matzoh flour together to
Matzoh flour	2	..	blend well. Fold in gently into the above in an overhand motion. Be sure it is folded in evenly. Do not overmix

Procedures to Follow

1. Deposit the sponge batter into paper-lined pans.
2. Bake as soon as the pans are filled with the mix.
3. Loaf pans should be filled slightly more than half full and baked 340° to 350°F.
4. Sheet cakes and jelly rolls should be baked at 380° to 385°F.

Note: For CHOCOLATE SPONGE SHEETS AND ROLLS, add 6 oz. of cocoa and reduce the potato starch and matzoh meal by 3 oz. each. Be sure to sift the cocoa in well before adding to the eggs.

It may be advisable to turn large sponge cakes or loaves over on a sugar-dusted pan immediately after baking. This will prevent very tender cakes from settling in the center.

Passover Sponge Cake #2

Ingredients	Lb.	Oz.	Mixing procedure
Sugar	6	..	Whip well until light and thick (marks of the
Salt	..	1	wire whip are seen)
Eggs	9		
Cake meal	3	..	Blend together and fold in gently
Potato starch	3	..	
Egg whites	3	..	Whip to a wet peak and fold gently into the
Sugar	1		above
Rind of 3 or 4 lemons			

This formula is especially valuable for the production of sponge cake loaves and larger cakes. It is also useful for sheets and jelly rolls.

Procedures to Follow

1. If the eggs are chilled or partially frozen, defrost and warm in a warm water bath. The warmed eggs will whip faster and provide greater volume.
2. Large cakes may also be made with a cinnamon sugar filling. Fill the pans half full. Sprinkle the batter with cinnamon sugar. Then fill the pans almost to the top.
3. Bake the cakes on double pans to prevent excessive bottom heat from scorching the bottom. Bake large units at 355°F. Smaller units and sheets are baked at higher temperatures.

Passover Honey Cake

Ingredients	Lb.	Oz.	Mixing procedure
Honey (approx. 3 qt.)	9	..	Blend together in the machine to remove lumps of honey and dissolve the sugar and salt
Sugar	3	..	
Eggs	5	..	
Salt	..	1½	
Water	2	..	Dissolve the baking soda in the water and mix into the above
Baking soda		4	
Vanilla (optional)		2	
Matzoh flour	4	..	Sift together and add to the above and mix in until smooth. Use flat beater
Potato starch	3	8	
Oil (vegetable)	2	..	Add the oil in a steady stream and mix in well
Diced fruits and orange peel	2	..	Add to the batter in the final stages of mixing and mix in well
Nuts	1		

Procedures to Follow

1. Deposit the batter into paper-lined loaf pans or larger pans. Large pans and thicker cakes will require a lower baking temperature. The pans should be filled slightly less than ½ full.
2. The tops of the cakes may be sprinkled with sliced almonds.
3. Bake large cakes at 285° to 300°F. Smaller loaf cakes may be baked at 325°F. Be sure the cakes spring back gently to the touch before removing from the oven.

Passover Honey Cake #2

Ingredients	Lb.	Oz.	Mixing procedure
Honey	6 (2 qts.)	..	Warm the sugar and honey to a liquid state
Sugar	2	8	
Eggs	8	..	Whip with the honey until light and fluffy
Cake meal	2	8	Blend the dry ingredients together and fold gently into the above
Potato starch	2	..	
Cocoa (for darker color)		3	
Cinnamon	..	½	
Oil	1	..	Fold in gently into the above
Egg whites	2	..	Whip to a wet peak and fold
Sugar	..	8	in gently into the above

Procedures to Follow

1. Deposit the batter into paper-lined loaf pans, large, deep pans, or deep layer cake pans. Garnish the top with slices of almonds.

2. Bake on double pans at 345°F. Larger units should be baked at lower temperatures. The center of the cakes should spring back gently to the touch when baked.

3. Baked cakes may be turned over on dusted parchment paper or cloths when removed from the oven. This will prevent any tendency to settle in the center.

Passover Nut Cake

Ingredients	Lb.	Oz.	Mixing procedure
Almond paste	1	..	Cream all the ingredients until soft and light.
Sugar	3	..	Scrape the sides of the kettle to remove
Salt	..	1	lumps
Shortening	3	..	
Vanilla	..	1	
Almond flavor	..	½	
Eggs	4	..	Add the eggs in 4 stages and cream well after each addition
Cake crumbs	2	..	Sift together and fold into the above
Ground nuts (filberts)	2		
Potato starch	1		
Egg whites	2	..	Whip to a soft or wet peak. Fold gently into
Sugar	1	..	the above

Procedures to Follow

1. Deposit the mix into a large, deep pan that has a pre-baked bottom. Line the bottom with raspberry or apricot jam before depositing. Be sure the pan is high enough to keep the mix from running over.

2. If desired two sheet pans may be used for two separate cakes. The mix may be deposited into the two sheet pans lined with parchment paper.

3. Bake the deep pan at 325°F. The two single sheet pans are to be baked at 340° to 350°F.

4. Single sheets baked on paper may be sandwiched together with jam after they have cooled. The top may be smeared with jam and sprinkled with nuts.

Passover Coconut Cake

Ingredients	Lb.	Oz.	Mixing procedure
Sugar	4	..	Cream together until soft and light. The or-
Salt	..	1	ange peel and the cherries will provide an
Shortening	4	..	orange color effect
Vanilla	..	1	
Candied orange peel	1	..	
Candied cherries	..	8	
Eggs	4	..	Add in 4 stages and cream in well after each addition
Macaroon coconut (unsweetened)	4	8	Blend the coconut and flour-potato starch to- gether. Add to the above and blend in well
Matzoh flour	..	8	
Potato starch	..	8	

Procedures to Follow

1. Deposit the mix into a high pan which contains a pre-baked short dough bottom, or, if desired, two regular sheet pans can be used, each containing a baked bottom. The baked bottoms may be smeared with orange or apricot jam before depositing the mix.
2. The deep single pan should be baked at 325°F.
3. Thinner sheet pans may be baked at 350°F.

Note: For a lighter coconut cake, whip 1 lb. 8 oz. of egg whites with 8 oz. of sugar to a wet peak. Fold the whipped whites into the cake batter gently. This will increase the volume of the cake and make it necessary to use two pans.

Passover Almond Sponge Cake

Ingredients	Lb.	Oz.	Mixing procedure
Sugar	3	..	Place these ingredients into the machine and
Almond or macaroon paste	3	..	work into a smooth paste with a flat beater. Add the eggs gradually. Remove and place in
Salt	..	½	a separate bowl
Eggs	1	8	
Eggs	1	8	Whip until light. Gradually add the almond
Egg yolks	3		mix in 4 stages and whip up well until thick
Matzoh flour	1	6	Blend together and fold into the above
Potato starch	1	8	

Passover Nut Sponge Cake

Ingredients	Lb.	Oz.	Mixing procedure
Sugar	3	..	Blend to smooth paste with a flat beater and
Salt	..	1	remove from the machine to separate bowl
Almond or macaroon paste	3		
Eggs	1	8	
Eggs	1	8	Whip the eggs until thick. Add the almond
Egg yolks	3		mix in 4 stages and whip in well
Ground nuts (filberts)	2	..	Blend together and fold into the above lightly. Do not overmix
Matzoh flour	1		
Potato starch	1	4	
Egg whites	2	..	Whip to a soft peak and fold into the above
Sugar	...	12	

Procedures to Follow

1. Deposit these cakes into paper lined loaf pans or large, deep pans.
2. Bake at 325°F.

Passover Eclair and Shell Mix

Note: This mix can be used for cream puff and eclair shells. It is also quite popular for making the round, French cruller type rings which are used for special Passover rolls. These rings or rolls may be sprinkled with chopped onions and oil as for an onion roll specialty. They may also be dusted with confectionery sugar or iced with a fondant-type icing.

Ingredients	Lb.	Oz.	Mixing procedure
Vegetable oil	1	..	Place into a bowl and bring to a rolling boil
Water	2		
Salt	..	1	
Matzoh flour	1	4	Add in a steady stream to the above stirring constantly. Mix to smooth paste
Eggs	2	4	Allow the cooked paste to cool slightly. Add the eggs to the paste in 4 or 5 stages and mix well after each addition. The mix should have the same consistency as the regular eclair mix

Procedures to Follow

1. Bag out the mix as usual on paper-lined pans.
2. Bake at 380–385°F until the shells are crisp and dry. Be careful not to remove from the oven too soon.
3. The eclair or cream puff shells should be filled with the custard preparation that has been thickened with potato starch. Be sure to cook the custard well to prevent the starch from separating or retrograd-

ing. Or, if desired, whipped cream may be used to fill the eclairs and cream puffs.

Passover Short Dough (For Cake Bottoms or Cookies)

Ingredients	Lb.	Oz.	Mixing procedure
Sugar	6	..	Mix these ingredients to a smooth paste with
Salt	..	1½	the flat beater
Almond or macaroon paste	1	..	
Eggs	..	8	
Shortening	6	..	Add to the above and mix to a smooth paste.
Honey (½ quart)	1	8	Scrape the sides of the kettle
Vanilla	..	2	
Eggs	3	8	Add the eggs in 4 stages and blend in well after each addition
Potato flour	6	..	Sift the flour and starch together with the
Matzoh flour	6	..	baking soda. Add to the above and mix in
Baking soda	..	¼	lightly to a dough. Avoid overmixing

Procedures to Follow

1. The dough should be chilled before using. This will make it easier to handle and to roll.
2. This dough can be used for cookies as well as for the bottoms of cakes. It lends itself well to the making of fruit cakes in large sheet pans.

Note: To make a Streusel type of topping from this dough, add extra matzoh flour to a portion of the dough after it is freshly mixed and before it is chilled. Rub together to get the lumpy or mealy effect. Use this as the regular topping for fruit cakes and other uses where streusel topping is used.

Passover Brownies

Ingredients	Lb.	Oz.	Mixing procedure
Sugar	4	..	Whip these ingredients until light and thick
Salt	..	1	in consistency as for sponge cake
Eggs (part yolks)	2	..	
Honey		4	
Cocoa (dark, natural)	..	12	Sift the cocoa, flour, and starch together. Add to the above and mix smooth. Add the
Matzoh flour	1	..	nuts and fold in
Potato starch	1	..	
Nuts (pecans or walnuts)	1	8	
Melted shortening	2		Add the melted shortening in a steady stream
Vanilla	..	1	and blend in until smooth. Add the vanilla and blend in smooth

Procedures to Follow

1. The mix may be deposited into two parchment paper-lined pans and baked as thin, candy- or cookie-type brownies; or the entire mix can be placed into one deeper sheet pan and baked as a regular brownie that is higher. This brownie will be chewy and maintain its softness. The top of the brownie may be sprinkled with nuts before baking and the baked brownie can be sliced immediately after baking. This is especially important if the brownies are thin and served as cookies.
2. The thicker or single sheet brownie may be iced with a chocolate fudge icing after it is cool and then sliced.
3. Bake the brownies at 345 to 350°F. for the thicker sheet. The thin sheets may be baked at 365°F.

Passover Almond Macaroons

Ingredients	Lb.	Oz.	Mixing procedure
Sugar	1	4	Place these ingredients into the mixing machine and mix until smooth
Confectionery sugar	1	4	
Salt	..	½	
Almond or macaroon paste	4	..	Scrape the bowl to remove any lumps
Vanilla	..	1	
Egg whites	..	8	
Egg whites		12	Add about 8 oz. of the egg whites and mix smooth. Add the additional whites if the mix is too stiff

Procedures to Follow

1. The mix should be medium stiff and should be bagged out on paper-lined pans.
2. Garnish the tops of the cookies with nuts, cherries, mixed fruits, etc.
3. Allow the cookies to dry well at shop temperature before baking. The crust formed will cause the tops of the cookies to crack during baking. This improves the appearance of the cookies.
4. For chocolate macaroons, add approximately 4 oz. of dark cocoa to the mix. You may have to add a little more egg whites to the mix to allow for the tightening effect of the cocoa on the mix.
5. You may use the FRENCH MACAROON recipe on page 432 for additional varieties and for an explanation of how to handle this type of cookie.

PASSOVER SPECIALTIES (SOME USING ALMOND MACAROON MIX)

Lattice Top Sponge Almond Sheet Cake

Invert a baked sponge or sponge almond sheet cake about 1 to 1½ in. thick. On the smooth bottom, now the top of the cake, bag out a lattice-top design so that the squares of almond macaroon mix are about 1½ in. square. Be sure to bag out a border around the edge of the cake about ¼ in. in from the edge. Allow the top to dry well. Before baking, smear the sides of the cake with jam or jelly and apply sliced almonds or ground nuts to the jam so that it sticks to the sides of cake. Fill each of the squares on top of the cake with raspberry or apricot jam. You may use several varieties of jam or fruit filling for variety and multi-color. Bake the sheet at 375°F. until golden brown. Wash the top of the cake with hot syrup-wash or apricot coating that has been heated with syrup. You may sprinkle the top with green colored coconut for added color.

Mirrors or Passover Jelly Tarts

Roll out the Passover short dough and cut out round discs of dough. Bake these cookie discs very lightly (just a little crust color). Turn the cookies over and then use the almond macaroon mix to bag a circle around the edge of the cookie. Allow the mix to dry and then bake at 375°F. until light brown. Wash the macaroon edge with hot syrup as soon as removed from the oven. Fill the centers with jam or jelly after the cookies have cooled.

Passover Bar Cookies (Also known as Railroad Cookie Strips)

Roll out the Passover short dough about ¼ in. thick. Cut strips of dough about 1½ to 2 in. wide and almost the length or size of the width of a sheet pan. Place the strips on a parchment paper-lined pan and space each strip of dough about ½ in. apart. Bake these strips lightly. Allow the strips to cool and then bag out the Almond macaroon mix along the sides of the strip. Use a French tube or star tube. You may also bag a strip down the center. Allow the macaroon mix to dry. Bake the strips again at 375°F. until golden brown. Wash the macaroon top with hot syrup or apricot coating wash. When cool fill the spaces between the rows of macaroon topping with jam or jelly. Stripe the tops of the cookies with fine strips of warm fondant. Allow the icing to dry before slicing into cookie strips.

Almond Horns

Refer to the recipe on page 430 and 431 in the text.

Nut Bars

Refer to the recipe and procedure in the text pages 431–432.
Be sure to use the Passover Short Dough for the bottom for the nut bar pan.

Almond Tarts

Use the Passover Short Dough to line the tart pans. Refer to the recipe on page 429, but substitute 2 oz. of matzoh flour for the 2 oz. of cake flour.

Chocolate Almond Macaroons

Refer to the recipe and procedure on pages 435 and 436 in the text.

Macaroon Cup Cakes

Refer to the recipe and procedure on page 452 in the text.

Passover Cocoanut Macaroons

Ingredients	Lb.	Oz.	Mixing procedure
Macaroon cocoanut	8	..	Place all the ingredients into a bowl and stir together until blended. Place on a baker's cooking stove and heat until warm and the mix is medium stiff (it will hold shape when bagged out). It may be necessary to add more egg whites
Sugar	8	..	
Salt	..	1	
Vanilla	..	1	
Honey (¾ qt.)	2	4	
Melted shortening	1	8	
Egg whites	4		
	(approx.)		

Procedures to Follow

1. For CHOCOLATE MACAROONS (cocoanut) add 6 oz. of dark, natural cocoa to the recipe and increase the egg whites by 6 to 8 oz.
2. BE SURE TO STIR THE MIX CONSTANTLY WHILE WARMING. This will avoid scorching the bowl and the formation of burned pieces throughout the mix.
3. Bag out the warm mix with a plain or star tube on paper-lined pans. Space the macaroons about 1 in. apart to allow for mild spread during baking.
4. If the macaroons are to be garnished with cherries or other topping, do this as soon as the macaroons are bagged out.
5. Allow the macaroons to dry until a crust is formed on the outside.
6. Bake at 375° to 380°F. until golden brown. DO NOT OVER BAKE.
7. The bottoms of the macaroons may be dipped in sweet chocolate after they have cooled.

(The recipe for COCOANUT MACAROONS on pages 434 and 435 may also be used for variety.)

Passover Mandel Bread (Bar Cookie)

Ingredients	Lb.	Oz.	Mixing procedure
Almond or macaroon paste	1	..	Blend these ingredients together to a smooth paste
Sugar	2	..	
Salt	..	½	
Eggs	..	8	
Shortening	1	..	Add the shortening to the above and cream in well
Eggs	..	12	Add the eggs in 2 stages and cream in well
Vanilla	..	1	
Walnuts or pecans filberts	1	..	Add and stir in slightly
Diced mixed fruits	1		
Matzoh flour	1	4	Sift together, add to the above and mix smooth
Potato starch	..	6	

Procedures to Follow

1. The mix may be scaled into one pound pieces and shaped into an oval shape. These should be placed on paper-lined pans and spaced about 3 in. apart to allow for some spread.
2. The tops of the bars may be egg washed lightly and sprinkled with nuts and sugar before baking.
3. Melted chocolate may be striped through the mix and the bars then made up with a marbled effect. Cocoa or chocolate may be mixed into half the mix and then mixed or rolled up for a striped effect.
4. The mix may be scaled into larger pieces and rolled into long, thin strips and baked as for bar cookies. The strips are then sliced into bars as for cookies. Bake the bar cookies as soon as made up at 375°F.

Passover Almond Roll Cookies (Schnitten)

Ingredients	Lb.	Oz.	Mixing procedure
Almond or macaroon paste	12	..	Add the egg whites to the sugar and almond paste in 2 or 3 stages and blend smooth. The mix is quite thick now
Sugar	6	..	
Salt	..	½	
Egg whites (approx.)	2	..	
Shortening	2	..	Add to the above and blend in. Do not cream the shortening
Lemon juice	..	4	
Almond flavor	..	1	Add and mix smooth
Matzoh flour	3	..	
Egg whites (approx.)	1	..	Add enough egg whites to form a firm, plastic mix (similar to an icebox cookie)
Chopped glazed cherries (optional) may be added	2	..	

Procedures to Follow

1. Divide the mix into the desired pieces and color each piece as you wish.
2. The colored pieces may be combined as for a bull's eye ice box cookie. Roll out one piece of the mix about ¼ in. thick. Brush them lightly with egg whites. Roll out another colored piece into a round roll about 1 in. in diameter and place it in the center of the rolled out part of the mix. Cover the roll now and roll out to about a thickness of about 1 in.
3. Scale pieces about 1 lb 8 oz. and place on a paper-lined pan. Wash the top with egg yolk and allow to dry well. Wash again with yolks before baking.
4. Bake at 350° F. until brown and the top cracks slightly
5. The strips may be brushed with hot apricot coating after baking and sprinkled with nuts. Slice into cookie sections about ½ to 1 in. wide.

Passover Nut Slices, Nut Topping

Ingredients	Lb.	Oz.	Mixing procedure
Butter	1	..	Place these ingredients into the kettle and
Sugar	1		place on a medium fire to boil. Stir constantly to prevent scorching. Bring to a rolling boil and remove from the fire
Honey	1		
Sliced filberts	2	8	

Procedures to Follow

1. Prepare a BAKED Passover short dough bottom that is about ¼ in. thick. Try to have the bottom of even thickness and baked a light, golden brown.
2. Be sure the bottom is cool before placing the nut topping on it. It is advisable to grease the sides of the pan to keep the topping from sticking to the pan.
3. Be sure to spread the BOILED NUT TOPPING evenly over the baked bottom. Allow the topping to cool and then dry.
4. Cut the cookies into rectangular strips about 1 in. wide and 2 in. long.
5. These cookies may be dipped at either end in melted sweet chocolate and allowed to dry.
6. They may be cut into small squares or triangular shapes. These cookies may be striped with chocolate and served or sold as is. They may also be dipped in melted chocolate or fudge and then dipped into toasted, ground filberts.

Passover Hazel Nut Cookies

Ingredients	Lb.	Oz.	Mixing procedure
Egg whites	2	. .	Whip the whites to a froth. Add the sugar in
Sugar	4	4	a slow, steady stream and whip to a wet peak
Toasted, ground nuts	2	. .	Blend the nuts, starch, and flour together and
Potato starch	. .	4	fold lightly into the beaten whites and sugar
Matzoh flour	. .	1	

Procedures to Follow

1. Bag out the mix on paper-lined pans with a bag and plain tube. The cookies should be small and equal in size.
2. Bake the cookies at 370°F. until light brown around the edges. DO NOT OVER BAKE. These cookies continue to bake or dry after they are removed from the oven.
3. These cookies are generally sandwiched together with apricot or other jam or jelly. The cookies may also be sandwiched with a chocolate or fudge filling.
4. The cookies may then be finished by striping with sweet chocolate, or dipping part of the cookie into melted, sweet chocolate and allowed to dry.
5. These cookies may be bagged out in finger or long shape and also sandwiched together after baking. These cookies may be striped with chocolate or dipped at either or both ends.

Marzipan for Fruits

Marzipan fruits and other vegetable shapes are specialty items for Passover. They are colorful and add sales value to the display of other cookies and cakes.

Ingredients	Lb.	Oz.	Mixing procedure
Almond paste	2	. .	Place all ingredients in the machine and mix
Clover (light) honey	. .	4	at slow speed to a smooth consistency. If too
Confectionery sugar	1	12	soft, add more confectionery sugar or potato
Potato starch	. .	1	starch. If too firm, add a small amount of
Egg whites (variable)	. .	4	egg whites
Rum flavor	. .	½	
Lemon rind (optional) of 1 lemon			

Procedures to Follow

1. Keep the marzipan covered at all times when not in use. This will avoid crustation. A damp cloth is advisable.

2. Refer to pages 396 to 398 for procedures to follow in forming or shaping a variety of fruits and other shapes.

Salami Type Pastry

Ingredients	Lb.	Oz.		Mixing procedure
Sugar	6	. .		Boil the sugar and honey over a low flame to
Honey	6			the soft crack stage (approx. 275°F.)
(2 qts.)				
Almond paste or	12	. .		Add sufficient jam to soften the almond
macaroon paste				paste. Add enough red color to provide for a
Red color	. .	1	. .	reddish appearance. Add the boiled honey
Apricot jam	. .			and mix in slow speed. Add the ground nuts
(variable)				and filbert pieces and mix in slow speed to a
Ground nuts	8			firm consistency. As the honey syrup cools,
(toasted)				the salami batter will become firmer. It
Filbert pieces	2			may be necessary to add additional raspberry
Raspberry or				or apricot jam to soften.
apricot jam				

Procedures to Follow

1. Place the batter on a clean and lightly oiled section of the work bench or marble top table.
2. Shape the pieces of salami batter into rolls about 2½ inches in diameter. Roll the pieces in light wax paper.
3. Units or pieces may be sliced at an angle to provide the appearance of salami.

CHAPTER 36

"Natural" Type Breads and Bakery Food Products

The growth of "natural" and health-type foods has had a decided impact upon the baking industry. Variety breads and other bakery food products have increased in sales volume within the past decade. The impact has been equally great upon the retail baker and larger bakery plants. Variety of breads has expanded with a concentration upon the use of whole and natural grains and other natural ingredients. The combination of grains, syrups, seeds, raisins, nuts, fruits, and vitamin supplements have made possible the varieties presently marketed. The consumer has been exposed to a concentration of publicity of the values of the more nutritious contents of the "natural" bread varieties. This has led to an increase in sales of variety breads and has enabled the bakers to expand their bakery foods product line.

With this growth of variety breads, has been a parallel expansion of prepared mixes and flour blends that make production of these products a more efficient and stream-lined process. Such flour blends as "Granola" and similar multi-cereal flour blends are available to the retail baker as well as the larger bread producers. Special varieties have been developed by individual producers and marketed with great success. Many retail bakers have joined in the production of these health-type breads and have revised formulas for these breads to meet consumer demands. The trend of natural bread specialties has expanded into other bakery foods. These include soft rolls, special rolls and breads, sweet rolls and buns, doughnuts, and quickbreads.

This section provides a wide sampling of formulas that will encompass most of the popular and growing areas of "natural" and "health-type" breads and bakery products. The formulas have been tested and proven to be of productive value. The baker may make revisions of the formulas by increasing the amount of whole grains, variety of grains and seeds, addition of natural syrups, fruits, nuts, and vitamin supplements. Variety of breads and related bakery foods are also dependant upon the size, shape, and packaging of the products. There are fundamental and basic considerations in the production of yeast-raised breads and other yeast-raised bakery products that are of the health-type variety. Such factors as dough conditioning, dough mixing, machining and moulding, proofing, and baking as they apply to the production of these specialty products, must be given careful consideration. A brief evaluation and explanation of these factors follow.

YEAST-RAISED "NATURAL" BREADS AND RELATED BAKERY FOODS

Natural grains, whole grains, protein-enriched flours, natural syrups, fruits, nuts, and seeds, are basic ingredients for the "natural" bread varieties. While they rarely exceed 25 per cent of the total weight of the flour used, they tend to increase the protein content and nutritional values of bakery products. They also contribute greatly to the shelf life of the baked products. For example, use of honey, molasses, and other natural syrups will increase the moisture retention (hygroscopic) capacities of the product. Small percentages of soy flour contribute to reduction in staling while increasing protein values. Whole grains and bran increase absorption and retention of moisture, thus adding to shelf life.

Most formulas for natural breads call for a small increase in shortening or fat content for more shortness and tenderness of crumb. Use of skim milk, brewers yeast, butter, and other natural ingredients add food value and contribute to longer shelf life.

Yeast-raised products will require a stronger (high gluten) flour to carry the enrichment ingredients. While flours such as soy, rye, whole grain, bran, and others may contain high percentages of protein, they are lacking in gluten-forming proteins. In order to obtain a well-piled loaf of fine grain and texture, it is necessary to use a high gluten patent or common (clear) flour to support the enrichment grains and other ingredients and maintain a vigorous fermentation. The baker is cautioned about the use of excessive percentages of enrichment flours and grains. For example, excessive use of soy flour to increase protein will also have a slackening effect on the dough, and will impart the special taste and flavor of the soy flour to the baked product. This is not readily acceptable to the consumer. Sound and careful production judgment will be necessary by the baker in making changes in formulation.

Proper dough mixing and dough temperatures are important. Because of the use of coarse grains, whole grains, bran, and similar enrichment products, doughs should be mixed in slower speeds. This is especially important in the final development stage. The coarse grains may have a tearing effect on the developing gluten in the dough. A high mixing speed may also cause over-development with a complete slackening of the dough and a product that is lacking in volume and having poor quality texture and grain.

Amount of adjustment in mixing speeds and times is affected by the type and percentage of coarse grain as well as the consistency of the dough. Stiffer or firmer doughs must have a slower mixing speed. Doughs that have presoaked and softened grains will be softer and may be mixed at a slightly increased speed. Doughs that are made with conditioned sours, such as sour rye bread, or doughs made with dry sour cultures have a lower pH (higher degree of acidity) are usually mixed at medium speed to avoid overmixing.

This is especially necessary when a high percentage of coarse grains and seeds is used.

Dough temperatures should be maintained slightly cooler than usual. A dough temperature of 76 to 78°F. is best in that a slower conditioning of the dough takes place. This will avoid over-conditioning and possible tearing of the extended gluten by coarse and whole grains. Doughs should be conditioned so that they are slightly on the "young" side. This will maintain the strength of the gluten. While there may be slight buckiness, this will be overcome during the preliminary proofing period, and will maintain the ability to mold and machine the units without extensive tearing. Of course, machine adjustments will have to be made so that the rollers are sufficiently apart to avoid the tearing effect.

Natural or health-type products should be given slightly less than full proof before baking. Proofing should be accomplished over a longer period at slightly reduced proofing temperatures. This will avoid greater pressure on the gluten of doughs and the consequent possibility of a tearing effect on the outside of the dough. Units that have three-quarter proof will spring back with a slight firmness when touched gently. At this point, breads and other units may be cut, washed, garnished, and otherwise treated without chance of falling back due to collapse of the gluten structure. Breads and other units that have been cut or garnished at ¾ proof are usually given slightly more proof before being loaded into the oven for baking.

Most yeast-raised bread specialties will require the injection of steam into the oven from before loading until the breads have fully risen. This will promote maximum oven spring during the early stages of baking. Harder crusted breads, such as the French, Italian, sour rye, and others, will require a more forceful injection of steam prior to loading and during the early stages of baking. Softer type breads and bakery products will require minimal steam.

Enriched, health-type breads will require slightly longer baking periods and slightly lower baking temperatures. In many instances, the oven temperature is lowered during the final stages of baking. This is to insure complete baking through the interior and a firming of the side walls of the loaf to prevent collapse or shrinking during cooling of the baked loaves. Natural type breads are richer, some more than others, and require longer baking. The higher percentages of fat, natural syrups, special grains and seeds, nuts and fruits require this longer bake to insure a thorough bake. Oven temperatures and crust colors are factors to be considered. The formulation of the recipe will regulate the baking process.

With each of the formulas presented, suggestions will be made regarding the factors mentioned. They will be brief but of significance in relation to the production of the specific bakery food. The baker is urged to make judgments in production that relate to the conditions under which the variety products are produced.

The several formulas for enriched, multi-grain, dark rye breads and for the lighter type of party rye breads that follow require the use of fermented sour rye sponge doughs or the use of prepared dry sour cultures. For the preparation and maintenance of a perpetual or continuing sour rye sponge dough refer to pages 101 and 102 for procedures to follow. When using a dry sour culture, it is advisable to follow the instructions provided by the manufacturer. Adjustments may be made by the baker to meet special product requirements.

Old Fashioned Dark Sour Rye Bread

Ingredients	Lb.	Oz.	Mixing procedure
Fermented and conditioned sour rye sponge dough	6	..	Mix at slow speed for 8 to 10 min. to further soften the bran particles and wheat kernels
Salt	..	5	
Molasses (dark)	..	8	
Water (cool)	3	..	
Pumpernickel flour	1	8	
Whole wheat flour	1	..	
Whole wheat kernels (pre-soak and drain)	..	8	
Wheat germ	..	2	
Caramel color (optional)	..	2	
Yeast (variable)	..	8	Dissolve the yeast and set aside. Add the flour and stir slightly
Water	1	4	
Clear flour (strong first clear)	8	..	Add the yeast solution and mix to a dough. Add the shortening and develop the dough at slow or medium speed
Shortening	..	3	

Procedures to Follow

1. Mixing time: Variable 10 to 15 min.
2. Dough temperature: 78–80° F.
3. Dough consistency: Medium stiff. This dough should be slightly softer than the usual dough made for pumpernickel bread. The bran and whole grain kernels will tend to absorb moisture during fermentation and cause the dough to stiffen slightly during this period.
4. Allow the dough to relax for about 30 min. before scaling and rounding.

Note: Units that are machined for makeup should be given a slightly longer preliminary proofing period to avoid tearing during moulding. It is also advisable to adjust the compression boards and curling rolls to a slightly open position to avoid tearing.

5. Proof the made up units to ¾ proof. Units may then be washed and garnished with bran or cracked wheat. Units may also be cut for variety.
6. If units are baked in loaf pans, it will require approximately 1½ lb. of dough to completely fill the average 1-lb. white bread loaf pan. Special units may be baked in smaller loaf pans. Units may also be baked in regular long or round rye shapes and baked directly on the hearth or oven grid.
7. Baking temperature: approximately 425°F. Steam should be injected into the oven about 3 to 5 min. before loading the breads into the oven. Allow the moist steam to continue until the loaves have had full oven spring and have started to firm up (approximately 10 to 15 min. depending upon the size of the loaf). The average baking time for the 1-lb. loaf is 45 to 50 min. It is advisable to lower the oven temperature to 385°F. during the final stages of baking to insure thorough bake and to avoid excessively dark crust color. Larger and smaller loaves will require changes in baking time.
8. For variation, a small amount of the rye sour dough may be softened with water and gently smeared over the loaf when ¾ proofed.

Note: Whole grain wheat kernels should be soaked for 2 to 3 hr.

Old Fashioned Dark Sour Rye Bread Made with Sour Culture

Note: The dry sour culture replaces the fermented sour rye sponge dough. This requires an increase in the amount of water and rye flour. Most sour cultures contain added salt, thus requiring a slight reduction in the amount of salt used in the dough.

Ingredients	Lb.	Oz.	Mixing procedure
Dry sour culture	1	..	Blend the sour culture with the flours and salt
Salt	..	3½	
Light rye (cream) flour	2	8	Add the remaining ingredients and mix in slow speed for about 10 min. to dissolve the dry ingredients and soften the bran and kernels
Pumpernickel flour	1	4	
Whole wheat kernels (pre-soaked)	..	12	
Whole wheat flour	1	..	
Wheat germ	..	2	
Caramel color (optional)	..	2	
Molasses (dark)	..	8	
Water	5	..	
Yeast (variable)	..	8	Dissolve the yeast and set aside
Water	1	4	
Clear flour (strong first clear)	8	8	Add the flour and stir slightly. Add the yeast and mix to a dough. Add the shortening and develop in slow speed
Shortening	..	3	

Procedures to Follow

1. Mixing time: approximately 12 to 15 min.
2. Dough temperature: 80°F.
3. Dough conditioning: Follow instructions provided by the manufacturer of the dry sour culture. It normally takes about 30 to 45 min. to relax and condition the dough before scaling and rounding when using a sour culture. Make up the same as regular sour dough bread.

Light Rye or Party Rye Bread

Ingredients	Lb.	Oz.	Mixing procedure
Fermented sourdough (rye sponge dough)	5	..	Mix at slow speed for about 10 min. to dissolve dry ingredients and distribute the sourdough
Water	3	..	
Salt	..	4	
Malt (non-diastatic)	..	6	
Potato flour	..	6	
Soy flour (defatted)	..	4	
Caraway seeds (optional)	..	½ to 1	
Yeast (variable)	..	5	Dissolve the yeast and set aside. Add the flour
Water	1	8	and mix slightly. Add the yeast and mix to a dough. Add the shortening and develop the dough. Use a slow or medium speed to avoid overmixing
Clear flour (strong first clear)	8	6	
Shortening	..	3	

Procedures to Follow

1. Dough temperature: 80 to 82°F.
2. Dough conditioning: Relax dough for approximately 30 to 40 min. and scale and round units.
3. Scale the units approximately 1 pound. Relaxed units should be rolled out in a long strip form about 12 in. in length. This dough is stiffer than the usual rye dough.
4. Proof to about ¾ proof. The units may be washed and cut before baking.
5. Bake at 425°F. Inject steam before loading the oven and continue for the next 10 to 12 min. after breads are in oven.
6. When using a dry sour culture to replace the sour rye sponge dough, follow instructions provided on the package.

Note: The use of celery salt, garlic powder, onion powder is suggested for variety.

7. The dough may be made darker or given a pumpernickel effect by adding sugar color (burnt sugar) to darken the dough. The combination of both light and dark color regular party rye doughs are often used to make a spiral effect in the baked bread. For example, an 8-oz. piece of light dough and an 8-oz. piece of the darker (pumpernickel type) dough are moulded together. The flattened pieces of dough are placed together after passing through the rollers and are then moulded into an internal spiral effect.

8. The baked breads are about 2 in. in diameter and are sliced very thin for the party or cocktail rye bread. The added flavorings allow for increased variety. These breads are usually double wrapped and are often merchandised from the freezer.
9. This bread dough may be used for production of special rye rolls and production of miniature loaves for the restaurant trade. They may be made in the round, oval, and the long shape.

American Light Rye Bread

This enriched bread is especially useful to the baker who does not maintain a continuing or perpetual sour rye sponge. The formula recommends the use of sour rye culture to replace the fermented sour rye sponge dough.

Ingredients	Lb.	Oz.	Mixing procedure
Sour rye culture (variable)	..	4–6	Mix all ingredients for approximately 6 min. to thoroughly dissolve and distribute ingredients
Salt	..	2½	
Malt (non-diastatic)	..	2	
Molasses	..	2	
Potato flour	..	12	
Rye flour (cream of rye)	1	8	
Caraway seeds (optional)	..	1	
Water	3	..	
Yeast (variable)	..	6	Dissolve the yeast and set aside
Water	1	8	
First clear flour	6	4	Add the flour and mix lightly. Add the yeast and mix to a dough. Add the shortening and develop. Use medium speed for final development
Shortening	..	3	

Procedures to Follow

1. Dough temperature: 78 to 80°F.
2. Fermentation time: One full rise (approximately 45 min.). Take to scaler-rounder.
3. Allow a full intermediate proof or resting period after rounding (15 min.). Shape into long (sandwich type), round, or bake in Pullman pans for the square sandwich shape.
4. Proof to slightly more than ¾ proof and bake at 415°F. with steam in the oven. The dough may be used for light rye rolls.

Home-Style Bread

The formula for this bread is enriched with natural ingredients and will result in a loaf that is compact, with close grain, smooth texture, and having long shelf life. A variety of bread shapes may be made from this dough. The dough may also be used to produce a variety of enriched soft buns or rolls. These will be explained after the formula and procedures for production and handling are presented.

Ingredients	Lb.	Oz.	Mixing procedure
Yeast (variable)	. .	8	Dissolve and set aside
Water	1	. .	
Sugar	. .	4	Mix at low speed to dissolve and disperse all
Salt	. .	3	ingredients
Dry skim milk	. .	6	
Clover honey	. .	5	
Butter (margarine or shortening may be used)	. .	3	
Eggs	. .	6	
Soy flour (defatted)	. .	4	
Wheat germ	. .	2	
Water	5	. .	
Bread flour (12 to 14% protein)	8	4	Add the flour and mix lightly. Add the yeast solution and mix to a dough. Add the shortening and develop dough
Shortening	. .	3	

Procedures to Follow

1. Dough temperature: 78–80° F.
2. Fermentation of dough: First punch 1½ hr. Second punch ½ hr. Rest 10 to 15 min. and take to bench or scaler-rounder.
3. Preliminary proofing period: approximately 15 to 20 min. and send to molder or hand shape breads on the bench.
4. Proofing: Give the units ¾ proof and then wash and sprinkle tops with sesame seeds or dust with cake flour or rye flour for the home made appearance. The units are then given a slightly longer proof.
5. Bake at 400° F. with steam injected into the oven before loading. Allow steam to continue until oven spring is complete and the crust shows slight color. Reduce oven temperature to 385° F. for the final few minutes of baking.
6. For the thin sliced pullman loaves, cross-twist or cross-grain the dough strip before placing into the pullman pans. Scale according to size of the pan. Be sure to use enough dough so that the full pan is filled with dough and baked bread. Remove the pan covers soon after baking to avoid sweating.
7. The old-fashioned or home-style loaf may be made by twisting two strips together and then placing in pans. The strip of dough may be divided

into two separate sections which are placed together into the pan and baked as a split top loaf.

8. Section loaves may be made by rounding six pieces of dough (equal to 1 lb. 2 oz. for the 1-lb. loaf) and placing 3 on each side of the pan.

9. Round loaves may be made in the cloverleaf style by placing four rounded dough units into a pie shape aluminum foil pan. These units may be dusted with flour after they have been proofed and before baking.

10. The plain round loaf may be baked in pie tins and cut across when ¾ proof. These loaves may be garnished with seeds or dusted with flour before baking.

11. Rolls or buns may be scaled about 3½ lb. per press and then rounded or oval-shaped for variety buns and soft rolls.

Cinnamon Tea Loaf

The formula that follows is enriched. The baker has the option of increasing the enrichment ingredients. Changes may be made by increasing the amount of cinnamon and raisins in the filled units. Variety may be increased by changes in size and shape of the pans in which the units are baked.

Ingredients	Lb.	Oz.	Mixing procedure
Sugar	..	12	Blend well to distribute all ingredients
Salt	..	3	
Dry skim milk	..	6	
Soy flour (defatted)	..	4	
Potato flour	.:	3	
Wheat germ	..	2	
Clover honey	..	3	
Malt (non-diastatic)	..	3	
Shortening	..	14	
Egg yolks	..	6	
Water	4	..	Add and mix in
Yeast (variable)	..	10	Dissolve the yeast
Water	2	..	
Bread flour	9	4	Add the flour mix lightly. Add the yeast and mix until almost fully developed. Add the raisins during the final stage of dough development
Raisins (optional) (pre-soaked and drained)	2	..	

Procedures to Follow

1. Dough temperature: Approximately 78–80°F.
2. First punch: approximately 1½ hr (will vary with yeast and temperature). Second rise: approximately 45 to 60 min. Do not punch. Take to bench or send to divider-rounder.

3. Make-up of breads: Units may be scaled 1 lb. for the average 1-lb. loaf of white bread size pan, if the dough is made without raisins. If dough contains raisins, scale 1 lb. 2 oz. The dough may be scaled into 8 to 10 1-lb pieces and formed into rectangular shape. Relax the dough for about 15 to 20 min. and send through the sheeter to about $\frac{1}{4}$ in. thickness or roll out on the bench. Brush the surface with water and sprinkle with raisins and cinnamon sugar and roll up and seal as for cinnamon buns.

4. Scale pieces cut from the long strip according to pan size. Breads made without the cinnamon sugar filling are usually brushed with melted butter or fat after baking and rolled in cinnamon sugar.

5. Bread units should be given slightly more than $\frac{3}{4}$ proof. The tops of the units may be brushed with egg wash for a shiny brown crust color after baking. These breads are usually brushed with a syrup wash as soon as they are baked. They are later striped with a fondant type icing while still slightly warm.

6. Baking: Bake at 375 to 380°F. These loaves require a low baking temperature because of the richness of the dough. Larger loaves will require a longer baking period and at a lower baking temperature.

7. Variety may be increased by using colorful aluminum foil pans. These may be in a smaller loaf form or in a round and slightly tapered form.

Granola (Many Grains) Bread

This type of health bread is composed of a variety of grains the most popular of which is oatmeal. Originally, granola was primarily a cereal, but larger bakeries and manufacturers of prepared mixes encouraged the growth of this bread variety. Retail bakers purchase the prepared granola blend and add additional ingredients such as natural syrups to further enhance the taste and flavor. The formula that follows may be changed by adding or subtracting or substituting ingredients. The baker has the choice of preparing his own cereal blend for enrichment.

Ingredients	*Lb.*	*Oz.*	*Mixing procedure*
Brown sugar	..	6	Mix all ingredients in slow speed for 10 min. to dissolve and soften grain and bran particles
Salt	..	3	
Dry skim milk	..	4	
Wheat germ	..	2	
Soy flour (defatted)	..	3	
Potato flour	..	4	
Rolled oats	..	10	
Cornmeal (yellow)	..	6	
Pumpernickel flour	..	10	
Malt (non-diastatic)	..	3	
Molasses	..	4	
Water	4	..	
Yeast (variable)	..	10	Dissolve and set aside
Water	2	..	Add the flour and mix slightly. Add the yeast and mix to a dough. Add the shortening and develop the dough at slow or medium speed
Whole wheat flour	1	2	
Bread flour	6	..	
Vegetable shortening	..	6	

Raisins are an optional ingredient. They may be used in varying amounts. The raisins should be pre-soaked and drained and added in the final stage of dough development.

Procedures to Follow

1. Dough temperature: 78–80°F.
2. First rise and punch: approximately 1½ hr. (variable). Second rise: approximately 30 min. and take to bench without punching. The dough should be kept slightly on the "young" side for better machining or bench make up. Send to divider or rounder or to bench for scaling and rounding.
3. This specialty bread may be made in a variety of sizes and shapes. The average 1-lb. white bread loaf pan will require 20 oz. of dough for a well risen baked loaf. Many bakers use smaller loaf pans and scale the dough accordingly.
4. Preliminary proofing: approximately 20 min. (allow complete relaxation of the rounded units before molding).
5. Adjust rollers to a slightly open position to avoid a tearing effect. Dusting flour should be minimal since the dough is slightly stiffer and will have a tendency to dry or crust slightly.
6. The molded units may be rolled in oats before panning. The units may be washed with water when ¾ proof and then sprinkled with oats, sesame seeds, bran, or a blend of several coarse grains for appearance.

7. Units should be given a slow proof (temperature approximately 90° F. with a humidity of approximately 85%) to prevent tearing of the dough due to a forced or rapid proofing. Units may be cut and garnished when ¾ proof and then be given a slight, additional proof before baking.

8. Bake at 390 to 400° F. with mild steam injected into the oven. Allow the steam to continue until oven spring is complete and the crust takes on a light crust color. Reduce the oven temperature to 375° F. during the final few minutes of baking.

Sourdough Bread

The old fashioned sourdough bread is, as the name indicates, a bread made from sourdough. This is very much like a sponge dough that has been fermented and then kept in a state whereby it will serve as the fermenting agent when fresh ingredients and flour are added to make a larger dough for bread. The dough is never completely used up for bread. There is always a sourdough base of dough retained for the building of another dough. Thus, it is like a perpetual sourdough that is maintained for the old-fashioned sour rye breads and dark breads of German variety. In the preparation of sourdough or building of the dough with the sour dough base, an approach similar to rye sours is used. The stages of sour dough development are longer for the sourdough bread. The bacterial development of lactic and acetic acids takes place at a slower rate and there is a lower pH developed. This accounts for the special flavor and sourdough taste in the baked bread.

The use of sourdough cultures is now quite popular. The prepared dry cultures save considerable time and space in that sourdough development is replaced by the cultures. The sourdough cultures contain the necessary fungal enzymes, dough conditioners, salt, sugar, lactic and other acids normally present in the sourdough. There are variables in the contents of the different sourdough cultures. The baker should follow the instructions provided by the manufacturer. However, the baker may make adjustments in fermentation time based upon the conditions he may use. This would apply to water temperature, shop temperature, percentage of yeast used, and other factors controlling fermentation. The formula for sourdough "freshings" and procedures may be adjusted for development of degree of pH and sourdough flavoring. A formula using a typical sourdough culture will also be provided.

Sourdough Bread

Ingredients	Lb.	Oz.	Mixing procedure

A. First Sour Build

Water	3	..	Dissolve the yeast in the water. Add the flour and mix to a smooth sponge dough
Yeast (variable)	..	4–6	
First clear flour	4	..	

Allow the sponge dough to rise well and then fall back by itself. Do not punch the sponge dough

B. Second Sour Build

			Add the water to the first freshing and mix well to break up. Add the flour and mix to
Water	3	..	a smooth sponge dough
First clear flour	4	..	

Allow the sponge dough to rise and fall back by itself. For larger production needs, the amount of water and flour may be increased proportionately to make for a larger second freshing.

Note: Some bakers will continue sour sponge development via a third and final build and will then increase the amount of this sourdough base used for the final dough.

C. Final Dough Preparation

Conditioned sourdough	12	..	Add these ingredients to the sourdough sponge and mix well to break up the sponge and dissolve the dry ingredients
Sugar	..	6	
Salt	..	5	
Malt (non-diastatic)	..	6	
Water	2	..	
Yeast (variable)	..	8	Dissolve the yeast and set aside. Add the flour
Water	2	..	and mix lightly. Add the yeast and mix to a dough. Add shortening and develop the dough. Mix the dough on medium speed to avoid overmixing and overdevelopment, which may cause a tearing effect and dough wetness or sticking
Bread flour	9	..	
Shortening	..	4	

Procedures to Follow

1. Dough temperature: 80–82°F.
2. Dough conditioning: Allow dough to rise well (about 45 min.) and take to bench or scaler-rounder.

3. Scale according to size and shape of the loaves. The average long loaf will be scaled at 1 lb. Demi or small loaves will be scaled 8 oz.

4. Units are placed on cornmeal dusted peels and given a slow proof. The dough is on the stiff side, as compared with Italian or French breads, and must be proofed slowly. A rapid proof will tend to cause a tearing effect. Units should be given ¾ proof and then washed and cut. This practice is used for the Vienna shaped loaves. Long French type breads may be left uncut or cut as desired. The units are given slightly more proof.

5. Baking: Inject mild steam into the oven before loading the oven. Peel the breads onto the hearth with sufficient space between loaves for expansion. Allow the steam to continue until oven spring is complete and slight crust color starts to form. Oven temperature should be 425°F. Bake so that the loaves have a dry, crisp crust.

Sourdough Bread Using Dry Culture

Ingredients	Lb.	Oz.	Mixing procedure
Salt	..	4	Blend the salt, culture, and flour. Dissolve yeast in part of water. Add balance of water and stir slightly. Add yeast and mix to a dough. Add shortening and develop dough
Sourdough culture	1	..	
Bread flour	13	8	
Yeast (variable)	..	8	
Water	8	..	
Shortening	..	3	

Handle dough as for the regular sourdough made with sour base.

Oatmeal Bread

Oat grains are highly nutritious and are used extensively in many bread varieties as a nutritional supplement. While small percentages are used in other breads, this formula for oatmeal bread contains approximately 24 per cent oatmeal. Because of this, bakers will often presoak the oatmeal for a lengthy period to soften the oat grains. This will reduce moisture absorption during fermentation and make for easier mixing and dough development. However, this process is time-consuming. In the following formula, it is recommended that the oats be mixed without a presoak to speed up mixing and preparation as well as to maintain a more nut-like taste and flavor in the baked bread.

Ingredients	Lb.	Oz.	Mixing procedure
Yeast (variable)	..	8	Dissolve the yeast and set aside
Water	2	..	
Sugar	..	4	Mix all ingredients together for 10 to 12 min. in
Salt	..	3	slow or medium speed to dissolve and hydrate
Dry skim milk	..	4	the ingredients
Oatmeal (rolled oats)	2	..	
Soy flour (defatted)	..	3	
Water	4	..	
Malt (non-diastatic)	..	3	
Honey (clover)	..	3	
Molasses	..	4	
Bread flour	8	4	Add the flour and mix slightly
Shortening	..	8	Add the yeast solution and mix to a dough. Add the shortening and develop dough on slow speed

Procedures to Follow

1. Dough temperature: 78–80°F.
2. First rise and punch: 1½ hr. (approximate time). Second rise: 30 to 40 min. (Do not punch a second time.)
3. Take to bench or scaler-rounder.

Note: Oatmeal bread may be made in several varieties. A smaller pan loaf or a round pan or pie tin may be used for round loaves. Scale dough accordingly.

4. Preliminary proofing period: 15–20 min. Allow for complete relaxation to avoid tearing during molding. Adjust rollers and plates to eliminate friction or bind which may cause the dough to tear.
5. Proofing: Give units ¾ proof and then wash with water and sprinkle with oatmeal flakes. The round units may be cut for variety. Allow slightly more proof before baking.
6. Bake at 400°F. with moist steam injected into the oven before loading the bread. Continue the moist steam until oven spring is completed and the crust takes on a mild crust color. Reduce the oven temperature to 375°F. during final stages of baking. This is to insure complete bake with firm side walls.

Note: For added variety, raisins (pre-soaked) may be added to the dough during the final stages of dough development. Some bakers may also add bran flakes and wheat germ to the dough for further nutritional value through increased protein.

7. The dough may be used for oatmeal roll specialties. The rolls may be shaped in round, oval, or simple twist (knot) form. Dough presses for rolls are usually scaled 3 to 3½ lb. per press. The rolls are garnished with oatmeal flakes when ¾ proof. Bake the rolls at 400°F. with a small amount of moist steam injected into the oven.

Potato Home-Style Bread

These breads are made with potato flour and NOT potato starch. The potato flour contains the important nutrients and provides for a soft, tender crumb, and prolonged shelf-life. The loaves may be made in regular loaf form or in the old-fashioned round form. This dough will also produce soft, light, and tender rolls.

Ingredients	Lb.	Oz.	Mixing procedure
Yeast (variable)	..	8	Dissolve and set aside
Water	2	..	
Sugar	..	5	Blend together at slow speed to dissolve ingre-
Salt	..	3	dients
Malt (non-diastatic)	..	3	
Potato flour	..	8	
Dry skim milk	..	5	
Soy flour (defatted)	..	2	
Water	4	..	
Bread flour	8	12	Add the flour and mix slightly. Add the yeast and mix to a dough. Add the shortening and develop the dough at slow or medium speed
Shortening	..	6	

Procedures to Follow

1. Dough temperature: 78–80°F.
2. First rise and punch: 1 hr. and 15 min. (approximate time). Second rise: 30 to 40 min. Do not punch. Take to bench or scaler-rounder.
3. Keep this dough slightly on the young side. It will handle and machine better since the dough tends to form a slight crust or skin formation.
4. Scale as for regular white pan bread. Adjust weight to meet pan size and shape.
5. Give units ¾ proof. Wash and cut if desired. Dust with cake or rye flour.
6. Bake with moist steam at 390 to 400°F.

Raisin Wheat Bread

Breads may be enriched by the addition of fruits and nuts as well as the use of variety grains. A combination of all enrichment ingredients is receiving growing acceptance by the consumer. While raisin breads have been popular, they are now enriched with added grains for further enrichment.

The following formula is basic, and may be further enriched by the addition of ingredients that provide added proteins and vitamins.

Ingredients	Lb.	Oz.	Mixing procedure
Water	2	. .	Dissolve the yeast and set aside
Yeast (variable)	. .	8	
Sugar	. .	4	Mix all ingredients in slow speed for 10 min. to
Salt	. .	3	dissolve ingredients and to hydrate the cracked
Dry skim milk	. .	3	wheat
Malt (non-diastatic)	. .	2	
Molasses	. .	4	
Honey (clover)	. .	3	
Soy flour (defatted)	. .	2	
Cracked wheat	1	8	
Water	4	. .	
Whole wheat flour	1	. .	Add the flour and mix slightly
Bread flour	6	8	Add the yeast solution and mix to a dough. Add the shortening and develop to a smooth dough. Mix at slow or medium speed. Add the raisins in the final stages of mixing and dough development
Shortening	. .	6	
Raisins (pre-soaked) (variable)	3	. .	

Procedures to Follow

1. Dough temperature: 78–80°F.
2. First rise and punch: 1½ hr. (approximately). Second rise: 30 to 40 min. Do not punch. Take to bench or divider-rounder. Adjust the pressure plates and rollers to a slightly open position to avoid tearing of the dough due to the bran particles and the raisins.
3. Scale the dough units 20 oz. for the average 1-lb. loaf of pan bread. Smaller pans are often used for a baked loaf weighing one pound. The units may be baked in special round pans or pie tins. Colorful aluminum foil pans are often used, and are merchandised with the baked bread in them.
4. Proofing and baking: The breads are given ¾ proof and washed lightly with water. The breads may then be garnished with bran flakes or coarse cracked wheat.
5. The breads are baked with mild, wet steam injected into the oven. Oven temperature should be 390–400°F. The oven temperature should be reduced to approximately 375°F. during the final stages of baking to insure a well baked loaf and to control the crust color.

Note: Raisin juice is often used in these breads to increase the nutritional values and improve the taste. The water in which the raisins are soaked may be used as part of the water used in the dough. A portion of the raisins may be crushed or ground and added to the juice.

Whole Grain Wheat Bread

Ingredients	Lb.	Oz.	Mixing procedure
Yeast (variable)	..	10	Dissolve the yeast and set aside
Water	2	..	
Sugar	..	6	Mix at slow speed for 10 to 12 min. to dissolve
Salt	..	3½	the dry ingredients and to soften the coarse
Dry skim milk	..	4	grains
Wheat germ	..	2	
Bran flour (bran flakes may be used)	..	8	
Whole wheat berries (pre-soaked)	..	8	
Cracked wheat flour	2	..	
Malt (low diastatic strength)	..	3	
Honey (clover)	..	4	
Water	5	..	
Whole wheat flour	1	..	Add the flour and mix slightly
Bread flour (high gluten)	7	..	Add the yeast solution and mix to a dough. Add the shortening and develop the dough at slow speed. Mixing time will be approximately 10 to 12 min. Do not overmix. This will avoid stickiness and slackening of the dough
Shortening	..	7	

Note: The whole wheat berries may soak overnight, or at least for several hours in order to soften the outer bran and maintain a whole grain. This will allow for a nutlike appearance and flavor in the baked loaf. The cracked wheat flour may be pre-soaked in a small amount of measured (about 1 lb.) water. The water will be absorbed and the bran softened. The amount of pre-soaking water absorbed is to be deducted from the formula requirements.

Procedures to Follow

1. Dough temperature: This dough should be kept on the cool side. (76–78°F. is advisable.) This will avoid a rapid fermentation and possible tearing of the dough and gluten structure.
2. First rise and punch: approximately 1½ hr. (variable, depending on dough temperature and environment). Second rise: approximately

40 min. Do not punch. Take to bench or divider rounder. Keeping the dough slightly on the "young" side is advisable to avoid tearing during molding.

3. Preliminary proofing: Allow approximately 20 min. for complete relaxation before molding by hand or sending through the molder. Adjust pressure plates and rollers to allow for the large percentage of bran, cracked wheat, and whole wheat berries. Close pressure will have a tearing effect. Some additional dusting flour may be necessary.

4. Proofing: The units are to be given a slow proof (90°F. and approximately 85 per cent relative humidity). This will avoid possible tearing during proof caused by the coarse grains and bran. Proof the units to ¾ proof. The units are then brushed lightly with water and dusted with bran flakes.

5. Baking: Bake with mild, wet steam injected into the oven. Oven temperature 410°F. Continue the steam until oven spring is complete and crust starts to show a slight crust color. The temperature should be reduced to approximately 380°F. during the final stages of baking. This will insure a thorough bake and firmer side walls to avoid collapse of bread sides or shrinkage. Remove the breads from the pans as soon as the breads are removed from the oven.

Old-Fashioned Cheese Bread

Cheese bread is becoming quite popular as a specialty loaf. Its popularity is greatest when used as a cocktail-type bread specialty. The use of cheddar-type cheese, enriched grains, firmness of grain and texture, and special appeal when toasted, contribute to popularity. The loaves may be made in the long, thin, sandwich form, or baked in a narrow loaf pan form. The breads are sliced very thin after baking for use with spreads, dips, and other specialties.

Ingredients	Lb.	Oz.	Mixing procedure
Yeast (variable)	..	8	Dissolve the yeast and set aside
Water	2	..	
Sugar	..	6	Mix in slow speed for 6 to 8 min. to dissolve dry
Salt	..	3	ingredients and hydrate grains
Dry skim milk	..	6	
Soy flour (defatted)	..	3	
Potato flour	..	4	
Wheat germ	..	3	
Water	4	..	
Bread flour (high gluten)	9	8	Add the flour and mix slightly. Add the yeast and mix to a dough. Add the shortening and develop the dough. The grated cheese is added in the final stages of dough development.
Shortening	..	6	
Grated cheddar cheese (Dry American cheese may be used)	1	2	

Procedures to Follow

1. A firm, dry cheddar or American cheese should be used. The cheese will soften during the fermentation period. The dough will assume a slight yellowish color, depending upon the color of the cheese and the degree of hardness of the cheese when grated.
2. Final development of the dough should be done at slow speed. This will avoid build-up of excessive friction causing a smearing effect by the cheese. It will also maintain a cooler dough temperature. The dough should be stiffer than that for ordinary white pan bread. There will be a slight softening or slackening of the dough during fermentation. This effect is also induced by the lower pH of the dough due to the addition of the cheese.
3. Dough temperature: 76 to 79°F.
4. First rise and punch: approximately 1½ hr. Second rise: 40 min. Do not punch. Take dough to bench or send to divider rounder.
5. Allow for a slightly longer intermediate proofing period (20 min.). This will allow for easier molding. A slight crust will form but can easily be worked into the molding of the bread. It is advisable to check for sufficient dusting flour to avoid stickiness.
6. Proofing: The units should be given slightly more than ¾ proof.
7. Bake at 410°F. with mild, moist steam injected into the oven. Maintain the steam until complete oven spring is completed and a slight crust color is indicated. Reduce the oven temperature to 375°F. during the final stages of baking to insure a solid bake with strong side walls to the bread loaf.

8. Loaves may be made in smaller loaf pans or round aluminum foil pans for variety. Loaves may be lightly brushed with water and sprinkled with sesame seeds or other garnish before baking.

Italian Wheat Bread

Ingredients	Lb.	Oz.	Mixing procedure
Yeast (variable)	..	8	Dissolve the yeast and set aside
Water	2	..	
Salt	..	4½	Mix in slow speed for 10 to 12 min. to dissolve
Dry sour culture (optional)	..	3	dry ingredients and to hydrate grains
Malt (low diastatic)	..	4	
Soy flour (defatted)	..	4	
Bran flour or pumpernickel flour	·	8	
Wheat germ (toasted)	..	3	
Wheat gluten	..	4	
Whole wheat grains (optional) pre-soaked	..	8	
Water	7	..	
Whole wheat flour	3	..	Add the flour and mix lightly. Add the yeast solution and mix to a dough. Add the shortening and develop dough at slow or medium speed
Bread flour (high gluten)	10	..	
Shortening	..	5	

Procedures to Follow

1. Dough temperature: 78–80°F.
2. First rise and punch: approximately 1½ hr. Second rise: 45 min. Do not punch again if dry sour culture is used. The culture will relax the gluten and dough will condition faster.

Note: The bread flour should be of high gluten variety in order to support the added grains and allow for a well risen loaf when baked.

3. Preliminary proofing: Allow approximately 20 min. for complete relaxation of the rounded units. This will allow for easier molding with less chance of tearing the dough.
4. The units may be scaled in varying weights depending upon the size and shape of the units. The long-oval shaped bread is customary. Loaves may vary from 20 oz. to the smaller 10-oz. size. The units for the long

or hoagie type rolls may be scaled at 4 oz. each. Shaped or molded units are placed on corn meal dusted boards before proofing.

5. Proofing: The units should be proofed at a slower rate than is regular Italian bread. This will prevent tearing of the dough due to the coarse grains and bran particles in the dough. Units should be given no more than ¾ proof before they are washed or brushed with water and then cut across either diagonally or through the center of the loaf. The units may then be garnished with sesame seeds or dusted with bran flakes. Slightly more proof may be given before baking.

6. Baking: Units are placed upon peels or the dusted peels are attached to poles for peeling into the oven. The peels may have handles for direct peeling into the oven. Bake at 415 to 420°F. with steam injected into the oven for a few minutes before loading the bread. Allow the steam to continue until breads are fully expanded and then show a slight crust color formation. Oven temperature should be reduced to 385°F. during the final stages of baking. The units should have a crisp, firm outer crust and sound hollow when baked.

Natural Hard-Type Rolls

These rolls are enriched with added grains to provide additional natural proteins and vitamins. The use of egg whites further increases the protein content and makes for a crispier type of roll.

Ingredients	Lb.	Oz.	Mixing procedure
Yeast (variable)	..	10	Dissolve the yeast and set aside
Water	2	..	
Sugar	..	10	Mix all ingredients at slow speed for approxi-
Salt	..	4	mately 10 min. to dissolve the dry ingredients
Dry skim milk	..	4	and to hydrate the coarse grains
Malt (low diastatic)	..	6	
Soy flour (defatted)	..	4	
Wheat germ (toasted)	..	2	
Wheat gluten	..	4	
Bran flour	..	8	
Vegetable oil	..	12	
Egg yolks	..	8	
Egg whites	..	12	
Water	6	4	
Bread flour (high gluten) (variable)	15	..	Add the flour and mix slightly. Add the yeast and develop the dough in slow or medium speed

Procedures to Follow

1. Dough temperature: 80 to 82°F.
2. First rise and punch: 1½ to 2 hr. (variable with temperature and amount of yeast used). Second rise: approximately 40 min. Do not punch. Take to bench or divider-rounder. This dough will be slightly on the young side to allow bench or makeup time for the variety of rolls to be made.
3. Scaled dough presses may vary in weight from 2½ to as much as 5 lb. in weight. This will allow for the makeup of the smaller restaurant or cocktail size rolls as well as the larger Kaiser, salt stick, and water roll types.
4. Preliminary proofing: Allow the presses of dough to relax about 20 min. before dividing into individual dough units to be made into rolls. This will allow for easier makeup without tearing of machined units. During makeup the sheeter rollers may have to be opened slightly to prevent tearing. Use sufficient dusting flour to avoid sticking and possible tearing.
5. Hard rolls to be baked on the hearth or oven grid are usually placed on cornmeal dusted peels for direct peeling into the oven. Others are placed on sheet pans for proofing and baking.
6. Proofing and baking: Units are given slightly more than ¾ proof. The rolls that are garnished may be brushed lightly with water and then garnished with seeds. Hard rolls, such as Kaiser rolls, are placed face down on seeds sprinkled at the bottom of the roll box or seeded peel. These are turned face up before being peeled into the oven. Salt sticks and caraway-garnished sticks are usually washed with water and garnished with seeds before proofing. Bake the rolls at 420°F. with steam injected into the oven before the rolls are peeled into the oven. Allow the steam to continue until the rolls have had full oven spring and have taken on a light crust color. The oven temperature may be reduced slightly during final baking to insure a crisp crust.

Enriched Challah (Egg) Bread

This egg bread specialty is enriched with use of grains that contain large percentages of protein and provide a longer shelf-life by slowing the rate of moisture transfer to the crust of the baked loaf.

Ingredients	Lb.	Oz.	Mixing procedure
Yeast (variable)	..	12	Dissolve the yeast and set aside
Water	2	..	
Sugar	1	8	Mix in slow speed for about 6–8 min. to dissolve
Salt	..	5	all ingredients and hydrate grains
Soy flour (defatted)	..	4	
Potato flour	..	4	
Wheat germ (toasted)	..	4	
Vegetable oil	1	8	
Egg yolks	2	8	
Egg whites	1	..	
Water	6	..	
Bread flour (high gluten) (variable)	18	..	Add the flour and mix slightly. Add the yeast and develop in slow speed

Procedures to Follow

1. The dough should be of a stiffer consistency than that for hard rolls. Check the dough consistency before final development for the addition of more flour. It is easier to add flour or water before the dough is fully developed.
2. Dough temperature: 78–80°F.
3. Dough conditioning: First punch 1½ to 2 hr. Relax 30 to 40 min. and take to bench or divider rounder. Refer to pages 105 and 106 for makeup (braiding), proofing, and baking procedures.

Wheat Bread Sticks

This is a formula for an enriched bread stick containing several different grains for enrichment and increased nutritional value.

Ingredients	Lb.	Oz.	Mixing procedure
Yeast (variable)	..	6	Dissolve the yeast and set aside
Water	2	..	
Salt	..	3	Mix in slow speed for 6 to 8 min. to dissolve the
Dry skim milk	..	2	dry ingredients and hydrate the coarse grains
Soy flour (defatted)	..	2	
Bran flour or flakes	..	8	
Wheat germ	..	2	
Wheat gluten	..	2	
Malt (non-diastatic)	..	3	
Water	4		
Whole wheat flour	2	..	Add the flour and mix slightly. Add the yeast and mix to a dough. Add the shortening and develop the dough in slow speed
Bread flour (high gluten)	6	..	
Margarine	..	12	
Butter or shortening	..	8	

Procedures to Follow

1. This is a stiff dough. A check should be made for proper consistency soon after the shortening is added and before the dough is fully developed. At this point, it is easier to add more flour or to add more water to obtain the desired dough consistency.

2. Dough temperature: 80 to 82°F. Use cool water to avoid a high dough temperature due to friction in mixing.

3. Dough conditioning: First rise and punch 1½ to 2 hr. Rest dough approximately 40 min. to a second rise and take to the bench or scaler-divider. Do not round up the scaled and divided units.

4. For bench preparation, scale the dough into presses weighing no more than 3 lb. per press. For smaller bread sticks, scale the presses of dough less.

5. The presses are rounded and then allowed to relax for 20 to 30 min. since this is a stiff dough.

6. Divide the presses in the dough divider (36 units of dough). Each unit may then be divided again for smaller bread sticks. The units may also be sent through sheeter to form strips and the strips then cut in half. Little or no flour is necessary for rolling out the strips of dough. In fact, the dough should be slightly moist so that the rolled out stick can be rolled in sesame seeds or other type of garnish before being placed on pans.

7. The bread sticks are placed on pans and spaced about 1 in. apart depending upon the size and thickness of the bread stick. Thinner sticks may be placed closer together. The bread sticks are given a slow proof

and no more than ¾ proof.   If given more or full proof, the sticks will flatten and lose the roundness of shape they should have.

8. Bread sticks are baked in a moderate oven at 390–400°F.   This will allow for a thorough bake, crispness of the bread stick, and maintain a light, golden crust color.   Avoid rapid baking at high temperatures which will cause dark crust colors and softness and collapse of the bread sticks after baking.

Note: Special flavorings may be used in the dough or as a garnish.   For example, garlic salt or celery salt, onion powder blended with salt, and sesame seeds are some of the varieties that can be made.   These are usually placed on the sticks after they are shaped and the variety may be changed.   This will enable the baker to make several varieties from the one dough.

Wheat Grain Bagels

These bagels are enriched with variety grains and natural syrup.   They do not have to be boiled and may be made with variety toppings.   These bagels lend themselves well to freezing and retarding for baking as required.

Ingredients	Lb.	Oz.	Mixing procedure
Yeast (variable)	..	8	Dissolve and set aside
Water	2	..	
Sugar	..	8	Blend ingredients in slow speed to dissolve dry
Salt	..	3	ingredients and to hydrate the coarse grains
Dry skim milk	..	5	
Shortening	..	8	
Malt (non-diastatic)	..	3	
Molasses	..	6	
Soy flour (defatted)	..	4	
Cracked wheat (bran or pumpernickel flour may be substituted)	1	4	
Sour rye culture (dry) (optional)	..	6	
Water	4	..	
Sugar color (variable)			
Whole wheat flour	1	8	Add the flour mix slightly
Bread flour (high gluten) (variable)	9	..	Add the yeast solution and develop the dough in slow speed

Procedures to Follow

1. Dough temperature: 80 to 82°F.   (Keep dough cool.)
2. Allow dough to relax about 45 min. and take to bench for makeup.

3. Scale the dough into presses. The size of the bagel will determine the weight of the press of dough. The average size is approximately 4 lb. 8 oz. per press. Smaller bagels require a lesser amount of dough. Very large or "jumbo" bagels may be scaled at 5½ lb. per press.

4. Because the dough is stiff, little or no dusting flour is necessary. The bench should be free of dusting flour. In fact, if a slight crust forms on the units of dough, it will be necessary to moisten the bench with water when shaping the bagels.

5. The bagels are made by rolling out each unit of dough with the palms of the hands and then sealing the edges in the palm of one hand. It is important to have all the gas pockets removed when rolling the strip of dough. The dough strip should be of even thickness for proper shape of the bagel.

6. The bagels may be dipped into a variety of toppings for greater bagel variety (onion topping, garlic salt, sesame seeds, poppy seeds, left plain or garnished lightly with coarse salt).

7. The bagels are then placed on parchment paper-lined pans and spaced about 1½ in. apart. The bagels may be placed in the retarder or freezer at this point.

8. Units that are to be baked soon after makeup are to be given no more than ¾ proof and baked 410–420 °F.

Natural Egg-Wheat Bread

This dough will result in an enriched and flavorful loaf. The added egg yolks and other enriching ingredients will provide for added volume, smooth grain and texture, and improved keeping qualities. The baker has the option of adding raisins, nuts, dried fruits, and natural grain seeds for further enrichment and variety.

Ingredients	Lb.	Oz.	Mixing procedure
Yeast	..	10	Dissolve the yeast and set aside
Water	2	..	
Sugar	1	..	Soften the butter and margarine and then blend
Salt	..	3	all ingredients together to a smooth, soft con-
Dry skim milk	..	6	sistency
Soy flour (defatted)	..	2	
Wheat germ	..	2	
(toasted)			
Honey (clover)	..	6	
Butter or margarine	..	10	
Shortening	..	8	
Ground nutmeg	..	⅛	
Ground cinnamon	..	¼	
Egg yolks	1	..	Add in two stages and blend in
Water	4	..	Add and stir slightly
Bread flour	9	..	Add the flour and mix lightly. Add the yeast and develop to a smooth dough
Whole wheat flour	2	..	
Raisins (optional, variable, and pre-soaked)	3	..	Add the raisins in the final stages of dough development

Note: The water in which the raisins were soaked may be used to replace part of the water in the dough.

Procedures to Follow

1. This dough should be slightly stiffer than regular white pan bread dough. This will allow for greater volume and enable the dough to support the added raisins, fruits, nuts, etc.
2. Dough temperature: 80 to 82°F.
3. Dough conditioning: First punch—approximately 1½ hr. Allow the dough to rise well again but do not punch. Take to the divider-rounder or to the bench for makeup.
4. Preliminary proofing period of approximately 20 min. should be allowed for complete relaxation of the rounded units before molding the loaves.
5. The dough units may be made up into various sizes and shapes. For the average 1-lb. loaf of baked bread pan size, use 16 oz. of dough. Units may be scaled into smaller sizes. Colorful aluminum foil pans of various sizes and shapes may be used. Round units should be docked or stippled before proofing to avoid formation of large holes or blisters during baking. Twisting or cross-graining strands of dough for loaf pan breads will provide for a more stable structure.

6. Proof the breads to ¾ proof and then wash the tops of the loaves with egg wash or milk. The tops may then be garnished with chopped nuts, bran, or other toppings. The units may then be given slightly more proof.

7. Bake at 370–380°F. Larger units will require a lower baking temperature. Smaller and flatter units will require a slightly higher baking temperature. Loaves are considered baked when they have a slightly hollow sound when tapped. They will also spring back quite firmly to the touch. The average one-pound loaf will require about 45 min. for proper bake. Remove the loaves from the pans soon after they are baked.

Protein Coffee Cake

The protein enrichment ingredients added to the formula for this dough will increase the nutritional value. The flakes of bran and wheat germ will not have a discoloring effect. In fact, the addition of enriched filling ingredients will blend well with the cereal grains. The use of egg whites in the dough will further increase the protein content as well as provide for greater volume.

Ingredients	Lb.	Oz.	Mixing procedure
Yeast (variable)	..	12	Dissolve the yeast and set aside
Water	2	..	
Sugar	1	..	Blend all ingredients to a smooth consistency
Brown sugar	..	8	
Salt	..	2½	
Dry skim milk	..	8	
Soy flour (defatted)	..	3	
Wheat germ (toasted)	..	3	
Bran flour	..	8	
Honey (clover)	..	6	
Cinnamon (ground)	..	¼	
Nutmeg	..	¼	
Butter or margarine	1	4	
Shortening	1	..	
Egg yolks	1	4	Add the eggs in three stages and blend in well
Egg whites	..	12	
Water	2	8	Add to the above and stir slightly. Add the flour and mix lightly. Add the yeast and develop to a smooth dough
Vanilla	..	1	
Bread flour	6	8	
Cake or pastry flour	2	..	

Note: This dough should be slightly softer than the usual sweet roll dough. The bran and wheat germ will tend to absorb moisture during fermentation and dough conditioning.

Procedures to Follow

1. Dough temperature: 80–82°F.
2. Dough conditioning: This dough is rich in sugar, fat, eggs, etc. Thus, additional time for conditioning will be required. This may be reduced by additional yeast and increased water temperature. The first rise and punch will be approximately 2 hr. Allow the dough to rise once again and take to the bench for makeup.
3. Makeup of Units: A complete variety of enriched coffee cakes may be made from this dough. Size of the pans and shape of the pans will determine scaling weights of the dough units. Approximately 20% may be added for the weight of the fillings to be used to fill the units. A blend of chopped nuts, mixed fruits, toasted chopped nuts, grain seeds and bran as a blend, cinnamon sugar, and other fillings (see formulas to follow), will add to the weight. The colorful aluminum foil pans may be used for a variety of sizes and shapes. The baked units are merchandised with the pans.
4. Madeup units are washed with either egg wash or a blend of melted butter, margarine, and shortening. The tops may be garnished with any of the filling blends or the special crumb topping (see formula to follow). Allow the units slightly more than ¾ proof and bake in a moderate oven (350 to 360°F.). Larger units will require a lower temperature. Smaller units can be baked at a slightly higher temperature. The eggs and other enrichment ingredients will make for a large oven spring during the first 10 to 15 min. of baking. This should take place slowly to avoid possible collapse. The units should be baked through thoroughly to avoid side wall collapse and possible shrinkage of the baked unit.

Special Topping, Filling, and Syrup Glaze

A. *Crumb Topping*

Ingredients	Lb.	Oz.	Mixing procedure
Brown sugar	1	..	Blend these ingredients together until soft and smooth
Salt	..	¼	
Honey (clover)	..	4	
Cinnamon	..	½	
Shortening (butter or margarine)	1	4	
Wheat germ (toasted)	..	2	
Cake flour	1	..	Sift the flours. Blend in other ingredients. Add to the above and rub together with palms of the hand or mix at slow speed to form small lumps
Bread flour	1	..	
Bran flakes (optional)	..	2	
Sunflower seeds or toasted chopped nuts	..	6	

If topping is too dry, add melted shortening or butter. If too moist, add a small amount of bread flour and rub together gently. The topping may be forced through a coarse sieve to form uniform lumps.

B. *Special Syrup Wash*

This wash is to be used on products that have been egg-washed, and baked with a nut or cereal bran topping or left plain. It will provide a lustre or shine if applied warm or hot to the baked product.

Ingredients	Lb.	Oz.	Mixing procedure
Granulated sugar	5	..	Stir well to dissolve the sugar. Bring to a boil and boil for 2 or 3 min.
Honey (clover)	..	8	
Water	3	8	
Juice and rind of 2 oranges	..	..	Add to the boiling syrup and boil for 3 min. stirring well
Juice and rind of 2 lemons	..	..	

Note: Avoid extended boiling. This will evaporate part of the water and thicken the syrup. This may lead to crystallization.

C. *Special Filling for Coffee Cakes*

The ingredients listed in the formula are a special blend. They may be changed or adjusted to meet the special requirements of the baker. The special nutritional values of this filling may be used as a part of the merchandising publicity.

Ingredients	Lb.	Oz.
Sugar	5	..
Cinnamon	..	3
Wheat germm (toasted)	..	6
Bran flakes	..	8
Sesame seeds	..	4
Sunflower seeds	..	4
Toasted, chopped peanuts	..	12
Toasted, chopped nuts (variety)	..	12

Mixing procedure

Sift the sugar and cinnamon together for proper blend. Add other ingredients and mix to an even blend

Note: Raisins that have been pre-soaked and drained and other dried mixed fruits may be added. It is advisable to brush the surface of the rolled-out dough units with melted butter or margarine or egg wash before sprinkling the filling over the surface. This will make adherence of the filling better and make handling easier. The use of dried crumbs from stale cakes or sweet breads and rolls is advisable. The crumbs may be blended into the filling or added to the filling when sprinkled over the surface of the dough.

Refer to pages 137–139 and 174–183 for additional information and guidance in the makeup of a variety of coffee cake products.

Date Nut Loaf

This bread is a specialty-enriched loaf and should be merchandised as such. The use of dates, variety nuts, and other enriching ingredients provides for an increase in nutritional values. The baker may adjust the amounts and variety of ingredients as well as the size and shape of the loaf.

Ingredients	Lb.	Oz.	Mixing procedure
Yeast (variable)	..	12	Dissolve the yeast and set aside
Water	2	..	
Brown sugar	..	8	Blend all ingredients together well
Salt	..	3	
Dry skim milk	..	6	
Shortening (butter or margarine may be used)	..	12	
Malt (non-diastatic)	..	3	
Honey (clover)	..	3	
Bran flour	..	8	
Wheat germ (toasted)	..	2	
Wheat gluten (optional)	..	2	
Egg yolks	..	8	
Water	4	..	Add the water and mix lightly
Whole wheat flour	1	8	Add the flour and mix lightly
Bread flour	8	4	Add the yeast and develop the dough. Add the dates and nuts in the final stages of dough development
Chopped dates (granulated pieces may be used)	1	8	
Toasted nut pieces (fine chop) (peanuts, pecans, walnuts)	1	8	

Procedures to Follow

1. Dough temperature: 78–80°F.
2. Dough conditioning: First rise and punch approximately 1½ hr. Second rise approximately 40 min. Do not punch. Take to bench or divider-rounder.
3. Preliminary proofing period approximately 20 min. for complete relaxation. This will allow for easier molding with less chance of tearing due to the nuts, dates and grains.
4. Scale the units in accordance with type and size of pan. The average 1-lb. loaf of white bread pan will require approximately 20 oz. of dough. This may vary depending upon the amount of dates and nuts added to the dough.
5. Give the units ¾ proof before washing with either egg wash or melted fat or butter and then garnishing. The units may be left with a plain top or garnished with finely chopped nuts, bran flakes, wheat germ, etc. The units may be given slightly more proof before baking.

6. Bake the units at 400 to 410°F. with a mild amount of moist steam injected into the oven during the first minutes of baking. Steam may be discontinued after oven spring has been completed. The average 1-lb. loaf will require a full 45 min. of baking time for a solid bake. This is necessary to prevent wall collapse and shrinkage after baking.

Note: Granulated dried dates may be used to replace the fresh dates. This is advantageous in that these dates will not smear during the final dough development. It will be necessary to increase the water by approximately 6 to 8 oz. to allow for increased absorption by the dried date pieces.

Enriched Frozen Dough

Frozen doughs can be specially prepared doughs, often using fermented sweet yeast doughs as a base, that are leavened by both yeast and baking powder. The dough is quite rich in sugar, eggs, fat, and lends itself well to the addition of special grains and other nutritious ingredients. The dough is conditioned before use by refrigerating and the madeup units may be further conditioned by retarding or freezing and baking as production requires.

Ingredients	Lb.	Oz.	Mixing procedure
Yeast (variable)	..	8–	Dissolve the yeast and set aside
	..	12	
Water	2	..	
Conditioned sweet yeast dough or coffee cake dough	6	..	Blend all ingredients in this stage well to break up and distribute the conditioned dough and to soften the flakes and other cereal grains
Sugar	2	..	
Salt	..	2	
Dry skim milk	..	12	
Soy flour (defatted)	..	4	
Wheat germ (toasted)	..	6	
Bran flour	1	4	
Honey (clover)	..	8	
Baker's cheese	2		
Shortening	1	8	
Butter or margarine	2	..	
Egg yolks	2	..	Add the eggs in 3 stages and blend well
Egg whites	1	..	
Vanilla	..	2	Add the vanilla and blend in. Sift the flour and baking powder together. Add and mix lightly. Add yeast and develop dough
Bread flour (variable)	4	8	
Baking powder	..	2	

Procedures to Follow

1. Dough temperature: 76–78°F. Keep the dough cool.
2. *Special Notes:* Cottage cheese may be used to replace the bakers cheese. A slight increase in flour will be necessary because of the added moisture content of the cheese. If no conditioned dough base is used, increase the amount of yeast used and increase the baking powder by ½ to 1 oz. The dough requires time for conditioning. This is usually done by placing the dough in the retarder for a day. The yeast will act slowly, and conditioning and mellowing of the gluten in the dough takes place. The cheese will tend to lower the pH and this will also have a softening or conditioning effect upon the dough. The dough may then be placed in the freezer if makeup is to be postponed.
3. The dough may be made up into units similar to those made from Danish pastry dough. Fillings may be those used in the enriched coffee cake dough units or babkas. The fillings will blend well with the bran flakes and wheat germ so that these grains may lose their appearance and yet increase the nutritive value of the product. Refer to pages 156–165 for information and procedures for the makeup of variety Danish pastries. These and similar units may be made from the frozen dough.
4. Madeup units may be brushed with melted butter or margarine and garnished with a variety of toppings, such as toasted chopped nuts, bran, wheat germ, special crumb topping, etc., before baking or placing the units in the retarder or freezer for later baking.
5. Units should be given a very slow or moderate proof without excessive use of steam in the proof box. In fact, if time permits, a slow proof at shop temperature may be best. This will avoid possible tearing of the dough and gaseous expenditure by the action of the baking powder.
6. The units, depending upon the size, are baked at 390°F. The units should have a mild crispness to the crust when baked. Units are usually dusted lightly with confectionery sugar when cool.

Sweet Wheat Rolls

This whole wheat and grain-enriched dough can be used for many of the sweet roll varieties and soft buns. The dough may also be used for a variety of filled buns and sweet rolls.

Ingredients	Lb.	Oz.	Mixing procedure
Yeast (variable)	..	8	Dissolve the yeast and set aside
Water	2	..	
Sugar	1	2	Blend all ingredients together to a smooth
Salt	..	2½	consistency
Dry skim milk	..	8	
Soy flour (defatted)	..	2	
Wheat germ	..	3	
Honey (clover)	..	6	
Potato flour	..	4	
Bran flour	..	4	
Shortening	1	6	
Yolks	..	8	Add in two stages and blend well
Whole eggs	..	8	
Water	2	8	Add and mix in lightly
Vanilla extract	..	1	
Lemon flavor	..	1	
Whole wheat flour	2	..	Add the flour and mix lightly
Bread flour	5	4	Add the yeast and develop the dough

Note: If raisins (pre-soaked) and mixed fruits are to be added to the dough, as for hot cross buns, they should be added in the final stages of dough development.

Procedures to Follow

1. Dough temperature: 78–80°F. Dough should be kept on the cool side because of the make-up time factor.
2. Dough conditioning: First rise and punch approximately 1½ hr. Allow dough to rise well once again and take to bench or divider rounder for scaling and makeup preparation.
3. For units to be made into cinnamon buns and other types of sweet rolls requiring the dough to be rolled out, the units of dough may be scaled into pieces weighing from 4 to 8 lb. These dough units are formed into rectangular shapes and allowed to relax before rolling. These units may also be retarded for makeup at a later time. Dough presses for rounded varieties or pocket type varieties may be scaled from 2½ to 3½ lb. per press, depending upon the size required. Refer to pages 140–154 for bun varieties and for information regarding their makeup. The enriched filling and topping listed with the Grandmother's loaf may be used for further enrichment of the sweet roll varieties.
4. Madeup units should be given ¾ proof and then washed and garnished or filled. The units may then be given slightly more proof before baking.
5. Units should be baked at approximately 400°F. Smaller units will require less time for baking.

6. Note is made of the fact that the bran flakes and other grains will not be obvious in the cinnamon-filled buns or rolls. In the plain variety, the bran particles will be slightly noticeable but will also impart a nut-like flavor and taste to the product.
7. Baked units that do not have a crumb topping may be washed with special syrup wash and then iced with a simple icing or fondant.

Combination Wheat Biscuits

The term "combination" refers to the fact that these specially enriched biscuits are leavened by yeast and baking powder and baking soda. This makes possible a light, fine-grained, and tender biscuit containing the enriching grains, honey, and molasses in the formula.

Ingredients	Lb.	Oz.	Mixing procedure
Yeast (variable)	..	6	Dissolve the yeast and set aside
Water	2	..	
Sugar	..	12	Blend these ingredients to a smooth consis-
Salt	..	2½	tency
Dry skim milk	..	8	
Shortening	1	4	
Wheat germ (toasted)	..	3	
Soy flour (defatted)	..	4	
Honey (clover)	..	4	
Molasses	..	4	
Cinnamon	..	¼	
Baking soda	..	½	
Eggs (yolks)	..	8	Add the eggs in 2 stages and blend well
Whole eggs	..	4	
Water	2	..	Add and mix lightly
Whole wheat flour	1	..	Sift the flours and baking powder. Add the flour and mix lightly. Add the yeast and develop to a smooth dough. Add the raisins in the final stage of dough development
Bran flour	..	8	
Bread flour	4	..	
Cake or pastry flour	1	4	
Baking powder	..	2¼	
Raisins (optional) pre-soaked)	2	..	

Procedures to Follow

1. Dough temperature: 78–80°F. Keep the dough on the cool side. This will tend to control the gassing effect of the chemical leavening agents used in the dough.

2. Dough conditioning: Allow the dough to relax for 20 to 30 min. before sheeting or rolling out on the bench.

3. At this time, large units of dough may be shaped into rectangular shape and retarded.

4. The sheeted or rolled out dough should be about ½ in. thick and the biscuits cut out. The scrap dough should be blended with part of the fresh or unrolled dough and sheeted again and biscuits cut out. The remaining dough should be formed into a rectangular shape together with the scrap dough.

5. Allow the dough to relax for about 15 min. before sheeting again. The biscuits may be cut into squares with a pastry wheel to avoid remaining scrap dough.

6. Biscuits may be washed with egg wash or brushed with melted butter or margarine. The biscuits may then be garnished with bran flakes, sesame seeds, sunflower seeds, cinnamon sugar, or just left plain.

7. Allow the biscuits to rise slightly (½ proof) before baking. Bake at 400 to 410°F. Smaller biscuits may be baked at a higher temperature to prevent overbaking or drying out. The biscuits will have considerable oven spring in that the leavening effect of the yeast and chemical leavening will jointly release the gas causing the biscuits to rise and expand. The baking soda will work with the natural acids present in the honey and molasses. This will cause a leavening effect as well as partially reduce the pH.

Wheat Muffins

Ingredients	Lb.	Oz.	Mixing procedure
Sugar	..	14	Blend these ingredients to a soft, smooth consistency
Salt	..	1	sistency
Dry skim milk	..	6	
Molasses (dark)	..	12	
Honey (clover)	..	4	
Soy flour (defatted)	..	2	
Wheat germ (toasted)	..	2	
Shortening	..	12	
Cinnamon	..	¼	
Eggs	..	12	Add in 2 stages and cream in
Water	3		Dissolve the baking soda in the water and stir in
Baking soda	..	1	in
Whole wheat flour	..	12	Blend the flours. Add and stir into the above
Bran flour	..	8	
Cake flour	1	4	Sift the flours and baking powder. Add and mix smooth
Bread flour	1	2	mix smooth
Baking powder	..	1¼	
Raisins (pre-soaked)	1	..	Add and mix into the above in the final stages of mixing. Avoid overmixing
Chopped nuts (toasted)	..	8	
Diced mixed fruits (optional)	..	8	

Note: The batter will be quite soft and may lead to overmixing. This is to be avoided to eliminate a stringy gluten development. Adjustment may be made in the amount of bran and other enrichment grains and ingredients added.

Procedures to Follow

1. The batter is usually dropped out into well greased muffin pans. Finger-type pans or tart pans may be used. Some bakers may prefer to use cup cake liners rather than grease muffin pans. Colorful liners are attractive.
2. When using an automatic dropper, be sure the raisins and nuts are well distributed in the batter. A slight adjustment in the liquid content may be necessary if the batter stands for a period before dropping out.
3. The whole grains and bran will tend to absorb liquid and have a tendency to bind or tighten the mix.
4. This batter may be used for loaves baked in small, rectangular pans or in large sheet pans. The baked sheet pan muffin batter is usually cut into squares while still warm and served.

5. The muffins, sheet, or loaves may be garnished with bran flakes, sesame seeds, diced fruits, and similar toppings before baking.
6. Muffins should be baked at 390 to 400°F. Larger units are baked at a slightly lower temperature. The average muffin will take approximately 15 min. to bake and will spring back gently to the touch when gently depressed in the center.

Granola Muffins

Ingredients	Lb.	Oz.	Mixing procedure
Brown sugar	1	8	Blend these ingredients to a soft, smooth con-
Salt	..	1¼	sistency
Dry skim milk	..	6	
Soy flour (defatted)	..	3	
Wheat germm (toasted)	..	3	
Potato flour	..	4	
Oatmeal (rolled oats)	..	6	
Honey (clover)	..	8	
Shortening	1	2	
Eggs	1	8	Add the eggs in 3 stages and cream well after each addition. Dissolve the baking soda in the water and stir into the above
Water	2	..	
Baking soda	..	¼	
Whole wheat flour	..	12	Blend the flours and cinnamon and mix lightly
Yellow cornmeal (coarse)	..	12	into the above
Cinnamon	..	½	
Water	2	..	Sift the flour and baking powder together.
Vanilla	..	1	Add alternately with the water-vanilla and mix
Cake flour	3	4	smooth
Baking powder	..	3	

Note: Raisins, toasted, ground or chopped nuts, sunflower seeds, diced fruits may be added in the final stages of mixing.

Procedures to Follow

1. Deposit the batter in greased muffin pans or paper lined pans.
2. Garnish with nuts, fruits, seeds.
3. Bake at 400°F. Remove the muffins from the pans while still slightly warm.

Enriched Irish Bread and Scones

This is a standard formula for Irish soda bread and scones that has been protein-enriched with addition of protein grains.   The baker may further enrich the formula with the addition of raisins, fruits, sunflower seeds, and other enriching ingredients.   The units may be made up into regular scones, round breads that are scored or cut, or made into round, flat units that are cut or sectioned in triangles.

Ingredients	Lb.	Oz.	Mixing procedure
Sugar	1	2	Blend these ingredients to a smooth consis-
Salt	..	1½	tency
Dry skim milk	..	8	
Soy flour (defatted)	..	3	
Potato flour	..	3	
Wheat germ	..	2	
(toasted)			
Bran flour	..	3	
Shortening	1	2	
Honey (clover)	..	6	
Baking soda	..	2	
Eggs	1	..	Add in 3 stages and cream in
Water	4	4	Add and mix in lightly
Bread flour	4	12	Sift the flours and cream of tartar together.
Cake flour	2	..	Add and mix to a smooth dough
Cream of tartar	..	3	
(tartaric acid)			
Raisins and mixed	4	..	Add in the final stage of mixing
fruits and nuts			
(optional)			

Procedures to Follow

1. The size of the pan will determine the weight of each of the units. Usually, 7-in. pans will require approximately 1 lb. of dough.   Smaller round pie tins may be used and these are scaled less.   Units that are flatter and divided into triangles to be broken apart as scones may be scaled according to the size of the pan.   The units may also be placed on parchment paper lined sheet pans and spaced four or six units to a sheet pan.   Be sure there is at least 2 to 3 in. of space between each unit when placing on the pans.
2. Round up the scaled units and allow them to relax for about 15 to 20 min.
3. Roll out the units to approximately ¾ in. thickness and place into the individual pans or on the larger sheet pans.   Be sure the thickness is even. With a hand scraper make 6 to 8 cuts into each of the units cutting almost through to the bottom.   This will allow for separation after baking.   Units

that are to be baked as whole breads are rolled thicker and then cut across the top.

4. The tops of the scones are washed with either egg wash or melted butter or margarine before baking. The round breads are scored across and brushed with egg wash or milk before dusting lightly with cake flour. This will provide for a more home-made effect.

5. Allow the units to relax for 15 to 20 min. before baking at approximately 425°F. The high temperature is required to get the maximum leavening at a rapid rate to cause the raising effect and light, porous grain and texture. Egg-washed units may have the oven temperature reduced slightly in the final stages of baking to avoid a dark crust color formation. Units are considered baked when they spring back to the touch when depressed gently in the center.

Home-Style Wheat Doughnuts

These doughnuts are leavened by yeast and baking powder. They are enriched with the added proteins contained in the grains and special flours. A variety of shapes may be made from this dough which will increase the merchandising value of the variety. Refer to pages 208–222 for information regarding the production of variety doughnuts.

Ingredients	Lb.	Oz.	Mixing procedure
Yeast (variable)	. .	8	Dissolve the yeast and set aside
Water	2	. .	
Sugar	. .	8	Blend the ingredients in this stage together to
Salt	. .	2	a smooth consistency
Dry skim milk	. .	6	
Soy flour (defatted)	. .	3	
Potato flour	. .	4	
Wheat germ	. .	2	
Shortening	1	4	
Honey (clover)	. .	6	
Eggs (part yolks)	1	. .	Add in 2 stages and blend
Water	2	. .	Add and mix in lightly
Vanilla	. .	2	
Cake flour	2	8	Sift the flours and baking powder together.
Bread flour	5	4	Add and mix lightly. Add the yeast and de-
Baking powder	. .	2	velop to a smooth dough

Note: This dough will be rolled out on the bench or sent through the sheeter and then cut into doughnuts. The dough must be of medium stiff consistency to avoid stickiness and excessive use of dusting flour. The dough should be checked for consistency in the final stages of mixing to determine the need for additional liquid or flour.

Procedures to Follow

1. Dough temperature: 78–80°F. Dough should be kept on the cool side. It may be advisable to chill the dough before rolling or sheeting.
2. Dough conditioning: Allow the dough to relax for approximately 30 min. to permit yeast activity and increased pH to mellow the gluten. This will make rolling or sheeting easier.
3. Roll or sheet the dough to about ⅜ to ½ in. thickness and then cut out the doughnuts for the ring shape variety. Smaller or miniature doughnuts should be rolled out thinner. If the centers are to be fried for merchandising as doughnut balls, they should be removed while the doughnuts are picked up and placed on pans.
4. The scrap dough should be blended with the remaining unrolled dough and scaled into presses weighing from 2½ to 3 lb. per press. They may be scaled at a lesser or greater weight depending upon the size required. The divided press units (36 per press) may be shaped into twist, bowtie, longjohn units.
5. The regular dough may also be formed into units of 4 to 6 pounds and of rectangular shape. After relaxing, these dough units may be rolled out or sheeted to about ½ in. thickness and then cut into rectangular shapes with a pastry wheel about 1½ inches wide and 4 inches long or longer. These are used for doughnut eclairs.
6. Allow the doughnuts to relax from 20 to 30 min. They will feel mildly gassy (about ½ proof).
7. Fry at 380–385°F. BE SURE TO CHECK FOR PROPER FRYING FAT TEMPERATURE BEFORE PLACING DOUGHNUTS INTO FAT.
8. The doughnuts may be finished in a variety of icings or coatings.

Wheat Grain Doughnuts

This is a cake-type doughnut leavened chemically. While the dough is usually rolled out on the bench or sheeted before cutting out the doughnuts, the formula may be adjusted so that it may be automatically dropped into the frying fat through the doughnut dropper. This will require a slight increase in the liquid and an adjustment in the ratio of bread flour to cake flour (50% of each suggested).

Ingredients	Lb.	Oz.	Mixing procedure
Brown sugar	1	4	Blend the ingredients to a smooth consis-
Salt	..	1½	tency
Dry skim milk	..	8	
Bran flour	..	3	
Wheat germ (toasted)	..	3	
Soy flour (defatted)	..	3	
Potato flour	..	4	
Shortening	..	12	
Molasses	..	12	
Cinnamon	..	½	
Baking soda	..	½	
Eggs (part yolks)	1	..	Add in 2 stages and blend in well
Water	4	..	Add and mix in lightly
Vanilla	..	1½	
Whole wheat flour	2	8	Sift the flours together for an even blend with
Bread flour	2	..	the baking powder. Add and mix to a smooth
Cake flour	1	8	dough
Baking powder	..	5	

Procedures to Follow

1. The dough is removed and divided into two equal pieces and formed into rectangular shape.
2. Allow the dough units to relax for about 20 min. and then roll out on the bench or send through the sheeter.
3. If a die cutter (multiple cutter) is used be sure to adjust the cutters to cut through the dough completely. Use sufficient dusting flour to avoid sticking. Cut the doughnuts about ⅜ to ½ in. thick.
4. Dough centers are removed when the doughnuts are separated and fried as separate doughnut balls for merchandising.
5. Scrap dough is worked lightly into fresh dough or blended with other scrap dough. After the second rolling or sheeting, it is advisable to remix the scrap dough when a fresh doughnut dough is mixed. This will avoid doughnuts that are tough and have poor volume when fried.
6. Allow the cut out doughnuts to relax for 15 to 20 min. and then fry (doughnuts on travelling belts should be timed accordingly before dropping into the hot fat). Doughnuts sent through the automatic dropper into the hot fat should be checked for cutting consistency and evenness when coming out of the dropper. Adjustment in dough or batter consistency may be advisable for a smooth even cut or drop.
7. Since these doughnuts are sweeter (more sugar and molasses) they should be fried at a slightly lower frying temperature (375 to 380°F). This will avoid a very dark crust color. Frying time is about the same as for regular

cake doughnuts (45 to 60 sec. on each side). It is advisable to check the doughnuts periodically for proper frying internally.

8. These doughnuts may be finished by rolling in cinnamon sugar or coating with a blend of confectionery sugar and starches.

Enriched Cake Doughnuts

This formula may be adjusted for bench type rolling by increasing the dough consistency through the addition of flour. Primarily, this formula is for direct dropping into the frying fat. Adjustment may have to be made to meet the machining operation of the dropper.

Ingredients	Lb.	Oz.	*Mixing procedure*
Sugar	3	..	Blend the dry ingredients with a part of the eggs to blend to a smooth consistency
Salt	..	2½	
Dry skim milk	..	8	
Soy flour (defatted)	..	4	
Wheat germ (toasted)	..	4	
Nutmeg (optional)	..	½	
Shortening	..	10	
Egg yolks	1	..	Add the remaining eggs in 3 stages and blend
Whole eggs	1	..	in
Water (variable)	5	..	Add half the water and flavor and mix light-
Vanilla	..	1½	ly
Lemon flavor	..	1	
Cake flour	7	..	Sift the flours and baking powder together.
Bread flour	3	..	Add and mix lightly. Add the balance of the
Baking powder	..	6	water and mix to a smooth batter

Procedures to Follow

1. Fry the doughnuts at 380–385°F.
2. If the batter remains standing for awhile before dropping out, it is advisable to mix lightly to remove gas pocket formation which will result in uneven dropping and uneven doughnut size.
3. The doughnuts may be finished in a variety of ways for merchandising.

QUICK BREADS

Quick breads that are enriched with added cereals, grains, seeds, nuts and fruits, are popular in the natural and enriched food marketing sections of bakeshops and supermarkets. They are chemically leavened, and production of the quick bread specialties is rapid. Variations in size, shape, and colorful packaging make these products attractive to the consumer. Bakers, large and small, are now producing these special breads with increasing sales.

Basic Quick Bread

Ingredients	Lb.	Oz.	Mixing procedure
Sugar	2	8	Blend these ingredients to a soft, smooth con-
Salt	..	1	sistency
Dry skim milk	..	6	
Soy flour (defatted)	..	2	
Wheat germ (toasted)	..	2	
Bran flour	..	6	
Shortening	1	..	
Butter or margarine	..	12	
Honey (clover)	..	8	
Egg yolks	..	12	Add the eggs in 3 stages and cream in well
Whole eggs	..	12	
Water	3	..	Add alternately with the flour
Vanilla	..	1	
Cake flour	4	6	Sift the flour and baking powder together.
Baking powder	..	3½	Add alternately with the water and mix until smooth

Note: If raisins, dried fruits, and nut pieces are to be added for variety, replace 1 lb. of the cake flour with 1 lb. of bread flour. This will provide for an increase in consistency and support. Thus, sinking of fruits and nut pieces to the bottom of the baked loaf or quick bread will be avoided.

Procedures to Follow

1. Pans should be filled approximately ½ full or just slightly more. Units that are filled much beyond the halfway mark may tend to peak in the center. They may also run over the sides of the pan during baking. Scale the amount of batter into each pan after establishing the exact weight desired for each size pan used. Adjust the automatic dropper-scaler and check pans for weight periodically. Special aluminum foil pans are often used and the quick breads are merchandised with the pans.
2. Quick breads are usually garnished on top before baking. This is to identify the type of quick bread as well as adding to the nutritive value. For example, bran flakes, sunflower seeds, sesame seeds, and dried fruits are used to distinguish types.
3. The quick breads are baked at moderate temperatures approximately 375°F. Larger units or deeper (higher) units will require a lower temperature. Smaller units baked in shallow pans are baked at slightly higher temperatures. Very often, shallow pans may be placed on sheet pans to avoid a strong bottom or dark bottom crust color.

4. A variety of different quick breads may be made from the basic quick bread batter by adding a variety of nuts, raisins, and fruits, as well as special fillings such as peanut butter. The following are suggested quick bread varieties that may be produced from the basic quick bread mix.

Prune Quick Bread

Sweet, pitted prunes weighing approximately 3 lb. should be soaked for about 15 min. in cool water and drained. Chop the prunes finely and add to the batter in the final stages of mixing. Sour pitted prunes will create a tart taste. Replace 1 lb. of the cake flour with 1 lb. of bread flour for better support of the chopped prunes.

Raisin-Nut Quick Bread

Two to three pounds of pre-soaked raisins and approximately 2 lb. of toasted, chopped peanuts are added in the final stages of mixing. The water used for soaking the raisins may replace part of the water in the formula. The "raisin juice" contains some of the nutrients extracted from the raisins. Other types of chopped nuts (pecans, walnuts) that have been toasted may be used. The raisins and nuts are mixed into the batter in the final stages of mixing. Replace some of the cake flour with bread flour to support the fruits and nuts. Bake at a slightly lower oven temperature depending upon size and shape of the pans.

Date-Nut Quick Bread

Add approximately 2 lb. of chopped, pitted dates and 1½ lb. of toasted, chopped nuts to the batter in the final stages of mixing. It is advisable to toss the nuts together with the dates to separate large clumps and make distribution even during the final mixing. Garnish the tops of the quick breads with chopped nuts before baking. It is also advisable to add approximately ½ oz. of cinnamon to the batter for taste variety and flavor.

Apricot-Nut Quick Bread

Soak approximately 2 to 3 lb. of dried apricots in cool water for about ½ hour. Drain the apricots and chop into fine pieces. Add 1½ lb. of toasted, chopped nuts to the apricots and toss or mix lightly to blend. Add to the basic batter in the final stages of mixing. Add some bread flour (pound for pound) to replace some of the cake flour.

Peanut Butter Quick Bread

One pound of fine, creamy peanut butter is creamed into the batter with the sugar, shortening and other ingredients in the first stage of mixing. If a chunky, or coarse peanut butter is used, it is best added with the first stage of the water that is added before the flour is added. In addition, approximately 1 lb. of chopped dates and one pound of chopped, toasted nut pieces may be added with the peanut butter for variety.

While other quick breads may be made from the basic batter, those requiring increased additions of bran, wheat grains, coarse grains, syrups such as molasses and honey in larger amounts, are best made with a separate and special formulation. The formulas that follow are those requiring special cereals and grains and a separate formula is provided for each. Bakers may make revisions to meet special consumer demands. These will often mean the addition of more or a greater variety of grains, flavors, and spices. Experiment is encouraged in this respect.

Wheat-Grain Quick Bread

Ingredients	Lb.	Oz.	Mixing procedure
Brown sugar	1	4	Blend these ingredients together to a soft, smooth consistency
Salt	..	1	
Dry skim milk	..	8	
Soy flour (defatted)	..	3	
Wheat germ (toasted)	..	4	
Rye meal (coarse pumpernickel flour)	..	6	
Shortening	1	..	
Molasses	1	8	
Cinnamon	..	½	
Eggs (part yolks)	..	12	Add in 2 stages and cream in
Water	4	..	
Baking soda		1½	Dissolve the soda in the water
Bran flour	1	..	Sift the flour and baking powder together. Add the bran and blend. Add alternately with the water and mix smooth
Bread flour	1	4	
Cake flour	1	4	
Baking powder	..	1	
Raisins (optional)	2	..	Add in final stages of mixing

Note: The batter will be quite soft and perhaps difficult to drop out by hand. The batter will get thicker as it stands since the bran and other grains will absorb liquid.

Procedures to Follow

1. Drop out into greased muffin pans or paper-lined muffin pans. The tops may be garnished with bran flakes before baking. For the loaf pans, fill the pans no more than half full.
2. Bake at 370 to 375°F.
3. Bake on double pans to avoid a dark bottom crust formation.

Banana Quick Bread

Ingredients	Lb.	Oz.	Mixing procedure
Sugar	1	8	Blend these ingredients to a soft, smooth con-
Salt	..	1	sistency
Dry skim milk	..	4	
Wheat germ (toasted)	..	4	
Soy flour (defatted)	..	2	
Bran flour	..	4	
Honey (clover)	..	8	
Shortening	1	4	
Baking soda	..	½	
Egg yolks	..	12	Add the eggs in 3 stages and cream in well
Whole eggs	..	12	
Mashed ripe bananas	4	..	Add the bananas and vanilla and blend in
Vanilla	..	1	
Cake flour	2	..	Sift the flours and baking powder together.
Bread flour	2	3	Add to the above and mix smooth
Baking powder	..	2½	

Note: Ripe bananas, even over-ripe bananas, should be used. They supply a better taste and flavor to the product. Green bananas should not be used. Dried bananas or banana flakes may be used. Follow the instructions for using the banana flakes or powder before adding to the mix.

Procedures to Follow

1. Additional moisture may be required when using the flakes. For variety, add 1½ pounds of toasted chopped nuts to the batter.
2. Deposit the batter into variety loaves or round pans.
3. Bake at 360–370° F. depending upon the size and depth of the pan.

Corn-Meal Quick Bread

Ingredients	Lb.	Oz.	Mixing procedure
Sugar	1	8	Blend these ingredients to a soft, smooth con-
Salt	..	1½	sistency
Dry skim milk	..	8	
Soy flour (defatted)	..	4	
Wheat germm (toasted)	..	4	
Bran flour	1	..	
Honey (clover)	1	..	
Cinnamon	..	½	
Shortening	1	8	
Egg yolks	1	..	Add the eggs in 3 stages and cream in well
Whole eggs	..	8	
Water	4	8	Add half the water and mix lightly
Vanilla (optional)	..	1	
Yellow cornmeal	1	8	Sift the flours and baking powder and blend with the corn meal. Add alternately with the water and mix smooth
Bread flour	1	..	
Cake flour	2	8	
Baking powder	..	4½	

Note: Yellow corn meal is preferred to the white corn meal. It provides for a yellow tinge or color and its coarseness provides for better taste and flavor of corn.

Procedures to Follow

1. Deposit batter into loaf pans or round pans. Individual aluminum foil pans make for better merchandising.
2. Bake the units at 380 to 385°F. depending on the size of the pan and thickness of the unit.
3. This batter may be used for baking corn bread in sheet pans or for corn muffins baked in muffin tins.

Pizza[1]

At one time, pizza was sold only through pizzerias. Today, with its increasing popularity, it is also sold through restaurants, grocery stores, bars, and bakeries.

Pizza is a food of many variations. We discuss here some of the major differences.

Most people classify pizzas by the variations in crust. For instance, there are thick crust pizzas and thin crust pizzas; round pizzas and square; rich (high shortening content) dough and lean dough. Typically, the thick crust or deep pan pizza is known as the Sicilian pizza and the thin crust pizza is called the neapolitan pizza.

The "basic pizza crust" is a lean bread dough made from high-gluten flour, water, sugar, salt, shortening, and yeast. The last four ingredients are generally less than four percent each. However, in recent years, many pizza bakers have been experimenting with additional ingredients and, also, have been increasing the sugar/shortening content for a richer dough.

Different methods can be utilized for "rolling out" the crust. Of course, the most basic method is by hand pressing, slapping, and spinning the dough from a ball shape to the round thin crust or skin, as it is sometimes called. For uniformity in dough thickness, a rolling pin can be used. If exact uniformity is desired, a dough roller or sheeter is necessary. The dough can be scaled and rounded into balls several hours in advance of rolling or it can be held in a large batch. With the large batch method, pieces of dough are pulled from the batch, run through a sheeter, and then cut to the shape of the pan immediately prior to baking.

Traditionally, a pizza was made on a wooden peel and then slid onto a stone hearth, or the oven deck. Cornmeal, sprinkled on the peel prior to laying down the dough, allowed the baker to slide the pizza from the peel onto the deck. Today, many bakers have eliminated the use of cornmeal. In its place the baker uses a pan, screen, or silicone-treated paper.

The sauce is made from tomato sauce, paste, or puree, or a combination thereof. Typical spices for pizza sauce are oregano, basil, fennel, thyme, black pepper, white or red pepper, garlic, and onion. Some pizza bakers simmer the sauce with the spices.

The traditional cheese for pizza is mozzarella. However, bakers frequently blend in other cheeses such as Muenster, brick, and Monterey jack.

Almost anything can go on top of pizza. Some of the common toppings are pepperoni or pizza sausage, ham, fresh pork sausage (Italian sausage), mushrooms, onions, green peppers, hamburger, olives, bacon, and anchovies.

Thin crust pizzas are usually baked at 550°F; thick crust at about 450°F. Generally, a pizza is considered done when the bottom crust is golden-brown.

Source: John D. Correll, President, Pizzuti's, Inc., Canton, Michigan.

Lean Pizza Dough

Ingredients	Lb.	Oz.	mixing procedure
Water (warm— 80°F)	6	..	Dissolve sugar, salt and yeast in warm water. Let yeast bloom 10–20 min.
Salt	..	2½	
Yeast (granulated)	..	8	
Vegetable oil	..	2½	Add to yeast solution
Bread flour (high gluten)	10	..	Add to yeast solution and mix/knead for 10 min. on low speed

Procedures to Follow

1. If necessary after mixing, add additional flour to increase firmness of the dough. When lifted, the finished dough should just slightly pull away from the sides of the bowl.
2. Bench rest 15 min.
3. Divide and round into balls. To prevent crusting, brush with oil. A 12-in. round pizza requires a 10-oz. ball of dough; a 14-in. pizza, a 13-oz. ball; a 16-in. pizza, an 18-oz. ball.

Pizza Sauce

Ingredients	Lb.	Oz.	Mixing procedure
1 No. 10 can of tomato sauce	..	..	Mix together all ingredients. For thicker sauce, add tomato paste.
Salt	..	1	
Granulated sugar	..	½	
Ground black pepper	..	¼	
Whole basil	..	1/20	
Whole oregano	..	1/20	
Garlic powder	..	½	
Ground Romano	..	⅓	

Procedures to Follow

1. Use sauce in the following amounts: for a 12-in. round pizza, use 3 oz. of sauce; for a 14-in. pizza, 4½ oz. sauce; for a 16-in. pizza, 6 oz. of sauce.
2. Add ground or shredded mozzarella cheese in the following proportions: for a 12-in. round pizza, 4 oz. cheese; for a 14-in. pizza, 5½ oz. cheese; for a 16-in. pizza, 7½ oz. cheese.

Appendix

Approximate Baking Temperature for Bakery Products

Product	Temperature, °F.
Bread and Rolls	
Heavy rye bread	425–430
Pan bread	400–410
Vienna bread	400–425
Vienna rolls and hard rolls	425–430
Raisin bread	385–395
Challah	350
Sweet rolls	400–410
Cakes	
High-ratio cake	
Layers	365–370
Sheets	365–375
Loaves	365–370
Cups	370–380
Sponge cake	
Layers	375–385
Sheets	375–385
Loaves	360–375
Cups	370–380
Jelly roll	400–410
Wine cake	
Layers	375–385
Sheets	375–385
Loaves	365–375
Cups	375–385
Angel cake	
Small (6 × 3 in.)	370–380
Large (9 × 3$^1/_2$ in.)	360–365
Pound cake	
Small (1 lb.)	370–375
Medium	360–365
Large	350–360
Extra-large	330–340
Cheese cake	
French-type	370–380
California	325–340
Cookies	
Sugar, Oatmeal, Lemon, Chocolate	400–410
Molasses, Fruit bars, Butter	380–385
Cocoanut and Almond Macaroons	375–385
Kisses	275
Pies	
Fruit pies	425–450
Sweet Yeast Products	
Buns	400–415
Danish	385–400
Puff pastry	400–410

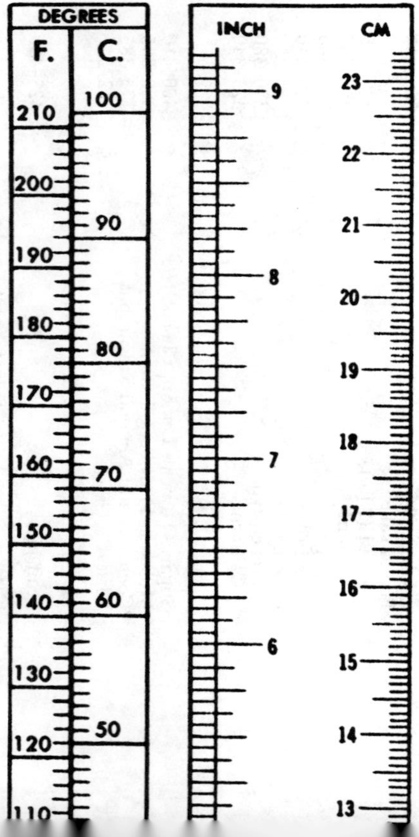

Conversion Factors

Length

1 centimeter	....	0.394 inch
1 inch	....	2.540 centimeters
1 meter	....	3.2808 feet
1 foot	....	0.305 meter
1 meter	....	1.0936 yards
1 yard	....	0.9144 meter
1 kilometer	....	0.62137 mile
1 mile	....	1.60935 kilometers

Area

1 square centimeter	....	0.1550 square inch
1 square inch	....	6.452 square centimeters
1 square meter	....	10.764 square feet
1 square foot	....	0.09290 square meter
1 square meter	....	1.1960 square yards
1 square yard	....	0.8361 square meter
1 square kilometer	....	0.3861 square mile
1 square mile	....	2.590 square kilometers
1 acre (U.S.)	....	4840 square yards

Volume

1 cubic centimeter	....	0.0610 cubic inch
1 cubic inch	....	16.3872 cubic centimeters
1 cubic meter	....	35.314 cubic feet
1 cubic foot	....	0.02832 cubic meter
1 cubic meter	....	1.3079 cubic yards
1 cubic yard	....	0.7646 cubic meter

FIG. A.1.   CONVERSION FACTORS

Capacity

1 milliliter	0.03382 ounce (U.S. liquid)
1 ounce (U.S. liquid)	29.573 milliliters
1 milliliter	0.2705 dram (U.S. Apothecaries;
1 dram (U.S. Apothecaries) . . .	3.6967 milliliters
1 liter	1.05671 quarts (U.S. liquid)
1 quart (U.S. liquid)	0.94633 liter
1 liter	0.26418 gallon (U.S. liquid)
1 gallon (U.S. liquid)	3.78533 liters

Mass

1 gram	15.4324 grains
1 grain	0.0648 gram
1 gram	0.03527 ounce (Avoirdupois)
1 ounce (Avoirdupois) . . .	28.3495 grams
1 gram	0.03215 ounce (Troy)
1 ounce (Troy)	31.10348 grams
1 kilogram	2.20462 pounds (Avoirdupois)
1 pound (Avoirdupois)	0.45359 kilogram

Power

1 watt	0.73756 foot pound per second
1 foot pound per second	1.35582 watts
1 watt	0.056884 BTU per minute
1 BTU per minute	17.580 watts
1 watt	0.001341 horsepower (U.S.)
1 horsepower (U.S.)	745.7 watts
1 watt	0.01433 kilogram-calorie per minute
1 kilogram-calorie per minute	69.767 watts
1 watt	1×10^7 ergs per second
1 lumen	0.001496 watt

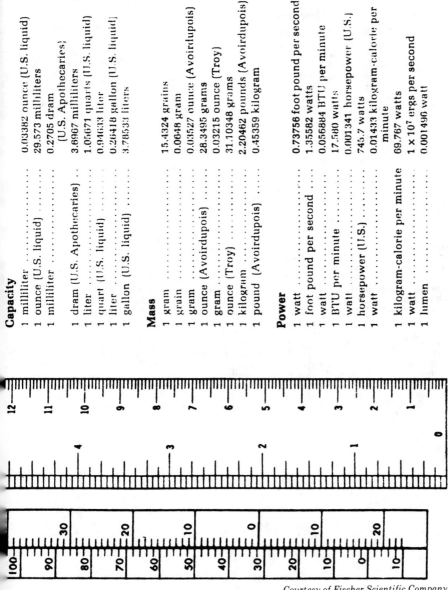

Courtesy of Fischer Scientific Company

BAKER'S CONVERSION TABLE

Ingredient	Measurement[1] Lb.	Oz.
Whole eggs, 10	1	..
Egg whites, 16	1	..
Egg yolks, 25	1	..
Whole eggs, 1 quart	2	..
Whites or yolks, 1 qt.	2	..
Water, 1 qt.	2	..
Milk, 1 qt.	2	..
Oil, 1 qt.	2	..
Buttermilk, 1 qt	2	..
Honey, 1 qt.	2	12
Invert sugar, 1 qt.	2	12
Molasses, 1 qt.	2	14
Malt syrup, 1 qt.	2	15
Glucose, 1 qt	2	15
Sugar, 1 bag	100	..
Chocolate, 1 bar	10	..

[1] 16 oz. = 1 lb.

CONVERSION TABLE FOR SMALL BATCHES

Baking powder	1 oz. = 2$^1/_2$ tbsp.	Lemon rind	1 oz. = 4 tbsp.
Baking soda	1 oz. = 2 tbsp.	Mace, ground	1 oz. = 4 tbsp.
Cake crumbs	3 oz. = 1 cup	Milk, liquid	1 lb. = 2 cups
Cardamom, ground	1 oz. = 5 tbsp.	Milk, powdered	1 lb. = 4 cups
Chocolate, grated	1 oz. = 4 tbsp.	Oil, vegetable	8 oz. = 1 cup
Cinnamon, ground	1 oz. = 4$^1/_2$ tbsp.	Orange rind	1 oz. = 4 tbsp.
Cocoa	1 lb. = 4$^1/_4$ cups	Salt	1 oz. = 2 tbsp.
Cream of tartar	1 oz. = 3 tbsp.	Shortening	1 lb. = 2$^1/_2$ cups
Eggs, whole (10)	1 lb. = 2 cups	Sugar, brown	1 lb. = 3 cups
Eggs, whites (18)	1 lb. = 2 cups	Sugar, granulated	1 lb. = 2$^1/_4$ cups
Eggs, yolks (24)	1 lb. = 2 cups	Sugar, confectionery	1 lb. = 3$^1/_2$ cups
Flour, sifted	1 lb. = 4$^1/_2$ cups	Vanilla	1 oz. = 2 tbsp.
Honey	12 oz. = 1 cup	Water	1 lb. = 2 cups
Lemon juice	1 oz. = 2 tbsp.	Yeast	$^1/_2$ oz. = 1 small cake

Glossary

GENERAL TERMS

Bag out
To press product out of a conical canvas bag onto baking pans in the desired forms

Beat or whip
To whip air into a liquid mass such as eggs, sweet cream, or gelatine solution until the desired lightness is obtained

Blend
To fold or mix two materials together to obtain equal distribution

Caramelization
The burning of sugar

Coagulate
To clot or curdle

Cream
To rub shortening usually with sugar or flour in order to incorporate air

Crystallization
The reforming of sugar into crystals

Fry
To cook in fat

Gelatinize
To convert into a jelly-like substance

Greasing
The process of applying shortening to the inside of a pan with a brush for the purpose of preventing the mixture from adhering to the pan when baked

Leavening
A substance which will produce aeration before or during baking. It creates a gas which is released when coming in contact with a liquid, and heat

Scrape down
To scrape the batter from the sides of the kettle so that it may blend with the batter in the center

BREAD BAKING TERMS

Absorption
The ability of a flour to absorb water, measured by the quantity of water absorbed to produce the proper consistency

Adding
The process of increasing

Blending flours
The process of mixing flours for the purpose of obtaining the desired characteristics

Bread box
A square wooden box 40 × 40 × 4 in. in which the rounded dough or molded loaves of bread are allowed to proof

Cleave or round
To shape a piece of dough into a smooth special form

Cutting
The act of cutting the top crust of the loaf to allow the gas to escape while baking

Developing dough
The act of mixing the dough to a smoother state by added mixing

Dissolving
The process of liquefying

Dusting
The act of spraying flour or cornmeal

Fermentation	The chemical reaction of the ingredients used in the making of dough which causes the forming of a gas, carbon-dioxide, in the dough which in turn causes the dough to expand
Folding or punching	The act of forcing the gas out of dough by folding one part of the dough over the other
Gluten	The rubbery, elastic substance found in flour when water is added
Humidity	The water vapor or water content of the air
Hygroscopic	The ability to draw moisture from the air
Incorporating	The act of mixing or blending one ingredient with another
Knead	To work into a mass or to develop dough by added mixing
Leavening	A substance which will produce gas to cause aeration within a product. In bread yeast
Measuring	The act of determining the amount of liquid ingredient
Mixing	The act of blending into one mass
Molding	The act of forming the loaf of bread
Peel	A flat board fastened to the end of a long or short pole and used for placing bakery products in the oven and taking them out again
Peeling	The act of putting bread or bakery products in the oven by means of a peel
Pouring	To empty as a liquid, out of a vessel or kettle
Preliminary proofing	A short period of fermentation after the dough has been scaled and rounded
Press out	To divide a piece of dough into a specified number of pieces by means of a press machine
Proof	The last stage of fermentation before baking
Roll box	The same type of box as the bread box but with half the height. Used for molded rolls or doughnuts
Scaling	The act of weighing materials
Sifting	Running material through a sieve
Steaming	The act of injecting steam into the oven while baking
Stippling or Docking	Piercing the loaf by means of a straight piece of heavy wire for the purpose of letting the gas escape while being baked
Stirring	The act of agitation, used in dissolving

CAKE BAKING TERMS

Breaking down	Overcreaming of ingredients, causing weakened products which collapse
Decorating or Trimming	The art of inscribing fancy inscriptions or designs on cakes
Dry	A condition found in the product due to its low liquid content or the degree to which it was baked
Folding	The act of gently incorporating or mixing flour into the mix
Gradually	The act of proceeding by stages
Grainy	A rough harsh condition

Ice	The act of applying a sugar preparation to the products
Invert	The act of turning the pan upside down
Light and firm	That degree of lightness and stability usually applied to the whipping of eggs and sugar
Moist	The product's ability to keep moist, which keeps the product fresher longer
Shrinking	The act of contracting or becoming wrinkled
Soggy	A condition in which the liquid content gives the product an excess amount of moisture
Stiff-meringue	Egg-whites and sugar whipped to a light, firm mass
Stirring	The act of agitation
Streaky	A condition in which discolored narrow bands appear
Texture	The inside grain or degree of smoothness in a product
Volume	That degree of size obtained by the mixture upon its being baked
Wet peak	Usually a mixture of eggs and sugar whipped to the point where the mixture forms a peak that is wet and has a tendency to fold over
Temperature	The degree of heat or coldness
Tempering	To modify or regulate the temperature of the water to meet requirements
Washing	The act of applying a liquid over bread and other products by means of a brush

A MESSAGE TO THE APPRENTICE BAKER

The course of study appearing in this Appendix of *Practical Baking* was prepared for you, keeping in mind the skilled baker which you will strive to ultimately become, and, knowing the importance of directing your steps toward that goal during the critical first six months of your training.

The critical first six months of your training will provide you with the opportunity to really explore the baking trade and to help determine where you may find your own particular niche in it. Explore it well and progress is assured. But, how well and rapidly you progress will depend upon you, more than the instructor, and the interest you personally evoke in becoming a skilled baker. Here are some suggestions which should be helpful in putting your best foot forward toward that ultimate goal:

(1) In order to learn the trade at a regular rate you must be present on the job regularly and punctually. Absence and lateness make it impossible to follow an organized training program. So help your instructor to help you learn the trade by being punctual and attentive.

(2) Listen carefully and follow instructions carefully when you are being shown "how" and while the "why" is being explained to you. If you do not understand clearly and completely, *ask* to be shown again. Try to avoid error and spoilage because you were afraid to ask. Your instructor will appreciate your asking questions and learning to perform well.

(3) Do not become discouraged. The skilled baker who is your instructor spent years learning and developing his skills. You will too. Keep at it. Repetition develops skill.

(4) You will be asked to do work that is simple and requires little skill. Remember, that clean pans and a clean shop are a part of the formation of good, clean working habits. Also, good, clean working habits are a requirement of local health laws governing bakery operations.

(5) It is very important that you practice safety in all you do on the job. An injured worker is nonproductive to himself and the job. Be particularly careful in the first weeks of your training until you develop safe habits of work.

(6) You will be required to attend a formal school program where you will receive additional trade practice and related trade information. The school instruction will help you perform better on the job. It will also be possible for you to exchange job experiences and trade information with the instructor and other apprentice bakers.

(7) Read the assignments in this textbook carefully. By so doing, you will develop a better understanding of what you are doing on the job. Later, even as an experienced baker, this textbook will serve you well as a good reference book throughout your career years.

(8) At the outset of your training period, develop the reading habit. Almost everything you read pertaining to the baking trade will, in future years, furnish you with a storehouse of valuable information that can become one of your greatest assets. Reading everything you can find relative to the baking trade will provide a source of continuing self-help and a lifetime education program that you will never regret having started in your apprentice days. Following the course of study in this Appendix is a List of Suggested Supplemental Reading that will be helpful to you.

WILLIAM J. SULTAN

A MESSAGE TO THE INSTRUCTOR

The apprentice baker has made a decision to learn the baking trade. To really find out whether he has made a wise decision, he must be given the opportunity to work in the major areas or divisions of the trade. This will enable him through instruction and experience to explore and determine whether he has made a proper choice.

The suggested first six months course of study appearing in this Appendix will serve you, the skilled baker-teacher, as a flexible guide for training on-the-job apprentices. The sequence of jobs are based upon the practical concept of "learning by doing from the simple to the complex." The sequence of jobs as outlined in the guide may be adjusted to any special needs reflected in the production needs of an employer. Educationally, the apprentice should experience all the jobs and job skills listed.

A simple pattern of organization is followed in the development and presentation of the course outlined: specific periods for skill development with selected trade divisions make it easy for both the instructor and apprentice to follow. The instructor providing the related trade information at school will be able to follow the on-the-job training and directly relate his instruction. Actually, it is a teaching-learning flow chart to be followed by all involved.

Even though *Practical Baking* is the recommended reference text throughout the suggested course of study because it is written with a direct and practical approach to the apprentice and stresses all major areas of the baking trade and industry, instructors and apprentices are advised to refer to all other publications published for further supplementary reading, such as the List of Suggested Supplemental Reading which you will find at the end of the course of study.

The suggested course of study may be used as is or adjusted to meet special training program needs at the secondary high school or junior college levels. It may be adjusted for inclusion into a comprehensive food preparation and service program. Selected areas may be utilized to meet special training needs.

In its present form, a full year of training would be required to adequately cover the entire course, based upon 15 hr. weekly of shop instruction and application.

A bona fide three year apprenticeship in baking will require additional courses of study to meet the needs of an expanded and more complex trade training program. Special course outline guides will be needed for selected specialized areas of training such as cake finisher and conditor, bread and roll baker, oven man, cake and pastry baker, and others. Upon satisfactory completion of this six months course of training, the apprentice should be permitted to select an area of trade specialization if he shows special aptitude and skill in any area.

Discovery of such special aptitudes and skills in apprentices under your supervision certainly is one of the most rewarding aspects of teaching. It affords you, the instructor, great opportunity to impart your skills, knowledge, and understanding of the baking trade to your apprentice students so that they, like yourself, may become masters of the trade. To help do this most successfully, may I remind you of the following pointers:

(1) Be patient while teaching. Some apprentices will learn faster than others. Speed and accuracy comes with teaching and experience.

(2) Teaching means "showing how" as well as "telling why." Show by demonstrating. Take a small part at a time in the beginning. If error or slow-

ness results, remember that you may not have shown and explained clearly. Repeat the demonstration and be understanding and helpful.

(3) Make the apprentice feel that he *will* learn. Use a positive approach. An encouraging word, a pat on the back, go well with good and effective teaching.

(4) Allow the apprentice to repeat certain jobs and job skills over and over so that he develops the "feel" of the dough or other preparations and materials he is working with.

(5) Follow the course outlines as best you can. If production requirements specialize more in one trade area than in others, then have the apprentice specialize on the job and get the additional instruction at school. Let the school work with you and you cooperate with the school in the total training program.

(6) It is strongly recommended that you check the progress of the apprentice with the skills and training outlined in the course of study.

(7) You will find it beneficial to study your own copy of *Practical Baking* to help you explain the "why" and the "how" of the job. In fact, you may find yourself brushing up on information that you once knew quite well but is now a bit hazy through lack of use.

(8) Finally, let your sound experience and judgment as a baker help the apprentice to decide which areas of the trade he is best suited for. You will get to know his strong points as he works and develops under your guidance and instruction. Encourage those with potential to become masters of the entire trade of baking.

(9) A periodic evaluation of the progress of the apprentice and consultation with the agency or coordinator of the area program is important to the apprentice and to the success of the total program. Your cooperation will be respected and appreciated.

WILLIAM J. SULTAN

Apprentice Baker on-the-Job Training Program

A Course of Study and Training for the First Six months Covering Orientation and Probationary Period (1,000 hrs)

Weeks 1 and 2

STRESS SANITATION AND SAFETY   STRESS REPETITION FOR SKILL

Trade Area Job: Orientation	Tools and Equipment to Be Used	Specific Job Skills to Be Developed
Tools	Bench scraper	Clean and grease pans
Equipment (small)	Work benches	Clean machines and equip-
Equipment (major)	Variety pans	ment
Ovens	Grease brushes	Identify raw materials
Mixers	Greasing equipment	Fill material bins
Refrigerators	Bowl knives	Store new delivery of material
Freezers	Vienna knife	(inventory)
Equipment for bread	Cutting cake knives	Load racks with pans
production	Sink	Remove baked products from
Raw materials	Mixing machines	pans and racks
Safety practices	Ovens	Scale raw materials using a
Sanitation	Racks	baker's scale
Personal	Proof box racks	Care and storage of perish-
Production	Fermentation room	ables: refrigerator storage;
Work routines	Racks	freezer storage; defrost eggs
Work schedule	Dough dividers	and other frozen ingredients·
Related instruction: The	Major equipment for yeast-	Remove unbaked units from
"why" of the job	raised goods	the work bench
School routine (if school	in large bakery	Wash and store small tools and
program exists)	plants	equipment
		Use pan washing machines

Related Trade Discussion and/or Study

Knowledge of facts concerning basic raw materials used in baking trade (pp. 1–48)
Glossary of bakery terms (see p. 462)

Baker's Conversion Tables (see p. 461)
Local health laws
State regulations
Safety regulations

Notes

TRAINING PROGRAM (*Continued*)

Weeks 3 and 4

Trade Area Job: Bread and Rolls	Tools and Equipment to Be Used	Specific Job Skills to Be Developed
(See text pp. 1–35, 54–60 and 71–74) Variety Soft Rolls (molded and twisted) Hamburger rolls Frankfurter rolls Finger rolls Single knot rolls Double knot rolls Figure "8" rolls Snail rolls	Baker's scale Automatic scalers Dough mixers Vertical Horizontal Flour sifter Automatic flour blender Dough divider (press machine) Automatic divider and rounder Dough strand molder Automatic panners Frankfurter pans Baking pans and racks Bench scraper Wash brushes Steam or proof box Ovens Steam generator or boiler and controls	Scale ingredients Prepare a yeast solution Mix a soft roll dough Punch a dough Scale fermented dough Divide dough Round up rolls by hand Shape Frankfurter rolls Shape finger rolls Shape strands of dough Twist single knot roll Twist double knot roll Twist figure "8" roll Twist snail-shaped roll Prepare egg wash Wash the rolls Place the rolls on pans Proof rolls Peel (place pans in oven) Load and unload pan racks Remove baked products on pans from oven Check rolls for proper bake and crust color

Related Trade Discussion and/or Study

Baking trade terms applied to yeast-raised products (see Glossary p. 462)

Identification of basic raw materials used in baking

Proper dough mixing

Care and use of dough divider

Function of basic raw materials used in manufacture of yeast-raised products: sugar, salt, flour, water, yeast, eggs, etc. (Review pp. 1–35)

Notes

TRAINING PROGRAM (*Continued*)

Weeks 5 and 6

Trade Area Job: Bread and rolls	Tools and Equipment to Be Used	Specific Job Skills to Be Developed
(See text pp. 29–33, 70, 74–77, and 80–82) Pan bread varieties Plain top pan bread White Mountain bread Slit-top bread Pullman bread	Scale and automatic scalers (large plant) Dough mixers Automatic dough scalers and rounders Baker's bench scale Overhead proofer (in large plant production) Dough molders and shapers (automatic) Bench scrapers Bread pans Bread boxes Vienna knife Proof box Pan racks Steam generator or boiler Ovens and peels Racking on racks Bread cooler (automatic in large plants)	Round units of scaled dough by hand Prepare bread pans Shape pan bread Place bread into pans Proof bread Use steam in the oven Bake pan bread Prepare a sponge for a sponge-type of dough Mix a sponge into dough Shape two-twist Pullman bread Prepare Pullman pans Bake Pullman bread Cut top of a split-top bread Dust bread with flour for White Mountain effect Shape a round-shaped split-top bread Bake split-top and White Mountain bread Use a peel Shift pans in the oven Bake out pan breads

Related Trade Discussion and/or Study

Purposes of fermentation
Factors that affect fermentation: to speed up; to slow down
Purpose of the sponge in yeast-raised doughs

Comparison of straight doughs and sponge doughs
Function of steam in baking
Common bread faults: their causes and corrections

Notes

TRAINING PROGRAM (Continued)
Weeks 7 and 8

Trade Area Job: Sweet Yeast Goods	Tools and Equipment to Be Used	Specific Job Skills to Be Developed
(See pp. 51–60, 134–154)	Scales for ingredients	Mix bun or sweet roll dough
Buns and sweet rolls	Automatic scalers (in large	Shape and pan crumb buns
Crumb buns	plant production)	Prepare Streussel topping
Cinnamon sticks	Dough mixers	Apply Streussel topping
Raisin-cinnamon buns	Fermenting room, or dough	Make cake crumbs from stale
Butterfly buns	troughs or bowls	dried products
Round-filled buns	Dough divider and rounder	Prepare crumb filling
Open cheese pocket	Dough sheeter	Shape cinnamon stick buns
Twist buns	Hand tools	Proof buns
Horseshoe buns	Rolling pins (large and	Bake buns
Bowtie-twist buns	small)	Finish Streussel and cinnamon
Preparation and use of	Bench scraper	stick buns
Streussel topping	Wash brush	Roll out sweet bun dough
Cheese filling	Bench brush	Apply cinnamon bun filling
Cinnamon sugar	Pastry wheel	Roll up, seal filled dough
Prepared fruit, and	Syrup wash brush	Cut dough into buns
other fillings and top-	Icing equipment (auto-	Shape butterfly buns
pings	matic in large plants)	Place buns on pans
Prepare syrup wash	Pans	Prepare and apply syrup wash
Prepare simple icing	Proof box	and simple icing
	Racks	Shape round buns, prepare
	Ovens	them for filling
	Aluminum foil baking pans	Shape open pocket buns
	for special production	Fold rolled out dough into
		three layers
		Shape twist, horseshoe and
		bowtie-twist buns

Related Trade Discussion and/or Study

The different stages of fermentation: primary, secondary, panary
Comparison of bun dough and bread dough
The proof box: (a) purpose and function; (b) operation: temperature and humidity

How to test for proof of yeast-raised products
Dough temperature and fermentation
Factors affecting bun production
Common bun faults: causes and corrections

Notes

TRAINING PROGRAM (*Continued*)

Weeks 9 and 10

Trade Area Job: Biscuits and Muffins	Tools and Equipment to Be Used	Specific Job Skills to Be Developed
(See pp. 17–20, 191–207, 310–311) Plain biscuits Raisin biscuits Cinnamon biscuits Combination biscuits Plain muffins Corn muffins Whole wheat muffins Fruit-filled muffins	Scales for ingredients Automatic scalers and temperers (large plants) Mixers (vertical) Automatic droppers Bench scrapers Pastry wheel Bun divider Muffin pans Racks Steam generator Ovens Cooling racks Refrigerators and defrosters for frozen fruits	Mix a biscuit dough Roll out dough for cutting Cut out biscuits Work in scrap dough Place biscuits on pans Wash and bake biscuits Mix a creamed type of batter Prepare muffin tins Drop batter into muffin tins by hand Operate automatic muffin or cup cake dropper Incorporate raisins and fruits into plain muffin batter Bake muffins Mix a combination biscuit dough Condition a combination biscuit dough (partial fermentation) Proof or relax combination biscuits before baking Mix a whole wheat muffin Mix corn bread Deposit corn bread into pans Bake Southern corn bread

Related Trade Discussion and/or Study

Review creaming method of mixing
Review Glossary terms which apply to cake mixing (p. 462)
Storage of baking pans; cleaning and sanitation

Common biscuit faults and causes
Study of whole wheat flour (uses)
Study of corn meal (types and uses)
Common muffin faults and causes

Notes

Weeks 11 and 12

Trade Area Job: Pie and Pastry	Tools and Equipment to Be Used	Specific Job Skills to Be Developed
(See pp. 225–235, 249–261)	Ingredient and bench scales	Mix pie crust dough
Pie crust doughs (variations)	Automatic scalers	Prepare a variety fruit filling
Variety fruit fillings	Mixers	Use prepared fruit fillings using cold process thickeners
Pies	Bowl knives	Divide pie crust into proper size for tops and bottoms
Apple	Scrapers	Roll out pie bottoms and tops
Pineapple	Refrigerators	Place dough into pie tins
Cherry	Baker's confectionery stove and utility cook stove	Fill the pies with filling
Blueberry	Steam pressure cooker	Close and finish pies
Lattice-type pies	Fruit defrosters	Bake the pies
Crumb-topped pies	Rolling pins	Use automatic pie dough and pie filling equipment
Pie crust turnovers	Pastry wheel	Rework scrap pie dough
	Automatic pie shell machine	Roll out pie crust for turnovers
	Automatic fruit depositer and pie filler	Cut the dough into squares
	Automatic sealing and spray wash machines	Fill the squares
	Pans	Shape the turnovers
	Racks	Pan and bake the turnovers
	Ovens	Finish the turnovers
	Freezer for unbaked and baked pies	Store baked and unbaked pies in the freezer

Related Trade Discussion and/or Study

Variations in pie crust dough recipes

Methods of mixing pie crust dough

Refrigeration of pie crust doughs

Methods of preparing canned fruit fillings

Preparation of frozen fruit fillings

Preventing fruit filling spoilage

Corn starch and other thickening agents

Variety fruit fillings and filling pies

Care of leftover fillings and pie dough

Notes

TRAINING PROGRAM (*Continued*)

Weeks 13 and 14

Trade Area Job: Cakes	Tools and Equipment to Be Used	Specific Job Skills to Be Developed
(See pp. 12–13, 22–23, 39–43, 44–48, 310–320, 325–328, and 460 for baking temperatures)	Ingredient scales	Mix a creamed-type wine cake batter
Wine cake cup cakes	Automatic scalers	Drop out cup cakes (review)
Plain iced	Mixing machines	Apply crumb topping
Crumb topped	Timer controls for mixing	Bake cup cakes
Simple or fondant icing	Cup cake pans	Use automatic dropper (review)
Drop cakes	Automatic pan washers and automatic greasing equipment	Prepare flat-type or simple icings
Metropolitans	Dropping machines	Prepare fondant for use
High-ratio cup cakes	Pan racks	Adjust a wine cake mix for drop cakes
Yellow	Ovens	Prepare pans for drop cakes
Chocolate	Icing pots	Bag out or drop out the drop cakes for size, shape, and spacing
White	Double boilers and icing warmers	Use automatic dropper
Fudge icings	Confectionery stoves	Bake drop cakes
Buttercream icing	Cooking kettles	Ice cup cakes
Butterfly cup cakes	Refrigerators	Ice drop cakes with knife
Fudge-topped cup cakes	Bowl knife	Prepare fudge icings
	Bowl scrapers	Prepare buttercream icing
	Storage room equipment	Finish cup cakes with fudge icing
	Finishing room	Finish metropolitans
	Marble-topped bench	Finish butterfly cup cakes

Related Trade Discussion and/or Study

Rules and methods for making variety icings

Defrosting frozen eggs

Study of cake flour and pastry flour

Comparison of cake and bread flours

Blending of flours

Common cup cake and drop cake faults and causes

Notes

TRAINING PROGRAM (*Continued*)

Weeks 15 and 16

Trade Area Job: Fried Products	Tools and Equipment to Be Used	Specific Job Skills to Be Developed
(See pp. 5–10 and 208–222)	Ingredient scales and automatic scaling	Mix dough for yeast-raised doughnuts (review)
Yeast-raised doughnuts	Mixing machines	Condition or ferment the
Ring doughnuts	Fermentation rooms	dough (review fermentation)
Jelly doughnuts	Fermentation troughs and	tion)
Twist doughnut varieties	bowls	Roll out dough for ring doughnuts
World's Fair or Combination doughnuts	Dough dividers and rounders	nuts
Longjohn	Automatic droppers	Shape jelly doughnuts
Bowtie variety	Frying kettle	Shape variety twist doughnuts
Cake-type doughnuts	Confectionery-baker's	Use automatic rounders
Plain doughnuts	stove and racks	Fry doughnuts
Whole wheat doughnuts	Automatic frying equipment	Fill jelly doughnuts
Chocolate doughnuts	ment	Glaze doughnuts
	Pan racks and coolers	Finish doughnuts with cinnamon sugar or confectionery
	Icing pots and icing equipment	sugar
	ment	Ice doughnuts with variety
	Glazing racks and dryers	icings
	Jelly pumps	Mix World's Fair doughnut
	Automatic doughnut finishing equipment	mix
	ing equipment	Condition the dough for use
	Refrigerator	Shape longjohn doughnuts
	Freezer	Shape bowtie doughnuts
	Packaging equipment (large plant production)	Prepare whole wheat doughnuts
		nuts
		Prepare chocolate doughnuts
		Use automatic doughnut droppers and fryers
		Use prepared doughnut mixes

Related Trade Discussion and/or Study

Types of fat used for frying
Safety and sanitation in frying
The use of variety frying equipment

Yeast-raised doughnut faults and causes
Leavening of variety doughnuts
Cake doughnut faults and causes

Notes

TRAINING PROGRAM (*Continued*)

Weeks 17 and 18

Trade Area Job: Cookies	Tools and Equipment to Be Used	Specific Job Skills to Be Developed
(See pp. 11–16 and 401–417)	Ingredient scales and automatic scalers	Mix sugar cookie dough
Cut-out cookie varieties	Mixing machines	Roll out cookie dough
Sugar cookies	Pastry bags and assorted	Use a cookie cutter
Short bread	pastry tubes	Cut dough with a pastry wheel
Bagged cookies (Variety shapes)	Pans	Put topping on cookie before baking
Plain tube	Automatic cookie dropper and wire cutter	Pan cookies
Star tube	Racks	Bake sugar and short dough cookies
French tube	Storage (variety toppings and garnishes)	Finish sugar and short dough cookies
Sandwich-type cookies	Double boiler for icings and chocolate	Mix lemon snap cookies
Variety finish	Ovens	Mix chocolate drop cookies
Prebaked finish	Refrigerator	Bag out cookies with a plain tube
Dipped finish	Finishing room for chocolate finish	Garnish and bake large drop out cookie varieties
Striped finish	Display pans	Prepare vanilla and chocolate jumble mix
		Bag out assorted large jumbles with star tube
		Garnish and bake jumble cookies
		Prepare a French butter cookie mix
		Prepare a button or sandwich cookie mix
		How to bag out star shape, pear shape, stick shape, rosette shape cookies
		How to fill sandwich cookies

Related Trade Discussion and/or Study

Qualities of a short dough for cookies
Use of cocoa and chocolate in baking
Variety toppings for cookies

Common short dough cookie faults and causes
Care and use of pastry bags and tubes
Bag-out cookie faults and common causes

Study and use of variety eggs in baking

Notes

Training Program (*Continued*)

Weeks 19 and 20

Trade Area Job: Bread and rolls	Tools and Equipment to Be Used	Specific Job Skills to Be Developed
(See pp. 17–23, 54–60, 61– 65, 78–80, 105–106. 120–122) French bread French rolls Italian bread Italian rolls Twisted egg bread 4 twist bread 5 twist bread 6 twist bread Kaiser rolls	Ingredient scales and automatic scaling equipment Dough mixers Dough troughs and fermentation rooms Automatic scaler and rounder Automatic shaper or molder Bench scale Bread and roll boxes Bench scraper Bench brush Dough divider for rolls Strip-making machine for twisted bread Vienna knives for cutting tops of breads Bread pans Peels Proofing and oading racks Ovens Steam generators Wash brushes Bread baskets Cooling equipment Wrapping equipment	Mix French bread dough Ferment the dough (review) Shape French bread Shape French oval rolls Mix Italian bread dough Shape variety Italian breads (long shape, round shape) Shape Italian rolls and Italian bread sticks Box, or place the shaped bread on peels Test for proof Cut breads before baking Peel breads and rolls into oven Bake the breads Test the breads for bake Unload the ovens Rack the breads Mix an egg bread Shape tapered dough strip Braid the twist breads Wash breads with egg wash Proof and bake egg breads Mix Kaiser roll dough Use Kaiser roll machine Shape Kaiser rolls by hand

Related Trade Discussion and/or Study

Use of rye flour for bread and roll makeup
Use of malt in bread and roll doughs
Increasing and decreasing a recipe
Expressing a recipe in percentage form

Comparison of hearth and pan-baked breads
Study of wheat and flour
Composition of flour
Gluten and its importance in bread and roll production
Common bread faults and causes

Notes

TRAINING PROGRAM (*Continued*)

Weeks 21 and 22

Trade Area Job: Danish Pastry and Puff Pastry	Tools and Equipment to Be Used	Specific Job Skills to Be Developed
(See pp. 134–139, 154 169, 240–245)	Ingredient scales and automatic scaling equipment	Mix a Danish pastry dough
Danish pastry varieties	Dough mixers (vertical)	Prepare and roll in fat
Cheese pockets	Automatic dough roller and	Prepare cheese filling
Open prune pockets	sheeter	Shape cheese pockets
Snecks (cinnamon)	Large rolling pin	Shape open pockets
Butter horns	Refrigerators	Shape snecks
Crescent horns	Freezers	Wash and proof Danish
Assorted custard twists	Bowl knives	Garnish Danish
Sticks (cigar shapes)	Pans	Prepare almond filling
Miniatures	Pastry wheel	Shape Danish horns
Small rings	Automatic dough divider	Make variety Danish twists
Puff pastry varieties	and filler	Make small Danish rings
Turnovers	Wash brush	Make miniature Danish
Fruit baskets	Stippler or docker	Make Danish sticks (cigars)
Apple dumplings	Steam pressure cooker	Pan variety Danish
Patty shells	Baker's stove	Bake Danish varieties
Napoleons	Kettles for cooking	Finish baked Danish pastries
	Proofer or proof box	Prepare Danish for freezer
	Ovens	Defrost frozen Danish
	Racks	Make puff pastry dough
	Cooler	Shape puff pastry turnovers
	Icing pots and automatic icing applicator	Make fruit baskets
		Make apple dumplings
		Make patty shells
		Make Napoleons
		Finish Napoleons (review cooking custard filling)

Related Trade Discussion and/or Study

Practices and operations in making Danish pastry dough and varieties
Leavening of Danish pastry units
Retarding and freezing Danish pastry
Common Danish pastry faults and causes

Practices and operations in making puff pastry dough and varieties
Leavening of puff pastry products
Use of cream of tartar or other acids in puff pastry
Common puff pastry faults and causes

Notes

TRAINING PROGRAM (*Continued*)

Weeks 23 and 24

Trade Area Job: Layer Cakes and Cake Finishing	Tools and Equipment to Be Used	Specific Job Skills to Be Developed
(See pp. 1–4, 24–28, 36–43, 310–324, 330–332, 338–360, 370–374)	Scales and scaling equipment	Mix a high-ratio cake using blending method
High-ratio cakes	Automatic droppers	Prepare layer cake pans
Yellow layer cake	Pan washers and pan greasers (automatic)	Deposit batter into pans
Chocolate layer cake	Mixing machines	Use automatic droppers or batter depositors
White layer cake	Bowl knives	Prepare eggs for sponge cake
Buttercream, fudge, and marshmallow icing	Bowl scrapers	Mix a sponge cake batter
Cakes made with the whipping method	Batter spreaders	Fold in flour and butter
	Variety pans for special cakes (angel food)	Mix a chiffon cake batter
Sponge cake	Icing pans and pots	Combine egg whites with rest of the batter
Butter sponge cake	Racks	Pan a jelly roll batter
Angel cake	Ovens	Bake a jelly roll
Chiffon cake	Refrigerators	Fill and roll a jelly roll
Jelly roll	Freezers	Bake high-ratio sponge type layer cakes
Chocolate roll	Double boilers	Mix a wonder cake
Cakes made with the creaming and whipping method	Confectioner's stove	Add chocolate to a wonder or other marbled type of cake
	Turntable	
Pound cake	Icing racks	Prepare baked layers for finishing
Wonder cake	Storage equipment	Finish layers with fondant, fudge, and buttercream icings
	Display materials and equipment	
	Cleaning equipment	Finish layers using turntable and a pastry bag and tube
	Pastry bags and tubes	Finish layers with a bowl knife

Related Trade Discussion and/or Study

Methods of mixing variety cakes
Sugar and its uses in baking
Milk and its uses in baking (types, preparation, storage)

High-ratio cake faults and causes
Whipped cake faults and causes
Balancing of creamed cakes and high-ratio cakes

Notes

Suggested Supplementary Reading

TEXTBOOKS

DE RENZO, D. J. 1975. Bakery Products—Yeast Leavened. Noyes Data Corp., Park Ridge, N.J.

DE RENZO, D. J. 1975. Doughs and Baked Goods. Noyes Data Corp., Park Ridge, N.J.

D'ERMO, D. 1962. The Modern Pastry Chef's Guide to Professional Baking. Harper & Row, Publishers, New York.

ESCOFFIER, A. 1941. Escoffier Cookbook. Crown Publishing Co., New York.

FANCE, W. F. 1969. Breadmaking and Flour Confectionery, 2nd Edition. Avi Publishing Co., Westport, Conn.

INGLETT, G. E. 1974. Wheat: Production and Utilization. Avi Publishing Co., Westport, Conn.

MATZ, S. A. 1968. Cookie and Cracker Technology. Avi Publishing Co., Westport, Conn.

MATZ, S. A. 1970. Cereal Technology. Avi Publishing Co., Westport, Conn.

MATZ, S. A. 1972. Bakery Technology and Engineering, 2nd Edition. Avi Publishing Co., Westport, Conn.

POMERANZ, Y. 1971. Wheat Chemistry and Technology. American Association of Cereal Chemists, St. Paul, Minn.

POMERANZ, Y., and SHELLENBERGER, J. A. 1971. Bread Science and Technology. Avi Publishing Co., Westport, Conn.

PRATT, C. D. 1970. Twenty Years of Confectionery and Chocolate Progress. Avi Publishing Co., Westport, Conn.

PYLER, E. J. 1973. Baking Science and Technology, 2nd Edition, Vol. I and II. Seibel Publishing Co., Chicago.

SMITH, L. L., and MINOR, L. J. 1974. Food Service Science. Avi Publishing Co., Westport, Conn.

SMITH, W. H. 1972. Biscuits, Crackers and Cookies, Vol. 2. Applied Science Publishers, Barking, Essex, England.

VAN EGMOND, D. 1974. School Foodservice. Avi Publishing Co., Westport, Conn.

MANUAL

SULTAN, W. S. 1976. Practical Baking Manual for Instructors and Students. Avi Publishing Co., Westport, Conn.

TRADE PUBLICATIONS

Bakers' Digest, 4049 Peterson Ave., Chicago, Ill. 60646.

Bakery Production and Marketing, Gorman Publishing Co., 3460 John Hancock Ctr., Chicago, Ill. 60611.

Baking Industry, Putnam Publishing Co., 430 N. Michigan Ave., Chicago, Ill. 60611.

Baking Today, Sosland Publishing Co., 4800 Main St., Kansas City, Mo. 64112.

Milling and Baking News, Sosland Publishing Co., 4800 Main St., Kansas City, Mo. 64112.

Index